CompTIA A+® Review Guide

Third Edition

Exam 220-901
Exam 220-902

CompTIA A+® Review Guide

Third Edition

Exam 220-901
Exam 220-902

Troy McMillan

SYBEX®
A Wiley Brand

Senior Acquisitions Editor: Kenyon Brown
Development Editor: Kelly Talbot
Technical Editor: Robin Abernathy, Ian Seaton, and Scott Johnson
Production Editor: Christine O'Connor
Copy Editor: Kim Wimpsett
Editorial Manager: Mary Beth Wakefield
Production Manager: Kathleen Wisor
Associate Publisher: Jim Minatel
Book Designers: Judy Fung and Bill Gibson
Proofreaders: Scott Klemp and Jen Larsen, Word One New York
Indexer: Robert Swanson
Project Coordinator, Cover: Brent Savage
Cover Designer: Wiley
Cover Image: Getty Images, Inc./Jeremy Woodhouse

For my wife Heike, who makes all the hard work worth it.

Acknowledgments

Special thanks go out to Kelly Talbot for keeping me on schedule and ensuring all the details are correct. Also, I'd like to thank Robin Abernathy and Ian Seaton for the excellent technical edit that saved me from myself at times. Finally, as always, I'd like to acknowledge Kenyon Brown for his continued support of all my writing efforts.

About the Author

Troy McMillan writes practice tests, study guides, and online course materials for Kaplan IT Cert Prep, while also running his own consulting and training business. He holds more than 30 industry certifications and also appears in training videos for Oncourse Learning and Pearson Press. Troy can be reached at mcmillantroy@hotmail.com.

Contents at a Glance

Contents

CompTIA.

Becoming a
CompTIA Certified
IT Professional is Easy

It's also the best way to reach greater
professional opportunities and rewards.

Why Get CompTIA Certified?

Growing Demand

Labor estimates predict some
technology fields will
experience growth of over 20%
by the year 2020.* CompTIA
certification qualifies the skills
required to join this workforce.

Higher Salaries

IT professionals with
certifications on their resume
command better jobs, earn
higher salaries and have more
doors open to new multi-
industry opportunities.

Verified Strengths

91% of hiring managers
indicate CompTIA certifications
are valuable in validating IT
expertise, making certification
the best way to demonstrate
your competency and
knowledge to employers.**

Universal Skills

CompTIA certifications are
vendor neutral—which means
that certified professionals can
proficiently work with an
extensive variety of hardware
and software found in most
organizations.

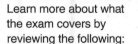 Learn > Certify > Work

| Learn more about what the exam covers by reviewing the following: | Purchase a voucher at a Pearson VUE testing center or at CompTIAstore.com. | Congratulations on your CompTIA certification! |

**Learn more about what
the exam covers by
reviewing the following:**

- Exam objectives for
  key study points.

- Sample questions for a general
  overview of what to expect
  on the exam and examples
  of question format.

- Visit online forums, like LinkedIn,
  to see what other IT professionals
  say about CompTIA exams.

**Purchase a voucher at a
Pearson VUE testing center
or at CompTIAstore.com.**

- Register for your exam at a
  Pearson VUE testing center:

- Visit pearsonvue.com/CompTIA to
  find the closest testing center to you.

- Schedule the exam online. You will
  be required to enter your voucher
  number or provide payment
  information at registration.

- Take your certification exam.

**Congratulations on your
CompTIA certification!**

- Make sure to add your
  certification to your resume.

- Check out the CompTIA
  Certification Roadmap to plan
  your next career move.

Learn more: Certification.CompTIA.org/aplus

* Source: CompTIA 9th Annual Information Security Trends study: 500 U.S. IT and Business Executives Responsible for Security
** Source: CompTIA Employer Perceptions of IT Training and Certification
*** Source: 2013 IT Skills and Salary Report by CompTIA Authorized Partner

Introduction

The A+ certification program was developed by the Computing Technology Industry Association (CompTIA) to provide an industry-wide means of certifying the competency of computer service technicians. The A+ certification is granted to those who have attained the level of knowledge and troubleshooting skills that are needed to provide capable support in the field of personal computers. CompTIA is a widely respected industry leader in this area.

CompTIA's A+ exam objectives are periodically updated to keep the certification applicable to the most recent hardware and software. This is necessary because a technician must be able to work on the latest equipment. The most recent revisions to the objectives—and to the whole program—were introduced in 2015 and are reflected in this book.

This book and the Sybex *CompTIA A+ Complete Study Guide* (both the Standard and Deluxe Editions) are tools to help you prepare for this certification—and for the new areas of focus of a modern computer technician's job.

What Is A+ Certification?

The A+ certification program was created to offer a wide-ranging certification, in the sense that it's intended to certify competence with personal computers from many different makers/vendors. Everyone must take and pass two exams: 220-901 and 220-902.

You don't have to take the 220-901 exam and the 220-902 exam at the same time. The A+ certification isn't awarded until you've passed both tests. For the latest pricing on the exams and updates to the registration procedures, call Pearson VUE at (877) 551-7587. You can also go to Pearson VUE for additional information or to register online at www.pearsonvue.com/comptia. If you have further questions about the scope of the exams or related CompTIA programs, refer to the CompTIA website at www.comptia.org.

Who Should Buy This Book?

If you want to acquire a solid foundation in personal-computer basics and your goal is to prepare for the exams by filling in any gaps in your knowledge, this book is for you. You'll find clear explanations of the concepts you need to grasp and plenty of help to achieve the high level of professional competency you need in order to succeed in your chosen field.

If you want to become certified as an A+ holder, this book is definitely what you need. However, if you just want to attempt to pass the exam without really understanding the basics of personal computers, this guide isn't for you. It's written for people who want to acquire skills and knowledge of personal-computer basics.

How to Use This Book

We've included several learning tools in the book. These tools will help you retain vital exam content as well as prepare to sit for the actual exams.

Exam Essentials   Each chapter includes a number of exam essentials. These are the key topics that you should take from the chapter in terms of areas on which you should focus when preparing for the exam.

Chapter Review Questions   To test your knowledge as you progress through the book, there are review questions at the end of each chapter. As you finish each chapter, answer the review questions and then check your answers—the correct answers are in the Appendix. You can go back to reread the section that deals with each question you got wrong to ensure that you answer correctly the next time you're tested on the material.

Interactive Online Learning Environment and Test Bank

The interactive online learning environment that accompanies *CompTIA A+ Complete Review Guide: Exams 220-901 and 220-902, Third Edition,* provides a test bank with study tools to help you prepare for the certification exam—and increase your chances of passing it the first time! The test bank includes the following:

Sample Tests   All the questions in this book are provided, including the **Chapter Tests** that include the review questions at the end of each chapter. In addition, there are four **Practice Exams**. Use these questions to test your knowledge of the study guide material. The online test bank runs on multiple devices.

Flashcards   One set of questions is provided in digital flashcard format (a question followed by a single correct answer). You can use the flashcards to reinforce your learning and provide last-minute test prep before the exam.

Other Study Tools   A glossary of key terms from this book and their definitions are available as a fully searchable PDF.

Go to http://sybextestbanks.wiley.com to register and gain access to this interactive online learning environment and test bank with study tools.

Tips for Taking the A+ Exams

Here are some general tips for taking your exams successfully:

- Bring two forms of ID with you. One must be a photo ID, such as a driver's license. The other can be a major credit card or a passport. Both forms must include a signature.

- Arrive early at the exam center so you can relax and review your study materials, particularly tables and lists of exam-related information.

- Read the questions carefully. Don't be tempted to jump to an early conclusion. Make sure you know exactly what the question is asking.

- Don't leave any unanswered questions. Unanswered questions are scored against you.

- There will be questions with multiple correct responses. When there is more than one correct answer, a message at the bottom of the screen will prompt you to either "Choose two" or "Choose all that apply." Be sure to read the messages displayed to know how many correct answers you must choose.

- When answering multiple-choice questions you're not sure about, use a process of elimination to get rid of the obviously incorrect answers first. Doing so will improve your odds if you need to make an educated guess.

- On form-based tests (nonadaptive), because the hard questions will eat up the most time, save them for last. You can move forward and backward through the exam.

- For the latest pricing on the exams and updates to the registration procedures, visit CompTIA's website at www.comptia.org.

Performance-Based Questions

CompTIA has introduced performance-based questions on the latest A+ exams. These are not the traditional multiple-choice questions with which you're probably familiar. These questions require the candidate to know how to perform a specific task or series of tasks. More than likely the candidate will be presented with a scenario and will be asked to complete a task. They will be taken to a simulated environment where they will have to perform a series of steps and will be graded on how well they complete the task.

CompTIA A+ 900 Series Exam Objectives

CompTIA goes to great lengths to ensure that its certification programs accurately reflect the IT industry's best practices. The company does this by establishing Cornerstone Committees for each of its exam programs. Each committee comprises a small group of IT professionals, training providers, and publishers who are responsible for establishing the exam's baseline competency level and who determine the appropriate target audience level.

Once these factors are determined, CompTIA shares this information with a group of hand-selected subject-matter experts (SMEs). These folks are the true brainpower behind the certification program. They review the committee's findings, refine them, and shape them into the objectives you see before you. CompTIA calls this process a Job Task Analysis (JTA).

Finally, CompTIA conducts a survey to ensure that the objectives and weightings truly reflect the job requirements. Only then can the SMEs go to work writing the hundreds of questions needed for the exam. And, in many cases, they have to go back to the drawing board for further refinements before the exam is ready to go live in its final state. So, rest assured, the content you're about to learn will serve you long after you take the exam.

 Exam objectives are subject to change at any time without prior notice and at CompTIA's sole discretion. Please visit the certification page of CompTIA's website at www.comptia.org for the most current listing of exam objectives.

CompTIA also publishes relative weightings for each of the exam's objectives. The following tables list the objective domains and the extent to which they're represented on each exam.

220-901 Exam Domains	% of Exam
1.0 Hardware	34%
2.0 Networking	21%
3.0 Mobile Devices	17%
4.0 Hardware and Network Troubleshooting	28%
Total	100%

220-902 Exam Domains	% of Exam
1.0 Windows Operating Systems	29%
2.0 Other Operating Systems and Technologies	12%
3.0 Security	22%
4.0 Software Troubleshooting	24%
5.0 Operational Procedures	13%
Total	100%

The following sections show the objectives beneath each of these in more detail.

CompTIA 220-901 Exam Objectives

1.0 Hardware

1.1 Given a scenario, configure settings and use BIOS/UEFI tools on a PC.

- Firmware upgrades – flash BIOS
- BIOS component information
  - RAM
  - Hard drive
  - Optical drive
  - CPU
- BIOS configurations
  - Boot sequence
  - Enabling and disabling devices
  - Date/time
  - Clock speeds
  - Virtualization support
  - BIOS security (passwords, drive encryption: TPM, LoJack, secure boot)
- Built-in diagnostics
- Monitoring
  - Temperature monitoring
  - Fan speeds
  - Intrusion detection/notification
  - Voltage
  - Clock
  - Bus speed

1.2 Explain the importance of motherboard components, their purpose, and properties.

- Sizes
  - ATX
  - Micro-ATX
  - Mini-ITX
  - ITX
- Expansion slots
  - PCI

- - PCI-X
  - PCIe
  - miniPCI
- RAM slots
- CPU sockets
- Chipsets
  - North bridge
  - South bridge
- CMOS battery
- Power connections and types
- Fan connectors
- Front/Top-panel connectors
  - USB
  - Audio
  - Power button
  - Power light
  - Drive activity lights
  - Reset button
- Bus speeds

1.3 Compare and contrast various RAM types and their features.

- Types
  - DDR
  - DDR2
  - DDR3
  - SODIMM
  - DIMM
  - Parity vs. non-parity
  - ECC vs. non-ECC
  - RAM configurations
- Single channel vs. dual channel vs. triple channel
  - Single-sided vs. double-sided
  - Buffered vs. unbuffered
- RAM compatibility

1.4 Install and configure PC expansion cards.

- Sound cards
- Video cards
- Network cards
- USB cards
- FireWire cards
- Thunderbolt cards
- Storage cards
- Modem cards
- Wireless/cellular cards
- TV tuner cards
- Video capture cards
- Riser cards

1.5 Install and configure storage devices and use appropriate media.

- Optical drives
  - CD-ROM/CD-RW
  - DVD-ROM/DVD-RW/DVD-RW DL
  - Blu-ray
  - BD-R
  - BD-RE
- Magnetic hard disk drives
  - 5,400 rpm
  - 7,200 rpm
  - 10,000 rpm
- Hot-swappable drives
- Solid-state/flash drives
  - Compact flash
  - SD
  - Micro-SD
  - Mini-SD
  - xD
  - SSD
  - Hybrid
  - eMMC

- RAID types
  - 0
  - 1
  - 5
  - 10
- Tape drive
- Media capacity
  - CD
  - CD-RW
  - DVD-RW
  - DVD
  - Blu-ray
  - Tape
  - DVD DL

1.6 Install various types of CPUs and apply the appropriate cooling methods.

- Socket types
  - Intel: 775, 1155, 1156, 1366, 1150, 2011
  - AMD: AM3, AM3+, FM1, FM2, FM2+
- Characteristics
  - Speeds
  - Cores
  - Cache size/type
  - Hyperthreading
  - Virtualization support
  - Architecture (32-bit vs. 64-bit)
  - Integrated GPU
  - Disable execute bit
- Cooling
  - Heat sink
  - Fans
  - Thermal paste
  - Liquid-based
  - Fanless/passive

1.7 Compare and contrast various PC connection interfaces, their characteristics, and purpose.

- Physical connections
    - USB 1.1 vs. 2.0 vs. 3.0
- Connector types: A, B, mini, micro
    - FireWire 400 vs. FireWire 800
    - SATA1 vs. SATA2 vs. SATA3, eSATA
    - Other connector types
- VGA
- HDMI
- DVI
- Audio
- Analog
- Digital (optical connector)
- RJ-45
- RJ-11
- Thunderbolt
- Wireless connections
    - Bluetooth
    - RF
    - IR
    - NFC
- Characteristics
    - Analog
    - Digital
    - Distance limitations
    - Data transfer speeds
    - Quality
    - DRM
    - Frequencies

1.8 Install a power supply based on given specifications.

- Connector types and their voltages
    - SATA
    - Molex

- 4/8-pin 12v
- PCIe 6/8-pin
- 20-pin
- 24-pin
- Specifications
  - Wattage
  - Dual rail
  - Size
  - Number of connectors
  - ATX
  - Micro-ATX
  - Dual-voltage options

1.9 Given a scenario, select the appropriate components for a custom PC configuration to meet customer specifications or needs.

- Graphic/CAD/CAM design workstation
  - Multicore processor
  - High-end video
  - Maximum RAM
- Audio/video-editing workstation
  - Specialized audio and video card
  - Large fast hard drive
  - Dual monitors
- Virtualization workstation
  - Maximum RAM and CPU cores
- Gaming PC
  - Multicore processor
  - High-end video/specialized GPU
  - High-definition sound card
  - High-end cooling
- Home Theater PC
  - Surround sound audio
  - HDMI output
  - HTPC compact form factor
  - TV tuner

- Standard thick client
  - Desktop applications
  - Meets recommended requirements for selected OS
- Thin client
  - Basic applications
  - Meets minimum requirements for selected OS
  - Network connectivity
- Home Server PC
  - Media streaming
  - File sharing
  - Print sharing
  - Gigabit NIC
  - RAID array

1.10 Compare and contrast types of display devices and their features.

- Types
  - LCD
- TN vs. IPS
- Fluorescent vs. LED backlighting
  - Plasma
  - Projector
  - OLED
- Refresh/frame rates
- Resolution
- Native resolution
- Brightness/lumens
- Analog vs. digital
- Privacy/antiglare filters
- Multiple displays
- Aspect ratios
  - 16:9
  - 16:10
  - 4:3

1.11 Identify common PC connector types and associated cables.

- Display connector types
  - DVI-D
  - DVI-I
  - DVI-A
  - DisplayPort
  - RCA
  - HD15 (i.e., DE15 or DB15)
  - BNC
  - miniHDMI
  - miniDin-6
- Display cable types
  - HDMI
  - DVI
  - VGA
  - Component
  - Composite
  - Coaxial
- Device cables and connectors
  - SATA
  - eSATA
  - USB
  - FireWire (IEEE 1394)
  - PS/2
  - Audio
- Adapters and convertors
  - DVI to HDMI
  - USB A to USB B
  - USB to Ethernet
  - DVI to VGA
  - Thunderbolt to DVI
  - PS/2 to USB
  - HDMI to VGA

1.12 Install and configure common peripheral devices.

- Input devices
    - Mouse
    - Keyboard
    - Scanner
    - Barcode reader
    - Biometric devices
    - Game pads
    - Joysticks
    - Digitizer
    - Motion sensor
    - Touch pads
    - Smart card readers
    - Digital cameras
    - Microphone
    - Webcam
    - Camcorder
    - MIDI-enabled devices
- Output devices
    - Printers
    - Speakers
    - Display devices
- Input & Output devices
    - Touchscreen
    - KVM
    - Smart TV
    - Set-Top Box

1.13 Install SOHO multifunction device/printers and configure appropriate settings.

- Use appropriate drivers for a given operating system
    - Configuration settings
        - Duplex
        - Collate

- Orientation
- Quality
- Device sharing
  - Wired
    - USB
    - Serial
    - Ethernet
  - Wireless
    - Bluetooth
    - 802.11 (a,b,g,n,ac)
    - Infrastructure vs. ad hoc
  - Integrated print server (hardware)
  - Cloud printing/remote printing
- Public/shared devices
  - Sharing local/networked device via operating system settings
    - TCP/Bonjour/AirPrint
  - Data privacy
- User authentication on the device
- Hard drive caching

1.14 Compare and contrast differences between the various print technologies and the associated imaging process.

- Laser
  - Imaging drum, fuser assembly, transfer belt, transfer roller, pickup rollers, separate pads, duplexing assembly
  - Imaging process: processing, charging, exposing, developing, transferring, fusing and cleaning
- Inkjet
  - Ink cartridge, print head, roller, feeder, duplexing assembly, carriage and belt
  - Calibration
- Thermal
  - Feed assembly, heating element
  - Special thermal paper
- Impact
  - Print head, ribbon, tractor feed

- Impact paper
- Virtual
  - Print to file
  - Print to PDF
  - Print to XPS
  - Print to image

1.15 Given a scenario, perform appropriate printer maintenance.

- Laser
  - Replacing toner, applying maintenance kit, calibration, cleaning
- Thermal
  - Replace paper, clean heating element, remove debris
- Impact
  - Replace ribbon, replace print head, replace paper
- Inkjet
  - Clean heads, replace cartridges, calibration, clear jams

2.0 Networking

2.1 Identify the various types of network cables and connectors.

- Fiber
  - Connectors: SC, ST and LC
- Twisted Pair
  - Connectors: RJ-11, RJ-45
  - Wiring standards: T568A, T568B
- Coaxial
  - Connectors: BNC, F-connector

2.2 Compare and contrast the characteristics of connectors and cabling.

- Fiber
  - Types (single-mode vs. multi-mode)
  - Speed and transmission limitations
- Twisted pair
  - Types: STP, UTP, CAT3, CAT5, CAT5e, CAT6, CAT6e, CAT7, plenum, PVC
  - Speed and transmission limitations
  - Splitters and effects on signal quality

- Coaxial
  - Types: RG-6, RG-59
  - Speed and transmission limitations
  - Splitters and effects on signal quality

2.3 Explain the properties and characteristics of TCP/IP.

- IPv4 vs. IPv6
- Public vs. private vs. APIPA/link local
- Static vs. dynamic
- Client-side DNS settings
- Client-side DHCP
- Subnet mask vs. CIDR
- Gateway

2.4 Explain common TCP and UDP ports, protocols, and their purpose.

- Ports
  - 21 – FTP
  - 22 – SSH
  - 23 – TELNET
  - 25 – SMTP
  - 53 – DNS
  - 80 – HTTP
  - 110 – POP3
  - 143 – IMAP
  - 443 – HTTPS
  - 3389 – RDP
  - 137-139, 445 - SMB
  - 548 or 427 - AFP
- Protocols
  - DHCP
  - DNS
  - LDAP
  - SNMP
  - SMB
  - CIFS

- SSH
- AFP
- TCP vs. UDP

2.5 Compare and contrast various Wi-Fi networking standards and encryption types.

- Standards
  - 802.11 a/b/g/n/ac
  - Speeds, distances, and frequencies
- Encryption types
  - WEP, WPA, WPA2, TKIP, AES

2.6 Given a scenario, install and configure SOHO wireless/wired router and apply appropriate settings.

- Channels
- Port forwarding, port triggering
- DHCP (on/off)
- DMZ
- NAT/DNAT
- Basic QoS
- Firmware
- UPnP

2.7 Compare and contrast Internet connection types, network types, and their features.

- Internet connection types
  - Cable
  - DSL
  - Dial-up
  - Fiber
  - Satellite
  - ISDN
  - Cellular
- Tethering
- Mobile hotspot
  - Line-of-sight wireless Internet service

- Network types
  - LAN
  - WAN
  - PAN
  - MAN

2.8 Compare and contrast network architecture devices, their functions, and features.

- Hub
- Switch
- Router
- Access point
- Bridge
- Modem
- Firewall
- Patch panel
- Repeaters/extenders
- Ethernet over Power
- Power over Ethernet injector

2.9 Given a scenario, use appropriate networking tools.

- Crimper
- Cable stripper
- Multimeter
- Tone generator & probe
- Cable tester
- Loopback plug
- Punchdown tool
- Wi-Fi analyzer

3.0 Mobile Devices

3.1 Install and configure laptop hardware and components.

- Expansion options
  - Express card/34
  - Express card/54

- SODIMM
- Flash
- Ports/adapters
  - Thunderbolt
  - DisplayPort
  - USB to RJ-45 dongle
  - USB to Wi-Fi dongle
  - USB to Bluetooth
  - USB optical drive
  - Hardware/device replacement
- Keyboard
- Hard drive
  - SSD vs. hybrid vs. magnetic disk
  - 1.8in vs. 2.5in
- Memory
- Smart card reader
- Optical drive
- Wireless card
- Mini-PCIe
- Screen
- DC jack
- Battery
- Touchpad
- Plastics/frames
- Speaker
- System board
- CPU

3.2 Explain the function of components within the display of a laptop.

- Types
  - LCD
    - TTL vs. IPS
    - Fluorescent vs. LED backlighting
  - OLED

- Wi-Fi antenna connector/placement
- Webcam
- Microphone
- Inverter
- Digitizer

3.3 Given a scenario, use appropriate laptop features.

- Special function keys
  - Dual displays
  - Wireless (on/off)
  - Cellular (on/off)
  - Volume settings
  - Screen brightness
  - Bluetooth (on/off)
  - Keyboard backlight
  - Touch pad (on/off)
  - Screen orientation
  - Media options (fast forward/rewind)
  - GPS (on/off)
  - Airplane mode
- Docking station
- Physical laptop lock and cable lock
- Rotating/removable screens

3.4 Explain the characteristics of various types of other mobile devices.

- Tablets
- Smartphones
- Wearable technology devices
  - Smart watches
  - Fitness monitors
  - Glasses and headsets
- Phablets
- e-Readers
- Smart camera
- GPS

3.5 Compare and contrast accessories and ports of other mobile devices.

- Connection types
  - NFC
  - Proprietary vendor-specific ports (communication/power)
  - microUSB/miniUSB
  - Lightning
  - Bluetooth
  - IR
  - Hotspot/tethering
- Accessories
  - Headsets
  - Speakers
  - Game pads
  - Docking stations
  - Extra battery packs/battery chargers
  - Protective covers/water proofing
  - Credit card readers
  - Memory/MicroSD

4.0 Hardware and Network Troubleshooting

4.1 Given a scenario, troubleshoot common problems related to motherboards, RAM, CPU, and power with appropriate tools.

- Common symptoms
  - Unexpected shutdowns
  - System lockups
  - POST code beeps
  - Blank screen on bootup
  - BIOS time and settings resets
  - Attempts to boot to incorrect device
  - Continuous reboots
  - No power
  - Overheating
  - Loud noise
  - Intermittent device failure

- Fans spin – no power to other devices
- Indicator lights
- Smoke
- Burning smell
- Proprietary crash screens (BSOD/pin wheel)
- Distended capacitors
- Tools
  - Multimeter
  - Power supply tester
  - Loopback plugs
  - POST card/USB

4.2 Given a scenario, troubleshoot hard drives and RAID arrays with appropriate tools.

- Common symptoms
  - Read/write failure
  - Slow performance
  - Loud clicking noise
  - Failure to boot
  - Drive not recognized
  - OS not found
  - RAID not found
  - RAID stops working
  - Proprietary crash screens (BSOD/pin wheel)
  - S.M.A.R.T. errors
- Tools
  - Screwdriver
  - External enclosures
  - CHKDSK
  - FORMAT
  - File recovery software
  - Bootrec
  - Diskpart
  - Defragmentation tool

4.3 Given a scenario, troubleshoot common video, projector, and display issues.

- Common symptoms
  - VGA mode
  - No image on screen
  - Overheat shutdown
  - Dead pixels
  - Artifacts
  - Color patterns incorrect
  - Dim image
  - Flickering image
  - Distorted image
  - Distorted geometry
  - Burn-in
  - Oversized images and icons

4.4 Given a scenario, troubleshoot wired and wireless networks with appropriate tools.

- Common symptoms
  - No connectivity
  - APIPA/link local address
  - Limited connectivity
  - Local connectivity
  - Intermittent connectivity
  - IP conflict
  - Slow transfer speeds
  - Low RF signal
  - SSID not found
- Hardware tools
  - Cable tester
  - Loopback plug
  - Punchdown tools
  - Tone generator and probe
  - Wire strippers
  - Crimper
  - Wireless locator

- Command-line tools
  - PING
  - IPCONFIG/IFCONFIG
  - TRACERT
  - NETSTAT
  - NBTSTAT
  - NET
  - NETDOM
  - NSLOOKUP

4.5 Given a scenario, troubleshoot and repair common mobile device issues while adhering to the appropriate procedures.

- Common symptoms
  - No display
  - Dim display
  - Flickering display
  - Sticking keys
  - Intermittent wireless
  - Battery not charging
  - Ghost cursor/pointer drift
  - No power
  - Num lock indicator lights
  - No wireless connectivity
  - No Bluetooth connectivity
  - Cannot display to external monitor
  - Touchscreen non-responsive
  - Apps not loading
  - Slow performance
  - Unable to decrypt e-mail
  - Extremely short battery life
  - Overheating
  - Frozen system
  - No sound from speakers
  - GPS not functioning
  - Swollen battery

- Disassembling processes for proper re-assembly
  - Document and label cable and screw locations
  - Organize parts
  - Refer to manufacturer resources
  - Use appropriate hand tools

4.6 Given a scenario, troubleshoot printers with appropriate tools.

- Common symptoms
  - Streaks
  - Faded prints
  - Ghost images
  - Toner not fused to the paper
  - Creased paper
  - Paper not feeding
  - Paper jam
  - No connectivity
  - Garbled characters on paper
  - Vertical lines on page
  - Backed up print queue
  - Low memory errors
  - Access denied
  - Printer will not print
  - Color prints in wrong print color
  - Unable to install printer
  - Error codes
  - Printing blank pages
  - No image on printer display
- Tools
  - Maintenance kit
  - Toner vacuum
  - Compressed air
  - Printer spooler

CompTIA 220-902 Exam Objectives

1.0 Windows Operating Systems

1.1 Compare and contrast various features and requirements of Microsoft Operating Systems (Windows Vista, Windows 7, Windows 8, Windows 8.1).

- Features:
    - 32-bit vs. 64-bit
    - Aero, gadgets, user account control, BitLocker, shadow copy, system restore, ready boost, sidebar, compatibility mode, virtual XP mode, easy transfer, administrative tools, defender, Windows firewall, security center, event viewer, file structure and paths, category view vs. classic view, previous versions.
    - Side-by-side apps, Metro UI, Pinning, One Drive, Windows store, Multimonitor task bars, Charms, Start Screen, Power Shell, Live sign in, Action Center.
- Upgrade paths – differences between in-place upgrades, compatibility tools, Windows upgrade OS advisor

1.2 Given a scenario, install Windows PC operating systems using appropriate methods.

- Boot methods
    - USB
    - CD-ROM
    - DVD
    - PXE
    - Solid-state/flash drives
    - Netboot
    - External/hot-swappable drive
    - Internal hard drive (partition)
- Type of installations
    - Unattended installation
    - Upgrade
    - Clean install
    - Repair installation
    - Multiboot
    - Remote network installation
    - Image deployment
    - Recovery partition
    - Refresh/restore

- Partitioning
    - Dynamic
    - Basic
    - Primary
    - Extended
    - Logical
    - GPT
- Filesystem types/formatting
    - ExFAT
    - FAT32
    - NTFS
    - CDFS
    - NFS
    - ext3, ext4
    - Quick format vs. full format
- Load alternate third-party drivers when necessary
- Workgroup vs. domain setup
- Time/date/region/language settings
- Driver installation, software, and windows updates
- Factory recovery partition
- Properly formatted boot drive with the correct partitions/format

1.3 Given a scenario, apply appropriate Microsoft command-line tools.

- TASKKILL
- BOOTREC
- SHUTDOWN
- TASKLIST
- MD
- RD
- CD
- DEL
- FORMAT
- COPY
- XCOPY
- ROBOCOPY

- DISKPART
- SFC
- CHKDSK
- GPUPDATE
- GPRESULT
- DIR
- EXIT
- HELP
- EXPAND
- [command name] /?
- Commands available with standard privileges vs. administrative privileges.

1.4 Given a scenario, use appropriate Microsoft operating system features and tools.

- Administrative
  - Computer management
  - Device manager
  - Users and groups
  - Local security policy
  - Performance monitor
  - Services
  - System configuration
  - Task scheduler
  - Component services
  - Data sources
  - Print management
  - Windows memory diagnostics
  - Windows firewall
  - Advanced security
- MSCONFIG
  - General
  - Boot
  - Services
  - Startup
  - Tools

- Task Manager
  - Applications
  - Processes
  - Performance
  - Networking
  - Users
- Disk management
  - Drive status
  - Mounting
  - Initializing
  - Extending partitions
  - Splitting partitions
  - Shrink partitions
  - Assigning/changing drive letters
  - Adding drives
  - Adding arrays
  - Storage spaces
- Other
  - User State Migration tool (USMT)
  - Windows Easy Transfer
  - Windows Upgrade Advisor
- System utilities
  - REGEDIT
  - COMMAND
  - SERVICES.MSC
  - MMC
  - MSTSC
  - NOTEPAD
  - EXPLORER
  - MSINFO32
  - DXDIAG
  - DEFRAG
  - System restore
  - Windows Update

1.5 Given a scenario, use Windows Control Panel utilities.

- Internet options
  - Connections
  - Security
  - General
  - Privacy
  - Programs
  - Advanced
- Display/display settings
  - Resolution
  - Color depth
  - Refresh rate
- User accounts
- Folder options
  - View hidden files
  - Hide extensions
  - General options
  - View options
- System
  - Performance (virtual memory)
  - Remote settings
  - System protection
- Windows firewall
- Power options
  - Hibernate
  - Power plans
  - Sleep/suspend
  - Standby
- Programs and features
- HomeGroup
- Devices and Printers
- Sound
- Troubleshooting

- Network and Sharing Center
- Device Manager

1.6 Given a scenario, install and configure Windows networking on a client/ desktop.

- HomeGroup vs. WorkGroup
- Domain setup
- Network shares/administrative shares/mapping drives
- Printer sharing vs. network printer mapping
- Establish networking connections
    - VPN
    - Dialups
    - Wireless
    - Wired
    - WWAN (Cellular)
- Proxy settings
- Remote Desktop Connection
- Remote Assistance
- Home vs. Work vs. Public network settings
- Firewall settings
    - Exceptions
    - Configuration
    - Enabling/disabling Windows firewall
- Configuring an alternative IP address in Windows
    - IP addressing
    - Subnet mask
    - DNS
    - Gateway
- Network card properties
    - Half duplex/full duplex/auto
    - Speed
    - Wake-on-LAN
    - QoS
    - BIOS (on-board NIC)

1.7 Perform common preventive maintenance procedures using the appropriate Windows OS tools.

- Best practices
    - Scheduled backups
    - Scheduled disk maintenance
    - Windows updates
    - Patch management
    - Driver/firmware updates
    - Antivirus/antimalware updates
- Tools
    - Backup
    - System restore
    - Recovery image
    - Disk maintenance utilities

2.0 Other Operating Systems and Technologies

2.1 Identify common features and functionality of the Mac OS and Linux operating systems.

- Best practices
    - Scheduled backups
    - Scheduled disk maintenance
    - System updates/App store
    - Patch management
    - Driver/firmware updates
    - Antivirus/antimalware updates
- Tools
    - Backup/Time Machine
    - Restore/snapshot
    - Image recovery
    - Disk maintenance utilities
    - Shell/terminal
    - Screen sharing
    - Force Quit

- Features
  - Multiple desktops/Mission Controls
  - Keychain
  - Spot Light
  - iCloud
  - Gestures
  - Finder
  - Remote disk
  - Dock
  - Boot Camp
- Basic Linux commands
  - ls
  - grep
  - cd
  - shutdown
  - pwd vs. passwd
  - mw
  - cp
  - rm
  - chmod
  - cmkdir
  - chown
  - iwconfig/ifconfig
  - ps
  - q
  - su/sudo
  - apt-get
  - vi
  - dd

2.2 Given a scenario, set up and use client-side virtualization.

- Purpose of virtual machines
- Resource requirements
- Emulator requirements

- Security requirements
- Network requirements
- Hypervisor

2.3 Identify basic cloud concepts.

- SaaS
- IaaS
- PaaS
- Public vs. Private vs. Hybrid vs. Community
- Rapid elasticity
- On-demand
- Resource pooling
- Measured service

2.4 Summarize the properties and purpose of services provided by networked hosts.

- Server roles
    - Web server
    - File server
    - Print server
    - DHCP server
    - DNS server
    - Proxy server
    - Mail server
    - Authentication server
- Internet appliance
    - UTM
    - IDS
    - IPS
- Legacy/embedded systems

2.5 Identify basic features of mobile operating systems.

- Android vs. iOS vs. Windows
    - Open source vs. closed source/vendor specific
    - App source (play store, app store and store)
    - Screen orientation (accelerometer/gyroscope)

- Screen calibration
- GPS and geotracking
- Wi-Fi calling
- Launcher/GUI
- Virtual assistant
- SDK/APK
- Emergency notification
- Mobile payment service

2.6 Install and configure basic mobile device network connectivity and e-mail

- Wireless/cellular data network (enable/disable)
  - Hotspot
  - Tethering
  - Airplane mode
- Bluetooth
  - Enable Bluetooth
  - Enable pairing
  - Find device for pairing
  - Enter appropriate pin code
  - Test connectivity
- Corporate and ISP e-mail configuration
  - POP3
  - IMAP
  - Port and SSL settings
  - Exchange, S/MIME
- Integrated commercial provider e-mail configuration
  - Google/Inbox
  - Yahoo
  - Outlook.com
  - iCloud
- PRI updates/PRL updates/baseband updates
- Radio firmware
- IMEI vs. IMSI
- VPN

2.7 Summarize methods and data related to mobile device synchronization.

- Types of data to synchronize
  - Contacts
  - Programs
  - E-mail
  - Pictures
  - Music
  - Videos
  - Calendar
  - Bookmarks
  - Documents
  - Location data
  - Social media data
  - eBooks
- Synchronization methods
  - Synchronize to the cloud
  - Synchronize to the desktop
- Mutual authentication for multiple services
- Software requirements to install the application on the PC
- Connection types to enable synchronization

3.0 Security

3.1 Identify common security threats and vulnerabilities.

- Malware
  - Spyware
  - Viruses
  - Worms
  - Trojans
  - Rootkits
  - Ransomware
- Phishing
- Spear phishing
- Spoofing
- Social engineering

- Shoulder surfing
- Zero-day attack
- Zombie/botnet
- Brute forcing
- Dictionary attacks
- Non-compliant systems
- Violations of security best practices
- Tailgating
- Man-in-the-middle

3.2 Compare and contrast common prevention methods.

- Physical security
  - Lock doors
  - Mantrap
  - Cable locks
  - Securing physical documents/passwords/shredding
  - Biometrics
  - ID badges
  - Key fobs
  - RFID badge
  - Smart card
  - Tokens
  - Privacy filters
  - Entry control roster
- Digital security
  - Antivirus/antimalware
  - Firewalls
  - User authentication/strong passwords
  - Multifactor authentication
  - Directory permissions
  - VPN
  - DLP
  - Disabling ports
  - Access control lists
  - Smart card

- E-mail filtering
- Trusted/untrusted software sources
- User education/AUP
- Principle of least privilege

3.3 Compare and contrast differences of basic Windows OS security settings.

- User and groups
  - Administrator
  - Power user
  - Guest
  - Standard user
- NTFS vs. share permissions
  - Allow vs. deny
  - Moving vs. copying folders and files
  - File attributes
- Shared files and folders
  - Administrative shares vs. local shares
  - Permission propagation
  - Inheritance
- System files and folders
- User authentication
  - Single sign-on
- Run as administrator vs. standard user
- BitLocker
- BitLocker-To-Go
- EFS

3.4 Given a scenario, deploy and enforce security best practices to secure a workstation.

- Password best practices
  - Setting strong passwords
  - Password expiration
  - Changing default usernames/passwords
  - Screensaver required password
  - BIOS/UEFI passwords
  - Requiring passwords

- Account management
  - Restricting user permissions
  - Login time restrictions
  - Disabling guest account
  - Failed attempts lockout
  - Timeout/screen lock
- Disable autorun
- Data encryption
- Patch/update management

3.5 Compare and contrast various methods for securing mobile devices.

- Screen locks
  - Fingerprint lock
  - Face lock
  - Swipe lock
  - Passcode lock
- Remote wipes
- Locator applications
- Remote backup applications
- Failed login attempts restrictions
- Antivirus/antimalware
- Patching/OS updates
- Biometric authentication
- Full device encryption
- Multifactor authentication
- Authenticator applications
- Trusted sources vs. untrusted sources
- Firewalls
- Policies and procedures
  - BYOD vs. corporate owned
  - Profile security requirements

3.6 Given a scenario, use appropriate data destruction and disposal methods.

- Physical destruction
  - Shredder
  - Drill/Hammer

- Electromagnetic (degaussing)
- Incineration
- Certificate of destruction
- Recycling or repurposing best practices
  - Low level format vs. standard format
  - Overwrite
  - Drive wipe

3.7 Given a scenario, secure SOHO wireless and wired networks.

- Wireless specific
  - Changing default SSID
  - Setting encryption
  - Disabling SSID broadcast
  - Antenna and access point placement
  - Radio power levels
  - WPS
- Change default usernames and passwords
- Enable MAC filtering
- Assign static IP addresses
- Firewall settings
- Port forwarding/mapping
- Disabling ports
- Content filtering/parental controls
- Update firmware
- Physical security

4.0 Software Troubleshooting

4.1 Given a scenario, troubleshoot PC operating system problems with appropriate tools.

- Common symptoms
  - Proprietary crash screens (BSOD/pin wheel)
  - Failure to boot
  - Improper shutdown
  - Spontaneous shutdown/restart
  - Device fails to start/detected
  - Missing dll message

- Services fails to start
- Compatibility error
- Slow system performance
- Boots to safe mode
- File fails to open
- Missing NTLDR
- Missing Boot.ini
- Missing operating system
- Missing Graphical Interface
- Missing GRUB/LILO
- Kernel panic
- Graphical Interface fails to load
- Multiple monitor misalignment/orientation
- Tools
  - BIOS/UEFI
  - SFC
  - Logs
  - Recovery console
  - Repair disks
  - Pre-installation environments
  - MSCONFIG
  - DEFRAG
  - REGSRV32
  - REGEDIT
  - Event viewer
  - Safe mode
  - Command prompt
  - Emergency repair disk
  - Automated system recovery
  - Uninstall/reinstall/repair

4.2 Given a scenario, troubleshoot common PC security issues with appropriate tools and best practices.

- Common symptoms
  - Pop-ups

- Browser redirection
- Security alerts
- Slow performance
- Internet connectivity issues
- PC/OS lock up
- Application crash
- OS updates failures
- Rogue antivirus
- Spam
- Renamed system files
- Files disappearing
- File permission changes
- Hijacked e-mail
- Responses from users regarding e-mail
- Automated replies from unknown sent e-mail
  - Access denied
  - Invalid certificate (trusted root CA)
- Tools
  - Antivirus software
  - Antimalware software
  - Recovery console
  - Terminal
  - System restore/snapshot
  - Pre-installation environments
  - Event viewer
  - Refresh/restore
  - MSCONFIG/safe boot
- Best practice procedure for malware removal
  1. Identify malware symptoms
  2. Quarantine infected system
  3. Disable system restore (in Windows)
  4. Remediate infected systems
     a. Update antimalware software
     b. Scan and removal techniques (safe mode, pre-installation environment)

5. Schedule scans and run updates

6. Enable system restore and create restore point (in Windows)

7. Educate end user

4.3 Given a scenario, troubleshoot common mobile OS and application issues with appropriate tools.

- Common symptoms
  - Dim display
  - Intermittent wireless
  - No wireless connectivity
  - No Bluetooth connectivity
  - Cannot broadcast to external monitor
  - Touchscreen non-responsive
  - Apps not loading
  - Slow performance
  - Unable to decrypt e-mail
  - Extremely short battery life
  - Overheating
  - Frozen system
  - No sound from speakers
  - Inaccurate touchscreen response
  - System lockout
- Tools
  - Hard reset
  - Soft reset
  - Close running applications
  - Reset to factory default
  - Adjust configurations/settings
  - Uninstall/reinstall apps
  - Force stop

4.4 Given a scenario, troubleshoot common mobile OS and application security issues with appropriate tools.

- Common symptoms
  - Signal drop/weak signal
  - Power drain

- Slow data speeds
- Unintended Wi-Fi connection
- Unintended Bluetooth pairing
- Leaked personal files/data
- Data transmission overlimit
- Unauthorized account access
- Unauthorized root access
- Unauthorized location tracking
- Unauthorized camera/microphone activation
- High resource utilization
- Tools
  - Antimalware
  - App scanner
  - Factory reset/clean install
  - Uninstall/reinstall apps
  - Wi-Fi analyzer
  - Force stop
  - Cell tower analyzer
  - Backup/restore
- iTunes/iCloud/Apple Configurator
- Google sync
- One Drive

5.0 Operational Procedures

5.1 Given a scenario, use appropriate safety procedures.

- Equipment grounding
- Proper component handling and storage
  - Antistatic bags
  - ESD straps
  - ESD mats
  - Self-grounding
- Toxic waste handling
  - Batteries
  - Toner
  - CRT

- Personal safety
  - Disconnect power before repairing PC
  - Remove jewelry
  - Lifting techniques
  - Weight limitations
  - Electrical fire safety
  - Cable management
  - Safety goggles
  - Air filter mask
- Compliance with local government regulations

5.2 Given a scenario with potential environmental impacts, apply the appropriate controls.

- MSDS documentation for handling and disposal
- Temperature, humidity-level awareness, and proper ventilation
- Power surges, brownouts, blackouts
  - Battery backup
  - Surge suppressor
- Protection from airborne particles
  - Enclosures
  - Air filters/mask
- Dust and debris
  - Compressed air
  - Vacuums
- Compliance to local government regulations

5.3 Summarize the process of addressing prohibited content/activity and explain privacy, licensing, and policy concepts.

- Incident response
  - First response
- Identify
- Report through proper channels
- Data/device preservation
  - Use of documentation/documentation changes
  - Chain of custody

- Tracking of evidence/documenting process
- Licensing/DRM/EULA
    - Open source vs. commercial license
    - Personal license vs. enterprise licenses
- Personally Identifiable Information
- Follow corporate end-user policies and security best practices

5.4 Demonstrate proper communication techniques and professionalism.

- Use proper language – avoid jargon, acronyms, slang when applicable
- Maintain a positive attitude/project confidence
- Actively listen (taking notes) and avoid interrupting the customer
- Be culturally sensitive
    - Use appropriate professional titles, when applicable
- Be on time (if late contact the customer)
- Avoid distractions
    - Personal calls
    - Texting/social media sites
    - Talking to co-workers while interacting with customers
    - Personal interruptions
- Dealing with difficult customer or situation
    - Do not argue with customers and/or be defensive
    - Avoid dismissing customer problems
    - Avoid being judgmental
    - Clarify customer statements (ask open-ended questions to narrow the scope of the problem, restate the issue or question to verify understanding)
    - Do not disclose experiences via social media outlets
- Set and meet expectations/timeline and communicate status with the customer
    - Offer different repair/replacement options if applicable
    - Provide proper documentation on the services provided
    - Follow up with customer/user at a later date to verify satisfaction
- Deal appropriately with customer's confidential and private materials
    - Located on a computer, desktop, printer, etc.

5.5 Given a scenario, explain the troubleshooting theory.

- Always consider corporate policies, procedures, and impacts before implementing changes.

    1. Identify the problem
        - Question the user and identify user changes to computer and perform backups before making changes
    2. Establish a theory of probable cause (question the obvious)
        - If necessary, conduct external or internal research based on symptoms
    3. Test the theory to determine cause
        - Once theory is confirmed, determine next steps to resolve problem
        - If theory is not confirmed, re-establish new theory or escalate
    4. Establish a plan of action to resolve the problem and implement the solution
    5. Verify full system functionality and if applicable implement preventive measures
    6. Document findings, actions, and outcomes

CompTIA A+ 220-901

I

Hardware

COMPTIA A+ ESSENTIALS EXAM OBJECTIVES COVERED IN THIS CHAPTER:

✓ **1.1 Given a scenario, configure settings and use BIOS/UEFI tools on a PC.**

- Firmware upgrades – flash BIOS
- BIOS component information (RAM, hard drive, optical drive, CPU)
- BIOS configurations (boot sequence, enabling and disabling devices, date/time, clock speeds, virtualization support, BIOS security [passwords, drive encryption: TPM, LoJack, secure boot])
- Built-in diagnostics
- Monitoring (temperature monitoring, fan speeds, intrusion detection/notification, voltage, clock, bus speed)

✓ **1.2 Explain the importance of motherboard components, their purpose, and properties.**

- Sizes (ATX, micro-ATX, mini-ATX, ITX)
- Expansion slots (PCI, PCI-X, PCIe, miniPCI)
- RAM slots
- CPU sockets
- Chipsets (north bridge, south bridge)
- CMOS battery
- Power connections and types
- Fan connectors
- Front/top-panel connectors (USB, audio, power button, power light, drive activity lights, reset button)
- Bus speeds

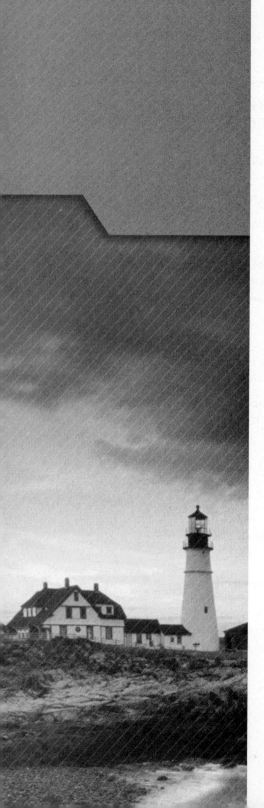

✓ **1.3 Compare and contrast various RAM types and their features.**

- Types (DDR, DDR2, DDR3, SODIMM, DIMM, parity vs. non-parity, ECC vs. non-ECC)
- RAM configurations (single channel vs. dual channel vs. triple channel)
- Single-sided vs. double-sided
- Buffered vs. unbuffered
- RAM compatibility

✓ **1.4 Install and configure PC expansion cards.**

- Sound cards
- Video cards
- Network cards
- USB cards
- FireWire cards
- Thunderbolt cards
- Storage cards
- Modem cards
- Wireless/cellular cards
- TV tuner cards
- Video capture cards
- Riser cards

✓ **1.5 Install and configure storage devices and use appropriate media.**

- Optical drives (CD-ROM/CD-RW, DVD-ROM/DVD-RW/DVD-RW DL, Blu-ray, BD-R, BD-RE)
- Magnetic hard drive drives (5,400 rpm, 7,200 rpm, 10,000 rpm, 15,000 rpm)
- Hot-swappable drives
- Solid-state/flash drives (Compact Flash, SD, micro-SD, mini-SD, xD, SSD, hybrid, eMMC)
- RAID types (0, 1, 5, 10)
- Tape drive
- Media capacity (CD, CD-RW, DVD-RW, DVD, Blu-ray, tape, DVD DL)

✓ **1.6 Install various types of CPUs and apply the appropriate cooling methods.**

- Socket types (Intel: 775, 1155, 1156, 1366, 1150, 2011, AMD: AM3, AM3+, FM1, FM2, FM2+)
- Characteristics (speeds, cores, cache size/type, hyperthreading, virtualization support, architecture [32-bit vs. 64-bit])
- Integrated GPU
- Disable execute bit
- Cooling (heat sink, fans, thermal paste, liquid-based, fanless/passive)

✓ **1.7 Compare and contrast various PC connection interfaces, their characteristics, and purpose.**

- Physical connections (USB 1.1 vs. 2.0 vs. 3.0, connector types [A, B, mini, micro])
- Firewire 400 vs. Firewire 800
- SATA1 vs. SATA2 vs. SATA3, eSATA
- Other connector types (serial, parallel, VGA, HDMI, DVI, audio [analog, digital/optical connector], RJ-45, RJ-11, Thunderbolt)
- Wireless connections (Bluetooth, RF, IR, NFC)
- Characteristics (analog, digital, distance limitations, data transfer speeds, quality, DRM, frequencies)

✓ **1.8 Install a power supply based on given specifications.**

- Connector types and their voltages (SATA, Molex, 4/8-pin 12v, PCIe 6/8-pin, 20-pin, 24-pin)
- Specifications (wattage, dual rail, size, number of connectors, ATX, micro-ATX, dual voltage options)

✓ **1.9 Given a scenario, select the appropriate components for a custom PC configuration to meet customer specifications or needs.**

- Graphic/CAD/CAM design workstation (multicore processor, high-end video, maximum RAM)
- Audio/video-editing workstation (specialized audio and video card, large fast hard drive, dual monitors)

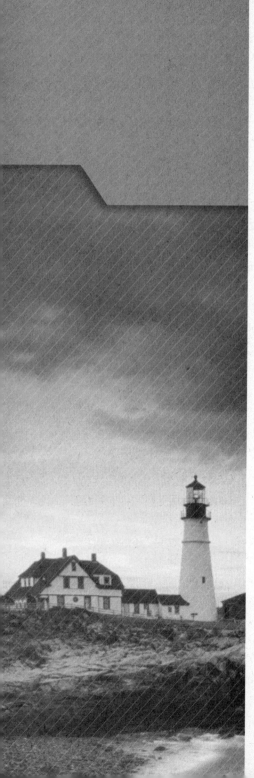

- Virtualization workstation (maximum RAM and CPU cores)
- Gaming PC (multicore processor, high-end video/specialized GPU, high-definition sound card, high-end cooling)
- Home theater PC (surround sound audio, HDMI, output, HTPC compact form factor, TV tuner)
- Standard thick client (desktop applications, meets recommended requirements for selected OS)
- Thin client (basic applications, meets minimum requirements for selected OS, network connectivity)
- Home server PC (media streaming, file sharing, print sharing, Gigabit NIC, RAID array)

✓ **1.10 Compare and contrast types of display devices and their features.**

- Types (LCD [TN vs. IPS, fluorescent vs. LED backlighting], plasma, projector, OLED)
- Refresh/frame rates
- Resolution
- Native resolution
- Brightness/lumens
- Analog vs. digital
- Privacy/antiglare filters
- Multiple displays
- Aspect ratios (16:9, 16:10, 4:3)

✓ **1.11 Identify common PC connector types and associated cables.**

- Display connector types (DVI-D, DVI-I, DVI-A, DisplayPort, RCA, HD-15 [i.e., DE-15 or DB-15], BNC, miniHDMI, miniDIN-6)
- Display cable types (HDMI, DVI, VGA, component, composite, coaxial)
- Device cables and connectors (SATA, eSATA, USB, FireWire [IEEE 1394], PS/2, audio)
- Adaptors and convertors (DVI to HDMI, USB A to USB B, USB to Ethernet, DVI to VGA, Thunderbolt to DVI, PS/2 to USB, HDMI to VGA)

✓ **1.12 Install and configure common peripheral devices.**

- Input devices (mouse, keyboard, scanner, barcode reader, biometric devices, game pads, joysticks, digitizer, motion sensor, touch pads, smart card readers, digital cameras, microphone, webcam, camcorder, MIDI-enabled devices)

- Output devices (printers, speakers, display devices)

- Input and output devices (touchscreen, KVM, smart TV, set-top box)

✓ **1.13 Install SOHO multifunction devices/printers and configure appropriate settings.**

- Using appropriate drivers for a given operating system

- Configuration settings (duplex, collate, orientation, quality)

- Device sharing (wired [USB, serial, Ethernet], wireless [Bluetooth, 802.11, infrastructure vs. ad hoc])

- Integrated print server (hardware)

- Cloud printing/remote printing

- Public/shared devices (sharing local/networked device via operating system settings [TCP/Bonjour/AirPrint], data privacy, user authentication on the device, hard drive caching)

✓ **1.14 Compare and contrast differences between the various print technologies and the associated imaging process.**

- Laser (imaging drum, fuser assembly, transfer belt, transfer roller, pickup rollers, separate pads, duplexing assembly)

- Inkjet (ink cartridge, print head, roller, feeder, duplexing assembly, carriage and belt, calibration)

- Thermal (feed assembly, heating element, special thermal paper)

- Impact (print head, ribbon, tractor feed, impact paper)

- Virtual (print to file, print to PDF, print to XPS, print to image)

✓ **1.15 Given a scenario, perform appropriate printer maintenance.**

- Laser (replacing toner, applying maintenance kit, calibration, cleaning)

- Thermal (replace paper, clean heating element, remove debris)

- Impact (replace ribbon, replace print head, replace paper)

- Inkjet (clean heads, replace cartridges, calibration, clear jams)

This chapter will focus on the exam topics related to PC hardware. It will follow the structure of the CompTIA A+ 220-901 exam blueprint, objective 1, and it will explore the 15 subobjectives that you will need to master before taking the exam.

1.1 Given a Scenario, Configure Settings and Use BIOS/UEFI Tools on a PC

PCs and other devices that use an operating system usually also contain firmware that provides low-level instructions to the device even in the absence of an operating system. This firmware, called either the Basic Input/Output System (BIOS) or the Unified Extensible Firmware Interface (UEFI), contains settings that can be manipulated as well as diagnostic utilities that can be used to monitor the device. This section discusses those settings and utilities. The topics addressed in objective 1.1 include the following:

- Firmware upgrades—flash BIOS
- BIOS component information
- BIOS configurations
- Built-in diagnostics
- Monitoring

Firmware Upgrades—Flash BIOS

Computer BIOSs don't go bad; they just become out of date or contain bugs. In the case of a bug, an upgrade will correct the problem. An upgrade may also be necessary when the BIOS doesn't support some component that you would like to install—a larger hard drive or a different type of processor, for instance.

Most of today's BIOSs are written to an electrically erasable programmable read-only memory (EEPROM) chip and can be updated through the use of software. Each manufacturer has its own method for accomplishing this. Check out the documentation for complete details. Regardless of the exact procedure, the process is referred to as *flashing* the BIOS. It means the old instructions are erased from the EEPROM chip and the new instructions are written to the chip.

UEFI is a standard firmware interface for PCs, designed to replace BIOS. Some advantages of UEFI include the following:

- Better security, which protects the pre-boot process
- Faster startup times and resuming from hibernation
- Support for drives larger than 2.2 TB
- Support for 64-bit firmware device drivers
- Capability to use BIOS with UEFI hardware

UEFI can also be updated by using an update utility from the motherboard vendor. In many cases, the steps are as follows:

1. Download the update file to a flash drive.
2. Insert the flash drive and reboot the machine.
3. Use the specified key sequence to enter the BIOS settings.
4. If necessary, disable secure boot.
5. Save the changes and reboot.
6. Reenter the BIOS settings.
7. Choose boot options, and boot from the flash drive.
8. Follow the specific directions with the update to locate the upgrade file on the flash drive.
9. Execute the file (usually by typing **flash**).
10. While the update is completing, ensure you maintain power to the device.

BIOS Component

At startup, the BIOS will attempt to detect the devices and components at its disposal. The information that it gathers, along with the current state of the components, will be available for review in the BIOS settings. Some of the components and the types of information available with respect to these devices and components are covered in this section.

You can view and adjust a computer's base-level settings through the CMOS Setup program, which you access by pressing a certain key at startup, such as F1 or Delete (depending on the system). The most common settings to adjust in CMOS include port settings (parallel, serial, USB), drive types, boot sequence, date and time, and virus/security protections. The variable settings that are made through the CMOS Setup program are stored in nonvolatile random access memory (NVRAM), while the base instructions that cannot be changed (the BIOS) are stored on an EEPROM chip. NVRAM is memory that does not lose its content when power is lost to the machine. Figure 1.1 shows an example of NVRAM on a motherboard.

FIGURE 1.1   NVRAM

RAM

Most systems today detect the random access memory (RAM) amount and speed automatically. Some motherboards can use different types of RAM, such as parity and nonparity, or different speeds, and the CMOS Setup program may provide the opportunity to change those settings. Increasingly, however, RAM settings are becoming a read-only part of CMOS Setup programs because the system will detect additional memory added or a change in memory type. This does not preclude you from ensuring you are installing the correct type of memory for the system.

Hard Drive

Some CMOS Setup programs have a feature that polls the IDE channels and provides information about the IDE devices attached to them. You can use this feature to gather the settings for a hard disk. However, most hard disks these days are fully Plug and Play, so they automatically report themselves to the CMOS Setup.

Hard drives can be autodetected by most systems if the IDE setting is set to Auto. The settings detected may include the drive's capacity; its geometry, meaning cylinders, heads, and sectors (CHS); and its preferred programmed input/output (PIO), direct memory access (DMA), or UltraDMA operating mode. You can also configure a hard drive by entering its CHS values manually, but doing so is almost never necessary anymore.

CHS is also called the *drive geometry* because together these three numbers determine how much data the disk can hold. Most CMOS Setup programs are able to automatically detect the CHS values.

Optical Drive

Optical drives, such as CD, CD-R, CD-RW, and DVD players, are also detected and reported by the BIOS. You can even set the computer to boot from one of these drives if desired (see the section "Boot Sequence" later in this chapter). When you do that, in most cases the drives will be listed as CD-ROM or CD-ROM/DVD.

CPU

In most modern systems, the BIOS detects the CPU type and speed automatically, so any CPU settings in CMOS Setup are likely to be read-only. Most operating systems provide utilities for gathering information about the CPU in the computer, but if the computer will not boot or there is no operating system, then viewing the CPU information in the BIOS can be a valuable option.

BIOS Configurations

When any of the changes listed in the following section are made to any of the BIOS configurations, it is important that the program be exited properly to save the changes. The CMOS Setup program includes an Exit command, with options that include Save Changes and Discard Changes. In most programs, Esc is a shortcut for exiting and discarding changes, and F10 is a common shortcut for exiting and saving changes.

Boot Sequence

Each system has a default boot order, which is the order in which it checks the drives for a valid operating system to which it can boot. Usually, this order is set for the hard disk and then CD-ROM, but these components can be placed in any boot order. For example, you might set CD-ROM first to boot from a Windows 7 Setup disk on a system that already contains an operating system. If you receive an error message when booting, always check the CD-ROM, and if a nonsystem disk is present, remove it and reboot.

Enabling and Disabling Devices

In CMOS Setup, you can enable or disable integrated components, such as built-in video cards, sound cards, or network cards. You may disable them in order to replace them with different models on expansion boards, for example.

You can also disable the onboard I/O ports for the motherboard, including parallel, serial, and USB. Depending on the utility, there may also be settings that enable or disable USB keyboard usage, Wake on LAN, or other special features.

In addition to enabling or disabling legacy parallel ports, you can assign an operational mode to the port. Table 1.1 lists the common modes for a parallel port. When you're troubleshooting parallel port problems, sometimes trying a different mode will help. Some legacy systems do not allow onboard devices to be disabled. If this is the case, if an onboard device fails, the entire motherboard may need to be replaced.

TABLE 1.1   Parallel port settings

Setting	Description	Use
Enhanced parallel port (EPP)	Supports bidirectional communication and transfer rates up to 2 Mbps	Newer inkjet and laser printers that can utilize bidirectional communication and scanners
Enhanced capabilities port (ECP)	Supports bidirectional communication (specified in the IEEE 1284 standard) and achieves transfer rates of 2.5 Mbps using direct memory access	Newer inkjet and laser printers that can utilize bidirectional communication, connectivity devices, and scanners
Standard parallel port (SPP, also called Centronics)	Supports bidirectional communication using unidirectional data lines	Older inkjet and laser printers and slower scanners

Date/Time

One of the most basic things you can change in CMOS Setup is the system date and time. You can also change this from within the operating system. When the PC is not keeping correct time or date when turned off, it is usually a CMOS battery issue and may include a warning that the battery is soon going to die. In the absence of the PC receiving time and date updates from a time server such as a Network Time Protocol (NTP) server, the time kept in the CMOS is the time source for the computer.

Clock Speeds

Clock speed is a measurement of the rate at which the clock signal oscillates; it is expressed in millions of cycles per second or megahertz. The motherboard must be set to utilize the proper clock settings for the CPU installed in the computer. The BIOS usually detects the type of CPU and automatically sets the proper timings. In some older systems, you may have to use jumpers to set the correct clock speed and CPU.

External Speed (Clock Speed)   The *clock speed*, or *external speed*, which is usually expressed in megahertz or gigahertz, is the speed at which the motherboard communicates with the CPU. It's determined by the motherboard, and its cadence is set by a quartz crystal (the system crystal) that generates regular electrical pulses.

Internal Speed   The *internal speed* is the maximum speed at which the CPU can perform its internal operations. This may be the same as the motherboard's speed (the external speed), but it's more likely to be a multiple of it. For example, a CPU may have an internal speed of 1.3 GHz but an external speed of 133 MHz. That means for every tick of the system crystal's clock, the CPU has 10 internal ticks of its own clock.

When the proper CPU speed is known, you must make sure the relationship between the speed of the CPU and that of the motherboard bus is correct. This is done with a value called the *multiplier*. Although the bus speed can also be manipulated, usually it is set to accommodate the required speed of the memory to be used, and so it is more likely you will be using the multiplier to achieve the proper relationship between the CPU speed and the bus speed.

For example, if you have a processor that has a CPU speed of 1.82 GHz, the proper settings for the BIOS would be a bus speed of 166 MHz and a multiplier of 11 (166 MHz × 11 = 1.826 GHz). So if the bus needed to be 166 MHz, you would set the multiplier for 11. On the other hand, if you changed the bus speed to 332 MHz (just a random example), the closest multiplier would be 5.5 to maintain 1.826 GHz (332 MHz × 5.5 = 1.826 GHz). When setting the speed of either is required, refer to the documentation from the CPU and motherboard.

Virtualization Support

Many computers, especially servers, host virtual machines (VMs). These are fully functional operating systems running in their own environment. In many cases, the motherboard and associated BIOS settings need no alteration to provide services to these VMs.

However, some of the newer virtualization products, for example, Microsoft Hyper-V, require that the motherboard support *hardware-assisted virtualization*. This is because in these cases the virtualization product is not installed on top of a regular operating system but is installed directly on bare metal—that is, as an integral part of the operating system, as in Windows Server 2012 R2.

The benefit derived from the virtualization product (also called a *hypervisor*) using hardware-assisted virtualization is it allows the hypervisor to dynamically allocate memory and CPU to the VMs as required. When the motherboard and the BIOS support this technology, you must ensure that it is enabled. Figure 1.2 shows an example of the settings.

FIGURE 1.2   BIOS virtualization

BIOS Security

A number of security features are built into most BIOSs. They include BIOS passwords, drive encryption, Trusted Platform Module (TPM), and LoJack. These items are discussed in this section.

BIOS Passwords   In most CMOS Setup programs, you can set a supervisor password. Doing so requires a password to be entered in order to use the CMOS Setup program, effectively locking out users from making changes to it. You may also be able to set a user password, which restricts the PC from booting unless the password is entered.

To reset a forgotten password, you can remove the CMOS battery to reset everything. There also may be a Reset jumper on the motherboard.

Drive Encryption   Many operating systems provide the ability to encrypt an entire volume or drive, protecting a mobile device's data in the event of theft. A good example of this is BitLocker, which is available in Windows Vista and Windows 7. The drives are encrypted with encryption keys, and the proper keys are required to boot the device and access the data.

BitLocker can be used with a TPM chip (discussed in the next section), but it is not required. When this feature is in effect with no TPM chip, the keys are stored on a USB drive that must be presented during startup to allow access to the drives. Without the USB drive holding the key, the device will not boot.

TPM Chips   When the device has a TPM chip present on the motherboard, additional security and options become available. First the chip contains the keys that unlock the drives. When the computer boots, the TPM chip unlocks the drive only after it compares hashes of the drive to snapshots of the drive taken earlier. If any changes have been made or tampering has been done to the Windows installation, the TPM chip will not unlock the drives.

Moreover, you can (and should) combine this with a PIN entered at startup or a key located in a USB drive. In this scenario, the computer will not start unless the hashes pass the test and the PIN or key is provided.

LoJack   LoJack is a product made by Absolute Software that allows you to remotely locate, lock, and delete the data on a mobile device when it is stolen. It is a small piece of software that embeds itself on the computer and is difficult to detect. Once activated, it stays in contact with a monitoring center, allowing you to send the commands to lock and delete data via the center. Not only can you protect the data in this fashion, but also it will gather forensic data that can help to locate the device and aid in its recovery.

Secure Boot   Secure Boot is a standard adopted by many venders that requires the operating system to check the integrity of all system files before allowing the boot process to proceed. By doing so, it protects against the alteration or corruption of these system files. As with any emerging technology, issues have already been discovered that can enable a hacker to not only bypass Secure Boot but to also change a key value in the settings that will "brick" the device (render it useless).

Built-in Diagnostics

Although you may not realize it, every time you start the computer, built-in diagnostics are at work. Every computer has a diagnostic program built into its BIOS called the *power-on self-test* (POST). When you turn on the computer, it executes this set of diagnostics. Many steps are involved in the POST, but they happen quickly, they're invisible to the user, and they vary among BIOS versions. The steps include checking the CPU, checking the RAM, checking for the presence of a video card, and so on. The main reason to be aware of the POST's existence is that if it encounters a problem, the boot process stops. Being able to determine at what point the problem occurred can help you troubleshoot.

One way to determine the source of a problem is to listen for a *beep code*. This is a series of beeps from the computer's speaker. The number, duration, and pattern of the beeps can sometimes tell you what component is causing the problem. However, the beeps differ depending on the BIOS manufacturer and version, so you must look up the beep code in a chart for your particular BIOS. Different BIOS manufacturers use the beeping differently. AMI BIOS, for example, relies on a raw number of beeps and uses patterns of short and long beeps.

Another way to determine a problem during the POST routine is to use a *POST card*. This is a circuit board that fits into an Industry Standard Architecture (ISA) or Peripheral Component Interconnect (PCI) expansion slot in the motherboard and reports numeric codes as the boot process progresses. Each of those codes corresponds to a particular component being checked. If the POST card stops at a certain number, you can look up that number in the manual that came with the card to determine the problem.

 BIOS Central is a website containing charts detailing the beep codes and POST error codes for many different BIOS manufacturers.

Monitoring

By viewing the information provided in the BIOS, basic monitoring of the many items can be done with varying degrees of certainty. It is simply a matter of navigating the menu-based BIOS program and locating the proper screen that provides the information. Examples are provided in the following sections.

Temperature Monitoring

Temperature is probably the most important item to monitor. When components like the CPU overheat, bad things start to occur, such as repeated reboots. Figure 1.3 shows an example of the values for the CPU. Technicians should retain baseline temperatures for these items. Baseline temperatures should include idle temperature and load temperature baselines. Intel processors run at a cooler temperature than AMD.

FIGURE 1.3 Temperature monitoring

Fan Speeds

The speed at which various fans are operating can also be displayed in the BIOS. There can be a CPU fan, as well as one or more system fans. (See Figure 1.3.) Programs are available that monitor this for you and can send alerts. This is particularly important for servers in a data center.

Intrusion Detection/Notification

It is also possible to enable intrusion detection, which will indicate to you whether the chassis has been opened. This may be referred to as the chassis intrusion detection or possibly the case open status, as shown in Figure 1.3, where this function has been disabled.

Voltage

You can also monitor and change the voltage settings in the BIOS. Be cautious in changing these settings because improper settings can damage the system or shorten the life of the CPU. Possible settings include the following:

- CPU voltage
- Memory voltage, which will typically be 1.5 volts
- Motherboard voltage
- Voltage of the graphics card

These are just a few examples. Figure 1.4 shows an example of these and many more voltage settings.

FIGURE 1.4   Voltage settings

Parameters	Setting	Current Va.
CPU Core	[Auto]	1.30V
CPU FSB	[Auto]	1.2V
Memory	[1.900V]	1.900V
nForce SPP	[Auto]	1.30V
nForce MCP	[Auto]	1.500V
HT nForce SPP <-> MCP	[Auto]	1.20V
nForce MCP Auxiliary	[Auto]	1.50V
GTLVREF Lane 0	[Auto]	+00mv
GTLVREF Lane 1	[Auto]	+00mv
GTLVREF Lane 2	[Auto]	+00mv
GTLVREF Lane 3	[Auto]	+00mv

Clock

The CMOS clock is located on the computer's motherboard and keeps time when the computer is off. The operating system gets its time from the BIOS clock at boot time. This clock can be set using the BIOS if it is not correct. Figure 1.5 shows the time setting.

FIGURE 1.5   Clock

Phoenix - Award WorkstationBIOS CMOS Setup Utility Standard CMOS Features		
Date (mm:dd:yy)	Nov 28 2011	Item Help
Time (hh:mm:ss)	15 : 4 : 23	

Bus Speed

The processor's ability to communicate with the rest of the system's components relies on the supporting circuitry. Part of the system board's underlying circuitry is called the *bus*. The computer's bus moves information into and out of the processor and other devices. A bus allows all devices to communicate with one another. The motherboard has several buses. The *external data bus* carries information to and from the CPU and is the fastest bus on the system. The *address bus* typically runs at the same speed as the external data bus and carries data to and from RAM. The address bus gives the address to which the data should go. The data bus uses the address supplied by the address bus and carries the data to the specified location. The PCI, AGP, and ISA interfaces also have their own buses with their own widths and speeds. With newer architectures, the system or front-side bus (FSB) connects the CPU to the north bridge (or memory) hub. The back-side bus (BSB) connects the CPU with the Level 2 (L2) cache, also called the *secondary* or *external* cache. The memory bus connects the north bridge (or memory) hub to RAM.

The bus speed, like the CPU speed, can also be set. (See the section on the relationship between the bus speed, the CPU speed, and the multiplier in the section "Clock Speeds.") Usually, this should be left alone because it is normally set to a setting proper for the memory, but it can be changed. In many systems, this must be done with jumpers on the motherboard.

Exam Essentials

Flash the BIOS or UEFI.   Understand the process for upgrading the BIOS or UEFI as the case may be. This usually involves running a program from the BIOS vendor that erases the instructions from the EEPROM chip and writes the new instructions to the same chip.

Identify components reported in the BIOS.   These include RAM, hard drives, optical drives, and the CPU. Information is listed for each, and changes can be made to selected settings for each component.

Describe available BIOS configurations.   The settings that can be made using the BIOS include the boot sequence, the enabling and disabling of devices, setting the date and time, adjusting clock speeds, enabling and disabling virtualization features if supported, and setting BIOS passwords.

Identify built-in diagnostic tools in the BIOS.   The power-on self-test is the most important diagnostic testing that occurs. It runs every time the PC is started and will report—either with a displayed error message or with beep tones—any problem components.

Monitor with the BIOS.   Utilize the BIOS display to monitor temperature, fan speeds, intrusion detection messages, voltage settings, the system clock, and bus speed settings.

1.2 Explain the Importance of Motherboard Components, Their Purpose, and Properties

The motherboard is the platform through which all the connected components communicate. The motherboard provides basic services needed for the machine to operate and provides communication channels through which connected devices such as the processor, memory, disk drives, and expansion devices communicate.

This section discusses those components. The topics addressed in objective 1.2 include the following:

▪ Sizes

▪ Expansion slots

▪ RAM slots

▪ CPU sockets

▪ Chipsets

▪ CMOS battery

▪ Power connections and types

▪ Fan connectors

- Front-panel connectors
- Bus speeds

> The figures in this section are representative of what can be expected. It all depends on the motherboard manufacturer. Consult the documentation for your motherboard.

Sizes

The spine of the computer is the *system board*, or *motherboard*. This component is made of green or brown fiberglass and is placed in the bottom or side of the case. It's the most important component in the computer because it connects all the other components of a PC together. On the system board you'll find the central processing unit (CPU), underlying circuitry, expansion slots, video components, RAM slots, and a variety of other chips. There are a number of different sizes or *form factors* of motherboards, which will be discussed in this section.

ATX

An older but still used form factor, Advanced Technology Extended (ATX), provided many design improvements over the previous version, the AT. These improvements include I/O ports built directly into the side of the motherboard, the CPU positioned so that the power-supply fan helps cool it, and the ability for the PC to be turned on and off via software. It uses a PS/2-style connector for the keyboard and mouse, which is rarely used today because USB keyboards are used. Newer ATX models have removed PS/2 connectors. The expansion slots are parallel to the narrow edge of the board. See Figure 1.6.

FIGURE 1.6   An ATX-style motherboard

Micro-ATX

The micro-ATX was released in 1997 for smaller—and typically cheaper—systems. It became popular in later years in low-cost PCs. The maximum size of a micro-ATX motherboard is 244 mm square, compared to 305 mm×244 mm for a standard ATX motherboard. The micro-ATX is backward compatible with the ATX. Micro-ATX motherboards have a maximum of four expansion slots and four DIMM slots.

Mini-ATX

The mini-ATX has dimensions of 15×15 cm (5.9×5.9 in) and is slightly smaller than the mini-ITX (discussed in the next section). It was originally part of the ATX specification but was removed after the introduction of micro-ATX. It uses less power, generates less heat, and fits into a single DIN space.

ITX

The Information Technology eXtended (ITX) motherboards—the mini-ITX, nano-ITX, and pico-ITX—were proposed by VIA Technologies. The mini-ITX fits in the same case as the micro-ATX; uses low power, which means it can be passively cooled (no fan); and has one expansion slot. The nano-ITX is even smaller; it is used for set-top boxes, media centers, and car computers. The pico-ITX is even smaller again, half the size of the nano-ITX. It uses daughter cards (extensions of the motherboard) to supply additional functionality.

Figure 1.7 compares common motherboard types and their sizes.

FIGURE 1.7   Motherboard sizes

ATX motherboard size comparison;
rear is on left.

▪ Flex-ATX (229 × 191 mm)

▪ Micro-ATX/Embedded-ATX (244 × 244 mm)

▪ Mini-ATX (284 × 208 mm)

▪ Standard-ATX (305 × 244 mm)

▪ Extended-ATX (EATX) (305 × 330mm)

▪ Workstation-ATX (WTX) (356 × 425 mm)

Expansion Slots

Expansion slots exist on a motherboard to allow for the addition of new interfaces to new technologies without replacing the motherboard. If expansion slots did not exist, you would have to buy a new motherboard every time you wanted to add a new device that uses an interface to the board that does not currently exist on the board. This section reviews various types of expansion slots.

PCI

The Peripheral Component Interconnect (PCI) bus is a fast (33 MHz), wide (32-bit or 64-bit) expansion bus that was a modern standard in motherboards for general-purpose expansion devices. Its slots are typically white. PCI devices can share interrupt requests (IRQs) and other system resources with one another in some cases. You may see two PCI slots, but most motherboards have gone to newer standards. Figure 1.8 shows some PCI slots.

FIGURE 1.8   PCI bus connectors

PCI cards that are 32-bit with 33 MHz operate up to 133 MBps, whereas 32-bit cards with 64 MHz operate up to 264 MBps. PCI cards that are 64-bit with 33 MHz operate up to 266 MBps whereas 64-bit cards with 66 MHz operate up to 538 MBps.

PCI-X

PCI-eXtended (PCI-X) is a double-wide version of the 32-bit PCI local bus. It runs at up to four times the clock speed, achieving higher bandwidth, but otherwise uses the same protocol and a similar electrical implementation. It has been replaced by the PCI Express (see the next section), which uses a different connector and a different logical design. There is also a 64-bit PCI specification electrically different but with the same connector as PCI-X.

There are two versions of PCI-X. Version 1 gets up to 1.06 GBps, and version 2 gets up to 4.26 GBps.

PCIe

PCI Express (PCIE, PCI-E, or PCIe) uses a network of serial interconnects that operate at high speed. It's based on the PCI system; you can convert a PCIe slot to PCI using an adaptor plug-in card, but you cannot convert a PCI slot to PCIe. Intended as a replacement for AGP and PCI, PCIe has the capability of being faster than AGP while maintaining the flexibility of PCI. There are four versions of PCIe: version 1 is up to 8 GBps, version 2 is up to 16 GBps, version 3 is up to 32 GBps, and final specifications for version 4 are still being developed. Figure 1.9 shows the slots discussed so far in this section.

FIGURE 1.9   PCI slots

miniPCI

Laptops and other portable devices utilize an expansion card called the miniPCI. It has the same functionality as the PCI but has a much smaller form factor. Unlike portable PCM-CIA cards, which are inserted externally into a slot, these are installed inside the case. Figure 1.10 shows a miniPCI card alongside a miniPCI Express card. Table 1.2 lists the specifications of all the slot types discussed in this section.

FIGURE 1.10   miniPCI

TABLE 1.2   PCI comparison

Type	Speeds
PCI 33 MHz 32-bit	133 MBps
PCI 33 MHz 64-bit	266 MBps
PCI 66 MHz 32-bit	264 MBps
PCI 66 MHz 64-bit	538 MBps
PCI-X version 1	1.06 GBps
PCI-X version 2	4.26 GBps

RAM Slots

RAM slots contain the memory chips. There are many and varied types of memory for PCs today. I'll discuss memory later in this chapter. PCs use memory chips arranged on a small circuit board. These circuit boards are called *single inline memory modules* (SIMMs) or *dual inline memory modules* (DIMMs). DIMMs utilize connectors on both sides of the board, whereas SIMMS utilize single connectors that are mirrored on both sides. DIMM is 64-bit and SIMM is 32-bit. There is also a high-speed type of RAM called *rambus dynamic RAM* (RDRAM), which comes on circuit boards called *rambus inline memory modules* (RIMMs).

Along with chip placement, memory modules also differ in the number of conductors, or pins, that the particular module uses. The number of pins used directly affects the overall size of the memory slot. Slot sizes include 30-pin, 72-pin, 168-pin, and 184-pin. Laptop memory comes in smaller form factors known as *small outline DIMMs* (SODIMMs). Figure 1.11 shows the form factors for the most popular memory chips. Notice that they basically look the same, but the memory module sizes are different.

FIGURE 1.11   Various memory module form factors

30-pin SIMM (3.5 n .75")   72-pin SIMM (4.25 n 1")

168-pin DIMM (5.375 n 1")

144-pin SoDIMM (2.625 n 1")   72-pin SoDIMM (2.375 n 1")

Memory slots are easy to identify on a motherboard. They're usually white and placed close together. The number of memory slots varies from motherboard to motherboard, but the appearance of the different slots is similar. Metal pins in the bottom make contact with the soldered tabs on each memory module. Small metal or plastic tabs on each side of the slot keep the memory module securely in its slot.

CPU Sockets

The CPU slot permits the attachment of the CPU to the motherboard, allowing the CPU to use the other components of the system. There are many different types of processors, meaning there are many types of CPU connectors.

The CPU slot can take on several different forms. In the past, the CPU slot was a rectangular box called a *pin grid array* (PGA) socket, with many small holes to accommodate the pins on the bottom of the chip. With the release of new and more powerful chips, additional holes were added, changing the configuration of the slot and its designator or number. Figure 1.12 shows a typical PGA-type CPU socket.

FIGURE 1.12   A PGA CPU socket

With the release of the Pentium II, the architecture of the slot went from a rectangle to more of an expansion-slot style of interface called a *single-edge contact cartridge* (SECC). This style of CPU slot includes Slot 1 and Slot 2 for Intel CPUs and Slot A for Athlon (AMD) CPUs. This type of slot looks much like an expansion slot, but it's located in a different place on the motherboard from the other expansion slots. Figure 1.13 shows an SECC.

FIGURE 1.13   SECC

Slot 1
connector

To see which socket type is used for which processors, examine Table 1.3. This list is not exhaustive. Some of the slots may fit processors that are not specifically listed.

TABLE 1.3   Socket types and the processors they support

Connector Type	Processor
Socket 1	486 SX/SX2, 486 DX/DX2, 486 DX4 Overdrive
Socket 2	486 SX/SX2, 486 DX/DX2, 486 DX4 Overdrive, 486 Pentium Overdrive
Socket 3	486 SX/SX2, 486 DX/DX2, 486 DX4 486 Pentium Overdrive
Socket 4	Pentium 60/66, Pentium 60/66 Overdrive
Socket 5	Pentium 75-133, Pentium 75+ Overdrive
Socket 6	DX4, 486 Pentium Overdrive
Socket 7	Pentium 75-200, Pentium 75+ Overdrive
Socket 8	Pentium Pro
Socket 370	Pentium III
Socket 423	Pentium 4
Socket 478	Pentium 4 and Celeron 4
SECC (Type I), Slot 1	Pentium II
SECC2 (Type II), Slot 2	Pentium III
Slot A	Athlon

TABLE 1.3   Socket types and the processors they support *(continued)*

Connector Type	Processor
Socket 603	Xeon
Socket 754	AMD Athlon 64
Socket 939	Some versions of Athlon 64
Socket 940	Some versions of Athlon 64 and Opteron
Socket LGA 775	Core 2 Duo/Quad
Socket AM2	Athlon 64 family (replacing earlier socket usage)
Socket F	OpteronShould be AMD Athlon 64 FX and AMD Opteron
Socket AM2+	AMD Athlon64, X2, Phenom, and Phenom II
Socket P	Intel Core2
Socket 441	Intel Atom
Socket LGA 1366/B	Intel Core i7, Xeon (35xx, 36xx, 55xx, 56xx series)
G1/G2/rPGA 988A/B	Intel Core i7, i5, i3, P6000, P4000
Socket AM3	AMD Phenom, Athlon II, Sempron
Socket H/LGA 1156	Intel Core i7, i5, Xeon, Penitium G5000, G1000
Socket G34	AMD Opteron 6000 series
Socket C32	AMD Opteron 4000 series
LGA 1150	Intel Haswell, Haswell Refresh, and Broadwell
Socket AM3+	AMD FX Vishera, AMD FX Zambezi, AMD Phenom II, AMD Athlon II, AMD Sempron
Socket FM2	AMD Trinity Processors
Socket FM2+	AMD Kaveri
LGA 1248	Intel Titanium 9300 series
LGA 1567	Intel Xeon 6500/7500 series
Socket H2/LGA 1155	Intel Sandy Bridge-DT
Socket R/LGA 2011	Intel Sandy Bridge B2 (also referred to as Xeon E5)
Socket FM1	AMD Llano (also referred to as A-series)

Chipsets

The *chipset* is the set of controller chips that monitors and directs the traffic on the motherboard between the buses. It usually consists of two or more chips. Motherboards use two basic chipset designs: the *north/south bridge chipset* and the *hub chipset*.

The hub chipset, a 2008 innovation, includes a memory controller hub (equivalent to the north bridge), an I/O controller hub (equivalent to the south bridge), and a SuperI/O chip.

North Bridge

The north bridge connects the system bus to the other relatively fast buses (AGP and PCIe). The north bridge typically handles communications between the CPU, RAM, and PCIe (or AGP) video cards and the south bridge. Figure 1.14 shows the location of the north and south bridges.

FIGURE 1.14   Location of bridges

South Bridge

The south bridge connects ISA, IDE, USB, audio, serial, the BIOS, the ISA bus, the IDE channels, and the interrupt controller. It handles all the computer's I/O functions. Figure 1.15 shows the relationship between the chipsets.

FIGURE 1.15   Chipsets

CMOS Battery

The CMOS chip must have a constant source of power to keep its settings. To prevent the loss of data, motherboard manufacturers include a small battery to power the CMOS memory. On modern systems, this is a coin-style battery, about the diameter of a U.S. dime and about as thick. Figure 1.16 shows the location of the CMOS battery.

FIGURE 1.16   CMOS battery

Power Connections and Types

A power connector allows the motherboard to be connected to the power supply. On an ATX, there is a single power connector consisting of a block of 20 holes (in two rows). On an AT, there is a block consisting of 12 pins sticking up; these pins are covered by two connectors with six holes each.

Figure 1.17 shows a versatile motherboard that has both kinds so you can compare them. The upper connector is for ATX, and the lower one is for AT.

FIGURE 1.17   Power connectors on a motherboard

When using the AT power connector, the power cable coming from the power supply will have two separate connectors, labeled P8 and P9. When you are attaching the two parts to the motherboard, the black wires on one should be next to the black wires on the other for proper function.

The 20-pin main connector from the power supply to the motherboard is standard for all ATX power supplies. In addition to this connector, many will include an auxiliary power connector of either four or six pins to provide additional power.

In 2004, the ATX 12V 2.0 (now 2.03) standard was passed, changing the main connector from 20 pins to 24. The additional pins provide +3.3V, +5V, and +12V (the fourth pin is a ground) for use by PCIe cards. When a 24-pin connector is used, there is no need for the optional four- or six-pin auxiliary power connectors.

Most power supplies have a recessed, two-position slider switch (often a red one) on the rear that is exposed through the case. Selections read 110 and 220, 115 and 230, or 120 and 240. This voltage selector switch is used to select the voltage level used in the country where the computer is in service. For example, in the United States, the power grid supplies anywhere from 110 VAC to 120 VAC. However, in Europe, for instance, the voltage supplied is double, ranging from 220 VAC to 240 VAC.

Fan Connectors

Connectors usually used for computer fans are called Molex connectors, and there can be several types. The following are some examples:

▪ A three-pin Molex connector is used when connecting a fan to the motherboard or other circuit board. Figure 1.18 shows the three-pin Molex.

FIGURE 1.18 Three-pin Molex

▪ A four-pin Molex connector includes an additional pin used for a pulse-width modulation signal to provide variable speed control. These connectors can be plugged into three-pin headers but will lose their fan speed control. Figure 1.19 shows the four-pin Molex connector.

FIGURE 1.19 Four-pin Molex

Front/Top-Panel Connectors

There are a number of interfaces, buttons, lights, and audio jacks in the front panel of the computer that must be connected to the board for power and functionality. This section discusses each of these and their respective methods of connection to the motherboard.

USB

When USB ports exist on the front panel (as they almost always do these days), they must be connected to the motherboard so that the connected USB device can communicate with the computer. This is done with a 10-pin connector located on the board, as shown in Figure 1.20.

FIGURE 1.20   Front-panel power connectors

Front-panel
USB

Front-panel
audio

Front-panel
connection
cluster

Audio

When audio plugs or jacks exist in the front panel, as they do in most computers now, they must be connected to the motherboard if you are using the integrated sound card. (Otherwise, they may connect directly to the sound card.) Figure 1.20 shows an example of the audio plug on the board.

Power Button

The power button located in the front panel must also be connected to the motherboard to communicate on and off to the computer. This connector is located along with the remaining connectors discussed in this section, clustered in a group on the motherboard in the section labeled "Front-panel connection cluster" in Figure 1.20.

Power Light

The power indicator light must also be provided with power and a connection to the board. It is also located in the section labeled "Front-panel connection cluster" in Figure 1.20.

Drive Activity Lights

The drive activity light, which indicates when a hard drive is being either read or written to, must have a connection to the motherboard both for power and to transmit the drive activity information. It is also located in the section labeled "Front-panel connection cluster" in Figure 1.20.

Reset Button

The reset button like all the other front-panel components, has a connection to the motherboard and is located in the section labeled "Front-panel connection cluster" in Figure 1.20.

Bus Speeds

Bus speeds were covered earlier in this chapter in the section "Monitoring" for subobjective 1.1.

Exam Essentials

Differentiate the motherboard form factors. The ATX is the oldest and largest of the motherboard sizes still being manufactured. The micro-ATX is for smaller and cheaper systems. The smaller ITX motherboards come in three sizes: the mini-ITX, the nano-ITX, and the pico-ITX.

Identify expansion slot types. PCI slots are the standard for general-purpose cards. The PCI-X provides higher bandwidth for servers. PCIe is a newer high-speed slot based on the PCI system. MiniPCI slots are used in laptops.

Describe RAM slots. Memory slots accept either single inline memory modules (SIMMs) or dual inline memory modules (DIMMs). DIMMs utilize connectors on both sides of the board, whereas SIMMs utilize single connectors that are mirrored on both sides. DIMM is 64-bit and SIMM is 32-bit. There is also a high-speed type of RAM called rambus dynamic RAM (RDRAM), which comes on circuit boards called rambus inline memory modules (RIMMs).

Locate the CPU socket on the motherboard. The CPU socket can take on several different forms. In the past, the CPU socket was a rectangular box called a PGA socket, with many small holes to accommodate the pins on the bottom of the chip. With the release of the Pentium II, the architecture of the socket went from a rectangle to more of an expansion-slot style of interface called an SECC.

Understand the function of the chipsets. The north bridge connects the system bus to the other relatively fast buses (AGP and PCIe). The south bridge connects ISA, IDE, USB, audio, serial, the BIOS, the IDA bus, the IDE channels, and the interrupt controller. It handles all the computer's I/O functions.

Utilize fan and power connections. A 20- or 24-pin main connector from the power supply to the motherboard is standard for all ATX power supplies. Fans connect with either three- or four-pin Molex connections.

Identify front connections. While the USB and audio jacks will be connected with 10-pin connectors, the remaining front-panel components will connect with much smaller plugs in a cluster in one area on the board.

1.3 Compare and Contrast Various RAM Types and Their Features

Physically, RAM is a collection of integrated circuits that store data and program information as patterns of 1s and 0s (on and off states) in the chip. Most memory chips require constant power (also called a *constant refresh*) to maintain those patterns of 1s and 0s. If power is lost, all those tiny switches revert to the off position, effectively erasing the data from memory. Some memory types, however, don't require a refresh.

This section discusses those RAM types and features. The topics addressed in objective 1.3 include the following:

- Types
- RAM configurations
- Single-sided vs. double-sided
- Buffered vs. unbuffered
- RAM compatibility

Types

There are many types of RAM. They differ in their speed, form factor, their ability to identify errors, and their bandwidth. Let's examine each type in detail.

SDRAM

Synchronous DRAM (SDRAM) is synchronized to the speed of the motherboard's system bus and works at half the speed of DDR. Synchronizing the speed of the systems prevents the address bus from having to wait for the memory because of different clock speeds. A 100 MHz clock signal produces 800 Mbps, and such memory modules are referred to as PC100. PC133, which replaced PC100, uses a 133 MHz clock to produce 1,067 Mbps of throughput.

The relationship between clock speed and throughput is always roughly 1:8. Thus, PC2700 modules are designed specifically for a motherboard with a speed of 333 MHz, and PC3200 modules are designed for a motherboard with a speed of 400 MHz.

SDRAM typically comes in the form of 168-pin DIMMs.

DDR

Double Data Rate (DDR) is clock-doubled SDRAM (covered in the previous section). The memory chip can perform reads and writes on both sides of any clock cycle (the up, or start, and the down, or ending), thus doubling the effective memory executions per second. So, if you're using DDR SDRAM with a 100 MHz memory bus, the memory will execute reads and writes at 200 MHz and transfer the data to the processor at 100 MHz. The advantage of DDR over regular SDRAM is increased throughput and thus increased overall system speed.

DDR2

The next generation of DDR SDRAM is Double Data Rate 2 (DDR2). This allows for two memory accesses for each rising and falling clock and effectively doubles the speed of DDR. DDR2-667 chips work with speeds at 667 MHz and are also referred to as PC2-5300 modules.

DDR3

The primary benefit of DDR3 over DDR2 is that it transfers data at twice the rate of DDR2 (eight times the speed of its internal memory arrays), enabling higher bandwidth or peak data rates. By performing two transfers per cycle of a quadrupled clock, a

64-bit-wide DDR3 module may achieve a transfer rate of up to 64 times the memory clock speed in megabytes per second. In addition, the DDR3 standard permits chip capacities of up to 8 GB. Table 1.4 lists the selected memory standards, speeds, and formats.

TABLE 1.4 Selected memory details

Module Standard	Speed	Format
DDR500	4,000 MBps	PC4000
DDR533	4,266 MBps	PC4200
DDR2-667	5,333 MBps	PC2-5300
DDR2-750	6,000 MBps	PC2-6000
DDR2-800	6,400 MBps	PC2-6400
DDR3-800	6,400 MBps	PC3-6400
DDR3-1600	12,800 MBps	PC3-12800

SODIMM

Portable computers (notebooks and subnotebooks) require smaller sticks of RAM because of their smaller size. One of the two types is small outline DIMM (SODIMM), which can have 72, 144, or 200 pins. A SODIMM was shown earlier in the chapter in Figure 1.11.

DIMM

Dual inline memory modules (DIMMs) are double-sided. DIMMs have separate connectors on both sides of the chip. They typically have 168 pins and are 64 bits in width. Figure 1.21 shows a DIMM. For comparison purposes, a DIMM and SODIMM were shown earlier in the chapter in Figure 1.11.

FIGURE 1.21 Dual inline memory module

Parity vs. Nonparity

RAM is supplied with no parity (8 data bits per byte) or with parity (8 data bits and 1 parity bit per byte, for a total of 9 bits per byte). If present, parity bits are used to determine whether data moving to and from memory has been corrupted or damaged (thus changed) in the transmission. You can identify parity SIMMs by counting the number of chips on the stick. If there are nine, it's parity RAM. If there are eight, it's nonparity.

When do you choose parity RAM? Usually, the motherboard requires either parity or nonparity RAM; a few motherboards will accept either. Nowadays, parity RAM is needed only in highly critical computing tasks because advances in RAM technology have created reliable RAM that seldom makes errors.

ECC vs. Non-ECC

Another type of RAM error correction is Error Correction Code (ECC). RAM with ECC can detect and correct errors. Like with parity RAM, additional information needs to be stored, and more processing needs to be done, making ECC RAM more expensive and a little slower than nonparity and parity RAM. Both ECC and parity memory work in ECC mode. However, ECC memory does not work in plain parity checking mode, meaning the extra bits cannot be individually accessed when ECC memory is used. This type of parity RAM is now obsolete. Most RAM today is non-ECC.

RAM Configurations

As I discussed earlier in this section, RAM can be either single-sided or double-sided. It can also use single, dual, or triple channels. In this section, I'll discuss the use of channels in RAM.

Single Channel vs. Dual Channel vs. Triple Channel

Utilizing multiple channels between the RAM and the memory controller increases the transfer speed between these two components. Single-channel RAM does not take advantage of this concept, but dual-channel memory does and creates two 64-bit data channels. Do *not* confuse this with DDR or double data rate. DDR doubles the rate by accessing the memory module twice per clock cycle.

This requires a motherboard that supports this and two or more memory modules. The modules go in separate color-coded banks, as shown in Figure 1.22.

FIGURE 1.22   Dual-channel memory slots

Triple-channel architecture adds a third memory module and reduces memory latency by interleaving or accessing each module sequentially with smaller bits of data rather than completely filling up one module before accessing the next one. Data is spread among the modules alternatingly with the potential to triple bandwidth as opposed to storing the data all on one module.

Single-Sided vs. Double-Sided

Earlier we discussed the difference between SIMMs and DIMMs. In review, SIMMs have connectors on one side, whereas DIMMs have connectors on both sides of the chip. DIMMs have twice the pins, meaning twice the contact with the motherboard, creating a larger interface with it and resulting in a wider data path.

Buffered vs. Unbuffered

Buffered memory or registered memory is memory that has a register between it and the memory controller. The register stores bits of information in such a way that systems can write to or read out all the bits simultaneously. This reduces the load on the controller and allows the device to support much more memory than would be possible otherwise. The other possible effect is an introduction of latency and a drop in performance, so you might think of this trade-off as gaining bandwidth (amount of memory) at a small cost of performance (transfer speed).

RAM Compatibility

RAM speed used to be expressed in nanoseconds but is also sometimes expressed in megahertz, like with CPUs. Faster memory can be added to a PC with slower memory installed, but the system will operate only at the speed of the slowest module present.

While you can mix speeds, you cannot mix memory types. For example, you cannot use SDRAM with DDR, and DDR cannot be mixed with DDR2. When looking at the name of the memory, the larger the number, the faster the speed. For example, DDR2-800 is faster than DDR2-533.

Exam Essentials

Identify the types of memory.   Types of memory include single data rate (SDRAM), double data rate (DDR), DDR2, and DDR3. These types differ in their data rate. Memory can also differ in packaging. There are SIMMS (single module) and DIMMs (double modules). They also can use either parity or ECC for error checking and can be single, dual, or triple channel, with multiple channels widening the path between the memory and the memory controller.

Follow RAM speed and compatibility guidelines.   Faster memory can be added to a PC with slower memory installed, but the system will operate only at the speed of the slowest module present. RAM types cannot be mixed.

1.4 Install and Configure PC Expansion Cards

Expansion cards allow you to add functionality to the PC. In the section "Expansion Slots," I covered the types of expansion slots that can be found on the motherboard. In this section, I'll discuss the types of cards and the functionality they provide. I'll also talk about installing them and configuring them properly.

Newer cards will install in the PCI or PCIe slots and will probably be detected by the operating system. If the operating system already contains the driver for the device in its preinstalled driver library, the process will be done as soon as you restart the PC. If it is not present in the driver cache, you will have to install the driver that came with it. These guidelines apply to all the expansion cards discussed in this section. The topics addressed in objective 1.4 include the following:

- Sound cards
- Video cards
- Network cards
- USB cards
- FireWire cards
- Thunderbolt cards
- Storage cards
- Modem cards
- Wireless/cellular cards
- TV tuner cards
- Video capture cards
- Riser cards

Sound Cards

Most computers these days come with an integrated sound card, but for more robust sound or advanced features, you may need to install a sound card. Sound cards can be either internal or external. Internal cards require opening the case and installing the card in a slot. External cards plug into the USB socket.

In some cases, an audio cable will be connected from the card to the CD-ROM. This is rarely required these days. Figure 1.23 shows the connectors present on most sound cards today.

FIGURE 1.23   Sound card connectors

Video Cards

PCs today also contain internal video cards, but like with sound cards, you can achieve better video quality with more expensive video cards. This is especially true when the video card has its own dedicated memory. In earlier times, most internal cards were vastly inferior to the cards you could buy, but that is much less the case today when users have learned to expect better video quality.

Newer operating systems, like Windows Vista and Windows 7, have helped raise the bar for internal cards as well in that they require a card with a minimum set of features and a minimum amount of dedicated RAM to appreciate the visual capabilities of the operating system.

Video cards can be installed in the AGP, PCI, and PCIe slots. At one point, the best choice was clear, and that was the AGP slot. However, the newer PCIe slots provide more bandwidth. AGP provides a wider data path because it's parallel, whereas PCIe is serial. But PCIe now goes up to 16,000 MBps as compared to AGP, which is 2,000 MBps. Figure 1.24 shows the AGP slot next to some slots you have already learned about.

FIGURE 1.24   AGP and PCI slots

Some of the special functions you may get with a more expensive video card are 3D imaging, MPEG decoding, and TV output (discussed later in this section). The ability to use multiple monitors is also built into many cards.

Network Cards

Network cards do exactly what you would think; they provide a connection for the PC to a network. In general, network interface cards (NICs) are added to a PC via an expansion slot or they are integrated into the motherboard, but they may also be added through a USB or PCMCIA slot (also known as PC card). The most common issue that prevents network connectivity is a bad or unplugged patch cable.

Network cards are made for Ethernet, fiber-optic, token ring (rarely used now), and 802.11 (wireless) connections. The Ethernet, token ring, and fiber-optic cards accept the appropriate cable, and the wireless cards have radio transmitters and antennas.

The most obvious difference in network cards is the speed of which they are capable. Most networks today operate at 100 MBps or 1 GBps. Regardless of other components, the PC will operate at the speed of the slowest component, so if the card is capable of 1 GBps but the cable is capable of only 100 MBps, the PC will transmit only at 100 MBps.

Another significant feature to be aware of is the card's ability to perform autosensing. This feature allows the card to sense whether the connection is capable of full duplex and to operate in that manner with no action required.

There is another type of autosensing, in which the card is capable of detecting what type of device is on the other end and changing the use of the wire pairs accordingly. For example, normally a PC connected to another PC requires a crossover cable, but if both ends can perform this sensing, that is not required. These types of cards are called auto-MDIX.

Serial and Parallel Cards

 The "Serial and Parallel Cards" section isn't part of the official objectives, but it is helpful to understand these additional concepts.

As discussed in the section "Video Cards," expansion cards and the slots they live in can be either serial or parallel. The difference is in how the bits are sent to and from the card. In standard parallel, these bits are sent eight at time using eight wires, one for each bit, whereas in serial the bits are sent one at a time down the same wire.

Serial has the following advantages over parallel:

- A serial link transmits less data per clock cycle but can achieve a higher data rate because it can be clocked considerably faster than parallel links. (Clock skew between different channels is not an issue because it is in parallel.)

- Fewer interconnecting cables occupy less space, allowing for better isolation of the channel from its surroundings.

- Crosstalk (which occurs when wires in the same cable interfere with one another) is less of an issue because there are fewer conductors in proximity.

- It is cheaper to implement. Serial card interfaces have fewer pins and are therefore less expensive.

USB Cards

Universal Serial Bus (USB) expansion cards are used to provide a USB connection (or an additional connection) to a PC that has none (pretty rare today). All modern motherboards today have at least two USB slots. Some of the advantages of USB include hot-plugging and the capability for up to 127 USB devices to share a single set of system resources. USB 1.1 runs at 12 Mbps, and USB 2.0 runs at 480 Mbps. Because USB is a serial interface, its width is 1 bit. USB 3.0 specifies a maximum transmission speed of up to 5 Gbps (625 MBps), which is more than 10 times as fast as USB 2.0 (480 Mbps or 60 MBps), although this speed is typically achieved only by using powerful, professional-grade or developmental equipment.

These cards are made to plug into PCI, PCIe, or PCMCIA slots (Chapter 3, "Mobile Devices," discusses laptops in more detail).

FireWire Cards

FireWire expansion cards, like USB cards, provide this connection when none is present or when more are required. Most new motherboards have a built-in IEEE 1394/FireWire port, although this port can be added with a PCI expansion board. It transfers data at 400 Mbps and supports up to 63 chained devices on a single set of resources. These cards also are made to plug into PCI, PCIe, or PCMCIA slots.

Thunderbolt Cards

Thunderbolt is an expansion card that was originally envisioned to use fiber cabling but was later adapted by Intel and Apple to copper. Thunderbolt controllers multiplex individual data lanes from connected PCIe and DisplayPort devices for transmission via one duplex Thunderbolt lane and then de-multiplex them for use by PCIe and DisplayPort devices on the other end, as depicted in Figure 1.25.

FIGURE 1.25   Thunderbolt cable

Devices can be daisy-chained on the line (up to 6). Thunderbolt devices and non-Thunderbolt devices can be connected, but the controller will treat them differently. It will provide a native DisplayPort signal with four lanes of output data at no more than 5.4 Gbps per Thunderbolt lane. When connected to a Thunderbolt device, the per-lane data rate becomes 10 Gbps, and the four Thunderbolt lanes are configured as two duplex lanes, with each 10 Gbps comprising one lane of input and one lane of output.

Thunderbolt card use has been restricted thus far to Apple devices, but the technology possesses a unique ability to handle audio and video in a way USB cannot. It remains to be seen if you will start seeing these interfaces on PCs in the near future.

Storage Cards

Storage cards plug into a slot (usually PCIe) and have storage devices attached to the card. Increasingly, these are solid-state drives (SSDs). This is like adding an external drive except it is added by placing the card in a slot inside the box.

The following are other ways these cards may be connected to the PC:

- Serial ATA SATA
- Serial-attached SCSI (generally found on servers)
- PCIe
- Fibre Channel (almost exclusively found on servers)
- USB
- Parallel ATA (IDE) interface (mostly replaced by SATA)
- (Parallel) SCSI

Modem Cards

Many PCs already have built-in modems and therefore will have an RJ-11 connector on the back in which to plug a phone line. However, modems can be added with an expansion card. This arrangement makes it possible to connect to your ISP through the phone line, an increasingly rare event that you might use only in an emergency since much faster and simpler connection methods are available. These are usually PCI or PCIe.

Wireless/Cellular Cards

A more likely modem connection you may use is one that connects to your mobile phone provider for wireless connectivity through the same system that your mobile phone uses. These can be either PCMCIA cards or USB devices. Figure 1.26 shows a PCMCIA card. They also are fully wireless versions, meaning there is no physical connection to a device. Your computers and mobile devices connect wirelessly to the card, and the card connects wirelessly to the cellular tower. These are becoming more common because of the ability to connect more than one device to the Internet.

FIGURE 1.26 PCMCIA 3G modem

TV Tuner Cards

TV tuner cards are designed to receive TV signals on the computer and usually contain a built-in video capture card (discussed more in the next section). The interfaces are most commonly either PCI or PCIe, but PCMCIA, ExpressCard, and USB devices also exist.

Video Capture Cards

Video capture is the process of converting an analog video signal to digital video. The resulting computer files create a digital video stream. This means that a video capture card takes input—such as that produced by an analog video camera—and converts it to a digital file. These cards usually come in PCI or PCIe format. Figure 1.27 shows an example of a PCI TV tuner card.

FIGURE 1.27 TV tuner card

Riser Cards

Although it isn't common, you may occasionally encounter a slim-line case, which is a desktop-orientation case that is shorter and thinner than a normal one—so short that normal expansion boards won't fit perpendicular to the motherboard. In such cases a riser card is installed, which sits perpendicular to the motherboard and contains expansion slots. The expansion cards can then be oriented parallel to the motherboard when installed. So, it's a card that hosts other cards. Figure 1.28 shows a riser card from two angles.

FIGURE 1.28   Riser card

Exam Essentials

Describe the installation process as it applies to Plug and Play expansion cards.   Newer cards will install in the PCI or PCIe slots and will probably be detected by the operating system. If the operating system already contains the driver for the device in its preinstalled driver library, the process will be done as soon as you restart the PC. If it is not present in the driver library, you will have to install the driver that came with it.

Differentiate each expansion card type.   Understand the function of each of the following card types:

- Sound cards
- Video cards
- Network cards
- Serial and parallel cards
- USB cards
- Thunderbolt cards
- FireWire cards
- Storage cards
- Modem cards
- Wireless/cellular cards
- TV tuner cards
- Video capture cards

Explain the purpose of riser cards.   Riser cards are used to provide expansions slot types that are not present on the system or that exist in insufficient numbers.

1.5 Install and Configure Storage Devices and Use Appropriate Media

Storage media hold the data being accessed, as well as the files the system needs to operate and the data that needs to be saved. The various types of storage differ in terms of capacity, the access time, and the physical type of media being used. This section covers the installation and configuration of various storage devices. The topics addressed in objective 1.5 include the following:

- Optical drives
- Magnetic hard drives
- Hot-swappable drives

- Solid-state/flash drives
- RAID types
- Tape drive
- Media capacity

Optical Drives

Optical drives work by using a laser rather than magnetism to change the characteristics of the storage medium. This is true for CD-ROM drives, DVD drives, and Blu-ray, all of which are discussed in the following sections.

CD-ROM

CD-ROM stands for Compact Disc Read-Only Memory. The CD-ROM media is used for long-term storage of data. CD-ROM media is read-only, meaning that once information is written to a CD, it can't be erased or changed. Access time for CD-ROM drives is considerably slower than for a hard drive. Standard CDs normally hold 650 MB to 700 MB of data and use the ISO 9660 standard, which allows them to be used in multiple platforms.

DVD-ROM

Because DVD-ROM drives use slightly different technology than CD-ROM drives, they can store up to 4.7 GB of data in a single-layer configuration. This makes DVDs a better choice than CDs for distributing large software bundles. Many software packages today are so huge that they require multiple CDs to hold all the installation and reference files. A single DVD, in a double-sided, double-layered configuration, can hold as much as 17 GB (as much as 26 regular CDs).

Blu-ray

Blu-ray recorders have been available since 2003, and they have the ability to record more information than a standard DVD using similar optical technology. In recent years, Blu-ray has been more synonymous with recording television and movie files than data, but the Blu-ray specification (1.0) includes two data formats: BD-R for write-once and BD-RE for rewritable media (more later in this section). BD-J is capable of more sophisticated bonus features than provided by standard DVD, including network access, picture-in-picture, and access to expanded local storage. With the exception of the Internet access component, these features are called Bonus View. The addition of Internet access is called BD Live.

In the official specification, as noted on the Blu-ray Disc Association website (http://us.blu-raydisc.com/), the *r* is lowercase. CompTIA favors the uppercase *R*.

The current capacity of a Blu-ray is 100 GB, with 400 GB on the horizon and an aim for 1 TB by 2015. As a final note, there was a long-running (but finally complete) battle between Blu-ray and HD DVD to be the format of the future, and Blu-ray won.

CD-RW

Compact Disc-ReWritable (CD-RW) media is a rewritable optical disc. A CD-RW drive requires more sensitive laser optics. It can write data to the disc but also has the ability to erase that data and write more data to the disc. It does this by liquefying the layer where the data resides (removing the reflectivity placed there by the writing process used to create the old data) and then creating new reflectivity in the same layer upon writing again that represents the new data. Two states of reflectivity are used to represent the 0s and 1s for the data. CD-RWs cannot be read in some CD-ROM drives built prior to 1997.

DVD-RW

As you might expect, the primary advantage of DVD-RW drives over DVD-R drives is the ability to erase and rewrite to a DVD-RW disc. In these drives, a layer of metal alloy on the disk is manipulated to erase and write the data, rather than burning into the disc itself, similar to the operation of CD-RW.

Dual-Layer DVD-RW

A dual-layer DVD-RW disc employs a second physical layer within the disc itself. The drive with dual-layer capability accesses the second layer by shining the laser through the first semitransparent layer.

BD-R

Blu-ray players have two data formats: BD-R for recording computer data and BD-RE for rewritable media. BD-R can be written to only one time.

BD-RE

Blu-ray Disc Recordable Erasable (BD-RE) can be erased and written to multiple times. Disc capacities are 25 GB for single-layer discs, 50 GB for double-layer discs, 100 GB for triple-layer discs, and 128 GB for quad-layer discs.

Magnetic Hard Drives

Before the development and use of SSDs, magnetic drives were—and are still as of this writing—the main type of hard drive used. The drive itself is a mechanical device that spins a number of disks or platters and uses a magnetic head to read and write data to the surface of the disks. One of the advantages of SSDs (discussed in the next section) is the absence of mechanical parts that can malfunction. Figure 1.29 shows the parts of a magnetic hard drive.

FIGURE 1.29 Magnetic hard drive

The basic hard disk geometry consists of three components: the number of sectors that each track contains, the number of read/write heads in the disk assembly, and the number of cylinders in the assembly. This set of values is known as CHS (for cylinders/heads/sectors). A *cylinder* is the set of tracks of the same number on all the writeable surfaces of the assembly. It is called a cylinder because the collection of all same-number tracks on all writable surfaces of the hard disk assembly looks like a geometric cylinder when connected vertically. Therefore, cylinder 1, for instance, on an assembly that contains three platters comprises six tracks (one on each side of each platter), each labeled track 1 on its respective surface. Figure 1.30 illustrates the key terms presented in this discussion.

FIGURE 1.30 CHS

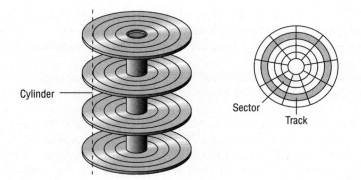

5,400 rpm

The rotational speed of the disk or platter has a direct influence on how quickly the drive can locate any specific disk sector on the drive. This locational delay is called *latency* and is measured in milliseconds (ms). The faster the rotation, the smaller the delay will be. A drive operating at 5,400 rpms will experience about 5.5 ms of this delay.

7,200 rpm

Drives that operate at 7,200 rpm will experience about 4.16 ms of latency. As of 2015, a typical 7,200 rpm desktop hard drive has a sustained data transfer rate up to 1,030 Mbps. This rate depends on the track location, so it will be higher for data on the outer tracks and lower toward the inner tracks.

10,000 rpm

At 10,000 rpm, the latency will decrease to about 3 ms. Data transfer rates also generally go up with a higher rotational speed but are influenced by the density of the disk (the number of tracks and sectors present in a given area).

15,000 rpm

Drives that operate at 15,000 rpm are higher-end drives and suffer only 2 ms of latency. These drives also generate more heat, requiring more cooling to the case. They also offer faster data transfer rates for the same areal density.

Hot-Swappable Drives

If a drive can be attached to the PC without shutting down the PC, then it is a hot-swappable drive. Drive types that are hot-swappable include USB, FireWire, SATA, and those that connect through Ethernet. You should always check the documentation to ensure that your drive supports this feature.

Solid-State/Flash Drives

Solid-state drives (SSDs) retain data in nonvolatile memory chips and contain no moving parts. Compared to electromechanical hard disk drives (HDDs), SSDs are typically less susceptible to physical shock, are silent, have lower access time and latency, but are more expensive per gigabyte.

Thumb drives are USB flash drives that have become extremely popular for transporting files. Figure 1.31 shows three thumb drives (also known as keychain drives) next to a pack of gum for size comparison.

Like with other flash drives, you can find these in a number of different size capacities. Many models include a write-protect switch to keep you from accidentally overwriting files stored on the drive. Most include an LED to show when they're connected to the USB port. Other names for thumb drives include travel drives, flash drives, and jump drives.

FIGURE 1.31 USB flash

Flash drives (which are solid state) have been growing in popularity for years and replacing floppy disks because of their capacity and small size. Flash technology is ideally suited for use not only with computers but also with many other things—digital cameras, MP3 players, and so on. This section discusses the various forms of these drives.

Compact Flash

Compact Flash (CF) cards are a widely used form of solid-state storage. There are two main subdivisions of CF cards: Type I (3.3-mm thick) and the thicker Type II (CF2) cards (5-mm thick). CF cards can be used directly in a PC card slot with a plug adaptor, used as an ATA (IDE) or PCMCIA storage device with a passive adaptor or with a reader, or attached to other types of ports such as USB or FireWire. Figure 1.32 shows a CF card.

FIGURE 1.32 SD and Compact Flash

Reader →

SD

Secure Digital (SD) cards are just one type of flash; there are many others. The maximum capacity of a standard SD card is 512 GB, and there are two other standards that go beyond this: SDHC can go to 32 GB and SDXC to 2 TB. Figure 1.32 shows a Compact Flash card (the larger of the two) and an SD card along with an eight-in-one card reader/writer. The reader shown connects to the USB port and then interacts with Compact Flash, Compact Flash II, Memory Stick, Memory Stick PRO, SmartMedia, xD-Picture cards, SD, and MultiMediaCards. The SD card specification defines three physical sizes, discussed in the following sections.

Micro-SD

Micro-SD is the smallest of the three. It is 11 mm × 15 mm × 1 mm.

Mini-SD

Mini-SD is the middle child of the three SD form factors. It is 20 mm × 21.5 mm × 1.4 mm.

xD

xD-Picture card is a flash memory card format, used mainly in older digital cameras. xD stands for Extreme Digital. xD cards are available in capacities of 16 MB up to 2 GB. Pictures are transferred from a digital camera's xD card to a PC by plugging the camera into the USB or IEEE 1394 (FireWire) cable or by removing the card from the camera and inserting it into a card reader.

SSD

A solid-state drive (SSD) is a form of flash drive that takes the place of a magnetic hard drive as the main storage device in the PC. Some SSDs use volatile RAM and external power or batteries to maintain the data after power is removed.

These drives access the data faster because there is no wait for the platters to spin up. Also, with no moving parts, there is less to go wrong with these drives, and they make no noise, like magnetic drives will do. Smartphones are an example of the growing number of devices that use solid-state storage, along with many laptops.

Hybrid

A hybrid drive is one in which both technologies, traditional mechanical and SSDs, are combined. This is done to take advantage of the speed of SSDs while maintaining the cost effectiveness of mechanical drives.

There are main approaches to this: dual-drive hybrid and solid-state hybrid. Dual-drive systems contain both types of drives in the same machine, and performance is optimized by the user placing more frequently used information on the SSD and less frequently accessed data on the mechanical drive. In some cases the operating system can create hybrid volumes using space in both drives.

An SSD, on the other hand, is a single storage device that includes solid-state flash memory in a traditional hard drive. Data that is most related to the performance of the machine is stored in the flash memory, resulting in improved performance. Figure 1.33 shows the two approaches to hybrid drives.

FIGURE 1.33   Hybrid drive approaches

eMMC

An Embedded Multi-Media Controller (eMMC) is a type of flash memory that is slower than solid state but also cheaper. It is often used in less expensive laptops and tablets. It's embedded into the board of the device and has more in common with an SD card than an SSD. Lower performance for lower price is an acceptable trade-off in devices such as cameras that don't demand the type of performance you get from an SSD, but eMMC may not be up to the task in a laptop or desktop machine.

Connection Types

Drives can be installed internally or can be connected externally to the PC. There are various options to connect the drives in both cases. This section discusses those options.

  The "Connection Types" section isn't part of the official objectives, but it is helpful to understand these additional concepts.

External

When a PC does not have the type of drive needed and has neither the internal connection type required nor the space inside the box to install the drive internally, external drives are made that can connect to the computer using several types of external interfaces. These connection types are discussed in this section.

USB

USB connections are probably the most widely used because of their inclusion on almost all front or back panels of computers these days. In fact, most have several USB slots, and it is simple to add more with a USB hub. USB drives also have the benefit of being Plug and Play, which makes them user friendly for setup.

FireWire

Although not as widely seen as USB or IEEE 1394, FireWire connections are also present on many computers. It transfers data at 400 Mbps and supports up to 63 chained devices on a single set of resources. It's hot-pluggable, like USB.

eSATA

eSATA provides a form of SATA meant for external connectivity. SATA (discussed more completely in the section "Internal SATA, IDE, and SCSI") is used for drive connections internally on many PCs. eSATA uses a more robust connector, longer shielded cables, and stricter (but backward-compatible) electrical standards. The interface resembles that of USB and IEEE 1394 (FireWire), but the cable cannot be as long, and the cable does not supply power to the device. The advantage it has over the other technologies is speed—it is approximately three times as fast as either FireWire or USB 2.0 (although USB 3.0 is faster).

Ethernet

There are drives that you connect to across the network or through Ethernet. These drives, also sometimes referred to as network-attached storage (NAS) devices, may also allow for wireless access, just as a laptop is capable of both wired and wireless communication. These devices are *not* seen as an attached device to the PC but rather as another device on the network, so they appear as a drive with shared folders as if you were connecting to a server. They only need to be on the same network as the PC.

Internal SATA, IDE, and SCSI

When drives are connected internally, there are several options, and the options available on your PC will be a function of how old it is and, in the case of SCSI, whether it is a computer designed to operate as a server.

IDE drives are the most common type of hard drive found in computers. But IDE is much more than a hard drive interface; it's also a popular interface for many other drive types, including CD-ROM, DVD, and Zip drives. IDE drives are easy to install and configure, and they provide acceptable performance for most applications. Their ease of use relates to their most identifiable feature—the controller is located on the drive itself.

The design of the IDE is simple: build the controller right on the drive and use a relatively short ribbon cable to connect the drive/controller to the IDE interface. This offers the benefits of decreasing signal loss (thus increasing reliability) and making the drive easier to install. The IDE interface can be an expansion board, or it can be built into the motherboard, as is the case on almost all systems today.

IDE generically refers to any drive that has a built-in controller. The IDE you know today is more properly called AT IDE; two previous types of IDE (MCA IDE and XT IDE) are obsolete and incompatible with it.

There have been many revisions of the IDE standard over the years, and each one is designated with a certain AT attachment (ATA) number—ATA-1 through ATA-8. Drives that support ATA-2 and higher are generically referred to as enhanced IDE (EIDE). Here are some of the highlights: With ATA-3, a technology called ATA Packet Interface (ATAPI) was introduced to help deal with IDE devices other than hard disks. ATAPI enables the BIOS to recognize an IDE CD-ROM drive, for example, or a tape backup or Zip drive. Starting with ATA-4, a new technology was introduced called UltraDMA, supporting transfer modes of up to 33 Mbps. ATA-5 supports UltraDMA/66, with transfer modes of up to 66 Mbps. To achieve this high rate, the drive must have a special 80-wire ribbon cable, and the motherboard or IDE controller card must support ATA-5. ATA-6 supports UltraDMA/100, with transfer modes of up to 100 Mbps.

If an ATA-5 or ATA-6 drive is used with a normal 40-wire cable or is used on a system that doesn't support the higher modes, it reverts to the ATA-4 performance level.

ATA-7 supports UltraDMA/133, with transfer modes of up to 150 Mbps and SATA.

ATA-8 made only minor revisions to ATA-7 and also supports UltraDMA/133, with transfer modes of up to 600 Mbps and SATA.

Table 1.5 lists the ATA standards and their details.

TABLE 1.5   ATA standards

Standard	Speed	Cable Type	New Feature
ATA 1	8.3 Mbps	40 wire	Multiword DMA
ATA 2	16.6 Mbps	40 wire	PIO mode
ATA 3	16.6 Mbps	40 wire	ATAPI
ATA 4	33 Mbps	40 or 80 wire	UltraDMA

TABLE 1.5   ATA standards *(continued)*

Standard	Speed	Cable Type	New Feature
ATA 5	66 Mbps	40 or 80 wire	UltraDMA 66
ATA 6	100 Mbps	40 or 80 wire	UltraDMA 100
ATA 7	150 Mbps	40 or 80 wire	UltraDMA 133
ATA 8	600 Mbps	40 or 80 wire	Hybrid drive capability

SATA drives are ATA drives that use serial transmission as opposed to parallel. They use a different cable because of this. It is not a ribbon cable but a smaller cable. Figure 1.34 shows the data cable and its connector.

FIGURE 1.34   Serial ATA data cable and connector

Small Computer System Interface (SCSI) is most commonly used for hard disks and tape drives, but it can connect a wide range of other devices, including scanners and CD drives. These devices reside on a single bus, which must be terminated on either end. Eight or sixteen devices can be attached to a single bus, depending on whether the SCSI bus is wide (0–15) or narrow (0–7) bus. There also is a host bus controller, which is usually plugged into a slot in the computer or can be integrated into the motherboard. Figure 1.35 shows an internal SCSI connector.

FIGURE 1.35   Internal SCSI connector

IDE Configuration and Setup (Master, Slave, Cable Select)

The primary benefit of IDE is that it's nearly universally supported. Almost every mother-board has IDE connectors.

A typical motherboard has two IDE connectors, and each connector can support up to two drives on the same cable. That means you're limited to four IDE devices per system unless you add an expansion board containing another IDE interface. In contrast, with SCSI (covered in the next section) you can have up to seven drives per interface (or even more on some types of SCSI).

Performance also may suffer when IDE devices share an interface. When you're burning CDs, for example, if the hard drive you are reading from is on the same cable as the CD drive you are writing to, errors may occur. SCSI drives are much more efficient with this type of transfer.

To install an IDE drive, do the following:

1. Set the master/slave jumper on the drive.

2. Install the drive in the drive bay.

3. Connect the power-supply cable.

4. Connect the ribbon cable to the drive and to the motherboard or IDE expansion board. Ensure that the master device is closest to the connection to the motherboard.

5. Configure the drive in BIOS Setup if it isn't automatically detected.

6. Partition and format the drive using the operating system.

Each IDE interface can have only one master drive on it. If there are two drives on a single cable, one of them must be the slave drive. This setting is accomplished via a jumper on the drive. Some drives have a separate setting for Single (that is, master with no slave) and Master (that is, master with a slave); others use the Master setting generically to refer to either case. The cable select setting will assume you have the primary drive first and secondary drive second on the cable. Figure 1.36 shows a typical master/slave jumper scenario, but different drives may have different jumper positions to represent each state. Today, the need for jumper settings has decreased because many drives can autodetect the master/slave relationship.

Most BIOS Setup programs today support Plug and Play, so they detect the new drive automatically at startup. If this doesn't work, the drive may not be installed correctly, the jumper settings may be wrong, or the BIOS Setup may have the IDE interface set to None rather than Auto. Enter BIOS Setup and find out. All you usually have to do is set the IDE interface to Auto and allow the BIOS to detect the drive.

FIGURE 1.36 Master/slave jumpers

1. Master
2. Slave (default setting)
3. Cable select

In BIOS Setup for the drive, you might have the option of selecting a DMA or PIO setting for the drive. Both are methods for improving drive performance by allowing the drive to write directly to RAM, bypassing the CPU when possible. For modern drives that support UltraDMA, neither of these settings is necessary or desirable.

When the drive is installed, you can proceed to partition and format it for the operating system you've chosen. Then, you can install your operating system of choice.

For a Windows 8 or 8.1 system, allow the Windows Setup program to partition and format the drive (when installing the operating system), or use the Disk Management utility in Windows to perform those tasks. To access Disk Management, from the Control Panel choose Administrative Tools and then Computer Management.

SCSI IDs (0–15)

The devices are identified by a unique SCSI ID. The SCSI ID of a device in a drive enclosure that has a backplane is set either by jumpers or by the slot in the enclosure the device is installed into, depending on the model of the enclosure. In the latter case, each slot on the enclosure's backplane delivers control signals to the drive to select a unique SCSI ID. It is important that all devices have unique IDs. The bootable hard disk should be set with an ID of 0, and the host controller should be set at 7 or 15 in the case of 16-bit SCSI (it will be the highest number possible based on the SCSI width). Each end of the chain must be terminated.

In some cases, a single SCSI *target* (as they are called) may contain multiple drives within the unit. In these cases, the drives are differentiated with a second number called a logical unit number (LUN).

RAID Types

RAID stands for Redundant Array of Independent Disks. It's a way of combining the storage power of more than one hard disk for a special purpose such as increased performance or fault tolerance. RAID is more commonly done with SCSI drives, but it can be done with

IDE or SATA drives. Several types of RAID are covered in the following sections. Because of the methods used to provide fault tolerance, the total amount of usable space in the array will vary, as discussed in each section.

RAID 0

RAID 0 is also known as *disk striping*. This is technically not RAID because it doesn't provide fault tolerance. Data is written across multiple drives, so one drive can be reading or writing while the next drive's read/write head is moving. This makes for faster data access. However, if any one of the drives fails, all content is lost. In RAID 0, since there is no fault tolerance, the usable space in the drive is equal to the total space on all the drives. So if the two drives in an array have 250 GB each of space, 500 GB will be the available drive space.

RAID 1

RAID 1 is also known as *disk mirroring*. This is a method of producing fault tolerance by writing all data simultaneously to two separate drives. If one drive fails, the other drive contains all the data and may also be used as a source of the data. However, disk mirroring doesn't help access speed, and the cost is double that of a single drive. Since RAID 1 repeats the data on two drives, only one half of the total drive space is available for data. So if two 250 GB drives are used in the array, 250 GB will be the available drive space.

RAID 5

RAID 5 combines the benefits of both RAID 0 and RAID 1 and is also known as *striping with parity*. It uses a parity block distributed across all the drives in the array, in addition to striping the data across them. That way, if one drive fails, the parity information can be used to recover what was on the failed drive. A minimum of three drives is required. RAID 5 uses $1/n$ (n = the number of drives in the array) for parity information (for example, one-third of the space in a three-drive array), and only 1 ($1/n$) is available for data. So if three 250 GB drives are used in the array (for a total of 750 GB), 500 GB will be the available drive space.

RAID 10

RAID 10 is also known as RAID 1+0. Striped sets are mirrored (a minimum of four drives, and the number of drives must be even). It provides fault tolerance and improved performance but increases complexity. Since this is effectively a mirrored stripe set and a stripe set gets 100 percent use of the drive without mirroring, this array will provide half of the total drive space in the array as available drive space. For example, if there are four 250 GB drives in a RAID 10 array (for a total of 1,000 GB), the available drive space will be 500 GB.

Tape Drive

Another form of storage device is the tape backup. Tape backup devices can be installed internally or externally and use a magnetic tape medium instead of disks for storage. They hold much more data than most other media but are also much slower. They're primarily used for archival storage.

Tape drives can be connected with SCSI, Fibre Channel, SATA, USB, FireWire, or other interfaces.

One of the disadvantages of tape drives in the past has been the sequential manner in which data is located on the tape. That issue may become a thing of the past. In 2010, IBM introduced the Linear Tape File System (LTFS), which allows you to access files on tape in the same way as on a disk filesystem.

Media Capacity

One of the common ways that storage options are compared is capacity. The capacity ranges of each option are briefly discussed here:

CD   Standard CDs normally hold 650–700 MB of data and use the ISO 9660 standard, which allows them to be used in multiple platforms.

CD-RW   Like CDs, CD-RWs normally hold 650–700 MB of data.

DVD-RW   The capacity of DVD-RW depends on whether it is single or dual layer. A single-layer DVD-RW holds about 4.7 GB (the same as a DVD-R), and a dual-layer DVD-RW will hold 8.5 GB.

DVD   DVDs can have up to four layers, can be either single- or double-sided, and can come in about 10 different types or generations. All affect the capacity. The range of capacities available is from 4.7 GB (DVD-5 single-sided, single-layer) to 17.08 GB (DVD-18, double-sided, double-layer, which results in four layers total).

Blu-ray   As mentioned earlier in the section "Optical Drives," the current capacity of a Blu-ray disc is 100 GB, with 400 GB on the horizon, and an aim for 1 TB by 2015.

Tape   The current maximum capacity of a standard tape drive is 10 TB. Sony has a new cassette tape that will hold 185 TB of data.

DL DVD   As described in the section on DVD capacity, a double-layer (DL) DVD's capacity is influenced by the type or generation of DVD and whether it is single or double sided. Single-sided DL (which results in a total of two layers) in DVD-10 holds up to 9.4 GB, and a double-sided DL (which results in a total of four layers) in DVD-18 holds up to 17.08 GB.

Exam Essentials

Identify and differentiate the optical drive options for the long-term storage of data.   Those options include CD-ROM, DVD-ROM, and Blu-Ray. When the ability to erase and rewrite to the disk is required, the options include CD-RW, DVD-RW, dual-layer (DL) DVD-RW, and Blu-ray Disc Recordable Erasable (BD-RE).

Describe the types of interfaces to connect a drive to the system.   Drives can be connected externally using USB, FireWire (IEEE 1394), eSATA, and Ethernet. Internally the connection types are SATA, IDE, and SCSI.

Appreciate the importance of the Master/Slave settings for IDE.   Each IDE interface can have only one master drive on it. If there are two drives on a single cable, one of them must be the slave drive. This setting is accomplished via a jumper on the drive.

Describe the operations of the SCSI bus.   SCSI devices reside on a single bus, which must be terminated on either end. Up to 8 or 16 devices can be attached to a single bus, depending on whether the SCSI bus is wide (0–15) or narrow (0–7). There also is a host bus controller, which is usually plugged into a slot in the computer or integrated into the motherboard.

Identify the advantages and disadvantage to both magnetic and solid-state drive operations.   SSDs retain data in nonvolatile memory chips and contain no moving parts. Compared to electromechanical HDDs, SSDs are typically less susceptible to physical shock, are silent, have lower access time and latency, but are more expensive per gigabyte.

List the capacities of various storage systems.   These range from 650 MB for a CD-Rom up to 17 GB for a double-sided DL DVD.

Identify the pros and cons of various RAID options.   RAID 0 provides only performance enhancement, whereas RAID 1 and RAID 5 provide fault tolerance. RAID 10 provides both performance enhancement and fault tolerance. The cost for these options is the use of multiple hard drives in various arrangements.

1.6 Install Various Types of CPUs and Apply the Appropriate Cooling Methods

The CPU is the brain of the PC and has evolved over the years both in the slots available to connect it to the PC and in its capabilities. With the addition of more processing power came the introduction of more heat in the case and the development of more advanced cooling methods. This section covers these issues as well. The topics addressed in objective 1.6 include the following:

- Socket types
- Characteristics
- Architecture
- Cooling

Socket Types

Sockets are the interface with which CPUs are plugged into the motherboard. These sockets have evolved over the years along with the changes in CPU architecture and design. There are three form factors for CPU chips: pin grid array (PGA), single-edge contact cartridge (SECC), and land grid array (LGA). The PGA style is a flat square or rectangular ceramic chip with an array of pins in the bottom. The actual CPU is a silicon wafer embedded inside that ceramic chip. The SECC style is a circuit board with the silicon wafer mounted on it. The circuit board is then surrounded by a plastic cartridge for protection; the circuit board sticks out of the cartridge along one edge. This edge fits into a slot in the motherboard.

The market leader in chip manufacturing is Intel Corporation, with Advanced Micro Devices (AMD) gaining market share in the home PC market. This section discusses various socket types you may encounter.

Intel: LGA 775, 1155, 1156, 1366, 1150, 2011   Earlier in this chapter, Table 1.3 listed the various Intel CPU slots and sockets you may find in a motherboard and explained which CPUs will fit into them.

AMD: AM3, AM3+, FM1, FM2, FM2+   Table 1.3 also listed the various AMD CPU slots and sockets you may find in a motherboard and explained which CPUs will fit into them. These later-generation AMD sockets were launched as the successor to Socket AM2+. In 2009 AMD3 was released alongside the initial grouping of Phenom II processors designed for it. The principal change from AM2+ to AM3 is support for DDR3 SDRAM. The AM3+ socket has been designed for the AMD FX series Zambezi processors based on the Bulldozer architecture. Socket FM2 is a CPU socket launched in September 2012. Motherboards using the FM2 utilize AMD's new A85X chipset. The FM2+ uses three PCI Express cores: one 2×16 core and two 5×8 cores, for a total of 64 lanes.

Characteristics

CPUs can be compared and contrasted on the basis of a number of characteristics. These characteristics ultimately define the ability of the CPU to perform its main role of processing as well as its ability to provide more advanced features to the PC. These characteristics are discussed in this section.

Speeds

Speeds were discussed earlier in this chapter in the section "1.1 Given a Scenario, Configure Settings and Use BIOS/UEFI Tools on a PC."

Cores

CPUs can have a single-core, dual-core, quad-core, and even dual-quad-core (eight CPUs total). When multiple cores exist, they operate as individual processors, so the more the better. The largest boost in performance will likely be noticed in improved response time while running CPU-intensive processes, such as virus scans, ripping/burning media (requiring file conversion), or file searching.

The addition of more cores does not have a linear effect on performance. The potential impact of multiple cores also depends on the amount of cache or memory present to serve the CPU. When a computer is designed for the processor, this will have been taken into consideration, but when adding a multicore processor to a PC, it is an issue to consider. Cache or memory is discussed in the next section.

Dual-Core Processors

Dual-core processors, available from Intel as well as AMD, essentially combine two processors into one chip. Instead of adding two processors to a machine (making it a multiprocessor system), you have one chip splitting operations and essentially performing as if it's two processors in order to get better performance. A multicore architecture simply has multiple, completely separate processor dies in the same package, whether it's dual core, triple core, or quad core. The operating system and applications see multicore processors in the same way that they see multiple processors in separate sockets. Both dual-core and quad-core processors are common cases for the multicore technology. Most multicore processors from Intel come in even numbers, whereas AMD's Phenom series can contain odd numbers (such as the triple-core processor).

Cache Size/Type

A *cache* is an area of extremely fast memory used to store data that is waiting to enter or exit the CPU. The *Level 1 cache*, also known as the *L1* or *front-side cache*, holds data that is waiting to enter the CPU. On modern systems, the L1 cache is built into the CPU. The *Level 2 cache*, also known as the *L2* or *back-side cache*, holds data that is exiting the CPU and is waiting to return to RAM. On modern systems, the L2 cache is in the same packaging as the CPU but on a separate chip. On older systems, the L2 cache was on a separate circuit board installed in the motherboard and was sometimes called *cache on a stick* (COAST).

On some CPUs, the L2 cache operates at the same speed as the CPU; on others, the cache speed is only half the CPU speed. Chips with full-speed L2 caches have better performance. Some newer systems also have an *L3 cache*, which is external to the CPU. It sits between the CPU and RAM to optimize data transfer between them.

Hyperthreading

One of the improvements offered since the Pentium 4 is *hyperthreading* technology. This feature enables the computer to multitask more efficiently between CPU-demanding applications. An advantage of hyperthreading is improved support for multithreaded code, allowing multiple threads to run simultaneously and thus improving reaction and response time.

Virtualization Support

When using virtualization technology (discussed in the "BIOS Configurations" section earlier, under "Virtualization Support"), a fuller realization of its benefits can be achieved when the processor supports this concept.

The benefit derived from this support is to allow the virtualization product (also called a *hypervisor*) to use hardware-assisted virtualization. This allows the hypervisor to dynamically allocate CPU to the VMs as required. Both AMD and Intel offer CPUs that support hardware virtualization.

Architecture

CPUs can be either 32-bit or 64-bit. This value describes what is called the *word size* of the processor. Having 64 bits offers two important benefits. Data can be processed in larger chunks, which also means with greater precision. Moreover, the system can point to or address a larger number of locations in physical memory. A key consideration is the operating system. If the operating system is not 64 bit, you cannot take advantage of the 64-bit processor.

Integrated GPU

A graphics processing unit (GPU) is a specialized circuit designed to rapidly manipulate and alter memory to accelerate the building of images in a frame buffer intended for output to a display. It improves the graphic abilities of the PC when this feature is present in the CPU.

Some visual features provided by operating systems such as Windows Vista and Windows 7 are unavailable unless the CPU has dedicated graphics memory or a GPU. For example, the Aero view in Vista and Windows 7 requires a card capable of DirectX, which is a technology that requires the DirectCompute API, which in turn requires a GPU.

Disable Execute Bit

The NX bit (No-eXecute) is a technology used in CPUs to segregate areas of memory for use either for storing processor instructions (code) or for storing data. Execute Disable Bit (EDB) is an implementation of this security feature in some Intel CPUs that helps to reduce vulnerability to malware. In AMD, this feature is called Enhanced Virus Protection. When malware attempts to insert code in the buffer, the processor disables code execution, preventing damage and worm propagation. The operating system must support this feature, and it must be enabled in the system BIOS.

Cooling

CPUs produce heat, and the more powerful the CPU the more heat it produces. Heat is an enemy to the PC in general because it causes problems such as random reboots. Methods of cooling the CPU and in turn the overall interior of the case have evolved with the increasing need to remove this heat. This section covers options that are used.

In methods of cooling, technology that transfers heat away from components uses thermoelectric cooling, and components that perform this function are called Peltier components. Heat sinks, cooling fans, and cooling fins are Peltier components. Liquid cooling, on the other hand, cools not by transferring heat away from components but by circulating a cool liquid around them.

Heat Sink

The cooling can be either active or passive. A *passive heat sink* is a block of heat-conductive material that sits close to the CPU and wicks away the heat into the air. An *active heat sink* contains a fan that pulls the hot air away from the CPU. The heat sink sits atop the CPU, in many cases obscuring it from view entirely.

Fans

Active heat sinks have a fan that sits atop the heat sink. It pulls the heat out of the heat sink and away from it. Then the case fan shunts the heat out the back or side of the case.

Thermal Paste

Most *passive heat sinks* are attached to the CPU using a glue-like thermal compound (called *thermal glue*, *thermal compound*, or *thermal paste*). This makes the connection between the heat sink and the CPU more seamless and direct. Thermal compound can be used on active heat sinks too, but generally it isn't because of the possibility that the fan may stop working and need to be replaced. Thermal compound improves thermal transfer by eliminating tiny air pockets between the heat sink and CPU (or other device like a north bridge or video chipset). Thermal compound provides both improved thermal transfer and adds bonding for heat sinks when there are no mounting holes to clamp the heat sink to the device to be cooled.

Liquid-Based

Liquid-Based Cooling cases are available that use circulating water rather than fans to keep components cool. These cases are typically more expensive than standard ones and may be more difficult for a technician untrained in this technology to work on, but they result in an almost completely silent system.

Issues with Liquid-Based Cooling machines can include problems with hoses or fittings, the pump, or the coolant. A failure of the pump can keep the liquid from flowing and cause the system to overheat. A Liquid-Based Cooling system should also be checked every so often for leaks or corrosion on the hoses and fittings, and the reservoir should be examined to make sure it is full and does not contain contaminants. Liquid-Based Cooling is more expensive, less noisy, and more efficient than Peltier components.

Fanless/Passive

Fanless or passive cooling systems are those that either use a highly efficient heat sink or use some type of Liquid-Based Cooling to keep the CPU cool. Some use a thermal heat pipe in which liquid is turned to vapor at the hot end, moves as a vapor down the pipe, and then turns back into liquid at the cool end, where it is cycled around to the hot end and the process starts again.

Exam Essentials

Identify the CPU socket types you may encounter.   These include but are not limited to Intel LGA, 775, 1155, 1156, and 1366, as well as AMD 940, AM2, AM2+, AM3, AM3+, FM1, and F.

Define the characteristic of CPUs.   CPUs can differ based on speed, number of cores, cache size and type, hyperthreading support, virtualization support, architecture (32-bit vs. 64-bit), and integrated GPU support.

Understand the various options available to reduce CPU heat.   These options include heat sinks, fans, thermal paste, and liquid cooling.

1.7 Compare and Contrast Various PC Connection Interfaces, Their Characteristics, and Purpose

When using various modes of connection to the PC, you should understand the characteristics of those connections. This includes the types inside the case as well as the ones that appear on the back or front panel and those that are provided as a result of adding an expansion card into a slot that includes a new connector type on the back panel. The topics addressed in objective 1.7 are as follows:

- Physical connections
- Connector types
- Wireless connections
- Characteristics

Physical Connections

Many different types of cables and connectors have been developed over the years to connect devices to the PC. Some have been around almost as long as the PC, whereas many others have made their appearance only in the last few years. This section discusses the physical characteristics of each of these connection methods, along with the operational characteristics, such as the speed and maximum cable length.

USB 1.1 vs. 2.0 vs. 3.0

USB is an expansion bus type that is used almost exclusively for external devices. All motherboards today have at least two USB ports. Some of the advantages of USB include hot-plugging and the capability for up to 127 USB devices to share a single set of system resources. A USB port requires only one IRQ for all USB devices that are connected to it, regardless of the type or number of devices. USB 1.1 runs at 12 Mbps and USB 2.0 runs at 480 Mbps.

USB 3.0 has transmission speeds of up to 5 Gbps, significantly reduces the time required for data transmission, reduces power consumption, and is backward compatible with USB 2.0. Because USB is a serial interface, its width is 1 bit. It is useful to note, however, that a USB 2.0 device will perform at 2.0 speeds even when connected to a 3.0 port.

By utilizing USB hubs in conjunction with the USB ports available on the local machine, you can connect up to 127 of these devices to the computer. You can daisy-chain up to four external USB hubs to a USB port. *Daisy chaining* means that hubs are attached to each other in a line. A USB hub will not function if it is more than four hubs away from the root port.

Connector Types: A, B, Mini, Micro

USB connectors come in two types and two form factors or sizes. The type A connector is what is found on USB hubs, on host controllers (cards that are plugged into slots to provide USB connections), and on the front and back panels of computers. Type B is the type of USB connector found on the end of the cable that plugs into the devices.

The connectors also come in a mini version and a micro version. The micro version is used on mobile devices, such as mobile phones, GPS units, PDAs, and digital cameras, whereas the mini is found in applications described in the previous paragraph. The choice between a standard A and B and a mini A and B will be dictated by what is present on the device. The cables used cannot exceed 5 meters in length. Figure 1.37 shows, from left to right, a standard Type A, a mini Type A, a standard Type B, and a mini Type B. Some manufacturers have chosen to implement a mini connector that is proprietary, choosing not to follow the standard.

FIGURE 1.37   USB connectors

FireWire 400 vs. FireWire 800

Some newer motherboards have a built-in IEEE 1394/FireWire socket, although this socket in the past was more commonly provided on a PCI expansion board. It transfers data at 400 Mbps and supports up to 63 chained devices on a single set of resources. It's hot-pluggable, like USB. Figure 1.38 shows the connections on a FireWire card.

FIGURE 1.38   Connections on a FireWire card

FireWire 400 (IEEE 1394a) is the original standard that operates up to 400 Mbps with a maximum cable length of 4.5 meters. Now, however, there are cables that will support 10 meters.

FireWire 800 (IEEE 1394b) uses a different encoding scheme that allows it to go up to 800 Mbps. It also can use a cable up to 10 meters.

SATA1 vs. SATA2 vs. SATA3, eSATA

Connections for storage devices can be either SATA or IDE. IDE was the only option early on, and then SATA came on the scene. SATA came out as a standard and was first adopted in desktops and then laptops. Whereas ATA had always been an interface that sends 16 bits at a time, SATA sends only one bit at a time. The benefit is that the cable used can be much smaller, and faster cycling can actually increase performance. SATA uses a seven-wire cable that can be up to 1 meter in length. eSATA cables can be up to 2 meters. Figure 1.39 shows the SATA and eSATA connectors.

FIGURE 1.39   SATA and eSATA

eSATA

SATA

Table 1.6 lists the speeds of the options.

TABLE 1.6 SATA speeds

Standard	Transfer Speed
SATA 1.0	150 MBps
SATA 2.0	300 MBps
SATA 3.0	600 MBps
SATA 3.2	1,969 MBps
eSATA	6 GBps

Other Connector Types

A computer's peripheral ports are the physical connectors outside the computer. Cables of various types are designed to plug into these ports and create a connection between the PC and the external devices that may be attached to it. A successful IT technician should have an in-depth knowledge of ports and cables.

Because the peripheral components need to be upgraded frequently, either to keep pace with technological change or to replace broken devices, a well-rounded familiarity with the ports and their associated cabling is required.

Unless a peripheral device connects directly to the motherboard, it must use a port. Ports can be distinguished from one another by three factors:

- Bits of data simultaneously conveyed
- Data transmission speed
- Type of connector

Serial

A serial cable (and port) uses only one wire to carry data in each direction; all the rest are wires for signaling and traffic control.

Common bit rates include 1,200; 2,400; 4,800; 9,600; 14,400; 19,200; 38,400; 57,600; and 115,200 bits per second. The connector used for serial is a D-shaped connector with a metal ring around a set of pins. These are named for the number of pins/holes used: DB-25, DB-9, HD-15 (also known as DB-15), and so on. Figure 1.40 shows DB-25, DB-15, and DB-9. HD-15 is covered in the section "VGA."

Parallel

A parallel cable uses eight wires to carry bits of data in each direction, plus extra wires for signaling and traffic control. The most common port of this type before the conversion of most printers to USB was the parallel printer port.

FIGURE 1.40   DB-25, DB-15, and DB-9

It sends data 8 bits at a time (in parallel) and uses a cable with a male DB-25 connector at the computer and a 36-pin Centronics male connector at the printer. Figure 1.40 shows a DB-25 connector, and Figure 1.41 shows a Centronics. Its main drawback is its cable length. Older-style Centronics parallel cables can sometimes be up to 15 feet long, although 9 feet to 12 feet is more common. Depending on the mode of operation, it can provide up to 2.5 MBps of bandwidth. IEEE-1284, a newer bidirectional standard, can go up to 30 feet.

FIGURE 1.41   Centronics

Optical

Optical ports are beginning to appear on motherboards to accept a Toshiba Link (TOSLINK) cable. This cable is used to connect consumer audio gear that comes with the cable. These cables have several form factors but the most common is the digital connector using a rectangular EIAJ/JEITA RC-5720 connector. This connector and the plug on the computer are shown in the graphic below.

VGA

This is the traditional connector for the display of a computer, and it is shaped like a *D*. It has three rows of five pins each, for a total of 15 pins. This is also often called the HD-15 (also known as DB-15) connector. A VGA cable carries analog signals. The cable length utilized will affect the resolution achieved: 1024×768 would operate more effectively with 30 feet or less of cable length. As the need for resolution increases, the allowable maximum cable length decreases. Figure 1.42 shows a VGA port.

FIGURE 1.42   VGA port

HDMI

High-Definition Multimedia Interface (HDMI) connectors are used to connect compatible digital items (DVD players and conference room projectors, for example). The Type A connector has 19 pins and is backward compatible with DVI. Type B connectors have 29 pins and aren't backward compatible with DVI, but they support greater resolutions. Type C connectors are a smaller version of Type A for portable devices. Type D is an even smaller micro version that resembles a micro-USB connector. Type E is planned for use in automotive applications. HDMI theoretical cable length limit is 25. Figure 1.43 shows all HDMI types.

FIGURE 1.43   HDMI connectors

There are several versions of HDMI, as described in Table 1.7.

TABLE 1.7   HDMI versions

Version	1.0	1.1	1.2	1.3	1.4	2.0
Maximum throughput (Gbps)	3.96	3.96	3.96	10.2	10.2	6
Maximum color depth (bit/px)	24	24	24	48	48	48
Maximum audio throughput (Mbps)	36.86	36.86	36.86	36.86	36.86	49.152

DVI

There are several types of Digital Video Interface (DVI) pin configurations, but all connectors are D-shaped. The wiring differs based on whether the connector is single-linked or dual-linked (extra pins are used for the dual link). DVI differs from everything else in that it includes both digital and analog signals at the same time, which makes it popular for LCD and plasma TVs. Figure 1.44 shows DVI connectors. Maximum cable length is 16 feet (5 meters). These connectors are covered in more detail in the section "Identify Common PC Connector Types and Associated Cables."

FIGURE 1.44   DVI connectors

DVI-I (Single Link)

DVI-I (Dual Link)

DVI-D (Single Link)

DVI-D (Dual Link)

DVI-A

Audio

Audio connectors (sound) can be analog or digital. The most common connectors are called a mini-TRS connector. There are usually two of these, one for headphones (or speakers) and the other for a microphone (or line in). Figure 1.45 shows a 3.5-mm plug.

FIGURE 1.45   TRS connector

RJ-45

A registered jack (RJ) is a plastic plug with small metal tabs, like a telephone cord plug. Numbering is used in the naming: RJ-11 has two metal tabs, and RJ-14 has four. RJ-45 has eight tabs and is used for Ethernet 10 BaseT/100 BaseT networking. The maximum cable length is 100 meters but can vary slightly based on the category of cabling used. Figure 1.46 shows RJ-11 (left) and RJ-45 (right) connectors.

FIGURE 1.46   RJ-11 and RJ-45

RJ-11

An RJ-11, as described earlier and shown in Figure 1.46, is a standard connector for a telephone line and is used to connect a computer modem to a phone line. It looks much like an RJ-45 but is noticeably smaller.

Thunderbolt

Thunderbolt is a connector type that we introduced earlier in this chapter in the section "Audio." For more information, see that section. Figure 1.47 shows the Thunderbolt cable and connector.

FIGURE 1.47   Thunderbolt connector and cable

Wireless Connections and Their Quality

Wireless connections, once considered a luxury, are now becoming a standard expected by users. There are several forms of wireless communication that serve very different purposes. These connection types differ in their speed, the distance at which they can operate, and the frequencies they use. This section discusses three common types of wireless communication and their applications.

Bluetooth

Bluetooth is a type of wireless that creates what is called a personal area network (PAN). Bluetooth is a radio frequency technology that can connect a device to a computer at a range of about 35 feet. It operates in the 2.4 GHz band, which is the same band as 802.11b/g. Version 2.0 offers 3 Mbps (with actual throughput of 2.1 Mbps).

IR

Infrared technology requires direct line of sight and has been used for printers in the past. It can operate at a distance of 5 meters and can offer up to 4 Mbps. It is being replaced with Bluetooth over time.

RF

Radio frequency (RF) describes any of the technologies, like Bluetooth, that use radio waves. This also includes 802.11 WLAN technologies. These operate in two frequencies: 802.11b/g in the 2.4 GHz range and 802.11a and 802.11ac in the 5.0 GHz range. 802.11n can operate in both. These connections are used for networking. The ranges, speeds, and frequencies of these technologies are covered later in the section "Speed, Distance Limitations, and Frequencies."

NFC

Near field communications (NFC) is a wireless technology that allows smartphones and other equipped devices to communicate when very near one another or when touching. NFC operates at slower speeds than Bluetooth but consumes far less power and doesn't require pairing. It also does not create a PAN like Bluetooth; rather, the connections are point-to-point. NFC can operate up to 20 cm at a transfer rate of 0.424 Mbps.

NFC is also a standard managed by the ISO and uses tags that are embedded in the devices. NFC components include an initiator and a target; the initiator actively generates an RF field that can power a passive target. This enables NFC targets to take simple form factors such as tags, stickers, key fobs, or cards that do not require batteries.

Characteristics

This section will discuss the characteristics of PC connection interfaces.

Analog vs. Digital Transmission

Audio and video can be delivered in either analog or digital form. For video this means that there are two connector types you may find on the PC for connecting the display (or monitor). Both types are discussed next.

VGA vs. HDMI

VGA connections and cables are analog in nature, and I've pretty much said all there is to say about this connector type. HDMI is an interface for transmitting encrypted uncompressed digital data. When these connections are available, they are preferable to using the VGA connector, but they require the use of an HDMI cable between the computer and the display. When compared to HDMI, VGA cannot deliver the high resolutions that HDMI can.

Speed, Distance Limitations, and Frequencies

Table 1.8 compares the speed and distance limitations of the wireless technologies discussed.

TABLE 1.8   Distances, speeds, and frequencies

Technology	Maximum Outdoor Range	Maximum Indoor Range	Maximum Speed	Frequency
Bluetooth	10 m/35 ft	10 m/35 ft	3 Mbps	2.4 GHz
IR	5 m/15 ft	5 m/15 ft	4 Mbps	33-40 GHz or 50-60 GHz
802.11	100 m/330 ft	20 m/66 ft	2 Mbps	2.4 GHz
802.11a	120 m/390 ft	35 m/115 ft	54 Mbps	5.0 GHz
802,11ac	35 m/115 ft	35 m/115 ft	6.933 Gbps	5.0 GHz
80211b	140 m/460 ft	35 m/115 ft	11 Mbps	2.4 GHz
802.11g	140 m/460 ft	38 m/125 ft	54 Mbps	2.4 GHz
802.11n	250 m/820 ft	70m/230 ft	600 Mbps	2.4 and 5.0 GHz

Digital Rights Management

With the rapid increase in wireless usage of all types, the concern for controlling the leakage of data from an organization and the illegal sharing of content wirelessly is rising. The

Open Mobile Alliance (OMA) created a system called OMA digital rights management (DRM) that provides a way for content creators to set enforced limits on the use and duplication of their content by customers. This system has been implemented in more than 500 mobile phone models at the time of this writing.

Exam Essentials

Identify the characteristics of connector types on most PCs.   These include but are not limited to USB, SATA, eSATA, FireWire, serial, parallel, VGA, HDMI, DVI, audio, RJ-45, and RJ-11.

Describe the difference in the operation of VGA and HDMI transmission.   VGA connections and cables are analog in nature, whereas HDMI is an interface for transmitting digital data.

List the speed, distance, and frequency of wireless connections.   For device connections, Bluetooth offers up to 2.1 Mbps at about 35 feet, and infrared transmits at 4 Mbps at 5 meters. For networking, 802.11b operates at 11 Mbps, 802.11g at 54 Mbps, 802.11n at up to 600 Mbps, and 80211ac at up to 6 Gbps. The 802.11a maximum indoor range is 100 meters, or 300 feet, and the maximum outdoor range is 350 meters, or 1,200 feet. The 802.11b maximum indoor range is 150 meters, or 492 feet, and the maximum outdoor range is 500 meters, or 1,640 feet. For 802.11g and 802.11ac, the maximum indoor range is 150 meters, or 492 feet, and the maximum outdoor range is 500 meters, or 1,640 feet.

1.8 Install a Power Supply Based on Given Specifications

The power supply provides a number of connectors for various devices as well as a plug for the motherboard. It is important to understand these connector types and to appreciate the power drawn by various devices. Knowledge of the power needs of the devices can allow the technician to choose a power supply that provides the total power needs of the PC. The topics addressed in objective 1.8 include the following:

- Connector types and their voltages
- Specifications

Connector Types and Their Voltages

When selecting a power supply, two issues become important. You need to supply the total wattage required by all the devices and the motherboard of the PC, and you must ensure that it has the connector types required by your devices. This section discusses the voltage requirements of various connector types.

To determine the wattage a device draws, multiply voltage by current. For example, if a device uses 5 amps of +3.3 V and 0.7 amps of +12 V, a total of 25 watts is consumed. Do this calculation for every device installed. Most devices have labels that state their power requirements.

SATA

The SATA power connector is 15 pins, with 3 pins designated for 3.3 V, 5 V, and 12 V and with each pin carrying 1.5 amps. This results in a total draw of 4.95 watts + 7.5 watts + 18 watts, or about 30 watts. Figure 1.48 shows the SATA power connector (the data cable was shown earlier in Figure 1.34).

FIGURE 1.48   SATA power connector

Molex

A Molex connector is used to provide power to drives of various types. It has four pins, two of which have power (one 12 V and the other 5 V). These are standard for IDE (PATA) or older SCSI drives. The total power demands are from 5 to 15 watts for IDE and 10 to 40 watts for SCSI. The four-pin Molex connector was shown earlier in Figure 1.19.

Four/Eight-Pin 12 V

With the introduction of the Pentium 4, the motherboard required more power. Supplemental power connections were provided to the motherboard in 4-, 6- (discussed later in this section), or 8-pin formats. These were in addition to the 20-pin connector (discussed later in this section) that already provided.

There is a four-pin square mini version of the ATX connector, which supplies two pins with 12 V, and an eight-pin version (two rows) that has four 12 V leads. These connect to other items, such as the processor, or to other components, such as a network card that may need power that exceeds what can be provided with the ATX connection to the board. Figure 1.49 shows the eight-pin version and the four-pin square mini version.

FIGURE 1.49 Eight-pin and four-pin 12 V

PCIe Six/Eight-Pin

PCIe slots also draw more power and require power in addition to the main 20-pin connector (discussed next). These additional connectors can be six pins and may also contain an additional two-pin connector on the side for cases where the connection required is eight-pin.

20-Pin

The main ATX connector, referenced earlier, is a 20-pin connector. The four pins carrying power are 3.3 V, 3.3 V, 5 V, and 5 V. This allows the motherboard to pull about 20 to 30 watts. Figure 1.50 shows the 20-pin ATX.

FIGURE 1.50 20-pin ATX

24-Pin

The 24-pin ATX connector is simply the 20-pin connector discussed earlier along with the extra 4-pin connector on the side. This provides the four pins carrying power as discussed earlier plus an additional four pins with 5 V standby, 12 V, 12 V, and 3.3. Figure 1.51 shows the 24-pin ATX.

FIGURE 1.51   24-pin ATX

Specifications

When purchasing the power supply, you must take into account issues such as wattage, number of connectors, physical size or form factor, and plug types. This section addresses these considerations.

Wattage

When the wattage needs of each device and of the motherboard and CPU are totaled, you will know the wattage that the power supply must provide. A power supply has a rated output capacity in watts, and when you fill a system with power-hungry devices, you must make sure that maximum capacity isn't exceeded. Otherwise, problems with power can occur, creating lockups or spontaneous reboots. Most power supplies provide between 250 watts and 1,200 watts. It's always a good idea to have more than the minimum required for the devices that are present so that additional devices can be added in the future.

Dual-Rail

Dual-rail power supplies are ones that use multiple wires or "rails" to supply the power rather than a single wire. While some think this will increase the amount of power that can be provided, that is not true. In fact, single rails deliver more power, but you are sending more current over a single wire, which can overheat the wires. Manufacturers typically group several wires together and apply the current limit to the entire group. Almost all high-power supplies claim to implement separate rails.

Size

The physical dimension of the power supply must also be considered. The slot where the power supply goes in the PC will be the limiting factor. The thin form has been optimized for small and low-profile micro-ATX and FlexATX system layouts. The long, narrow profile of this power supply fits easily into low-profile systems.

Number of Connectors

The power supply can come with any combination of the power connector types discussed earlier in this section. A quick inventory of the connectors that you need will assist you in ensuring that the power supply you purchase has the connectors required.

ATX

If the motherboard is an ATX (the larger motherboard), the power needs of the system will probably be higher than that of a micro-ATX. In that case, ensure that the supply is designed for an ATX system and can provide the higher requirements.

Micro-ATX

Micro-ATX boards are smaller and designed to operate with power supplies of a lower wattage rating. As you add more USB devices or put the board in a larger case with more internal devices, a larger power supply may become necessary.

Dual-Voltage Options

Most power supplies have the ability to accept input of either 110 or 220 volts. Some expensive power supplies can autosense and do not need to be set manually; however, most have to be set manually, and you want to set the switch to the correct voltage setting or you could cause damage. Figure 1.52 shows the typical position of this switch.

FIGURE 1.52   Voltage switch

Exam Essentials

Identify common power connector types and their voltages.   These include but are not limited to SATA, Molex, 4- to 8-pin 12 V, PCIe 6- to 8-pin, 20-pin, 24-pin, and floppy connectors.

Understand the specifications of power supplies.   Differentiate power supplies by wattage, size, number of connectors, and design (ATX or mini-ATX).

Describe a dual-wattage power supply.   This is a supply that can be set to accept either 110 volts or 220 volts.

1.9 Given a Scenario, Select the Appropriate Components for a Custom PC Configuration to Meet Customer Specifications or Needs

In many cases, an off-the-shelf computer does not fill the needs of a customer. In these cases, a unit must be custom built to accommodate their specific needs. This section describes some common custom configurations and options to meet specific needs. The topics addressed in objective 1.9 include the following:

- Graphic/CAD/CAM design workstation
- Audio/video-editing workstation
- Virtualization workstation
- Gaming PC
- Home theater PC
- Standard thick client
- Thin client
- Home server PC

Graphic/CAD/CAM Design Workstation

Computers used for graphic design, computer-aided design (CAD) applications, and computer-aided manufacturing (CAM) require much more horsepower than the standard PC. Specifically, they require multiple or more powerful processors, more robust video cards, and significantly more memory. In this section, these needs are discussed.

Multicore Processor

The resource-intensive applications used with graphics, CAD, and CAM require high-end multicore processors. For example, to run a 64-bit version of Autodesk AutoCAD software, requirements are an AMD Athlon 64 with SSE2 technology, AMD Opteron processor with SSE2 technology, Intel Xeon processor with Intel EM64T support and SSE2 technology, or Intel Pentium 4 with Intel EM64T support and SSE2 technology.

Streaming Single Instruction, Multiple Data Extensions 2 (SSE2) technology is the latest version of a technology that provides additional instructions to the CPU that allows it to perform a single instruction on multiple pieces of data. Moreover, to do 3D modeling (which is graphic intensive), an Intel 4 processor or AMD Athlon 3.0 GHz or greater is required. If a dual-core Intel or AMD dual-core processor is used, then it can be 2.0 GHz.

Keep in mind these are only the minimums. For good performance, these minimums should be exceeded.

High-End Video

As you can imagine, the video demands of graphics such as 3D are much higher than those of common office applications. Continuing with the example of AutoCAD 2012, this requires a 1,280×1,024 true-color video display adaptor with 128 MB of its own memory or greater and Pixel Shader 3.0 or greater, and it should be a Microsoft Direct3D-capable workstation-class graphics card. Note that the graphics card *itself* should have a minimum of 128 MB of RAM for its operations.

Maximum RAM

There can never be enough RAM, and in the case of CAD/CAM and graphics, the minimum (using the same example) is 2 GB of RAM. When the minimum to run the software is 2 GB, you need much more than that for good performance.

Audio/Video-Editing Workstation

As I go over the requirements of these specialty solutions, you may notice a recurring theme: RAM, CPU, and graphics. It's no different with an audio- or video-editing machine. These are the components that are saddled with the workload and will be the ones that require boosting above what would be used on a standard workstation.

With audio and video editing, however, additional components can make the workstation more productive to the user. This section discusses those items.

Specialized Audio and Video Card

Many video- and audio-editing software packages come with a special capture card that works in concert with the accompanying software to provide ease of use. For example, it might be an internal PCI card that captures video from any analog or DV source. You can also output video to a VCR or an analog or DV camcorder from this card. They still require (you guessed it) a high-end audio and video card as well and plenty of memory and a processor that may not have quite the requirements of CAD/CAM but still should be 2.4 GHz or higher.

Large, Fast Hard Drive

Your hard drive should be at least 7,200 RPM. You will also want at least two drives if not three. When doing audio, use one for the operating system and programs and a second drive for audio files. When doing video, consider a third drive used exclusively for video files.

Even better, consider a RAID setup. Many motherboards include a SATA RAID controller built in. Use RAID 0 to enhance performance (see the section "RAID Types").

Dual Monitors

Especially when doing video editing, a second monitor is well worth the money and the desk real estate. You may need to read or refer to something on one screen while using the other for the editing software. The material could be tutorials or source material.

It also may be that you move your tools (for example, Photoshop tools) to one screen so they don't clutter the image you are working on.

Virtualization Workstation

A virtualization workstation is also called a *virtualization host*. The VMs that reside on this operating system are called *guest* operating systems. The host operating system and the guest must all share the total amount of RAM and CPU that the host machine possesses. This section discusses these issues.

Maximum RAM and CPU Cores

The amount of RAM that is required depends on the number of VMs that you anticipate operating at the same time, not how many exist on the desktop. Total the memory requirements of each VM that will be open at the same time, in addition to the requirements of the host operating system. That should be the minimum. Then add more for overhead to ensure performance.

The memory issue is not something you can fudge. If there is not enough memory, the VM will not start, and you will be notified with an error message that there is insufficient memory.

With regard to CPU, it should be dual- if not quad-core, and multiple CPUs would be even better.

Gaming PC

Gaming PCs may place the highest demands on the system of any specialty PC discussed here because the machines are in competition with other machines. The skill of the player is certainly a big factor in success, but at some point the user with the more powerful PC is going to be able to raise the level of the game through hardware.

Multicore Processor

When it comes to the processor, the question becomes "How much do you want to spend?" Just as a comparison (prices change daily!), for more than $600 you can get the Intel Core i7-3930K. (There is also the i7-3960X for $1,000.) Also keep in mind that multiple processors or multicore processors will always improve the gaming experience.

High-End Video/Specialized GPU

When playing a game, it is critical that the action you are seeing (and reacting to) is rendered to the screen as quickly as possible. With gaming machines, dual GPU cards are often used. The higher-end cards also require water cooling of GPUs. In fact, the faster cards all need water cooling (covered later in this section).

High-Definition Sound Card

When you're considering the features of a sound card, you want those features to be performed in hardware. Anytime these functions are performed in software, it simply means the main CPU is going to get the workload. Also, you want to go with a high-definition card. The following are things to consider:

- Using the PCI Express slot (better bandwidth) is better than using the PCI slot.

- Make sure the card has its own onboard memory (less work for the main CPU).

- If you are using a Mac, a Thunderbolt card is the way to go.

High-End Cooling

With all the heat being generated by the CPUs and GPUs, fans may not be sufficient to remove the heat. Water-cooling systems will cool the system better and will be quieter as well. Cooling kits circulate water through the case in tubes that enter and exit the box to a unit where the water is cooled again (think of the cooling system in your car). Figure 1.53 shows a cooling system.

FIGURE 1.53   Cooling system

Home Theater PC

A home theater PC (HTPC) is a convergence device. It uses software to bring together video, photo, music playback, television content, and even video recording to a single computer interface. Many operating systems today include this software. To take advantage of its capabilities, however, additional components need to be in place. This section discusses some of the components that will enhance the experience.

Surround Sound Audio

Surround sound speaker systems can add to the experience of the home theater PC. A numbering system has been developed that indicates the number and type of speakers present. The common setups are 2.1, 4.1, 5.1, 6.1, and 7.1. The number on the left is the total number of speakers, and the number on the right is the number of subwoofers (bass).

Don't forget, you will need places to plug these speakers into the system. So, a new card with additional plugs may be called for, or a new-generation external sound processor that can plug into the USB slot may be the solution.

HDMI Output

In some cases, you want to direct the content from your PC to a more suitable viewing device such as your big-screen TV. That is best accomplished with an HDMI plug from the PC to the TV. If the PC does not have multiple outlets for video, you may need to get a graphics card that provides these outlets. If you do that, make sure the card has an HDMI plug. If you are lucky, there will be one of these plugs present on the PC. Figure 1.54 shows an HDMI plug.

FIGURE 1.54   HDMI plug

HTPC Compact Form Factor

An HTPC that appears in the small form factor is one that is smaller in size and shape when compared to a regular PC while still providing the capabilities required. In some cases, they are cubical in shape, and in other cases they resemble a DVR or mini audio receiver. Other changes to the layout include placing all ports in the front. Figure 1.55 shows an example.

FIGURE 1.55   Compact form factor

TV Tuner

If you want to receive TV signals on the HTPC, you will need a TV tuner card. These can be installed internally in a slot, or they can be external units connected with the USB port. They also can be analog, digital, or both (although broadcast analog TV has been discontinued in the United States since 2009). If recording the TV content is required, the card must also be a video capture card.

In cases where it is desired to watch one stream of content while recording another stream, a card that has two tuners in it must be used. These are called *combo tuners*.

Standard Thick Client

When discussing thin and thick clients, you should understand that a thick client is a PC that has all the capabilities of a standard PC. It runs all applications locally from its own hard drive. A thin client (discussed in the next section) is one that has minimal capabilities and runs the applications (and perhaps even the operating system itself) from a remote server.

Desktop Applications

A thick client has the applications installed locally and will need to have sufficient resources to support the applications. Applications state these requirements in the documentation. With a thick client, since all application support will come from the local machine, these requirements must be met to use the software.

Meets Recommended Requirements for Selected Operating System

A standard thick client will need to provide all the hardware requirements of the installed operating system. This is because unlike the thin client (discussed in the next section) none of the processing will be offloaded to a server. It all must be supplied by the thick client. Requirements for various operating systems are covered in Chapter 5, "Windows Operating Systems," and Chapter 6, "Other Operating Systems and Technologies."

Thin Client

A thin client is a PC with minimal resources. Such a system is responsible only for receiving the processed output of an operating system and application running on a server and rendering the output in the screen.

The latest example of this is a computer running the Windows Thin PC (WinTPC) operating system, which is designed to run on older hardware.

Basic Applications

Some applications are created to function in a client-server architecture. When these are used in a thin client, the client side of the application operates on the thin client but requires minimal system resources. The server side of the application performs all the processing, and the client side simply renders the output to the display and transmits keystrokes to the server.

Meets Minimum Requirements for Selected Operating System

Even thin client operating systems have minimum requirements. Follow the documented requirements to ensure good performance. In many cases, older computers that are of no use because thick clients are suitable candidates to be thin clients.

Network Connectivity

Most traditional thin clients come with a NIC built in. They require the same settings that any networked device does, including IP address, subnet mask, and default gateway. These can be static configuration, or the device can receive these through DHCP.

Home Server PC

Many homes and small offices have a network of computers to rival a small enterprise. In these cases, sometimes it makes sense to centralize the location of resources for both ease of use and security of information. There are even home server operating systems made, but that is not required to make a PC a home server. This section discusses some common roles of a home server.

Media Streaming

The home server can act as a streaming media server to other computers in the home network if the operating system provides this capability. An example of such an operating system is Windows Home Server. Once the streaming feature is enabled, other systems can use their Windows Media Players to connect to any shared content and stream that content to the other PC. One of the benefits of this is centralized storage of the content and reduced duplication of the content on other machines in the network. This type of server should have plenty of disk space and memory.

File Sharing

For the same reasons that centralized storage of media content reduces content duplication in the network, so can file sharing from a home server. Another great benefit of this is a central location to perform regular backups of the files so that this does not need to be done on all the other machines in the network. This server should have plenty of disk space.

Print Sharing

Centralized control of printing can also be done with a home server. The machine can be the print server for all home printers. When done this way, printer permissions can be used to control who does what to the printers as well as whose print jobs get priority in a crunch. Print servers needs extra memory.

Gigabit NIC

When a machine is acting as the home server for all these functions, the network card will be busy. For that reason, it is probably a good idea to ensure that it is a Gigabit NIC, which allows it to operate 10 times faster than the standard 100 MB NIC. Make sure that the cabling supports 1 GB, or you will be wasting your time and money.

RAID Array

To speed the access to data or to provide fault tolerance to any data stored on the home server, consider using multiple hard drives and implementing a RAID 0, RAID 1, or RAID 5 hard disk system. See the section "RAID Types."

Exam Essentials

Describe the specific requirements of specialty workstations. These include but are not limited to graphic, CAD, CAM, audio/video editing, virtualization, gaming, home theater, and home server systems.

Identify the difference between a thick and a thin client. A thick client runs the operating system and applications from the local hard drive, whereas a thin client runs these components from a remote server.

1.10 Compare and Contrast Types of Display Devices and Their Features

The possibilities for displaying the content from a PC used to consist of two options, cathode ray tube (CRT) technology found in television sets or the liquid crystal display (LCD) technology found on all laptop, notebook, and palmtop computers. That is no longer the case. Now this output can be directed to a number of different devices employing several technologies. This section discusses these options. The topics addressed in objective 1.10 include the following:

- Types
- Refresh/frames rate
- Resolution
- Native resolution
- Brightness/lumens
- Analog vs. digital
- Privacy/antiglare filters
- Multiple displays
- Aspect ratios

Types

Today, users need to redirect the content from the PC to other devices besides the regular monitor. Even within the monitor category, various technologies are employed to present content to a user from a computer device. This section discusses devices to which computer content may be directed, along with competing technologies for rendering the content.

LCD

LCDs have almost completely replaced CRTs as the default display type for both laptops and desktops. Two major types of LCDs are used today: active matrix screens and passive matrix screens. Their main differences lie in the quality of the image. Both types use some kind of lighting behind the LCD panel to make the screen easier to view. One or more small fluorescent tubes are used to backlight the screen.

Passive Matrix   A passive matrix screen uses a row of transistors across the top of the screen and a column of them down the side. It sends pulses to each pixel at the intersection of each row and column combination, telling it what to display. Passive matrix displays are becoming obsolete because they're less bright and have poorer refresh rates and image quality than active matrix displays. However, they use less power than active matrix displays do.

Active Matrix   An active matrix screen uses a separate transistor for each individual pixel in the display, resulting in higher refresh rates and brighter display quality. These screens use more power, however, because of the increased number of transistors that must be powered. Almost all notebook PCs today use active matrix. A variant called thin-film transistor (TFT) uses multiple transistors per pixel, resulting in even better display quality.

TN vs. IPS

There are two major LCD technologies used in LCDs. This section discusses the pros and cons of each.

Twisted Nematic (TN)   Twisted nematic (TN) is the older of the two major technologies for flat-panel displays. While it provides the shortest response time, high brightness, and draws less power than competing technologies, it suffers from poor quality when viewed from wide angles. It suffers color distortions when viewed from above or from the sides.

In-Plane Switching (IPS)   This is a newer technology that solves the issue of poor quality at angles other than straight on. It also provides better color quality. However, it has much slower response time and is more expensive. Newer versions like Super-IPS (SIPS) make improvements on the response time.

Fluorescent vs. LED Backlighting

LCDs can use two kinds of backlighting: LED-based and fluorescent. Fluorescent is an older technology and consists of a fluorescent tube connected to a voltage inverter board that provides power to the backlight. LED-based is a newer technology and uses a matrix of LEDs for the backlighting. Table 1.9 compares the two technologies.

TABLE 1.9   Fluorescent and LED

Characteristic	Fluorescent	LED
Size	Thicker and heavier	Thinner and lighter
Cost	Cheaper	More expensive
Power	High power consumption and heat generation	Lower power consumption and heat generation
Brightness	Lower	Higher
Lifespan	Shorter	Longer

LED

LED-based monitors are still LCDs (they still use liquid crystals to express images onscreen), but they use a different type of backlight than what is normally used. Several types of backlights are used with LED.

The most common for computers is white LEDs (WLEDs). Using a special diffuser, the light is spread to cover the entire screen. A more expensive type is RGB LED. Instead of using WLEDs on one edge of the screen, with RGB LCD layers, like the previous technology, RGB LEDs are aligned all over the panel matrix. Each LED is capable of red-, green-, or blue-colored light. This gives the display more accurate color than WLEDs. Finally, there is WLED on a flat array, covering the entire screen (like an RGB LED using only WLEDs). Currently, it's used only in LED-backlit HDTVs. As you've seen, however, computer output can be directed to the HDTV screen.

Plasma

Plasma displays utilize small cells containing ionized gases, similar to what is used in fluorescent lamps. They have the advantage of high-quality picture, wider viewing angles, and less motion blur—but they have the disadvantage of screen burn-in and high energy requirements.

They have mainly been used for TV displays but now can be purchased simply as display monitors that accept output from a variety of devices, including PCs.

Projector

In the business world, it is frequently necessary to share the desktop with others in a meeting. This is easily accomplished by directing the output of the PC to a projector. The projector can be plugged into the same connector as the monitor, and in most cases both can be used at the same time. Some projectors require an HDMI connector.

OLED

Organic light-emitting diode (OLED) technology uses a layer of organic compound with emissive electroluminescent qualities to emit light in response to an electric current. This organic layer resides between two electrodes. Although it uses no backlight, it results in a higher-contrast ratio than an LCD in low-light conditions.

This technology is currently expensive, and the materials used have a limited life span. As of this writing, 17-inch models with LED technology run close to $5,000.

Refresh/Frame Rate

A monitor's refresh rate specifies how many times in one second the scanning beam of electrons redraws the screen. The phosphors stay bright for only a fraction of a second, so they must constantly be hit with electrons to stay lit. Given in draws per second, or hertz (Hz), the refresh rate affects how much energy is being put into keeping the screen lit. Most people notice a flicker in the display at refresh rates of 75 Hz or lower because the phosphors begin to decay to black before they're revived; increasing the refresh rate can help reduce eyestrain by reducing the flickering. CRTs experienced a refresh flicker that was often visible to the naked eye. This is no longer a problem with newer LCD monitors.

The frame rate, or frame frequency, is the frequency at which an imaging device produces unique consecutive images called *frames*. It is a description of the number of frames per second that the card writes to the buffer, while the refresh rate refers to how often the screen is drawn from the data coming from the buffer. That means the refresh rate depends on the display, and the frame rate depends on the application writing data to the buffer.

If the application writes data at a rate faster than the display can refresh, then some visual data will be lost because screen buffer updates will be overwritten by the application before the display refresh occurs. This results in what is typically called screen *tearing*.

Resolution

The resolution of a monitor is the number of horizontal and vertical pixels that are displayed. Most monitors allow for two or more resolutions, and you can pick the one to use in the desktop settings of the operating system. On a CRT, the vertical hold (V-hold) setting can be tweaked to make the image appear properly in the monitor.

Display resolutions include the following:

VGA   Video graphics array is a 320×200 resolution and uses analog technology.

XGA   Extended graphics array has been around since 1990. It's a 1,024×768 resolution that offers fixed-function hardware acceleration for 2D tasks.

SXGA+   Super extended graphics array is a 1,400×1,050 resolution commonly used on 14- or 15-inch laptops. It's typically considered the maximum resolution that video projectors will work with.

UXGA   Ultra-extended graphics array is a 1,600×1,200 resolution and is the next step in the monitor-resolution evolution.

WUXGA   Widescreen ultra-extended graphics array is a resolution of 1,920×1,200 with a 16:10 screen aspect ratio. It's also a standard for use with television sets, at a slightly different ratio.

Native Resolution

The native resolution of a display refers to its single fixed resolution. An LCD cannot change resolution to match the signal being displayed like a CRT monitor can, meaning that optimal display quality can be reached only when the signal input matches the native resolution. Most LCD monitors are able to inform the PC of their native resolution.

Brightness/Lumens

Contrast ratio is a measurement of the brightness of the LCD panels. A general rule of thumb is the greater the contrast ratio, the brighter the display can be, and thus a rating of 3,000:1 is preferred over 800:1.

You can adjust the brightness by using the controls that are usually found on the front of the monitor, but keep in mind that these adjustments will be less refined than if you use a calibration program. Standard symbols are used to represent brightness; the location and operation of these controls vary from monitor to monitor. Use the documentation that came with your monitor.

Analog vs. Digital

As described in the section "VGA vs. HDMI," VGA connections and cables are analog in nature, and HDMI and DVI are interfaces for transmitting encrypted uncompressed digital data.

CRT monitors require the signal information in analog. In those cases, the video adaptor converts digital data into analog. DVI and HDMI maintain the information in digital format through the process with no need for conversion. Some DVI connectors will support both analog and digital.

Privacy/Antiglare Filters

Privacy and antiglare filters fit over the front of a display screen and either reduce the glare on the screen or, in the case of privacy filters, make it difficult if not impossible to read the monitor unless you are squarely in front of it, which helps to reduce eavesdropping or shoulder surfing. In situations where high-security information will be displayed on the desktop, a privacy filter may be called for. When the workstation is facing sunlight, an antiglare filter may be beneficial.

Multiple Displays

Most PCs allow you to use multiple monitors as long as there is a display card installed for each. Although this can be useful for running a window for each monitor, one of the most common uses is the Presenter View in Microsoft PowerPoint. When chosen, this allows a different view of the slideshow to be shown on the main monitor (typically a projector) than what is shown on the secondary monitor (such as presenter notes, the next slide that is set to appear, and so forth). Multiple displays can present the same desktop on both displays (mirroring) or can be set up as a large single desktop, which is called extending the desktop. Multiple displays are beneficial in any cases where many windows or documents need to open at the same time, especially if copying and pasting may be called for between the windows.

Aspect Ratios

Aspect ratio describes the proportional relationship between its width and its height and is usually expressed as a ratio such as 16:9, where the first value is the width and the second is the length. Keep in mind the values are not inches or centimeters or any other absolute value, but describe the proportional relationship between the two. Three standard aspect ratios are discussed here:

4:3 At one time most monitors had a 4:3 aspect ratio. This continued until about 2006.

16:10 Starting about 2006, the 16:10 aspect ratio began to replace the 4:3 aspect ratio, as the use of "square" monitors began to decline.

16:9   In about 2008, this ratio, sometimes referred to as *sixteen-nine* began to replace both 16:10 and 4:3. By 2010, virtually all manufacturers had moved to 16:9.

Exam Essentials

Identify the common technologies used on devices that display computer output.   These include but are not limited to LCD, LED, plasma, and OLED displays. Projectors are included as well.

Describe the settings and characteristics of various display types.   Understand refresh rate, resolution, native resolution, and brightness.

Describe the differences between analog and digital display.   The video adaptor converts digital data into analog. DVI and HDMI maintain the information in digital format through the process with no need for conversion.

1.11 Identify Common PC Connector Types and Associated Cables

A wide variety of connector types and cables are used to hook together the parts and pieces of a PC system. This section briefly reviews the connectors and cables that have been covered and discusses others for the first time. The topics addressed in objective 1.11 include the following:

- Display connector types
- Display cable types
- Device cables and connectors
- Adaptors and converters

Display Connector Types

Connecting the monitor to the PC can be accomplished with many different connector types. In this section, for those types that have been covered earlier, I'll provide a reference to the section discussing them.

DVI-D

DVI connectors can come in several forms. You may remember that DVI can sometimes do analog and digital at the same time. DVI-D (the *D* stands for digital) connectors supply digital signals only. These can also come in a single- or dual-link format. A dual-link format allows for a second data link.

DVI-I

A DVI-I connector (the *I* stands for integrated) has pins that can provide analog and digital. These can also come in a single- or dual-link format.

DVI-A

A DVI-A connector (the *A* stands for analog) has pins that can provide analog and digital. This type comes in a single-link format only. Figure 1.56 shows the various types of DVI plugs discussed in this section.

FIGURE 1.56   DVI connectors

DVI-I (Single Link)

DVI-I (Dual Link)

DVI-D (Single Link)

DVI-D (Dual Link)

DVI-A

DisplayPort

DisplayPort is a digital interface standard produced by the Video Electronics Standards Association (VESA), used for audio and video. The interface is primarily used to connect a video source to a display device such as a computer monitor or television set. It resembles a USB connector (see Figure 1.57).

FIGURE 1.57   DisplayPort

RCA

RCA plugs are sometimes used for audio and video in the same way that mini-TRS connectors are (see the "Audio" section under "Other Connector Types"). They are nearly the same size but look quite different. Figure 1.58 shows a set of these connectors.

FIGURE 1.58   RCA plugs

HD-15 (Examples: DE-15 or DB-15)

The DB-15 plug is the standard VGA plug that has been around since the earliest displays. It was discussed in the section "Serial" under "Other Connector Types." Figure 1.59 shows an example.

FIGURE 1.59   DB-15

BNC

Bayonet Neill–Concelman (BNC) connectors are sometimes used in the place of RCA connectors for video electronics, so you may encounter these connectors, especially when video equipment connects to a PC. In many cases, you may be required to purchase an adaptor to convert this to another form of connection because it is rare to find one on the PC. Figure 1.60 shows male and female BNC connectors.

FIGURE 1.60 BNC

Male

Female

miniHDMI

The miniHDMI is a small form-factor version of HDMI. It is intended for portable devices such as a camcorder. Cables that are made to connect a portable device to a PC will have a miniHDMI connector on one end and a standard HDMI (type A) connector on the other. A miniHDMI connector (type C) was shown in Figure 1.43.

miniDIN-6

MiniDIN connectors come with a number of different pin arrangements and are used in various applications. A six-pin version, miniDIN-6, is used to connect to some projectors and speaker systems. When connecting those devices to the PC, you may encounter this plug. As with the BNC connector, it may require a converter to a connection type that exists on the PC, such as USB. Figure 1.61 shows a six-pin miniDIN.

FIGURE 1.61 Six-pin miniDIN

Display Cable Types

Cables must match the connector. This section provides a quick survey of the cables that go with the various connectors.

HDMI HDMI cables are rated by the resolution they can provide. Category 2 (also called *high speed*) provides better resolution than Category 1. These also differ in acceptable length. Category 1 is best at 5 meters, whereas Category 2 can be up to 15 meters.

DVI When purchasing DVI cables, you should make note of the connector type that exists on the PC. The cable connector must be the same type as the PC. Review the section "Display Connector Types."

VGA   VGA cables are quite common and come in lengths up to 50 feet. They have an HD-15 (or DB-15a) female connector on one end and a DB-15 male connector on the other.

Component   Component video is a video signal that has been split into two or more component channels. It is transmitted or stored as three separate signals. There will typically be three color-coded plugs on the cable that connect to the same color plug on the PC or the video device.

Composite   Composite video combines the signal into one line-level signal, so there is one plug on the connector, usually an RCA plug.

Coaxial   When BNC cables are used, the cable type will be coaxial. See the BNC section in "Display Connector Types."

Device Cables and Connectors

As with display connectors, there are a wide variety of connector and cable types for the other devices in the PC. This includes internal devices as well as peripherals. In this section, the most common connectors are discussed along with the pin-outs. In many cases, the number of pins and their arrangement is the only way to differentiate two connector types with common form factors. In cases where the connector has been discussed, a reference is provided to the section where the connector was discussed. Following that section is one on cable types.

SATA   Internal SATA storage devices have a 7-pin data connection and a 15-pin power connection. Those connections sit next to one another on the SATA device, as shown in Figure 1.62.

FIGURE 1.62   SATA connections

eSATA   External SATA devices use receptacles rarely found in PCs as of this writing. An eight-pin eSATA connector is shown next to an internal SATA connector in Figure 1.63.

FIGURE 1.63   eSATA connections

eSATA connectors

Standard internal
SATA connectors

USB   USB connectors were discussed in the section "Front-Panel Connectors."

FireWire (IEEE 1394)   IEEE 1394 (FireWire) was discussed in the section "FireWire Cards," and the connectors on the PC were shown in Figure 1.38.

PS/2   Though rarely used anymore, some PCs may still have a PS/2 connector for the mouse and the keyboard. These have been replaced for the most part with USB mice and keyboards. Figure 1.64 shows the PS/2 connectors.

FIGURE 1.64   PS/2

Audio   TRS audio connectors were discussed in the section "Audio" and shown in Figure 1.45. RCA connectors were covered in the section "RCA" and shown in Figure 1.58.

Device Cable Types

Cables must match the connector. This section provides a quick survey of the cables that go with the various connectors.

SATA   Internal SATA storage devices have 7-pin data cables and a 15-pin power cable. Figure 1.65 shows a SATA data cable.

FIGURE 1.65   SATA data cable

eSATA   eSATA cables may be either flat or round and can be only 2 meters in length. An eSATA connector was shown in Figure 1.63.

USB   USB cables were discussed in the section "USB 1.1 vs. 2.0 vs. 3.0," and the micro and mini versions were displayed in Figure 1.37.

IEEE 1394   IEEE 1394 (FireWire) was discussed in the section "FireWire 400 vs. FireWire 800." The cables look very much like USB cables.

Adaptors and Converters

In many cases, you will need to attach a device to a computer on which the correct connectors is not present. In these cases, there are adaptors (converters) and connectors that can be used to connect the device to a connector type for which it was not designed. In this section, you'll look at some of the more common of these.

DVI to HDMI

These adaptors connect from HDMI to DVI and come in a number of gender combinations (male DVI to female HDMI, male DVI to male HDMI, female DVI to male HDMI, and so on) and as either a cable or simply an inline connector. Figure 1.66 shows an inline connector.

FIGURE 1.66   HDMI to DVI

USB A to USB B

These adaptors will connect the A end of a USB connection to the B end of a USB cable. Figure 1.67 shows an example of one of these inline converters.

FIGURE 1.67   USB A to USB B

USB to Ethernet

These converters allow you to use a USB port as a network interface. They come both as cables and as inline connectors. Figure 1.68 shows an example of a USB to Ethernet adaptor.

FIGURE 1.68 USB to Ethernet

DVI to VGA

In cases where you need to convert DVI to VGA, you can use a DVI to VGA adaptor. These come as a cable or inline connectors and also come in a variety of gender combinations. Figure 1.69 shows an example of the ends of this adaptor.

FIGURE 1.69 DVI to VGA

Thunderbolt to DVI

The Thunderbolt connector is typically found only in Apple products, but if you need to connect from a Thunderbolt interface to a DVI, this adaptor is what you need. Figure 1.70 shows an inline connector.

FIGURE 1.70 Thunderbolt to DVI

PS/2 to USB

There aren't too many computers still in use that have a PS/2 connector for the keyboard and mouse, but if the need arises (or if you have an old PS/2 keyboard or mouse that you need to connect to a USB port), these adaptors are what you need. They come in versions that will solve either connectivity issue. Figure 1.71 shows a version that connects a PS/2 keyboard into a USB port.

FIGURE 1.71   PS/2 to USB

HDMI to VGA

Another quite common need is to adapt HDMI to VGA. The one pictured in Figure 1.72 connects an HDMI-compatible device to a monitor or projector with a VGA port.

FIGURE 1.72   HDMI to VGA

Exam Essentials

Identify display connectors, their associated cables, and the maximum cable lengths.   This includes but is not limited to DVI in all variants, DisplayPort, RCA, HD-15 (or DB-15), BNC, miniHDMI, and miniDIN-6.

Identify other device connectors, their associated cables, and the maximum cable lengths.   This includes but is not limited to SATA, eSATA, USB, IEEE 1394, PS/2, and audio.

1.12 Install and Configure Common Peripheral Devices

Installing devices is much easier today than it was at one time. In most cases, the device is detected and set up for you by the operating system as soon as you plug it in. This section discusses any deviations from that along with any special issues related to a particular device type. The topics addressed in objective 1.12 include the following:

▪ Input devices

▪ Output devices

▪ Input and output devices

Input Devices

Input devices allow you to communicate with the PC either by clicking an item or by using the keyboard. This category also includes devices that allow you to import information into the system in other ways. This section discusses the installation of each device.

Mouse

Mice are typically USB devices these days and require you only to plug them in; in moments they are functional. In some rare cases (especially for a mouse with special capabilities), you may need to install a driver for the mouse. These types typically have a CD you can access that will install those drivers for you.

Keyboard

Keyboards can be treated the same as mice. Follow the guidelines in the section on mice.

Scanner

Scanners are used to convert paper documents or photographs to digital files so they can be stored on a PC and transmitted as files across the network. The installation process is much like a print device. Because so many of these now are USB, plugging them in will install the driver. In cases where that does not work (usually when it is a new model and the operating system is older), use the installation disc to install the driver.

Barcode Reader

Barcode readers read and input codes used to identify products. They are used in warehouses and at retail checkouts. Once you plug the device into either the serial or the USB connector, you need to install the software that comes with the reader. Use the installation disc that comes with the reader.

Microphone

Microphones are simple to install. Typically, all you do is plug them into the mini-TRS connector. There are usually two of these: one for headphones (or speakers) and the other for a microphone (or line in). In some systems, you may be prompted to specify the mic or line in when you plug in a headset. A 3.5-mm plug was shown in Figure 1.45.

Biometric Devices

Biometric devices allow for inputting information used to authenticate or identify a user to the system. That input may be a retina scan or a fingerprint, for example. Use the installation disc that comes with the device. In most cases, you should install the software before you plug in the device (usually USB). During the installation process of the software, at some point you will be told to connect the device. Follow the instructions.

Game Pads

You may begin to notice a pattern. Game pads are also usually USB and install in the same way as biometric devices and barcode readers. Install the software and connect the device when instructed. One additional thing you may need to do with the game pad is to calibrate it. Once it's installed, locate the device in Control Panel in the correct section (usually Game Controllers), open the properties of the device, and click the option Calibrate. Follow the instructions. This will make it operate correctly. Some game pads require a DB-15 serial port, as shown in Figure 1.73.

FIGURE 1.73   DB-15 game port

GAME

Joysticks

Joysticks use the same guidelines and instructions as game pads and usually the same connectors.

Digitizer

Digitizers are pad-like devices that allow you to write and draw on the pad and input that to a digital file. Treat the installation of these devices in the same way as the other devices in this section. Install the software first and connect the digitizer when instructed to do so.

Motion Sensor

Motion sensors can be used to allow control of the computer using hand gestures. It allows you to control an operating system with your hands and fingers and never touch a mouse or keyboard. It also can be used in PC gaming when developers integrate these controls in their games as they build them. Figure 1.74 shows a USB-based motion sensor. The device is a small rectangular cube that you plug into your computer via the USB drive. To install these, you simply connect them and if the operating system does not have the drivers, provide these drivers during installation.

FIGURE 1.74   Motion sensor

Touchpads

While touchpads come on laptops, you can also buy add-on touchpads. These allow you to perform basic mouse functions on the device. In most cases, they use a USB connector. To install them, you simply connect them and if the operating system does not have the drivers, provide these drivers during installation. Figure 1.75 shows an external touchpad and a laptop.

FIGURE 1.75   Touchpads

desktop
touchpad

laptop
touchpad

Smart Card Readers

Smart card readers are used to accept input from a smart card, which is a credit card–sized piece of plastic that can be used to input credentials securely. They are small and usually USB based, as shown in Figure 1.76. To install them, you simply connect them and if the operating system does not have the drivers, provide these drivers during installation.

FIGURE 1.76   Smart card reader

Digital Cameras

Digital cameras usually connect to the PC with a USB cable. In many cases, the operating system comes with software that may detect the camera and assist you in accessing the pictures and moving them to the computer. In other instances, you may want to install software that came with the camera. Doing so will often allow you to take fuller advantage of the features the camera offers. SD cards can be used to transfer images from the camera if a cable is not available.

Microphone

Follow the instructions in the earlier section "Input Devices." In some cases, the connector on the microphone may not be one that is present on the PC. You may be able to purchase a converter to match the input on the PC.

Webcam

First install the software that came with the webcam (sound familiar?) and then connect the webcam to the USB port when instructed. If the webcam has been out for some time and the operating system is new, it may be possible to just plug in the camera and let the operating system set it up.

Camcorder

Treat camcorders like cameras for the purpose of installation. If the camcorder is an older analog model, you will need to install a signal digitizer. If you have a TV tuner card present, it can perform the conversion.

MIDI-Enabled Devices

Musical Instrument Digital Interface (MIDI) is an industry specification for encoding, storing, synchronizing, and transmitting musical performance information, basically allowing you to digitally record a musical instrument.

The MIDI controller (usually an instrumental keyboard) connects to the PC using MIDI cables, which use a five-pin DIN connector. Since most computers don't have these, you may need to buy a MIDI-to-USB converter cable. Some specialized sound cards come with a MIDI port.

To use the controller, you install the software and then connect the MIDI device. The software will install the driver for the device. Once that is taken care of, install the recording software of choice. If the installation of the device went correctly, the recording software should recognize the MIDI controller and allow you to record from it.

Output Devices

Output devices allow you to print, listen to, or view information from the PC. The installation of these devices is remarkably like that of input devices.

Printers

Printers and their installation are covered in the "Compare and Contrast Differences Between the Various Print Technologies and the Associated Imaging Process" section later in this chapter.

Speakers

Installing speakers is more a matter of connecting them properly than installing them. Usually, one of the speakers will connect to a power source and the other will connect to the powered speaker. Once they are connected to a power source, connect the speaker cable to the proper plug in the PC. These plugs will be marked with icons that indicate which is for a microphone and which is for speakers.

Display Devices

Before connecting or disconnecting a monitor, ensure that the power to both the PC and the monitor is off. Then, connect a VGA (DB-15) cable from the monitor to the PC's video card, and connect the monitor's power cord to an AC outlet. If a better connection is available (DVI, for example), use it.

Input and Output Devices

There are also several dual-purpose input/output devices.

Touchscreen

Touchscreen monitors allow you to interact with the screen instead of using the mouse. These monitors may require installing a driver to function. Use the CD that comes with the device to install the driver. Touchscreens also require calibration. Most vendors include calibration software with the installation disc.

KVM

A keyboard, video, and mouse (KVM) device allows you to plug multiple PCs (usually servers) into the device and to switch easily back and forth from system to system using the same mouse, monitor, and keyboard. The KVM is actually a switch that all the systems plug into. There is usually no software to install. Just turn off all the systems, plug them all into the switch, and turn them back on; then you can switch from one to another using the same keyboard, monitor, and mouse device connected to the KVM switch.

Smart TV

A smart TV is one with integrated Internet and Web 2.0 features. These devices can provide Internet TV (receiving a TV signal from an Internet connection), online interactive media, over-the-top content (content that arrives from a third party), as well as on-demand streaming media and home networking access. "Installing" a smart TV really consists of connecting it to the Internet, which can be done in several ways.

- Some devices have an Ethernet jack on the back of the TV, and you can use that option.
- Other devices have wireless capability, and you need to connect the smart TV to your home wireless network.
- Some will allow you to connect to the Internet though a gaming console.
- Finally, you can connect some to a computer or laptop that in turn has Internet access.

Set-Top Box

Another option for getting content to a TV is to use a set-top box. These are appliances that contain a TV-tuner input and display output to a television set or other display device. Some can accept input from multiple sources (cable, satellite, and so on). They are used in cable television, satellite television, and over-the-air television systems. The exact manner in which they are installed and the specific connectors they require to be on the TV vary, so it is important to determine beforehand if the set-top box can be used with the TV based on the connectors present on both devices.

Exam Essentials

Install input devices.   These include the mouse, keyboard, scanner, barcode reader, biometric devices, game pads, joysticks, digitizer, motion sensor, touchpads, smart card readers, digital cameras, microphone, webcam, camcorder, and MIDI-enabled devices.

Install output devices.   These include printers, speakers, and display devices. Take appropriate precautions if encountering an LCD.

Install devices that are both input and output.   These include but are not limited to touch-screen devices, KVMs, smart TVs, and set-top boxes.

1.13 Install SOHO Multifunction Devices/ Printers and Configure Appropriate Settings

Printers are one of the most common elements in any computing environment, from home to office. The range they cover is phenomenal—everything from a free printer included by a vendor with the purchase of a PC up to a monolith in a large office churning out hundreds of pages a minute. Regardless of where a printer falls in that spectrum, they are all the same in that they must be installed and properly configured to be of use. Moreover, most printing devices today are multifunction devices. They print, scan, and fax in various combinations.

The topics addressed in objective 1.13 include the following:

- Using appropriate drivers for a given operating system
- Configuration settings
- Device sharing
- Integrated print server (hardware)
- Cloud printing/remote printing
- Public/shared devices

Printing Components

Printing components are not a topic of objective 1.13, but they are something that will be helpful for you to understand in the real world. In addition to the physical body of the printer, components and consumables are associated with it. Components include the following:

Memory   As a general rule, the more memory a laser printer has, the better. The memory is used to hold the print jobs in the printer queue; the more users and the larger the print jobs, the more memory you'll want. Dot-matrix and inkjet printers contain little memory, the former using only a buffer to hold a few characters.

Drivers   These are the software components of the printer—allowing the device to communicate with the operating system. It's important to always have the correct and most current drivers for the greatest efficiency. The printer drivers vary based on the operating system being used on the client computer, and if a printer is attached to more than one operating system, you have to make sure you have the appropriate driver for each operating system in use.

Firmware   Although drivers can be updated, firmware rarely is. Firmware is installed on the printer and can be thought of as the operating system for that device.

Consumables for printers are those items you must change as you use the printer—the variable items that get consumed and must be replenished. These include toner (or ink, depending on the type of printer you're using) and paper. Be sure to always order and use the correct grade of consumables that are recommended for your machine. For example, don't use inkjet media in a laser printer or you will run the risk of the laser printer's fuser melting it.

Using Appropriate Drivers for a Given Operating System

Besides understanding the printer's operation, for the exam you need to understand how these devices talk to a computer. The driver software controls how the printer processes the print job. When you install a printer driver for the printer you are using, it allows the computer to print to that printer correctly (assuming you have the correct interface configured between the computer and printer). Also keep in mind that drivers are specific to the operating system, so you need to select the one that is both for the correct printer and for the correct operating system.

An interface is the collection of hardware and software that allows the device to communicate with a computer. Each printer, for example, has at least one interface, but some printers have several to make them more flexible in a multiplatform environment. If a printer has several interfaces, it can usually switch between them on the fly so that several computers can print at the same time.

Configuration Settings

You need to be familiar with the various settings that are available and what these settings do. This section covers the more common settings, features, and characteristics of printers.

Duplex   An optional component that can be added to printers (usually laser but also inkjet) is a duplexer. This can be an optional assembly added to the printer, or built into it, but the sole purpose of duplexing is to turn the printed sheet over so it can be run back through the printer and allow printing on both sides.

Collate   Collating is the process of arranging the output of a print job so that multiple individual sets of the output are in proper order. A collator is a unit that if present on the printer will allow the printer to collate.

Orientation   The orientation of a document refers to how the printed matter is laid out on the page. In the landscape orientation, the printing is written across the paper turned on its long side, while in portrait the paper is turned up vertically and printed top to bottom.

Quality   Print quality is a description of the look of the printing, its sharpness, and its color depth. It is impacted by the quality of the paper, the speed of the printing process, and the resolution settings. It can also be affected by the DPI setting. This setting controls the size of objects on the screen and therefore their quality. As you increase the size of an object, its quality will usually decrease a bit.

Device Sharing

Printer sharing covers the hardware technologies involved in getting the information to and from the computer. There are several types, which can be broken into two broad categories: wired and wireless.

Wired

The wired forms of connection this exam test on are USB, parallel, serial, and Ethernet. Each is addressed in the sections that follow.

USB   The most popular type of printer interface as this book is being written is USB. It's the most popular interface for just about every peripheral. The benefits for printers are that it has a higher transfer rate than either serial or parallel and it automatically recognizes new devices. USB is also fully Plug and Play, and it allows several printers to be connected at once without adding ports or using up additional system resources.

Serial   This is the traditional RS-232 serial port found on most PCs. The original printer interface on the earliest computers, it has fallen out of favor and is seldom used anymore for printing because it's so slow.

Ethernet   Most large-environment printers (primarily laser and LED printers) have a special interface that allows them to be hooked directly to a network. These printers have a NIC and ROM-based software that let them communicate with networks, servers, and workstations.

Wireless

The wireless forms of connection included on this exam are Bluetooth, 802.11x, and Infrared (IR). Each is addressed in the sections that follow.

Bluetooth   Bluetooth is an infrared technology that can connect a printer to a computer at a short range; its absolute maximum range is 100 meters (330 feet), and most devices are specified to work within 10 meters (33 feet). When printing with a Bluetooth-enabled device (like a PDA or mobile phone) and a Bluetooth-enabled printer, all you need to do is get within range of the device (that is, move closer), select the print driver from the device, and choose Print. The information is transmitted wirelessly through the air using radio waves and is received by the device.

802.11 (a, b, g, n, ac)   A network-enabled printer that has a wireless adaptor can participate in a wireless Ethernet (IEEE 802.11b, a, g, n, or ac) network, just as it would as a wired network client.

Infrastructure vs. ad hoc   The architecture of the wireless network may affect the way you set up a wireless printer. In ad hoc mode, all devices communicate directly in a peer-to-peer fashion. This means that each user who accesses the wireless printer will establish their own connection to the wireless printer, and they need to ensure they are in the same IP network with the printer as well as the same WLAN. In infrastructure mode, the wireless network is using an access point (AP), and all communication goes through the AP. In this case, the printer must be set up to automatically connect to the AP so it is on the same network as the wireless clients that need to use the printer.

Integrated Print Server (Hardware)

A print server is a popular option for adding a printer to the network and not adding a host computer. To be a print server, the NIC in the printer differs from a NIC in a computer in that it has a processor on it to perform the management of the NIC interface and it is made by the same manufacturer as the printer.

To qualify as a print server, when someone on the network prints, the print job goes directly to the printer and not through any third-party device. This tends to make printing to that printer faster and more efficient—that NIC is dedicated to receiving print jobs and sending printer status to clients.

Cloud Printing/Remote Printing

While printing remotely to a printer over the Internet has been available for a number of years, cloud printing is a new service being offered by cloud vendors. In a cloud arrangement, you connect your printer to the vendor's cloud, and then the printer is available to you anywhere you can get Internet access, just as cloud-based resources are available anywhere you can get Internet access.

While not required, cloud vendors encourage the use of cloud-ready printers in this arrangement. These are printers that need no PC to connect to the Internet. It makes the process of connecting to the cloud print server much simpler.

Another option is to create a VPN connection to your home network. Once connected to the home network over the VPN, you should be able to connect to and print to the printer as if you were sitting in your home office.

Public/Shared Devices

All operating systems allow you to share a local printer or connect over the network to one that has been shared. To connect to a printer in Windows 8.1, choose Start ➤ Control Panel ➤ Devices And Printers, and it will show the currently recognized printers (see Figure 1.77) and allow you to add new ones.

FIGURE 1.77   Devices And Printers

The image of a check box on the first instance of the Samsung M 2070 shows that it is the current default printer, and the image of two people on the second instance of the device means that it is shared. Clicking Add A Printer (at the top of the dialog box) starts the wizard shown in Figure 1.78.

FIGURE 1.78 Adding a printer

Sharing Local/Networked Device via Operating System Settings

To share a local/networked printer via the Windows operating systems, right-click the icon for the printer (beneath Devices And Printers or Printers And Faxes, depending on your operating system) and choose Printer Properties. Next, click the Sharing tab.

Select Share This Printer and provide a name that the printer will be known by on the network. This is the name that will appear when adding a new network printer on a client, and it can also be referenced by the entire qualified name using the syntax \\host\ share_name.

TCP A TCP printer is one that is not shared by a computer but one that has its own network card and IP address. To share them, you must create a TCP port on the computer from which you would like to print that points to the IP address of the printer. Then when adding the printer, select the TCP port you created instead of selecting a local port (USB, and so on) like you would do if setting up a printer that is connected locally.

Bonjour   Bonjour is an Apple technology that discovers devices on a network. It can also be used to facilitate the sharing of a printer in the network. While it can work with Windows, the steps for using it on a Mac are as follows:

1. Click the System Preferences icon in the Dock to open the System Preferences window.

2. Click Print And Scan in the Hardware section to open the Print And Scan window.

3. Click the + button under the Printers list box to open the Add window.

4. Click the Default tab to display the list of available printers. Choose the name of the network printer from the list of printers. The system automatically searches for and installs the appropriate driver for the printer.

5. If the system cannot find a printer driver, click the Use box and manually select it from the pop-up menu. Click Add to automatically make the printer available in the printer queue.

AirPrint   AirPrint is the Apple technology for printing wirelessly to a printer in the network. Many printers come ready to support AirPrint. One important thing to note is that AirPrint does not support printing directly to the wireless printer; it must be done through an AP. This means that you can use this technology only in a WLAN where an AP is present.

Data Privacy

In any scenario where users are sharing a device, data privacy is an issue. There are several things that can be done to protect the privacy of data sent to the printer.

- Ensure that all users are authenticated to the device (discussed in the next section).

- Ensure that users are given only the rights to the device they need to perform their job.

- Consider the use of data loss prevention (DLP). These services can be used to control the printing, emailing, sharing, or deleting of documents.

- Make use of the auditing features to maintain an awareness of who does what and when they do it.

User Authentication on the Device

While nearly all enterprise-grade multifunction devices support user authentication, it may be easier and make more sense in a large network to perform this on the print server and use domain credentials to take advantage of single sign-on. In any case, user authentication forms the bedrock for auditing.

Hard Drive Caching

It is also important to realize that most enterprise-grade multifunction devices have hard drives and cache information on those hard drives. You must take steps to protect that data; it can be stolen from the hard drive, either by remote access or by extracting the data once the drive has been removed.

Options for securing the data on the device include the following:

Encryption   Encodes the data stored on the hard drive so that it cannot be retrieved even if the hard drive is removed from the machine.

Overwriting   Changes the values of the bits on the disk that make up a file by overwriting existing data with random characters. By overwriting the disk space that the file occupied, its traces are removed, and the file can't be reconstructed as easily.

Exam Essentials

Be familiar with the possible interfaces that can be used for printing.   The types generally fall into two categories: wired (USB, parallel, Ethernet) and wireless (Bluetooth and 802.11x).

Know how to install printers.   The manufacturer is the best source of information about installing printers. You should, however, know about the wizards available in Windows as well.

Know how to share printers.   This includes how to share in Windows and by using AirPrint and Bonjour.

1.14 Compare and Contrast Differences Between the Various Print Technologies and the Associated Imaging Process

This objective tests your knowledge of five types of printers: laser, inkjet (sometimes called *ink dispersion*), thermal, impact, and virtual. Make certain you understand the imaging process associated with each of these printer types and—in particular—can name the steps in the laser imaging process. The A+ certification exams have traditionally focused heavily on laser printers, but you can expect to also see questions about other printer types. The topics covered in subobjective 1.14 include the following:

- Laser
- Inkjet
- Thermal
- Impact
- Virtual

Printer Introduction

Although it is not a topic for objective 1.14, it is helpful to know that printers may be differentiated from one another in several ways, including the following:

Impact vs. Nonimpact   Impact printers physically strike an inked ribbon and therefore can print multipart forms; nonimpact printers deliver ink onto the page without striking it. Dot matrix is impact; all the other printers you need to know for the exam are nonimpact.

Continuous Feed vs. Sheet Fed   Continuous-feed paper feeds through the printer using a system of sprockets and tractors. Sheet-fed printers accept plain paper in a paper tray. Dot matrix is continuous feed; everything else is sheet fed.

Line vs. Page   Line printers print one line at a time; page printers compose the entire page in memory and then place it all on the paper at once. Dot matrix and inkjet are line printers; laser is a page printer.

Laser

Laser printers are referred to as *page printers* because they receive their print job instructions one page at a time. They're sheet-fed, nonimpact printers. Another name for a laser printer is an *electrophotographic* (EP) printer.

LED printers are much like laser printers except they use light-emitting diodes (LEDs) instead of lasers. Their process is similar to that of laser printers.

An EP (laser) printer consists of the following major components:

Printer Controller   This is a large circuit board that acts as the motherboard for the printer. It contains the processor and RAM to convert data coming in from the computer into a picture of a page to be printed.

Imaging Drum   The toner cartridge and drum are typically packaged together as a consumable product that contains the toner. Toner is a powdery mixture of plastic resin and iron oxide. The plastic allows it to be melted and fused to the paper, and the iron oxide allows it to be moved around via positive or negative charge. Toner comes in a cartridge, like the one shown in Figure 1.79.

FIGURE 1.79   An EP toner cartridge

The drum is light sensitive; it can be written to with the laser scanning assembly. The toner cartridge in Figure 1.79 contains the print drum, so every time you change the toner cartridge, you get a new drum. In some laser printers, the drum is a separate part that lasts longer, so you don't have to change it every time you change the toner.

There are quite a few images included with this discussion. You need not memorize the images for the exam; they are included to help make concepts that may seem difficult more easily explainable.

Primary Corona (Charge Corona)   This applies a uniform negative charge (around $-600V$) to the drum at the beginning of the printing cycle.

Laser Scanning Assembly   This uses a laser beam to neutralize the strong negative charge on the drum in certain areas, so toner will stick to the drum in those areas. The laser scanning assembly uses a set of rotating and fixed mirrors to direct the beam, as shown in Figure 1.80.

FIGURE 1.80   The EP laser scanning assembly (side view and simplified top view)

Paper Transport Assembly (Transfer Belt, Transfer Rollers)   This moves the paper through the printer. The paper transport assembly consists of a motor and several rubberized rollers and transfer belts. These rollers are operated by an electronic stepper motor. See Figure 1.81 for an example.

FIGURE 1.81   Paper transport rollers

Pickup Rollers   Pickup rollers are rubber wheels that grab the paper and feed it in. When these parts get old, they lose their ability to grip the paper, so they should be checked and changed regularly.

Separate Pads   These pads are used to separate sheets in a stack of printing paper. It does this as the paper passes over them by creating friction that separates the paper. These pads are usually 2 to 3 inches wide, and when they start to wear out, they lose their ability to create friction, and you start getting two and three sheet at a time pulled through.

Transfer Corona   This applies a uniform positive charge (about +600V) to the paper. When the paper rotates past the drum, the toner is pulled off the drum and onto the paper. Then the paper passes through a static eliminator that removes the positive charge from it (see Figure 1.82). Some printers use a transfer corona wire; others use a transfer corona roller.

FIGURE 1.82   The transfer corona assembly

High-Voltage Power Supply (HVPS)   This delivers the high voltages needed to make the printing process happen. It converts ordinary 120V household AC current into high-DC voltages used to energize the primary and transfer corona wires (discussed later).

DC Power Supply   This delivers lower voltages to components in the printer that need much lower voltages than the corona wires do (such as circuit boards, memory, and motors).

Fusing Assembly   This melts the plastic resin in the toner so that it adheres to the paper. The fusing assembly contains a halogen heating lamp, a fusing roller made of Teflon-coated aluminum, and a rubberized pressure roller. The lamp heats the fusing roller, and as the paper passes between the two rollers, the pressure roller pushes the paper against the hot fusing roller, melting the toner into the paper (see Figure 1.83).

FIGURE 1.83   The fusing assembly

Duplex Assembly Duplex assemblies were discussed in the section "Duplex" earlier in this chapter.

Imaging Process

The laser (EP) print process consists of six steps. Here are the steps in the order you'll see them on the exam:

Step 1: Conditioning In the *conditioning* step (Figure 1.84), a special wire (called a *primary corona* or *charge corona*) within the EP toner cartridge (above the photosensitive drum) gets a high voltage from the HVPS. It uses this high voltage to apply a strong, uniform negative charge (around –600VDC) to the surface of the photosensitive drum.

FIGURE 1.84   The conditioning step of the EP process

Charge corona wire

EP drum

Step 2: Writing In the *writing* step of the EP process, the laser is turned on and scans the drum from side to side, flashing on and off according to the bits of information the printer controller sends it as it communicates the individual bits of the image. In each area where the laser touches the photosensitive drum, the drum's charge is severely reduced from –600VDC to a slight negative charge (around –100VDC). As the drum rotates, a pattern of exposed areas is formed, representing the image to be printed. Figure 1.85 shows this process.

FIGURE 1.85   The writing step of the EP process

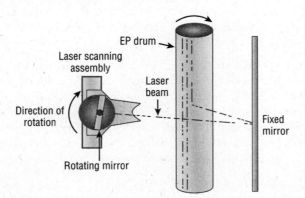

EP drum

Laser scanning assembly

Laser beam

Direction of rotation

Fixed mirror

Rotating mirror

At this point, the controller sends a signal to the pickup roller to feed a piece of paper into the printer, where it stops at the registration rollers.

Step 3: Developing   Now that the surface of the drum holds an electrical representation of the image being printed, its discrete electrical charges need to be converted into something that can be transferred to a piece of paper. The EP process's *developing* step accomplishes this (Figure 1.86). In this step, toner is transferred to the areas that were exposed in the writing step.

FIGURE 1.86   The developing step of the EP process

A metallic *developing roller* or *cylinder* inside an EP cartridge acquires a –600VDC charge (called a *bias voltage*) from the HVPS. The toner sticks to this roller because there is a magnet located inside the roller and because of the electrostatic charges between the toner and the developing roller. While the developing roller rotates toward the photosensitive drum, the toner acquires the charge of the roller (–600VDC). When the toner comes between the developing roller and the photosensitive drum, the toner is attracted to the areas that have been exposed by the laser (because these areas have a lesser charge of –100VDC). The toner also is repelled from the unexposed areas (because they're at the same –600VDC charge and like charges repel). This toner transfer creates a fog of toner between the EP drum and the developing roller.

The photosensitive drum now has toner stuck to it where the laser has written. The photosensitive drum continues to rotate until the developed image is ready to be transferred to paper in the next step.

Step 4: Transferring   At this point in the EP process, the developed image is rotating into position. The controller notifies the registration rollers that the paper should be fed through. The registration rollers move the paper underneath the photosensitive drum, and the process of transferring the image can begin with the *transferring* step.

The controller sends a signal to the corona wire or corona roller (depending on which one the printer has) and tells it to turn on. The corona wire/roller then acquires a strong *positive* charge (+600VDC) and applies that charge to the paper. The paper, thus charged, pulls the toner from the photosensitive drum at the line of contact between the roller and the paper because the paper and toner have opposite charges. Once the registration rollers move the paper past the corona wire, the static-eliminator strip removes all charge from that line of the paper. Figure 1.87 details this step. If the strip didn't bleed this charge away, the paper would attract itself to the toner cartridge and cause a paper jam.

FIGURE 1.87   The transferring step of the EP process

The toner is now held in place by weak electrostatic charges and gravity. It won't stay there, however, unless it's made permanent, which is the reason for the fusing step.

Step 5: Fusing   In the next step, the *fusing* step, the toner image is made permanent. The registration rollers push the paper toward the fuser rollers. Once the fuser grabs the paper, the registration rollers push for only a short time more. The fuser is now in control of moving the paper.

   As the paper passes through the fuser, the fuser roller melts the polyester resin of the toner, and the rubberized pressure roller presses it permanently into the paper (Figure 1.88). The paper continues on through the fuser and eventually exits the printer.

FIGURE 1.88   The fusing step of the EP process

Step 6: Cleaning In the last part of the laser print process, a rubber blade inside the EP cartridge scrapes any toner left on the drum into a used-toner receptacle inside the EP cartridge, and a fluorescent lamp discharges any remaining charge on the photosensitive drum (remember that the drum, being photosensitive, loses its charge when exposed to light). See Figure 1.89.

FIGURE 1.89 The cleaning step of the EP process

A color laser is much like a regular laser printer except that multiple passes over the page are made, one for each ink color. Consequently, the printing speed is rather low.

The EP cartridge is constantly cleaning the drum. It may take more than one rotation of the photosensitive drum to make an image on the paper. The cleaning step keeps the drum fresh for each use. If you didn't clean the drum, you would see ghosts of previous pages printed along with your image.

The actual amount of toner removed in the cleaning process is quite small. The cartridge will run out of toner before the used toner receptacle fills up.

Putting It All Together

Figure 1.90 summarizes all the EP process printing steps. First, the printer uses a rubber scraper to clean the photosensitive drum. Then the printer places a uniform, negative, –600VDC charge on the photosensitive drum by means of a charge corona. The laser paints an image onto the photosensitive drum, discharging the image areas to a much lower voltage (–100VDC). The developing roller in the toner cartridge has charged (–600VDC) toner stuck to it. As it rolls the toner toward the photosensitive drum, the toner is attracted to (and sticks to) the areas of the photosensitive drum that the laser has discharged. The image is then transferred from the drum to the paper at its line of contact by means of the corona wire (or corona roller) with a +600VDC charge. The static-eliminator strip removes the high, positive charge from the paper, and the paper, now holding the image, moves on. The paper then enters the fuser, where the fuser roller and the pressure roller make the image permanent. The paper exits the printer, and the printer starts printing the next page or returns to its ready state.

An optional component that can be added to printers (usually laser but also inkjet) is a duplexer. This can be an optional assembly added to the printer, or built into it, but the sole purpose of *duplexing* is to turn the printed sheet over so it can be run back through the printer and allow printing on both sides.

FIGURE 1.90 The EP print process

Inkjet

Inkjet printers are one of the most popular types in use today. This type of printer sprays ink on the page to print text or graphics. It's a nonimpact, sheet-fed printer. Figure 1.91 shows an ink cartridge.

FIGURE 1.91 A typical ink cartridge

There are two kinds of inkjet printers: *thermal* and *piezoelectric*. These terms refer to the way the ink is sprayed onto the paper. A thermal inkjet printer heats the ink to about 400 degrees Fahrenheit, creating vapor bubbles that force the ink out of the cartridge. Thermal inkjets are also sometimes called *bubble jets*. A piezoelectric printer does the same thing but with electricity instead of heat.

Inkjet printers are popular because they can print in color and are inexpensive. However, their speed isn't quite as good as that of a laser printer, and the per-page cost of ink can be higher than for a laser printer. Therefore, most businesses prefer laser printers for their main printing needs, perhaps keeping one or two inkjet printers around for situations requiring color printing. Components of an inkjet printer are covered in the following sections.

Ink Cartridge

These cartridges contain the ink. Some cartridges contain the print head for that color of ink; you get a new print head each time you replace the cartridge. On other printer models, the ink cartridge is just an ink reservoir, and the heads don't need replacing.

Print Head

The print head has a series of nozzles from which the ink is sprayed onto the paper. They may be attached to the ink cartridge, or those two components may be separate. In cases where they are one piece, you will be getting a new print head each time you get a new ink cartridge.

Roller

Just as on a laser printer, rollers are used to pull the paper in from the tray or feeder and advance the paper when the print head assembly is ready for another pass. As is the case with any rollers, they will need to be replaced when they lose their ability to "grab" the paper.

Feeder

The feeder looks like a tray and is where you load paper. It is from here that it is pulled into the printer when a new sheet is required. These feeders do not usually hold as much paper as a tray in a printer will.

Duplexing Assembly

A duplexing assembly performs the same function on an inkjet printer that it does on a laser printer, which is to flip a sheet over to print on the back side.

Carriage and Belt

The carriage holds the ink cartridges, and it uses a belt to move the entire piece across the paper as it is printing. As it prints, it uses ink from the various cartridges in whatever proportion is necessary to create the desire colors.

Calibration

Calibrating an inkjet printer is the process of ensuring that there is proper alignment of the cartridges to one another and to the paper so that high quality is maintained. When a printer gets out of calibration, the print quality will decline. When a new cartridge is loaded, the printer will usually perform a calibration, but you may need to do this manually from time to time, especially on printers that are not used often enough to require a cartridge change as often as a calibration may be required.

On an inkjet printer, calibration is more commonly known as *head alignment*. The printer will automatically try to align ink cartridges each time they are replaced (or installed). If you want to make sure they are in the right place, most printers allow you to print an alignment page from the maintenance menu.

If characters are not properly formed or are appearing as straight lines along the margin (usually the left), you can use the maintenance menu settings to align the ink cartridges.

Thermal

Thermal printers can be found in many older fax machines (most newer ones use either inkjet or laser printing) that print on a waxy paper that comes on a roll; the paper turns black when heat passes over it. These are also found on many handheld package tracking and point-of-sale (POS) devices such as credit card terminals. Thermal printers work by using a print head the width of the paper. When it needs to print, the print head heats and cools spots on the print head. The paper below the heated print head turns black in those spots. As the paper moves through the printer, the pattern of blackened spots forms an image on the page of what is being printed.

Another type of thermal printer uses a heat-sensitive ribbon instead of heat-sensitive paper. A thermal print head melts wax-based ink from the ribbon onto the paper. These are called *thermal transfer* or *thermal wax-transfer* printers.

Thermal direct printers typically have long lives because they have few moving parts. However, the paper is somewhat expensive, doesn't last long, and produces poorer-quality images (that tend to fade over time) than most of the other printing technologies.

There are some deviations of thermal printing that exist. They're all high-end color graphics printers designed for specialty professional usage. Here are four popular ones:

Thermal Wax Transfer   This is a color, nonimpact printer that uses a solid wax. A heater melts the wax and then sprays it onto the page, somewhat like an inkjet. The quality is very high, but so is the price.

Dye Sublimation   This is another color, nonimpact line printer. This one converts a solid ink into a gas that is then applied to the paper. Color is applied in a continuous tone, rather than individual dots, and the colors are applied one at a time. The ink comes on film rolls. The paper is expensive, as is the ink. Print speeds are low. The quality is extremely high.

Feed Assembly   Feed assemblies, commonly called *feeders*, are available to allow you to feed in the media you are printing on (paper, cards, and so on). Some feeders allow you to switch between multiple feeds, which is helpful if you need to alternate printing on different types of stock.

Heating Element   The heating element for a thermal printer is what generates the heat and does the actual printing. It is often the most expensive component of the printer.

Special Thermal Paper

To print with a thermal printer, you need to use heat-sensitive paper designed for the thermal printer as opposed to paper for any other type of printer. Rolls of thermal paper are available in a variety of sizes and colors.

Impact

A dot-matrix printer is an impact printer; it prints by physically striking an inked ribbon, much like a typewriter. It's an impact, continuous-feed printer.

The print head on a dot-matrix printer consists of a block of metal pins that extend and retract. These pins are triggered to extend in patterns that form letters and numbers as the print head moves across the paper. Early models, known as near letter-quality (NLQ), printed using only nine pins. Later models used 24 pins and produced much better letter-quality (LQ) output.

The main advantage of dot matrix is its impact (physical striking of the paper). Because it strikes the paper, you can use it to print on multipart forms. Nonimpact printers can't do that. Dot-matrix printers aren't commonly found in most offices these days because of their disadvantages, including noise, slow speed, and poor print quality.

 Dot-matrix printers are still found in many warehouses, and other businesses, where multipart forms are used or where continuous feed is required.

Key elements of an impact printer are discussed in the sections that follow.

Print Head   The pins in the print head are wrapped with coils of wire to create a solenoid and are held in the rest position by a combination of a small magnet and a spring. To trigger a particular pin, the printer controller sends a signal to the print head, which energizes the wires around the appropriate print wire. This turns the print wire into an electromagnet, which repels the print pin, forcing it against the ink ribbon and making a dot on the paper.

Ribbon   The ribbon is like that on an old typewriter. Most impact printers have an option to adjust how close the print head rests from the ribbon. So if your printing is too light, you may be able to adjust the print head closer to the ribbon. If it's too dark or you get smeared printing, you may be able to move the print head back.

Tractor Feed   The tractor feed unit feeds in the continuous feed paper. This paper has holes running down both edges.

Impact Paper

An impact printer uses continuous feed paper fed to it by the tractor feed unit.

Virtual

There is also virtual printing that is not really printing at all but a way to convert a document to a particular format. There a number of ways this conversion can take place.

Print to File

Print to file is quite an old concept by now but still available as an option when printing. When you do this, the information that would normally be sent to the printer is saved, usually as a `.prn` file. It is a way to avoid the printing process from within an application (which may be time-consuming or inconvenient) and print it (convert it) once and then save the file so that whenever you need a copy, you can simply send that to the printer.

Print to PDF

If you can print to file, you can print to PDF. In applications that support this feature, it will be an option presented when you select to print. When you select this option, it produces an Adobe PDF instead of a printout. It is a convenient format because you can still print them later, search them, and send them, and when you do send them, you can be certain that the way the document appears to you will be the way it does to the recipient, regardless of the device type on which they are viewing it.

Print to XPS

An XPS document is a standardized open format and is Microsoft's answer to the PDF. It is always offered as a printer type in Windows. It will be called a Microsoft XPS Document Writer and will appear with other printers in the printer's folder, as shown in Figure 1.92.

FIGURE 1.92   Microsoft XPS Document Writer

When your file is converted, it will appear with an `.opxs` file extension (Open XPS). While Microsoft encourages the use of these documents and of the default XPS device and offers more support for it then for PDF, the document type is not as widely supported elsewhere as the PDF.

Print to Image

Finally, printing to an image is somewhat like scanning because it creates an image of the document. This typically requires a third-party application. Many of the applications that will create a PDF, such as Nitro PDF Writer, will also allow for you to convert those formats to a .jpg file.

Exam Essentials

Identify the components of laser printers.   These include the imaging drum, fuser assembly, transfer belt, transfer roller, pickup rollers, separate pads, and duplexing assembly.

Describe the function of the components of an inkjet printer.   These include the ink cartridge, print head, roller, feeder, duplexing assembly, carriage, and belt.

Identify examples of using a virtual printer.   These include print to file, print to PDF, print to XPS, and print to image.

1.15 Given a Scenario, Perform Appropriate Printer Maintenance

Most printing problems today are because of either improper configuration or actual physical problems that arise from the poor maintenance of the printer. As far as configuration goes, the Windows architecture is such that when a client wants to print to a network printer, a check is first done to see whether the client has the latest printer driver. If it doesn't—as judged by the print server—the new driver is sent from the server to the client, and then the print job is accepted. This is an enormous help to the administrator because when a new driver comes out, all the administrator must do is install it on the server, and the distribution to the clients becomes automatic. The printers covered in subobjective 1.15 include the following:

- Laser
- Thermal
- Impact
- Inkjet

This objective tests your knowledge of some of the basic operations of printers. The emphasis, however, is on detecting and solving problems with them. If you truly want to show your expertise with printers, CompTIA offers another certification, PDI+, which is meant for that purpose.

General Maintenance

Beyond what is covered in subobjective 1.15, it is important to know good principles of general printer maintenance. To keep your printers working efficiently and extend their life as much as possible, you should start by creating a log of scheduled maintenance as outlined by the vendor's guidelines and then make certain this maintenance log is adhered to. For many printers, the scheduled maintenance includes installing maintenance kits. Maintenance kits typically include a fuser, transfer roller, pickup rollers (for the trays), separation rollers, and feed rollers.

 After installing the maintenance kit, you need to reset the maintenance counter as explained in the vendor's documentation.

Pay a great deal of attention to the ambient surroundings of the printers as well. High temperature, high humidity, and high levels of dust and debris can negatively affect the life of the printer and the quality of print jobs. Always make certain you use recommended supplies. It may be cheaper to buy off-brand supplies that aren't intended for your equipment, but you're taking a gamble with shortening the life of your printer and decreasing the quality of your output.

Some general preventive maintenance includes the following:

- Never reuse paper in a laser printer that has been through the printer once. Although it may look blank, you're repeating the charging and fusing process on a piece of paper that most likely has *something* already on it.

- Change the toner when needed. You should recycle; most toner manufacturers participate in a recycling program of some type. The toner cartridge should never be exposed to light for longer than a few minutes; it usually comes sealed in a black plastic light-resistant bag.

- Clean any toner that accidentally spills into the printer with a dry, lint-free cloth. Bear in mind that spilled toner in the paper path should clear after you run a few blank pages through. If toner gets on your clothes, wipe them with a dry cloth and wash them with cold water (hot water works like the fusing process to set them into the material).

- Clean any paper shreds, dust, or dander that gets deposited in the printer. Pressurized air is the most effective method of removal.

- Keep the drum in good working order. If it develops lines, replace it.

- Install the maintenance kit when needed and reset the page count. The maintenance kit (sometimes called a *fuser kit*) typically includes a fusing assembly, rollers, and separation pads. A printer that displays a message similar to "Perform Printer Maintenance" indicates the printer has reached its maintenance interval and a maintenance kit needs to be installed.

▪ Don't be afraid to cycle the power for an unresponsive printer. Turning it off, leaving it off for one minute to clear, and then turning it back on can solve a great many problems.

▪ For inkjet and impact printers, you should periodically clean the print head.

While the previous list is a good rule of thumb, for this objective CompTIA wants you to be familiar with maintenance for three types of printers: laser, thermal, and impact. The following sections will look at each of those.

Laser

Just as laser printers are the most complicated of the types (and offer the most capabilities), they also have the most things that can go awry. A thermal fuse is included to keep the system from overheating, and if it becomes faulty, it can prevent the printer from printing. Many high-capacity laser printers also include an ozone filter to prevent the corona's ozone output from reaching too high a level. On these printers, the filter should be changed as part of regular maintenance.

Other common problems and solutions are as follows:

Paper Jams While paper jams can be caused by numerous problems, two common ones are the paper not feeding correctly and moisture. To correct improper feeds, make sure you set the alignment guides for the paper you are using and verify the paper is feeding in straight. Keep paper from getting any moisture before feeding into the printer because moisture often causes pages to stick together and bind. Paper jams can also be caused by using paper that is not approved for the printer—particularly thick cardstock.

 One employee routinely had problems with a printer each time he went to print on high-quality paper—a problem experienced by no one else. Upon close examination, it turned out that each time he chose to print to the expensive paper, he counted the number of sheets he loaded into the printer—counting that involved licking his finger and then touching each page. A simple directive to stop doing this solved the problem.

Regardless of the cause of a paper jam, you need to always fully clear the printer of any traces of paper (torn or whole) before attempting to print again.

Error Codes Many laser printers include LCDs for interaction with the printer. When error codes appear, refer to the manufacturer's manuals or website for information on how to interpret the codes and solve the problem causing them.

Out-of-Memory Error While PCs now may need a minimum of 1 GB of RAM to run at a base level, it is not uncommon to find printers that still have only 4 MB or 8 MB of memory. If you are routinely running out of memory on a printer, add more memory if possible, and replace the printer when it is no longer possible to do so.

Lines and Smearing   Lines and smearing can be caused by the toner cartridge or the fuser. Try replacing the toner first (and cleaning any that may have spilled). If this does not fix the problem, replace the fuser.

Blank Pages Print   Verify that there is toner in the cartridge. If it's an old cartridge, you can often shake it slightly to free up toner once before replacing. If it's a new cartridge, make sure the sealing tape has been removed from the cartridge prior to placing it in the printer.

WARNING   Be careful when doing this operation. Someone who has asthma or who is sensitive to microfine particles could be adversely affected by the toner.

Dark Spots Print   The most likely culprit is too much toner. Run blank pages through the printer to clean it.

Garbled Pages Print   Make sure you're using the right printer driver in your application.

Ghosted Images Print   Ghosting—repeating text or images on the page—is usually caused by a bad cartridge. There can be damage to the drum or charging roller, and if there is, replacing the cartridge will help with the problem.

No Connectivity   If a network printer is not able to receive jobs, it can be an issue with the IP address that it has (or, more correctly, does not have). Often the printer will need to be manually assigned an IP address to make sure that it has the same one each time. Read the manufacturer's documentation for assigning an IP address to the printer and walk through the steps to do so.

NOTE   Never overlook the obvious. Connectivity problems also occur when the printer is turned off.

Print-Quality Problems   See whether your printer has the ability to turn Resolution Enhancement Technology (RET) on and off. This is what allows the printer to use partial-sized dots for images that are rounded. If it's turned off, turn it back on. If there are small marks or defects in the same spot on every page printed, the most likely culprit is a scratch on the drum.

Replacing Toner   Toner represents the consumable within the laser printer. Toner cartridges are used by laser printers to store toner. Use toner that is recommended for your printer. Using bad supplies could ruin your printer and void your warranty. Remove the toner before moving or shipping a printer to avoid spills.

Applying a Maintenance Kit   Maintenance kits are marketed by the manufacturer. Each kit varies in contents based on the printer in question but typically consists of a fuser, transfer roller, and feed/separation rollers. A counter on the laser printer often identifies when the maintenance kit is needed, and you can reset the counter after applying the new kit.

Calibration   With laser printers and inkjets, there is often a need to calibrate. Calibration is the process by which the result produced matches what was created. All the hardware, including the monitor, scanner, and printer, need to match on color, margins, and so forth.

The calibration process is different for each manufacturer but is usually similar to the following:

1. During installation of the software, you are asked (by the installation wizard) if you want to calibrate now (say Yes).

2. The printer prints multiple sets of numbered lines. Each set of lines represents an alignment instance, and you are asked which set looks the best.

3. You enter the set number and click OK. In some cases, the alignment ends here. In other cases, the alignment page is reprinted to verify that the settings are correct, and you are given a chance to change.

4. You exit the alignment routine.

Cleaning   It is important to keep the printer and the area around it clean. Each time you replace the toner or perform any maintenance, be sure to clean the debris.

Thermal

The amount of maintenance required on a thermal printer pales in comparison to laser since there are no moving parts to speak of. The following sections look at the key items to be aware of related to thermal printers as you study for the exam.

Replace Paper   Replace the thermal paper as it is needed; be sure to keep the feed area clean of paper slivers and other debris.

Clean Heating Element   Before even looking at a heating element, always unplug the printer and make certain it is cool. Thermal printer cleaning cards, cleaning pens, and kits are available and recommended for cleaning.

Remove Debris   Keep the printer free of dust and debris. Any particulates that get into the printer can interfere with the paper feeding properly or can affect the print quality. Use compressed air or computer vacuum to remove any debris.

Impact

A dot-matrix print head reaches high temperatures, and care must be taken to avoid a user or technician touching it and getting burned. Most dot-matrix printers include a temperature sensor to tell whether the print head is getting too hot. The sensor interrupts printing to let the print head cool down and then allows printing to start again. If this sensor becomes faulty, it can cause the printer to print a few lines, stop for a while, print more, stop, and so on. The following sections look at the key items to be aware of related to impact printers as you study for the exam.

Replace Ribbon   A common culprit with poor printing is the ribbon. A tight ribbon, or one that isn't advancing properly, will cause smudges or overly light printout. To solve this problem, replace the ribbon.

Replace Print Head   The print head should never be lubricated, but you can clean off debris with a cotton swab and denatured alcohol. Print pins missing from the print head will cause incomplete images or characters or white lines running through the text. This can be remedied by replacing the print head.

If the print head isn't at fault, make certain it's close enough to the platen to make the right image. The print head can be moved closer and farther from the platen (the surface on which typing occurs) depending on the thickness of the paper and other considerations.

Replace Paper   Preventive maintenance includes not only keeping the print head dry and clean but also vacuuming paper shreds from inside the machine. This should be done more often if needed but always when you replace the paper.

Inkjet

While inkjet printers use a different technology to print, they require many of the same maintenance procedures. These are discussed briefly in this section.

Clean Heads   Two maintenance task apply to the print heads. If your colors don't look the same or your blacks are getting a bronze look, you need to clean the nozzles. This can be done with the head cleaning cycle, which will clear out the nozzles. The second task is head alignment. If you see white repeating lines or a grid-like pattern in the printing, the head is misaligned. While some newer printers have an automatic alignment and cleaning function, you may need to do this manually using the printer documentation.

Replace Cartridges   When ink runs low (and most printers will alert you before you run out), you must remove the old cartridge and replace it with a new one. The procedure is as follows:

1. Open the printer cover and locate the button that is used to place the cartridge in the replacement position.
2. Open the cover that may be over the cartridge.
3. Grasp and remove the empty cartridge.
4. Take the new cartridge out of its packaging.
5. Place the new cartridge in the empty position left by the old cartridge. It should "click" into place.
6. Replace the cartridge cover.
7. Use the same button you used to place the cartridge into the replacement positon to move it back to the home position.

Calibration   Calibration is a task usually performed by accessing the properties of the printer and looking for the calibration function either on the General tab or on the Advanced tab. Just select it, and the printer will perform a calibration. It is also useful to know that in most cases a calibration is done whenever you replace one of the cartridges.

Clear Jams   While keeping in mind that many paper jams are a result of using poor-quality paper, there will be times you suffer jams with good paper. To clear a jam, do the following:

1. Check the paper tray. If you see a piece protruding from where the paper is picked up, pull it out gently.

2. If there is still a jam, remove the rear access door and look into the printer. If you see any paper stuck inside, pull it out, making sure you get all the pieces out.

3. Check the front door of the printer and see whether any pieces are stuck in that section; if so, gently pull them out.

4. At any point in this process you can select the resume button, and if you have cleared the jam, the print process will resume.

Exam Essentials

Know how to interact with printers.   Know that the Properties page for each, available from Windows, allows you to interact with them, but many printers also include advanced utilities that go beyond basic interaction.

Know the common printing problems listed.   Understand the most common problems that occur in an environment.

Know the importance of running scheduled maintenance.   Scheduled maintenance can prolong the life of your equipment and help ensure that your output continues to live up to the quality you expect.

Understand the importance of a suitable environment.   If you want your equipment to last as long as possible and deliver quality, you should pay attention to the environment in which you place it.

Review Questions

You can find the answers in the Appendix.

1. Which if the following is a standard firmware interface for PCs, designed to replace BIOS.
   A. UEFI
   B. NVRAM
   C. CMOS
   D. CHS

2. Which if the following is memory that does not lose its content when power is lost to the machine.
   A. CMOS
   B. NVRAM
   C. CHS
   D. SDRAM

3. Which if the following is also called the drive geometry?
   A. EEPROM
   B. SDRAM
   C. CHS
   D. CMOS

4. Which of the following NOT an example of an optical drive?
   A. CD
   B. CD-R
   C. DVD
   D. ROM

5. Where do you change the boot sequence?
   A. BIOS/UEFI settings
   B. Control Panel
   C. Jumper settings
   D. Command prompt

6. What value represents the relationship between the speed of the CPU and that of the motherboard bus?
   A. divisor
   B. multiplier
   C. gradient
   D. correlation

7. Which of the following is required to take the most advantage of drive encryption technologies?

   A. Lo jack

   B. Secure boot

   C. TPM chip

   D. POST card

8. Which of the following allows you to remotely locate, lock, and delete the data on a mobile device when it is stolen?

   A. Lo jack

   B. TPM chip

   C. POST card

   D. Secure Boot

9. Which of the following is a standard adopted by many venders that requires the operating system to check the integrity of all system files before allowing the boot process to proceed?

   A. PXE boot

   B. Secure Boot

   C. POST boot

   D. Bootcheck

10. What is the name for the set of diagnostic steps the computer undertakes when you first boot it up?

   A. PXE

   B. CHS

   C. POST

   D. PRE

Chapter

2

Networking

COMPTIA A+ EXAM OBJECTIVES COVERED IN THIS CHAPTER:

✓ **2.1 Identify the various types of network cables and connectors.**

- Fiber (Connectors: SC, ST and LC)

- Twisted Pair (Connectors: RJ-11, RJ-45, Wiring Standards: T568A, T568B)

- Coaxial (Connectors: BNC, F-connector)

✓ **2.2 Compare and contrast the characteristics of connectors and cabling.**

- Fiber (Types single-mode vs. multi-mode, Speed and transmission limitations)

- Twisted Pair (Types: STP, UTP, CAT3, CAT5, CAT5e, CAT6,CAT 6E, CAT7, plenum, PVC, Speed and transmission limitations, Splitters and effects on signal quality)

- Coaxial (Types: RG-6, RG-59, Speed and transmission limitations, Splitters and effects on signal quality)

✓ **2.3 Explain the properties and characteristics of TCP/IP.**

- IPv4 vs. IPv6

- Public vs. private vs. APIPA/link local

- Static vs. dynamic

- Client-side DNS settings

- Client-side DHCP

- Subnet mask vs. CIDR

- Gateway

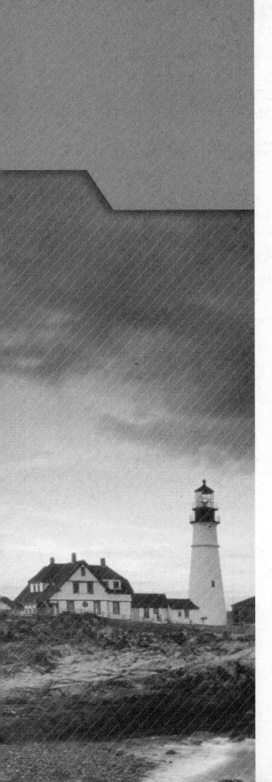

✓ **2.4 Explain common TCP and UDP ports, protocols, and their purpose.**

- Ports (21—FTP, 22—SSH, 23—Telnet, 25—SMTP, 53—DNS, 80—HTTP, 110—POP3, 143—IMAP, 443—HTTPS, 3389—RDP, 137-139, 445—SMB, 548 or 427—AFP)
- Protocols (DHCP, DNS, LDAP, SNMP, SMB, CIFS, SSH, AFP)
- TCP vs. UDP

✓ **2.5 Compare and contrast various Wi-Fi standards and encryption types.**

- Standards (802.11 a/b/g/n/ac, Speeds, distances, and frequencies)
- Encryption types (WEP, WPA, WPA2, TKIP, AES)

✓ **2.6 Given a scenario, install, and configure SOHO wireless/wired router and apply appropriate settings.**

- Channels
- Port forwarding, port triggering
- DHCP (on/off)
- DMZ
- NAT/DNAT
- Basic QoS
- Firmware
- UPnP

✓ **2.7 Compare and contrast Internet connection types, network types, and their features.**

- Internet Connection Types (Cable, DSL, Dial-up, Fiber, Satellite, ISDN, Cellular (Tethering, Mobile Hotspots), Line of sight wireless Internet service)
- Network Types (LAN, WAN, PAN, MAN)

✓ **2.8 Compare and contrast network architecture devices, their functions, and features.**

- Hub
- Switch
- Router

- Access point
- Bridge
- Modem
- Firewall
- Patch Panel
- Repeaters/extenders
- Ethernet Over Power
- PoE injector

✓ **2.9 Given a scenario, use appropriate networking tools.**

- Crimper
- Cable stripper
- Multimeter
- Tone generator and probe
- Cable tester
- Loopback plug
- Punchdown tool
- Wi-Fi analyzer

CompTIA offers a number of other exams and certifications on networking (Network+, Server+, and so on), but to become A+ certified, you must have good knowledge of basic networking skills. Not only do you need to know the basics of cabling and connectors, but you also need to know how to install and configure a wireless/wired router, apply appropriate settings, and use some basic tools. There are nine objectives for this domain.

2.1 Identify the Various Types of Network Cables and Connectors

You're expected to know the basic concepts of networking as well as the different types of cabling that can be used. For the latter, you should be able to identify connectors and cables from figures even if those figures are crude line art (think shadows) appearing in pop-up boxes.

For this exam you must know the three specific types of network cables (fiber, twisted pair, and coaxial) and the connectors associated with each. Fiber is the most expensive of the three and can run the longest distance. A number of types of connectors can work with fiber, but three you must know are SC, ST, and LC.

Twisted pair is commonly used in office settings to connect workstations to hubs or switches. It comes in two varieties: unshielded (UTP) and shielded (STP). The two types of connectors commonly used are RJ-11 (four wires and popular with telephones) and RJ-45 (eight wires and used with xBaseT networks—100BaseT, 1000BaseT, and so forth). Two common wiring standards are T568A and T568B.

Coaxial cabling is not as popular as it once was, but it's still used with cable television and some legacy networks. The two most regularly used connectors are F-connectors (television cabling) and BNC (10Base2 and so on).

Fiber

Fiber-optic cabling is the most expensive type of those discussed for this exam. Although it's an excellent medium, it's often not used because of the cost of implementing it. It has a glass core within a rubber outer coating and uses beams of light rather than electrical signals to relay data (see Figure 2.1). Because light doesn't diminish over distance the way electrical signals do, this cabling can run for distances measured in kilometers with transmission speeds from 1 Gbps up to 100 Gbps or higher.

FIGURE 2.1   Fiber-optic cable

Inner insulation (cladding)

Optical fiber

Outer insulation

Connectors: SC, ST, and LC

Often, fiber is used to connect runs to wiring closets where they break out into UTP or other cabling types, or as other types of backbones. Fiber-optic cable can use either ST, SC, or LC connectors. ST is a barrel-shaped connector, whereas SC is squared and easier to connect in small spaces. The LC connector looks similar to SC but adds a flange on the top (much like an RJ-45 connector) to keep it securely connected. Figure 2.2 shows the fiber connectors.

FIGURE 2.2   Fiber connectors ST, SC, and LC

ST   SC   LC

In addition to these listed in the A+ objectives, other connectors are used with fiber. FC connectors may also be used but are not as common. MT-RJ is a popular connector for two fibers in a small form factor.

Twisted Pair

There are two primary types of twisted-pair cabling (with categories beneath each that are addressed in the "2.2 Compare and Contrast the Characteristics of Connectors and Cabling"): shielded twisted pair (STP) and unshielded twisted pair (UTP). In both cases, the cabling consists of pairs of wires twisted around each other, as shown in Figure 2.3.

UTP offers no shielding (hence the name) and is the network cabling type most prone to outside interference. The interference can be from a fluorescent light ballast, electrical motor, or other such source (known as *electromagnetic interference* [EMI]) or from wires being too close together and signals jumping across them (known as *crosstalk*). STP adds a foil shield around the twisted wires to protect against EMI.

FIGURE 2.3   Twisted-pair cable

Connectors: RJ-11, RJ-45

STP cable uses an IBM data connector (IDC) or universal data connector (UDC) to connect to token ring networks. It can also be used in Ethernet networks where EMI is an issue. While you need to know STP for the exam, you are not required to have any knowledge of the connectors associated with it. You must, however, know that most UTP cable uses RJ-45 connectors, which look like telephone connectors (RJ-11) but have eight wires instead of four. Figure 2.4 shows both RJ-45 (left) and RJ-11 (right) connectors.

FIGURE 2.4   RJ-45 and RJ-11 connectors

Wiring Standards: T568A, T568B

Two wiring standards are commonly used with twisted-pair cabling: T568A and T568B (sometimes referred to simply as 568A and 568B). These are telecommunications standards from TIA and EIA that specify the pin arrangements for the RJ-45 connectors on UTP or STP cables. The number 568 refers to the order in which the wires within the CAT5 cable are terminated and attached to the connector. The signal is identical for both.

T568A was the first standard, released in 1991. Ten years later, in 2001, T568B was released. Figure 2.5 shows the pin number assignments for the 568A and 568B standards. Pin numbers are read left to right, with the connector tab facing down. Notice that the pinouts stay the same, and the only difference is in the color coding of the wiring.

The bottom line here is that if the same standard is used on each end, the cable will be a crossover cable, and if a different standard is used on either end, it will be a straight-through cable.

Mixing cables can cause communication problems on the network. Before installing a network or adding a new component to it, make sure the cable being used is in the correct wiring standard.

FIGURE 2.5   Pin assignments for T568A and T568B

Coaxial

Coaxial cable, or *coax*, is one of the oldest media used in networks. Coax is built around a center conductor or core that is used to carry data from point to point. The center conductor has an insulator wrapped around it, a shield over the insulator, and a nonconductive sheath around the shielding. This construction, depicted in Figure 2.6, allows the conducting core to be relatively free from outside interference. The shielding also prevents the conducting core from emanating signals externally from the cable.

Before you read any further, accept the fact that the odds are incredibly slim that you will ever need to know about coax for a new installation in the real world (with the possible exception of RG-6, which is used from the wall to a cable modem). If you do come across it, it will be in an existing installation, and one of the first things you'll recommend is that it be changed. That said, you do need to know about coax for this exam.

Connectors: BNC, F-connector

Connections to a coax occur through a wide variety of connectors, often referred to as *plumbing*. These connectors provide a modular design that allows for easy expansion. The three primary connections used in this case are the T-connector, the inline connector, and the terminating connector (also known as a *terminating resistor* or *terminator*). Figure 2.7 shows some of these common connectors in a coaxial cable–based network.

FIGURE 2.6   Coaxial cable construction

Center pin

BNC connector

Center conductor

Braid

Sheath

Center insulator

FIGURE 2.7   Common BNC connectors

BNC male connector

BNC inline connector

BNC female connector

BNC T-connector

In addition to these, there are *F-connectors* (commonly called *F-type connectors*). These are screw-on connectors used to attach coaxial cable (including RG-59 and RG-6) to devices. They have a nut on the connection that provides something to grip as the connection is tightened by hand (or, if necessary, pliers to aid with disconnecting). F-connectors are most commonly associated with connecting Internet modems to cable or satellite Internet service provider (ISP) equipment. However, F-type connectors are also used to connect to some proprietary peripherals.

Coax supports both baseband and broadband signaling. *Baseband* signaling means that a single channel is carried through the coax, and *broadband* refers to multiple channels on the coax. Figure 2.8 illustrates this difference. Baseband signaling is similar in concept to a speaker wire. The speaker wire in your stereo connects one channel from the amplifier to the speaker. Broadband is similar to the cable TV connection in your home. The cable from the cable company carries hundreds of channels. Your TV set uses a tuner to select the channel you choose to watch.

FIGURE 2.8   Baseband versus broadband signaling

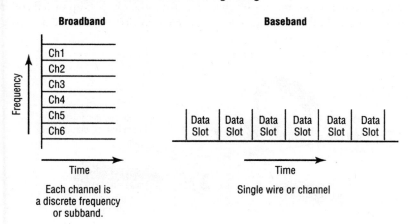

In a coax network, some type of device must terminate all the coax ends. Figure 2.9 shows this termination process in more detail. Coax is present in many older networks and tends to provide reliable service once it's installed. However, if a terminator, NIC, T-connector, or inline connector malfunctions or becomes disconnected, the entire segment of wire in that network will malfunction, and network services will cease operation. Coax tends also to become brittle over time, and it can fail when handled. In addition, coax is expensive per foot when compared to UTP cable. These are the primary reasons that coax is falling from favor as a primary network medium.

FIGURE 2.9   Network termination in a coax network

Coax has two primary vulnerabilities from a security perspective. The most common is the addition of a T-connector attached to a network *sniffer*. This sniffer would have unrestricted access to the signaling on the cable. The second and less common method involves a connection called a *vampire tap*. A vampire tap is a type of connection that hooks directly into a coax by piercing the outer sheath and attaching a small wire to the center conductor or core. This type of attachment allows a tap to occur almost anywhere in the network. Taps can be hard to find because they can be anywhere in the cable. Figure 2.10 shows the two common methods of tapping a coax cable. The T-connector is a standard connector that can be used any place there is a connector on the cable. An inductive pickup or RF collar can be placed around a coaxial cable to capture any stray RF that isn't blocked by the coax's shield.

FIGURE 2.10   A vampire tap and a T-connector on a coax

Table 2.1 lists the cabling types discussed and various attributes of each.

TABLE 2.1   Cable types

Characteristic	Fiber-optic	Unshielded twisted pair	Coaxial
Cost	Expensive	Least expensive	Rarely used
Flexibility	Fair	Most flexible	Fair
Ease of installation	Difficult	Very easy	Moderate
Interference	Not susceptible	Susceptible	Not as susceptible as UTP
Connectors	ST/SC/LC	RJ-45	BNC for Ethernet F-connector for cable modem

Exam Essentials

Know the network cable types.   UTP is the cheapest type of cable to implement, but it's also the weakest. STP is more expensive, but it isn't subject to EMI. Fiber-optic cabling is the most expensive and most difficult to implement, but it offers the greatest combination of speed and distance. Coaxial typically exists in legacy installations with the exception of cable modems.

Know the cable connectors.   Fiber connections include ST, SC, and LC connectors. Twisted-pair cabling uses RJ-45 connectors and can differ in pin-outs based on whether the wiring standard used is T568A (old) or T568B (newer). Coaxial cabling uses either BNC or F-connectors.

2.2 Compare and Contrast the Characteristics of Connectors and Cabling

The previous section introduced cabling and the connectors used with each type. This objective builds on that and reexamines each of the three major types (fiber, twisted-pair, and coaxial) and looks at some of the characteristics of each with an emphasis on speed and transmission limitations.

Fiber cabling comes in two major types: single-mode (SMF) and multi-mode (MMF). The speed of fiber makes it a wonderful choice for network implementations, but the cost still remains prohibitive in many situations. Twisted-pair cabling, which is available unshielded (UTP) or shielded (STP), comes in a number of types—known as categories (CAT3, CAT5, and so forth). As a general rule, the higher the category of twisted-pair cabling, the greater the speed possible. Coaxial cabling comes in a number of types, with RG-6 and RG-59 being the two to know for the exam.

Fiber

Because fiber-based media use light transmissions instead of electronic pulses, such problems as EMI, crosstalk, and attenuation become nonissues. Fiber gets around the limitations on almost everything else except cost and is well suited for transferring data, video, and voice transmissions. Since anyone trying to access data signals on a fiber-optic cable must physically tap into the medium, it is the most secure of all cable media.

Types (Single-Mode vs. Multi-mode)

Two types of fiber-optic cable are available: single-mode and multi-mode. As the name implies, single-mode uses a single direct beam of light, thus allowing for greater distances and increased transfer speeds. With multi-mode, a lot of light beams travel through the cable, bouncing off the cable walls; this weakens the signal, reducing the length that the data signal can travel.

The most common types of fiber-optic cable include the following:

- 8.3 micron core/125 micron cladding single-mode
- 50 micron core/125 micron cladding multi-mode
- 62.5 micron core/125 micron cladding multi-mode

Speed and Transmission Limitations

Table 2.2 lists the speed and transmission limitations for the most common fiber-optic implementations.

TABLE 2.2   Fiber speeds and limitations

Characteristic	100BaseFX	1000BaseSX	1000BaseLX	10GBaseER
Speed	100 Mbps	1000 Mbps	1000 Mbps	10,000 Mbps
Distance (multi-mode)	412 meters	220 to 550 meters	550 meters	(not used)
Distance (single-mode)	10,000 meters	(not used)	5 km	40 km

Twisted Pair

Twisted-pair cabling is most often used in 100BaseT/1000BaseT networks.

Types

There are different grades, which are given as categories, and as you may guess, the higher the grade, the more expensive the cabling and the higher the data rate it can support. You do not need to know all of the categories for the exam, but the ones you do need to know are described in the following sections.

STP   Shielded twisted pair (STP) differs from unshielded twisted pair (UTP) only in the presence of the shielding, which resembles aluminum foil directly beneath the outer insulation. The shielding adds to the cost of the cable, and a rule of thumb based on current prices is that STP is twice as expensive as UTP for the same length of cable.

UTP   Unshielded twisted pair (UTP) is the most popular twisted-pair cabling in use.

CAT3   CAT3 transmits data at speeds up to 10 Mbps with a possible bandwidth of 16 MHz. It contains four twisted pairs of wires with three twists per foot. This is the lowest-level cabling you can safely use in a network. For many years, it was the standard used, but since cabling today considers 100 Mbps to be a minimum, CAT3 has been pushed to legacy installations.

CAT5   CAT5 transmits data at speeds up to 100 Mbps and was used with Fast Ethernet (operating at 100 Mbps) with a transmission range of 100 meters. It contains four twisted pairs of copper wire to give the most protection. Although it had its share of popularity (it's used primarily for 10/100 Ethernet networking), it is now an outdated standard. Newer implementations use the 5e standard.

CAT5e   CAT5e transmits data at speeds up to 1 Gbps (1000 Mbps). Category 5e cabling can be used up to 100 meters, depending on the implementation and standard used and provides a minimum of 100 MHz of bandwidth. It also contains four twisted pairs of copper wire, but they're physically separated and contain more twists per foot than Category 5 to provide maximum interference protection.

CAT6   CAT6 transmits data at speed up to 10 Gbps, has a minimum of 250 MHz of bandwidth, and specifies cable lengths up to 100 meters (using CAT6a). It contains four twisted pairs of copper wire and is used in 10GBaseT networks. Category 6 cable typically is made up of four twisted pairs of copper wire, but its capabilities far exceed those of other cable types. Category 6 twisted pair uses a *longitudinal separator*, which separates each of the four pairs of wires from each other and reduces the amount of crosstalk possible.

CAT6e   While not an official standard, many vendors now offer a CAT6e cable and market them as providing better performance, which may be true, but whatever improvement there is will vary from vendor to vendor since there is no official standard. They are designed to double transmission frequency to 500 MHz. Moreover, by wrapping it in grounded foil shielding, full 10 Gigabit Ethernet speeds can be reached without sacrificing the maximum cable length of 100 meters.

CAT7   Another cable specification not recognized by TIA/EIA is CAT7. By shielding individual wire pairs and the cable as a whole, 10 Gigabit Ethernet can be extended over 100 meters of copper cabling. Moreover, the twisting of the pairs and the number of turns per unit length increase RF shielding and protect from crosstalk.

PVC   The outer insulation that covers most network cables—the part you touch when you handle the cable—is a plastic known as PVC (an acronym for polyvinyl chloride). While inexpensive and easy to work with, PVC gives off a poisonous gas when burned. In places where this may be a problem, plenum cable must be run.

Plenum   Plenum cable is a specific type of cable that is rated for use in plenum spaces. Plenum spaces are those in a building used for heating and air-conditioning systems. Most cable cannot be used in the plenum because of the danger of fire (or the fumes the cables give off as they burn). Plenum cable is fire-rated and meets the necessary standards, which makes it OK to use in these locations. It replaces PVC with a Teflon-like material.

Speed and Transmission Limitations

Table 2.3 lists the speed and transmission limitations for the most common twisted-pair implementations.

TABLE 2.3   Twisted-pair speeds and limitations

	CAT3	CAT5	CAT5e	CAT6	CAT6e	CAT7
Speed	16 Mbps	100 Mbps	1000 Mbps	10/100/1000 Mbps and 10 Gbps	10/100/1000 Mbps and 10 Gbps	10/100/1000 Mbps and 10 Gbps
Limitation	Ineffective for higher-speed networks; often found in older 10BaseT networks	Range of 100 meters	Range of 100 meters	Range of 100 meters	Range of 100 meters	Range over 100 meters

Splitters and Effects on Signal Quality

It is possible to connect a splitter to a single port in a wall outlet and then connect two devices to the splitter. However, considering that this works by using all eight wires (four for each device), it cannot be done when using a higher-speed connection that uses all eight wires. Moreover, it does not eliminate the requirement for two ports on the switch or hub to which the cable from the wall outlet connects. You must also have a second splitter on that end and split the connection again to the two ports. Otherwise, only one device can function at a time.

With regard to the effect on signal quality, you may experience some degradation because the wire pairs being used by the two devices are within the same physical cable and may interfere with one another. When connected to a hub on the far end, this may be worse because of the potential for collisions between the two devices.

Coaxial

Several types of coax exist, and usually each has a specific use. The exam expects you to know two types.

Types

While the exam will probably require you to know only two of these types of coaxial cables, in this section I'll cover three of the most common types of coaxial cable.

RG-6   This is often used for cable TV and cable modems. RG-6 can run longer distances than RG-59 and support digital signals.

RG-59   This is used to generate low-power video connections. The RG-59 cable cannot be used over long distances because of its high-frequency power losses. In such cases, RG-6 cables are used instead.

RG-58   Not specifically listed in the objectives, but something you should know is that RG-58 is the type traditionally used in Thin Ethernet networks (10Base2). Thick coax (10Base5) utilized RG-8, was used primarily for backbone cable, and could be run through plenum spaces since it offered significant resistance to EMI and crosstalk and could run in lengths up to 500 meters. Thick coax offered speeds up to 10 Mbps—too slow for today's network environments.

 There are two types of RG-58 used in legacy Thin Ethernet implementations. RG-58/U has a solid core, whereas RG-58A/U has a stranded wire core.

Speed and Transmission Limitations

Table 2.4 lists the speed and transmission limitations for the most common coax implementations.

TABLE 2.4   Coax speeds and limitations

Characteristic	RG-6	RG-59
Speed	Not used in networking	Not used in networking
Limitation	Cannot be used over long distances (supports digital signals)	Cannot be used over long distances (supports only analog)

Splitters and Effects on Signal Quality

Splitters are often used to send the signal from a coaxial cable to multiple locations in a house or office. When you do this, it does affect the signal quality. The amount of degradation is related to where you perform the split. Consider the diagram in Figure 2.11.

In this scenario there are two splitters. One is placed just after the cable enters the house and splits the signal between the cable modem and the TV. Since there are multiple TVs, a second splitter has been inserted. The loss of signal will be greater at the second split than at the first split. So if you going to introduce a splitter, do so as close to the main signal line as possible.

FIGURE 2.11 Locations for splitting coaxial cable in your house

Exam Essentials

Know the types available for each media.   The two types of fiber available are single-mode and multi-mode. The types of twisted pair you need to know are all UTP related: CAT3, CAT5, CAT5e, and CAT6. Coax cabling includes RG-6 (TV and cable modems) and RG-59 (video). The cables also come in either single-mode (SMF) or multi-mode (MMF) versions.

Know the speeds of CAT cabling.   CAT3 transmits data at speeds up to 10 Mbps. CAT5 transmits data at speeds up to 100 Mbps. CAT5e transmits data at speeds up to 1000 Mbps (1 Gbps). CAT6 transmits data at speeds up to 10 Gbps.

2.3 Explain the Properties and Characteristics of TCP/IP

The protocol of the Internet is TCP/IP, and because of this, TCP/IP has become the de facto protocol of most networks as well. Far from the only networking protocol available, TCP/IP meets the needs of most organizations and is becoming more and more the one protocol suite that administrators must understand in order to do their jobs.

A *host* is any machine or interface that participates in a TCP/IP network—whether as a client or a server. Every interface on a TCP/IP network that must be issued an IP address is considered a host. Those addresses can be manually entered or provided dynamically to the host by a Dynamic Host Configuration Protocol (DHCP) server. (If IPv4 is in use, the addresses fall into three classes—A, B, and C.) The other values needed, besides the

IP address, are the subnet mask (identifying the scope of the network on which the host resides) and the default gateway (the router interfacing with the outside world). Since memorizing complex numerical addresses can be difficult to do, the Domain Name System (DNS) is used to translate hostnames into IP addresses as needed.

IP Class

Although there is no official IP class objective, it is helpful to understand IP classes in the real world, and knowing about them also enriches your understanding of various CompTIA objectives.

IPv4 addresses (IPv6 is discussed later) are 32-bit binary numbers. Because numbers of such magnitude are difficult to work with, they're divided into four octets (8 bits) and converted to decimal. Thus, 01010101 becomes 85. This is important because the limits on the size of the decimal number are because of the reality that they're representations of binary numbers. The range must be from 0 (00000000) to 255 (11111111) per octet, making the lowest possible IP address 0.0.0.0 and the highest 255.255.255.255. Many IP addresses aren't available because they're reserved for diagnostic purposes, private addressing, or some other function.

Three classes of IP addresses are available for assignment to hosts; they're identified by the first octet. Table 2.5 shows the class and the range the first octet must fall into to be within that class. The entire 127.0.0.0 network is missing because that network has been set aside or reserved for diagnostics.

TABLE 2.5 IP address classes

Class	Range
A	1–126
B	128–191
C	192–223

Five classes exist. Class D (multicast) and Class E (experimental) are not assigned to hosts.

Class A If you're given a Class A address, then you're assigned a number such as 125. With a few exceptions, this means you can use any number between 0 and 255 in the second field, any number between 0 and 255 in the third field, and any number between 0 and 255 in the fourth field. This gives you a total number of hosts that you can have on your network in excess of 16 million. The default subnet mask is 255.0.0.0.

Class B If you're given a Class B address, then you're assigned a number such as 152.119. With a few exceptions, this means you can use any number between 0 and 255 in the third field and any number between 0 and 255 in the fourth field. This gives you a total number of hosts that you can have on your network in excess of 65,000. The default subnet mask is 255.255.0.0.

Class C   If you're given a Class C address, then you're assigned a number such as 205.19.15. You can use any number between 1 and 254 in the fourth field, for a total of 254 possible hosts (0 and 255 are reserved). The default subnet mask is 255.255.255.0.

The class, therefore, makes a tremendous difference in the number of hosts your network can have. In most cases, the odds of having all hosts at one location are small. Assuming you have a Class B address, will there be 65,000 hosts in one room, or will they be in several locations? Most often, it's the latter.

IPv4 vs. IPv6

IPv4 uses a 32-bit addressing scheme that provides for more than 4 billion unique addresses. Unfortunately, there are a lot of IP-enabled devices added to the Internet every day—not to mention, not all of the addresses that can be created are used by public networks (many are reserved, in classes D and above and are unavailable for public use). This reduces the number of addresses that can be allocated as public Internet addresses.

IPv6 offers a number of improvements, the most notable of which is its ability to handle growth in public networks. IPv6 uses a 128-bit addressing scheme, allowing a huge number of possible addresses: 340,282,366,920,938,463,463,374,607,431,768,211,456. Table 2.6 compares IPv4 to IPv6.

 In IPv6 addresses, repeating zeros can be left out so that colons next to each other in the address indicate one or more sets of zeros for that section.

TABLE 2.6   IPv4 vs. IPv6

Feature	IPv4	IPv6
Loopback address	127.0.0.1	0:0:0:0:0:0:0:1 (::1)
Private ranges	10.0.0.0 172.16.0.0 to 172.31.0.0 192.168.0.0	FEC0:: (proposed)
Autoconfigured addresses	169.254.0.0	FE80::

Public vs. Private vs. APIPA/Link Local

Within each of the three major classes of IP addresses, there is a range set aside for *private addresses*. These are addresses that do not communicate directly with the Internet (often using a proxy server or network address translation to do so), so each host's address needs to be unique only within the realm of that network. Table 2.7 lists the private address ranges for Class A, B, and C addresses.

TABLE 2.7   Private address ranges

Class	Range
A	10.0.0.0 to 10.255.255.255
B	172.16.0.0 to 172.31.255.255
C	192.168.0.0 to 192.168.255.255

Automatic Private IP Addressing (APIPA) is a TCP/IP feature Microsoft added to its operating systems. If a DHCP server cannot be found and the clients are configured to obtain IP addresses automatically, the clients automatically assign themselves an IP address, somewhat randomly, in the 169.254.*x.x* range with a subnet mask of 255.255.0.0. This allows them to communicate with other hosts that have similarly configured themselves, but they are unable to connect to the Internet. If a computer is using an APIPA address, it will have trouble communicating with other clients if those clients do not use APIPA addresses.

In IPv6, there is a type of address called a link local address that in many ways is like an APIPA address in that the device will generate one of these addresses for each interface with no intervention from a human, as is done with APIPA. The scope of the address is also the same, in that it is not routable and is good only on the segment the device is located on.

However, as is the case with APIPA addresses, if two devices connected to the same segment generate these addresses, they will be in the same network, and the two devices will be able to communicate. This is because the devices always generate the address using the same IPv6 prefix (the equivalent of a network ID in IPv4), which is FE80::/64. The remainder of the address is created by spreading the 48-bit MAC address across the last 64 bits yielding an IPv6 address that looks like the one shown here:
FE80::2237:06FF:FECF:67E4/64

Static vs. Dynamic

The two methods of entering address information for a host are static and dynamic. Static means that you manually enter the information for the host and it does not change. Dynamic means that DHCP is used for the host to lease information from.

Client-Side DNS Settings

As stated earlier, every computer, interface, or device on a TCP/IP network is issued a unique identifier known as an *IP address* that resembles 192.168.12.123. Because of the Internet, TCP/IP is the most commonly used networking protocol today. You can easily see that it's difficult for most users to memorize these numbers, so hostnames are used in their place. *Hostnames* are alphanumeric values assigned to a host; any host may have more than one hostname.

For example, the host 192.168.12.123 may be known to all users as Gemini, or it may be known to the sales department as Gemini and to the marketing department as Apollo9. All that is needed is a means by which the alphanumeric name can be translated into its IP address. There are a number of methods of doing so, but for this exam, you need to know only one: DNS. On a large network, you can add a server to be referenced by all hosts for the name resolution. The server runs DNS and resolves fully qualified domain names (FQDNs) like www.entrepreneurshipcamp.com into their IP address. Multiple DNS servers can serve an area and provide fault tolerance for one another. In all cases, the DNS servers divide their area into zones; every zone has a primary server and any number of secondary servers. DNS works with any operating system and any version.

   FQDNs identify the host and information about it.

Client-Side DHCP

Dynamic Host Configuration Protocol (DHCP) falls into a different category. Whereas DNS resolves names to IP addresses, DHCP issues IP configuration data.

Rather than an administrator having to configure a unique IP address for every host added on a network (and *default gateway* and *subnet mask*), they can use a DHCP server to issue these values. That server is given a number of addresses in a range that it can supply to clients.

For example, the server may be given the IP range (or *scope*) 192.168.12.1 to 192.168.12.200. When a client boots, it sends out a request for the server to issue it an address (and any other configuration data) from that scope. The server takes one of the numbers it has available and leases it to the client for a length of time. If the client is still using the configuration data when 50 percent of the lease has expired, it requests a renewal of the lease from the server; under normal operating conditions, the request is granted. When the client is no longer using the address, the address goes back in the scope and can be issued to another client.

DHCP is built on the older Bootstrap Protocol (BOOTP) that was used to allow diskless workstations to boot and connect to a server that provided them with an operating system and applications. The client uses broadcasts to request the data and thus—normally—can't communicate with DHCP servers beyond their own subnet (broadcasts don't route). A DHCP Relay Agent, however, can be employed to allow DHCP broadcasts to go from one network to another.

While the primary purpose of DHCP is to lease IP addresses to hosts, when it gives the IP address, it also often includes the additional configuration information as well: DNS server, router information, and so on.

Subnet Mask vs. CIDR

Subnetting your network is the process of taking the total number of hosts available to you and dividing it into smaller networks. When you configure TCP/IP on a host, you typically need only give three values: a unique IP address, a default gateway (router) address, and a subnet mask. Table 2.8 shows the default subnet mask for each class of network.

 Purists may argue that you don't need a default gateway. Technically this is true if your network is small and you don't communicate beyond it. For all practical purposes, though, most networks need a default gateway.

TABLE 2.8   Default subnet values

Class	Default subnet mask
A	255.0.0.0
B	255.255.0.0
C	255.255.255.0

When you use the default subnet mask, you're allowing for all hosts to be at one site and not subdividing your network. This is called *classful* subnetting. Any deviation from the default signifies that you're dividing the network into multiple subnetworks, which is called classless subnetting.

The problem with classful subnetting is that it allows for only three sizes of networks: Class A (16,777,216 hosts), Class B (65,536 hosts), and Class C (254 hosts). Two of these are too large to operate efficiently in the real world, and when enterprises were issued public network IDs that were larger than they needed, many public IP addresses were wasted. For this reason and simply to allow for the creation of smaller networks that operate better, the concept of classless routing, or Classless Interdomain Routing (CIDR), was born.

Using CIDR, administrators can create smaller networks called subnets, by manipulating the subnet mask of a larger classless or major network ID. This allows you to create a subnet that is much closer in size to what you need, thus wasting fewer IP addresses and increasing performance in each subnet. The increased performance is a function of the reduced broadcast traffic generated in each subnet.

Gateway

A *gateway* can have two meanings. In TCP/IP, a gateway is the address of the machine to send data to that is not intended for a host on this network (in other words, a default gateway). A gateway is also a physical device operating between the Transport and Application layers of the OSI model that can send data between dissimilar systems. The best example of the latter is a mail gateway—it doesn't matter which two networks are communicating; the gateway allows them to exchange e-mail.

A gateway, as it is tested on the exam, is the server (router) that allows traffic beyond the internal network. Hosts are configured with the address of a gateway (called the default gateway), and if they need to correspond with a host outside the internal network, the data is sent to the gateway to facilitate this. When you configure TCP/IP on a host, one of the fields that should be provided is a gateway field, which specifies where data not intended for this network is sent in order to be able to communicate with the rest of the world.

Exam Essentials

Know the IP classes.   Class A addresses range from 0 to 126, Class B from 128 to 191, and Class C from 192 to 223. Within each class, there are private address ranges. Class A's private range is from 10.0.0.0 to 10.255.255.255, Class B is from 172.16.0.0 to 172.31.255.255, and Class C is from 192.168.0.0 to 192.168.255.255.

Understand what APIPA is.   Automatic Private IP Addressing (APIPA) is a TCP/IP feature for clients that cannot find a DHCP server but are configured to get their address from DHCP. The clients automatically assign themselves an IP address, somewhat randomly, in the $169.254.x.x$ range with a subnet mask of 255.255.0.0.

2.4 Explain Common TCP and UDP Ports, Protocols, and Their Purpose

Communication across a TCP/IP-based network takes place using various protocols, such as FTP to transfer files, HTTP to view web pages, and POP3 or IMAP to work with e-mail. Each of these protocols has a default port associated with it, and CompTIA expects you to be familiar with them for this exam.

Both TCP and UDP use port numbers to listen for and respond to requests for communication using various protocols. There are a number of protocols and their port numbers that you must know for this exam, as well as the differences between TCP and UDP.

Ports

There are two transport layer protocols in the TCP/IP stack. TCP provides guaranteed, connection-oriented delivery, while UDP provides nonguaranteed, connectionless delivery.

Each protocol or service uses one of the two transport protocols (and in some cases both). There will be additional information later in this chapter on TCP and UDP.

TCP and UDP both use port numbers to listen for and respond to requests for communications. RFC 1060 defines *common ports* for a number of services routinely found in use, and these all have low numbers—up to 1,024. You can, however, reconfigure your service to use another port number (preferably much higher) if you're concerned about security and you don't want your site to be available to anonymous traffic.

21—FTP   File Transfer Protocol (FTP) is both a TCP/IP protocol and software that permits the transferring of files between computer systems. Because FTP has been implemented on numerous types of computer systems, files can be transferred between disparate systems (for example, a personal computer and a minicomputer). It uses ports 20 and 21 by default. It can be configured to allow or deny access to specific IP addresses and can be configured to work with exceptions. While the protocol can be run within most browsers, a number of FTP applications are available, with FileZilla (`http://filezilla-project.org/`) being one of the most popular.

22—Secure Shell (SSH)   Secure Shell is a remote administration tool that can serve as a secure alternative to using Telnet to remotely access and configure a device like a router or switch. While requiring a bit more setup than Telnet, it provides an encrypted command-line session for managing devices remotely.

23—Telnet   Telnet is a protocol that functions at the application layer of the OSI model, providing terminal-emulation capabilities. Telnet runs on port 23 but has lost favor to SSH because Telnet sends data—including passwords—in plain-text format.

25—SMTP   Simple Mail Transfer Protocol (SMTP) is a protocol for sending e-mail between SMTP servers. Clients typically use either IMAP or POP to access their e-mail server and use SMTP to send e-mail. SMTP uses port 25 by default.

53—DNS   As mentioned earlier, DNS is the Domain Name System, and it is used to translate hostnames into IP addresses. DNS is an example of a protocol that uses both UDP and TCP.

80—HTTP   Hypertext Transfer Protocol (HTTP) is the protocol used for communication between a web server and a web browser. It uses port 80 by default.

110—POP3   The Post Office Protocol (POP) is a protocol for receiving e-mail from a mail server. The alternative to POP (which runs on port 110) is IMAP.

143—IMAP   Internet Message Access Protocol (IMAP) is a protocol with a store-and-forward capability. It can also allow messages to be stored on an e-mail server instead of downloaded to the client. The current version of the protocol is 4 (IMAP4), and the counterpart to it is Post Office Protocol (POP). IMAP runs on port 143.

443—HTTPS   Hypertext Transfer Protocol over Secure Sockets Layer (HTTPS) is a protocol used to make a secure connection. It uses port 443 by default.

3389—RDP   Remote Desktop Protocol (RDP) is used in a Windows environment to make remote desktop communications possible.

137-139 (UDP ports 137, 138 & TCP ports 137, 139), 445—SMB   Server Message Block (SMB) is an application layer protocol used to provide shared access to resources. It is primary used in Windows systems with the latest version being 3.02, which was released to support Windows 8.1 and Windows Server 2012R2. It operated as a client-server application.

548— or 427—AFP   Apple Filing Protocol (AFP) is a proprietary resource sharing protocol by Apple, one of several it supports. It uses port 548 or 427 for communication. The latest version, 3.4, was introduced with the OS Mountain Lion system.

Just associating each protocol with a port doesn't do much good. You should also know what the protocol is used for. The following sections look at each of the ports in the table and explain a bit about them.

Protocols

There are a number of protocols that CompTIA lists for this objective. Among them are DHCP and DNS, which were covered fully in the discussion of objective 2.3. The others are as follows:

LDAP   Lightweight Directory Access Protocol (LDAP) is a protocol that provides a mechanism to access and query directory services systems. These directory services systems are most likely to be Microsoft's Active Directory but could also be Novell Directory Services (NDS). Although LDAP supports command-line queries executed directly against the directory database, most LDAP interactions are via utilities such as an authentication program (network logon) or a search engine that locates a resource in the directory.

SNMP   Simple Network Management Protocol (SNMP) is a protocol that facilitates network management functionality. It is not, in itself, a network management system (NMS), simply the protocol that makes NMS possible.

SMB   Server Message Blocks (SMBs) are used to share access to resources. While the newest versions of SMB (versions 30 and 30.2) are proprietary to Microsoft, compatible versions are available in Linux operating systems, allowing them to still share the printers, files, and other resources that have been made available across the network.

CIFS   Common Internet File System (CFIS) is a cross-platform implementation of SMB that became the native file system in Windows starting with Windows 2000. It is also supported on many other systems such as Unix, Mac OS, and IBM.

SSH   The Secure Shell (SSH) application replaces Telnet and provides the same functionality while increasing security. SSH runs on port 22 and encrypts the transmitted data, including the password.

AFP   Apple Filing Protocol (AFP) was discussed in the section "Ports."

TCP vs. UDP

Operating at the transport layer of the TCP/IP stack are two key protocols: *Transmission Control Protocol* (TCP) and *User Datagram Protocol* (UDP). The biggest difference between these two is that one is connection based (TCP) and the other works in the absence of a dedicated connection (UDP). Both are needed and serve key roles.

If you are sending credit card information to a website, you need a dedicated connection between your host and the server, so TCP handles that task. An example of UDP is DHCP. When a client sends a request for any DHCP server listening to give it an address, it is not requiring a dedicated communication.

Exam Essentials

Know the default ports.   There are a number of protocols you need to know the default ports for: FTP (20/21), Telnet (23), SMTP (25), DNS (53), HTTP (80), POP3 (110), IMAP (143), HTTPS (443), and RDP (3389).

Know what the protocols do.   In addition to the protocols for which ports are given, know as well DHCP, DNS, LDAP, SNMP, SMB, CIFS, SSH, and AFP.

2.5 Compare and Contrast Various Wi-Fi Networking Standards and Encryption Types

More and more, networks are using wireless as the medium of choice. It is much easier to implement, reconfigure, upgrade, and use than wired networks. Unfortunately, there can be downsides, with security being one of the largest.

The 802.11 standard applies to wireless networking, and there have been many versions/types of it released; the main ones are a, b, g, and n. Encryption has gone from very weak (WEP) to much stronger with increments along the way, including WPA, WPA2, and implementations of TKIP and AES.

Standards

The IEEE 802.11x family of protocols provides for wireless communications using radio frequency transmissions. The frequencies in use for 802.11 standards are the 2.4 GHz and 5 GHz frequency spectrums. Several standards and bandwidths have been defined for use in wireless environments, and they aren't extremely compatible with each other.

802.11a   The *802.11a* standard provides wireless LAN bandwidth of up to 54 Mbps in the 5 GHz frequency spectrum. The 802.11a standard also uses orthogonal frequency division multiplexing (OFDM) for encoding rather than FHSS or DSSS.

802.11b   The *802.11b* standard provides for bandwidths of up to 11 Mbps (with fallback rates of 5.5, 2, and 1 Mbps) in the 2.4 GHz frequency spectrum. This standard is also called *Wi-Fi* or *802.11 high rate*. The 802.11b standard uses only DSSS for data encoding.

802.11g   The *802.11g* standard operates in the 2.4 GHz frequency spectrum. This offers a maximum rate of 54 Mbps and is backward compatible with 802.11b.

802.11n   The goal of the 802.11n standard is to significantly increase throughput in both the 2.4 GHz and 5 GHz frequency ranges. The baseline goal of the standard was to reach speeds of 100 Mbps, but given the right conditions, it is estimated that the 802.11n speeds might be able to reach 600 Mbps. In practical operation, 802.11n speeds will be much slower. It is also backward compatible with 802.11 a/b/g.

802.11ac   The 802.11ac standard builds upon the features of 802.11n and improves on them in the following ways:

- Wider channels (40 MHz, 80 MHz, and 160 MHz)
- New modulation (256 Quadrature amplitude modulation (QAM), which has the potential to provide a 30 percent increase in speed)
- More spatial streams (up to eight spatial streams)
- Improved MIMO and beamforming with the use of multi-user MIMO, allowing an AP to transmit a signal to multiple client stations on the same channel simultaneously if the client stations are in different physical areas

With 802.11ac, which operates only in the 5 GHz frequency range, it is possible to achieve a data rate of almost 2 Gbps if the AP and the station have enough antennas.

Three technologies are used to communicate in the 802.11 standard.

Direct-Sequence Spread Spectrum (DSSS)   DSSS accomplishes communication by adding the data that is to be transmitted to a higher-speed transmission. The higher-speed transmission contains redundant information to ensure data accuracy. Each packet can then be reconstructed in the event of a disruption.

Frequency-Hopping Spread Spectrum (FHSS)   FHSS accomplishes communication by hopping the transmission over a range of predefined frequencies. The changing or hopping is synchronized between both ends and appears to be a single transmission channel to both ends.

Orthogonal Frequency Division Multiplexing (OFDM)   OFDM accomplishes communication by breaking the data into subsignals and transmitting them simultaneously. These transmissions occur on different frequencies or subbands.

The mathematics and theories of these transmission technologies are beyond the scope of this book and far beyond the scope of this exam.

Speeds, Distances, and Frequencies

Table 2.9 compares the speed, distance, and frequency of each of the 802.11 standards.

TABLE 2.9   Comparison of 802.11 standards

Standard	Speed	Distance (indoors)	Frequency
802.11a	Up to 54 Mbps	Up to 115 feet	5 GHz
802.11b	Up to 11 Mbps	Up to 115 feet	2.4 GHz
802.11g	Up to 54 Mbps	Up to 125 feet	2.4 GHz
802.11n	Up to 600 Mbps	Up to 380 feet	2.4 GHz/5 GHz
802.11ac	Up to 6.9 Gbps	Up to 115 feet	5 GHz

Encryption Types

There are a number of wireless encryption "types" you need to know for the A+ exam. These are WEP, WPA, WPA2, TKIP, and AES.

Let's take a closer look at each.

WEP   *Wired Equivalent Privacy* (WEP) is a standard that was created as a first stab at security for wireless devices. Using WEP-encrypted data to provide data security has always been under scrutiny for not being as secure as initially intended. WEP is vulnerable because of weaknesses in the way the encryption algorithms are employed. These weaknesses allow the algorithm to potentially be cracked in as few as five minutes using available PC software. This makes WEP one of the most vulnerable protocols available for security.

WPA   The *Wi-Fi Protected Access* (WPA) and *Wi-Fi Protected Access 2* (WPA2) technologies were designed to address the core problems with WEP. These technologies implement the 802.11i standard. The difference between WPA and WPA2 is that the former implements most—but not all—of 802.11i in order to be able to communicate with older wireless cards (which might still need an update through their firmware to be compliant), while WPA2 implements the full standard and is not compatible with older cards.

WPA2   WPA2 implements the full 802.11i standard for security and is not compatible with older wireless cards.

TKIP   WPA was able to increase security by using a *Temporal Key Integrity Protocol* (TKIP) to scramble encryption keys using a hashing algorithm. The keys are issued an integrity check to verify they have not been modified or tampered with during transit. While a good solution, it was far from perfect. Corporate security today favors WPA2 since it replaces TKIP with Counter Mode with Cipher Block Chaining Message Authentication Code Protocol (CCMP).

AES   CCMP uses 128-bit Advanced Encryption Security (AES) with a 48-bit initialization vector, making it much more difficult to crack and minimizing the risk of a replay attack.

> **WARNING**
>
> Never assume that a wireless connection is secure. The emissions from a wireless portal may be detectable through walls and for several blocks from the portal. Interception is easy to accomplish, given that RF is the medium used for communication. Newer wireless devices offer data security, and you should use it. You can set newer WAPs and wireless routers to nonbroadcast. This is also sometimes called *disabling the broadcast* of the SSID. Given the choice, you should choose to use WPA2, WPA, or WEP at its highest encryption level in that order.

Exam Essentials

Understand wired and wireless connectivity.   Networks work the same whether there is a physical wire between the hosts or that wire has been replaced by a wireless signal. The same order of operations and steps are carried out regardless of the medium employed.

Know the capabilities and limitations of the 802.11x network standards.   The current standards for wireless protocols are 802.11, 802.11a, 802.11b, 802.11g, 802.11n, and 802.11ac.

Know the vulnerabilities of wireless networks.   The primary method of gaining information about a wireless network is a site survey. Site surveys can be accomplished with a PC and an 802.11 card. Wireless networks are subject to the same attacks as wired networks.

2.6 Given a Scenario, Install and Configure a SOHO Wireless/Wired Router and Apply Appropriate Settings

Small office and home office (SOHO) networks can be created easily today and relatively inexpensively. You can choose to do so with or without wires. While there isn't a hard-and-fast rule on what the limit is for a SOHO network, the term is generally used for networks of 10 or fewer workstations.

One of the biggest differences between SOHO networks and larger local area networks (LANs) is the way they connect to the outside world. While a LAN would never connect in today's world through an ADSL connection, it is still common in a SOHO network.

This section will look at the connection types and possibilities that exist for small networks, as well as some of the basics of network configuration. While a number of topics in this section are not part of the official objectives, they are included because they are both important and helpful to your understanding.

MAC Filtering

One way to increase security is to implement *MAC filtering*. Every network card has a unique 48-bit address assigned to it—half of which identifies the vendor of the card and the other half of which acts like a serial number. When MAC filtering is implemented, you identify each host by this number and determine specifically which addresses are allowed access to the network. While a great security tool, bear in mind that it is identifying the NIC and not the person sitting at that machine, so it cannot ever be the only form of authentication employed.

 An example of a MAC address is 00-21-6A-2C-89-3C.

Channels (1–11)

Wireless routers can be set to use different channels, which are numbered 1 through 11 (1, 6, and 11 are those commonly used in the United States). Each channel represents a different frequency. You can change the channel to avoid interference—either from another network nearby or from devices also using that frequency.

The channel change is made only on the router because each client should automatically detect and change to the new channel.

SSID Broadcast (On/Off)

Many networks will regularly broadcast their name (known as an *SSID broadcast*) to announce their presence. For security reasons, you should change the SSID from its default value (if one is preconfigured) and disable broadcasts where possible. Disabling the broadcasts prevents snooping eyes from seeing that the network is there but does not affect operations in any other way—clients simply need to specify the name of the network without having the assistance of seeing it.

Wireless Encryption

Domain 2.5, which preceded this one, is focused solely on wireless encryption. Information is not repeated here to avoid needless repetition, but you are advised to read it there.

Port Forwarding/Triggering

A firewall can be hardware- or software-based. At its simplest, firewall configuration is accomplished by configuring ports and rules. A *port* is an interface that is used to connect to a device and is identified by number. Throughout this book, many well-known ports have been discussed by their number (SMTP on port 25, for example).

When you use a service, the default port is implied, but you can always change the *port assignment* if you want to increase security. For example, when you attempt to connect to a website, you'll use port 80 by default. (A socket is the combination of the IP address and the port number. If you were accessing a website at 192.168.0.100, the combination of these two elements would give you a socket; the full address and port description would then be 192.168.0.100:80.)

The assignment can be changed so that a server offers the web service at a port other than the default, such as 8080. If that is done, the service can be accessed by the client by specifying the socket: http://192.168.0.100:8080.

Port forwarding (also known as port mapping) is the act of mapping one port to another. This is essentially the same as what NAT does, and it allows external users to access the private LAN. This is useful when you want to allow only some external users (partners, for example) to be able to access the network resources remotely. These ports can be left open all the time or turned on only when needed. If the latter is the case, this is known as *port triggering*. With triggering, an inbound attempt at connection triggers the opening of an outbound port, and communication is now possible. Obviously, the trigger is activated only after all authentication measures have been successfully met.

Another aspect of firewall configuration is the establishment of rules. The *rules* are criteria given for what is allowed to pass through or connect to the network. These rules are typically accept- or deny-based (but can be configured to include exceptions). For example, you may choose to deny all connections except those specifically allowed; this is much better than the alternative of allowing all except those specifically denied, which creates a security nightmare.

Rules can typically be created based on the following:

- Direction, which can be inbound or outbound

- Protocol source, which can be either TCP (connection-based) or UDP (connectionless)

- Address source

- Port

- Destination address

- Destination port

If you want to limit all of any one criterion—for example, all destination ports—most firewalls allow you to use the value any for this purpose.

DHCP (On/Off)

This chapter has discussed DHCP a few times already. It serves a useful purpose of issuing IP addresses and other network-related configuration values to clients to allow them to operate on the network. The router can perform this function on a SOHO network and simplify the administrator's life.

From a security standpoint, however, having the router do this can present a serious concern. Since the values can be issued to any wireless device that comes within range, it is possible that a rogue machine could be issued these values and then be allowed on the network. In the interest of security, I recommend that the DHCP feature be turned off on the router and IP addresses (along with other networking values) manually entered for the clients.

DMZ

The networking equivalent of a security zone is a network security zone. They perform the same function. If you divide a network into smaller sections, each zone can have its own security considerations and measures—just like a physical security zone. This arrangement allows layers of security to be built around sensitive information. The division of the network is accomplished by implementing virtual LANs (VLANs) or instituting demilitarized zones (DMZs).

A *demilitarized zone* (DMZ) is an area where you can place a public server for access by people you might not trust otherwise. By isolating a server in a DMZ, you can hide or remove access to other areas of your network. You can still access the server using your network, but others aren't able to access further network resources. This can be accomplished using firewalls to isolate your network.

When establishing a DMZ, you assume that the person accessing the resource isn't necessarily someone you would trust with other information. By keeping the rest of the network from being visible to external users, this lowers the threat of intrusion in the internal network.

 Any time you want to separate public information from private information, a DMZ is an acceptable option.

The easiest way to create a DMZ is to use a firewall that can transmit in three directions.

- To the internal network
- To the external world (Internet)
- To the public information you're sharing (the DMZ)

From there, you can decide what traffic goes where; for example, HTTP traffic would be sent to the DMZ, and e-mail would go to the internal network.

NAT/DNAT

Network address translation (NAT) creates a unique opportunity to assist in the security of a network. Originally, NAT extended the number of usable Internet addresses. Now it allows an organization to present a single address to the Internet for all computer connections. The NAT server provides IP addresses to the hosts or systems in the network and tracks inbound and outbound traffic.

A company that uses NAT presents a single connection to the network. This connection may be through a router or a NAT server. The only information that an intruder will be able to get is that the connection has a single address.

NAT effectively hides your network from the world, making it much harder to determine what systems exist on the other side of the router. The NAT server effectively operates as a firewall for the network. Most new routers support NAT; it provides a simple, inexpensive firewall for small networks.

 It's important to understand that NAT acts as a proxy between the local area network (which can be using private IP addresses) and the Internet. Not only can NAT save IP addresses, but it can also act as a firewall.

Most NAT implementations assign internal hosts private IP address numbers and use public addresses only for the NAT to translate to and communicate with the outside world. The private address ranges, all of which are addresses that are nonroutable, are as follows:

- 10.0.0.0–10.255.255.255
- 172.16.0.0–172.31.255.255
- 192.168.0.0–192.168.255.255

 In addition to NAT, port address translation (PAT) is possible. Whereas NAT can use multiple public IP addresses, PAT uses a single one and shares the port with the network. Because it is using only a single port, PAT is much more limited and typically used only on small and home-based networks. Microsoft's Internet Connection Sharing is an example of a PAT implementation.

Destination network address translation (DNAT) is a technique for transparently changing the *destination* IP address of an end route packet and performing the inverse function for any replies.

Also known as Transparent Traffic Forwarding, DNAT provides a facility to send HTTP user traffic to another destination, such as a centralized content filter, authentication server, or some other external location, based on defined criteria; it accomplishes a similar goal as port forwarding.

WPS

Wi-Fi Protected Setup (WPS) simplifies the security configuration of small home networks by implementing WPA2 encryption and allowing new devices to join the network by pressing a button on the router instead of having to enter a complicated passphrase. When a new device (called an *enrollee*) needs to join, you simply press the button on the access point and the registrar enrolls the device. The access point itself can be the registrar (common), or it can pass the information on to a server that does the actual enrollment (not common).

Basic QoS

Quality of Service (QoS) describes the strategies used to manage the flow of network traffic. A network administrator can use QoS to manage the amount of bandwidth provided to applications that are latency sensitive (those that don't function well with lags—voice and video, for example).

One way QoS accomplishes this is by prioritizing latency-sensitive applications over latency-insensitive ones and then doing priority queuing. Traffic is placed in order based on its importance on delivery time. All data is given access, but the more important and latency-sensitive data is given higher priority.

Firmware

Like many hardware devices, wireless access points, wireless routers, and wireless controllers use *firmware* to manage the hardware in the device. In many cases, the firmware version will determine the features and functions that are available on the device. For this reason you create a plan to monitor the vendor website for any firmware updates that are issued.

Firmware updates either correct something that isn't working or add additional functionality to the device. The most critical firmware updates are those that address and correct security vulnerabilities. These are updates you *don't* want to miss because otherwise your device has a security vulnerability.

UPnP

Universal Plug and Play (UPnP) is a protocol that lets computers, printers, and other devices make themselves easily discoverable to a network router. Promoted by the UPnP Forum, a computer industry initiative, it is available on many wireless APs and routers. While it makes it easier to connect devices, it does have security issues.

In several studies it has been shown that more than 6,900 network-aware products from 1,500 companies at 81 million IP addresses responded to their discovery requests on the Internet. Depending on the security posture of the device, many of those devices can be accessed or manipulated. For this reason, many have called for disabling this feature on wireless routers or APs.

Exam Essentials

Know the difference between port forwarding and port triggering.   Port forwarding is the act of mapping one port to another (essentially the same as what NAT does). Port triggering involves turning on ports only when they are needed.

Understand MAC filtering.   When MAC filtering is implemented, you identify each host by this number and determine specifically which addresses are allowed to access the network.

2.7 Compare and Contrast Internet Connection Types, Network Types, and Their Features

Your network can connect to the Internet in a number of ways. This can range from the slow dial-up connection that is established only when you need it to be established to a high speed fiber connection that is always on. This section looks at many of the options available and all that you need to know for this objective on the A+ exam.

When discussing ways to connect to the Internet, most of the discussion is on broadband network techniques. It is imperative that you understand the various types of networks, including broadband. The sections that follow will focus on the key issues associated with connecting to the Internet.

Cable

Two of the most popular methods of connecting to the Internet today are using DSL or a cable. Instead of the service coming from a telephone company as with DSL, cable service is provided by the cable provider, and a *cable modem* is used. While speeds vary based on the number of users the cable company is servicing, as a general rule cable-based broadband service is faster than DSL.

DSL

Digital Subscriber Line (DSL) uses existing phone lines with a DSL modem and a network card. A standard RJ-45 connector is used to connect the network card to the DSL modem, and a phone cord with RJ-11 connectors is used to connect the DSL modem to the phone jack. Multiple types of DSL exist; the most popular are *high bit-rate DSL* (HDSL), *symmetric DSL* (SDSL), *very high bit-rate DSL* (VHDSL), *rate-adaptive DSL* (RADSL), and *asymmetric DSL* (ADSL). The latter provides slower upload than download speed and is the most common for home use. While speeds may vary depending on the quality of the connection and the equipment used, Table 2.10 shows the most common upload and download speeds for the various flavors of DSL.

TABLE 2.10   DSL speeds

Type	Upload	Download
ADSL	1 Mbps	8 Mbps
ADSL2	1.3 Mbps	12 Mbps
ADSL2+	1.3 Mbps	24 Mbps
SDSL	4.5 Mbps	4.5 Mbps
VHDSL	3 Mbps	55 Mbps

Dial-up

Whereas broadband holds great promise for high-speed connections, there are many people (quite a few in rural areas) who cannot take advantage of this. Thankfully, one of the first methods of remote access, dial-up networking, is still in existence. With dial-up, you add a modem to your computer and connect to an Internet service provider (ISP) over the existing phone lines, also known as the *Plain Old Telephone System* (POTS). With a good connection, you can transmit and receive at 56 Kbps.

Fiber

Fiber-optic cabling provides excellent speed and bandwidth but is expensive. Not only are the cables that you use costly, but the light-emitting/receiving hardware costs also make this an expensive undertaking. Because of the cost involved, fiber is often an option for businesses only when it comes to broadband access.

Fiber to the Home (FTTH) is an attempt some communities are undertaking to offer high-speed connectivity to residential dwellings as well. Verizon's FiOS, a similar implementation, runs single-mode optical fiber to homes and includes phone and television service along with Internet access.

Satellite

Whereas the other broadband technologies discussed require the use of physical wiring, with satellite broadband the service provider sends a microwave signal from a dish to an orbiting satellite and back. One satellite can service many receivers, so this is commonly known as *point-to-multipoint* technology. As a general rule, satellite connections are slower than the other broadband technologies you need to know for the exam, and they are adversely affected by weather and atmospheric conditions.

With satellite, download speed is much faster than upload speed.

ISDN

Integrated Services Digital Network (ISDN) is a WAN technology that performs link management and signaling by virtue of packet switching. The original idea behind it was to let existing phone lines carry digital communications by using multiplexing to support multiple channels.

Cellular

Mobile devices have made cellular networking popular, though they are not the only devices capable of using networking; for example, a cellular modem can also be quickly added to a laptop. Cellular networks use a central access point (a cell tower) in a mesh network design. For a long time, two competing standards were the *Global System for Mobile Communications* (GSM) and the *Code Division Multiple Access* (CDMA); the latest technology is Long Term Evolution (LTE), which is used in 4G networks.

> Most cellular phone companies now have specialized wireless routers that are used to create mobile hotspots. These cards act as stand-alone routers to the Internet using the cellular phone network.

Tethering

Tethering is the process of connecting a device to a smartphone or tablet with a cellular connection for the purpose of using the Internet connection on the cellular device. Connecting to the phone or tablet with the other device can be done using 802.11, Bluetooth, or a physical connection using a cable, for example through USB.

Mobile Hotspot

When the devices using the Internet connection on the cellular device are connected wirelessly using 802.11, it is sometimes called a *mobile hotspot*. This is also the term used for devices that are capable of acting as a hotspot for surrounding Wi-Fi devices. The mobile hotspot device may get its Internet access through either cellular or 802.11.

Line-of-Sight Wireless Internet Service

Line-of-sight wireless, as the name implies, requires you to have a direct line of vision between your location and the ISP. Because this uninterrupted path must be maintained, distances are quite short, and this method is not widely used.

Network Types

You should know the terminology used for networking as well as the major topologies that are available. Networks consist of servers and clients. A *server* is a dedicated machine offering services such as file and print sharing. A *client* is any individual workstation accessing the network. A *workstation* is a client machine that accesses services elsewhere (normally from a server).

Networks differ in size and scope. The size of the network on which servers and clients operate can range significantly.

LAN

A *local area network* (LAN) is a network that is geographically confined within a small space—a room, a building, and so on. Because it's confined and does not have to span a great distance, it can normally offer higher speeds.

With Ethernet, you can often use the network type to compute the required length and speed of your cabling. For example, 100BaseT tells you three things:

- **100:** The speed of the network, 100 Mbps.
- **Base:** The technology used (either baseband or broadband).
- **T:** Twisted-pair cabling. In the case of 10BaseT, it's generally UTP.

When you configure a network, one of the first places to turn your attention is the routers and access points—they are the hardware components on which network access can rely. Because these devices must always be able to be found, I suggest that you not use DHCP to issue them addresses but that you configure their addresses statically.

To increase security, devices should be behind a firewall, and you should always change the administrative username and password that comes preconfigured with these devices to ones that adhere to stringent password policies (mixture of uppercase and lowercase alphabet, numbers, and special characters), and you should keep the firmware updated.

With wireless access points, you should change the SSID from its default value (if one is preconfigured) and disable broadcasts. MAC filtering can be used on a wireless network, for example, to prevent certain clients from accessing the Internet. You can choose to deny service to a set list of MAC addresses (and allow all others) or allow service only to a set of MAC addresses (and deny all others).

WAN

A *wide area network* (WAN) is a collection of two or more LANs, typically connected by routers, and dedicated leased lines (not to mention complicated implementations). The geographic limitation is removed, but WAN speeds are traditionally less than LAN speeds.

PAN

A *personal area network* (PAN) is a LAN created by personal devices. Often, personal devices include networking capabilities and can communicate directly with one another. Wireless technologies have introduced a new term: *wireless personal area network* (WPAN). WPAN refers to the technologies involved in connecting devices in close proximity to exchange data or resources. An example is connecting a laptop with a PDA to synchronize an address book. Because of their small size and the nature of the data exchange, WPAN devices lend themselves well to ad hoc wireless networking. Ad hoc wireless networks are those that have devices connect to each other directly, not through a wireless access point.

MAN

Occasionally, a WAN will be referenced as a *metropolitan area network* (MAN) when it is confined to a certain geographic area, such as a university campus or city. No formal guidelines dictate the differences between a MAN and a WAN; technically, a MAN *is* a WAN. Perhaps for this reason, the term *MAN* is used less frequently than *WAN*. If any distinction exists, it's that a MAN is smaller than a WAN. A MAN is almost always bigger than a

LAN and usually is smaller than or equal to a WAN. MANs utilize an ISP or telecommunications (telco) provider.

Exam Essentials

Know the differences between Internet connection types.   Many technologies can be used to obtain Internet access. DSL and cable are two of the most popular for SOHO networks and require modems. DSL service is provided by the telephone provider in the area, and cable service is provided by the area cable television provider.

Understand ISDN's purpose.   The original idea behind it was to let existing phone lines carry digital communications by using multiplexing to support multiple channels.

Know the various types of networks.   A network is a collection of computers that can interact with one another and share files and resources. The network may be peer-to-peer or client-server. LANs are confined to local, whereas WANs expand that limit.

2.8 Compare and Contrast Network Architecture Devices, Their Functions, and Features

To make a network, you need a number of devices. The most common of those devices are tested on the A+ exam and discussed in this section.

Networks are built using a number of devices. Know those that are covered in this section to be able to answer questions on their functions and features when presented with them on the A+ exam.

Hub

Hubs are used in networks that use twisted-pair cabling to connect devices, and they can be used to join segments into larger networks. Hubs direct data packets to all devices connected to the hub, regardless of whether the data package is destined for the device. This makes them inefficient by nature and can create a performance bottleneck on busy networks. In its most basic form, a hub does nothing except provide a pathway for the electrical signals to travel along. Such a device is called a *passive* hub. Far more common nowadays is an *active* hub, which, as well as providing a path for the data signals, regenerates the signal before it forwards it to all the connected devices. In addition, an active hub can buffer data before forwarding it. However, a hub does not perform any processing on the data it forwards, nor does it perform any error checking.

Switch

Like hubs, *switches* are the connectivity points of an Ethernet network. Devices connect to switches via twisted-pair cabling, one cable for each device. The difference between hubs and switches is in how the devices deal with the data they receive. Whereas a hub forwards the data it receives to all the ports on the device, a switch forwards it to only the port that connects to the destination device. It does this by learning the MAC address of the devices attached to it and then by matching the destination MAC address in the data it receives.

Router

A *router* is used to connect LANs together; you can even use a router to connect dissimilar topologies that use the same protocol because physical specifications don't apply. A router can be a dedicated hardware device or a computer system with more than one network interface and the appropriate routing software. All modern network operating systems include the functionality to act as a router.

Access Point

Access points (APs) are transmitter and receiver (transceiver) devices used to create a wireless LAN (WLAN). APs typically are a separate network device with a built-in antenna, transmitter, and adapter. APs use the wireless infrastructure network mode to provide a connection point between WLANs and a wired Ethernet LAN. APs also typically have several ports, giving you a way to expand the network to support additional clients.

Depending on the size of the network, one or more APs might be required. Additional APs are used to allow access to more wireless clients and to expand the range of the wireless network. Each AP is limited by a transmission range—the distance a client can be from an AP and still obtain a usable signal. The actual distance depends on the wireless standard being used and the obstructions and environmental conditions between the client and the AP.

Bridge

Bridges are used to divide larger networks into smaller sections. Bridges accomplish this by sitting between two physical network segments and managing the flow of data between the two. By looking at the MAC address of the devices connected to each segment, bridges can elect to forward the data (if they believe that the destination address is on another interface) or block it from crossing (if they can verify that it is on the interface from which it came).

Modem

A *modem*, short for modulator/demodulator, is a device that converts the digital signals generated by a computer into analog signals that can travel over conventional phone lines. The modem at the receiving end converts the signal back into a format that the computer can understand.

Modems can be used as a means to connect to an ISP or as a mechanism for dialing up a LAN. Modems can be internal add-in expansion cards or integrated with the motherboard, external devices that connect to a system's serial or USB port, PCMCIA cards designed for use in laptops, or proprietary devices designed for use on other devices, such as portables and handhelds.

Firewall

A *firewall* is a server that sits between the internal network and the rest of the world and filters what goes between the two. While the filter can be done on programs, most are done on ports since applications and protocols use ports that are recognized. Open ports are those that allow traffic, whereas closed ports are those that block traffic. The firewall can be software- or hardware-based, and most incorporate both. The firewall may incorporate a proxy, a gateway, and a filter.

Patch Panel

A *patch panel* is a device to which the cables running through the walls from the hosts are connected. Then shorter cables called *patch cables* run from the patch panel to the switch or hub. Three types of patch panels are shown in Figure 2.12.

FIGURE 2.12   Patch panels

(JPE004F) Patch panel type A

(JPE005F) Patch panel type B

(JPE006F) Patch panel type C

Repeaters/Extenders

A repeater or extender is a device that regenerates any signal that goes through it. It can be used to extend a cable run that exceeds the maximum allowable distance. For example, if you needed to run a cable with a maximum allowable length of 100 meters for 150 meters, you could put a repeater between two 75 feet lengths of cable, and the problem would be solved. Figure 2.13 illustrates the use of a repeater.

FIGURE 2.13   Repeater

Ethernet over Power

Ethernet over Power is a technology designed to allow for the sending of Ethernet frames over the power lines in a facility. In Figure 2.14, a device called a *power line Ethernet bridge* plugs into the wall outlet, and then the devices or a switch are plugged into the bridge. This eliminates the need to install costly power outlets and leverages the existing power lines in the building.

FIGURE 2.14   Ethernet over Power

Power over Ethernet Injector

Many times when installing devices, the device needs to be located far from an available power outlet. On switches that support Power over Ethernet (PoE), the switch can supply power on the same data cable used to connect to the device. So if you get the device within 100 meters of a switch, you can eliminate the need to install costly power outlets.

A PoE injector is a device that can be used to provide PoE to a device when the switch does not support PoE. It plugs into the wall, then a line providing data and PoE is run to the device and another cable runs to the switch, as shown in Figure 2.15.

FIGURE 2.15   Power over Ethernet

Exam Essentials

Know the two types of hubs.   Hubs can be passive or active. If the hub does nothing except provide a pathway for the electrical signals to travel along, it is passive. It if regenerates the signal, it is considered active.

Be able to recognize a firewall.   A firewall is a server that sits between the internal network and the rest of the world and filters what goes between the two.

2.9 Given a Scenario, Use Appropriate Networking Tools

To create a network and solve problems with it, you need a toolbox. While some of the tools you use will be in the form of software, many others are hardware, and those are the ones this objective focuses on.

No networking administrators worth their pay would try to troubleshoot a problem without a set of tools. The tools that should be readily on hand include a crimper for fixing connectors, a multimeter for checking signals, a toner probe to find breaks in a cable, a cable tester, a loopback plug, and a punchdown tool.

Crimper

Wire *crimpers* look like pliers but are used to attach media connectors to the ends of cables. For instance, you use one type of wire crimper to attach RJ-45 connectors on unshielded twisted-pair (UTP) cable. You use a different type of wire crimper to attach Bayonet Neill-Concelman (BNCs) to coaxial cabling.

Cable Stripper

A *cable stripper* is used to remove the outer covering of the cable to get to the wire pairs within. You place the end of the cable in the mouth of the device, close the mouth, and then circle the cable, cutting away the outer sheath without damaging the wire pairs within. Figure 2.16 shows a cable stripper.

FIGURE 2.16   Cable stripper

Multimeter

A *multimeter* combines a number of tools into one. There can be slight variations, but a multimeter always includes a voltmeter, an ohmmeter, and an ammeter (and is sometimes called VOM as an acronym). With one basic multimeter, you can measure voltage, current, and resistance (some will even measure temperature).

A multimeter has a display, terminals, probes, and a dial to select various measurement ranges. A digital multimeter has a numeric digital display, and an analog has a dial display.

Inside a multimeter, the terminals are connected to different resistors, depending on the range selected.

Toner Generator and Probe

A *toner probe* has two parts: the tone generator (called the *toner*) and the tone locator (called the *probe*). The toner sends the tone, and at the other end of the cable, the probe receives the toner's signal. This tool makes it easier to find the beginning and end of a cable. The purpose of the toner probe is to generate a signal that is transmitted on the wire you are attempting to locate. At the other end, you press the probe against individual wires. When it makes contact with the wire that has the signal on it, the locator emits an audible signal or tone.

A toner probe can be used to find breaks in a cable.

Cable Tester

Cable testers (sometimes called *media testers*) are used to verify that the cable you are using is good. Commonly used with network cabling, you can perform many of the same tests with a multimeter. Any tool that facilitates the testing of a cable can be deemed a cable tester, but a media tester allows administrators to test a segment of cable, looking for shorts, improperly attached connectors, or other cable faults. All media testers have a way of telling you whether the cable is working correctly and where the problem in the cable might be.

Loopback Plug

Also called wrap plugs, *loopback plugs* take the signal going out and essentially echo it back. This allows you to test ports to make certain they're working correctly.

To simply test an implementation of TCP/IP on a host, you can always use the loopback address of 127.0.0.1. This is often used with ping (discussed in Chapter 6, "Other Operating Systems and Technologies.")

Punchdown Tool

Punchdown tools are used to attach twisted-pair network cable to connectors within a patch panel. Specifically, they connect twisted-pair wires to the insulation displacement connector (IDC).

Wi-Fi Analyzer

A *Wi-Fi analyzer* is a tool that gathers information of all sorts about the RF medium in the area. These may be handheld hardware devices or software that is installed on a laptop that uses the wireless card in the laptop to gather information. These analyzers vary widely in what type of information they are capable of generating and the price point.

The following are among the functions that these analyzers offer:

- Noise and inference detection and location
- Channel information
- Signal strength
- List of APs in the area

Exam Essentials

Know the tools for working with networks.   A good administrator's toolbox will include wire crimpers, a multimeter, a toner probe, cable tester, loopback plugs, and a punchdown tool.

Know the two parts of a toner probe.   A toner probe has two parts: the tone generator (the toner) and the tone locator (the probe).

Review Questions

You can find the answers in the Appendix.

1. Which the following is NOT a fiber connector?
   A. ST
   B. LC
   C. BNC
   D. SC

2. Which cabling type offers no protection against EMI or RFI?
   A. STP
   B. UTP
   C. Fiber
   D. Thicknet

3. Which connector type is used for a modem connection?
   A. RJ-45
   B. RJ-11
   C. BNC
   D. SC

4. Which wiring combination creates a crossover cable?
   A. T568A and T568B
   B. T568A and T568A
   C. T568B and T568B
   D. T568A and T568C

5. Which signaling method uses a single channel in the coaxial cable?
   A. broadband
   B. wideband
   C. narrow band
   D. baseband

6. Which fiber standard will operate up to 550 meters?
   A. 100BaseFX
   B. 1000BaseSX
   C. 1000BaseLX
   D. 10GBaseER

7. Which twisted pair cable category will have a maximum speed of 100 Mbps?

   A. CAT3

   B. CAT5

   C. CAT5e

   D. CAT6

8. Which twisted pair cable category uses a longitudinal separator, which separates each of the four pairs of wires from each other and reduces the amount of crosstalk possible?

   A. CAT3

   B. CAT5

   C. CAT5e

   D. CAT6

9. What type of coaxial cable is used in the type traditionally used in Thin Ethernet networks?

   A. RG-9

   B. RG-59

   C. RG-58

   D. RG-8

10. Which of the following is a Class B address?

   A. 192.168.5.5

   B. 10.6.6.3

   C. 172.6.8.9

   D. 201.69.3.2

Chapter

3

Mobile Devices

COMPTIA A+ 220-901 EXAM OBJECTIVES COVERED IN THIS CHAPTER:

✓ **3.1 Install and configure laptop hardware and components.**

- Expansion options (ExpressCard/34, ExpressCard/54, SoDIMM, flash, ports/adaptors [Thunderbolt, DisplayPort, USB to RJ-45 dongle, USB to Wi-Fi dongle, USB to Bluetooth, USB to optical drive])

- Hardware/device replacement (keyboard, hard drive [2.5 vs. 3.5, SSD vs. hybrid vs. magnetic disk], memory, smart card reader, optical drive, wireless card, mini-PCIe, screen, DC jack, battery, touchpad, plastics/frames, speaker, system board, CPU)

✓ **3.2 Explain the function of components within the display of a laptop.**

- Types (LCD [TTL vs. IPS, fluorescent vs. LED backlighting], OLED)

- Wi-Fi antenna connector/placement

- Webcam

- Microphone

- Inverter

- Digitizer

✓ **3.3 Given a scenario, use appropriate laptop features.**

- Special function keys (dual displays, wireless [on/off], cellular [on/off], volume settings, screen brightness, Bluetooth [on/off], keyboard backlight, touchpad [on/off], screen orientation, media options [fast forward/rewind], GPS [on/off], airplane mode)

- Docking station

- Physical laptop lock and cable lock

- Rotating removable screen

✓ **3.4   Explain the characteristics of various types of other mobile devices.**

- Tablets

- Smartphones

- Wearable technology devices (smart watches, fitness monitors, glasses, and headsets)

- Phablets

- e-Readers

- Smart camera

- GPS

✓ **3.5   Compare and contrast accessories and ports of other mobile devices.**

- Connection types (NFC, proprietary vendor-specific ports [communication/power], microUSB/miniUSB, Lightning, Bluetooth, IR, hotspot/tethering)

- Accessories (headsets, speakers, game pads, docking stations, extra battery packs/battery chargers, protective covers/waterproofing, credit card readers, memory/microSD)

This chapter will focus on the exam topics related to mobile devices. I will follow the structure of the CompTIA A+ 220-901 exam blueprint, objective 3, and cover the five subobjectives that you will need to master before taking the exam.

3.1 Install and Configure Laptop Hardware and Components

Whether you choose to call them laptops, notebooks, tablets, or something different is mostly a matter of semantics. In this section, I'll discuss some of the basic components of laptops and their installation (when possible and called for). In many cases, the components are the same as in a desktop computer, and I discussed them already. I'll focus now on those that are different. The following are the topics addressed in exam objective 3.1:

- Expansion options
- Hardware/device replacement

Expansion Options

A portable computer must provide all the functionality of a desktop counterpart yet be able to withstand travel, run in the absence of AC power, and be much smaller and more compact. When you get right down to it, there is not a great deal of difference between laptop and desktop computers, with the exception that laptops are more difficult to disassemble, and form factors on items such as motherboards, memory, and hard drives become important. In this section, I will discuss (and in some cases simply review) the options available to expand the functionality of a laptop, and I'll cover the type of memory packages used in laptops.

ExpressCard/34

The ExpressCard standard is an alternative to the use of PC Cards. ExpressCards are inserted into a slot that will accept either of two form factors. Neither card type is installed or configured as such; they are simply plugged into the slot if present on the laptop.

The ExpressCard/34 is 34 mm wide with a connector that runs the full width of the card. The cards are 75 mm long (10.6 mm shorter than CardBus) and 5 mm thick. In some cases, the functionality provided by the card requires the thickness of the card to be more than 5 mm, such as when it must provide a port or an antenna. ExpressCard slots may be either 34 mm or 54 mm wide. The 54 mm slot (covered in the next section) will accept either card, whereas the 34 mm slot will accept only a 34 mm card. Having said that, the connector on both card types is 34 mm. The maximum transmission speeds are as follows:

- 280 Mbps effective (USB 2 mode)
- 1.6 Gbps effective (PCIe 1 mode)
- 3.2 Gbps effective (PCIe 2 or USB 3 mode)

ExpressCard/54

By using a guide at the rear of the slot, the 54 mm slot will accept both card form factors. Adaptors are made for connecting an ExpressCard/34 card to a CardBus (but not 16-bit PC Card) slot.

Both the 34 mm and 54 mm versions of these cards are used in the same way PC Cards are—that is, to provide functionality that does not presently exist on the laptop. They could be used to add an 802.11 wireless connection or access to a mobile phone network, for example. Figure 3.1 shows both types of ExpressCards and a PC Card for comparison.

FIGURE 3.1   Laptop expansion cards

SoDIMM

For space reasons, memory modules that are used in desktops cannot be used in laptops. Laptop memory comes in smaller form factors known as small outline DIMMs (SoDIMMs). Figure 3.2 shows the form factor for 144-pin and 72-pin SoDIMMS compared to memory modules used in desktops. Notice that they basically look the same but the memory module sizes are different. The most common sizes are 512 MB and 1 GB. They are also available in 4 GB and 8 GB sizes. The speeds of these modules range from 677 MHz to 1,333 MHz. They can have 72, 144, or 200 pins.

FIGURE 3.2   SoDIMMS, SIMMs, and DIMMs

30-pin SIMM (3.5×.75")   72-pin SIMM (4.25×1")

168-pin DIMM (5.375×1")

144-pin SoDIMM (2.625×1")   72-pin SoDIMM (2.375×1")

Another option is the MicroDIMM, which has either 172 pins (DDR) or 214 pins (DDR2). These modules are slightly shorter than the SoDIMM and slightly wider. They do not use the same slots. Keep in mind that many manufacturers have proprietary memory, which means it does not conform to a standard and that you will have to buy the memory from them. Consult the documentation in all cases.

To install laptop memory, follow these steps:

1. Turn off the computer.
2. Disconnect the computer and any peripherals from their power sources, and remove any installed batteries.
3. Remove the screws holding the memory door in place.
4. Use your fingers to gently separate the plastic tabs holding the memory module in place. The module should pop up so you can grab it.
5. Align the notch in the new memory module to the one in the connector.

6. Insert the new memory module into the socket at a 45-degree angle. Once full contact is made, press the module down. It should click into place.

7. Replace the memory door and fasten the screws.

Some laptops have the memory under the keyboard, so you might need to remove the keyboard to get to it.

Once the memory is installed, there really is no configuration, but you should check System Tools ➤ System Information to ensure that the memory has been recognized by the system at reboot.

Flash

Flash memory is a type of solid-state storage (covered in Chapter 1, "Hardware") that is beginning to be considered not only as an option for additional storage in a laptop but as a replacement for the hard drive. The advantages are reduced heat, lower power consumption, less noise, and better reliability since you have no moving parts. The disadvantages are higher cost and less capacity. The Lenovo IdeaPad (called the Yoga) released in 2012 will cost about $1,200 with solid-state drives (SSDs) up to 256 GB. A similar model by the same manufacturer with a 500 GB hard drive will be only $700.

While all flash drives are solid state, not all solid-state drives are flash drives.

Ports/Adaptors

In many cases, you need to connect a device to a laptop that requires a port type not present on the laptop. In scenarios like these, you need adaptors like the ones I discussed in Chapter 1 in the section "Compare and Contrast Various PC Connection Interfaces, Their Characteristics and Purpose." In this section, I'll briefly review these adaptors. I'll also discuss the use of other components discussed in Chapter 1's "Thunderbolt" section. Here I'll cover how they are used in laptops.

Thunderbolt   As I said in Chapter 1, Thunderbolt ports are most likely to be found on Apple laptops, but they are now showing up on others as well. Figure 3.3 shows a Thunderbolt port on an HP laptop. Notice the "thunderbolt" icon next to the port. For more information on Thunderbolt, see the section "Thunderbolt Cards" in Chapter 1.

FIGURE 3.3   Thunderbolt port

DisplayPort   As you learned in Chapter 1, DisplayPort is a digital interface primarily used to connect a video source to a display device such as a computer monitor or television set. It resembles a USB connector and is displayed next to one in Figure 3.3. It is between a Thunderbolt port on the left and a USB port on the right. It has an icon that looks like a *D* with one arrow pointing up and another pointing down to its left. For more information on DisplayPort, see the section "DisplayPort" in Chapter 1. The latest version of DisplayPort is 1.3, approved on September 15, 2014. This standard increases overall transmission bandwidth to 32.4 Gbps with the new HBR3 mode featuring 8.1 Gbps per lane (up from 5.4 Gbps with HBR2 in version 1.2), totaling 25.92 Gbps with overhead removed.

USB to RJ-45 Dongle   This adaptor allows you to use a USB port on a laptop to connect an Ethernet cable to the device. It can be useful when the device has a bad Ethernet port or if it lacks one. One of these is shown in Figure 3.4.

FIGURE 3.4   USB to RJ-45 dongle

USB to Wi-Fi Dongle   This adaptor allows you to use the USB port to connect an 802.11 wireless adaptor to the laptop. In the early days of 802.11 this was usually done with a PCMCIA card (the slots for which are no longer found on new laptops), but now it is much simpler with USB to Wi-Fi adaptors. One of these is shown in Figure 3.5.

FIGURE 3.5   USB to Wi-Fi dongle

USB to Bluetooth Dongle   When you need to allow Bluetooth access to a laptop that lacks this, you can use a USB to Bluetooth dongle. One of these is shown in Figure 3.6.

FIGURE 3.6   USB to Bluetooth dongle

USB Optical Drive   While many laptops come with an optical drive, some do not. In cases where there is no internal optical drive, you can use the USB port to connect an external optical drive, one of which is shown in Figure 3.7.

FIGURE 3.7   USB to external optical drive

Hardware/Device Replacement

Replacing hardware and devices in a laptop can be a challenge because of the size limitations. The best way to determine the proper disassembly method is to consult the documentation from the manufacturer.

Some models of notebook PCs require a special T-8 Torx screwdriver. Most PC toolkits come with a T-8 bit for a screwdriver with interchangeable bits, but you may find that the T-8 screws are countersunk in deep holes so that you can't fit the screwdriver into them. In such cases, you need to buy a separate T-8 screwdriver, available at most hardware stores or auto parts stores.

 Many laptop manufacturers will consider a warranty void if an unauthorized person opens a laptop case and attempts to repair a laptop.

Prepare a clean, well-lit, flat work surface; assemble your tools and manuals; and ensure that you have the correct parts. Shut down the PC, unplug it, and detach any external devices such as an external keyboard, mouse, or monitor. In this section, with these general guidelines for opening the laptop in mind, you'll look at replacing various components of a laptop. Always ensure that you have grounded yourself before working with computer components of any kind. Use an antistatic wristband and attach it to the case.

Keyboard

When replacing the keyboard, one of the main things you want to keep in mind is to *not* damage the data cable connector to the system board. With the laptop fully powered off and unplugged from the wall, remove the battery.

Examine the screws on the back of the laptop. Ideally, icons indicating which screws are attached to the keyboard will be available. If not, look up the model online and determine which of the screws are attached to the keyboard.

Remove the screws with a T-8 or Phillips-head screwdriver. With the laptop turned back over, open it. If the keyboard is tucked under any plastic pieces, determine whether those pieces need to have screws removed to get them out of the way; if so, remove the screws and the plastic pieces. In some cases, there may just be clamps that are easily removed.

With any plastic covers out of the way, remove any screws at the top and remove the keyboard itself from top to bottom. There should be a thin, but wide, data cable to the system board at the bottom.

    This is the piece to be careful with!

Take a pick and lift the plastic connectors that hold this data cable in place. Remove the data cable. Take the new keyboard and slip the data cable back in between the plastic connectors on the system board. Ensure it's all the way in.

Put the plastic connector back into place and make sure it's holding the data cable in. Position the keyboard into place and refasten the keyboard in place at the top, replacing any screws that were there before.

Replace any plastic pieces that were covering the keyboard, turn the laptop over, and replace all of the keyboard screws. When you replace the battery and turn it on, check the functionality. If the keyboard doesn't work, the main component to check is the data connector.

Hard Drive

To change the hard drive, turn the laptop upside down and look for a removable panel or a hard drive release mechanism. Laptop drives are usually accessible from the bottom or side of the chassis. Release the drive by flicking a lock/unlock button and/or removing a screw that holds the drive in place.

You may be required to remove the drive from a caddy or detach mounting rails from its sides. Attach the rails or caddy to the new drive using the same screws and washers. If required, remove the connector attached to the old drive's signal pins and attach it to the new drive. Make sure it's right side up and do not force it. Damaging the signal pins may render the drive useless.

Reverse your steps to place the drive (and caddy if present) into the case. Replace the screws and start the laptop. The system should recognize the drive. If you or the customer created a bootable backup disc or a complete image disc (before the drive failed, by the way), place it in the optical drive and follow the instructions for restoring the data. You may have to update a driver or two, but you should otherwise be ready to go.

2.5 Inch vs. 3.5 Inch

The 2.5-inch hard drives are smaller (which makes them attractive for a laptop where space is at a minimum), but in comparison to 3.5-inch hard drives, they have less capacity and cache, and they operate at a lower speed. Whereas 3.5-inch drives often can store up to 3 TB of data and have as much as 64 MB of cache, 2.5-inch drives usually store only 1 TB of data and use up to 16 MB of cache.

Moreover, whereas 2.5-inch drives operate from 5,400 to 7,200 RPM, 3.5-inch drives can operate from 7,200 to 10,000 RPM. However, 2.5-inch drives use about half the power (again, good for a laptop) of a 3.5-inch drive (2.5 W rather than 5 W).

The 1.8-inch drive is the smallest of the three I'm discussing here and is rarely seen anymore. It was originally used in subnotebooks and audio players. It has the least capacity of the three, with the largest up to 320 GB. It has only two platters, each of which can hold 220 GB maximum.

SSD vs. Hybrid vs. Magnetic Disk

Although many devices still use a magnetic disk hard drive as discussed in the previous section, most laptop vendors are moving to using either solid-state drives or hybrid drives, which are a combination of magnetic disk and solid-state technology.

The advantage of solid-state drives is that they are not as susceptible to damage if the device is dropped, and they are, generally speaking, faster because no moving parts are involved. They are, however, more expensive, and when they fail, they don't typically give some advanced symptoms like a magnetic drive will do.

Hybrid storage products have a magnetic disk and some solid-state memory. These drives monitor the data being read from the hard drive, and they cache the most frequently accessed bits to the high-speed NAND flash memory. These drives tend to cost slightly more than traditional hard drives (but far less than solid-state drives), but the addition of the SSD memory for cached bits creates a surprising improvement in performance. This improvement will not appear initially because the drive must "learn" the most frequently accessed data on the drive.

Memory

There should be a panel used for access to the memory modules. If the panels are not marked (many are not), refer to your laptop instruction manuals to locate the panel on the bottom.

Remove any screws holding the panel in place, remove the panel from the laptop, and set it aside. If removing an existing memory module, remove it by undoing the module clamps, gently lifting the edge of the module to a 45-degree angle, and then pulling the module out of the slot.

Align the notch of the new module with that of the memory slot and gently insert the module into the slot at a 45-degree angle. With all pins in the slot, gently rotate the module down flat until the clamps lock the module into place.

Replace the memory access panel, replace any screws, and power up the system. When the computer is powered back up, it may be necessary to go into the computer BIOS to let the system properly detect the new RAM that has been installed in the computer. Please refer to the user manual for the computer system for any additional information.

Smart Card Reader

Smart card readers come in both internal and external versions. External versions will most likely plug into a USB port and replacing them is easy; all you do is plug them in. It is possible that you may need to install a driver for the device, and if so, you should use the installation utility that came with the device if there is one. There are also external readers that use the ExpressCard slot.

Internal readers will reside in a drive bay like a hard drive or optical drive would. You will remove the hard drive, optical drive, and keyboard screws first, and then you'll remove the screws that hold the bottom case on the laptop. There will also be some screws marked P or P1 inside the case that you will remove. Once they are removed, turn the laptop over and remove the keyboard screws, keyboard, and the palm rest cables. Don't forget to unplug both the keyboard and the palm rest cables! Underneath you will now be able to access the smart card reader. Unplug the reader, remove the screw holding it in, and remove it. Place the new reader in the same place and reverse these steps.

Optical Drive

Replacing an optical drive is usually easier than replacing a hard drive or memory. Remove the screw that secures the optical drive to the bottom of the notebook. Grasp the edge of the optical drive bezel and slide the optical drive out of the base enclosure. Insert the new optical drive into the base enclosure until the connector is seated and replace the screw that secures the optical drive to the bottom of the notebook.

Wireless Card

Both 802.11 and Bluetooth wireless cards that are built in can be replaced if they go bad. Sometimes they reside near the memory, so open the same panel that holds the memory. In other cases (such as a Dell Inspiron), you have to remove the memory, keyboard, optical drive, and hand rest to get to it. The Bluetooth card may be located in the same place, or it may be located at the edge of the laptop with its own small panel to remove. Consult your documentation.

Once you've found either type of wireless card, disconnect the two antenna contacts from the card. Do *not* pull by the wire; pull by the connector itself. Remove any screws from the wireless card and gently pull out the card from the slot. Insert the replacement card into the slot at a 45-degree angle, replace the screws, and reconnect the antenna to the adaptor. Replace the parts you were required to remove to get to the card, reversing your steps carefully.

Mini-PCIe

Since many of the wireless cards are mini-PCIe, replacing any other card in this format will follow the same procedure, with the exception of removing and reconnecting the antenna cables. You can find the location of the card in the documentation. Make sure that the new card is firmly inserted into the slot after removing the old card.

Screen

The screen is one of the more involved parts to replace, which is why many people throw a laptop away when the screen gets damaged. It's possible to replace a damaged screen, but you have to remove a lot of parts to do so. Start by removing the battery and then hold the power on for 10 seconds to drain the power out of the capacitors.

Remove all the screws on the back of the unit and then turn the laptop over. Remove the speaker bezel and you will see six wires coming from the old screen to the laptop. Remove the keyboard (see the instructions in the section "Keyboard"). Under the keyboard, locate where these six wires connect, and disconnect them. Make note of what went where so you can replace them correctly when you reconnect the new screen.

Remove the screws that are holding the old screen to the hinges of the laptop. Position the new screen in place and screw it into the hinges. Reroute the six wires coming from the new screen through any holes or spaces that lead them to their connection points. These are usually for the video cable, mic jacks, and wireless antenna. Reconnect the keyboard and reinstall it. Replace all parts that were required to get at the keyboard and replace all screws on the back of the unit.

These are general guidelines for this replacement, and you should always check the documentation for any departures from this general approach.

DC Jack

Replacing a bad DC jack usually requires soldering. If this is not a skill you possess, just replace the motherboard. If you want to attempt it, remove all the parts to get to the motherboard. In some cases, the old DC jack can still be used; it just needs to have the old solder removed and replaced. If that is not the case, remove the old DC jack by unsoldering it from the connector. Then put the new jack in place and solder it to the connectors. Replace all the parts and pieces you removed to get to the board. In general, a bad DC jack usually means a new board.

Battery

Replacing the battery in a laptop is simply a matter of removing the battery storage bay, removing the old battery from the bay, inserting the new battery into the bay, and replacing the bay. Determining the battery type for the replacement will probably take longer than the replacement procedure. In fact, many users carry extra batteries for situations where they know they will need to use the laptop for longer than the battery life (such as a long plane trip) and change the battery as needed.

Touchpad

This is another repair where many parts must be removed just to get to the piece to be replaced. Remove all the covers from the back of the system first. This may include those for the hard drive, RAM, and wireless card compartments. Remove the RAM, hard drive, and wireless card. Take the screw holding the CD-ROM in place and remove it as well.

Turn the laptop back over, open the lid, and remove any plastic pieces in the way of the keyboard. Remove the keyboard (see the section "Keyboard"). Disconnect the video and antenna cables from the motherboard (see the section "Screen"). Remove the Phillips-head screws from the LCD hinges and then remove the LCD.

Disconnect the touchpad cable from the motherboard. Separate the upper casing assembly from the bottom casing and set it aside. Remove the touchpad from the upper casing assembly. Install the new touchpad by reversing the previous steps.

Plastics/Frames

In the course of explaining some of the replacement procedures in this section, several times I have mentioned plastic pieces that either hold something in place or cover something. These pieces may be held in place by screws, or they may use snaps. In either case, it is easy to damage these parts (especially the snaps) in the disassembly or assembly process. If this occurs, consult the documentation for the laptop. Even these pieces will have part numbers and can be ordered. It's easier to just take great care not to damage them in the first place. The best way to prevent damage to these pieces from happening is to *never* force a piece in place. If you meet resistance, back out and try to determine what the obstruction is.

Speaker

To replace speakers, first follow the earlier instructions to remove the hard drive, the battery pack, and all the screws holding the body together. Lift the screen up and separate it from the body (see the section "Screen"). Do *not* remove the wires connecting the screen to the motherboard.

Separate the two pieces of plastic body frame to view the inside of the laptop. Locate the speakers, using the documentation if necessary. Unscrew the speakers and note where they connect to the motherboard. Disconnect the old speakers and connect the new ones to the same location as where the old speakers were removed. Replace all the parts in the reverse order you removed them.

System Board

Replacing the system board requires removing all parts discussed to this point since they all are either in the way of or connected to the motherboard. Once that is done, open the processor access door if there is one on the machine. If the processor is removable and one did not come with the new motherboard, remove it and set it aside in a safe place.

Disconnect any remaining wires that are connected to the motherboard. Unplug any cards, such as the video card, that are not built directly into the motherboard. Locate the mounting screws for the motherboard and unscrew them. Remove the old motherboard, mount the new unit and reassemble the parts in reverse order.

CPU

If the CPU is not built into the motherboard, it can be replaced. If it is built in, then you will be replacing the motherboard as well. If you are upgrading the processor and not simply replacing it, make sure your BIOS will support the new processor. It may be that you need to flash the BIOS to support the new CPU. You can determine this at the website of either the CPU maker or the laptop. This is important!

Follow the earlier instructions to remove the case, keyboard, and display. This will allow you to separate the two parts of the case. Remove the graphic card and note where it plugs back in. Remove the heat sink from the top of the CPU by removing the screws holding it in place.

Remove the single screw holding the CPU in place and pull it out. Insert the new CPU in place and replace the screw. (In some cases, it is not a screw but a locking bar.) Place some thermal grease between the CPU and the heat sink. Replace the heat sink and its screws. Reverse your steps to reattach all the other parts and pieces.

In some cases, you may encounter a laptop that allows you to get at this from the bottom without removing the keyboard and display. This is why it is best to follow the specific directions in the documentation to save unnecessary component removal.

Exam Essentials

Describe the options available to expand the functionality of a laptop.   Understand the differences between 34-pin and 54-pin ExpressCards. Describe the memory options for a laptop (SoDIMMs) and the relative advantages and disadvantages of solid-state drives.

List the steps to install or replace laptop components.   This includes but is not limited to keyboards, hard drives, memory, optical drives, wireless cards, mini-PCIe cards, screens, DC jacks, batteries, touchpads, speakers, system boards, and CPUs.

3.2 Explain the Function of Components Within the Display of a Laptop

The display of a laptop contains more components than you may expect. In this section, I'll discuss these components and, in some cases, cover competing technologies. The following are the topics addressed in exam objective 3.2:

- Types
- Wi-Fi antenna connector/placement
- Webcam
- Microphone
- Inverter
- Digitizer

Types

Laptop displays can use several technologies. These were covered in Chapter 1 (all of them can be used in a desktop as well). This section contains a quick review of these display types and their characteristics as they apply to laptops.

LCD

Two major types of liquid crystal displays (LCDs) are used today: active matrix screens and passive matrix screens. Their main differences lie in the quality of the image. Both types use some kind of lighting behind the LCD panel to make the screen easier to view. For more information on both active and passive LCDs displays, see the section "Compare and Contrast Types of Display Devices and Their Features" in Chapter 1.

TTL vs. IPS Displays   In Chapter 1, you learned about two types of LCDs displays, twisted nematic (TN) and in-plane switching (IPS). You may also run across the term *TTL display*. TTL refers to transistor-transistor logic and refers to a special type of digital circuit. When that term is attached to a display, it means that the display accepts digital input.

Fluorescent vs. LED   LCDs can use two kinds of backlighting: LED-based and fluorescent. For more information, see the section "Fluorescent vs. LED Backlighting" in Chapter 1.

LED

Light-emitting diode (LED)-based monitors are still LCDs (they still use liquid crystals to express images onscreen), but they use a different type of backlight than what is normally used. Several types of backlights are used with LED, including white LED (WLED), RGB LED, and WLED on a flat array. For more information on all three LED display types, see the section "Compare and Contrast Types of Display Devices and Their Features" in Chapter 1.

OLED

An organic light-emitting diode (OLED) is another type of LED technology. It uses an emissive electroluminescent layer of organic compounds that emit light in response to an electric current. For more information, see the section "Compare and Contrast Types of Display Devices and Their Features" in Chapter 1.

An interesting characteristic of these displays is their flexibility and transparency. This means they can roll up for storage (like a mat) and you can see through the display to objects behind the display. These displays are now available but quite expensive.

Plasma

Plasma displays utilize small cells containing ionized gases, similar to what is used in fluorescent lamps. They have the advantage of high-quality picture, wider viewing angles, and less motion blur, but they have the disadvantage of screen burn-in and high energy requirements.

Because of the high energy requirements, using plasma for laptops is a challenge; however, laptop makers are working to reduce the power consumption of plasma to bring this technology to wider use.

Wi-Fi Antenna Connector/Placement

The wireless antenna is located in the display. You may recall that when replacing a laptop screen, you encountered a number of wires coming from the screen to the laptop body. One of these is the cable that connects the wireless antenna (located in the display) with the wireless card located in the body of the laptop.

The antennas that are in the display usually work quite well. In any specific situation you may improve your signal by moving the laptop around. This changes the polarization of the antenna and may cause it to line up better to the incoming signal.

Webcam

Many displays today, especially laptop displays, have a webcam built in. They come ready to go with all drivers preinstalled and nothing to configure or set up. If you need to replace the webcam, you will have to disconnect the laptop lid (which holds the display) from the base, remove the screw covers and screws holding the display bezel in place, and remove the bezel. After removing the screws holding the mounting rails to the hinges, remove the LED screen from the lid assembly. Now you can get at the camera, but first carefully remove the tape that holds the camera cable in place and remove it and the camera. Attach the replacement cable to the new camera, install the new camera, and reverse these steps.

Microphone

While many desktop systems lack a built-in microphone, almost all laptops have one. In some cases this microphone will be located on the laptop bottom, but in many cases it will be in the display next to the webcam or off to the side. If you need to replace it, you will need to take the same steps to get inside the display that you took for the webcam.

When you unhook the lid from the bottom, you will need to unplug several things from the board, and one of those will be the microphone cable. If the microphone is not working (which it probably isn't or you wouldn't be replacing it), take a moment to inspect the cable. Sometimes the cable can be cut by the constant opening and closing of the case (it shouldn't, but sometimes it does happen). You may be able to repair the cable without replacing the microphone.

If that is not the case, remove the microphone and cable and replace both with the new mic and cable. Reverse the steps to get into the display, reconnect the cables to the board, and put the back on the bottom.

Inverter

An inverter is a component that takes DC power and converts it to a form that can be used by the LCD screen. It is implemented as a circuit board that is located behind the LCD. If problems with flickering display or dimness occur, the inverter is a prime suspect.

If the inverter needs to be replaced, you should be aware that it may contain stored energy, so it may need to be discharged to be safe.

Digitizer

Digitizers read pressure applied to the surface of the display and are what make touch-screens work. In some cases, they work with a stylus or small pen-like device, or you simply touch the screen with your finger. The digitizer is a thin piece of clear material that fits on top of the display. It has its own cable just as the display itself does. If it gets cracked, which often happens, it can be replaced without replacing the display itself. Typically when you perform this replacement, you will have to open the display lid, as I covered earlier, and separate the digitizer from the display. It is usually glued to the display, and you can use a hair dryer to heat the glue to make removing it easier. When you need to put the new digitizer in, you may need to reheat the glue on the display to stick them back together.

Exam Essentials

Differentiate the types of displays available in laptops.   Two major types of LCDs are used today: active matrix screens and passive matrix screens. LED-based monitors are still LCDs, but they use a different type of backlight than what is normally used. An OLED is another type of LED technology. It uses an emissive electroluminescent layer of organic compounds that emit light in response to an electric current. Because of the high energy requirements, using plasma for laptops is a challenge.

Describe the location and operational characteristics of the wireless antenna in a laptop.   The wireless antenna is located in the display. Moving the laptop changes the polarity of the antenna and may result in a better signal.

Identify the location and function of the inverter.   An inverter is a component that takes DC power and converts it to a form that can be used by the LCD screen. It is implemented as a circuit board behind the LCD.

3.3 Given a Scenario, Use Appropriate Laptop Features

Because of the nature of their physical implementation, laptops have some features not found in desktops and some issues that need to be handled differently than with desktops. In this section, I will discuss some of these features and issues along with the use of some special function keys. The following topics are addressed in exam objective 3.3:

- Special function keys
- Docking station
- Physical laptop lock and cable lock
- Rotating/removable screens

Special Function Keys

Special function keys exist in both desktops and laptops, but in laptops function keys exist that may not be present in desktops. In the lower-left corner of the keyboard is a key with blue text on it that says Fn. When this key is held, other keys with a similar blue marking (such as F1, F2, and so on) will perform a different function than their normal function. This section describes some of the most common uses of these keys, although manufacturers sometimes implement these keys differently, so you should consult the documentation.

Dual Displays

When additional displays are connected to the laptop (for example, a projector or second monitor), holding down the Fn key and pressing the appropriate function key (located on the top row of the keyboard) will move the active screen from display to display (or display to a projector) and then to a setting where all monitors have the same output. Normally, the F key that you press has an image of a monitor on it. This is valuable when making a presentation or when you would like to direct the image to the projector or the laptop screen. It is also worth noting that some laptop keyboards have the F1 key on the top line marked with an icon of a laptop display and another screen. If this is the case, this key is used to toggle between dual-monitor settings rather than the Fn and F8 keys.

Wireless (On/Off)

There is also a function key that will turn the wireless off and on. Consult the documentation to determine which key does this. Many laptops now have an antenna icon just above the blue text on F2 (or maybe another key in the top line). In that case, you do not have to hold the Fn key to use it. If wireless does not work (especially if the system is telling you to turn the wireless on), check this setting. It is easy to hit this key and disable the wireless!

Cellular (On/Off)

Just as you can turn off the wireless (802.11) connection, you can also turn off the cellular (WWAN) connection (if one exists on the device). Because integrated cellular connections are still fairly new, you will probably need to refer to the device's documentation to identify the exact key.

Volume Settings

On the top row where the keys labeled F1–F12 are located, there are usually a couple of keys (usually F8 and F9) that have icons on them that look like speakers. These keys can be used to raise and lower the volume of the sound. If the icon is blue, you have to hold down the Fn key. Otherwise, you do not need to use the Fn key to activate them. (As a matter of fact, if you hold down the Fn key and use the F8 key, you may be changing the location of the display output, as described in the section "Dual Displays.") If these keys are not present, consult the documentation for the key to use in conjunction with Fn to lower and raise the volume. Most laptops also include a mute button marked as such.

Screen Brightness

On the top row where the keys labeled F1–F12 are located, there are usually a couple of keys (usually F4 and F5) that have icons on them that look like suns with arrows pointing up and down, respectively. They could also be located on the lower right on the keyboard. These keys can be used to increase and decrease the brightness of the display. As with the volume settings described in the previous section, you do not need to use the Fn key to activate them. If these keys are not present, consult the documentation for the key to use in conjunction with Fn to increase and decrease the brightness.

Bluetooth (On/Off)

In most cases, the same key that turns 802.11 wireless off and on also does the same for Bluetooth. See the section "Wireless (On/Off)."

Keyboard Backlight

Some keyboards come with backlighting. These models will usually allow you to turn the backlighting on and off by using the Fn key in combination with another key, such as the Z key on some models. Consult the documentation to determine which key combination will perform this function.

Touchpad (On/Off)

While touchpads provide you with a way to operate without a mouse, there are cases when you don't want to use the touchpad and it gets in your way when typing. In other cases, the touchpad does not work simply because it has been turned off. So, how do you enable and disable the touchpad? It can be done using either software or hardware.

In some cases, you may find there is a touchpad icon in the notification area. If there is, you can right-click or double-click it, and in the settings you should find an enable and disable feature. If there is no icon, it may be possible to go to the mouse settings in Control Panel and find touchpad settings. Finally, you can always open Device Manager and enable and disable the touchpad from here.

There also is usually a way to physically enable and disable the touchpad. This varies from laptop to laptop. For example, on a Lenovo, you hit a location in the upper-right corner of the touchpad and it acts as a toggle switch between on and off. Consult the documentation that came with the laptop, or look on the vendor's website.

Screen Orientation

The screen orientation refers to the position of the image on the screen. This is changed by "rotating" the screen. For example, if you rotated the screen 180 degrees, the image would be upside down. Rotating the screen can be done either by using the display settings or in some cases by using a special key combination. In most cases, if you right-click the desktop, you will find the option to rotate in various ways in the menu. It may also be under the Graphics Options menu, as shown in Figure 3.8.

FIGURE 3.8   Screen orientation

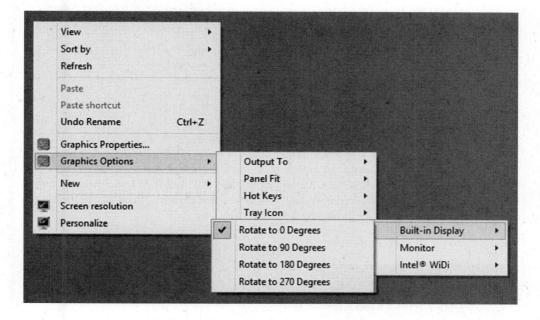

It could be that a special key combination can be used as well. On many models, you can use the Shift+Alt+arrow keys to cycle through the four positions (right side up, on one side, upside down, and on the other side).

Media Options (Fast-Forward/Rewind)

Many laptops also offer keys that are used with your media players. For example, you can fast-forward (or go to the next track), rewind (go to the last track), and stop the player. These keys may have a special location, or they may be included as function keys at the top of the keyboard (the ones that say F1, F2, and so on). If they are in the function keys, you will need to hit the Fn key at the bottom of the keyboard and hold it down as you use the function keys. In Figure 3.9, they are located at the top of the keyboard.

FIGURE 3.9 Media keys

GPS (On/Off)

Many devices now come with a built-in GPS feature. You can enable and disable the GPS using the privacy settings in Windows. While you will probably find it is enabled by default, you can disable it in Windows 8.1 by bringing up the Charms bar. At the bottom, choose the Settings charm. Tap or click the Change PC Settings link and then select Privacy on the left. Choose Location. On this page you can select to either turn it off completely or turn it off for certain applications, as shown Figure 3.10.

FIGURE 3.10 Location tracking

Airplane Mode

Airplane mode is a mode that suspends many of the device's signal-transmitting functions. It's called airplane mode because it disables the transmission of signals that interfere with aircraft signaling (or so they say). Enabling and disabling this mode can be done either in Windows or in some cases by using a special key on the keyboard.

To enable and disable it in Windows 8.1, navigate to the PC settings, as discussed in the "GPS (On/Off)" section. In the PC settings, select Network. Then select Airplane Mode. On the right you will see a button to toggle between on and off, as shown in Figure 3.11. There will be separate controls for Wi-Fi and Bluetooth.

FIGURE 3.11   Airplane mode

On many laptops this can also be done using one of the function keys. If this feature is present on the laptop, the key will have an airplane icon on it. Use it as you would any function key to toggle between off and on.

Docking Station

Some notebook PCs have optional accessories called *docking stations* or *port replicators*. They let you quickly connect/disconnect with external peripherals and may also provide extra ports that the notebook PC doesn't normally have.

A docking station essentially allows a laptop computer to be converted to a desktop computer. When plugged into a docking station, the laptop has access to things it doesn't have stand-alone—the network, a workgroup printer, and so on. The cheapest form of docking station (if it can be called that) is a port replicator. Typically, you slide a laptop into the port replicator, and the laptop can then use a full-sized monitor, keyboard (versus the standard 84 keys on a laptop), mouse, and so on. Extended, or enhanced, replicators add other ports not found on the laptop, such as PC slots, sound, and more. The most common division between port replicators and docking stations is that port replicators duplicate the ports the laptop already has to outside devices, and the docking station expands the laptop to include other ports and devices that the laptop does not natively have.

Laptops can support Plug and Play at three levels, depending on how dynamically they're able to adapt to changes.

Cold Docking   The laptop must be turned off and back on for the change to be recognized.

Warm Docking   The laptop must be put in and out of suspended mode for the change to be recognized.

Hot Docking   The change can be made and is recognized while running normal operations.

Each docking station works a little differently, but there is usually a button you can press to undock the notebook from the unit. There may also be a manual release lever in case you need to undock when the button is unresponsive. Moreover, the docking station must be purchased from the same vendor you purchased the laptop from because docking stations are vendor and model specific.

Physical Laptop Lock and Cable Lock

Laptops can be easily stolen. Therefore, they come with a lock slot to which a cable lock can be attached. Figure 3.12 shows the lock slot, and Figure 3.13 shows the connected lock (sometimes called a Kensington lock).

FIGURE 3.12   Lock slot

Rotating/Removable Screen

Many mobile devices today have a removable screen. While it appears that the screen is removable, you are actually unhooking the keyboard because the computer is contained in the display. With the keyboard detached, you can use the device as a tablet, and with the keyboard attached, you can interact with the device as you would a laptop.

FIGURE 3.13   Connected lock

Many of these same devices will also allow for the rotation of the screen when it is attached to the keyboard. This might be a rotation within the frame of the screen, or it could be a rotation in a circle.

Exam Essentials

Describe the purpose of special function keys.   In the lower-left corner of the keyboard is a key with blue text on it that says Fn. When this key is held, other keys with a similar blue marking (such as F1–F12) will perform a different function than their normal function.

Differentiate between docking stations and port replicators.   A docking station essentially allows a laptop computer to be converted to a desktop computer. Extended, or enhanced, replicators add other ports not found on the laptop, such as PC slots, sound, and more. The most common division between port replicators and docking stations is whether the peripheral provides network access and expands the laptop's capabilities.

Describe approaches to the physical security of a laptop.   Laptops come with a lock slot to which a cable lock can be attached. Also, there is a lock on some models for the lid of the laptop.

3.4 Explain the Characteristics of Various Types of Other Mobile Devices

At one time, the term *mobile devices* referred only to notebook laptops, tablets, and PDAs. Today this category includes all sort of devices that at one time were only ideas. In this section, you'll look at digital devices that have had their capabilities greatly expanded, such as smart cameras that have become essentially computers with a lens, and smart watches and fitness monitors that almost become part of their owner. The following are the topics covered in exam objective 3.4:

- Tablets
- Smartphones
- Wearable technology devices
- Phablets
- E-readers
- Smart cameras
- GPS

Tablets

Tablet devices have been in existence in some form or fashion since the early 1990s. Early on they were proprietary devices that didn't have a lot in common with desktop computers, but increasingly the two form factors have gravitated toward one another; now, many new tablets run the same operating systems that are run on desktop systems. Having said that, most tablet computers run one of three operating systems: Android, iOS, or Windows 8.1.

The tablet market was changed significantly with the release of the iPad by Apple. It was the most successful tablet ever at its time of release, and the devices set the standard for others to meet. Today, typical features of tablets include the following:

- Cameras (in some cases dual)
- GPS
- Handwriting recognition
- Solid-state hard drives
- 3G and 4G mobile support

Tablet devices today use touchscreen displays rather than keyboards, although keyboards can be attached. Some such as the Microsoft Surface can be attached and detached at will from a keyboard that also acts as a stand and a cover for the device. In most cases, they require applications written for the platform, although the Surface can run the Windows 8.1 operating system and thus can also run regular desktop applications.

Smartphones

As phones have become smarter and smarter, they more and more resemble computers rather than phones. Today's smartphones are really computers that can make calls. They have touchscreen interfaces, an onscreen keyboard that can be brought up to input data, and sometimes even motion sensors and mobile payment mechanisms.

Moreover, the drive by organizations and individuals to create applications for these devices has exploded. Every week it seems someone has designed and created an application that turns the phone into some new gadget! Because of this phenomenon, the smartphone has become almost part of the body to several younger generations of users.

Most of these devices run either the iOS or Android operating system, although Microsoft continues to release Windows phones that run a special Windows OS for the device. The latest is Windows 8.1, and there will be a Windows 10 version as well.

Wearable Technology Devices

Since the days of Dick Tracy's futuristic phone watch, we have waited for wearable technology to arrive, and it has. In this section, I'll survey some of the latest examples of digital devices created to be worn.

Smart Watches

Smart watches that are computers on your wrist have arrived! Although the jury is still out on the long-term viability of the smart watch, when Apple introduced one in 2015, most in the industry began to take the devices seriously. These devices run either proprietary operating systems or Android. The Apple model runs an operating system called Watch OS.

These devices are typically paired to a smartphone for the purpose of accessing calls and messages, and they contain GPS features as well. The following are some of the features you may find in these smart watches:

- Anti-lost alert
- Time display
- Call vibration
- Caller ID
- Answer call
- Micro-USB input port

Fitness Monitors

While many smart watches can also act as fitness monitors, there is a class of devices that specializes in tracking your movement. Fitness monitors read your body temperature, heart rate, and blood pressure. They do this while also tracking where you are for the purpose of determining the distance you ran or walked and the time it took to do so.

Some of the devices, called *fitness trackers*, are wrist bands that can track the information discussed and communicate wirelessly to an application located on a computer. One of these is shown in Figure 3.14. Other, more sophisticated units combine a strap that goes around the chest with a watch or band that collects the information gathered by the sensors in the band.

FIGURE 3.14   Fitness tracker

Glasses and Headsets

By now, everyone has heard about and probably seen Google Glass, the most well-known and recognizable computing device worn as glasses. Just in case you haven't, Figure 3.15 shows a drawing of the glasses. While the devices caused quite a stir, Google announced in early 2015 that sales to individuals would cease for two years while the technology is improved.

FIGURE 3.15   Google Glass

While worn as glasses, there is a small screen just to the side of one of the eyes that houses the computer screen (think Cyborg). The user can view the screen at any time by just casting a glance to the screen. Many promising uses have been proposed for the devices, with a number in the healthcare field. Although sales of the devices to individuals was halted, sales to organizations that have or are working to find ways to use the glasses continue.

Another similar device that is not based on glasses but around a headset format is the HC1 headset computer by Zebra. It can respond to voice commands and body movements. One of these is shown in Figure 3.16.

FIGURE 3.16　　Headset computer

Phablets

Phablets comprise a new category of mobile device that combine the size of a phone with the capability of a tablet. While larger than a smartphone, they are smaller than a tablet. Sales of these devices exceeded those of laptops and desktop computers in 2014, signaling a shift in how computers are used.

These devices typically use the same or similar operating systems as smartphones but provide a larger screen. They may also include a stylus for interacting with the screen, as shown in Figure 3.17.

FIGURE 3.17   Phablet

E-readers

While these devices typically have Internet access and can be used for Internet browsing, the main job these devices were created for is reading. These devices have proven to be more popular with older users because younger users seem to have grown up reading everything on a computer and see no reason for another device. Older users, on the other hand, who are still struggling with the move from reading printed material to reading on a device like the idea of a device dedicated to enhancing their reading experience.

The Kindle was the first of these devices to garner widespread acceptance. The Nook soon followed. Both enjoyed good sales until other rivals began to enter the market. Sales of these devices is now in decline because of the aging of the main customer base. The following are some of the features found in these devices:

- Touchscreens
- Buttons for turning pages
- Editing tools
- Wireless networking
- Text-to-speech support
- Digital rights management support

Smart Cameras

Smart cameras are cameras that have not only the ability to capture an image but also the ability to extract information from the image and even make decisions based on that information. Some typical uses are as follows:

- Unattended surveillance
- Noncontact measurements
- Part sorting and identification

- Code reading and verification
- Detection of position and rotation of parts for robot guidance and automated picking
- Biometric recognition and access control
- Robot guidance
- Automated inspection for QA

GPS

A global positioning system (GPS) uses satellite information to plot the global location of an object and use that information to plot the route to a second location. GPS devices are integrated into many of the mobile devices discussed already and are used for many things, but when I use the term for a stand-alone device, I am usually referring to a navigation aid.

These aids have grown in sophistication over time and now not only can plot your route but also help you locate restaurants, lodging, and other services along the way. Another use for these devices includes tracking delivery vehicles and rental cars.

Exam Essentials

Describe the common features of tablets.   These features include cameras (in some cases dual), GPS, handwriting recognition and solid-state hard drives support.

Identify the most common smartphone operating systems.   The operating systems used in Smartphones include iOS, Android, and Windows 8.1.

Describe some items that are considered wearable technology.   Wearable technology includes smart watches, fitness monitors, Google Glass, and headset computers.

3.5 Compare and Contrast Accessories and Ports of Other Mobile Devices

Mobile devices in many cases have the same connection types and ports as laptop and desktop computers, but the accessories can vary somewhat. In this section, you'll look at the types of ports and accessories you will find on mobile devices. Specifically, I will cover the following topics:

- Connection types
- Accessories

Connection Types

While mobile devices do use some of the same ports and connection methods, they also use a few that you will not encounter on most laptop and desktop devices. This section covers connection types.

NFC

Near Field Communication (NFC) is a short-range technology that allows mobile devices to establish radio communication by touching one another or by coming in close proximity to one another. The technology was first used in Radio Frequency ID (RFID) tagging and was implemented on mobile devices first as a way to share short-range information and later as a method to make payments at a point of sale. It operates by reading tags, which are small microchips with antennae that can in some cases only be read and other cases can be read and written to. For more information on NFC, see the section "NFC" in Chapter 1.

A mobile device must have the support for NFC built in, and many already do. Special applications are available that make it easy to use the technology in various ways.

- Making point-of-sale payments
- Reading information stored in tags in posters and advertisements
- Communication between toys used in gaming
- Communication with peripherals

Proprietary, Vendor-Specific Ports (Communication/Power)

Many mobile devices have proprietary ports that they use either for power or for communication. While this was widespread at one point, vendors have gradually moved toward using standard physical implementations of both power and communication ports. While I can't cover all of these, I can present the best examples, which are the ports used by Apple in its devices.

Apple uses what it calls the Lightning connector for power. Although it makes an adaptor for this connector to convert it to mini-USB (see the next section), it doesn't encourage its use because of the limitations the adaptor places on the functionality of the proprietary connector.

The following are other examples of proprietary connectors:

- The Sony-Ericsson power connector looks like USB but is not.
- Nokia and Motorola have used coaxial in some power connectors.

For the most part, you will find that many vendors have chosen to adopt standard connection types for both power and communication.

Micro-USB/Mini-USB

The two most common ports found on mobile devices are micro-USB and mini-USB. Both are small form-factor implementations of the USB standard, the latest of which is USB 3.1. In Figure 3.18, the mini-USB and micro-USB connectors are compared to the regular USB connector.

FIGURE 3.18   USB form factors

Lightning

Earlier I discussed the Lightning connector from Apple. This is an eight-pin connector that while not standard has advantages over USB, according to Apple. The following are some of these advantages:

- It can supply more power.
- It can be inserted either way.
- It is physically more durable than USB.
- It can detect and adapt to connected devices.

  Figure 3.19 shows a Lightning connector next to a USB cable.

FIGURE 3.19   Lightning connector and USB

Bluetooth

Mobile devices also support Bluetooth wireless connections. For more information on Bluetooth, see the section "Bluetooth" in Chapter 1.

IR

While infrared (IR) connectors were once common on mobile devices, they disappeared only to reappear recently. This slow wireless method can convert your mobile device to a remote control! For more information on IR, see the section "IR" in Chapter 1.

Hotspot/Tethering

Another way that many mobile devices can connect to other devices is through a hotspot or when tethered to another device. Many mobile devices have the ability to act as an 802.11 hotspot for other wireless devices in the area. There are also devices dedicated solely to performing as a mobile hotspot.

When one mobile device is connected to another mobile device for the purpose of using the Internet connection, it is said to be *tethered* to the device providing the access. While use of this connection can be done by using 802.11, it can also be done connecting through Bluetooth or a USB cable between the devices. Typically this will incur an additional charge from your provider.

Accessories

Mobile devices require a lot of accessories to take advantage of many of the features they provide. While many of these are also commonly used with desktop and laptop devices, some are much more likely to be used with mobile devices. In this section, you'll take a brief look at the types of accessories you may find attached to a mobile device.

Headsets

Headsets provide the ability to take your conversation offline or to listen to your music in private. They can be connected both through a wired connection, usually a 3.55 mm audio connector or USB, and by using Bluetooth to pair the device with the headset.

Speakers

Speakers are used in the same fashion as headsets. They can also be connected using the same options that include using USB, using a 3.55 mm audio plug, or by pairing the speakers with the devices using Bluetooth. This includes the speaker systems in many cars, which can now be paired with the devices using Bluetooth as well.

Game Pads

People seem to love to kill time playing games on their smartphones and other mobile devices, but they may find their level of enjoyment increased by connecting the devices to a game controller offering them many more input options. These controllers look like any game controller, which can differ based on the game being played and the type of input required for the game.

These controllers can also be small, some fitting on a keychain. They typically are paired to the mobile device using the Bluetooth connection. Some of the newer game controllers for this purpose can be set on a table and the mobile device plugs physically into a slot or holder on the controller, making a connection with the controller. Figure 3.20 shows the layout of a typical game controller.

FIGURE 3.20   Smartphone game controller

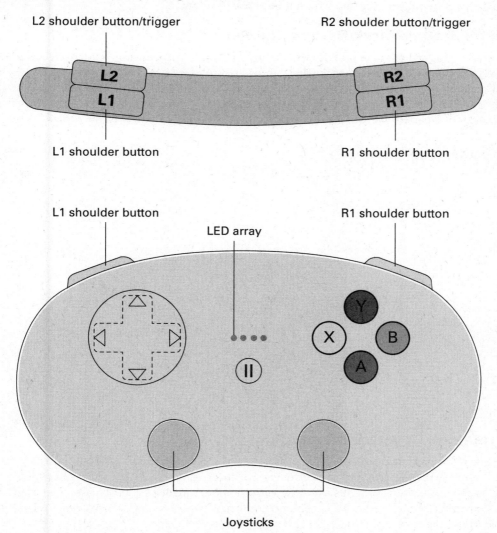

Docking Stations

Docking stations include those used to hold the device and connect the device to a computer for synchronization. They also are made to hold the device and connect it to speakers. The stations typically look like the charging stations used to hold the early wireless landlines.

Moreover, since a new generation of users has used a smartphone for everything and may never have used a device any larger than a laptop, it is inevitable that docking stations used to connect PC peripherals to smartphones will be created. These devices will serve the same function as docking stations for laptops. At the time of this writing, the solutions created so far are proprietary and have not been widely adopted.

Extra Battery Packs/Battery Chargers

Batteries are the lifeline of mobile devices. For a device to stay constantly connected, many users purchase extra battery packs that can be used to power the devices when the battery is dead and no power outlet is available. Some of these packs simply provide power to the device, while others store power used to charge the device's battery. Figure 3.21 shows an example of a battery pack that can be charged while providing power to the device.

FIGURE 3.21 Battery pack

Protective Covers/Waterproofing

While much work has been done to make mobile devices more sturdy and durable, they are still somewhat delicate pieces of electronics. For this reason, an entire industry has sprung up to provide protective covers for the devices. Some are made of a hard plastic material and protect the device from all but the worst impacts, while others go further and provide waterproofing as well.

Credit Card Readers

Mobile devices can also accept connections from external credit card readers. Some of these physically connect to the smartphone, and others can communicate with the phone using Bluetooth. Many of them use the same jack used for the headphones. There is usually software that has to be installed on the device as well and a processing agreement established with a provider. Figure 3.22 shows the Square reader.

FIGURE 3.22   Square credit card reader

Memory/MicroSD

Secure digital (SD) cards are a type of flash memory. Micro-SD is the smallest of three standards. Many mobile devices have MicroSD slots or ports on them that allow you to connect one to the device. This allows you either to access data on the memory card or to move information to the memory card from the smartphone. For more information on MicroSD, see the section "Solid-State/Flash Drives" in Chapter 1.

Exam Essentials

Describe the most common connection types found on mobile devices.   These include Near Field Communication, proprietary ports, microUSB, miniUSB, Lightning, Bluetooth, and infrared.

Identify the most common mobile device accessories.   Mobile devices will accept gamepads, headsets, speakers, docking stations, battery packs and chargers, and credit card readers. They can also use protective covers and waterproof containers to protect them.

Review Questions

You can find the answrs in the Appendix.

1. What is the maximum transmission speed of an ExpressCard in PCIe2 mode?
   A. 280 Mbit/s
   B. 512 Mbit/s
   C. 1.6 Gbits/s
   D. 3.2 Gbits/s

2. What type of memory goes in a laptop?
   A. DIMM
   B. RIMM
   C. SODIMM
   D. SIMM

3. Which memory type can be used in laptops?
   A. MicroDIMM
   B. RIMM
   C. DIMM
   D. SIMM

4. Which interface is natively found only in Apple devices?
   A. USB
   B. Serial
   C. Thunderbolt
   D. PS/2

5. What port type has an icon that looks like a D with one arrow pointing up and another pointing down to its left?
   A. USB
   B. Thunderbolt
   C. DisplayPort
   D. RJ-45

6. What special screwdriver is typically required to work on a notebook?
   A. phillips head
   B. T-8 Torx
   C. hex
   D. metric

7. What is the easiest thing to damage when removing a laptop keyboard?

   A. the keys

   B. the data cable

   C. the plastic cover

   D. the plastic screws

8. If damaged which component can render the hard drive useless?

   A. the caddy

   B. the rails

   C. signal pins

   D. chassis

9. What size hard drive goes in a laptop?

   A. 1.5 Inch

   B. 2.0 Inch

   C. 2.5 Inch

   D. 3.5 Inch

10. Which is NOT an advantage of solid state drives?

   A. cheaper

   B. not as susceptible to damage

   C. faster

   D. no moving parts

Chapter 4

Hardware and Network Troubleshooting

COMPTIA A+ 220-901 EXAM OBJECTIVES COVERED IN THIS CHAPTER:

✓ **4.1 Given a scenario, troubleshoot common problems related to motherboards, RAM, CPU, and power with appropriate tools.**

- Common symptoms (unexpected shutdowns, system lock-ups, POST code beeps, blank screen on bootup, BIOS time and settings resets, attempts to boot to incorrect device, continuous reboots, no power, overheating, loud noise, intermittent device failure, fans spin: no power to other devices, indicator lights, smoke, burning smell, proprietary crash screens [BSOD/pinwheel], distended capacitors)

- Tools (multimeter, power supply tester, loopback plugs, POST card/USB)

✓ **4.2 Given a scenario, troubleshoot hard drives and RAID arrays with appropriate tools.**

- Common symptoms (read/write failure, slow performance, loud clicking noise, failure to boot, drive not recognized, OS not found, RAID not found, RAID stops working, proprietary crash screens [BSOD/pinwheel], S.M.A.R.T. errors)

- Tools (screwdriver, external enclosures, CHKDSK, format, file recovery software, Bootrec, Diskpart, defragmentation tool)

✓ **4.3 Given a scenario, troubleshoot common video, projector, and display issues.**

- Common symptoms (VGA mode, no image on screen, over-heat shutdown, dead pixels, artifacts, color patterns incorrect, dim image, flickering image, distorted image, distorted geometry, burn-in, oversized images and icons)

✓ **4.4 Given a scenario, troubleshoot wired and wireless networks with appropriate tools.**

- Common symptoms (no connectivity, APIPA/link local address, limited connectivity, local connectivity, intermittent connectivity, IP conflict, slow transfer speeds, low RF signal, SSID not found)

- Hardware tools (cable tester, loopback plug, punch down tools, tone generator and probe, wire strippers, crimper, wireless locator)

- Command-line tools (PING, IPCONFIG/IFCONFIG, TRACERT, NETSTAT, NBTSTAT, NET, NETDOM, NSLOOKUP)

✓ **4.5 Given a scenario, troubleshoot and repair common mobile device issues while adhering to the appropriate procedures.**

- Common symptoms (no display, dim display, flickering display, sticking keys, intermittent wireless, battery not charging, ghost cursor/pointer drift, no power, Num Lock indicator lights, no wireless connectivity, no Bluetooth connectivity, cannot display to external monitor, touchscreen non-responsive, apps not loading, slow performance, unable to decrypt email, extremely short battery life, overheating, frozen system, no sound from speakers, GPS not functioning, swollen battery)

- Disassembling processes for proper re-assembly (document and label cable and screw locations, organize parts, refer to manufacturer resources, use appropriate hand tools)

✓ **4.6 Given a scenario, troubleshoot printers with appropriate tools.**

- Common symptoms (streaks, faded prints, ghost images, toner not fused to the paper, creased paper, paper not feeding, paper jam, no connectivity, garbled characters on paper, vertical lines on page, backed up print queue, low memory errors, access denied, printer will not print, color prints in wrong print color, unable to install printer, error codes, printing blank pages, no image on printer display)

- Tools (maintenance kit, toner vacuum, compressed air, printer spooler)

This chapter will focus on the exam topics related to hardware and network troubleshooting. I will follow the structure of the CompTIA A+ 220-901 exam blueprint, objective 4, and cover the six subobjectives that you will need to master before taking the exam.

4.1 Given a Scenario, Troubleshoot Common Problems Related to Motherboards, RAM, CPU, and Power with Appropriate Tools

While problems can occur with the operating system with little or no physical warning, that is rarely the case when it comes to hardware problems. Your senses will often alert you that something is wrong based on what you hear, smell, or see. This section discusses common issues with the main players. The following are the topics addressed in exam objective 4.1:

- Common symptoms
- Tools

Common Symptoms

Once you have performed troubleshooting for some time, you will notice a pattern. With some exceptions, the same issues occur over and over and usually give you the same warnings each time. This section covers common symptoms or warning signs. When you learn what these symptoms are trying to tell you, it makes your job easier.

Unexpected Shutdowns

It doesn't get any more obvious that something is wrong when the computer just shuts down on its own. In some cases, a blue screen on the display with a lot of text precedes this shutdown. If that occurs, the problem is related to operating system and may not involve a hardware issue. Operating system issues related to the Blue Screen of Death are covered in the section "Proprietary Screen Crashes" later in this chapter.

One common reason for shutdowns is overheating. Often when that is the case, however, the system reboots itself rather than just shutting down. Reboots are covered later in this section.

Always check the obvious, such as the power cable and the source of power. Check to see whether a breaker flipped in the power box as well. Checking these items is an example of starting the process at the physical layer. If the computer is plugged into a power strip or UPS that has a fuse or breaker, check to see whether the fuse blew or the breaker flipped because of a power surge.

System Lockups

Sometimes the system just freezes up and will not respond to any keyboard input or mouse clicks. The difference between a blue screen and a system lockup is whether the dump message that accompanies a blue screen is present. With a regular lockup, things just stop working. As with blue screens, lockups have been greatly reduced with more recent versions of the Microsoft operating systems (a notable exception may occur with laptops, which go to hibernate and then occasionally do not want to exit this mode). If lockups occur, you can examine the log files to discover what was happening (such as a driver loading) and take steps to correct it.

From a hardware standpoint, freezes or lockups can be caused by the following:

Memory Problems   Memory problems include a bad or failing memory chip, using memory that's too slow for the system, or using applications that require more memory than is present in the computer. Replace and upgrade the memory as required.

Virus or Malware   If the system freezes and there is still significant hard drive activity occurring, a virus could be present. Scan the system, preferably from an external source such as a flash drive or CD.

Video Driver   Bad video drivers can sometimes cause a lockup. Update the video driver. In the case of a driver you just updated, you can roll back the driver to the old driver until you can obtain a new version of the driver that does not cause issues.

POST Code Beeps

During the bootup of the system, a power-on self-test (POST) occurs, and each device is checked for functionality. If the system boots to the point where the video driver is loaded and the display is operational, any problems will be reported with a numeric error code.

If the system cannot boot to that point, problems will be reported with a beep code. Although each manufacturer's set of beep codes and their interpretation can be found in the documentation for the system or on the website of the manufacturer, one short beep always means everything is OK. Some examples of items tested during this process include the following:

- RAM
- Video card
- Motherboard

To interpret the beep codes in the case where you cannot read the error codes on the screen, use the chart provided at www.computerhope.com/beep.htm.

During startup, problems with devices that fail to be recognized properly, services that fail to start, and so on, are written to the system log and can also be viewed with Event Viewer. If no POST error code prevents a successful boot, this utility provides information about what's been going on system-wise to help you troubleshoot problems. Event Viewer shows warnings, error messages, and records of things happening successfully. You can access it through Computer Management, or you can access it directly from the Administrative Tools in Control Panel.

Blank Screen on Bootup

When the screen is blank after bootup and there are signs that the system has power and some functionality (perhaps you can hear the fan or see lights on the system), the problem could lie in several areas. Consider these possibilities:

- Make sure the monitor is on. It has a power switch, so check it.
- If you hear the fan but the system doesn't boot, it could be the power to the motherboard. Check and reseat the power cable to the motherboard.
- Make sure the cable from the monitor to the system is connected properly and try changing it out with a known good cable.
- Try a known good video card to rule out a bad card.
- Ensure that the brightness setting is set high enough.
- In cases where a laptop has been used to direct output to a second display, ensure that the image is being sent to the main display and not just to the external monitor.

BIOS Time and Settings Resets

If you find that you are continually resetting the system time, it could be that the CMOS battery is dying. In the absence of an external time source, the time in the BIOS is where the system gets its cue for the date and time. Change the CMOS battery and the problem should be solved.

Attempts to Boot to Incorrect Device

When multiple volumes or partitions exist on the computer or there are multiple hard drives and maybe CD/DVD and floppy drives as well, there are multiple potential sources for the boot files. If the system delivers an "operating system not found" message, it could be that the system is looking in the wrong location for the boot files.

The boot order is set in the BIOS. Check the boot order and ensure that it is set to boot to the partition, volume, and hard drive where the boot files are located. If the device still has a floppy drive, check first whether there is a floppy in the floppy drive. When the system is running down the list of potential sources of boot files, in all other cases if it looks in a location and finds no boot files, it will move on to the next location in the list. However, if a floppy is in the floppy drive and it checks the floppy drive and no boot files are present, it does not proceed but stops and issues the nonsystem disk message.

Boot problems can also occur with corruption of the boot files or missing components (such as the NTLDR file being "accidentally" deleted by an overzealous user). Luckily, during the installation of the OS, log files are created in the %SystemRoot% or %SystemRoot%\ Debug folder (C:\WINNT and C:\WINNT\DEBUG or C:\Windows and C:\Windows\Debug, depending on the operating system). If you have a puzzling problem, look at these logs to see whether you can find error entries there. These are primarily helpful during installation. For routine troubleshooting, you can activate boot logging by selecting Enable Boot Logging from the Windows Advanced Options menu to create an ntbtlog.txt log file in the %systemroot% folder.

Continuous Reboots

If the system reboots on its own, consider the following possibilities:

- Electrical problems such as brownouts (not a total loss of power but a sag in the power level) or blackouts can cause reboots.

- Power supply problems can cause reboots as well. The power supply continually sends a Power_Good signal to the motherboard, and if this signal is interrupted, the system will reset.

- Overheating is also a big cause of reboots. When CPUs get overheated, a cycle of reboots can ensue. Make sure the fan is working on the heat sink and the system fan is also working. If required, vacuum the dust from around the vents.

- As overheating plays a large role in reboots, ensure a laptop is sitting on a flat surface that allows for proper cooling (not on a bed, pillow, or other soft surface).

No Power

Power problems usually involve the following issues and scenarios:

- Check the power cord, and if it's plugged into a power strip or UPS, ensure the strip is plugged in (and if it has a breaker, check to see whether it was tripped by a surge or whether the switch that turns off the entire strip has been inadvertently turned to the off position). In the case of a UPS, check whether the UPS battery is dead.

- Try replacing the power supply with a known good unit to see whether the power supply failed.

Overheating

Under normal conditions, the PC cools itself by pulling in air. That air is used to dissipate the heat created by the processor (and absorbed by the heat sink). When airflow is restricted by clogged ports, a bad fan, and so forth, heat can build up inside the unit and cause problems. Chip creep—the unseating of components—is one of the more common byproducts of a cycle of overheating and cooling of the inside of the system.

Since the air is being pulled into the machine, excessive heat can originate from outside the PC as well because of a hot working environment. The heat can be pulled in and cause the same problems. Take care to keep the ambient air within normal ranges (approximately 60–90 degrees Fahrenheit) and at a constant temperature.

Replacing slot covers is vital. Computers are designed to circulate air with slot covers in place or cards plugged into the ports. Leaving slots on the back of the computer open alters the air circulation and causes more dust to be pulled into the system.

Loud Noise

When it comes right down to it, there are not a lot of moving parts within a PC. When you hear noise, you can begin to readily narrow down the possible culprits. The most common are the fan and the hard drive. No matter what is responsible, you will want to take immediate steps to shut down the machine and start the replacement process. Change each component you suspect with a known good replacement until the noise stops.

Intermittent Device Failure

One of the most vexing issues to troubleshoot is one that comes and goes. When presented with this type of behavior, consider the following possibilities:

- Try replacing the problem component with a known good one.
- A bad motherboard can cause these types of problems when there are issues with its circuitry. Try replacing the motherboard with a known good motherboard.

Fans Spin: No Power to Other Devices

This issue was discussed in the section "Blank Screen on Bootup."

Indicator Lights

Many of the components in the system have an indicator light that should be in a specific state during normal operation. Status lights are often found on the network interface card (NIC) as well as on the front of a desktop model and in the display area of a laptop.

On the NIC, a display other than a green light can indicate that there are problems with the network; more important, though, the lack of any light can indicate that the card itself has gone bad.

The hard drive, CD-ROM, and tape or DVD drive lights will be on when activity is occurring and will blink accordingly. The power light should be a steady green.

Smoke

Smoke is never a good thing. Shut the system down immediately to prevent further damage. This is usually a burning or overheating component, usually the CPU.

Burning Smell

A burning smell usually accompanies smoke but could be present after the smoke has ended because the burning component is now dead. Try to identify the damaged component through a visual inspection; if that is not possible, try to determine the damaged component by replacing parts one by one until functionality returns.

Proprietary Screen Crashes

Some operating systems have a proprietary method of notifying the user that the worst may have just happened. In this section you'll look at two of the most widely known methods.

BSOD

Once a regular occurrence when working with Windows, blue screens (also known as the Blue Screen of Death) have become much less frequent. Occasionally, systems will lock up, and you can usually examine the log files to discover what was happening when this occurred and then take the necessary steps to correct it. For example, if you see that a driver or application was loading before the crash, you can begin to isolate it as a possible problem. The details included in the BSOD error that comes up can help in troubleshooting the problem. It is often easy to query Microsoft's Knowledge Base with the first part of the BSOD error to discover the component causing the problem. Often, the Knowledge Base article gives a detailed explanation of how to fix the problem as well.

In more recent versions of Windows (Windows 7, 8, and 8.1), information from such crashes is written to XML files by the operating system. When the system becomes stable, a prompt usually appears asking for approval to send this information to Microsoft. The goal that Microsoft has in collecting this data is to be able to identify drivers that cause such problems and work with vendors to correct these issues.

Better-known error messages include the following:

Data_Bus_Error This error is described on the Microsoft website: "The most common cause of this error message is a hardware problem. It usually occurs after the installation of faulty hardware, or when existing hardware fails. The problem is frequently related to defective RAM, L2 RAM cache, or video RAM. If hardware has recently been added to the system, remove it and test to see if the error still occurs."

Unexpected_Kernel_Mode_Trap This error is described on the Microsoft website: "If hardware was recently added to the system, remove it to see if the error recurs. If existing hardware has failed, remove or replace the faulty component. Run hardware diagnostics supplied by the system manufacturer, especially the memory scanner, to determine which hardware component has failed. For details on these procedures, see the owner's manual for your computer. Setting the CPU to run at speeds above the rated specification (known as overclocking the CPU) can also cause this error."

Page_Fault_in_nonpaged_area   This error is described on the Microsoft website: "This Stop message usually occurs after the installation of faulty hardware or in the event of failure of installed hardware (usually related to defective RAM, either main memory, L2 RAM cache, or video RAM). If hardware has been added to the system recently, remove it to see if the error recurs. If existing hardware has failed, remove or replace the faulty component. Run hardware diagnostics supplied by the system manufacturer. For details on these procedures, see the owner's manual for your computer."

irq1_not_less_or_equal   This error is described on the Microsoft website: "This Stop message indicates that a kernel-mode process or driver attempted to access a memory address to which it did not have permission to access. The most common cause of this error is an incorrect or corrupted pointer that references an incorrect location in memory. A pointer is a variable used by a program to refer to a block of memory. If the variable has an incorrect value in it, the program tries to access memory that it should not. When this occurs in a user-mode application, it generates an access violation. When it occurs in kernel mode, it generates a STOP 0x0000000A message. If you encounter this error while upgrading to a newer version of Windows, it might be caused by a device driver, a system service, a virus scanner, or a backup tool that is incompatible with the new version."

machine_check_exception   This error is described on the Microsoft website: "This behavior occurs because your computer processor detected and reported an unrecoverable hardware error to Windows XP." To do this, the processor used the Machine Check Exception (MCE) feature of Pentium processors or the Machine Check Architecture (MCA) feature of some Pentium Pro processors. The following factors may cause this error message:

- System bus errors
- Memory errors that may include parity or error correction code (ECC) problems
- Cache errors in the processor or hardware
- Translation lookaside buffers (TLB) errors in the processor
- Other CPU vendor-specific detected hardware problems
- Vendor-specific detected hardware problems

Because Microsoft has ended support for XP, the best approach is to upgrade the operating system.

Pinwheel

While Microsoft users have the BSOD to deal with, Apple users have similarly come to have the same negative feelings about the Pinwheel of Death (PWOD). This is a multicolored pinwheel mouse pointer (shown in Figure 4.1) that signifies a temporary delay while the system "thinks." In the death scenario, waiting until doomsday will yield no relief to the user.

FIGURE 4.1   Pinwheel

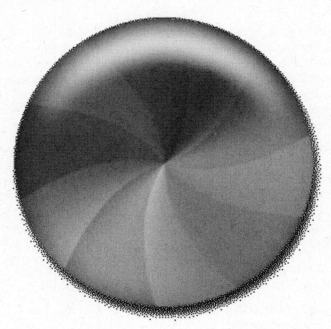

In many cases, the situation may not be as dire as it appears. It can be that a single application is holding the device captive. If this is the case, either clicking the desktop or bringing another application to the front will return control to the user. While that will solve the issue for the moment, there was some reason why that application caused the lockup, and it will probably occur again. Two things can be done to prevent this from occurring again.

First, it could be that the system permissions associated with the application and the files it uses have gotten corrupted. You can use Disk Utility to perform a "permissions repair," which restores file or folder permissions to the state the OS and applications expect them to be in.

Second, it may help to clear the dynamic link editor cache. This is a cache of recently used entry points to the dynamic link library. If this cache gets corrupted, it can cause the SPOD. To clear the cache, follow these steps:

1. Launch Terminal, located at /Applications/Utilities/.

2. At the Terminal prompt, enter the following command. Please note this is a single line; some browsers may show this command spanning multiple lines.

   ```
   sudo update_dyld_shared_cache -force
   ```

3. Press Enter or Return.

4. Enter the administrator account password.

5. Terminal may display warnings about mismatches in the dlyd cache. These are normal, and you can proceed.

On the other hand, if you are experiencing this spinning wheel at startup, the problem is more severe. It means that the system is corrupted. The recovery options will be found by booting to the recovery hard drive, which is a partition created for this purpose in OS X 10.7 Lion or 10.8 Mountain Lion. To do this, start the device, and after the chime, press and hold Command+R until a menu appears. Then select to boot to the recovery partition. Figure 4.2 shows the menu that will appear. You have four options:

- Restore the system from a Time Machine backup, in which you select Restore From Time Machine Backup. Then use a backup to restore the system.

- Boot to the Apple servers, which can be done only on newer systems. To do this, select Reinstall OS X. Of course, this will require an Internet connection to be working.

- Get Help Online, which will allow you to use Safari to browse to the Apple support site. This will require an Internet connection to be working as well. To do this, select Get Help Online.

- Repair the hard drive and permissions, in which you select Disk Utility from the menu. Click the First Aid tab and select Repair.

FIGURE 4.2   OS X Utilities

Distended Capacitors

A swollen or distended capacitor on the motherboard does not always indicate a failed or failing capacitor, but at the least it indicates one that is in poor health and should be replaced. A distended capacitor will look normal on the side, but the top of it will be swollen a bit, and there may be brown residue coming out of the top of the capacitor. This is caused by gassing of the electrolyte, meaning the electrolyte has been broken down into gas and no longer contributes to the capacitance of the capacitor. The symptoms of this are a system that reboots intermittently and will start only intermittently or not at all.

While replacing a failed capacitor is not easy and in some cases not worth the time and effort when compared with replacing the motherboard, to replace a failed capacitor, follow these steps:

1. Locate the failed capacitor. Look for those that exhibit any of the physical symptoms shown in Figure 4.3.

FIGURE 4.3 Failed capacitors

Normal capacitor

2. Procure a replacement capacitor. It should have the following:
   - The same voltage
   - The same or larger capacity
   - The same external size

   While you can use a capacitor that has a higher voltage or a larger capacity, it is best to use one that matches the one you are replacing.

3. Remove the battery from the board.

4. Use a soldering iron to heat the connection to the board until you can remove the old capacitor. Be careful not to heat the board so much that you damage the connections of other components.

5. Clean the remaining hole, and if necessary, use a pin to enlarge the hole for the new capacitor.

6. Insert the new capacitor. Heat solder and allow it to flow into the hole to seal. Try to keep the remaining drop on the outside as small as possible.

Tools

There are troubleshooting tools that you should be familiar with that can aid you. This section discusses some of the most important tools.

Multimeter

Multimeters were discussed in Chapter 2, "Networking." To review, these can be used to check voltages found on power plugs coming from the power supply to ensure the proper voltage is being delivered to the hard drive, motherboard, and other components. If that is not the case, components will not function properly and could be damaged.

Power Supply Tester

Inexpensive devices called *power supply testers* can go a bit beyond simply checking the voltage of the power cables. One of the things these devices can check is the proper operation of the Power_Good signal. If this signal is not working correctly, the computer will not boot from the power button but will do so when you press Ctrl+Alt+Del.

Loopback Plugs

Loopback plugs are used to test the functionality of various types of ports, but their most common use is to test a network card. These plugs send a signal out of the card and then loop it back into the same card to test its operation. They look like an RJ-45 connector without the cable.

POST Card/USB

POST cards are plugged into one of the slots in the computer, and when the computer is booting, the card will generate error codes on an LED. These codes serve a similar purpose as the beep codes discussed in the section "POST Code Beeps." In some cases, the system is incapable of generating the codes. These cards for laptops connect to an external port such as the mini-PCI slot or LPT Printer port. They receive their power from a USB cable when connected to the printer port.

Exam Essentials

Describe the common symptoms of hardware problems.   These symptoms include unexpected shutdowns, lockups, and reboots; POST code beeps; blank screens on bootup; loss of system timekeeping; attempts to boot to an incorrect device; overheating; loss of power; loud noises; intermittent device failures; smoke; a burning smell; and BSODs.

Identify tools used in troubleshooting.   These tools include but are not limited to multimeters, power supply testers, loopback plugs, and POST cards.

4.2 Given a Scenario, Troubleshoot Hard Drives and RAID Arrays with Appropriate Tools

Hard drives must be operational for the system to function, and hard drive arrays such as RAID introduce an additional level of complexity. This section discusses issues with hard drives and RAID arrays. The topics addressed in exam objective 4.2 include the following:

- Common symptoms
- Tools

Common Symptoms

Hard drives and RAID arrays typically exhibit symptoms before they fail. Learning to read these clues is critical to troubleshooting. This section discusses the most common of these clues and symptoms.

Read/Write Failure

Read/write failures occur when areas of the hard drive require repeated attempts before successful reads or writes occur. This is because these areas are at least partially damaged, although perhaps not enough for these areas to be marked as bad sectors.

Slow Performance

Another symptom of hard drive issues is slow access to the drive. Oddly, one of the potential causes of this is insufficient memory. When this is the case, it causes excessive paging. Another cause can be a drive that needs to be defragmented. A fragmented drive results in it taking much longer for all the parts of a file to be located before the file will open. Other issues that cause slow performance are controller cards that need updating, improper data cables, and slower devices sharing the same cable with the hard drive.

Loud Clicking Noise

A loud clicking noise, sometimes referred to as the *click of death*, is caused by the read/write heads making contact with the platters. After that happens, both the heads and the platters become damaged, and the system becomes unable to establish a successful starting point to read the drive. This is serious damage and cannot be repaired. Back up all the data if that's still possible. If the drive is beyond readable, the only option to recover the data is with the help of a professional data recovery service. At that point, you must balance the cost of the recovery with the value of the data. This is a case where performing regular backups saves the day!

Failure to Boot

A failure of the system to boot can be caused by a number of issues:

- Failure of the system to locate the boot files. See the section "Attempts to Boot to Incorrect Device."

- If you are presented with an "IDE drive not ready" at startup, the drive may not be spinning fast enough to be read. Enable or increase the hard disk predelay time.

- If you receive the message "Immediately back up all your data and replace your hard drive. A fault may be imminent," take it seriously. This means the drive is using Self-Monitoring, Analysis, and Reporting Technology (SMART) to predict a failure.

- The hard drive data cable or power cable may have become unseated. Sometimes even if the cable appears to be seated fine, reseating it can have a positive effect. Also ensure that the data cable has not been reversed.

Drive Not Recognized

If the system does not recognize the drive, the problem could be one of the following:

- The hard drive data cable or power cable may have become unseated. See the "Failure to Boot" section.

- If you just added a drive, ensure that both drives have not been set to master or slave and that the boot drive is set as master on the first channel.

- If the system uses SATA and you just added a drive, ensure that all the onboard SATA ports are enabled.

- If you just added a drive, ensure that there is no conflict between the new drive and another device.

- If you receive the "No boot device available, strike F1 to retry boot, F2 for setup utility" message, it could be incorrect drive geometry (probably not the case if this drive has been functioning properly before), bad CMOS battery, or inability to locate the active partition or master boot record.

OS Not Found

When you receive the "operating system not found" message, it's usually a software error rather than a hardware error. It could be that the master boot record cannot be located or the active partition cannot be located. These issues can be corrected in Windows by rebooting the computer into Recovery mode and executing one of several commands at the command line of the Recovery environment. See the "Recovery Console" section in Chapter 8, "Software Troubleshooting."

RAID Not Found

RAID can be either software or hardware based. When hardware-based RAID is implemented, a RAID controller card is installed into a slot and the RAID drives connect to that controller card. When the RAID array cannot be located, usually it's a problem with the controller card.

One item to check after you just installed the RAID controller card is that RAID is set in the BIOS. It is also possible that the computer has a built-in RAID controller. If that is the case, there will be ports for the drives in the motherboard. Ensure that the two hard drives (or three) are connected to the same port group.

If the RAID system has been operational, check all the cables connecting the drives to the motherboard, reseating them to ensure a good connection. Also ensure the BIOS is still set to RAID.

If there is no integrated RAID controller and the controller card is installed in a slot, ensure that the card is seated properly (maybe even try reseating it). Also ensure that all the drives are securely connected to the ribbon cable coming from the controller card.

RAID Stops Working

In some cases, one of the drives in the RAID array will cease to function and, depending on the type of RAID, can cause the entire array to be unavailable.

If this is a RAID 1 or a mirrored set, you should still be able to access the other drive. To determine which drive is bad, remove each drive one by one and reboot until you have identified the bad drive. Replace the bad drive and use the RAID software to rebuild the array.

If this is a RAID 5 array, follow the same procedure. The bad news is that if more than one drive has failed, you will not be able to rebuild the array. You will need to create the array again after replacing the bad drives and then restore the data from backup.

Once the bad drives have been replaced, the system may rearrange the drives such that the system cannot locate the drive with the operating system. Use the RAID setup program that you access during bootup to set the boot order of the drives in the array with the drive with the operating system first in the list.

Proprietary Screen Crashes

Earlier in this chapter I discussed the Blue Screen of Death (BSOD) and the Pinwheel of Death (PWOD). Use the guidelines in the next sections to approach these problems.

BSOD/Pinwheel

When presented with a Blue Screen of Death (BSOD) or the Pinwheel of Death (PWOD), it's often difficult to interpret the problem. Always try rebooting, which in many cases causes it to go away. When dealing with the ambiguity of the crash screen, it is often useful to ask yourself these questions:

- Did I just make any changes?
- Is there any component that has been exhibiting symptoms of a problem?

If you just changed a hard drive, made a hard drive configuration change, installed a new driver, or have been dealing with hard drive issues, you have reason to suspect these actions as the source of the crash. Try reversing the change you made and rebooting; if that helps, it indicates something faulty or detrimental about your change.

If you have multiple drives, try removing them one by one and observe the effect on the crash. Once you have located the drive causing the crash, begin to consider what the problem with the drive is or simply replace it, if no possible remedy comes to mind.

SMART Errors

SMART (Self-Monitoring, Analysis, and Reporting Technology; often written as S.M.A.R.T.) is a system included in hard drives and solid-state drives that detects and reports on drive reliability, with a goal of anticipating hardware failures. It requires software on the computer to read the data from the drives and performs its analysis during startup.

Errors reported by SMART should be accepted as predictions that the drive will soon fail, and you should back up all the data as soon as possible, even if the drive appears to be performing normally and passes other disk checks you may run. One error that you may be able to mitigate is overheating. If you can increase ventilation such that the error disappears, you are probably safe to continue using the drive.

Tools

Troubleshooting and working on hard drives requires some tools, both hardware and software. This section covers the tools used in the process of troubleshooting hard drives. The types of external enclosures encountered in the process of getting at the hard drives physically are also discussed.

Screwdriver

Screws of various sizes and types hold many parts of the PC together, from the case itself to internal hard drives in their drive bays. The following types of screwdrivers should be part of your toolkit when dealing with hard drive issues:

- Phillips screwdriver (nonmagnetic).
- Hex driver (looks like a screw driver with a head like a socket wrench). The most common size is the 3/16 inch, but you may also need the 1/4 inch ones as well.

 WARNING   Avoid using magnetic screwdrivers internally because the magnetic field can damage components.

External Enclosures

Before you can get to the hard drives, you have to open the external enclosure. Enclosure designs have evolved over the years, but this section covers one of the most common types and the approach to opening it.

Unfasten the computer's cover by removing any retaining screws at the back of the computer. Some cases don't have screws; instead, they have a sliding bar or latches that release the cover. Many of today's PCs can be completely disassembled without a single tool.

Then, remove the cover by sliding or lifting it. The exact procedure varies greatly depending on the case. Figure 4.4 shows an example for a desktop-style case.

FIGURE 4.4 Removing the enclosure

Pull cover back, then up, to remove.

Remove screws.

 Don't remove all the screws at the back of the computer! Some of these **WARNING** screws hold vital components (such as the power supply) to the case, and removing them will cause those components to drop into the computer.

CHKDSK

CHKDSK is an older MS-DOS utility that is used to correct logical errors in the FAT file-system. The most common switch for the chkdsk command is /F, which fixes the errors that it finds. Without /f, chkdsk is an information-only command.

Format

When implementing a new hard drive and creating new partitions or volumes, you must format the partition or volume before data can be written to it. You can do this for both FAT and NTFS partitions by using the Disk Management utility or by using the formatting function that is available during the installation of an operating system.

Another older option is to use the format command. It is executed at the command line and will not only format the volume or partition but will also erase all data, so you should be aware of that end result as well. To format the C: drive, you execute format c:.

File Recovery Software

In some cases, a hard drive cannot be saved, but the data can be recovered. Data recovery companies can recover data from some of the most damaged hard drives you can imagine, but the cost is high. Before going to those lengths to recover data from damaged drives or simply to recover data that may have been inadvertently deleted, consider using data recovery software. Popular examples are Data Rescue, Advanced Disk Recovery, and Recover My Files.

Bootrec

Bootrec.exe is a tool available on the installation DVD of Windows 7, 8, and 8.1 that can be used to repair the following:

- Master boot record (MBR)
- Boot sector
- Boot Configuration Data (BCD) store

It is a command-line tool that becomes available when you reboot to the installation CD; choose Repair Your Computer, select the problematic operating system, and choose System Recovery Options. In the options presented, choose Command Prompt. The command and its options are shown here:

- `bootrec/fixmbr`: Attempts to repair the master boot record
- `bootrec/fixboot`: Writes a new boot sector to the system partition
- `bootrec/scanos`: Scans the systems for supported installations and adds them to the list displayed at bootup
- `bootrec/rebuildbcd`: Completely rebuilds the BCD store

Diskpart

Diskpart is command-line Disk Management utility in Windows. It enables you to manage objects (disks, partitions, or volumes) by using scripts or direct input at a command prompt. It can perform all the functions that can be done with the Disk Management utility and quite a few that cannot be done with Disk Management. In many ways, it is an updated version of fdisk. It can be used to create and manage volumes on the drive.

Defragmentation Tool

Defragmentation tools are used to reorganize the physical location of the data on the hard drive so as to locate all pieces of a file together in the same place. When this is done, it improves the performance of the drive. All operating systems come with built-in defragmentation tools, and their operation can be scheduled for a time convenient to the user. This also frees the user (and the technician) from having to think about running the tool on a regular basis. Figure 4.5 shows the Drive Optimization tool in Windows 8.1. To arrive at this tool, swipe in from the right edge of the screen, tap Search (or if you're using a mouse, point to the upper-right corner of the screen, move the mouse pointer down, and click Search), enter Defragment in the search box, tap or click Defragment, and optimize your drives.

FIGURE 4.5 Drive Optimization tool

Exam Essentials

Identify the most common symptoms of hard drive issues. These include but are not limited to read/write failures, slow performance, loud clicking noises, boot failures, unrecognizable drives, missing operating systems, and Blue Screens of Death.

List symptoms of RAID array issues. These include missing arrays and RAID arrays that stop functioning.

Describe hardware troubleshooting tools. These include screwdrivers of various types and their proper use in opening the external enclosures and drive bays.

Use software troubleshooting tools. Utilize tools such as CHKDSK, format, and file recovery software.

4.3 Given a Scenario, Troubleshoot Common Video, Projector, and Display Issues

Video, projector, and display problems may not rate at the top of the priority list for technicians (unless the display is not functioning at all), but to a user, problems with their display may seem like a huge issue. This section discusses common video- and display-related symptoms and their possible sources. The topics addressed in exam objective 4.3 include the following:

- Common symptoms

Common Symptoms

Display monitors and projectors can exhibit a wide range of symptoms when video-related problems arise. Some are as obvious as no signal whatsoever, whereas other symptoms can be so slight as to almost defy detection. This section discusses common symptoms and some approaches to dealing with these issues.

VGA Mode

When a display ceases to function at the resolution level supported by the video card and reverts to 16-bit VGA mode (low resolution in Windows 7 and Vista), the problem is almost always video drivers. If the issue arises during the installation of a new video card, then the driver was not found in the cache of drivers provided with the operating system.

Even if the video card is Plug and Play, the driver must be present. If it is not, the computer will not be able to use the card and will revert to using VGA mode (low resolution in Windows 7). Another common problem associated with drivers is not having the current version—as problems are fixed, the drivers are updated, and you can often save a great deal of time by downloading the latest drivers from the vendor's site early in the troubleshooting process.

The easiest way to see or change drivers in Windows 7 or Windows 8.1 is to click the Driver tab in the Properties dialog box for the device. For example, to see the driver associated with the hard drive in Windows 7, double-click the hard drive in Device Manager (Start ➤ Control Panel ➤ Hardware And Sound ➤ Devices And Printers, and then click Device Manager in the Task list) and choose the Driver tab. Among other things, this shows the driver provider, date, version, and signer. You can choose to view details about it, update it, roll it back to a previous driver, or uninstall it. If the installation of the device resulted in VGA mode (low resolution in Windows 7), then you need to select Update Driver and point the system to the CD or local folder where the correct driver is located.

No Image Onscreen

When there is no image on the screen, the display is either dead or not receiving the signal from the computer. Check the cable from the back of the PC to the monitor, ensure it is tightly screwed in place, and reseat the cables if required. Also ensure that the monitor is plugged into a functional power outlet and that the brightness settings are high enough. Finally, for a laptop, you should use the appropriate Fn key to ensure that the signal isn't being sent to an external monitor.

To eliminate the video card as the problem, connect a known good display to the computer and see whether the same problem exists. If so, then the problem is not the display. If it works fine, the problem is the display. Displays do die and usually are not cost effective to repair. The usual solution is to replace the display.

If the card is the problem, try reseating it. If that provides no relief, insert a known good card. Operating in the same fashion as you did with the display, you can determine whether the video card is the problem.

Overheat Shutdown

When the video card is overheating, it can cause display problems and shutdowns. Overheating video cards usually exhibit symptoms like garbled output on the display or artifacts (covered later in this section). It also can result in flickers and flashes. In some cases, the display will cease functioning after being on a few seconds. After you restart the computer, the display again works for a few seconds and then fails.

When overheating is the problem, you must find the reason for the overheating. Clean all the dust out of the inside of the case and inspect all fans to ensure they are functioning—especially the fan on the video card if one is present. If the problem has been happening for some time, the card may have become damaged. Try using a different card and see whether the problem goes away. You may need to replace the video card.

Projectors

With respect to projectors, when the bulbs are overheating, they may shut down to cool down. Simply waiting until the bulb has cooled and then restarting the projector will usually solve the problem. It may also be helpful to inform the users that many projectors will not allow the bulb to be restarted soon after you turn it off, so they may want to consider that if they intend to restart the projector soon after shutting it down.

Dead Pixels

Pixels are the small dots on the screen that are filled with a color; as a group they present the image you see on the screen. Two conditions can occur with the pixels: stuck pixels and bad or dead pixels.

Stuck pixels have been filled with a color and are not changing as required to display changes in the image. Dead pixels are simply black with no color in them.

When there are few of these and they are not clustered in the same spot, you may not even be able to notice them. When they build to the point where they are noticeable, they cannot be fixed. You may be able to get some satisfaction from the manufacturer depending on how old the monitor is and the policy of the vendor.

Artifacts

Artifacts are visual anomalies that appear on the screen. They might be pieces of images left over from a previous image or a "tear in the image" (it looks like the image is divided into two parts and the parts don't line up).

Artifacts can be generated whenever hardware components such as the processor, memory chip, or cabling malfunction causing data corruption. It may be caused by physical damage, but the first thing to check is the overheating of the graphics processor or video card. Use the same techniques described in the section "Overheat Shutdown."

Color Patterns Incorrect

When the image displayed uses incorrect color patterns or is garbled, the root of the problem could depend on when the condition presents itself. If the screen looks fine during the POST but then goes bad when Windows starts to load, it probably is because of an incorrect setting of the video card. For example, it may be set to do something the card is incapable of doing. Restart in safe mode (which will cause the system to use the VGA driver) and check all the settings of the card while ensuring that it is not set for a resolution level for which the card is not capable. You may also try updating the driver if a new one is available.

If this problem occurs from the moment you turn the system on, the problem is hardware, and you should check the monitor, cable, and card, replacing each with a known good piece until you isolate the bad component.

Dim Image

If the image is fine but dim, first check the brightness setting, usually found in the front of the monitor. If this is a laptop, remember there are function keys that when hit inadvertently will dim the screen as well. Check that.

If it is an LCD, the backlight may be going bad. You learned earlier that these are pencil-sized lights that go behind the screen. They can be replaced on a laptop by following the procedure for opening the laptop lid (where the display resides) and replacing the backlight. Keep in mind that opening the case voids the warranty, so if you still have warranty left, make use of that option.

If it is the backlight on a desktop LCD, the backlight can be replaced for about $20, so it makes a repair worth doing if you want to open the monitor. Use the documentation or the vendor website for details on opening the case.

Projectors

When projectors have a dim image, it can be that the bulb is going bad. All bulbs have a stated lifetime that can be found in the documentation of the projector. The hours of lifetime that you find in the documentation have usually been stretched a bit, meaning toward the end of the lifetime the bulb will start to fade in brightness.

Flickering Image

When the image is flickering, check the cables and ensure they are seated properly. If that doesn't help, try different cables because it could be a problem with the cable itself.

Another possible reason is a mismatch between the resolution settings and the refresh rate. If this is the problem, it will occur only when using the higher resolutions. You should increase the refresh rate to support the higher resolutions.

While you won't see many CRT monitors, flickering on those can indicate a source of magnetic interference near the display, such as a radio. Degaussing CRT monitors can help.

Distorted Image

This behavior can be caused by problems with power. Try replacing the power cable, and if that doesn't help, try plugging the monitor into a different wall outlet. Sometimes other devices on the same line (air conditioner, refrigerator, and so forth) can cause problems for the supply of power to the monitor.

Distorted Geometry

Distorted geometry can occur in projectors. It's simpler to show the symptoms than it is to explain what causes it, but it is a defect in the optical lens system. Figure 4.6 shows the most common forms.

FIGURE 4.6   Geometric distortion

Pincushion   Barrel

There is usually a setting that can be used to compensate and correct the distortion. The setting is called the Keystone setting. You simply move the slider in this setting until the image is corrected. Figure 4.7 shows a sample of the correction buttons you may find on a projector remote.

FIGURE 4.7   Correction buttons on projector remote

Burn-in

Burn-in is a condition that affected CRT monitors and still affects plasma and OLED displays. LCDs are generally not affected. The condition occurs when images are left for extended periods of time on the screen. The early screen savers were designed to prevent this in unattended displays by displaying a constantly changing image.

Software and utilities can be used to remedy burn-in but will have little effect if the burn-in is severe. It is also useful to know that the display will be most susceptible to this when it is new in the first few hours of operation. DVDs can be purchased that will "break in" a screen, and in some cases they can even eliminate existing burn-in if it is not severe.

Oversized Images and Icons

When a user is experiencing oversized images and icons, it is typically a misconfigured setting. In the iOS operating system it could be that the zoom is on. In Windows 7 and 8.1 there is a slider on the Display settings page, as shown in Figure 4.8, that can be used to enlarge all items on the screen. This setting is called Change The Size Of All Items. Check this setting and adjust as required.

FIGURE 4.8   Change The Size Of All Items option

Exam Essentials

List the common symptoms of display problems and the appropriate troubleshooting technique for each.   These include but are not limited to reversion to VGA mode; no image; overheating; dead pixels; artifacts; incorrect color patterns; dim, flickering, or distorted image; discoloration (degaussing); and BSOD. Resolution techniques include updating drivers, degaussing, changing resolution settings, and replacing the monitor.

4.4 Given a Scenario, Troubleshoot Wired and Wireless Networks with Appropriate Tools

At one time, wireless networks were considered an extravagant and insecure addition to the enterprise network, but now users expect wireless access. No longer is it a business advantage; it is now a business requirement. This section discusses troubleshooting both wired and wireless networks. The topics addressed in exam objective 4.4 include the following:

- Common symptoms
- Hardware tools
- Command-line tools

Common Symptoms

Network problems, usually manifesting themselves as an inability to connect to resources, can arise from many different sources. This section discusses some common symptoms of networking issues.

No Connectivity

When no connectivity can be established with the network, your troubleshooting approach should begin at the physical layer and then proceed up the OSI model. As components at each layer are eliminated as the source of the problem, proceed to the next higher layer. A simple yet effective set of steps might be as follows:

1. Check the network cable to ensure it is the correct cable type (crossover or straight through) and that it is functional. If in doubt, try a different cable.

2. Ensure that the NIC is functional and TCP/IP is installed and functional by pinging the loopback address 127.0.0.1. If required, install or reinstall TCP/IP and/or replace or repair the NIC.

3. Check the local IP configuration and ensure that the IP address, subnet mask, and gateway are correct. If the default gateway can be pinged, the computer is configured correctly for its local network and the problem lies beyond the router or with the

destination device. If pings to the gateway are unsuccessful, ensure that the IP configurations of the router interface and the computer are compatible and in the same subnet.

When dealing with a wireless network, ensure that the wireless card is functional. The wireless card is easily disabled with a keystroke on a laptop and should be the first thing to check. If the network uses a hidden SSID, ensure that the station in question is configured with the correct SSID.

APIPA/Link Local Addresses

Automatic Private IP Addressing (APIPA) is a TCP/IP feature Microsoft added to its operating systems. If a DHCP server cannot be found, the clients automatically assign themselves an IP address, somewhat randomly, in the 169.254.*x.x* range with a subnet mask of 255.255.0.0. This allows them to communicate with other hosts that have similarly configured themselves, but they will be unable to connect to the Internet or to any machines or resources that have DHCP-issued IP addresses.

If the network uses DHCP for IP configuration and the computer with the connectivity issue has an APIPA address, the problem is one of these three things:

- The DHCP server is out of IP addresses.

- The DHCP server is on the other side of a router and there is no functional DHCP relay present or no IP helper address configured on the router—all of which is to say the DHCP request is not reaching the DHCP server.

- The computer has a basic connectivity issue preventing it from connecting to the network (see the section "No Connectivity").

In Chapter 2, you learned about a type of IPv6 address called a *link local address* that in many ways is like an APIPA address in that the device will generate one of these addresses for each interface with no intervention from a human, as is done with APIPA. The scope of the address is also the same, in that it is not routable and is good only on the segment where the device is located.

However, as is the case with APIPA addresses, if two devices that are connected to the same segment generate these addresses, they will be in the same network, and the two devices will be able to communicate. This is because the devices always generate the address using the same IPv6 prefix (the equivalent of a network ID in IPv4), which is fe80::/64. The remainder of the address is created by spreading the 48-bit MAC address across the last 64 bits, yielding an IPv6 address that looks like the following one:

FE80::2237:06FF:FECF:67E4/64

Limited Connectivity

In some cases, the computer has connectivity to some but not all resources. When this is the case, issues that may reside on other layers of the OSI model should come under consideration. These include the following:

Authentication Issues   Does the user have the permission to access the resource?

DNS Issues   You may be able to ping the entire network using IP addresses, but most access is done by name, not IP address. If you can't ping resources by name, DNS is not functional, meaning either the DNS server is down or the local machine is not configured with the correct IP address of the DNS server. If recent changes have occurred in the DNS mappings or if your connection to the destination device has recently failed because of a temporary network issue that has been solved, you may need to clear the local DNS cache using the `ipconfig/flushdns` command.

Remote Problem   Don't forget that establishing a connection is a two-way street, and if the remote device has an issue, communication cannot occur. Always check the remote device as well. Any interconnecting device between the computer and resource, such as a switch or router, should also be checked for functionality.

Local Connectivity

When a computer can communicate only on its local network or subnet, the problem is usually one of the following:

Incorrect Subnet Mask   Sometimes an incorrect mask will prevent all communication, but in some cases it results in successful connections locally but not remotely (outside the local subnet). The subnet mask value should be the same mask used on the router interface connecting to the local network.

Incorrect Default Gateway Address   If the computer cannot connect to the default gateway, it will be confined to communicating with devices on the local network. This IP address should be that of the router interface connecting to the local network.

Router Problem   If all users on the network are having connectivity problems, you likely have a routing issue that should be escalated to the proper administrators.

Intermittent Connectivity

When a connectivity issue comes and goes, it can be a hardware issue or a software issue. The following hardware components should be checked for functionality:

Network Cable   A damaged cable can cause intermittent connectivity.

Network Interface Card   If the NIC is not properly seated or has worked its way partially out of its slot, it can cause connections that come and go.

Interference   On a wireless network, cordless phones, microwave ovens, and other wireless networks can interfere with transmissions. Also, users who stray too far from the access point (AP) can experience a signal that comes and goes.

The following are software issues that can cause intermittent connectivity:

DHCP Issues   When the DHCP server is down or out of IP addresses, the problem will not manifest itself to those users who already have an IP address until their lease expires and they need a new address. In this case, some users will be fine and others will not, and then users who were fine earlier in the day may have problems later when their IP address lease expires.

DNS Problems   If the DNS server is down or malfunctioning, it will cause problems for DNS clients who need name resolution requests answered. For users who have already connected to resources in the last hour before the outage, connectivity to those resources will still be possible until the name to IP address mapping is removed from the client DNS resolver cache.

IP Conflict

IP address conflicts are somewhat rare when DHCP is in use, but they can still happen. DHCP servers and clients both check for IP duplication when the DHCP client receives an IP address, but the process doesn't always work. Moreover, if someone with a statically configured IP address connects to the network with the same address as another machine, a conflict will exist.

Regardless of how the conflict occurs, it must be resolved because until it is, one or possibly both computers with the same address will not be able to operate on the network. You can determine the MAC address of the computer with which you are experiencing the conflict by using the ping command followed by the arp -d command.

Slow Transfer Speeds

Slow transmission on the network can be caused by hardware and software issues. Some of the physical issues that can cause slow performance are as follows:

Interference Both wireless and wired networks can be affected by electromagnetic interference (EMI) and radio frequency interference (RFI). EMI will degrade network performance. This can be identified by the poor operation you may experience. Be sure to run cables around (not over) ballasts and other items that can cause EMI. RFI is a similar issue introduced by radio waves. Wireless networks suffer even more from both of these issues.

Incorrect Cabling The network can go only as fast as its weakest link. Using CAT3 cabling, for example, will only allow the network to operate at 10 Mbps even if all the network cards are capable of 10 Gbps.

Malfunctioning NIC Network interface cards (NICs) can malfunction and cause a broadcast storm. These broadcast packets fill the network with traffic that slows performance for all users. Use a protocol analyzer to determine the MAC address of the offending computer.

From a software standpoint, the following issues can result in less than ideal performance:

Router Misconfiguration If the router is not configured correctly, it can cause slow performance because of less than optimal routing paths. Escalate the issue to the appropriate administrators.

Switch Misconfiguration An improperly implemented redundant switch network can result in switching loops that cause slow performance. Escalate the issue to the appropriate administrators.

Low RF Signal

In a wireless network, the signal coming from the AP has a distance limit. With some variation by standard, this is about 300 feet. However, this distance is impacted by obstructions and interference in the area. The WLAN design should include a site survey that identifies these issues and locates APs and antenna types in such a way as to mitigate these effects.

It is also useful to know that APs and some client radios have a setting to control signal strength. It is not a normal practice to change the setting in a laptop wireless card, but it may be necessary to change the transmit level on an AP. In many cases, it is actually beneficial to reduce the transmit level of an AP in situations where it is interfering with other APs in your network or you want to limit the range of the signal to prevent it from leaving the building. This is especially true in high-density areas where several APs are collocated in the same area for increased throughput.

SSID Not Found

In an 802.11 WLAN, the service set identifier (SSID) is used as both a network name and in some cases the magic word that allows access to the network. One of the ways you can increase the security of a WLAN (not sufficient in and of itself but a good addition to a layered approach to WLAN security) is to "hide" the SSID. This is also referred to as disabling SSID broadcast. This is done by setting the AP to *not* list the SSID in the beacon frames. These frames contain the information that is used to populate the list of available wireless networks when you "scan" for wireless networks on your wireless device.

When the SSID is hidden, the *only* way a device can connect to the WLAN is to be configured with a profile that includes the SSID of the WLAN. While every operating system is slightly different, to do this in Windows 8.1, you follow these steps:

1. Open the Network and Sharing Center, as shown in Figure 4.9.

FIGURE 4.9 Network And Sharing Center

2. Select Set Up A New Connection Or Network, opening the dialog shown in Figure 4.10.

FIGURE 4.10   Set Up A New Connection Or Network

3. Select the option Manually Connect To A Wireless Network and click Next, opening the dialog shown in Figure 4.11.

FIGURE 4.11   Manually Connect To A Wireless Network

4. Complete the network name, security type, encryption type, and security key; check the box Connect Even If The Network Is Not Broadcasting; and click Next. Now the profile is complete and you should be able to connect to the "hidden" network. To make it easier for the user, you may also want to check the box Start This Connection Automatically.

Hardware Tools

You have a number of tools at your disposal when troubleshooting. Some of these tools have already been discussed, and some are new to the discussion. This section discusses some of the main ones.

Cable Tester

Commonly used with network cabling, cable testers are used to verify that the cable you are using is good. You can perform many of the same tests with a multimeter. Although trading a known good cable for a suspected bad cable is also acceptable, a cable tester can help determine exactly what's wrong with the cable.

Loopback Plug

Also called wrap plugs, loopback plugs take the signal going out and essentially echo it back. This allows you to test parallel, serial, and network ports to make certain they're working correctly. This is a good way to eliminate or implicate the NIC as a problem.

Punch-Down Tools

A punch-down tool is used when you are securing cables to the patch panel that have been run from the wall outlets into the switch room. A wire is prepositioned into a slotted post, and then the punch-down tool is pressed down on top of the wire, over the post. Once the required pressure is reached, the internal spring is triggered, and the blade pushes the wire into the slot, cutting the insulation and securing the wire. Figure 4.12 shows a punch-down tool.

FIGURE 4.12   Punch-down tool

Tone Generator and Probe

Toner probes (also called *tone generators*) are used to locate the correct cable coming into a patch panel from the wall outlet when either connections have not been labeled or the labels have been removed from the patch panel. They are two-piece units (sometimes called *fox* and *hound*) where one end sends a signal and the other end is used to locate the wires that contain the signal in the switch room. Figure 4.13 shows a set.

FIGURE 4.13   Toner probe

Wire Strippers

Wire strippers are used to prepare the end of a cable for the attachment of a connector. They are used to remove the plastic covering and any shielding to get to the wire pairs contained in a twisted-pair wire. This functionality is often included with the crimper (see the next section).

Crimper

A crimper is used to attach a connector to a cable by securing each wire (eight of them in a twisted-pair wire) to the proper connector in an RJ-45 connector. It usually also includes a stripper as well. Figure 4.14 shows a coaxial crimper.

FIGURE 4.14   Crimper

Wireless Locator

A wireless locator is a hardware device that scans all channels or a specified channel for any 802.11 WLANs that may be in the area. They can be used to find a WLAN and to determine whether the network is broadcasting its SSID and whether security is enabled on the WLAN. It also can be used during the implementation of a WLAN to identity the channels used by the existing WLANs in the area so that an unused channel can be selected to avoid interference.

Command-Line Tools

Several command-line tools can be quite helpful.

ping

The ping command makes use of the Internet Control Message Protocol (ICMP) to test connectivity between two devices. ping is one of the most useful commands in the TCP/IP. It sends a series of packets to another system, which in turn sends a response. The ping command can be extremely useful for troubleshooting problems with remote hosts.

The ping command indicates whether the host can be reached and how long it took for the host to send a return packet. On a LAN, the time is indicated as less than 10 milliseconds. Across WAN links, however, this value can be much greater. When the -a parameter is included, it will also attempt to resolve the hostname associated with the IP address. Figure 4.15 shows an example of a successful ping.

FIGURE 4.15   The ping command

```
C:\Users\tmcmillan>ping 10.88.2.103

Pinging 10.88.2.103 with 32 bytes of data:
Reply from 10.88.2.103: bytes=32 time<1ms TTL=128
Reply from 10.88.2.103: bytes=32 time<1ms TTL=128
Reply from 10.88.2.103: bytes=32 time<1ms TTL=128
Reply from 10.88.2.103: bytes=32 time<1ms TTL=128

Ping statistics for 10.88.2.103:
    Packets: Sent = 4, Received = 4, Lost = 0 (0% loss),
Approximate round trip times in milli-seconds:
    Minimum = 0ms, Maximum = 0ms, Average = 0ms
```

ipconfig/ifconfig

The ipconfig command is used to view the IP configuration of a device and, when combined with certain switches or parameters, can be used to release and renew the lease of an IP address obtained from a DHCP server and to flush the DNS resolver cache. Its most common use is to view the current configuration. Figure 4.16 show its execution with the /all switch, which results in a display of a wealth of information about the IP configuration.

FIGURE 4.16   Using `ipconfig`

```
C:\Users\tmcmillan>ipconfig/all

Windows IP Configuration

        Host Name . . . . . . . . . . . . : tmcmillan
        Primary Dns Suffix  . . . . . . . : alpha.kaplaninc.com
        Node Type . . . . . . . . . . . . : Hybrid
        IP Routing Enabled. . . . . . . . : No
        WINS Proxy Enabled. . . . . . . . : No
        DNS Suffix Search List. . . . . . : alpha.kaplaninc.com
                                            kaplaninc.com

Ethernet adapter Local Area Connection:

        Connection-specific DNS Suffix  . : alpha.kaplaninc.com
        Description . . . . . . . . . . . : Broadcom NetXtreme 57xx Gigabit Controlle
r
        Physical Address. . . . . . . . . : 00-1A-A0-E1-95-AB
        DHCP Enabled. . . . . . . . . . . : Yes
        Autoconfiguration Enabled . . . . : Yes
        Link-local IPv6 Address . . . . . : fe80::ada3:8b73:a66e:6bc0%10(Preferred)
        IPv4 Address. . . . . . . . . . . : 10.88.2.103(Preferred)
        Subnet Mask . . . . . . . . . . . : 255.255.254.0
        Lease Obtained. . . . . . . . . . : Monday, January 30, 2012 9:38:37 AM
        Lease Expires . . . . . . . . . . : Tuesday, January 31, 2012 9:38:37 AM
        Default Gateway . . . . . . . . . : 10.88.2.6
        DHCP Server . . . . . . . . . . . : 10.88.10.48
        DHCPv6 IAID . . . . . . . . . . . : 234887840
        DHCPv6 Client DUID. . . . . . . . : 00-01-00-01-14-EE-0F-98-00-1A-A0-E1-95-AB

        DNS Servers . . . . . . . . . . . : 10.88.10.48
                                            10.75.139.18
        NetBIOS over Tcpip. . . . . . . . : Enabled
```

`ipconfig` can be used to release and renew a configuration obtained from a DHCP server by issuing first the `ipconfig /release` command, followed by the `ipconfig /renew` command.

It is also helpful to know that when you have just corrected a configuration error (such as an IP address) on a destination device, you should ensure that the device registers its new IP address with the DNS server by executing the `ipconfig /registerdns` command.

It may also be necessary to clear incorrect IP address to hostname mappings that may still exist on the devices that were attempting to access the destination device. This can be done by executing the `ipconfig /flushdns` command.

If you are using a Linux or Unix system, the command is not `ipconfig` but `ifconfig`. Figure 4.17 shows an example of the command and its output. The `ifconfig` command with `-a` option shows all network interface information, even if the network interface is down.

tracert

The `tracert` command (called `traceroute` in Linux and Unix) is used to trace the path of a packet through the network. Its best use is in determining exactly where in the network the packet is being dropped. It will show each hop (router) the packet crosses and how long it takes to do so. Figure 4.18 shows a partial display of a traced route to `www.msn.com`.

FIGURE 4.17   `ifconfig`

FIGURE 4.18   Using tracert

```
C:\Users\tmcmillan>tracert www.msn.com

Tracing route to us.co1.cb3.glbdns.microsoft.com [70.37.131.153]
over a maximum of 30 hops:

  1    11 ms     1 ms     1 ms  10.88.2.6
  2     2 ms     2 ms     1 ms  208-47-7-130.dia.static.qwest.net [208.47.7.130]

  3     7 ms     7 ms     7 ms  frp-edge-04.inet.qwest.net [205.168.14.213]
  4     7 ms     7 ms     7 ms  frp-core-02.inet.qwest.net [205.171.22.49]
  5    22 ms    22 ms    22 ms  chx-edge-03.inet.qwest.net [67.14.38.1]
  6    22 ms    22 ms    23 ms  63-234-10-14.dia.static.qwest.net [63.234.10.14]

  7    23 ms    23 ms    23 ms  xe-0-1-2-0.ch1-16c-1b.ntwk.msn.net [207.46.43.20
4]
  8    24 ms    24 ms    24 ms  xe-0-1-0-0.ch1-96c-1a.ntwk.msn.net [207.46.46.13
3]
  9    34 ms    34 ms    34 ms  ge-2-1-0-0.ash-64cb-1b.ntwk.msn.net [207.46.45.1
4]
 10    38 ms    38 ms    38 ms  ge-4-0-0-0.nyc-64cb-1b.ntwk.msn.net [207.46.46.5
7]
 11    39 ms    38 ms    38 ms  xe-3-1-0-0.ewr-96cbe-1b.ntwk.msn.net [207.46.47.
2]
 12    39 ms       *     39 ms  xe-3-0-0-0.ewr-96cbe-1a.ntwk.msn.net [207.46.43.
250]
 13
```

netstat

The netstat (network status) command is used to see what ports are listening on the TCP/IP-based system. The -a option is used to show all ports, and /? is used to show what other options are available (the options differ based on the operating system you are using). When executed with no switches, the command displays the current connections, as shown in Figure 4.19.

FIGURE 4.19   Using netstat

```
C:\Users\tmcmillan>netstat

Active Connections

   Proto  Local Address          Foreign Address              State
   TCP    10.88.2.103:51273      64.94.18.154:https           ESTABLISHED
   TCP    10.88.2.103:51525      sratl060:microsoft-ds        ESTABLISHED
   TCP    10.88.2.103:51529      gmonsalvatge:microsoft-ds    ESTABLISHED
   TCP    10.88.2.103:51573      sjc-not18:http               ESTABLISHED
   TCP    10.88.2.103:51716      schexv02:2785                ESTABLISHED
   TCP    10.88.2.103:51720      schvoip01:epmap              ESTABLISHED
   TCP    10.88.2.103:51721      schvoip01:1297               ESTABLISHED
   TCP    10.88.2.103:51722      schvoip01:1299               ESTABLISHED
   TCP    10.88.2.103:51824      69.31.116.27:http            CLOSE_WAIT
   TCP    10.88.2.103:51965      dcalpsch2:1026               ESTABLISHED
   TCP    10.88.2.103:53865      cs219p3:5050                 ESTABLISHED
   TCP    10.88.2.103:53871      sip109:http                  ESTABLISHED
   TCP    10.88.2.103:62522      ord08s08-in-f22:https        ESTABLISHED
   TCP    10.88.2.103:62567      ord08s08-in-f22:https        CLOSE_WAIT
   TCP    10.88.2.103:62682      by2msg3010613:http           ESTABLISHED
   TCP    10.88.2.103:63554      baymsg1020213:msnp           ESTABLISHED
   TCP    10.88.2.103:63770      v-client-2b:https            CLOSE_WAIT
   TCP    10.88.2.103:63771      ec2-174-129-205-197:https    CLOSE_WAIT
   TCP    10.88.2.103:63772      v-client-2b:https            CLOSE_WAIT
   TCP    10.88.2.103:63773      65.55.121.231:http           ESTABLISHED
   TCP    10.88.2.103:63774      168.75.207.20:http           ESTABLISHED
   TCP    10.88.2.103:63777      65.55.17.30:http             ESTABLISHED
   TCP    10.88.2.103:63779      70.37.131.11:http            ESTABLISHED
   TCP    10.88.2.103:63781      65.124.174.56:http           ESTABLISHED
   TCP    10.88.2.103:63788      69.31.76.41:http             ESTABLISHED
   TCP    10.88.2.103:63791      207.46.140.46:http           ESTABLISHED
   TCP    10.88.2.103:63792      64.4.21.39:http              ESTABLISHED
   TCP    127.0.0.1:2002         tmcmillan:51543              ESTABLISHED
   TCP    127.0.0.1:19872        tmcmillan:51571              ESTABLISHED
   TCP    127.0.0.1:51543        tmcmillan:2002               ESTABLISHED
   TCP    127.0.0.1:51549        tmcmillan:51550              ESTABLISHED
   TCP    127.0.0.1:51550        tmcmillan:51549              ESTABLISHED
   TCP    127.0.0.1:51571        tmcmillan:19872              ESTABLISHED
   TCP    127.0.0.1:53869        tmcmillan:53870              ESTABLISHED
   TCP    127.0.0.1:53870        tmcmillan:53869              ESTABLISHED
   TCP    127.0.0.1:63557        tmcmillan:63574              ESTABLISHED
   TCP    127.0.0.1:63574        tmcmillan:63557              ESTABLISHED

C:\Users\tmcmillan>
```

nbtstat

Microsoft networks use an interface called Network Basic Input/Output System (NetBIOS) to resolve workstation names with IP addresses. The nbtstat command can be used to view NetBIOS information. In Figure 4.20 it has been executed with the -n switch, which will display the NetBIOS names that are currently known to the local machine. In this case, this local machine is aware only of its own NetBIOS names.

FIGURE 4.20   Using nbtstat

```
C:\Users\tmcmillan>nbtstat -n

Local Area Connection:
Node IpAddress: [10.88.2.103] Scope Id: []

                NetBIOS Local Name Table

        Name               Type          Status
    ─────────────────────────────────────────────
        TMCMILLAN    <00>  UNIQUE     Registered
        ALPHA        <00>  GROUP      Registered
        TMCMILLAN    <20>  UNIQUE     Registered
        ALPHA        <1E>  GROUP      Registered

VMware Network Adapter VMnet1:
Node IpAddress: [192.168.21.2] Scope Id: []
```

net

The net command is one of the most powerful on the Windows-based network, as illustrated by net use. The options that can be used with the command differ slightly based on the Windows operating system you are using; you can view a full list by typing **net /?**.

The net use command is used on Windows-based clients to connect or disconnect from shared resources. You can see what is currently shared by typing **net use** without any other parameters, as shown in Figure 4.21.

FIGURE 4.21   Typing net use lets you see what is currently shared.

```
C:\Users\tmcmillan>net use
New connections will be remembered.

Status      Local     Remote                  Network
─────────────────────────────────────────────────────────────────
OK          G:        \\srat1060\groups        Microsoft Windows Network
OK          M:        \\srat1060\pstpickup\tmcmillan
                                               Microsoft Windows Network
OK          P:        \\srat1060\personal\tmcmillan
                                               Microsoft Windows Network
OK          Z:        \\10.88.2.132\fun        Microsoft Windows Network
The command completed successfully.
```

netdom

The netdom command is a Windows tool used to manage Active Directory domains and trust relationships from the command line. It is built into the Windows Server 2008, Windows Server 2008 R2, Windows Server 2012, and Windows Server 2012 R2 and also becomes available if you have the Active Directory Domain Services Tools that are part of the Remote Server Administration Tools (RSAT) installed on a Windows client machine like Windows 8.1.

The following are some of the tasks that can be performed with this tool:

- Join a computer that runs Windows XP Professional, Windows Vista, Windows 7, Windows 8, and Windows 8.1 to a Windows Server 2008 R2, Windows Server 2008, Windows Server 2003, Windows 2000, or Windows NT 4.0 domain.
- Manage computer accounts for domain member workstations and member servers.
- Establish one-way or two-way trust relationships between domains.

The command syntax is as follows:

```
NetDom <Operation> [<Computer>] [{/d: | /domain:} <Domain>] [<Options>]
NetDom help <Operation>
```

Table 4.1 shows some of the more common commands.

TABLE 4.1 netdom commands

Command	Description
netdom add	Adds a workstation or server account to the domain
netdom *computername*	Safely renames Active Directory domain controllers as well as member servers
netdom join	Joins a workstation or member server to a domain
netdom move	Moves a workstation or member server to a new domain

nslookup

The nslookup command a command-line administrative tool for testing and troubleshooting DNS servers. It can be run in two modes, interactive and noninteractive. While noninteractive mode is useful when only a single piece of data needs to be returned, interactive allows you to query for either an IP address for a name or a name for an IP address without leaving nslookup mode. The command syntax is as follows:

```
nslookup [-option] [hostname] [server]
```

To enter interactive mode, simply type nslookup as shown next. When you do this, by default it will identify the IP address and name of the DNS server that the local machine is configured to use, if any, and then will go to the > prompt. At this prompt you can type either an IP address or a name, and the system will attempt to resolve the IP address to a name or the name to an IP address.

```
C:\> nslookup
   Default Server: nameserver1.domain.com
   Address: 10.0.0.1
   >
```

The following are other queries that can be run that may prove helpful when troubleshooting name resolution issues:

- Looking up different data types in the database (such as Microsoft records)
- Querying directly from another name server (different from the one the local device is configured to use)
- Performing a zone transfer

Exam Essentials

Identify common symptoms of network issues and their potential causes.   Examples include limited, intermittent, local only or no connectivity, APIPA addresses, IP conflict, slow transfer speeds, and low RF signal.

Identify hardware tools available to diagnose and repair network cables.   These include but are not limited to cable testers, loopback plugs, punch-down tools, toner probes, wire strippers, crimpers, and wireless locators.

Identify commands that let you identify network issues.   These include ping, ipconfig, tracert, netstat, nbtstat, net, netdom, and nslookup.

4.5 Given a Scenario, Troubleshoot and Repair Common Mobile Device Issues While Adhering to the Appropriate Procedures

Mobile devices have their own unique sets of issues that may not be encountered with desktop computers. This section discusses common issues and their solutions. Mobile devices require a different set of procedures for opening the case while protecting the integrity of the unit. The following topics are addressed in exam objective 4.5:

- Common symptoms
- Disassembling processes for proper reassembly

Common Symptoms

Not all mobile device issues are unique to mobile devices. They suffer from many of the same issues as desktop machines. However, some problems are unique to laptops and mobile devices or at least are more prone to occur with laptops, as you will learn in this section.

No Display

The backlight is the light in the device that powers the LCD screen. It can go bad over time and need to be replaced, and it can also be held captive by the inverter. The inverter takes the DC power the laptop is providing and boosts it up to AC to run the backlight. If the inverter goes bad, you can replace it on most models (it's cheaper than the backlight).

Before going to the trouble of opening the case, however, ensure that the screen has not been inadvertently dimmed to the off position with the Fn keys or that the system has not been set to direct the output to an external monitor.

Dim Display

As with a blank display, the backlight and inverter can cause dimming problems, but in most cases the screen has been dimmed inadvertently with the Fn keys. It is also possible that the switch on the laptop that tells the system the lid is closed may be held down by some obstruction. Check that as well.

Flickering Display

Flickering screens can be caused by video drivers. The first thing to try is updating the driver. Another cause can be a low screen-refresh rate. Make sure the rate is set according to the documentation. Keep in mind that if you set it incorrectly, another symptom that may appear is more than one image displaying with the top image appearing transparent.

Flickering can also be caused by a loose connection. You may remember that a cable connects the display to the motherboard. Open the lid as described in Chapter 3, "Mobile Devices," and reseat the cable.

Sticking Keys

Problems with keyboards can range from collecting dust (in which case you need to blow it out) to their springs wearing out. In the latter case, you can replace the keyboard (they cost about 10 times more than desktop keyboards) or choose to use an external one (provided the user isn't traveling and having to lug another hardware element with them). As you can imagine, spilled liquids are often the cause of sticking keys.

Intermittent Wireless

Most laptops today include an internal wireless card. This is convenient, but it can be susceptible to interference (resulting in low signal strength) between the laptop and the AP. Do what you can to reduce the number of items blocking the signal between the two devices, and you'll increase the strength of the signal. It is also possible that the cable that connects the antenna to the laptop needs to be reseated. Open the lid as described in Chapter 3.

Battery Not Charging

Most NiCad batteries build up memory, and that memory can prevent a battery from offering a full charge. The biggest issue with DC power problems is a battery's inability to power the laptop as long as it should. If a feature is available to fully drain the battery, you should use it to eliminate the memory (letting the laptop run on battery on a regular basis greatly helps). If you can't drain the battery and eliminate the memory effect, you should replace the battery.

Ghost Cursor/Pointer Drift

A second, or ghost, cursor can be caused when the laptop has a track pad that is too sensitive. Some laptops and tablets also vent warm air through the keyboard, and when the lid gets left down, it heats up the track pad and causes this type of cursor behavior. Updating the driver for the touchpad has been known to help this problem. Another approach is to disable the touchpad completely and use an external mouse.

Pointer drift occurs when the mouse cursor slowly drifts across the screen with no assistance from the user. In some cases, it occurs only on a second or third monitor and not the main monitor. If that is the case, there is a setting in the display properties that may solve the issue. In Windows 8.1, navigate to the display properties by right-clicking the display and select Preferences. Then in the menu at the bottom left of the resulting screen, choose Display. Then on the screen shown in Figure 4.22, select the check box next to the selection Let Me Choose One Scaling Level For All My Displays.

FIGURE 4.22 Addressing pointer drift

In other cases, the problem is not related to multiple monitors at all. If you find that it is occurring only with certain applications, it may be neither a pointer nor device problem at all but rather an application issue. Finally, on some laptops and other small devices that use trackpads, it may be that you or the user are leaving your hand resting on a part of the device very close to the trackpad and it is picking that up and causing the pointer to move.

No Power

In the absence of AC power, the device will attempt to run off the battery. This solution is good for a time, but AC power must be available to keep the battery charged and the laptop running. Most laptops have an indicator light showing whether AC power is being received, and the AC cord typically has an indicator light on it as well to show that it's receiving power. If no lights are lit on the cord or the laptop indicating that AC power is being received, try a different outlet or a different cord. Also try reseating the cord in the power adaptor. The cord between the wall and the adaptor is removable (to interchange for different countries' outlet types), and sometimes it comes loose from the brick.

The presence of AC can affect the action of the NIC. To conserve power, the NIC is often configured not to be active when running on DC power (see Figure 4.23). In some laptop models, you can access this dialog box through Start ➤ Control Panel ➤ Internal NIC Configuration. If power problems arise, ensure that this setting is enabled.

FIGURE 4.23 NIC settings

In Windows 7, 8, and 8.1, use Device Manager to set Allow The Computer To Turn Off This Device To Save Power in the Properties ➤ Power Management tab. Then use the Power Options to set the NIC to Maximum Power Saving.

Num Lock Indicator Lights

Sometimes the Num Lock indicator light does not function. This can be a hardware issue, but many times it is a case of not understanding the process for enabling and disabling Num Lock. In many laptops you simply hit the key once to turn it on and again to turn it off. However, on some devices, you must also use the Fn key simultaneously. Spilling liquids on the laptop can also cause these problems and usually requires taking the laptop in for service to clean the internal parts.

No Wireless Connectivity

When there is no wireless connectivity, it is usually one of two things:

- The wireless capability is disabled (enabling and disabling this function is usually done with a key combination or a Fn key) because this is easy to disable inadvertently. This can also be a hardware switch on the side, front, or back of the case.

- The wireless antenna is bad or the cable needs to be reseated.

No Bluetooth Connectivity

Bluetooth is also enabled and disabled with a key combination and can be disabled easily. The first thing to try is to reenable it. The second thing to try is to reseat the antenna cable. If all else fails, try a new antenna. Like the WLAN NIC, this can also be a hardware switch on the side, front, or back of the case.

Cannot Display to External Monitor

It's always possible that a hardware issue is causing an external monitor to not work when connected to a laptop; but, again, in most cases the problem is an incomplete understanding of the key combination to use to send the output to the external monitor.

On some laptops you need to use the Fn key in combination with keys on the top row; on other laptops you simply use the top row keys. Before spending too much time troubleshooting, consult the documentation and ensure you are using the correct procedure. In some models, this can also be controlled from the video control panel or from within PowerPoint or other presentation software.

Touchscreen Nonresponsive

Tablets, phablets, and smartphones use a touchscreen interface that eliminates the need for a keyboard. Touchscreen monitors use two technologies: touch flow and multitouch. Before we dive into solving a nonresponsive touchscreen, let's review these technologies.

Touch Flow

Touch flow, or TouchFLO, is a user interface feature designed by HTC. It is used by dragging your finger up and down or left and right to access common tasks on the screen. This movement is akin to scrolling the screen up and down or scrolling the screen left and right.

Multitouch

Multitouch allows the screen to recognize multiple simultaneous screen touches. This allows for movements such as those used for expanding or enlarging pictures with two fingers and then reducing them back again with the reverse movement.

The first thing that all documentation will tell you to try is to restart the device, and in many cases the documentation is not blowing smoke at you; it does actually solve the issue. Unfortunately, if the screen is broken or the wires are cut, this will not help, but you should always try this first.

Many devices, such as the Android operating system, have a Device Diagnostics tool, which can test, among other things, the touchscreen. To access this tool, a special key sequence is used on the same key pad where you dial phone numbers. When you hit the proper sequence (see the documentation), the menu for the tool will appear, as shown in Figure 4.24, which shows the menu for the Device Diagnostic tool for the Samsung S4. There are two tests found here that apply to the touchscreen, the TSP Dot Mode and the TSP Grid Mode.

FIGURE 4.24   Samsung Device Diagnostics menu

(SmartMobilePhoneSolutions.com)

1. Melody

2. Vibration

3. Speaker

4. Dimming

5. Camera

6. VT Camera

7. Bluetooth

8. TSP Dot Mode

9. TSP Grid Mode

10. Accelerometer Sensor

11. Proximity Sensor

12. Light Sensor

TSP Dot mode allows you to verify that the screen is reading your touch. It will place a dot on the screen everywhere you touch it where it is reading the input. The TSP Grid mode allows you to test each section or grid of the screen. You can drag your finger across the screen and identify any dead spots that may be present.

If the device passes both of these tests, you have no problem with the screen; you have an issue with software, not hardware. Try removing the battery while the device is on (soft reset). If the device doesn't allow this, it will typically have an operation you can execute called a *simulated battery pull*. If neither of these steps helps, the next step is to reboot the device to safe mode.

If booting to safe mode solves the issue, the issue lies in your application. It may be outdated or corrupt, so try reinstalling the latest version. If none of what I have discussed so far works, you are ready to get more extreme and perform a hard reset, which returns the device to the factory settings. Don't do this until you have backed up all the data on the device. Also, do not do this if the device exhibited any hardware issues when you ran the diagnostics test. You will need it to work properly when you finish the reset so you can set up the phone again.

If the device fails the diagnostic test, you have a hardware issue. If the damage is from liquids, submerge the phone in 99 percent isopropyl alcohol. Dry the phone completely and turn it on. This has actually fixed some phones with water damage. Unfortunately, in most cases, when the diagnostic test fails, you have to replace the screen.

These same options are also available with touchscreens on devices like the Microsoft Surface as well. The same general approach applies with some variation (clean screen, restart, recalibrate the screen, install the latest updates, restore from backup, refresh, reset). The terms *refresh* and *reset* mean the same here as when dealing with laptops and desktops.

Apps Not Loading

Many times after a user purchases an app or accesses a free application, the app does not appear to load and function. The following are some possible solutions:

- Close the problematic application and all other applications and start the process of opening the application anew. This process will be unique to the device. If you find the application to be missing when you attempt to restart it, download the app again.

- Restart the device. When the device has started, if you find the application to be missing, download the app again.

- Reauthorize the device. This means unauthorize the device to use the app and then authorize it again. This process will be unique to the device.

- Uninstall the app and then reinstall it.

Slow Performance

Many of the causes of slow performance in mobile devices are the same as the causes of slow performance in desktop machines. For the purposes of this discussion, I will focus on performance that deteriorates after being acceptable as opposed to system performance that is poor from the outset (which could be a matter of insufficient resources such as RAM). Here is a list of possibilities:

- The first thing to check is the presence of a virus. If the system seems to have an overabundance of disk activity, scan it for viruses, using a virus program that resides externally on a CD/DVD or memory stick.

- Defragment the hard drive or, in the case of a smartphone, the memory. The more fragmented the storage is, the slower the access will be.

- Check the space on the hard drive or memory. When the partition or volume where the operating system is located becomes full, performance will suffer. This is why it is a good idea to store data and applications on a different partition from that holding the system files.

- Ensure the latest updates are installed. In many cases, updates help to solve performance problems, so make sure they are current.

    Some specific tips for smartphones are as follows:

- Kill background apps that may be running.

- Keep all apps up to date.

- Turn off background data services such as Facebook, Twitter, and WeatherBug.

- On an Android device, turn off Google Services.

Unable to Decrypt Email

Some mobile devices have trouble decrypting encrypted emails either because the selected encryption mechanism does not work using the device's browser or because the device cannot locate the certificate and corresponding key required to decrypt the message. Some vendors, such as Trend Micro, have simply chosen to not support any mobile browsers because of the large number in existence. In a case such as this, you will receive a message such as this:

> Forward this email to m@zd.trendmicro.com and receive URLs to view the message on mobile devices.

Then an intermediate device will decrypt the email and send you a link, which is valid for a short period of time for you to view the email.

In other cases, the issue is the inability to locate the required certificate and key. The solution could be as simple as inserting a smart card containing the key. In other cases, you may need to install or reinstall the certificate and corresponding private key required to decrypt the messages. In other cases, it is an issue that can be solved by applying an operating system patch. Just one more reason for keeping all operating systems fully updated!

Finally, sometimes S/MIME is not enabled in the device. Many systems, such as BlackBerry, use S/MIME for encryption, and the receiving device must have this enabled.

Extremely Short Battery Life

There are a number of reasons that battery life is not what it should be in a mobile device. The following are some things that can drain a good battery:

- Leaving display brightness too high
- Constantly enabled wireless connections
- Constantly enabled location services
- Constantly enabled background data services

You may detect a trend in this list, and that is leaving things on! All of those services eat the battery. Setting the device to Airplane mode stops all of that battery sucking. Yes, you may have to manually turn it on to check email, but the convenience is eating the battery.

In other cases, the battery is nearing the end of its life. If using Airplane mode doesn't help, it's probably time for a new battery. All batteries have a limited number of recharges in them. Check the documentation of the device for guidance on this. If the battery does suddenly die shortly after a charge, it's a red flag.

Overheating

When a mobile device is getting hot (and I'm talking very hot here, not just warm), it can be the battery. If you find that is the source of the heat, replace the battery. Beyond that, some issues that can cause or contribute to overheating are as follows:

- Excessive gaming
- Excessive browsing
- Using the device while charging the device

On a laptop, excessive heat can indicate that the vents are blocked. It also can be a case of running too many things at once. Clean vents often and ensure they are not blocked when the device is on. Laptops need a hard, even surface so the vents can expel heat. This is why running a device on your lap produces so much heat.

Frozen System

Mobile devices can lock and become unresponsive just like desktop systems can and may do so for some the same reasons. But they have their own special set of issues that can cause this. The following are some things that you can try to prevent and/or unfreeze a system:

- Clear the application memory cache, which can be overloaded. Closing all applications or restarting the device can solve this issue.
- If the lockup occurred during texting, enable Airplane mode and then disable Airplane mode to force the device to reestablish the connection.

Many of the same issues that cause slow performance also cause lockups. Think of lockups as the next step after slowness. Therefore, some of the same tactics discussed in the section "Slow Performance" apply here as well.

No Sound from Speakers

When no sound is coming from the speakers of a device, start by checking the obvious.

- Is the volume on the device turned down?
- Is the device set on vibrate or to "no sound"?

If the obvious has been checked, then consider when this issue arises. If it arises only when accessing certain sites or when using certain apps, it's an issue with either site compatibility or with the application. In some cases, only taking out the battery and putting it back in (or using a function on the device that does the same) will solve an issue with an application.

If it occurs at all times, then try the following approaches:

- Refresh the device (saves your data but not your apps).
- Reset the device to factory defaults (back up all data!).
- Check for any updates you may have missed.

GPS Not Functioning

When location services do not appear to be working (these are the services that make the GPS feature work), keep the following principles in mind:

- Make sure it's on!
- Keep in mind it always works best outdoors rather than indoors.
- Check for Internet access. If you don't have that, you won't have GPS services.
- The first time you use the GPS service, it will take longer because it must find the GPS location.
- As always, the first thing to try is restarting he device.

The GPS performance on some mobile devices can also be affected by the position of your hand on the device. If your hand covers the antenna used for GPS, performance can be negatively affected. It also has been reported that certain UV-protected windshields can block GPS.

Swollen Battery

Just as swollen capacitors are a bad thing, so are swollen batteries. A swollen battery occurs when the battery's cells are overcharged because lithium-ion batteries react unfavorably to overcharging. When you encounter a swollen battery, the only solution is to replace it. But you should practice the following safe battery handling procedures when dealing with swollen batteries:

- Be careful not to puncture a swollen battery. The casing is under stress from the built-up gasses within.
- If the swollen state makes the battery difficult to remove, take the device to an expert for removal.

- If you are able to safely remove the swollen battery, store it in a safe cool container and take it to an authorized acceptance center. Do not throw it in the trash!

To avoid a swollen battery altogether, follow the guidelines in the section "Extremely Short Battery Life" to extend the life of batteries.

Disassembling Processes for Proper Reassembly

Disassembling a laptop in such a way that you end up with no leftover parts after the reassembly can be more of a challenge than with desktop machines. This section discusses best practices for this process.

Document and Label Cable and Screw Locations

With a desktop computer there is often plenty of empty space in the case. In a laptop, space is at a premium, and because of that, every screw is crucial! To avoid playing a guessing game about which screw goes where, you should create a map that tells you not only where each screw goes (and organize the screws by whatever naming convention you choose) but also where each cable plugs in. You should create this map as you disassemble the laptop and follow it carefully when reassembling it. Taking photos with your phone as you work can also suffice.

Organize Parts

As you disassemble the device, organize the parts in such a way that you can reverse your steps when it comes time to reassemble the laptop. Keep screws of the same type together and be careful about making assumptions about screws that appear to be the same kind. Keep all screws that hold a particular component in place together in the same place, perhaps in a cup or on a paper plate.

Another helpful idea is to maintain the parts in the same sequence in which they were taken off the laptop. This will help you remember which part must go back on before another, which may not be as obvious as you think when the time comes to put the laptop back together.

Refer to Manufacturer Resources

There is no better source of information about the idiosyncrasies of disassembling and reassembling a particular laptop model than the manufacturer documentation. No, it's not cheating to look at that! Each model's documentation has certain small tips that can save much time and grief.

Use Appropriate Hand Tools

Mobile device tools were discussed earlier in this chapter. The important message beyond what is provided there is to use the correct tools. If you render a screw useless by trying to take it out with the wrong kind of screwdriver, you will be wishing you had just bought the correct tool.

Exam Essentials

Identify common symptoms of mobile device issues. Some of the symptoms include a dim, flickering, or blank display; sticking keys; intermittent or nonexistent wireless or Bluetooth connectivity; battery and power issues; ghost cursors; problems with Num Lock indicator lights; and an inability to use an external monitor.

Describe proper disassembly and reassembly procedures. Use the following guidelines:

- Document and label cable and screw locations.
- Organize parts.
- Refer to manufacturer resources.
- Use appropriate hand tools.

4.6 Given a Scenario, Troubleshoot Printers with Appropriate Tools

In the real world, you'll find that a large portion of all service calls relate to printing problems. This section will give you some general guidelines and common printing solutions to resolve printing problems. The topics addressed in exam objective 4.6 include the following:

- Common symptoms
- Tools

Common Symptoms

There is no single shared device in the network that more users come in contact with and use every day than the printer. You may have to troubleshoot the common symptoms in this section on a daily basis, depending on your environment. Your ability to get a down printer working will make you more valuable to your employer.

Streaks

With laser printers, streaks usually indicate that the fuser is not fusing the toner properly on the paper. It could also be that the incorrect paper is being used. In laser printers, you can sometimes tell the printer that you are using a heavier paper. For dot matrix, you can adjust the platen for thicker paper.

If you can pick up a sheet from a laser printer, run your thumb across it, and have the image come off on your thumb, you have a fuser problem. The fuser isn't heating the toner and fusing it onto the paper. This could be caused by a number of things—but all of them can be taken care of with a fuser replacement. For example, if the halogen light inside the heating roller has burned out, that will cause the problem. The solution is to replace the fuser. The fuser can be replaced with a rebuilt unit, if you prefer. Rebuilt fusers are almost as good as new fusers, and some even come with guarantees. Plus, they cost less.

> The whole fuser may not need to be replaced. You can order fuser components from parts suppliers and then rebuild them. For example, if the fuser has a bad lamp, you can order a lamp and replace it in the fuser.

Another, similar problem happens when small areas of smudging repeat themselves down the page. Dents or cold spots in the fuser heat roller cause this problem. The only solution is to replace either the fuser assembly or the heat roller.

If an ink cartridge becomes damaged or develops a hole, it can put too much ink on the page, and the letters will smear. In this case, the solution is to replace the ink cartridge. (However, a small amount of smearing is normal if the pages are laid on top of each other immediately after printing.) Because damage is possible in the process, you need to be careful when refilling cartridges, and many manufacturers do not suggest using refilled cartridges at all.

With inkjet or dot-matrix printers, streaks can mean the printhead needs cleaning. If cleaning doesn't help, try replacing the cartridge (inkjet) or the ribbon (dot matrix).

Faded Prints

In laser printers, faded output usually indicates that the toner cartridge is just about empty. You can usually remove it, shake it, and replace it and then get a bit more life out of it before it is completely empty, but it is a signal that you are near the end.

Another possibility is that the ink cartridge has dried out from lack of use. That's why the manufacturers include a small suction pump inside the printer that primes the ink cartridge before each print cycle. If this priming pump is broken or malfunctioning, this problem will manifest itself, and the pump will need to be replaced.

For dot-matrix printers, faded printing means you need to replace the ribbon, which is the source of ink in those printer types.

Ghost Images

A problem unique to laser printers, *ghosting*, means you can see light images of previously printed pages on the current page. This is caused by one of two things: bad erasure lamps or a broken cleaning blade. If the erasure lamps are bad, the previous electrostatic discharges aren't completely wiped away. When the electrophotographic (EP) drum rotates toward the developing roller, some toner sticks to the slightly discharged areas. A broken cleaning blade, on the other hand, causes old toner to build up on the EP drum and consequently present itself in the next printed image.

Replacing the toner cartridge solves the second problem. Solving the first problem involves replacing the erasure lamps in the printer. Because the toner cartridge is the least expensive cure, you should try that first. Usually, replacing the toner cartridge will solve the problem. If it doesn't, you'll then have to replace the erasure lamps.

Toner Not Fused to the Paper

In laser printers, when the toner does not fuse properly to the paper, it will streak and smudge. See the section "Streaks" for more information.

Creased Paper

Creased paper is a sign of a paper jam inside the printer that, although not grinding the entire operation to halt (see the "Paper Jam" section later in this section), is mangling your paper. Approach this problem with the same techniques described in the section "Paper Jam."

Paper Not Feeding

When the paper is not feeding into the printer, it means the pickup rollers have hardened and lost their ability to pick up the paper. Replacing these rollers usually fixes the problem.

In some cases, it's not the rollers but the paper-feed sensor. It is designed to tell the printer when it is out of paper. Always try cleaning the sensor first before replacing it. High humidity can also cause the paper to not feed properly.

Paper Jam

Laser printers today run at copier speeds. As a result, their most common problem is paper jams. Paper can get jammed in a printer for several reasons. First, feed jams happen when the paper-feed rollers get worn. The solution to this problem is easy: replace the worn rollers.

If your paper-feed jams are caused by worn pickup rollers, there is something you can do to get your printer working while you're waiting for the replacement pickup rollers. Scuff the feed rollers with a pot scrubber pad (or something similar) to roughen up the feed rollers. This trick works only once. After that, the rollers aren't thick enough to touch the paper.

Another cause of feed jams is related to the drive of the pickup roller. The drive gear (or clutch) may be broken or have teeth missing. Again, the solution is to replace it. To determine whether the problem is a broken gear or worn rollers, print a test page, but leave the paper tray out. Look into the paper-feed opening with a flashlight, and see whether the paper pickup rollers are turning evenly and don't skip. If they turn evenly, the problem is more than likely worn rollers.

Worn exit rollers can also cause paper jams. These rollers guide the paper out of the printer into the paper-receiving tray. If they're worn or damaged, the paper may catch on its way out of the printer. These types of jams are characterized by a paper jam that occurs just as the paper is getting to the exit rollers. If the paper jams, open the rear door and see where the paper is. If the paper is close to the exit roller, the exit rollers are probably the problem.

The solution is to replace all the exit rollers. You must replace all of them at the same time, because even one worn exit roller can cause the paper to jam. Besides, they're inexpensive. Don't be cheap and skimp on these parts if you need to have them replaced.

Paper jams can be the fault of the paper. If your printer consistently tries to feed multiple pages into the printer, the paper isn't dry enough. If you live in an area with high humidity, this could be a problem. Some solutions are pretty far-out but may work (such as keeping the paper in a Tupperware-type airtight container or microwaving it to remove moisture). The best all-around solution, however, is humidity control and keeping the paper wrapped until it's needed. Keep the humidity around 50 percent or lower (but greater than 25 percent if you can in order to avoid problems with electrostatic discharge). Poor paper quality can also cause this problem.

Finally, a metal, grounded strip called the *static eliminator strip* inside the printer drains the corona charge away from the paper after it has been used to transfer toner from the EP cartridge. If that strip is missing, broken, or damaged, the charge will remain on the paper and may cause it to stick to the EP cartridge, causing a jam. If the paper jams after reaching the corona assembly, this may be the cause.

No Connectivity

A number of software issues can cause printer problems. Sometimes it's difficult to tell exactly where in the process the communication between the computer and the printer is breaking down. It could be that you are not establishing a connection with the printer, or it could be an incorrect setting or driver is preventing successful printing.

To determine whether it is a connectivity problem, ping the IP address of the printer. If you cannot ping the printer by IP address, that problem must be solved or all other troubleshooting of settings and drivers will be wasted effort. Use this simple test to rule out a network connectivity problem.

If the printer is connected directly to the computer (locally connected), then check the cables. If they check out, ensure that the printer port is enabled and that the correct driver for the printer is installed.

Garbled Characters on Paper

Many problems with a printer that won't work with the operating system or that prints the wrong characters can be traced to problems with its software. Computers and printers can't talk to each other by themselves. They need interface software to translate software commands into commands the printer can understand.

For a printer to work with a particular operating system, a driver must be installed for it. This driver specifies the page description language (PDL) the printer understands, as well as information about the printer's characteristics (paper trays, maximum resolution, and so on). For laser printers, there are two popular PDLs: Adobe PostScript (PS) and Hewlett-Packard Printer Control Language (PCL). Almost all laser printers use one or both of these.

If the wrong printer driver is selected, the computer will send commands in the wrong language. If that occurs, the printer will print several pages of garbage (even if only one page of information was sent). This "garbage" isn't garbage at all, but the printer PDL commands printed literally as text instead of being interpreted as control commands.

Vertical Lines on Page

Vertical lines can appear in either of two forms.

Vertical Black Lines on the Page

With laser printers, a groove or scratch in the EP drum can cause the problem of vertical black lines running down all or part of the page. Because a scratch is lower than the surface, it doesn't receive as much (if any) of a charge as the other areas. The result is that toner sticks to it as though it were discharged. Because the groove may go around the circumference of the drum, the line may go all the way down the page.

Another possible cause of vertical black lines is a dirty charge corona wire. A dirty charge corona wire prevents a sufficient charge from being placed on the EP drum. Because the EP drum has almost zero charge, toner sticks to the areas that correspond to the dirty areas on the charge corona wire.

The solution to the first problem is, as always, to replace the toner cartridge (or EP drum, if your printer uses a separate EP drum and toner). You can also solve the second problem with a new toner cartridge, but in this case that would be an extreme solution. It's easier to clean the charge corona with the brush supplied with the cartridge.

When dealing with inkjet printers, vertical black lines on the page can mean the print head needs cleaning or that the print cartridge needs to be replaced.

Vertical White Lines on the Page

With laser printers, vertical white lines running down all or part of the page are relatively common problems on older printers, especially ones that see little maintenance. They're caused by foreign matter (more than likely toner) caught on the transfer corona wire. The dirty spots keep the toner from being transmitted to the paper (at those locations, that is), with the result that streaks form as the paper progresses past the transfer corona wire.

The solution is to clean the corona wires. Some printers come with a small corona-wire brush to help in this procedure. To use it, remove the toner cartridge and run the brush in the charge corona groove on top of the toner cartridge. Replace the cartridge and use the brush to brush away any foreign deposits on the transfer corona. Be sure to put it back in its holder when you're finished.

For inkjet printers, clean the print head first (or run the built-in cleaning cycle) and then try replacing the cartridge. This behavior is usually because of dust or debris.

Backed-Up Print Queue

Sometimes the printer will not print and all attempts to delete print jobs or clear the print queue fail. It's almost as if the printer is just frozen. When this occurs, the best thing to do is restart the print spooler service on the computer that is acting as the print server. Unfortunately, all users will have to resend their print jobs after this, but at least the printer will be functional again.

Low Memory Errors

A printer can have several types of memory errors. The most common is insufficient memory to print the page. Sometimes you can circumvent this problem by doing any of the following:

- Turn off the printer to flush out its RAM and then turn it back on and try again.

- Print at a lower resolution. (Adjust this setting in the printer's properties in Windows.)

- Change the page being printed so it's less complex.

- Try a different printer driver if your printer supports more than one PDL. (For example, try switching from PostScript to PCL, or vice versa.) Doing so involves installing another printer driver.

- Upgrade the memory, if the printer allows.

Access Denied

Printers are considered resources just like files and folders, and as such can have permissions attached to them. When a user receives an access denied message, the user lacks the print permission. Typically, a printer that has been shared will automatically give all users the print permission, but when permissions have been employed to control which users can print to a particular printer, that default has been altered.

When checking permissions, keep in mind that in Windows, users may have permissions derived from their personal account and from groups of which they are a member. You must ensure that users have not been explicitly denied print permission through their accounts or through any groups of which they are members. A single Deny will prevent them from printing, regardless of what other permissions they may have to the printer.

Also, *print availability* or *print priority* can affect access to the printer. Print availability is used to permit certain users to print only during certain times. With print priority, print jobs from certain users or groups are assigned a higher priority than other users or groups. These settings, usually set by an administrator, can prevent or delay successful printing.

Printer Will Not Print

If your printer isn't spitting out print jobs, it may be a good idea to print a test page and see whether that works. The test page information is stored in the printer's memory, so there's no formatting or translating of jobs required. It's simply a test to make sure your printer hears your computer. In addition to the Windows Print Test Page button, try the built-in test function on the printer if your printer has one. While the Windows test verifies driver and connectivity, testing or printing at the print device tests the device itself.

When you install a printer, one of the last questions it asks you is if you want to print a test page. If there's any question, go ahead and do it. If the printer is already installed, you can print a test page from the printer Properties window. Just click the Print Test Page button and it should work. If nothing happens, double-check your connections and stop and restart the print spooler. If garbage prints, there is likely a problem with the printer's memory or the print driver.

In many cases, a printer will not print because either the printer is not on, it doesn't have power, or the print queue is stopped or paused. Printing a test page will identify these issues before they affect users.

Color Prints in Wrong Print Color

Incorrect colors or colors that are faint or washed out are often the result of a dirty print head, although it can also mean that one of the colors is running out. Head cleaning is a crucial operation that should be carried out at least once a month under normal usage. This is a procedure carried out in the properties or preferences of the printer (which may vary by printer).

You should not perform this procedure if the ink cartridges are low because it takes ink to do this. Check that first and, if they are low, replace any cartridges that need it and then run the head-cleaning procedure.

Unable to Install Printer

Installing a printer and attaching to a shared printer are two different operations in the Windows environment. Users with no administrative rights can attach to an existing shared printer, but installing a printer on the machine (which means that machine will function as the print server for that device) requires administrative permissions in the local machine. When an inability to install occurs, verify that you are logged into the computer with an administrator account.

Error Codes

Many laser printers include LCDs for interaction with the printer. When error codes appear, refer to the manufacturer's manuals or website for information on how to interpret the codes and solve the problem causing them.

Printing Blank Pages

When an inkjet printer prints blank pages, the issue is usually a clogged print head. When these types of printers sit for an extended period without use, the ink that may be in the print head dries out, clogging the head. Consequently, when you print, everything else in the process occurs correctly, but the ink cannot get through the clogged head and you get no ink on the paper. The solution is to clean the head and replace any cartridges that may be low.

Another reason for this can be an incorrect print driver. This is not a typical symptom of a bad driver, but can still be the solution in some printers. Try updating and/or downloading the driver if clogged ink cartridges are not the issue.

If it is a laser printer, check the following items:

- Empty toner cartridge
- Malfunctioning laser shutter (prevents creation of image in the drum)
- No voltage to the transfer roller (prevents transfer of toner from the drum to the paper)
- No bias charge on the drum (prevents transfer of toner to the drum)
- Defective laser scanner cable (prevents image creation on the drum)

No Image on Printer Display

When the display located on the physical printer is blank, it may be a formatter failure. While the failure of a formatter is not common, the solution, replacing the formatter, is not difficult. The formatter assembly is a self-contained unit that can be purchased and installed in the place of the bad formatter.

In some cases, the display may go into a sleep mode when not in use. If this is the case, touching the screen (if it is touchscreen) may wake it up. Make sure there is power to the unit, and if there is not, check the power supply. Finally, some screens have a brightness setting that may be set so low you can't read it, so consider that possibility as well.

Tools

Tools are available in the crusade to keep the printers working. This section discusses some of the most important tools that should be present in your toolkit.

Maintenance Kit

For many printers, the scheduled maintenance includes installing maintenance kits. Maintenance kits typically include components designed to wear out. For example, for laser printers, they contain a fuser, transfer roller, pickup rollers (for the trays), separation rollers, and feed rollers. For dot-matrix or inkjet printers, the components in the kit will be different.

 After installing the maintenance kit, you need to reset the maintenance counter as explained in the vendor's documentation.

Toner Vacuum

Sometimes accidents occur and toner gets spilled on the floor or carpet. You should never vacuum this up with a regular household vacuum cleaner. Toner particles may create static-electric charges when they rub against other particles or the interior of the vacuum or its hoses because of their electrostatic properties. If there is dust in the vacuum, static discharge can ignite it and create a small explosion. This may damage the vacuum cleaner or, worse, start a fire.

For spills into the printer, a special type of vacuum cleaner with an electrically conductive hose and a high-efficiency (HEPA) filter may be needed for effective cleaning. These are called electrostatic discharge-safe (ESD-safe) or toner vacuums. Similar vacuums should be used for cleaning up larger toner spills.

Compressed Air

Although compressed air is a good approach for cleaning out the inside of the case of a desktop computer, it's generally not a good idea to use compressed air to clean a printer.

Most manufacturers warn against this. If you insist on using compressed air, blow the dust out of the printer and not into it. A lint-free cloth is the best for removing dust when you can get at it.

Printer Spooler

The print spooler service controls the print queue. This service can be stopped and started to solve many software-related problems. Locate this service in the Services console and right-click it; you can first start and then stop the service. This can also be done at the command line using the `net stop spooler` and `net start spooler` commands.

Exam Essentials

Identify the most common symptoms of printing problems.   These include streaks, faded prints, ghost images, incompletely fused toner, creased paper, paper jams and feeding issues, no connectivity, garbled characters, vertical lines, print queue issues, low memory errors, permission issues, total print failure, and incorrect print colors.

List the tools used to address printer issues.   These tools include maintenance kits, toner vacuums, compressed air, and the printer spooler.

Review Questions

You can find the answers in the Appendix.

1. What is the most common reason for an unexpected reboot?
   - **A.** overheating
   - **B.** ESD damage
   - **C.** RFI
   - **D.** memory leak

2. Which if the following is typically not a cause of system lockups?
   - **A.** memory issues
   - **B.** virus
   - **C.** video driver
   - **D.** bad NIC driver

3. What process may generate beep cores during reboot?
   - **A.** SMART
   - **B.** POST
   - **C.** DCDIAG
   - **D.** BIOS

4. The system is not keeping the time correctly. What should you do?
   - **A.** reboot the machine
   - **B.** change the CMOS battery
   - **C.** change the boot order
   - **D.** replace the system clock

5. The system is rebooting unexpectedly and the system is NOT overheating. What other component could it be?
   - **A.** motherboard
   - **B.** power supply
   - **C.** CMOS battery
   - **D.** inverter

6. What should the ambient temperature be inside the case?
   - **A.** 60-90 degrees
   - **B.** 50-100 degrees
   - **C.** 30-70 degrees
   - **D.** 40-80 degrees

7. What is the proprietary screen crashes called in Windows?
   A. Pin wheel
   B. BSOD
   C. Bomb screen
   D. PSOID

8. Which operating system uses the pin wheel of death as a proprietary screen crash?
   A. Apple
   B. LINUX
   C. Windows
   D. UNIX

9. When procuring a replacement capacitor, which of the following need not match?
   A. voltage
   B. manufacturer
   C. same or larger capacity
   D. same external size

10. Which tool can be used to test a port?
    A. Power Supply Tester
    B. POST card
    C. Loopback plug
    D. multimeter

CompTIA A+
220-902

PART

II

Windows Operating Systems

COMPTIA A+ 220-902 EXAM OBJECTIVES COVERED IN THIS CHAPTER:

✓ **1.1 Compare and contrast various features and requirements of Microsoft operating systems (Windows Vista, Windows 7, Windows 8, Windows 8.1).**

- Features (32-bit vs. 64-bit, Aero, gadgets, user account control, BitLocker, shadow copy, system restore, ready boost, sidebar, compatibility mode, virtual XP mode, Easy Transfer, administrative tools, Defender, Windows Firewall, security center, event viewer, file structure and paths, category view vs. classic view, side-by-side apps, Metro UI, pinning, One Drive, Windows store, multimonitor taskbars, charms, start screen, PowerShell, live sign in, Action Center)

- Upgrade paths (differences between in-place upgrades, compatibility tools, Windows Upgrade OS Advisor)

✓ **1.2 Given a scenario, install Windows PC operating systems using appropriate methods.**

- Boot methods (USB, CD-ROM, DVD, PXE, solid-state/flash drives, NetBoot, external/hot-swappable drive, internal hard drive [partition])

- Types of installations (unattended installation, upgrade, clean install, repair installation, multiboot, remote network installation, image deployment, recovery partition, refresh/restore)

- Partitioning (dynamic, basic, primary, extended, logical, GPT)

- Filesystem types/formatting (ExFAT, FAT32, NTFS, CDFS, NFS, ext3, ext4, quick format vs. full format)

- Load alternate third-party drivers when necessary

- Workgroup vs. domain setup

- Time/date/region/language settings
- Driver installation, software, and Windows updates
- Factory recovery partition
- Properly formatted boot drive with the correct partitions/format

✓ **1.3   Given a scenario, apply appropriate Microsoft command-line tools.**

- TASKKILL
- BOOTREC
- SHUTDOWN
- TASKLIST
- MD
- RD
- CD
- DEL
- FORMAT
- COPY
- XCOPY
- ROBOCOPY
- DISKPART
- SFC
- CHKDSK
- GPUPDATE
- GPRESULT
- DIR
- EXIT
- HELP
- EXPAND
- [command name] /?
- Commands available with standard privileges vs. administrative privileges

✓ **1.4 Given a scenario, use appropriate Microsoft operating system features and tools.**

- Administrative (computer management, device manager, users and groups, local security policy, performance monitor, services, system configuration, task scheduler, component services, data sources, print management, Windows memory diagnostics, Windows Firewall, advanced security)

- MSCONFIG (general, boot, services, startup, tools)

- Task Manager (applications, processes, performance, networking, users)

- Disk management (drive status, mounting, initializing, extending partitions, splitting partitions, shrinking partitions, assigning/changing drive letters, adding drives, adding arrays, storage spaces)

- Other (User State Migration Tool [USMT], Windows Easy Transfer, Windows Upgrade Advisor)

- System utilities (REGEDIT, COMMAND, SERVICES.MSC, MMC, MSTSC, NOTEPAD, EXPLORER, MSINFO32, DXDIAG, DEFRAG, system restore, Windows Update)

✓ **1.5 Given a scenario, use Windows Control Panel utilities.**

- Internet options (connections, security, general, privacy, programs, advanced)

- Display/display settings (resolution, color depth, refresh rate)

- User accounts

- Folder options (view hidden files, hide extensions, general options, view options)

- System (performance [virtual memory], remote settings, system protection)

- Windows Firewall

- Power options (hibernate, power plans, sleep/suspend, standby)

- Programs and features

- HomeGroup

- Devices and printers

- Sound
- Troubleshooting
- Network and sharing center
- Device manager

✓ **1.6 Given a scenario, install and configure Windows networking on a client/desktop.**

- HomeGroup vs. WorkGroup
- Domain setup
- Network shares/administrative shares/mapping drives
- Printer sharing vs. network printer mapping
- Establish networking connections (VPN, dialups, wireless, wired, WWAN [cellular])
- Proxy settings
- Remote desktop connection
- Remote assistance
- Home vs. work vs. public network settings
- Firewall settings (exceptions, configuration, enabling/disabling Windows Firewall)
- Configuring an alternative IP address in Windows (IP addressing, subnet mask, DNS, gateway)
- Network card properties (half duplex/full duplex/auto, speed, wake-on-LAN, QoS, BIOS [on-board NIC])

✓ **1.7 Perform common preventive maintenance procedures using the appropriate Windows OS tools.**

- Best practices (scheduled backups, scheduled disk maintenance, Windows updates, patch management, driver/firmware updates, antivirus/antimalware updates)
- Tools (backup, system restore, recovery image, disk maintenance utilities)

The previous chapters mostly focused on the hardware and physical elements of the computing environment. You looked at the hardware that makes up a personal computer's and laptop's physical components, as well as networking, printers, and operational procedures. That completes the coverage of the topics on the 220-901 exam, and this chapter marks a departure from that.

In this chapter, the focus is on operating systems (OSs). To be specific, the focus is on Microsoft Windows operating systems, which you must know well for the 220-902 certification exam.

1.1 Compare and Contrast Various Features and Requirements of Microsoft Operating Systems (Windows Vista, Windows 7, Windows 8, and Windows 8.1)

While there are many operating systems available, this exam asks that you know the intricacies of only four that run on the personal computer, and all four are versions of Microsoft Windows: Windows Vista, Windows 7, Windows 8, and Windows 8.1.

This section contains numerous tables because of the nature of the information that it covers. It is imperative that you be familiar with Windows Vista, Windows 7, Windows 8, and Windows 8.1. Make certain you understand the features available in each of these versions of Windows as well as the editions that were made available for each of them. The topics covered in this chapter are as follows:

- Features
- Upgrade paths

Features

There are a number of features that separate one operating system—and even one edition of an operating system—from another. These features range from utilities that may or may not be present, up to whether the operating system is 32-bit or 64-bit. The sections that follow examine these features.

32-bit vs. 64-bit

The primary difference between 32-bit and 64-bit is the amount of data the processor (CPU) is able to process effectively. To run a 64-bit version of the operating system, you must have a 64-bit processor. To find out whether you are running the 32-bit or 64-bit version of Windows, you can look at the information shown in the System applet in the Control Panel in any of the Windows versions you need to know for this exam.

Aero, Gadgets, User Account Control, BitLocker, Shadow Copy, System Restore, Ready Boost, Sidebar, Compatibility Mode, Virtual XP Mode, Easy Transfer, Administrative Tools, Defender, Windows Firewall, Security Center, Event Viewer

There are a number of operating system features listed for this objective. Table 5.1 describes each of the features.

A Note About Procedures in This Chapter

Throughout this chapter are procedures that describe the path to locate a tool or utility. There are several views in which the Control Panel (which is frequently involved in these paths) can be set (Large Icons, Small Icons, Category View, and so on). Because you should be familiar with these views, I have used both views in the paths. In each procedure that had Control Panel tools as part of the path, I will tell you the view setting of Control Panel required for that path.

TABLE 5.1   Windows features

Feature	Significance
Aero	The Aero interface offers a glass design that includes translucent windows. It was new with Windows Vista.
Gadgets	These are mini programs, introduced with Windows Vista, that can be placed on the desktop (Windows 7) or on the Sidebar (Windows Vista), allowing them to run quickly and letting you personalize the PC (clock, weather, and so on). Windows 7 renamed these Windows Desktop Gadgets (right-click the desktop and click Gadgets in the context menu; then double-click the one you want to add). In 2011, Microsoft announced it is no longer supporting the development or uploading of new gadgets.
Sidebar	Windows Vista had an area known as the Sidebar designed for gadgets that could be placed on the desktop. Windows 7 did away with the Sidebar, and the gadgets are now placed directly on the desktop. Interestingly enough, though, sidebar.exe is the program that runs if any gadgets are installed.

Feature	Significance
User Account Control (UAC)	The UAC is intended to prevent unintentional or unauthorized changes to the computer by either prompting for permission to continue or requiring the administrator password before continuing. Changes to this from Windows Vista allow you to control how strict UAC intercedes.
BitLocker	What CompTIA calls BitLocker allows you to use drive encryption to protect files—including those needed for startup and logon. This is available with the Ultimate and Enterprise editions of Windows Vista and Windows 7 and the Pro and Enterprise editions of Windows 8 and 8.1. For removable drives, BitLocker To Go provides the same encryption technology to help prevent unauthorized access to the files stored on them.
Shadow Copy	The Volume Shadow Copy Service creates copies that you can recover from should a file be accidentally deleted or overwritten. Windows 7 adds to what Vista included by adding an interface for configuring storage used by volume shadow copies.
ReadyBoost	This feature allows you to use free space on a removable drive to speed up a system by caching content and is used when you are running low on available memory. In Windows 7, it can work with a USB drive, flash memory, SD card, or CompactFlash. Up to eight devices can employ ReadyBoost in Windows 7 (each needing a minimum of 256 MB of free space). ReadyBoost is configured from the ReadyBoost tab of the properties dialog box for the removable media device.
Compatibility Mode	Program Compatibility is included with Windows 7 to configure programs to believe they are running with an older version of Windows. Using Category view, choose Start ➢ Control Panel ➢ Programs and then click Run Programs Made For Previous Versions Of Windows.
Virtual XP Mode	Included with Windows 7 Professional, Enterprise, and Ultimate as well as Windows 8 is the ability to run applications in Windows XP Mode (XPM). This is a virtual client (emulating Windows XP Professional with Service Pack 3), which requires that you also download and install Windows Virtual PC to use. This can be downloaded from the Windows Virtual PC site at www.microsoft.com/windows/virtual-pc/. You should have 2 GB RAM and 15 GB hard drive space for each virtual Windows instance.
Easy Transfer	This feature can be used to migrate a few accounts from one OS to another (for a large number of accounts, Microsoft recommends using the User State Migration Tool [USMT]). It transfers both the accounts and the files and settings of the user. When transferring to Windows 7, you can download a version of Windows Easy Transfer in either the 32-bit or 64-bit version for Windows Vista from www.microsoft.com/downloads.

(continues)

TABLE 5.1 Windows features (*continued*)

Feature	Significance
Windows Firewall	Windows 7, as well as Windows Vista and Windows 8, incorporates Windows Firewall, which can be used to stop incoming and outgoing traffic. There are only three basic settings: On, Off, and Block All Incoming Connections.
Security Center	Rolled into the Action Center in Windows 7, this interface shows the status of, and allows you to configure, the firewall, Windows Update, virus protection, spyware and unwanted software protection, Internet security settings, UAC, and network access protection.
Defender	A free antimalware program included in Windows Vista, Windows 7, Windows 8, and Windows 8.1. Originally an antispyware program, in Windows 8 it was upgraded to include antivirus as well.

Four items are not shown in Table 5.1 because they are large enough to warrant more discussion than the table allows: System Restore, Administrative Tools, Event Viewer, and File Structure/Paths. Administrative Tools is a sizable portion of objective 1.4 and is not covered here to avoid needless repetition. The others are covered next.

System Restore

System Restore appears in Windows Vista, Windows 7, Windows 8, and Windows 8.1. It allows you to restore the system to a previous point in time. You can access this feature from Start ➤ All Programs ➤ Accessories ➤ System Tools ➤ System Restore to roll back as well as to create a restore point.

To create a restore point, you should access the System Protection tab of the System Properties dialog box. In Windows 7, that path using Category View is Start ➤ Control Panel ➤ System And Security ➤ System Protection ➤ System Restore. In Windows Vista, the path is Start ➤ All Programs ➤ Maintenance ➤ Backup And Restore Center ➤ Create A Restore Point Or Change Settings ➤ System Properties.

In Windows 8 and Windows 8.1, the path to System Restore is a bit more involved. Start by placing the cursor in the bottom-right corner of the screen and then click the Settings (gear) icon when the items appear on the right side of the screen. When another menu appears beneath that, select Change PC Settings.

You will then be presented with a menu on the left side of the screen; select Update And Recovery from this menu. When the submenu appears, select Recovery. At the next page, select Advanced Startup. This will restart the computer, and then you will land at the Advanced Startup screen. In the next three screens, select, in order, Troubleshooting, Advanced Options, and then System Restore. Once you've accessed System Restore, using it is no different from using it in Windows 7.

Event Viewer

Windows employs comprehensive error and informational logging routines. Every program and process theoretically could have its own logging utility, but Microsoft has come up with a rather slick utility, Event Viewer, which, through log files, tracks all events on a particular Windows computer. Normally, though, you must be an administrator or a member of the Administrators group to have access to Event Viewer.

The process for starting Event Viewer differs based on the operating system you are running, but always log in as an administrator (or equivalent). With Windows 7, using Small or Large icons view, choose Start ➤ Control Panel ➤ Administrative Tools ➤ Event Viewer; on earlier systems, choose Start ➤ Programs ➤ Administrative Tools ➤ Event Viewer (or you can always right-click the Computer desktop icon and choose Manage ➤ Event Viewer). In the resulting window (shown in Figure 5.1), you can view the System, Application, and Security log files. If you are running Windows 7, Windows 8, or Windows 8.1, you will also see log files available for Setup and Forwarded Events.

FIGURE 5.1   The opening interface of Event Viewer

- The System log file displays alerts that pertain to the general operation of Windows.
- The Application log file logs application errors.
- The Security log file logs security events such as login successes and failures.
- The Setup log will appear on domain controllers and will contain events specific to them.
- The Forwarded Events log contains events that have been forwarded to this log by other computers.

These log files can give a general indication of a Windows computer's health.

To access Event Viewer in Windows 8 and Windows 8.1, just type **event viewer** in the desktop Search box, and when the option for opening Event Viewer appears, select it.

One situation that does occur with Event Viewer is that the log files get full. Although this isn't really a problem, it can make viewing log files confusing because there are so many entries. Even though each event is time- and date-stamped, you should clear Event Viewer every so often. To do this, open Event Viewer, and in Windows 7, right-click the log, choose Properties, and click the Clear Log button; in earlier OSs, choose Clear All Events from the Log menu. Doing so erases all events in the current log file, allowing you to see new events more easily when they occur. You can set maximum log size by right-clicking the log and choosing Properties. By default, when a log fills to its maximum size, old entries are deleted in first in, first out (FIFO) order. Clearing the log, setting maximum log size, and setting how the log is handled when full are done in the Log Properties dialog, as shown in Figure 5.2.

FIGURE 5.2   Log Properties dialog

Log Properties - Application (Type: Administrative)

General | Subscriptions

Full Name:	Application
Log path:	%SystemRoot%\System32\Winevt\Logs\Application.evtx
Log size:	20.00 MB(20,975,616 bytes)
Created:	Wednesday, August 1, 2012 11:51:22 AM
Modified:	Monday, August 3, 2015 10:48:53 AM
Accessed:	Friday, November 2, 2012 11:29:35 AM

☑ Enable logging

Maximum log size (KB):   20480

When maximum event log size is reached:

◉ Overwrite events as needed (oldest events first)

◯ Archive the log when full, do not overwrite events

◯ Do not overwrite events (Clear logs manually)

Clear Log

OK   Cancel   Apply

You can save the log files before erasing them. The saved files can be burned to a CD or DVD for future reference. Often, you are required to save the files to CD or DVD if you are working in a company that adheres to strict regulatory standards.

In addition to just erasing logs, you can configure three different settings for what you want to occur when the file does reach its maximum size. The first option is Overwrite Events As Needed (Oldest Events First), which replaces the older events with the new entries. The second option is Archive The Log When Full, Do Not Overwrite Events, which will create another log file as soon as the current one runs out of space. The third option, Do Not Overwrite Events (Clear Logs Manually), will not record any additional events once the file is full.

File Structures and Paths

In the Windows environment, users are required to authenticate in some way (even if it is just as Guest) before gaining access to a user account. The operating system then uses a user profile to deliver the computer settings (theme, screen saver, and so on) that are configured for them. It is important to realize that the user account (which authenticates the user) and the user profile (which holds their settings) are two separate things—one is needed before the other.

Part of the user profile involves allowing each user to have a set of files that are specific to them. The same set of folders is automatically created for each user. While the address bar for a user often simply shows the location as edulaney, in reality the folder being viewed is beneath *%systemdrive%*\Users\ (usually C:\Users\).

> **NOTE** When settings need to apply to everyone who uses the machine, they can be placed in All Users instead of being copied beneath each user's folder set.

Whereas user files are placed in folders specific to them, system files are those used by the operating system and are used by all users. In all the operating systems you need to know for the exam, these files are beneath *%systemroot%*, and many, such as System32, appear in the default path. A number of files reside in this directory, with most residing in subdirectories.

> **NOTE** The variable *systemroot* (referenced as *%systemroot%*) is usually set to C:\Windows in the operating systems this exam focuses on. Because it is a variable, it can be changed to other values as well.

Temporary files are written to a system on an almost nonstop basis. The purpose behind these files is to hold any information that is needed for only a short time. In addition to temporary files used for print queues, you have cache from Internet sites and many other programs. You can manually pick files to delete, but one of the simplest solutions is to choose Properties for a drive and then click the General tab. A command button for the Disk Cleanup utility will appear, which you can use to delete most common temporary files, including the following:

- Downloaded program files
- Temporary Internet files
- Offline web pages

- Office setup files
- Recycle Bin contents
- Setup log files
- Temporary files
- Web client and publisher temporary files
- Temporary offline files
- Offline files
- Catalog files for the Content Indexer

The Program Files directory, beneath *%systemdrive%* (usually C:\), holds the files needed for each of the installed applications on a machine. Windows Vista also added a Program Data directory, which is hidden by default. It contains the settings needed for applications and works like the Local Settings folder did in previous operating systems. You will also find that any 64-bit version of Windows has two Program Files directories, one for 32-bit programs and another for 64-bit programs. The 32-bit program is called Program Files (x86). Keeping these two types of programs separate prevents placing any 32-bit restriction on 64-bit applications.

Category View vs. Classic View

In most of the operating systems you need to know for this exam, there are two ways of viewing the Control Panel and applets—Classic and Category views. CompTIA prefers the Classic view, but both will be used throughout the book, with the view used specified with each procedure.

Side-by-Side Apps

Windows 8.1 allows you to run a Metro application (also called at various times Tileworld apps and modern apps; these are apps you get at the Windows Store) and a desktop application at the same time, or up to four Metro apps at the same time, which on other devices such as a smartphone may not be possible.

To do this, you must split the screen into two parts, which can be done in two ways.

- If you have a keyboard, you can press Windows+< or Windows+>. The current app's window is now shoved to the left or right side. When you open a second app (from the Start screen or the app switcher), it fills the newly opened space.
- You can also drag the left edge of an open app and divide the screen.

Metro UI

In both Windows and Windows 8.1, the user interface is different from earlier versions of Windows. The Start menu was removed, and the desktop replaced with a new look called Metro. This look resembles the interface of a smartphone or tablet and represents the Microsoft vision of a common interface on all devices. Information, settings, and applications are housed in *tiles*. Figure 5.3 shows this look.

FIGURE 5.3   Start screen

This look received negative reaction from most desktop and laptop users and more positive reaction from those raised on the smartphone interface. Microsoft reacted by changing the name of the look to the Microsoft design language. While there were rumors of a return to the Start menu, Microsoft made the classic Start menu available in Windows 8.1 but by default stuck to its guns and continued to use a Start screen rather than a Start menu. (The Start screen is covered in the "Start Screen" section.)

Pinning

Pinning is the process of configuring an icon for a program on the taskbar so that it is easier to locate. It was introduced in Windows 7 and continued in Windows 8 and Windows 8.1, and for frequently used applications, it saves navigating through the Start menu or Start screen to locate the application.

To pin the program to the taskbar in Windows 7, do one of the following:

- If the program is running, right-click the program's button on the taskbar (or drag the button toward the desktop) to open the program's Jump List and then click Pin This Program To Taskbar.

- If the program is not running, click Start, find the program's icon, right-click the icon, and then click Pin To Taskbar.

To pin the program to the taskbar in Windows 8 and Windows 8.1, follow these steps:

1. Swipe in from the right edge of the screen and then tap Search. (If you're using a mouse, point to the lower-right corner of the screen, move the mouse pointer up, and then click Search.)

2. Enter the name of the program in the search box.

3. In the search results, swipe down on the program icon and then tap Pin To Taskbar (If you're using a mouse, right-click Internet Explorer and then click Pin To Taskbar.)

OneDrive

OneDrive is the cloud-based storage feature formerly known as SkyDrive that is Microsoft's answer to other cloud-based storage solutions such as Dropbox. User files that were stored in SkyDrive are still there, but in OneDrive. It is available in Windows 7, Windows 8, Windows 8.1, and Windows Vista with Service Pack 2 installed.

While the OneDrive desktop app must be installed on earlier versions of Windows (Vista, 7, and 8), this functionality is built into Windows 8.1. If you install the desktop app on a PC running Windows 8.1, Setup won't appear. A setting will be installed that lets you use Office to work on OneDrive documents with other people at the same time, but no other features will be installed.

OneDrive will appear with its own section in File Explorer, as shown in Figure 5.4, and you can work with the drive as you would any external drive. Users get 15 GB free and can add storage for a monthly fee.

FIGURE 5.4 OneDrive

Windows Store

The Windows Store is a site where you can purchase (in many cases the apps are free) Metro-style applications (the official name of the minute is Windows Store apps). It is available only to systems that can run these types of applications, which are Windows 8 and Windows 8.1 or Windows RT.

In Windows 8 and Windows 8.1, in many cases you may encounter a file that requires an application that is not present on the device. In the past, you could always right-click the file, select Open With, and choose an application or look for one on the Internet. A new option is to look in the Windows Store. In many cases, if you do so, you may be presented with a choice of options, some of which may be free. It is also possible that from time to time you may get notifications that an application you have needed in the past may now be available in the Windows Store as well.

Multimonitor Taskbar

Prior to Windows 8, if you set up multiple monitors, you could have the taskbar only on the primary monitor, which meant you have go back to that monitor (which may not be where you are currently engaged) to access the taskbar. In Windows 8 and 8.1, you can now have your taskbar on all monitors by selecting the option in the properties of the taskbar, as shown in Figure 5.5.

FIGURE 5.5   Enabling the multimonitor taskbar

Charms

Charms are a bit like icons and were introduced with Windows 8 and the Metro UI. They are organized on a Charms bar that will appear on the right side of the screen when invoked. With the mouse you bring up the bar by moving the cursor into the right corner of the desktop; on a touchscreen, you swipe from the right edge toward the center.

There are five charms there that are like doors to other lists of options. The five charms are Search, Share, Start, Devices, and Settings. The Start charm simply opens the Start screen, which replaces the Start menu. Figure 5.6 shows the Charms bar.

FIGURE 5.6   Charms bar

Start Screen

One of the more controversial changes that was made to the user interface with Windows 8 and Windows 8.1 was removing the Start menu and replacing it with the Start screen (shown previously in Figure 5.3). This is the screen that appears to be the future of all Windows operating systems, despite the resistance of many desktop and laptop users.

PowerShell

PowerShell is a powerful scripting tool that can be used to perform and therefore schedule and automate any function that can be done using other tools or the graphical interface. Functions are usually performed using cmdlets (pronounced "command-lets"), which are specialized .NET classes implementing a particular operation.

Windows Vista, Windows 7, Windows 8, and Windows 8.1 all include support for PowerShell. PowerShell Version 4.0 is integrated into Windows 8 and Windows 8.1, and the version of PowerShell in Windows 7 is updated when you add Service Pack 1. The version in Windows Vista can be updated only to version 2.0 and only when adding Service Pack 2.

Live Sign in

Another change Microsoft made with Windows 8.1 that was not well received was the use of Windows Live accounts as the logon account for the operating system. Although it is possible to designate a local account as the Administrator account during the installation or configuration of the operating system, Microsoft doesn't make the process simple and discourages the use of a local account at several points in the process.

The advantage to using a Microsoft account (this is any account used in the past to interact with Microsoft, such as a Hotmail, Xbox, or Office365 account) is that you can use to log into all your devices that are set up in this fashion with the account, and you can synchronize the desktop and data between the devices to make the experience on all devices as consistent as possible. Another advantage is that an account is required to get apps from the Windows Store. Moreover, some of the built-in apps require the use of a Windows Live account anyway (Calendar, Mail, and People).

The disadvantage is that if you have no Internet access, you can't be authenticated and validated by the Windows Live sign-in services. Luckily, Internet access is required only during the first time you log onto the device using your Windows Live account. After that, if you attempt to log in with no Internet access, you will be instructed to use the last password you used to log in. It will be looking for the last Windows Live password that was validated.

Action Center

The Action Center is part of the Windows Vista, Windows 7, Windows 8, and Windows 8.1 operating systems. This tool centralizes a number of security- and maintenance-related functions in one place. While the tool began life called the Windows Security Center in Windows Vista, its name was changed to Action Center in Windows 7.

Figure 5.7 shows the latest version of the Action Center in Windows 8.1. The Security section contains nine different security functions that can be monitored and configured from here, while the Maintenance section likewise contains six maintenance-related functions and tools.

FIGURE 5.7   Action Center

Upgrade Paths

There are several things to be aware of regarding upgrade paths, including the difference between in-place upgrades, compatibility tools, and the Windows Upgrade Advisor.

Differences Between In-Place Upgrades

One Windows operating system can often be upgraded to another, if compatible. With the case of Windows 7, it is even possible to upgrade from one edition of the operating system to another. When you are faced with a scenario in which you cannot upgrade, you can always do a clean installation. There's one more thing to consider when evaluating installation methods. Some methods work only if you're performing a clean installation and not an upgrade.

Table 5.2 lists the minimum system requirements for the various versions of Windows Vista.

TABLE 5.2   Windows Vista minimum hardware

Hardware	Minimum supported for all versions	Home Basic recommendation	Home Premium/Business/ Ultimate recommendation
Processor	800 MHz	1 GHz 32-bit (x86) or 64-bit (x64) processor	1 GHz 32-bit (x86) or 64-bit (x64) processor
Memory	512 MB	512 MB	1 GB

TABLE 5.2   Windows Vista minimum hardware *(continued)*

Hardware	Minimum supported for all versions	Home Basic recommendation	Home Premium/Business/Ultimate recommendation
Free hard disk space	15 GB free on a 20 GB drive	15 GB free on a 20 GB drive	15 GB free on a 40 GB drive
CD-ROM or DVD	CD-ROM	DVD-ROM	DVD-ROM
Video	SVGA	Support for DirectX 9 graphics and 32 MB graphics memory	Support for DirectX 9 with WDDM Driver, 128 MB of graphics memory; Pixel Shader 2.0 in hardware; 32 bits per pixel
Mouse	Required (but not listed as a requirement)	Required (but not listed as a requirement)	Required (but not listed as a requirement)
Keyboard	Required (but not listed as a requirement)	Required (but not listed as a requirement)	Required (but not listed as a requirement)
Internet access	Not listed as a requirement	Required	Required

Table 5.3 lists the minimum system requirements for the various versions of Windows 7.

TABLE 5.3   Windows 7 minimum hardware

Hardware	Minimum supported for all versions
Processor	1 GHz
Memory	1 GB for 32-bit; 2 GB for 64-bit
Free hard disk space	16 GB free for 32-bit; 20 GB free for 64-bit
CD-ROM or DVD	DVD-ROM
Video	DirectX 9 with WDDM 1.0 (or higher) driver
Mouse	Required (but not listed as a requirement)
Keyboard	Required (but not listed as a requirement)
Internet access	Not listed as a requirement

Table 5.4 lists the minimum system requirements for Windows 8, and Table 5.5 lists the minimum system requirements for Windows 8.1.

TABLE 5.4   Windows 8 minimum hardware

Hardware	Minimum supported for all versions of Windows 8
Processor	1 GHz with support for PAE, NX and SSE
Memory	1 GB for 32-bit; 2 GB for 64-bit
Free hard disk space	16 GB free for 32-bit; 20 GB free for 64-bit
CD-ROM or DVD	DVD-ROM
Video	DirectX 9 with WDDM 1.0 (or higher) driver

TABLE 5.5   Windows 8.1 minimum hardware

Hardware	Minimum supported for all versions of Windows 8.1
Processor	1 GHz with support for PAE, NX and SSE
Memory	1 GB for 32-bit; 2 GB for 64-bit
Free hard disk space	16 GB free for 32-bit; 20 GB free for 64-bit
CD-ROM or DVD	DVD-ROM
Video	DirectX 9 with WDDM 1.0 (or higher) driver

If there is one thing to be learned from Tables 5.3 through 5.5, it is that Microsoft is nothing if not optimistic. For your own sanity, though, I strongly suggest that you always take the minimum requirements with a grain of salt. They are minimums. Even the recommended requirements should be considered minimums. Bottom line: Make sure you have a good margin between your system's performance and the minimum requirements listed. Always run Windows on more hardware rather than less!

Certain features in Windows 7 have further hardware requirements that are listed here:

http://windows.microsoft.com/en-US/windows7/products/
system-requirements

The easiest way to see whether your current hardware can run Windows 7 is to download and run the Windows 7 Upgrade Advisor available here:

http://windows.microsoft.com/en-us/windows/downloads/
upgrade-advisor

You can also always check hardware in the Windows 7 Compatibility Center here:

www.microsoft.com/windows/compatibility/windows-7/en-us/
default.aspx

Upgrading to Windows Vista

With Windows Vista you can upgrade to various versions based on the operating system that you are coming from. Table 5.6 lists the upgrade paths for each Windows Vista version based on the operating system you are coming from. Those listed as "No" must be clean installations.

TABLE 5.6   Windows Vista upgrade options

Existing operating system	Vista Home Basic	Vista Home Premium	Vista Business	Vista Ultimate
Windows XP Home	Yes	Yes	Yes	Yes
Windows XP Professional	No	No	Yes	Yes
Windows XP Professional x64	No	No	No	No
Windows XP Media Center (2002 Edition)	No	No	No	No
Windows XP Media Center (2004 and 2005 Edition)	No	Yes	No	Yes
Windows XP Tablet PC	No	No	Yes	Yes
Windows Vista Home Basic	N/A	Yes	No	Yes

(continue)

TABLE 5.6 Windows Vista upgrade options *(continued)*

Existing operating system	Vista Home Basic	Vista Home Premium	Vista Business	Vista Ultimate
Windows Vista Home Premium	No	N/A	No	Yes
Windows Vista Business	No	No	N/A	Yes
Windows Vista Ultimate	No	No	No	N/A

For the exam, recognize that no version of Windows older than Windows XP can be upgraded to Windows Vista.

Note that Windows Vista Enterprise does not appear in Table 5.6 because it is typically done as a clean install. The only "upgrade" possibility with it is that it can be installed over Windows Vista Business. Note as well that where "N/A" appears in Table 5.6, it is always possible to do a repair installation or clean installation but not a true upgrade.

A clean installation is one that keeps no previous settings and copies over or removes the old operating system. An upgrade installation is one that keeps previous settings (usually related to accounts and configuration) from the older operating system. A repair installation involves keeping the same operating system and performing a reinstall of system files.

Upgrading to Windows 7

If you want to do an upgrade instead of a clean installation, review the upgrade options in Table 5.7 (it is worth pointing out again that a "No" does not mean you can't buy the upgrade version of Windows 7 but rather that you can't keep your files, programs, and settings).

TABLE 5.7 Windows 7 upgrade options

Existing operating system	Windows 7 Home Premium 32-bit	Windows 7 Home Premium 64-bit	Windows 7 Professional 32-bit	Windows 7 Professional 64-bit	Windows 7 Ultimate 32-bit	Windows 7 Ultimate 64-bit
Windows XP	No	No	No	No	No	No
Windows Vista Starter 32-bit	No	No	No	No	No	No

TABLE 5.7   Windows 7 upgrade options *(continued)*

Existing operating system	Windows 7 Home Premium 32-bit	Windows 7 Home Premium 64-bit	Windows 7 Professional 32-bit	Windows 7 Professional 64-bit	Windows 7 Ultimate 32-bit	Windows 7 Ultimate 64-bit
Windows Vista Starter 64-bit	No	No	No	No	No	No
Windows Vista Home Basic 32-bit	Yes	No	No	No	Yes	No
Windows Vista Home Basic 64-bit	No	Yes	No	No	No	Yes
Windows Vista Home Premium 32-bit	Yes	No	No	No	Yes	No
Windows Vista Home Premium 64-bit	No	Yes	No	No	No	Yes
Windows Vista Business 32-bit	No	No	Yes	No	Yes	No
Windows Vista Business 64-bit	No	No	No	Yes	No	Yes
Windows Vista Ultimate 32-bit	No	No	No	No	Yes	No
Windows Vista Ultimate 64-bit	No	No	No	No	No	Yes

The Enterprise versions play by different rules since they are licensed directly from Microsoft. In the case of Windows 7, both Windows Vista Business and Windows Vista Enterprise can be upgraded to Windows 7 Enterprise.

Those operating systems not listed in Table 5.7 do not include any upgrade options to Windows 7 and cannot be done with upgrade packages (you must buy the full version of Windows 7). An easy way to remember upgrade options for the exam is that you must have at least Windows Vista to be able to upgrade to Windows 7. In the real world, the Windows Vista machine should be running Service Pack 1 at a minimum, and you can always take an earlier OS and upgrade it to Vista SP1 and then upgrade to Windows 7.

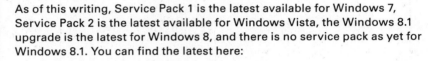

As of this writing, Service Pack 1 is the latest available for Windows 7, Service Pack 2 is the latest available for Windows Vista, the Windows 8.1 upgrade is the latest for Windows 8, and there is no service pack as yet for Windows 8.1. You can find the latest here:

http://windows.microsoft.com/en-US/windows/downloads/service-packs

In the past, all service packs used to be cumulative—meaning you needed to load only the last one. Starting with XP SP3, however, all Windows service packs released have been incremental, meaning that you must install the previous ones before you can install the new one.

Microsoft created the Windows 7 Upgrade Advisor to help with the upgrade to this operating system. You can download the advisor from http://windows.microsoft.com/upgradeadvisor. It will scan your hardware, devices, and installed programs for any known compatibility issues. Once it is finished, it will give you advice on how to resolve the issues found and recommendations on what to do before you upgrade. The reports are divided into three categories: System Requirements, Devices, and Programs.

After all incompatibilities have been addressed, the upgrade can be started from an installation disc or from a download (preferably to a USB drive). If the setup routine does not begin immediately on boot, look for the setup.exe file and run it. When the Install Windows page appears, click Install Now.

You'll be asked if you want to get any updates (recommended) and to agree to the license agreement. After you've done so, choose Upgrade for the installation type and follow the steps to walk through the remainder of the installation. I highly recommend that after the installation is complete, you run Windows Update to get the latest drivers.

New to Windows 7 is the ability at any time to upgrade from one edition of the operating system to a higher one (for example, from Home Premium to Professional) using the Windows Anytime Upgrade utility in the System And Security section of the Control Panel (it can also be accessed by clicking the Start button and choosing All Programs; scroll down the list and choose Windows Anytime Upgrade).

Upgrading to Windows 8

With Windows 8 you can upgrade based on the operating system that you are coming from. Table 5.8 lists the upgrade paths for each Windows version based on the operating system you are coming from. Those listed as "No" must be clean installations.

TABLE 5.8   Upgrade paths for Windows 8

Existing operating system	Windows 8	Windows 8 Pro	Windows 8 Enterprise
Windows 7 Starter	Yes	Yes	No
Windows 7 Home Basic	Yes	Yes	No
Windows 7 Home Premium	Yes	Yes	No
Windows 7 Professional	No	Yes	No
Windows 7 Ultimate	No	Yes	No
Windows 7 Pro (volume licensed)	No	No	Yes
Windows 7 Enterprise (volume licensed)	No	No	Yes
Windows 8 (volume licensed)	No	No	Yes

Upgrading to Windows 8.1

With Windows 8.1 you can upgrade based on the operating system that you are coming from. Table 5.9 lists the upgrade paths for each Windows version based on the operating system you are coming from. Those listed as "No" must be clean installations.

TABLE 5.9   Upgrade paths for Windows 8.1

Existing operating system	Windows 8.1	Windows 8.1 Pro	Windows 8.1 Enterprise
Windows 8	Yes	Yes	No
Windows 8 Pro	No	Yes	Yes
Windows 8 Pro with Media Center	No	Yes	Yes
Windows 8.1	No	Yes	No
Windows 8 Enterprise	No	No	No
Windows 8.1 Pro	No	No	Yes

Windows Upgrade OS Advisor

The Windows Vista Upgrade Advisor from Microsoft can be useful in any upgrade process. It will check your system, verify that it can run the desired operating system, and give you a report of any identified compatibility issues. There are also versions for Windows 7, Windows 8, and Windows 8.1.

To begin the upgrade, insert the DVD, and the Setup program should automatically begin (if it doesn't, run setup.exe from the root folder). From the menu that appears, choose Install Now and then select Upgrade when the Which Type Of Installation Do You Want? screen appears. Answer the prompts to walk through the upgrade.

Booting from the DVD is also possible but recommended only if the method just described does not work. When you boot, you will get a message upon startup that says Press Any Key To Boot From CD, and at this point you simply press a key. (Don't worry that it is a DVD and not a CD.)

Compatibility Tools

Beyond the Compatibility Mode discussed in the Table 5.1, several other features are available to enhance the compatibility of the operating system with the applications you are running. First there is the Windows Compatibility Center, a site you can access that will scan your device for compatible device drivers, app updates, and downloads. You just enter the name of the program, and it will tell you whether it is supported; if you need a driver or an update, it will provide it.

In some cases, it may not be possible to use an application without creating a shim, which is a small piece of software that communicates between the unsupported application and the operating system. This is done with an Application Compatibility toolkit. There are such toolkits for Windows Vista, Windows 7, Windows 8, and Windows 8.1. Their use is beyond the scope of this book.

Exam Essentials

Understand version and edition differences of Windows.   For each version of Windows (Windows Vista, Windows 7, Windows 8, and Windows 8.1), know how to group the editions (Home, Professional, and so on) according to similarity and explain how one group differs from the other.

Know the system requirements of Windows.   You should know the minimum system requirements for Windows Vista, Windows 7, and Windows 8.1.

Understand upgrading.   You should know that an installation overwrites any existing files, whereas an upgrade keeps the same data/application files.

1.2 Given a Scenario, Install Windows PC Operating Systems Using Appropriate Methods

The focus of this objective is on installing and configuring the Windows operating systems discussed in the previous section. Some of the topics that CompTIA lists here also appear beneath other objectives and they are touched on here only to avoid needless repetition. The topics covered in this section include the following:

- Boot methods
- Types of installations
- Partitioning
- Filesystem types/formatting
- Loading alternate third-party drivers when necessary
- Workgroup vs. domain setup
- Time/date/region/language settings
- Driver installation and software and Windows updates
- Factory recovery partition
- Properly formatted boot drive with the correct partitions/format

Boot Methods

You can begin the installation or upgrade process by booting from a number of sources. There are eight in particular that CompTIA wants you to be familiar with: USB, CD-ROM, DVD, PXE, solid-state or flash drives, NetBoot, external/hot swappable drives, and internal hard drives.

USB

Most systems will allow you to boot from a USB device, but you must often change the BIOS settings to look for USB first. Using a large USB drive, you can store all the necessary installation files on the one device and save the time of needing to swap media.

CD-ROM

The most commonly used for an attended installation is the CD-ROM/DVD boot (they are identical). Since Windows 7 and newer come only on DVD, though, CD-ROM applies to older operating systems and not this one.

DVD

A DVD boot is the most common method of starting an installation.

PXE

Booting the computer from the network without using a local device creates a *Preboot Execution Environment* (PXE). Once it is up, it is common to load the Windows Preinstallation Environment (WinPE) into RAM as a stub operating system and install the operating system image to the hard drive.

WinPE can be installed onto a bootable CD, USB, or network drive using the copype .cmd command. This environment can be used in conjunction with a Windows deployment from a server for unattended installations.

Solid-State/Flash Drives

If boot files and installation files are located on a solid-state drive or flash drive and the device is set to look on those drives for boot files, you can boot from these devices and install the operating system in the same way that you boot from a CD or DVD drive.

NetBoot

NetBoot is a method developed by Apple that allows an Apple device to boot from a network location rather than from the hard drive. The device uses DHCP to receive a network configuration and to receive the IP address of a TFTP server from which the device will download an operating system image from a server. This entire process is similar to the way an IP phone learns through DHCP the IP address of the server from which it downloads its configuration file.

NetInstall is a related Apple technology that uses a similar process to install an image on an Apple device. It is similar in concept to Windows Deployment Services.

External/Hot-Swappable Drives

Just as boot files can be located on a USB drive, CD, DVD, and flash drive, they can also be located on an external hard drive. Most of these drives are also hot-swappable (you can connect and remove them with the devices on). As always, you will probably have to alter the boot order of the device so that it looks on the external drive before the other drives if boot files are also located in these locations.

Internal Hard Drive (Partition)

Finally, the most common location of boot files is on the internal hard drive. These files are placed there during the installation and will be executed as long as the device is set to look for them there. By default most systems are set to look on the internal hard drive first, and even if the device is not set to look there first, it will eventually boot to those files if there are no boot files located on any of the other drives or boot sources.

Types of Installations

Operating system installations can be lumped into two generic methods: attended or unattended. During an attended installation, you walk through the installation and answer the questions as prompted. Questions typically ask for the product key, the directory in which you want to install the OS, and relevant network settings.

As simple as attended installations may be, they're time-consuming and administrator-intensive in that they require someone to fill in a fair number of fields to move through the process. Unattended installations allow you to configure the OS with little or no human intervention. Table 5.10 shows you four common unattended installation methods and when they can be used.

TABLE 5.10 Windows unattended installation methods

Method	Clean installation	Upgrade
Unattended Install	Yes	Yes
Bootable media	Yes	No
Sysprep	Yes	No
Remote install	Yes	No

Another decision you must make is which method you are going to use to access the Windows installation files. It is possible to boot to the installation DVD and begin the installation process. However, your system must have a system BIOS that is capable of supporting bootable media.

If you don't have a bootable DVD, you must first boot the computer using some other bootable media, which then loads the disk driver so that you can access the installation program on the DVD.

Creating an Image

Creating an image isn't actually an objective, but it is something important that you'll need to know how to do in the real world. Creating an image involves taking a snapshot of a model system (often called a *reference computer*) and then applying it to other systems (see the section "Image Deployment" later). A number of third-party vendors offer packages that can be used to create images, and you can use the system preparation tool, or *Sysprep*. The Sysprep utility works by making an exact image or replica of the reference computer (sometimes also called the *master computer*), to be installed on other computers. Sysprep removes the master computer's security ID (a process sometimes called *generalization*) and will generate new IDs for each computer the image is used to install.

All Sysprep does is create the system image. You still need a cloning utility to copy the image to other computers.

Perhaps the biggest caveat to using Sysprep is that because you are making an exact image of an installed computer (including drivers and settings), all the computers that you will be installing the image on need to be identical (or close) to the configuration of the master computer. Otherwise, you would have to go through and fix driver problems on every installed computer. Sysprep images can be installed across a network or copied to a CD or DVD for local installation. Sysprep cannot be used to upgrade a system; plan on all data on the system (if there is any) being lost after a format.

 Similar to Sysprep, ImageX is the preferred command-line utility for imaging Windows 7. You can find more information about it at http:// technet.microsoft.com/en-us/library/cc722145(v=ws.10).

Several third-party vendors provide similar services, and you'll often hear the process referred to as *disk imaging* or *drive imaging*. The third-party utility makes the image, and then the image file is transferred to the computer without an OS. You boot the new system with the imaging software and start the image download. The new system's disk drive is made into an exact sector-by-sector copy of the original system.

Imaging has major upsides. The biggest one is speed. In larger networks with multiple new computers, you can configure tens to hundreds of computers by using imaging in just hours, rather than the days it would take to individually install the OS, applications, and drivers.

Unattended Installation

Answering the myriad of questions posed by Windows Setup doesn't qualify as exciting work for most people. Fortunately, there is a way to answer the questions automatically: through an unattended installation. In this type of installation, an *answer file* is supplied with all the correct parameters (time zone, regional settings, administrator username, and so on), so no one needs to be there to tell the computer what to choose or to hit Next 500 times.

Unattended installations are great because they can be used to upgrade operating systems. The first step is to create an answer file. Generally speaking, you'll want to run a test installation using that answer file first before deploying it on a large scale because you'll probably need to make some tweaks to it. After you create your answer file, place it on a network share that will be accessible from the target computer. (Most people put it in the same place as the Windows installation files for convenience.)

Boot the computer that you want to install on using a boot disk or CD, and establish the network connection. Once you start the setup process, everything should run automatically.

Upgrade

An upgrade involves moving from one operating system to another and keeping as many of the settings as possible. An example of an upgrade would be changing the operating system on a laptop computer from Windows Vista to Windows 7 and keeping the user accounts that existed.

It is also possible to upgrade from one edition of an operating system to another—for example, from Windows 7 Professional to Windows 7 Ultimate. This is known as a Windows 7 *Anytime Upgrade*.

Clean Install

With a clean installation, you overwrite the operating system that existed on a machine and place a new one there. An example of a clean installation would be changing the operating system on a laptop from Windows Vista to Windows 7. The user accounts and other settings that existed with Windows Vista would be removed in the process and need to be re-created under Windows 7.

Repair Installation

A repair installation overwrites system files with a copy of new ones from the same operating system version and edition. For example, a laptop running Windows 7 is hanging on boot, and the cause is traced to a corrupted system file. A repair installation can replace that corrupted file with a new one (from the DVD or other source) without changing the operating system or settings (for configuration, accounts, and so on).

Multiboot

Multiple operating systems can exist on the same machine in one of two popular formats: in a multiboot configuration or in virtual machines. With a multiboot configuration, when you boot the machine, you choose which operating system you want to load of those that are installed. You could, for example, boot into Windows Vista, reboot and bring up Windows 7, reboot and bring up Windows 8, and test a software application you've created in each OS. It is possible, in this scenario, to have multiple editions of the same OS installed (Professional, Ultimate, and so forth) and choose which to boot into in order to test your application. The key to this configuration, however, is that you can have only one operating system running at a time.

An alternative to multiboot that has become more popular in recent years is to run virtual machines. You could boot into Windows 7, for example, and run a virtual machine of Windows Vista and one of Windows 8 and test your application in the three environments that are all running at the same time.

Remote Network Installation

Older Windows Server operating systems have a feature called Remote Installation Service (RIS), which allows you to perform several network installations at one time. Beginning with Windows Server 2003 SP2, RIS was replaced by Windows Deployment Service (WDS). This utility offers the same functionality as RIS.

A *network installation* is handy when you have many installs to do and installing by CD is too much work. In a network installation, the installation CD is copied to a shared location on the network. Then individual workstations boot and access the network share. The workstations can boot either through a boot disk or through a built-in network boot device known as a PXE ROM. Boot ROMs essentially download a small file that contains an OS and network drivers and has enough information to boot the computer in a limited fashion. At the least, it can boot the computer so it can access the network share and begin the installation.

Image Deployment

System images created with Sysprep and other tools can be deployed for installation on hosts across the network. The Windows Automated Installation Kit (AIK) can be useful for this purpose (http://technet.microsoft.com/library/dd349348.aspx).

Recovery Partition

In the past, many devices that were purchased with the operating system installed by the OEM came with recovery media that could be used to boot the device and recover or replace the operating system if needed. Now many come with an additional partition on the drive called a *recovery partition*. The users could use specific key sequence during bootup that would cause the device to boot to the recovery partition and make available tools to either recover the installation or replace it. The downside of this approach is that if the hard drive fails or if the partition is overwritten, the receiver partition is useless. In an effort to address this concern, many OEMs now make available recovery media if requested by the user.

Refresh/Restore/Reset

Windows 8 and 8.1 offer three methods of dealing with a device that either won't boot, is corrupted, or is simply performing badly. These two options are refresh and restore, and it is critical that you understand the consequences of each. When a refresh is performed, the user's data is unaffected, while the operating system is returned to the factory default state. While the data remains intact, any applications or programs that the user installed will be gone. All default applications that come with the system will remain, and any purchased from the Windows Store will remain as well. When a restore is performed, the system is retired to a point in time in the past. It removes no user data, but any configuration changes made or programs and service packs installed since that point in time will be gone. A third option is the reset, which removes all data and programs and reinstalls a fresh version of the operating system.

Partitioning

For a hard disk to be able to hold files and programs, it has to be partitioned and formatted. Partitioning is the process of creating logical divisions on a hard drive. A hard drive can have one or more partitions. Formatting is the process of creating and configuring a file allocation table (FAT) and creating the root directory. Several filesystem types are supported by the various versions of Windows, such as FAT16, FAT32, and NTFS (partitions are explored later in the discussion of disk management under objective 1.4).

The partition that the operating system boots from must be designated as *active*. Only one partition on a disk may be marked active. Each hard disk can be divided into a total of four partitions, either four primary partitions or three primary and one extended partition. Some of the other possibilities are examined in the following sections.

Dynamic

Partitions can be made dynamic, which—as the name implies—have the ability to be configured and reconfigured on the fly. The big benefit they offer is that they can increase in size (without reformatting) and can span multiple physical disks. Dynamic partitions can be simple, spanned, or striped.

Dynamic partitions that are simple are similar to primary partitions and logical drives (which exist on basic partitions, discussed next). This is often the route you choose when you have only one dynamic disk and want the ability to change allocated space as needed.

Spanned means that you want space from a number of disks (up to 32) to appear as a single logical volume to the users. A minimum of two disks must be used, and no fault tolerance is provided by this option.

Striped is similar to spanned in that multiple disks are used, but the big difference is that data is written (in fixed-size stripes) across the disk set in order to increase I/O performance. Although read operations are faster, a concern is that if one disk fails, none of the data is retrievable (like spanned, there is no fault tolerance).

Basic

With basic storage, Windows drives can be partitioned with *primary* or *logical* partitions. Basic partitions are a fixed size and are always on a single physical disk. This is the simplest storage solution and has been the traditional method of storing data for many years.

You can change the size of primary and logical drives by *extending* them into additional space on the same disk. You can create up to four partitions on a basic disk, either four primary or three primary and one extended.

Primary

A primary partition contains the boot files for an operating system. In older days, the operating system had to also be on that partition, but with the Windows versions you need to know for this exam, the OS files can be elsewhere as long as the boot files are in that primary partition.

Primary partitions cannot be further subdivided.

Extended

Extended partitions differ from primary in that they can be divided into one or more logical drives, each of which can be assigned a drive letter.

Logical

In reality, all partitions are logical in the sense that they don't necessarily correspond to one physical disk. One disk can have several logical divisions (partitions). A logical partition is any partition that has a drive letter.

> **NOTE** Sometimes, you will also hear of a logical partition as one that spans multiple physical disks. For example, a network drive that you know as drive H: might actually be located on several physical disks on a server. To the user, all that is seen is one drive, or H:.

GPT

Devices that use the Unified Extensible Firmware Interface (UEFI) specification (discussed in the section "1.1 Given a Scenario, Configure Settings and Use BIOS/UEFI Tools on a PC" in Chapter 1) instead of a BIOS also use a partitioning standard called GUID Partition Table (GPT). Since 2010, most operating systems support this and using a master boot record (MBR), which is the alternative method of booting to a legacy BIOS firmware interface. Today, almost all operating systems support it, and many *only* support booting from a GPT rather than MBR.

Moreover, it is also used on some BIOS systems because of the limitations of MBR partition tables, which was the original driver for the development of UEFI and GPT to begin with. MBR works with disks up to 2 TB in size, but it can't handle disks with more than 2 TB of space. MBR also supports only up to four primary partitions, so to have more than four, you had to make one of your primary partitions an "extended partition" and create logical partitions inside it. GPT removes both of these limitations. It allows up to 128 partitions on a GPT drive.

Filesystem Types/Formatting

New Technology Filesystem (NTFS) is available with all the versions of Windows you need to know for the exam, but all versions also recognize and support FAT16 and FAT32. The file table for the NTFS is called the Master File Table (MFT).

This section lists the major filesystems that are used with Windows and the differences among them.

ExFAT

Extended File Allocation Table (exFAT) is a Microsoft filesystem optimized for flash drives. It is proprietary and has also been adopted by the SD Card Association as the default filesystem for SDXC cards larger than 32 GB. The proprietary nature and licensing requirements make this filesystem difficult to use in any open source or commercial software. This filesystem is supported in Windows 7, Windows 8, and Windows 8.1. It is also supported in Windows Vista with either Service Pack 1 or Service Pack 2.

FAT32

FAT, which stands for File Allocation Table, is an acronym for the file on a filesystem used to keep track of where files are. It's also the name given to this type of filesystem, introduced in 1981. The largest FAT disk partition that could be created was approximately 2 GB. FAT32 was introduced along with Windows 95 OEM Service Release 2. As disk sizes grew, so did the need to be able to format a partition larger than 2 GB. FAT32 was based more on VFAT than on FAT16. It allowed for 32-bit cluster addressing, which in turn provided for a maximum partition size of 2 TB (2048 GB). It also included smaller cluster sizes to avoid wasted space (discussed later). FAT32 support is included in current Windows versions.

NTFS

Introduced along with Windows NT (and available on Windows 7, Vista, Windows 8, and Windows 8.1), NT File System (NTFS) is a much more advanced filesystem in almost every way than all versions of the FAT filesystem. It includes such features as individual file security and *compression*, RAID support, and support for extremely large file and partition sizes and disk transaction monitoring. It is the filesystem of choice for higher-performance computing.

CDFS

While not a filesystem that can be used on a hard drive, CD-ROM File System (CDFS) is the filesystem of choice for CD media and has been used with 32-bit Windows versions since Windows 95. A CD mounted with the CDFS driver appears as a collection.

NFS

Network File System (NFS) is a distributed filesystem protocol originally developed by Sun Microsystems. While it is supported on some Windows systems, it is primarily used on Unix-based systems; the SMB-based Common Internet File System (CIFS) is more common on Windows systems for access to resources on other devices. To support NFS, Windows systems make available the client for NFS. While the client for NFS is available in Windows Vista and Windows 7, the Services for the Network File System (NFS) feature is available only in the Windows 8 Enterprise edition. This feature is not available in Windows 8 and Windows 8 Pro editions.

ext3, ext4

ext3 and ext4 are Linux filesystems. While ext4 has the following advantages, it should be noted that it is not compatible with Windows, while ext3 is. The following are the strengths of ext4:

- It supports individual file sizes up to 16 TB.
- The overall maximum ext4 filesystem size is 1 EB (exabyte); 1 EB = 1024 PB (petabyte), and 1 PB = 1024 TB (terabyte).
- The directory can contain 64,000 subdirectories as opposed to 32,000 in ext3.

- You can mount an existing ext3 fs as ext4 fs (without having to upgrade it).

- It improves the performance and reliability of the filesystem when compared to ext3.

- In ext4, you also have the option of turning off the journaling feature.

Quick Format vs. Full Format

When you're installing any Windows OS, you will be asked first to format the drive using one of these disk technologies. Choose the disk technology based on what the computer will be doing and which OS you are installing.

To format a partition, you can use the FORMAT command. FORMAT.EXE is available with all versions of Windows. You can run FORMAT by using the command prompt or by right-clicking a drive in Windows Explorer and selecting Format. However, when you install Windows, it performs the process of partitioning and formatting for you if a partitioned and formatted drive does not already exist. You can usually choose between a *quick format* or a *full format*. With both formats, files are removed from the partition; the difference is that a quick format does not then check for bad sectors (a time-consuming process).

 Be extremely careful with the FORMAT command! When you format a drive, all data on the drive is erased.

Load Alternate Third-Party Drivers When Necessary

During the installation of Windows, it may be necessary to load a third-party driver that you update later. The goal during installation is to get the operating system up and running and in a state where you can interact with it. Some of the drivers included with media are not the latest from the vendor but can be used to complete the installation. Once installation is done, you can access the website of third-party vendors and download and then install the latest drivers.

Time/Date/Region Language Settings

During installation of the operating system, you are asked to choose the correct settings for the local time, date, and region. As was mentioned earlier, the goal during installation is to complete the process as quickly as possible, and you may need to tweak these settings later.

Once the installation is complete, there are a number of ways to change these values, the easiest of which is to right-click the clock in the lower-right corner of the taskbar and choose Adjust Date/Time. In the Control Panel, you can choose the Region And Language applet to configure date and time formats, as well as change language and location settings. Language interface packs (LIPs) are available that can be installed to modify what appears in wizards, dialog boxes, and such (see http://windows.microsoft.com/en-US/windows7/Install-or-change-a-display-language for more information).

Driver Installation, Software, and Windows Updates

During the installation process of Windows Vista, Windows 7, Windows 8, and Windows 8.1, you will be presented with the option to download any required updates and new driver packages that may have become available since the time the installation DVD was created. If the device will have an active Internet connection, you may want to take advantage of this because it will download the required files and make them part of the installation. If this is not an option, you can always perform this step by visiting Windows Update after the installation.

Properly Formatted Boot Drive with Correct Partitions/ Format

Clearly it important to properly create and format the boot drive prior to the installation. Please review the sections "Partitioning," "File System Types/Formatting," and "Quick Format vs. Full Format."

Other Concerns

This objective also lists a number of other topics that can be lumped into two areas: workgroup vs. domain, and factory recovery partitions. These reappear beneath other objectives within this domain and are not discussed here since they are explored elsewhere in this chapter.

Exam Essentials

Know the difference between basic and dynamic partitions.   Basic partitions are a fixed size and are always on a single physical disk. Dynamic partitions can increase in size (without reformatting) and can span multiple physical disks.

Be familiar with the various boot methods.   You can begin the installation or upgrade process by booting from a number of sources. There are four in particular that CompTIA wants you to be familiar with: USB, CD-ROM, DVD, and PXE. The most commonly used for an attended installation is the CD-ROM/DVD boot.

1.3 Given a Scenario, Apply Appropriate Microsoft Command-Line Tools

Although the exam is on the Windows operating systems, it tests many concepts that carry over from the Microsoft Disk Operating System (MS-DOS), which was discussed earlier. MS-DOS was never meant to be extremely friendly. Its roots are in CP/M, which was based on the command line, and so is MS-DOS. In other words, they all use long strings of commands typed in at the computer keyboard to perform operations. Some people prefer this type of interaction with the computer, including many folks with technical backgrounds (such as yours truly). Although Windows has left the full command-line interface behind, it still contains a bit of DOS, and you get to it through the command prompt.

Although you can't tell from looking at it, the Windows command prompt is actually a Windows program that is intentionally designed to have the look and feel of a DOS command line. Because it is, despite its appearance, a Windows program, the command prompt provides all the stability and configurability you expect from Windows. You can access a command prompt by running CMD.EXE.

A number of diagnostic utilities are often run at the command prompt. Since knowledge of each is required for the exam, they are discussed next in the order given. The commands in this section include the following:

- TASKKILL
- BOOTREC
- SHUTDOWN
- TASKLIST
- MD
- RD
- CD
- DEL
- FORMAT
- COPY
- XCOPY
- ROBOCOPY
- DISKPART
- SFC
- CHKDSK
- GPUPDATE
- GPRESULT
- DIR
- EXIT
- HELP
- EXPAND
- [command name] /?
- Commands available with standard privileges vs. administrative privileges

TASKKILL

The TASKKILL.EXE utility is used to terminate processes. Those processes can be identified by either name or process ID number (PID), and the process can exist on the machine where the administrator is sitting (the default) or on another machine, in which case you signify the other system by using the /S switch.

The /IM parameter is used to specify an image name of a process to kill and can include wildcard (*) characters. If the process ID number is used in place of the name, then the /PID switch is needed. The processes in question are the same that can be killed through the Task Manager.

BOOTREC

The BOOTREC.EXE utility can be run to interact with the MBR, boot sector, or boot configuration data (BCD) store.

To run the tool, you must boot from the installation disc, choose the Repair Your Computer option, and enter the Recovery Environment. Choose Command Prompt from System Recovery Options and then type **bootrec.exe**.

The options for BOOTREC are /FIXBOOT (to write a new boot sector), /FIXMBR (to write a new MBR), /REBUILDBCD (to rebuild the BCD store), or /SCANOS (to scan all disks for installations the Boot Manager menu is not listing).

SHUTDOWN

The SHUTDOWN.EXE utility can be used to schedule a shutdown (complete or a restart) locally or remotely. A variety of reasons can be specified and announced to users for the shutdown. Three parameters to be aware of are /S (turns the computer off), /R (restarts the computer), and /M (lets you specify a computer other than this one).

TASKLIST

The TASKLIST.EXE utility is used at the command line to see a list of all the running processes (and their process ID number), similar to what you see in the GUI by using Task Manager. By default, it shows the processes on the current machine, but the /S switch can be used to see the processes on a remote machine. /SVC will show the services hosted in each process, and you can use /U if you need to run the command as another user (/P allows you to specify a password associated with that user).

MD

The MD command is used to make directories. It's a shorthand version of the MKDIR command. Table 5.11 describes its use and switches (I discuss RD and CD next).

TABLE 5.11   CD, MD, and RD use and switches

Command	Purpose
CD *[path]*	Changes to the specified directory.
CD /D *[drive:][path]*	Changes to the specified directory on the drive.
CD ..	Changes to the directory that is up one level.
CD\	Changes to the root directory of the drive.
MD *[drive:][path]*	Makes a directory in the specified path. If you don't specify a path, the directory will be created in your current directory.
RD *[drive:][path]*	Removes (deletes) specified directory.
RD /S *[drive:][path]*	Removes all directories and files in the specified directory, including the specified directory itself.
RD /Q *[drive:][path]*	Quiet mode. It won't ask whether you're sure you want to delete the specified directory when you use /S.

RD

The RD command is used to remove directories. It's a shorthand version of the RMDIR commands. Table 5.11 describes its use and switches.

CD

The CD command is used to change (or display). It's a shorthand version of the CHDIR command. Table 5.11 describes its use and switches.

DEL

The DEL command is used to delete files and directories at the command line. Wildcards can be used with it. ERASE performs the same operations.

FORMAT

The FORMAT command is used to wipe data off disks and prepare them for new use. Before a hard disk can be formatted, it must have partitions created on it. (Partitioning was done in the DOS days with the FDISK command, but as I just mentioned, that command does not exist in Windows 7, Windows Vista, Windows 8, or Windows 8.1, having been replaced with DISKPART.) The syntax for FORMAT is as follows:

FORMAT [volume] [switches]

The *volume* parameter describes the drive letter (for example, D:), mount point, or volume name. Table 5.12 lists some common FORMAT switches.

TABLE 5.12   FORMAT switches

Switch	Purpose
/FS:[*filesystem*]	Specifies the type of filesystem to use (FAT, FAT32, or NTFS)
/V:[*label*]	Specifies the new volume label
/Q	Executes a quick format

There are other options as well to specify allocation sizes, the number of sectors per track, and the number of tracks per disk size. However, I don't recommend that you use these unless you have a specific need. The defaults are just fine.

So, if you wanted to format your D: drive as NTFS with a name of HDD2, you would type the following:

FORMAT D: /FS:NTFS /V:HDD2

WARNING   Before you format anything, be sure you have it backed up or be prepared to lose whatever is on that drive!

COPY

The COPY command does what it says: it makes a copy of a file in a second location. (To copy a file and remove it from its original location, use the MOVE command.) Here's the syntax for COPY:

COPY [filename] [destination]

It's pretty straightforward. There are several switches for COPY, but in practice they are rarely used. The three most used ones are /A, which indicates an ASCII text file; /V, which verifies that the files are written correctly after the copy; and /Y, which suppresses the prompt asking whether you're sure you want to overwrite files if they exist in the destination directory.

The COPY command cannot be used to copy directories. Use XCOPY for that function.

One useful tip is to use wildcards. For example, in DOS (or at the command prompt), the asterisk (*) is a wildcard that means everything. So, you could type **COPY *.EXE** to copy all files that have an .EXE extension, or you could type **COPY *.*** to copy all files in your current directory.

XCOPY

If you are comfortable with the COPY command, learning XCOPY shouldn't pose too many problems. It's basically an extension of COPY with one notable exception—it's designed to copy directories as well as files. The syntax is as follows:

XCOPY [source] [destination][switches]

There are 26 XCOPY switches; Table 5.13 lists some of the commonly used ones.

TABLE 5.13   XCOPY switches

Switch	Purpose
/A	Copies only files that have the Archive attribute set and does not clear the attribute. This is useful for making a quick backup of files while not disrupting a normal backup routine.
/E	Copies directories and subdirectories, including empty directories.
/F	Displays full source and destination filenames when copying.
/G	Allows copying of encrypted files to a destination that does not support encryption.
/H	Copies hidden and system files as well.
/K	Copies attributes. (By default, XCOPY resets the Read-Only attribute.)

TABLE 5.13   XCOPY switches *(continued)*

Switch	Purpose
/O	Copies file ownership and ACL information (NTFS permissions).
/R	Overwrites read-only files.
/S	Copies directories and subdirectories but not empty directories.
/U	Copies only files that already exist in the destination.
/V	Verifies each new file.

Perhaps the most important switch is /O. If you use XCOPY to copy files from one location to another, the filesystem creates a new version of the file in the new location without changing the old file. In NTFS, when a new file is created, it inherits permissions from its new parent directory. This could cause problems if you copy files. (Users who didn't have access to the file before might have access now.) If you want to retain the original permissions, use XCOPY /O.

ROBOCOPY

The ROBOCOPY command (Robust File Copy for Windows) is included with Windows 7, Windows 8, and Windows 8.1 and has the big advantage of being able to accept a plethora of specifications and keep NTFS permissions intact in its operations. The /MIR switch, for example, can be used to mirror a complete directory tree.

You can find an excellent TechNet article on how to use Robocopy at http://technet .microsoft.com/en-us/magazine/ec85e01678.aspx.

DISKPART

The DISKPART command shows the partitions and lets you manage them on the computer's hard drives. A universal tool for working with hard drives from the command line, it allows you to convert between disk types, extend/shrink volumes, and format partitions and volumes, as well as list them, create them, and so on. You can find a list of all the available commands at http://technet.microsoft.com/en-us/library/bb490893.aspx.

SFC

The System File Checker (SFC) is a command line–based utility that checks and verifies the versions of system files on your computer. If system files are corrupted, the SFC will replace the corrupted files with correct versions.

The syntax for the SFC command is as follows:

```
SFC [switch]
```

While the switches vary a bit between different versions of Windows, Table 5.14 lists the most common ones available for SFC.

TABLE 5.14   SFC switches

Switch	Purpose
/CACHESIZE=X	Sets the Windows File Protection cache size, in megabytes
/PURGECACHE	Purges the Windows File Protection cache and scans all protected system files immediately
/REVERT	Reverts SFC to its default operation
/SCANFILE (Windows 7 and Vista only)	Scans a file that you specify and fixes problems if they are found
/SCANNOW	Immediately scans all protected system files
/SCANONCE	Scans all protected system files once
/SCANBOOT	Scans all protected system files every time the computer is rebooted
/VERIFYONLY	Scans protected system files and does not make any repairs or changes
/VERIFYFILE	Identifies the integrity of the file specified and makes any repairs or changes
/OFFBOOTDIR	Does a repair of an offline boot directory
/OFFFWINDIR	Does a repair of an offline Windows directory

To run the SFC, you must be logged in as an administrator or have administrative privileges. If the System File Checker discovers a corrupted system file, it will automatically overwrite the file by using a copy held in the *%systemroot%*\system32\dllcache directory. If you believe that the dllcache directory is corrupted, you can use SFC /SCANNOW, SFC /SCANONCE, SFC /SCANBOOT, or SFC /PURGECACHE to repair its contents.

The C:\Windows\System32 directory is where many of the Windows system files reside.

If you attempt to run SFC, or many other utilities, from a standard command prompt in Windows Vista, for example, you will be told that you must be an administrator running a console session in order to continue. Rather than opening a standard command prompt, choose Start ➢ All Programs ➢ Accessories and then right-click Command Prompt and choose Run As Administrator. The UAC will prompt you to continue, and then you can run SFC without a problem.

CHKDSK

You can use the Windows CHKDSK utility to create and display status reports for the hard disk. CHKDSK can also correct filesystem problems (such as cross-linked files) and scan for and attempt to repair disk errors. CHKDSK can be run from the command line or you can use a version in Windows Explorer.

To use the non-command-line version, right-click the problem disk and select Properties. This will bring up the Properties dialog box for that disk, which shows the current status of the selected disk drive.

By clicking the Tools tab at the top of the dialog box and then clicking the Check Now button in the Error-Checking section, you can start CHKDSK.

GPUDATE

Configuration settings on Windows devices can be controlled through the use of policies. These policies can be applied on a local basis or on a domain and organizational unit basis when a device is a member of an Active Directory domain. When changes are made by an administrator to these policies, some types of changes will not take effect until the next schedule refresh time.

An administrator can force a device to update its policies after a change by executing the gpupdate command on the device. This is the syntax of the command:

```
gpupdate [/target:{computer|user}] [/force] [/wait:value] [/logoff] [/boot]
```

The parameters are as follows:

- `/target: { computer | user }`: Processes only the Computer settings or the current User settings. By default, both the computer settings and the user settings are processed.
- `/force`: Ignores all processing optimizations and reapplies all settings.
- `/wait: value`: Number of seconds that policy processing waits to finish. The default is 600 seconds. 0 means "no wait," and -1 means "wait indefinitely."
- `/logoff`: Logs off after the refresh has completed. This is required for those Group Policy client-side extensions that do not process on a background refresh cycle but that do process when the user logs on, such as user Software Installation and Folder Redirection. This option has no effect if there are no extensions called that require the user to log off.

- /boot: Restarts the computer after the refresh has completed. This is required for those Group Policy client-side extensions that do not process on a background refresh cycle but do process when the computer starts up, such as computer Software Installation. This option has no effect if there are no extensions called that require the computer to be restarted.

GPRESULT

Group policies can be applied to Windows devices at the local, OU, and domain levels, and when the policies are applied to the device, the results can be somewhat confusing because of variables that can affect how the policies interact with one another. If you need to determine the policies that are in effect for a particular device, you can execute the gpresult command on the device, and it will list the currently applied and defective polies. This is the command syntax:

```
gpresult [/s <COMPUTER> [/u <USERNAME> [/p [<PASSWORD>]]]] [/user
[<TARGETDOMAIN>\]<TARGETUSER>] [/scope {user | computer}]
{/r | /v | /z | [/x | /h] <FILENAME> [/f] | /?}
```

The parameters are as follows:

- /s <COMPUTER>: Specifies the name or IP address of a remote computer. Do not use backslashes. The default is the local computer.

- /u <USERNAME>: Uses the credentials of the specified user to run the command. The default user is the user who is logged on to the computer that issues the command.

- /p [<Password>]: Specifies the password of the user account that is provided in the /u parameter. If /p is omitted, gpresult prompts for the password. /p cannot be used with /x or /h.

- /user [<TARGETDOMAIN>\]<TARGETUSER>: Specifies the remote user whose data is to be displayed.

- /scope {user | computer}: Displays data for either the user or the computer. If /scope is omitted, gpresult displays data for both the user and the computer.

- [/x | /h] <FILENAME>: Saves the report in either XML (/x) or HTML (/h) format at the location and with the filename that is specified by the FILENAME parameter. This cannot be used with /u, /p, /r, /v, or /z.

- /f: Forces gpresult to overwrite the filename that is specified in the /x or /h option.

- /r: Displays summary data.

- /v: Displays verbose policy information. This includes detailed settings that were applied with a precedence of 1.

- /z: Displays all available information about Group Policy. This includes detailed settings that were applied with a precedence of 1 and higher.

DIR

The DIR command is simply used to view a listing of the files and folders that exist within a directory, subdirectory, or folder. The following is the syntax:

```
dir [Drive:][Path][FileName] […] [/p] [/q] [/w] [/d]
[/a[[:]attributes]][/o[[:]SortOrder]] [/t[[:]TimeField]] [/s] [/b]
[/l] [/n] [/x] [/c] [/4]
```

The parameters are as follows:

- [Drive:][Path]: Specifies the drive and directory for which you want to see a listing.
- [FileName]: Specifies a particular file or group of files for which you want to see a listing.
- /p: Displays one screen of the listing at a time. To see the next screen, press any key on the keyboard.
- /q: Displays file ownership information.
- /w: Displays the listing in wide format, with as many as five filenames or directory names on each line.
- d: Same as /w but files are sorted by column.
- i: Displays only the names of those directories and files with the attributes you specify.
- /o [[:]SortOrder]: Controls the order in which DIR sorts and displays directory names and filenames.
- /t [[:]TimeField]: Specifies which time field to display or use for sorting.
- /s: Lists every occurrence, in the specified directory and all subdirectories, of the specified filename.
- /b: Lists each directory name or filename, one per line, including the filename extension. /b does not display heading information or a summary. /b overrides /w.
- /l: Displays unsorted directory names and filenames in lowercase. /l does not convert extended characters to lowercase.
- /n: Displays a long list format with filenames on the far right of the screen.
- /x: Displays the short names generated for files on NTFS and FAT volumes. The display is the same as the display for /n, but short names are displayed after the long name.
- /c: Displays the thousand separator in file sizes.
- /4: Displays four-digit year format.

EXIT

EXIT is a command that can be used to quit the current batch script, quit the current subroutine, or quit the command processor (CMD.EXE). This is the syntax of the command:

```
EXIT [/B] [exitCode]
```

The parameters are as follows:

- /B: When used in a batch script, this option will exit only the script (or subroutine) but not CMD.EXE.

- exitCode: Sets the %ERRORLEVEL% to a numeric number. If quitting CMD.EXE, set the process exit code to no.

HELP

The HELP command does what it says: it gives you help. Actually, if you just type **HELP** and press Enter, your computer gives you a list of system commands you can type. Type the name of a command you want to know about after typing HELP. For example, type **HELP RD** and press Enter, and you will get information about the RD command.

EXPAND

The EXPAND command is used to open compressed update files. By using this command, you can open and review the update. This is the syntax of the command:

```
expand [-r] source [destination] [-d source.cab [-f:files]] [source.cab
[-f:filesdestination]]
```

The parameters are as follows:

- [-r]: Renames expanded files.

- [destination]: Specifies where files are to be expanded. If source is multiple files and -r is not specified, destination must be a directory. destination can consist of a drive letter and colon, a directory name, a filename, or a combination of any of these.

- [-d source.cab]: Displays a list of files in the source location. Does not expand or extract the files.

- [-f:files]: Specifies the files in a cabinet (.cab) file that you intend to expand. You can use wildcards (* and ?).

- source.cab: Specifies the files to expand. source can consist of a drive letter and colon, a directory name, a filename, or a combination. You can use wildcards (* and ?).

- [/?]: Displays help at a command prompt.

[command name] /?

You can also get help information by typing **/?** after a command.

The /? switch is slightly faster and provides more information than the HELP command. The HELP command provides information only for system commands (it does not include network commands). For example, if you type **help ipconfig** at a command prompt, you get no useful information (except to try /?); however, typing **ipconfig /?** provides the help file for the ipconfig command.

Commands Available with Standard Privileges vs. Administrative Privileges

In Windows Vista, Windows 7, Windows 8, and Windows 8.1, some commands are unavailable to a user logged in with a standard privilege account. This set of commands can be executed only if the user is logged on with an administrator account or possesses an administrative account and references it by using the runas command. When this command is used and references an administrative account, privileges for that command *only* are elevated.

This is the syntax of the runas command:

```
runas [{/profile | /noprofile}] [/env] [{/netonly | /savecred}]
[/smartcard] [/showtrustlevels] [/trustlevel] /user:<UserAccountName>
"<ProgramName> <PathToProgramFile>"
```

The parameters are as follows:

- /profile: Loads the user's profile. This is the default. This parameter cannot be used with the /netonly parameter.

- /no profile: Specifies that the user's profile is not to be loaded. This allows the application to load more quickly, but it can also cause a malfunction in some applications.

- /env: Specifies that the current network environment be used instead of the user's local environment.

- /netonly: Indicates that the user information specified is for remote access only. This parameter cannot be used with the /profile parameter.

- /savecred: Indicates if the credentials have been previously saved by this user. This parameter is not available and will be ignored on Windows Vista Home or Windows Vista Starter Editions. This parameter cannot be used with the /smartcard parameter.

- /smartcard: Indicates whether the credentials are to be supplied from a smartcard. This parameter cannot be used with the /savecred parameter.

- /showtrustlevels: Displays the trust levels that can be used as arguments to /trustlevel.

- /trustlevel: Specifies the level of authorization at which the application is to run. Use /showtrustlevels to see the trust levels available.

- /user:<UserAccountName> "<ProgramName> <PathToProgramFile>": Specifies the name of the user account under which to run the program, the program name, and the path to the program file. The user account name format should be <User>@<Domain> or <Domain>\<UserAccountName>.

Exam Essentials

Know the main command-line utilities.   Those discussed in this chapter include the ones CompTIA wants you to know for the exam. Among these are: /?, CD, CHKDSK, COPY, FORMAT, MD, RD, SFC, TRACERT, and XCOPY.

Know the switches for specified commands.   CompTIA expects you to know the switches for the most common utilities. Make sure you look at each command and utility listed in the objectives and the switches and parameters for each that have been listed in this section.

1.4 Given a Scenario, Use Appropriate Microsoft Operating System Features and Tools

This objective requires you to know how to work at the command line and run common command-line utilities available with the Windows-based operating systems, as well as use administrative tools. Some of the material here overlaps with other objectives, but you'll want to make certain you know each utility discussed.

Although most of the information presented about Windows utilities and administration should seem like second nature to you (on-the-job experience is expected for A+ certification), you should read these sections thoroughly to make certain you can answer any questions that may appear about them. The topics covered in this section include the following:

- Administrative tools
- MSCONFIG
- Task Manager
- Disk Management
- Other tools
- System utilities

Table 5.15 lists the administrative tools, and the purpose for each, that you need to know for this objective. The majority of these run in the Microsoft Management Console (MMC).

TABLE 5.15   Windows administrative tools

Tool	Purpose
Computer Management	The Computer Management Console is a power-packed interface and includes the following system tools: Device Manager, Event Viewer, Shared Folders, Performance/Performance Logs And Alerts (based on the OS you are running, you may also see Local Users And Groups, or Task Scheduler, here as well). Computer Management also has the Storage area, which lets you manage removable media, defragment your hard drives, or manage partitions through the Disk Management utility. Finally, you can manage system services and applications through Computer Management as well.
Device Manager	Device Manager shows a list of all installed hardware and lets you add items, remove items, update drivers, and more.

TABLE 5.15 Windows administrative tools (*continued*)

Tool	Purpose
Users And Groups	If Local Users And Groups is not visible in the left pane of MMC, choose File ➤ Add/Remove Snap-in and select Local Users And Groups from the list of possible snap-ins. You can choose to manage the local computer or another computer (requiring you to provide its address). The built-in groups for a domain are a superset of local groups.
	Local Users And Groups is not available for Windows 7 editions lower than Professional. In all other editions, you must manage user accounts using the User Accounts applet in the Control Panel, and you cannot create or manage groups. The default users created are Administrator, Guest, and the administrative account created during the install.
Local Security Policy	The Local Security Policy (choose Start and then enter `secpol.msc`) allows you to set the default security settings for the system. This feature is available only in Windows 7 Professional, Windows 7 Ultimate, Windows 7 Enterprise, Windows 8.1 Pro, Windows 8 Ultimate, Windows 8 Professional (old Business), and Windows 8 Enterprise editions.
Performance Monitor	Performance Monitor differs a bit in versions but has the same purpose throughout: to display performance counters. While lumped under one heading, two tools are available—System Monitor and Performance Logs And Alerts. System Monitor will show the performance counters in graphical format. The Performance Logs And Alerts utility will collect the counter information and then send it to a console (such as the one in front of the admin so they can be aware of the problem) or event log.
Services	This interface is listed, and discussed, with the Run line utilities later in this objective.
System Configuration	MSCONFIG, known as the System Configuration utility, helps you troubleshoot startup problems by allowing you to selectively disable individual items that normally are executed at startup. It works in all versions of Windows, although the interface window is slightly different among versions.
Task Scheduler	Task Scheduler allows you to configure jobs to automatically run unattended. For the run frequency, you can choose any of the following options: Daily, Weekly, Monthly, One Time Only, When The Computer Starts, or When You Log On.
	You can access a job's advanced properties any time after the job has been created. To do so, double-click the icon for the job in the Scheduled Tasks screen. In the resulting dialog box, you can configure such things as the username and password associated with the job, the actual command line used to start the job (in case you need to add parameters to it), and the working directory.
	At any time, you can delete a scheduled job by deleting its icon, or you can simply disable a job by removing the check mark from the Enabled box on the Task tab of the task's properties dialog box. For jobs that are scheduled to run, a picture of a clock appears in the bottom-left corner of the icon; jobs not scheduled to run do not have that clock.

(*continues*)

TABLE 5.15 Windows administrative tools (*continued*)

Tool	Purpose
Component Services	Component Services is an MMC snap-in that allows you to administer, as well as deploy, component services and to configure behavior such as security (Component Services is located beneath Administrative Tools).
Data Sources	ODBC Data Source Administrator (located beneath Administrative Tools) allows you to interact with database management systems.
Print Management	Available in Windows 7 and Windows Vista, Print Management (located beneath Administrative Tools) allows you to manage multiple printers and print servers from a single interface. Print Management is not available for Windows 7 in any edition lower than Windows 7 Professional. In all later editions of Windows (Vista, 8, 8.1), you must manage individual printers using the Printers applet in the Control Panel.
Windows Memory Diagnostic	The Windows Memory Diagnostic Tool (located beneath Administrative Tools) can be used to check a system for memory problems. For the tool to work, the system must be restarted. The two options that it offers are to restart the computer now and check for problems or wait and check for problems on the next restart. Upon reboot, the test will take several minutes, and the display screen will show which pass number is being run and the overall status of the test (percentage complete). When the memory test concludes, the system will restart again, and nothing related to it is apparent until you log in. If the test is without error, you'll see a message that no errors were found. If anything else is found, the results will be displayed.
Windows Firewall	Windows Firewall (Start ➤ Control Panel ➤ Windows Firewall) is used to block access from the network, and in Windows 7, it is divided into separate settings for private networks and public networks. While host-based firewalls are not as secure as other types of firewalls, this provides much better protection than previously and is turned on by default. It is also included in the Security component of the Action Center and can be tweaked significantly using the Advanced Settings.
Advanced Security	Continuing the discussion of Windows Firewall, once you click Advanced Settings, Windows Firewall with Advanced Security opens. Here, you can configure inbound and outbound rules as well as import and export policies and monitor. Monitoring is not confined only to the firewall; you can also monitor security associations and connection security rules. In short, Windows Firewall with Advanced Security is an incredibly powerful tool that builds on what Windows Vista started. Not only can this MMC snap-in do simple configuration, but it can also configure remote computers and work with Group Policy.

MSCONFIG

The MSCONFIG system configuration tool features different tabs based on the Windows version you are running, but the key ones are General, Boot, Services, Startup, and Tools.

General   On the General tab, you can choose the startup type. There are three sets of options: Normal, Diagnostic, and Selective. A normal startup loads all drivers and services, whereas a diagnostic startup loads only the basic drivers and services. Between the two extremes is the selective startup that gives you limited options on what to load. Figure 5.8 shows the General tab.

FIGURE 5.8   General tab

Boot   The Boot tab shows the boot menu and allows you to configure parameters such as the number of seconds the menu should appear before the default option is chosen and whether you want go to safe boot. You can toggle on/off the display of drivers as they load during startup and choose to log the boot, go with basic video settings, and similar options. Figure 5.9 shows the Boot tab.

Services   The Services tab shows the services configured and their current status. From here, you can enable or disable all and hide Microsoft services from the display (which greatly reduces the display in most cases). Figure 5.10 shows the Services tab.

FIGURE 5.9   Boot tab

FIGURE 5.10   Services tab

Startup The Startup tab shows the items scheduled to begin at startup, the command associated with them, and the location where the configuration is done (usually, but not always, in the Registry). From here, you can enable or disable all. If a particular startup item has been disabled in Windows 7 and Windows Vista, the date and time it was disabled will appear in the display. Figure 5.11 shows the Startup tab for Windows 7 and earlier.

FIGURE 5.11 Startup tab on Windows 7

This functionality has been moved to Task Manager in Windows 8 and Windows 8.1; Figure 5.12 shows the Startup tab.

Tools The Tools tab contains quick access to some of the most useful diagnostic tools in Windows. You can launch such items as the Registry Editor as well as many Control Panel applets, and you can enable or disable User Account Control (UAC). Figure 5.13 shows the Tools tab.

Task Manager

This tool lets you shut down nonresponsive applications selectively in all Windows versions. In current versions of Windows, it can do so much more. Task Manager allows you to see which processes and applications are using the most system resources, view network usage, see connected users, and so on. To display Task Manager, press Ctrl+Alt+Del and click the Task Manager button to display it. You can also right-click an empty spot in the taskbar and choose it from the pop-up menu that appears.

FIGURE 5.12   Startup tab on Windows 8.1

FIGURE 5.13   Tools tab

To get to the Task Manager directly in any of the Windows versions, you can press Ctrl+Shift+Esc.

In Windows Vista and Windows 7, Task Manager has six tabs: Applications, Processes, Performance, Networking, and Users. The Networking tab is shown only if your system has a network card installed (it is rare to find one that doesn't). The Users tab is displayed only if the computer you are working on is a member of a workgroup or is a stand-alone computer. The Users tab is unavailable on computers that are members of a network domain. In Windows 8 and 8.1, there is an additional tab called Details, and the Applications tab is replaced with the App History tab. Let's look at these tabs, in the order of their appearance, in more detail in Windows 8.1.

Applications

The Applications tab (shown in Figure 5.14) lets you see which tasks are open on the machine. You also see the status of each task, which can be either Running or Not Responding. If a task or application has stopped responding (that is, it's hung), you can select the task in the list and click End Task. Doing so closes the program, and you can try to open it again. Often, although certainly not always, if an application hangs, you have to reboot the computer to prevent the same thing from happening again shortly after you restart the application. You can also use the Applications tab to switch to a different task or create new tasks.

FIGURE 5.14   Applications tab

![Windows Task Manager screenshot showing the Applications tab with menu items File, Options, View, Windows, Help and tabs Applications, Processes, Services, Performance, Networking, Users. The Task list shows "RaceView - Internet Explorer" (Running) and "Set Network Location" (Running), with buttons End Task, Switch To, New Task. Status bar shows Processes: 94, CPU Usage: 21%, Physical Memory: 65%]

App History (Windows 8 and 8.1 Only)

The App history tab in Windows 8 and Windows 8.1 (shown in Figure 5.15) displays the history of the usage of Metro apps only.

FIGURE 5.15   App History tab

Processes

The Processes tab (shown in Figure 5.16) lets you see the names of all the processes running on the machine. You also see the user account that's running the process, as well as how much CPU and RAM resources each process is using. To end a process, select it in the list and click End Process. Be careful with this choice since ending some processes can cause Windows to shut down. If you don't know what a particular process does, you can look for it in any search engine and find a number of sites that will explain it.

FIGURE 5.16   Processes tab

You can also change the priority of a process in Task Manager's Processes display by right-clicking the name of the process and choosing Set Priority. The six priorities, from lowest to highest, are as follows:

Low   For applications that need to complete sometime but that you don't want interfering with other applications. On a numerical scale from 0 to 31, this equates to a base priority of 4.

Below Normal   For applications that don't need to drop all the way down to Low. This equates to a base priority of 6.

Normal   The default priority for most applications. This equates to a base priority of 8.

Above Normal   For applications that don't need to boost all the way to High. This equates to a base priority of 10.

High   For applications that must complete soon, when you don't want other applications to interfere with the application's performance. This equates to a base priority of 13.

Realtime   For applications that must have the processor's attention to handle time-critical tasks. Applications can be run at this priority only by a member of the Administrators group. This equates to a base priority of 24.

If you decide to change the priority of an application, you'll be warned that changing the priority of an application may make it unstable. You can generally ignore this option when changing the priority to Low, Below Normal, Above Normal, or High, but you should heed this warning when changing applications to the Realtime priority. Realtime means that the processor gives precedence to this process over all others—over security processes, over spooling, over everything—and is sure to make the system unstable.

Task Manager changes the priority only for that instance of the running application. The next time the process is started, priorities revert to that of the base (typically Normal).

Services

The Services tab (shown in Figure 5.17) lists the name of each running service, as well as the process ID associated with it, its description, its status, and its group. A button labeled Services appears on this tab, and clicking it will open the MMC console for Services, where you can configure each service. Within Task Manager, right-clicking a service will open a context menu listing three choices: Start Service, Stop Service, and Go To Process (which takes you to the Processes tab).

FIGURE 5.17 Services tab

Performance

The Performance tab (shown in Figure 5.18) contains a variety of information, including overall CPU usage percentage, a graphical display of CPU usage history, page-file usage in megabytes, and a graphical display of page-file usage.

FIGURE 5.18 Performance tab

This tab also provides you with additional memory-related information such as physical and kernel memory usage, as well as the total number of handles, threads, and processes. Total, limit, and peak commit-charge information also displays. Some of the items are beyond the scope of this book, but it's good to know that you can use the Performance tab to keep track of system performance. Note that the number of processes, CPU usage percentage, and commit charge always display at the bottom of the Task Manager window, regardless of which tab you have currently selected.

On Windows 7 this pane has a button marked Resource Monitor, which breaks down resource usage on a per-process basis.

Networking

The Networking tab (shown in Figure 5.19) provides you with a graphical display of the performance of your network connection. It also tells you the network adaptor name, link speed, and state. If you have more than one network adaptor installed in the machine, you can select the appropriate adaptor to see graphical usage data for that adaptor.

FIGURE 5.19   Networking tab

Users

The Users tab (shown in Figure 5.20) provides you with information about the users connected to the local machine. You'll see the username, ID, status, client name, and session type. You can right-click any connected user to perform a variety of functions, including sending the user a message, disconnecting the user, logging off the user, and initiating a remote-control session to the user's machine.

FIGURE 5.20   Users tab

Use Task Manager whenever the system seems bogged down by an unresponsive application.

Details Tab (Windows 8 and 8.1 Only)

The Details tab (shown in Figure 5.21) displays information about the processes that are running on the computer. A process can be an application that you start or subsystems and services that are managed by the operating system.

Disk Management

In Windows, you can manage your hard drives through the Disk Management component. To access Disk Management, access the Control Panel and double-click Administrative Tools. Then double-click Computer Management. Finally, double-click Disk Management.

The Disk Management screen lets you view a host of information regarding all the drives installed in your system, including CD-ROM and DVD drives. The list of devices in the top portion of the screen shows you additional information for each partition on each drive, such as the filesystem used, status, free space, and so on. If you right-click a partition in either area, you can perform a variety of functions, such as formatting the partition and changing the name and drive letter assignment. For additional options and information, you can also access the properties of a partition by right-clicking it and selecting Properties.

The basic unit of storage is the disk. Disks are partitioned (primary, logical, extended) and then formatted for use. With the Windows operating systems this exam focuses on, you can choose to use either FAT32 or NTFS; the advantage of the latter is that it offers security and many other features that FAT32 can't handle. Both Windows 7 and Windows Vista can be installed only in NTFS, but they will recognize FAT partitions.

FIGURE 5.21 Details tab

Name	PID	Status	User name	CPU	Memory (p...	Description
AcroRd32.exe	5468	Running	PNUT	00	4,092 K	Adobe Reader
AcroRd32.exe	1240	Running	PNUT	00	100,904 K	Adobe Reader
armsvc.exe	1548	Running	SYSTEM	00	512 K	Adobe Acrobat Up...
audiodg.exe	8412	Running	LOCAL SE...	00	7,380 K	Windows Audio De...
BTStackServer.exe	6140	Running	PNUT	00	4,608 K	Bluetooth Stack CO...
BTTray.exe	5400	Running	PNUT	00	2,480 K	Bluetooth Tray App...
CCleaner64.exe	7636	Running	PNUT	00	396 K	CCleaner
ClassicStartMenu.exe	4020	Running	PNUT	00	1,172 K	Classic Start Menu
conhost.exe	12188	Running	SYSTEM	00	308 K	Console Window H...
CSISYNCCLIENT.EXE	5984	Running	PNUT	00	4,416 K	Microsoft Office Do...
csrss.exe	736	Running	SYSTEM	00	1,308 K	Client Server Runti...
csrss.exe	816	Running	SYSTEM	00	1,480 K	Client Server Runti...
dasHost.exe	1752	Running	LOCAL SE...	00	1,280 K	Device Association ...
dirmngr.exe	1732	Running	SYSTEM	00	680 K	dirmngr.exe
Dropbox.exe	5596	Running	PNUT	00	100,808 K	Dropbox
dwm.exe	588	Running	DWM-1	00	17,848 K	Desktop Window M...
Energy Management...	4280	Running	PNUT	00	2,064 K	Lenovo Energy Ma...
explorer.exe	2764	Running	PNUT	00	67,772 K	Windows Explorer
FAHWindow64.exe	5500	Running	PNUT	01	628 K	File Association Hel...
FlashUtil_ActiveX.exe	11248	Running	PNUT	00	3,624 K	Adobe® Flash® Pl...
genie2_tray.exe	5360	Running	PNUT	00	1,504 K	genie2_tray.exe
googletalkplugin.exe	5728	Running	PNUT	00	6,168 K	Hangouts Plugin
GoogleUpdate.exe	2688	Running	SYSTEM	00	196 K	Google Installer

Task Manager — File Options View — Processes | Performance | App history | Startup | Users | **Details** | Services — Fewer details — End task

If you're using FAT32 and want to change to NTFS, the convert utility will allow you to do so. For example, to change the E: drive to NTFS, the command is `convert e: /FS:NTFS`.

Once the disk is formatted, the next building block is the directory structure, in which you divide the partition into logical locations for storing data. Whether these storage units are called directories or folders is a matter of semantics—they tend to be called *folders* when viewed in the graphical user interface (GUI) and *directories* when viewed from the command line.

Drive Status

The status of a drive can have a number of variables associated with it (System, Boot, and so on), but what really matters is whether it falls into the category of *healthy* or *unhealthy*.

As the title implies, if it is healthy, it is properly working, and if it is unhealthy, you need to attend to it and correct problems. In Figure 5.22 you can see in the Status column of Disk Management that all drives are healthy.

FIGURE 5.22   Status in Disk Management

Disk Management

File   Action   View   Help

Volume	Layout	Type	File System	Status	Capaci
	Simple	Basic		Healthy (Recovery Partition)	1000 M
	Simple	Basic		Healthy (EFI System Partition)	260 ME
	Simple	Basic		Healthy (OEM Partition)	1000 M
	Simple	Basic		Healthy (Recovery Partition)	450 ME
	Simple	Basic		Healthy (Recovery Partition)	20.00 G
LENOVO (D:)	Simple	Basic	NTFS	Healthy (Primary Partition)	25.00 G
Windows8_OS (C:)	Simple	Basic	NTFS	Healthy (Boot, Page File, Crash Du...	650.86

Disk 0
Basic
698.51 GB
Online

1000 ME Healthy	260 M Healtl	1000 ME Healthy	Windows8_OS (C 650.86 GB NTFS Healthy (Boot, Pac	450 ME Health	LENOVO (D: 25.00 GB NTF Healthy (Prin	20.00 GB Healthy (Recc

CD-ROM 0
DVD (E:)

■ Unallocated   ■ Primary partition

You can find a list of status states that are possible and require action at http://technet.microsoft.com/en-us/library/cc771775.aspx.

Mounting

Drives must be mounted before they can be used. Within Windows, most removable media (flash drives, CDs, and so forth) are recognized when attached and mounted. Volumes on basic disks, however, are not automatically mounted and assigned drive letters by default. To mount them, you must manually assign them drive letters or create mount points in Disk Management.

You can also mount from the command line using either the Diskpart or Mountvol utility.

Initializing

Initializing a disk makes it available to the disk management system, and in most cases the drive will not show up until you do this. Once the drive has been connected or installed, this should be done. Initializing the drive can be done at the command using diskpart or in the Disk Management tool. You need to know that initialization will wipe out the drive! To use diskpart to perform the initialization on 2 TB drives and smaller, follow these steps:

1. Open the Start menu, type **diskpart,** and press Enter.
2. Type **list disk** and press Enter.
3. Type **select disk X** (where X is the number your drive shows up as) and press Enter.
4. Type **clean** and press Enter.
5. Type **create partition primary** and press Enter.
6. Type **format quick fs=ntfs** and press Enter.
7. Type **assign** and press Enter.
8. Type **exit** and press Enter.

To use diskpart to perform the initialization on drives that are 2.5 TB drives and larger, follow these steps:

1. Open the Start menu, type **diskpart,** and press Enter.
2. Type **list disk** and press Enter.
3. Type **select disk X** (where X is the number your drive shows up as) and press Enter.
4. Type **clean** and press Enter.
5. Type **convert gpt** and press Enter.
6. Type **create partition primary** and press Enter.
7. Type **format quick fs=ntfs** and press Enter.
8. Type **assign** and press Enter.
9. Type **exit** and press Enter.

To use Disk Management, follow this procedure:

1. Install the drive and reboot the device.
2. In the search line, type **Disk Management** and press Enter. With the drive connected, you will get the pop-up box shown in Figure 5.23.
3. If you got the pop-up, choose either MBR or GPT and click OK.

If you didn't get the pop-up, then right-click and select to initialize the newly added drive under where it says Disk #, as shown in Figure 5.24.

Extending Partitions

It is possible to add more space to partitions (and logical drives) by extending them into unallocated space. This is done in Disk Management by right-clicking and choosing Extend or using the Diskpart utility.

FIGURE 5.23   Initialize disk pop-up

FIGURE 5.24   Initialize Disk option

Splitting Partitions

Just as you can extend a partition, you can also reduce the size of it. While generically known as *splitting* the partition, the menu option in Disk Management is Shrink. By shrinking an existing partition, you are creating another with unallocated space that can then be used for other purposes. You can shrink only basic volumes that use the NTFS filesystem (and space exists) or that do not have a filesystem.

Shrinking Partitions

It is also possible to shrink a volume from its size at creation. To do so in Disk Management, access the volume in question, right-click the volume, and select Shrink Volume, as shown in Figure 5.25.

FIGURE 5.25   Shrink Volume option

This will open another box that will allow you to control how much you want to shrink the volume, as shown in Figure 5.26.

Assigning/Changing Drive Letters

Mounting drives and assigning drive letters are two tasks that go hand-in-hand. When you mount a drive, you typically assign it a drive letter to be able to access it. Right-clicking a volume in Disk Management gives the option Change Drive Letter And Paths, as shown in Figure 5.27.

Adding Drives

When removable drives are added, the Windows operating system is configured, by default, to identify them and assign a drive letter. When nonremovable drives are added, you must mount them and assign a drive letter, as mentioned earlier.

Adding Arrays

Arrays are added to increase fault tolerance (using RAID) or performance (striping). Disk Management allows you to create and modify arrays as needed.

FIGURE 5.26   Setting the volume size

FIGURE 5.27   Changing the drive letter

Storage Spaces

Configuring storage spaces is a fault tolerance and capacity expansion technique that can be used as an alternative to the techniques described earlier when discussing dynamic volume types. It enables you to virtualize storage by grouping industry-standard disks into storage pools and then creating virtual disks called *storage spaces* from the available capacity in the storage pools. This means that, from a high level, you have to do three tasks to use storage spaces.

1. Create a storage pool, which is a collection of physical disks.

2. From the storage pool, create a storage space, which can also be thought of as a virtual disk.

3. Create one or more volumes on the storage space.

First let's look at creating the pool from several physical disks. Each of the disks must be at least 4 GB in size and should not have any volumes in them. The number of disks required depends on the type of resiliency you want to provide to the resulting storage space. Resiliency refers to the type of fault tolerance desired. Use the following guidelines:

- For simple resiliency (no fault tolerance), only a single disk is required for the pool.

- For mirror resiliency, two drives are required.

- For party resiliency (think RAID 5), three drives are required.

To create the pool, access the Control Panel using any of the methods discussed so far and click the applet Storage Spaces. On the resulting page, select the option Create A New Pool And Storage Space. On the Select Drives To Create Storage Pools page, the drives that are available and supported for storage pools will appear, as shown in Figure 5.28.

FIGURE 5.28   The Select Drives To Create A Storage Pool page

In this case, only one drive is eligible, so you can create only a simple type pool. Check the drive and click the Create Pool button at the bottom of the page. On the next page, give the space a name, select a drive letter, and choose the filesystem (NTFS or REFS), the resiliency type (in this case you can select only Simple), and the size of the pool. Figure 5.29 shows the pool as Myspace, with a drive letter of F, an NTFS filesystem, simple resiliency, and a maximum size of 100 GB. When you click Create Storage Space, the space will be created. Be aware that any data on the physical drive will be erased in this process!

FIGURE 5.29   Creating a storage space

When the process is finished, the new space will appear on the Manage Storage Spaces page. Now you have a pool and a space derived from the pool. The last step is to create a volume in the storage space. If you now access Disk Management, you will see a new virtual disk called Myspace. It will be a basic disk, but you can convert it to dynamic by right-clicking it and selecting Convert To Dynamic Disk. This will allow to you shrink or delete the existing volume if you desire.

Other (User State Migration Tool [USMT], Windows Upgrade Advisor, Windows Easy Transfer)

Several Microsoft tools can assist in the transfer from one operating system to another. This section discusses three of those tools.

User State Migration Tool

Microsoft Windows User State Migration Tool (USMT) allows you to migrate user file settings related to the applications, desktop configuration, and accounts. Version 4.0 works with Windows 7, is part of the Windows Automated Installation Kit (AIK), and can be found at http://technet.microsoft.com/en-us/library/dd560801(WS.10) .aspx. Version 3.0 works with Windows Vista. You can download this tool from http://technet.microsoft.com/en-us/library/cc722032.aspx. If all you are doing is a simple migration from one OS to another, you do not need this tool, but it is invaluable during large deployments.

Windows Easy Transfer

If you are migrating only a few accounts, Microsoft recommends *Windows Easy Transfer* instead of USMT. This tool works with Windows 7, Windows Vista, Windows 8, and Windows 8.1. When transferring to Windows 7, for example, a version of Windows Easy Transfer can be downloaded in either 32-bit or 64-bit version for Windows Vista from www .microsoft.com/downloads.

Windows Upgrade Advisor

The Windows Upgrade Advisor is a tool that you can use to determine whether a computer has the resources required to run a new operating system. There is a version of this tool for each of the operating systems discussed (Windows Vista, Windows 7, Windows 8, and Windows 8.1). The tool scans the computer and generates a report detailing any issues that may arise because of insufficient resources.

System Utilities

Table 5.16 lists the utilities CompTIA singles out as relevant to know for this section. All of these can be started from Start ➢ Run by entering their name and pressing Enter.

TABLE 5.16   System utilities

Utility	Purpose
MSCONFIG	Discussed previously, the MSCONFIG configuration utility is useful for looking at start-related settings.
REGEDIT	Used to open and edit the Registry. Regedit does not have save or undo features (though you can import and export); once you make a change, you've made the change for better or worse, and this is not a place to play around in if you're not sure what you're doing.
	The Registry is divided into five "hives" that hold all settings. The two main hives are HKEY_USERS (which contains settings for all users) and HKEY_LOCAL_MACHINE (which contains settings for the machine itself). HKEY_CURRENT_USER is a subset of HKEY_USERS holding information only on the current user. HKEY_CURRENT_CONFIG and HKEY_CLASSES_ROOT are both subsets of HKEY_LOCAL_MACHINE for the current configuration.
COMMAND	Starts a command prompt window intentionally designed to have the look and feel of a DOS command line. Because it is, despite its appearance, a Windows program, the command prompt provides all the stability and configurability you expect from Windows.
SERVICES.MSC	An MMC snap-in that allows you to interact with the services running on the computer. The status of the services will typically be either started or stopped, and you can right-click and choose Start, Stop, Pause, Resume, or Restart from the context menu. Services can be started automatically or manually, or they can be disabled. If you right-click the service and choose Properties from the context menu, you can choose the startup type as well as see the path to the executable and any dependencies.
MMC	Starts the management console, allowing you to run any snap-in (such as SERVICES.MSC).
MSTSC	Remote Desktop Connection Usage is used to configure remote desktop connections.
NOTEPAD	Starts a simple editor. You can edit a file that already exists or create a new one.
EXPLORER	Starts the Windows interface, allowing you to interact with files and folders.

(continues)

TABLE 5.16 System utilities (*continued*)

Utility	Purpose
MSINFO32	The System Information dialog box, this tool displays a thorough list of settings on the machine. You cannot change any values from here, but you can search, export, save, and run a number of utilities. It is primarily used during diagnostics because it is an easy way to display settings such as IRQs and DMAs.
DXDIAG	The DirectX Diagnostic tool (which has the executable name dxdiag) allows you to test DirectX functionality, with a focus on display, sound, and input. When started, you can also verify that your drivers have been signed by Microsoft. DirectX is a collection of APIs related to multimedia.
Defrag	Defrag is a tool that can be used to reorganize the data on a drive such that all parts of each file are located in the same place, improving performance.
System restore	System Restore is a tool that be used to create restore points, or snapshots of an system at certain points in time that can be returned to when a system gets corrupted. When a restore is performed, it leaves all data unaltered but returns the operating system settings to the state they were in when the restore point was created.
Windows Update	Windows is a tool that can be used to automate the process of checking for updates and patches. Once the feature is enabled, the system will check with the Update website for missing patches on a schedule and keep the device up-to-date. You have four choices when it comes to the update process: Install Updates Automatically: Downloads the updates and installs them when they are available Download Updates And Let Me Choose When To Install: Downloads the updates and notifies the user Check For Updates But Let Me Choose Whether To Download And Install Them: Just notifies the user an update is available Never Check For Updates: Stops all update notifications

Exam Essentials

Know the main administrative tools. Know the primary graphical tools for troubleshooting Windows and working with the operating system. These include the administrative tools, Device Manager, Task Manager, and others discussed.

Know the system utilities. These administrative tools, which can be started from the Run menu, are considered *run line utilities*. The commands include MSCONFIG, REGEDIT, COMMAND, SERVICES.MSC, MMC, MSTSC, NOTEPAD, EXPLORER, MSINFO32, and DXDIAG.

1.5 Given a Scenario, Use Windows Control Panel Utilities

The Control Panel is often the first place to turn for configuration settings. The applets contained within allow you to customize the system and personalize it for each user.

There are a number of applets that every version of Windows has in common, but CompTIA specifically singles out a number of them for you to know. The topics covered in this chapter include the following:

- Internet Options
- Display/Display Settings
- User Accounts
- Folder Options
- System
- Windows Firewall
- Power Option
- Programs And Features
- HomeGroup
- Devices And Printers
- Sound
- Troubleshooting
- Network And Sharing Center
- Device Manager

Internet Options

The configuration settings for Internet Options provide a number of Internet connectivity possibilities. The tabs here include General, Security, Privacy, Content, Connections, Programs, and Advanced.

General

On the General tab, as shown in Figure 5.30, you can configure the home page that appears when the browser starts or a new tab is opened. You can also configure the history settings, search defaults, what happens by default when new tabs are opened, and the appearance of the browser (colors, languages, fonts, and accessibility).

FIGURE 5.30 General tab

Security

On the Security tab, as shown in Figure 5.31, you can choose both a zone and security level for the zone. The zones include Internet, Local Intranet, Trusted Sites, and Restricted Sites. The default security level for most of the zones is between High and Medium-High, but you can also select lower levels.

Privacy

Privacy settings, as shown in Figure 5.32, allow you to configure the privacy level, choose whether you want to provide location information, use Pop-up Blocker, and disable toolbars (and extensions) when InPrivate Browsing starts.

FIGURE 5.31   Security tab

FIGURE 5.32   Privacy tab

Content

This tab isn't actually part of the objectives, but it is useful to understand. The Content tab contains Family Safety and Certificates information, as shown in Figure 5.33, which can be helpful for troubleshooting purposes.

FIGURE 5.33   Content tab

Connections

As the name implies, from this tab you can configure connections for an Internet connection, a dial-up or VPN connection, and LAN settings, as shown in Figure 5.34.

FIGURE 5.34   Connections tab

Programs

On the Programs tab, as shown in Figure 5.35, you specify which browser you want to be the default browser, what editor to use if HTML needs editing, and what programs to associate with various file types. You can also manage add-ons from here.

Advanced

On the Advanced tab, as shown in Figure 5.36, you can reset settings to their default options. You can also toggle configuration settings for granular settings not found on other tabs.

FIGURE 5.35 Programs tab

FIGURE 5.36 Advanced tab

Display

This dialog box lets you configure screensavers, colors, display options, and monitor drivers.

Resolution

The resolution settings vary based on the OS, but typically they range from Low (800 × 600) to High (1280 × 800).

Color Depth

Color depth is either the number of bits used to indicate the color of a single pixel, in a bit-mapped image or video frame buffer, or the number of bits used for each color component of a single pixel. In Windows Vista and Windows 7, this can be set on the Monitor tab of the properties of the adaptor, as shown in Figure 5.37.

FIGURE 5.37   Windows 7 color depth

In Windows 8 and 8.1, color depth, resolution, and refresh rate are all the same drop-down box and are found after clicking the List All Modes button on the Adapter tab of the display, as shown in Figure 5.38.

FIGURE 5.38   Windows 8.1 color depth, refresh rate, and resolution

Refresh Rate

The refresh rate is the number of times in a second that a display updates its buffer and is expressed in hertz. In Windows Vista and Windows 7, the refresh rate is set using a drop-down box just above the setting for color depth (see Figure 5.37). In Windows 8 and 8.1, the setting is located as described in the previous section, "Color Depth."

User Accounts

This dialog box lets you create and manage user accounts, parental controls, and related settings. The default users created are Administrator, Guest, and the administrative account created during the install.

Folder Options

This dialog box lets you configure the look and feel of how folders are displayed in Windows Explorer.

View Hidden Files

On the View tab, shown in Figure 5.39, beneath Advanced Settings, you can choose the option Show Hidden Files, Folders, And Drives, and this will allow you to see those items.

View Options

Along with the setting that allows you to hide or show file extensions and to show hidden files are a number of other settings that affect what you see when you use File Explorer (as shown in Figure 5.39).

FIGURE 5.39   View tab

The opposite of this—the default setting—is Don't Show Hidden Files, Folders, Or Drives. Radio buttons allow you to choose only one of these options.

A related check box that you should also clear in order to see all files is Hide Protected Operating System Files (Recommended). When this check box is cleared, those files will also appear in the view you are seeing.

Hide Extensions

On the View tab, shown in Figure 5.39, beneath Advanced Settings, you must clear the check box Hide Extensions For Known File Types in order for the extensions to be shown with the files.

General Options

You can configure the layout on the General tab of Folder Options (shown in Figure 5.40). Browsing options allow you to choose whether each folder will open in its own folder or the same folder. The Navigation Pane setting allows you to control what items are included in the tree structure that appears to the left when using File Explorer.

FIGURE 5.40   General tab

Always Show Icons, Never Thumbnails   Always show icons, rather than thumbnail previews of files. Use this setting if thumbnail previews are slowing down your computer.

Always Show Menus   Always show menus above the toolbar. Use this setting if you want access to the classic menus, which are hidden by default.

Display File Icon On Thumbnails   Always shows the icon for a file in addition to the thumbnail (for easier access to the related program).

Display File Size Information In Folder Tips   See the size of a folder in a tip when you point to the folder.

Hide Protected Operating System Files   See all system files that are usually hidden from view.

Hide Empty Drives In The Computer Folder   Show removable media drives (such as card readers) in the Computer folder even if they currently don't have media inserted.

Launch Folder Windows In A Separate Process   Increase the stability of Windows by opening every folder in a separate part of memory.

Restore Previous Folder Windows At Logon   Automatically open the folders that you were using when you last shut down Windows whenever you start your computer.

Show Drive Letters   Hide or show the drive letter of each drive or device in the Computer folder.

Show Encrypted Or Compressed NTFS Files In Color   Display encrypted or compressed NTFS files with unique color coding to identify them.

Show Pop-Up Description For Folder And Desktop Items   Turn off the tips that display file information when you point to files.

Show Preview Handlers In Preview Pane   Never show or always show the contents of files in the preview pane. Use this setting to improve the performance of your computer or if you don't want to use the preview pane.

Use Check Boxes To Select Items   Add check boxes to file views for easier selection of several files at once. This can be useful if it's difficult for you to hold down the Ctrl key while clicking to select multiple files.

When typing into list view, there are two radio buttons:

Automatically Type Into The Search Box   Automatically puts the cursor in the search box when you start typing

Select The Type Item In The View   Does not automatically put the cursor in the search box when you start typing

System

This utility allows you to view and configure various system elements. From within this one relatively innocuous panel, you can make a large number of configuration changes to a Windows machine. The different versions of Windows have different options available in this panel, but they will include some of the following: General, Network Identification, Device Manager, Hardware, Hardware Profiles, User Profiles, Environment, Startup/Shutdown, Performance, System Restore, Automatic Updates, Remote, Computer Name, and Advanced.

The General tab gives you an overview of the system, such as OS version, registration information, basic hardware levels (Processor and RAM), and the service pack level that's installed, if any.

Performance (Virtual Memory)

Performance settings are configured on the Advanced tab, as shown in Figure 5.41. Clicking the Settings button allows you to change the visual effects used on the system and configure Data Execution Prevention (DEP). You can also configure virtual memory on the Advanced tab. Virtual memory is the paging file used by Windows as RAM.

FIGURE 5.41 Advanced tab

Remote Settings

On the Remote tab, as shown in Figure 5.42, you can choose whether to allow Remote Assistance to be enabled.

System Protection

On the System Protection tab, as shown in Figure 5.43, you can choose to do a system restore as well as create a manual restore point and see the date and time associated with the most recent automatic restore point.

FIGURE 5.42   Remote tab

FIGURE 5.43   System Protection tab

Windows Firewall

As the name implies, the Windows Firewall applet can be used to manage the firewall included with the operating system. Figure 5.44 shows an example. In this case, the computer's firewall settings are being managed by the domain administrator. When the computer is outside of that network, the firewall settings are available to the user of the computer.

FIGURE 5.44 Windows Firewall

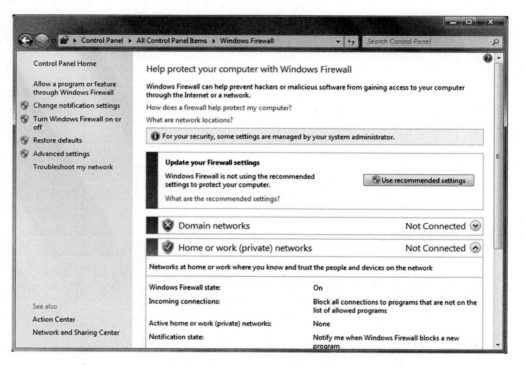

Power Options

Here you can configure different power schemes to adjust power consumption dictating when devices—the display and the computer—will turn off or be put to sleep. Through the Advanced Settings, you can configure the need to enter a password to revive the devices, as well as configure wireless adaptor settings, Internet options (namely, JavaScript), and the system sleep policy. Common choices include the following:

- **Standby** puts your computer into energy-saving mode, where it uses little power.
- **Hibernate** saves your workspace (all your open windows) and then turns the computer off.
- **Sleep/suspend** puts your computer into an even deeper energy-saving mode than Standby, where it uses even less power.

Power plans are collections of power settings that determine when various components in the device are shut down. There are some built-in plans available to you or you can create your own. There are three default plans: Balanced, which strikes a balance between performance and saving power; Power Saver, which errs on the side of saving power at the expense of performance; and High Performance, which errs on the side of performance over power saving. These options appear on the opening page when you open Power Options, as shown in Figure 5.45. To create a power, select Create A Power Plan from the tree menu on the left.

FIGURE 5.45   Power plans

Programs and Features

Formerly known as Add/Remove Programs, this tool allows you to manage the programs running on the machine and the Windows features as well. Windows Features are tools and utilities that come with the operating system that may or may not be installed and running. You can uninstall any program you have installed here. When you select Turn Windows Features On Or Off from the menu on the left, you get a box that allows you to enable and disable Windows features, as shown in Figure 5.46.

FIGURE 5.46 Programs and features

HomeGroup

In Windows 7, Windows 8, and Windows 8.1, but not Windows Vista, is an applet called HomeGoup. The purpose of HomeGroup (Start ≻ Control Panel ≻ HomeGroup) is to simplify home networking (the sharing of files and printers). Figure 5.47 shows the Homegroup applet for a device that is not currently connected to its home network. Windows 7 Starter can only join a HomeGroup, while all other editions of Windows 7 can both join and create a HomeGroup. The location must be set to Home.

Shared files can include libraries (a big feature of Windows 7). All computers participating in the HomeGroup must be running Windows 7, Windows 8, or Windows 8.1, and the network cannot extend outside of the small group.

Devices and Printers

While Windows Vista still makes use of the Add Printer Wizard, in Windows 7, Windows 8, and Windows 8.1 the Devices And Printers applet is now where printers and other devices are managed. This tool is divided into three sections with printers in one, multimedia devices in another, and other devices in a third, as shown in Figure 5.48. To manage any device, you right-click the device and select its properties. The printers also can be double-clicked, and you can see what's printing, manage the print queue, and adjust additional settings.

FIGURE 5.47 HomeGroup

FIGURE 5.48 Devices And Printers applet

Sound

While Windows Vista still uses Hardware And Sound, the Windows 7, Windows 8, and Windows 8.1 operating systems have a Control Panel item called Sound that is used to manage all sound settings. You can manage the input devices (microphones, lines in) and the output devices (speakers, headphones) in one place. Moreover, you can enable and disable the various Windows sounds that you hear when certain events occur. Figure 5.49 shows the Sound applet.

FIGURE 5.49 Sound applet

Troubleshooting

Available only in Windows 7, Windows 8, and Windows 8.1, this applet (Start ➢ Control Panel ➢ Troubleshooting) is used to provide a simple interface to attack many common problems. All links preceded by a shield require administrator permissions to run and are often tied to UAC prompts before continuing. Most of the problems found will be "automatically fixed" without any prompts. For example, clicking the link Improve Power Usage will start the Power Troubleshooter and then fix problems that it identifies. Clicking the link to get help from a friend brings up Remote Assistance, allowing someone to connect to this computer. You can also offer to be the one helping another. Figure 5.50 shows this applet.

FIGURE 5.50   Troubleshooting applet

Network and Sharing Center

In Windows Vista, two applets were used to manage network settings, Network Connections and the Network Setup Wizard. In Windows 7, Windows 8, and Windows 8.1, all the settings that were available there have been combined in an applet called Network And Sharing Center, where many sharing functions have also been relocated. While most of the tools are dedicated to creating and managing both wireless and wired network connections, as you will see when I discuss sharing in detail in the section "3.3 Compare and Contrast Differences of Basic Windows OS Security Settings" in Chapter 7, some Advanced sharing functions are available in this applet. Figure 5.51 shows this applet.

Device Manager

Device Manager was discussed in several sections so far including Table 5.15 on Windows administrative tools and the section "1.4 Given a Scenario, Use Appropriate Microsoft Operating System Features and Tools" earlier in this chapter. Figure 5.52 shows this applet.

FIGURE 5.51 Network And Sharing Center applet

FIGURE 5.52 Device Manager

Exam Essentials

Be able to name the common Control Panel applets.   While there are others, these include Display, Folder Options, Internet Options, Power Options, Security Center, System, User Accounts, and Windows Firewall.

Understand and apply the default options.   These include Standby, Hibernate, and Sleep. Also be capable of creating any custom power plans you may require.

1.6 Given a Scenario, Install and Configure Windows Networking on a Client/Desktop

CompTIA offers a number of exams and certifications on networking (Network+, Server+, and so on), but to become A+ certified, you must have good knowledge of basic networking skills as they relate to the Windows operating system.

It's important to know how network addressing works and the features offered in the Windows operating systems to simplify configuration. CompTIA expects you to have a broad range of knowledge in this category on some obscure features (such as QoS). The topics covered in this chapter include the following:

- HomeGroup vs. a workgroup
- Domain setup
- Network shares/administrative shares/mapping drives
- Printer sharing vs. network printer mapping
- Establishing networking connections
- Proxy settings
- Remote Desktop Connection
- Remote Assistance
- Home vs. work vs. public network settings
- Firewall settings
- Configuring an alternative IP address in Windows
- Network card properties

HomeGroup vs. Workgroup

As you learned in objective 1.5, HomeGroup offers a simplified way to set up a home network. It allows you to share files (including libraries) and prevent changes from being made to those files by those sharing them (unless you give them permission to do so).

All computers participating in the HomeGroup must be running Windows 7, Windows 8, or Windows 8.1 and the network can never grow beyond a limited size. While all editions of Windows 7 can join a HomeGroup, not all can create a HomeGroup. Windows 8 and Windows 8.1 clients can do both.

An alternative to make sharing easier in the home is to add all the computers to a peer-to-peer network. A peer-to-peer network, one of two network types you can create in Windows (also known as a workgroup), consists of a number of workstations (two or more) that share resources among themselves. The resources shared are traditionally file and print access, and every computer has the capacity to act as a workstation (by accessing resources from another machine) and as a server (by offering resources to other machines).

The other network type is client-server (or a domain). The primary distinction between workgroups and client-server networks is where security is controlled: locally on each workstation or centrally on a server. A domain is a centrally managed group of computers and physical proximity does not matter; the computers within a domain may all be on the same LAN or spread across a WAN.

The advantage of a peer-to-peer network is that the cost is lower; you need only add cards and cables to the computers you already have if you're running an operating system that allows such modifications. With a server-based network, you must buy a server—a dedicated machine—and thus the costs are higher. It's never recommended that a peer-to-peer network be used for more than 10 workstations because the administration and management become so significant that a server-based network makes far greater sense.

Domain Setup

In a domain (also known as a *client-server network*), users log on to the server by supplying a username and password. They're then authenticated for the duration of their session. Rather than requiring users to give a password for every resource they want to access (share-level), security is based on how they authenticated themselves at the beginning of their session. This is known as *user-level* security, and it's much more powerful than share-level security.

To join a computer to a domain, use the following procedures in Vista:

1. Open Control Panel (Start ➢ Control Panel).
2. Select System And Maintenance.
3. Click the System section.
4. In the Computer Name, Domain, And Workgroup Settings section, click the Change Settings link.
5. If you're prompted by the User Account Control module to continue, click Continue.
6. In the Computer Name tab of the properties, click the Change button.
7. In the Member Of section, select Domain, enter the name of the domain, and click OK.

8. You'll be prompted for an account with rights to join the computer to the domain. Enter the details and click OK.

9. Click OK to the welcome dialog box.

10. Click OK to the notice that the machine will be rebooted.

11. Click Close to the dialog box.

12. Click Restart Now to the restart prompt.

To join a computer to a domain, use the following procedures in Windows 7:

1. Open System by clicking the Start button, right-clicking Computer, and then clicking Properties.

2. Under Computer Name, Domain, And Workgroup Settings, click Change Settings. If you're prompted for an administrator password or confirmation, type the password or provide confirmation.

3. Click the Computer Name tab and then click Change.

4. Under Member Of, click Domain.

5. Type the name of the domain that you want to join and then click OK.

You will be asked to type your username and password for the domain. Once you are successfully joined to the domain, you will be prompted to restart your computer. You must restart your computer before the changes take effect.

To join a computer to a domain, use the following procedures in Windows 8 and 8.1:

1. Open System by swiping in from the right edge of the screen, tapping Search (or if you're using a mouse, pointing to the upper-right corner of the screen, moving the mouse pointer down, and then clicking Search), entering **System** in the search box, and tapping or clicking System.

2. Under Computer Name, Domain, And Workgroup Settings, click Change Settings. You might be asked for an admin password or to confirm your choice.

3. Click Network ID and follow the steps on your screen. You will select a domain and enter the fully qualified name of the domain.

Network Shares/Administrative Shares Mapping Drives

Network shares can be mapped to drives to appear as if the resources are local. The NET USE command is used to establish network connections via a command prompt. For example, to connect to a shared network drive and make it your M drive, you would use the syntax **net use m: \\server\share**. Figure 5.53 shows an example of mapped drives. This can also be done in File Explorer, as shown in Figure 5.54.

NET USE can also be used to connect to a shared printer: net use lpt1: \\ printername.

FIGURE 5.53 Mapped network drives

```
C:\>net use
New connections will be remembered.


Status         Local      Remote                 Network

Disconnected J:           \\Flint\Group          Microsoft Windows Network
OK           P:           \\fargo\home\eadulaney  Microsoft Windows Network
Disconnected S:           \\Flint\Group          Microsoft Windows Network
The command completed successfully.


C:\>_
```

FIGURE 5.54 Mapping a drive

An administrative share is one that is hidden to those file browsing. To connect to these drives, you must reference the name of the drive. While you can create a hidden drive at any time simply by adding a dollar sign at the end of its name, there are some default administrative drives.

Table 5.17 gives information on the default administrative drives.

TABLE 5.17   Default Administrative Drives

Share name	Location	Purpose
ADMIN$	%SystemRoot%	Remote administration
IPC$	N/A	Remote interprocess communication
print$	%SystemRoot%\System32\ spool\drivers	Access to printer drivers
C$, D$, E$ and so on	The root of any drive	Remote administration

Printer Sharing vs. Network Printer Mapping

In Chapter 1 in the section "Public/Shared Devices," you learned how to share a printer that is connected locally to a computer. It is also possible to connect to a network printer that is one that is not tied to a computer but has its own IP address and probably built-in print server. To connect or map a user's device to one of these devices, follow the procedure to add a shared printer, and on the page you normally enter the UNC path to the shared printer, select the option Add A Printer Using A TCP/IP Address Or Hostname, as shown in Figure 5.55, and click Next.

FIGURE 5.55   Adding a printer using a TCP/IP address

Enter the IP address or the hostname of the printer, as shown in Figure 5.56, and click Next.

FIGURE 5.56   Adding the printer IP address

If the IP address is correct and can be reached, the printer driver will download, and the printer will be added to the printer's area of Control Panel.

Establishing Networking Connections

When configuring the connection method for accessing the Internet, the three choices Windows offers are This Computer Connects Directly To The Internet, This Computer Connects Through A Residential Gateway Or Another Computer, and Other. If you choose the first option, you can turn on Internet Connection Sharing (ICS) and allow this machine to serve as a proxy. The network connection you configure can be wireless or wired, dial-up, or a VPN.

VPN   A virtual private network (VPN) is used when you want to connect from a remote location (such as home) to the company's network (authenticating the user and encrypting the data).

Dialups   Dial-up connections are used when a modem must be used to gain access. Typically, the dial-up connection is to an Internet service provider (ISP) and used in remote locations where faster forms of access are not available.

Wireless   A wireless connection uses one of the 802.11 technologies, along with encryption (discussed in Chapter 7, "Security") to connect to the network.

Wired   A wired connection uses a wire to connect the computer to the network. Typically, this is an Ethernet cable, such as 100BaseT (discussed in Chapter 2, "Networking"), which connects to a hub or switch and offers network access to the host.

WWAN (Cellular)   A wireless wide area network (WWAN) connection is one that uses cellular to connect the host to the network. A wireless service provider (such as AT&T, Sprint, or T-Mobile) will provide a card that is plugged into the host to make the cellular connection possible.

The choices will vary slightly based on the version of Windows you are using, but those commonly available are shown in Table 5.18.

TABLE 5.18 Network connection options

Option	Purpose
Connect To The Internet	Use for connection to a proxy server or other device intended to provide Internet access. This includes wireless, broadband, and dial-up.
Set Up A Wireless Router Or Access Point	If the wireless device will be connected to this machine, this is the option to use.
Manually Connect To A Wireless Network	If you have a wireless network already in place and the device (such as the router) is not directly connected to this machine, then use this option.
Set Up A Wireless Ad Hoc (Computer-To-Computer) Network	This is meant for peer-to-peer resource sharing via wireless network cards and typically a temporary connection.
Set Up A Dial-Up Connection	If you live in the middle of nowhere and the only way to access a network is by using a dial-up modem, then this is the option to select.
Connect To A Workplace	If you are needing to dial into a VPN from a remote location, this is the option to use.

Regardless of which option you choose, you will need to fill out the appropriate fields for the device to be able to communicate on the network. With TCP/IP, required values are an IP address for the host, subnet mask, address for the gateway, and DNS information.

Proxy Settings

Proxy settings identify the proxy server to be used to gain Internet access. The proxy server is responsible for making the Internet access possible and may utilize Network Address Translation (NAT) to translate between the public network (Internet) and the private network (on which the host sits). These settings are configured in Internet Options, as shown in Figure 5.57, using the LAN Settings button in the Connections tab, which opens the dialog shown in Figure 5.57.

FIGURE 5.57   LAN settings

Local Area Network (LAN) Settings

Automatic configuration

Automatic configuration may override manual settings. To ensure the use of manual settings, disable automatic configuration.

☑ Automatically detect settings

☐ Use automatic configuration script

Address

Proxy server

☑ Use a proxy server for your LAN (These settings will not apply to dial-up or VPN connections).

Address: 192.1698.12.4   Port: 80   Advanced

☑ Bypass proxy server for local addresses

OK   Cancel

Remote Desktop Connection

Remote Desktop, which is not included in the Home editions of the operating systems, allows members of the Administrators group to gain access to the workstation. (You can specifically allow other users as well.) By default, Remote Desktop is not enabled on Windows 7 or Windows Vista, but you can enable it from Remote Settings in the Control Panel applet System And Security. To enable Remote Desktop connections in Windows Vista and Windows 7, follow these steps:

1. Right-click the Computer icon and choose Properties, or you can type **system** into the Start menu search box and then find the entry for System.

2. Click the Remote Settings link on the left side.

3. Select one of the two options allowing Remote Desktop connections, as shown in Figure 5.58.

   To enable Remote Desktop connections in Windows 8 and 8.1, follow these steps:

1. Open the desktop Control Panel and find the System panel there, or you can search for *Remote Access* in the Start menu or Start screen.

2. Click Allow Remote Access To Your Computer.

3. When the System Properties dialog box appears, select to allow Remote Desktop connections, as shown in Figure 5.59.

FIGURE 5.58   Enabling Remote Desktop in Windows Vista and 7

FIGURE 5.59   Enabling Remote Desktop in Windows 8

Remote Assistance

Remote Assistance is a tool that allows you to connect to a remote computer to provide assistance to another user currently logged into that computer. When you connect via Remote Assistance, you do not have to log into that computer; instead, invitations are sent from the host computer to you so you can take over the computer. You can use the remote computer (the host computer) as if you are sitting in front of it. The user on the other end can watch your activities onscreen. At any time, either user can terminate the session. To configure this feature, follow these steps:

1. Type **Remote**.
2. Click Settings under the Search box.
3. Click Allow Remote Assistance Invitations To Be Sent From This Computer. The System Properties dialog box appears, with the Remote tab showing.
4. Click Allow Remote Assistance Connections To This Computer, as shown in Figure 5.60.
5. Click OK.

A user on the host computer can now send an invitation to you to allow you to connect to that computer for repair or training purposes.

FIGURE 5.60   Enabling Assistance in Windows 8 and 8.1

Home vs. Work vs. Public Network Settings

In Windows 7, Windows Vista, and Windows 8, when you make a new connection, you are asked to identify whether it is a home network, work network, or public network. If you choose one of the first two, *network discovery* is on by default, allowing you to see other computers and other computers to see you. If you choose Public, network discovery is turned off. In Figure 5.61, you can see that the device is connected to a public network.

FIGURE 5.61   Public network

Firewall Settings

Windows Firewall (Start ➤ Control Panel ➤ Windows Firewall) is used to block access from the network. In Windows 7, it is divided into separate settings for private networks and public networks.

Exceptions

Exceptions are configured as variations from the rules. Windows Firewall will block incoming network connections except for the programs and services that you choose to allow through. For example, you can make an exception for Remote Assistance to allow communication from other computers when you need help (the scope of the exception can be set to allow any computer, only those on the network, or a custom list of allowed addresses you create). Exceptions can include programs as well as individual ports.

Configuration

Most of the configuration is done as network connection settings. You can configure both ICMP and Services settings. Examples of ICMP settings include allowing incoming echo requests, allowing incoming router requests, and allowing redirects. Examples of services often configured include an FTP server, Post-Office Protocol Version 3 (POP3), and web server (HTTP).

Enabling/Disabling Windows Firewall

On the General tab of Windows Firewall, it is possible to choose the radio button Off (Not Recommended). As the name implies, this turns Windows Firewall completely off. The other radio button option, On (Recommended), enables the firewall. You can also toggle the check box Don't Allow Exceptions. This option should be enabled when you're connecting to a public network in an unsecure location (such as an airport or library), and it will then ignore any exceptions that were configured.

Configuring an Alternative IP Address in Windows

Windows 7, Windows Vista, and Windows 8 and 8.1 all allow the use of an alternate IP address. This is an address that is configured for the system to use in the event the first choice is not available. The first choice can be either a dynamic or static address, and the alternate is used only if the primary cannot be found or used, such as when the DHCP server is down.

The Properties dialog box for each instance of IPv4—on any of the Windows operating systems this exam focuses on—contains an Alternate Configuration tab. To make changes, you must click it.

IP Addressing

Two radio buttons appear on the Alternate Configuration tab, as shown in Figure 5.62: Automatic Private IP Address and User Configured. The default is the first, meaning that the alternate address used is one in the APIPA range ($169.254.x.x$). Selecting User Configured requires you to enter a static IP address to be used in the IP address field. The entry entered must be valid for your network for it to be usable (see Chapter 2 for more information on IP addressing).

Subnet Mask

When you select the User Configured radio button on the Alternate Configuration tab, you must enter a value in the Subnet Mask field. This value must correspond with the subnet values in use on your network and work with the IP address you enter in the field above (see Chapter 2 for more information on subnet addresses).

FIGURE 5.62   APIPA

Internet Protocol Version 4 (TCP/IPv4) Properties

General | Alternate Configuration

If this computer is used on more than one network, enter the alternate IP settings below.

◉ Automatic private IP address
○ User configured

IP address:
Subnet mask:
Default gateway:

Preferred DNS server:
Alternate DNS server:

Preferred WINS server:
Alternate WINS server:

☐ Validate settings, if changed, upon exit

OK   Cancel

DNS

When you select the User Configured radio button on the Alternate Configuration tab, you should enter values in the fields Preferred DNS Server and Alternate DNS Server. These entries are needed in order to translate domain names into IP addresses (see Chapter 2 for more information on DNS).

Gateway

When you select the User Configured radio button on the Alternate Configuration tab, you must enter a value in the Default Gateway field. This value must correspond with the subnet values and the IP address you enter in the fields above. This address identifies the router to be used to communicate outside the local network (see Chapter 2 for more information on default gateways).

Network Card Properties

Like other devices, network cards can be configured to optimize performance. Configuration is done through the Properties dialog box for each card.

Half Duplex/Full Duplex/Auto

Duplexing is the means by which communication takes place.

- With *full duplexing*, everyone can send and receive at the same time. The main advantage of full-duplex over half-duplex communication is performance. NICs can operate twice as fast in full-duplex mode as they do normally in half-duplex mode.

- With *half duplexing*, communications travel in both directions, but in only one direction at any given time. Think of a road where construction is being done on one lane—traffic can go in both directions but in only one direction at a time at that location.

- With *auto duplexing*, the mode is set to the lowest common denominator. If a card senses another card is manually configured to half duplex, then it also sets itself at that.

Duplexing is set using the Advanced tab on the Properties of the network card, as shown in Figure 5.63.

FIGURE 5.63   Setting speed and duplex

Speed

The speed allows you to configure whether the card should run at its highest possible setting. You often need to be compatible with the network on which the host resides. If, for example, you are connecting a workstation with a 10/100BaseT card to a legacy network, you will need to operate at 10 MBps to match the rest of the network. This is done along with duplex, as shown in Figure 5.63.

Wake-on-LAN

Wake-on-LAN (WoL) is an Ethernet standard implemented via a card that allows a "sleeping" machine to awaken when it receives a wakeup signal.

QoS

Quality of Service (QoS) implements packet scheduling to control the flow of traffic and help with network transmission speeds. No properties can be configured for the service itself.

BIOS (Onboard NIC)

While some older devices may have network cards installed in slots, most devices now have integrated or built-in network interfaces on the motherboard. While these interfaces will be recognized and set up automatically, if you find you do not see an integrated interface when you go to Network And Sharing, you may need to enable the interface in the BIOS. The steps to locate this setting are specific to the BIOS on the machine, but if you identify the BIOS vendor and the version, you should be able to look up the steps on the BIOS vendor website.

Exam Essentials

Know what values are needed for network connectivity.   Regardless of which network access method you choose, you will need to fill out the appropriate fields for the device to be able to communicate on the network. With TCP/IP, required values are an IP address for the host, subnet mask, address for the gateway, and DNS information.

Understand the purpose of HomeGroup.   The HomeGroup feature was added to Windows 7 as a simplified way to set up a home network. It works only with Windows 7 and allows you to share files (including libraries) and resources.

1.7 Perform Common Preventive Maintenance Procedures Using the Appropriate Windows OS Tools

Taking care of your company's desktop and laptop computers can extend their life and save considerable money. Most of the actions necessary to maintain laptops fall under the category of what is reasonable, and you would undoubtedly think of them on your own.

Best practices exist to define what should be done to keep systems maintained. The first section under this objective focuses on the best practices related to preventive maintenance, and the second section explores the tools used to put many of those practices into play. The topics covered in this chapter include the following:

- Best practices
- Tools

Best Practices

Preventive maintenance is more than just manipulating hardware; it also encompasses running software utilities on a regular basis to keep the filesystem fit. These utilities can include scheduled backups, check disks, defragmentation, and updates.

Scheduled Backups

Backups are duplicate copies of key information, ideally stored in a location other than the one where the information is currently stored. Backups include both paper and computer records. Computer records are usually backed up using a backup program, backup systems, and backup procedures.

The primary starting point for disaster recovery involves keeping current backup copies of key data files, databases, applications, and paper records available for use. Your organization must develop a solid set of procedures to manage this process and ensure that all key information is protected. A security professional can do several things in conjunction with systems administrators and business managers to protect this information. It's important to think of this problem as an issue that is larger than a single department.

The information you back up must be immediately available for use when needed. If a user loses a critical file, they won't want to wait several days while data files are sent from a remote storage facility. Several types of storage mechanisms are available for data storage.

Working Copies *Working copy* backups—sometimes referred to as *shadow copies*—are partial or full backups that are kept on the premises for immediate recovery purposes. Working copies are frequently the most recent backups that have been made.

Typically, working copies are intended for immediate use. These copies are often updated on a frequent basis.

Many filesystems used on servers include *journaling*. Journaled filesystems (JFSs) include a log file of all changes and transactions that have occurred within a set period of time (such as the last few hours). If a crash occurs, the operating system can look at the log files to see which transactions have been committed and which ones haven't. This technology works well and allows unsaved data to be written after the recovery and the system (usually) to be successfully restored to its condition before the crash.

Onsite Storage *Onsite storage* usually refers to a location on the site of the computer center that is used to store information locally. Onsite storage containers are available that allow computer cartridges, tapes, and other backup media to be stored in a reasonably protected environment in the building.

Onsite storage containers are designed and rated for fire, moisture, and pressure resistance. These containers aren't *fireproof* in most situations, but they're *fire-rated*: a fireproof container should be guaranteed to withstand damage regardless of the type of fire or temperatures, whereas fire ratings specify that a container can protect the contents for a specific amount of time in a given situation.

If you choose to depend entirely on onsite storage, make sure the containers you acquire can withstand the worst-case environmental catastrophes that could happen at your location. Make sure as well that those containers are in locations where you can easily find them after the disaster and access them (near exterior walls, and so on).

Offsite Storage   *Offsite storage* refers to a location away from the computer center where paper copies and backup media are kept. Offsite storage can involve something as simple as keeping a copy of backup media at a remote office, or it can be as complicated as a nuclear-hardened high-security storage facility. The storage facility should be bonded, insured, and inspected on a regular basis to ensure that all storage procedures are being followed.

Determining which storage mechanism to use should be based on the needs of the organization, the availability of storage facilities, and the budget available. Most offsite storage facilities charge based on the amount of space you require and the frequency of access you need to the stored information.

Three methods exist to back up information on most systems.

Full Backup   A *full backup* is a complete, comprehensive backup of all files on a disk or server. The full backup is current only at the time it's performed. Once a full backup is made, you have a complete archive of the system at that point in time. A system shouldn't be in use while it undergoes a full backup because some files may not get backed up. Once the system goes back into operation, the backup is no longer current. A full backup can be a time-consuming process on a large system.

Incremental Backup   An *incremental backup* is a partial backup that stores only the information that has been changed since the last full or incremental backup. If a full backup were performed on a Sunday night, an incremental backup done on Monday night would contain only the information that changed since Sunday night. Such a backup is typically considerably smaller than a full backup. This backup system requires that each incremental backup be retained until a full backup can be performed. Incremental backups are usually the fastest backups to perform on most systems, and each incremental tape is relatively small.

Differential Backup   A differential backup is similar in function to an incremental backup, but it backs up any files that have been altered since the last full backup; it makes duplicate copies of files that haven't changed since the last differential backup. If a full backup was performed on Sunday night, a differential backup performed on Monday night would capture the information that was changed on Monday. A differential backup completed on Tuesday night would record the changes in any files from Monday and any changes in files on Tuesday. As you can see, during the week each differential backup would become larger; by Friday or Saturday night, it might be nearly as large as a full backup. This means the backups in the earliest part of the weekly cycle will be very fast, and each successive one will be slower.

When these backup methods are used in conjunction with each other, the risk of loss can be greatly reduced. You should never combine an incremental backup with a differential backup. One of the major factors in determining which combination of these three methods to use is time—ideally, a full backup would be performed every day. Several commercial backup programs support these three backup methods. You must evaluate your organizational needs when choosing which tools to use to accomplish backups.

Almost every stable operating system contains a utility for creating a copy of configuration settings necessary to reach the present state after a disaster. As an administrator, you must know how to do backups and be familiar with all the options available to you.

Scheduled Disk Maintenance

Several additional maintenance operations can be used on a regular basis to prevent performance issues that will arise from simply using the devices. This section covers two important performance-enhancing maintenance tasks.

Scheduled Check Disks

I recommend that in addition to backups you also regularly run CHKDSK. You can so by manually running the tool, or you can configure Task Scheduler to run it on a routine basis.

To manually run it, you can start chkdsk.exe in a command window, or you can right-click the drive in My Computer, choose Properties, click the Tools tab, and select Check Now.

Scheduled Defragmentation

Defragmenting the disk moves the files on the disk so the data is contiguously located when possible. Both volume and file fragmentation occurs as files continue to grow through normal usage, and thus defragmentation should be done on a regular basis.

Just as you can right-click a drive in My Computer, choose Properties, and click the Tools tab to start a CHKDSK routine, you can also start defragmentation from here by selecting Defragment Now. The Task Scheduler can be used to schedule the program (Defrag.exe or Dfrgntfs.exe) to regularly run.

Windows Updates

Windows Updates were discussed in the section "Driver Installation, Software and Windows Updates." After the installation, however, you should configure the system to regularly check for and install updates. To do this in Windows Vista, follow these steps:

1. Open the Start menu. Choose All Programs ➤ Windows Update.
2. Click Change Settings.

To turn on automatic updating with Automatic Install, follow these steps:

1. Select Install Updates Automatically (Recommended).
2. Under Recommended Updates, check the Include Recommended Updates When Downloading, Installing, Or Notifying Me About Updates check box.
3. Under Update Service, check the Use Microsoft Update check box.

To turn on automatic updating without Automatic Install, follow these steps:

1. Select either Download Updates But Let Me Choose Whether To Install Them or Check for Updates But Let Me Choose Whether To Download And Install Them.

2. Under Recommended Updates, check the Include Recommended Updates When Downloading, Installing, Or Notifying Me About Updates check box.

3. Under Update Service, check the Use Microsoft Update check box.

To turn off Automatic Updating, follow these steps:

1. Select Never Check for Updates (Not Recommended).

2. Click OK.

3. Click Continue For UAC prompt.

4. Close the Windows Update window when done.

To configure Windows Update in Windows 7, Windows 8, and Windows 8.1, follow these steps:

1. In Control Panel, open the Windows Update window.

2. Click or tap Change Settings from the left pane.

3. In the Important Updates section, in the drop-down box select from one of the following:

   - Install Updates Automatically
   - Download Updates But Let Me Choose Whether To Install Them
   - Check For Updates But Let Me Choose Whether To Download And Install Them
   - Never Check For Updates

Patch Management

Windows Update can be configured in Windows 7 and Windows Vista to also look for and install updates to other Microsoft software programs installed on the machine. You should make a practice of routinely checking with vendors of other programs you use for patches they release, many of which address issues of security and functionality.

Always check the patches on test machines before applying them to production machines—they may occasionally disrupt or affect operations your company relies on.

Driver/Firmware Updates

Device drivers are the software stubs that allow devices to communicate with the operating system. Called *drivers* for short, they're used for interacting with printers, monitors, network cards, sound cards, and just about every type of hardware attached to the PC. One of the most common problems associated with drivers isn't having the current version. As problems are fixed, the drivers are updated, and you can often save a great deal of time by downloading the latest drivers from the vendor's site early in the troubleshooting process. The easiest way to change drivers in Windows is to right-click the device in Device Manager and select Update Driver Software, as shown in Figure 5.64.

FIGURE 5.64 Updating a driver

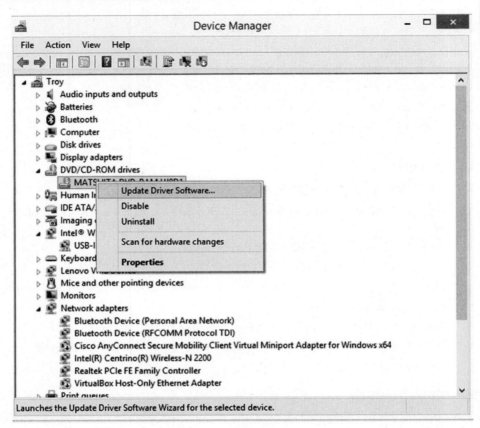

Any software that is built into a hardware device is called *firmware*. Firmware is typically in flash ROM and can be updated as newer versions become available. An example of firmware is the software in a laser printer that controls it and allows you to interact with it at the console (usually through a limited menu of options).

Firmware and driver updates are often released by hardware vendors. You should routinely check their sites for patches and updates that you need to download and install.

Antivirus/Antimalware Updates

While malware will be discussed extensively in Chapter 7, antivirus and antimalware updates should be regularly updated (with particular interest paid to the definition files). While steps and options to configure these updates are unique to each product, with respect to the built-in Windows tools, such as Windows Defender, those definitions will be updated along with other updates you receive from Windows Update.

Tools

A number of tools are available to ensure the safety of your data and the operating system. This section discusses five tools you need to know about: Backup, Check Disk, Defrag, System Restore, and Recovery Image.

Backup

The Backup utility allows you to create the backups discussed regarding best practices earlier. To access this tool in Windows Vista, follow these steps:

1. Click Start.
2. Click Control Panel.
3. Double-click Backup And Restore Center.
4. Click Back Up Files.
5. When the User Account Control dialog box opens, click Continue.
6. Decide where you want to save your backup.
7. Choose the option that you want to use to back up.
8. Click Next.
9. On the Which Disks Do You Want To Include In The Backup? dialog box, select the disks you want to back up.
10. Click Next.
11. On the Which File Types Do You Want To Include In The Backup? dialog box, uncheck any files types you do not want to back up.
12. Click Next.
13. Select how often you want your backups to happen.
14. Click Save Settings And Start Backup.
15. Insert blank media into the appropriate drive. When prompted, insert each new disc and label each one as instructed.

To perform this in Windows 7, follow these steps:

1. Right-click the drive and select Properties. Then click the Tools tab and click the Back Up Now button.
2. In the Back Up Or Restore Your Files window, click the link to set up a backup.
3. Windows will search for a suitable drive to store the backup, or you can also choose a location on your network.
4. Select either of the following:
   - Let Windows Choose (What To Backup)
   - Let Me Choose (What To Backup)
5. If you chose Let Me Choose, select the files and folder to include in the backup.

6. Review the backup job and make sure everything looks correct.

7. Schedule the days and times the backup occurs.

8. Save the backup settings and start the backup.

In Windows 8 and 8.1, backups are done through the File History tool. To do this, you have to set up a drive for File History. Follow these instructions:

1. Swipe in from the right edge of the screen and then tap or Search or point to the lower-right corner of the screen, move the mouse pointer up, and then click Search.

2. Enter **File History settings** in the search box, and then tap or click File History settings.

3. Tap or click Select A Drive, and choose the network or external drive you want to use.

4. Select Turn On File History.

> File History only backs up copies of files that are in the Documents, Music, Pictures, Videos, and Desktop folders and the OneDrive files available offline on your PC. If you have files or folders elsewhere that you want backed up, you can add them to one of these folders.

System Restore

To access the System Restore tool, choose the System applet in the Control Panel and then the System Protection tab (see Figure 5.65). By clicking the System Restore button, you can revert to an earlier restore point and circumvent problems that have recently occurred with system settings or corrupted files.

From here, you can also manually create a restore point, configure what is included in a restore point, and specify how much space you are allowing to be used for saving these files (setting the space to 0 percent effectively disables the creation of restore points).

Recovery Image

A *recovery image*, also known as a *system image*, is an image that includes all the drives required for Windows to run as well as default system settings, programs, and files. If you replace a failed hard drive in a workstation, you can use the recovery image to replicate the initial settings (you can't choose individual items to restore) and then turn to the backups to bring the system back up-to-date.

Many OEM vendors include a recovery image with new systems they ship. That image may be on a recovery disc (CD or DVD) or on a partition that can be accessed after POST. Obviously, vendors prefer the partition approach since it saves shipping any physical item, but it is of no use at all in the event of a full failure of the hard drive.

FIGURE 5.65   The System Restore option

Disk Maintenance Utilities

Several tools are available in Windows to help keep the disk system operating at peak performance. While I discussed scheduling CHKDSK and the graphical version of Defrag in the section "Scheduled Disk Maintenance," in this section I will talk a bit more in depth about these tools.

Check Disk

Check Disk is a Windows graphical utility for finding and fixing logical errors and optionally for checking each sector of the physical disk and relocating any readable data from damaged spots.

Check Disk isn't a menu command on the Start menu. To run it, display the Properties box for a hard disk and then select the Check Now button in the Error-Checking section of the Tools tab, as shown in Figure 5.66.

FIGURE 5.66   The Tools tab for a hard drive

OS (C:) Properties

| Security | Previous Versions | Quota |
| General | Tools | Hardware | Sharing |

Error-checking

This option will check the drive for errors.

Check now...

Defragmentation

This option will defragment files on the drive.

Defragment now...

Backup

This option will back up files on the drive.

Back up now...

OK   Cancel   Apply

Do not be confused by CHKDSK—an old MS-DOS utility used to correct logical errors in the FAT. The most common switch for the CHKDSK command is /F, which fixes the errors that it finds. Without /F, Chkdsk acts as an "information only" utility.

Defrag

Disk Defragmenter reorganizes the file storage on a disk to reduce the number of files that are stored noncontiguously. This makes file retrieval faster because the read/write heads on the disk have to move less.

There are two versions of Disk Defragmenter: a Windows version that runs from within Windows and a command-line version (DEFRAG.EXE). In addition to being on the Tools tab (shown in Figure 5.66), the Windows version is located on the System Tools submenu on the Start menu (Start ➤ All Programs ➤ Accessories ➤ System Tools ➤ Disk Defragmenter).

The available switches for the command-line version of DEFRAG.EXE in Windows 8.1 include the following:

- /A: Perform analysis on the specified volumes.
- /C: Perform the operation on all volumes.
- /D: Perform a traditional defrag (this is the default).
- /E: Perform the operation on all volumes except those specified.
- /H: Run the operation at normal priority (the default is low).
- /K: Perform slab consolidation on the specified volumes.
- /L: Perform a retrim on the specified volumes.
- /M: Run the operation on each volume in parallel in the background.
- /O: Perform the proper optimization for each media type.
- /T: Track an operation already in progress on the specified volume.
- /U: Print the progress of the operation on the screen.
- /V: Print verbose output containing the fragmentation statistics.
- /X: Perform free space consolidation on the specified volumes.

Exam Essentials

Know the importance of running scheduled maintenance.   Scheduled maintenance can prolong the life of your equipment and help ensure that your output continues to live up to the quality you expect.

Know how to access System Restore.   To access the System Restore tool, choose the System applet in the Control Panel and then select the System Protection tab.

Review Questions

You can find the answers in the Appendix.

1. Which of the following is an interface that offers a glass design that includes translucent windows?

    A. Sidebar

    B. Aero

    C. Metro

    D. Start screen

2. Which of the following are mini programs, introduced with Windows Vista, that can be placed on the desktop (Windows 7) or on the Sidebar (Windows Vista)?

    A. Gadgets

    B. Metro apps

    C. Widgets

    D. Shims

3. Which feature applies to removable drives?

    A. Compatibility mode

    B. Shadow coy

    C. BitLocker to Go

    D. UAC

4. Which feature requires you to download Windows Virtual PC to use?

    A. Easy Transfer

    B. Virtual XP mode

    C. Hyper-V

    D. ReadyBoost

5. Which feature is beneficial when you are running low on available memory?

    A. XP Mode

    B. Shadow copy

    C. East Transfer

    D. ReadyBoost

6. In which tool has the Security center been rolled in Windows 7?

    A. Action Center

    B. Control Panel

    C. Windows Firewall

    D. Defender

7. Which Windows log in Event viewer displays alerts that pertain to the general operation of Windows?

   A. Application

   B. System

   C. Security

   D. Forwarded Events

8. What is the name of the user interface in Windows 8 and 8.1?

   A. Aero

   B. Metro

   C. Sidebar

   D. Start

9. What is the process of configuring an icon for a program on the taskbar so that it is easier to locate?

   A. nailing

   B. posting

   C. pinning

   D. taping

10. What feature was formerly called SkyDrive?

   A. CloudDrive

   B. DriveBox

   C. OneDrive

   D. HomeDrive

Chapter

6

Other Operating Systems and Technologies

COMPTIA A+ 220-902 EXAM OBJECTIVES COVERED IN THIS CHAPTER:

✓ **2.1 Identify common features and functionality of the Mac OS and Linux operating systems.**

- Best practices (scheduled backups, scheduled disk maintenance, system updates/app store, patch management, driver/firmware updates, antivirus/antimalware updates)

- Tools (backup/Time Machine, restore/snapshot, image recovery, disk maintenance utilities, shell/terminal, screen sharing, force quit)

- Features (multiple desktops/Mission Control, Key Chain, Spot Light, iCloud, gestures, Finder, Remote Disk, Dock, Boot Camp)

- Basic Linux commands (ls, grep, cd, shutdown, pwd vs. passwd, mv, cp, rm, chmod, cmkdir, chown, iwconfig/ifconfig, ps, q, su/sudo, apt-get, vi, dd)

✓ **2.2 Given a scenario, setup and use client-side virtualization.**

- Purpose of virtual machines

- Resource requirements

- Emulator requirements

- Security requirements

- Network requirements

- Hypervisor

- PRI updates/PRL updates/baseband updates

- Radio firmware

- IMEI vs. IMSI

- VPN

✓ 2.7 Summarize methods and data related to mobile device synchronization.

- Types of data to synchronize (contacts, programs, email, pictures, music, videos, calendar, bookmarks, documents, location data, social media data, eBooks)

- Synchronization methods (synchronize to the cloud, synchronize to the desktop)

- Mutual authentication for multiple services

- Software requirements to install the application on the PC

- Connection types to enable synchronization

While the overwhelming percentage of devices you will come into contact with will be Windows devices, you will also encounter other operating systems. The Linux operating system and the Mac OS are increasingly found in enterprise networks in situations where their strengths can be leveraged. There are also many other technologies that you may not be directly managing, but you should still be familiar with them and understand their purpose. This chapter will focus on these areas.

2.1 Identify Common Features and Functionality of the Mac OS and Linux Operating Systems

In your career, you are almost certain to come in contact with both the Linux and Mac OS operating systems (since 2001 the Mac OS system has been called OS X, so you may consider those terms interchangeable). Despite that these systems constitute only a small percentage of the total number of devices found in the enterprise, the proponents of both of these systems are cult-like in their devotion to both operating systems. Linux is probably used more often, in part because many proprietary operating systems that reside on devices such as access points, switches, routers, and firewalls are Linux-based. In this section of the chapter, you will be introduced to some of the common features and functions in these operating systems. The subobjectives covered in this section include the following:

- Best practices
- Tools
- Features
- Basic Linux commands

Best Practices

Like with any operating system, Linux and Mac OS will function better and with more reliability with the proper care. This section will discuss some of the best practices that have been developed over the years for using these operating systems.

Scheduled Backups

In Linux, backups of data can be scheduled using the `rsync` utility from the command line. While there is another utility, cp, that can be used, `rsync` prevents unnecessary copying when the destination file has not been changed. It also can operate locally and remotely. It also encrypts the transfer. The basic syntax is as follows, where the a switch tells `rsync` to work in "archive" mode:

```
rsync -a [source dir] [destination dir]
```

As with any command-line utility, you can create batch files and schedule these backups.

In Mac OS, you can also use `rsync`, but another tool is available. With Time Machine, you can back up your entire Mac, including system files, apps, music, photos, e-mails, and documents. When Time Machine is enabled, it automatically backs up your Mac and performs hourly, daily, and weekly backups of your files.

Scheduled Disk Maintenance

Because Linux systems manage the disk differently than Windows, they need no defragmentation. There is a maintenance task you may want to schedule in Linux. From time to time you should run a filesystem checker called `fsck`. This is a logical filesystem checker.

The Mac OS needs defragmentation in only a small number of cases. If the user creates large numbers of multimedia files and the drive has been filling for quite some time, the system may benefit from defragmentation. However, in most cases, this is not required.

One task that is beneficial to execute from time to time is to check the health of the disk using the Disk Utility's Verify Disk functionality. While many disk operations (including the use of Time Machine) require booting to a different drive to perform the operation on the drive in question, Disk Utility can perform a live verification without doing this.

System Updates/App Store

Many of the versions of Linux now make updates much easier than in the past. Both Ubuntu and Fedora offer a GUI tool (shocking!) for this. In Ubuntu, for example, choosing System ➤ Administration and then selecting the Update Manager entry will open Update Manager. When it opens, click the Check button to see whether there are updates available. Figure 6.1 shows a list of available updates.

Of course, you can still do this from the command line. Follow these steps:

1. Open a terminal window.

2. Issue the command **sudo apt-get upgrade**.

3. Enter your user's password.

4. Look over the list of available updates and decide whether you want to go through with the entire upgrade.

5. When the desired updates have been selected, press the Install Updates button.

6. Watch as the update happens.

FIGURE 6.1 Ubuntu Update Manager

In Mac OS, updates can come either directly from Apple or from the Apple Store. To make updates automatic, access Software Update preferences, where you can set it to daily, monthly, or weekly, as shown in Figure 6.2.

FIGURE 6.2   Software Update preferences

Patch Management

While in the past patch management in Linux and Mac OS presented more of a challenge than with Windows, today the same tool used to manage patches with Windows (System Center Configuration Manager) can now be used to patch additional systems such as Linux and Mac. There are also third-party tools such as Spacewalk that can manage updates.

Driver/Firmware Updates

Updating drivers and firmware in Linux can be done either during the installation or afterward. Some versions such as Red Hat recommend installing first and then performing the upgrade. While the upgrade process varies from version to version, in Ubuntu either you can wait until a new version of the OS is released (which is once every six months) and get the update from the Software Update Center, or you can access what is called a *personal package archive* (PPA). These PPAs are repositories containing drivers that can be easily made available to the Ubuntu Update Manager by adding the PPA to the local system. Once added, the drivers will appear as available when you access the local Ubuntu Update Manager, as shown in Figure 6.3.

In Red Hat, driver and firmware updates download the driver update RPM package from the location specified by Red Hat or your hardware vendor. Then locate and double-click the file that you downloaded. The system might prompt you for the root password, after which it will present the Installing packages box, shown in Figure 6.4. Then click Apply.

FIGURE 6.3   Update Manager with PPA

FIGURE 6.4   Installing packages

On Mac OS, firmware and driver updates are obtained from the Apple Support site. After downloading the update, the system will restart, and while a gray screen appears, the update will be applied.

Antivirus/Antimalware Updates

All the major antivirus and antimalware vendors create products for both Mac and commercial versions of Linux. Updates to the engines and definitions for these applications are done in a similar fashion to Windows. Checks for updates can be scheduled just as is done in Windows.

Tools

Tools exist to perform maintenance, some of which I have already mentioned. This section will cover some of these utilities and functions.

Backup/Time Machine

For all Linux versions, backup tools are available for free and for a fee. You can also use the tar and cpio command-line utilities to construct full or partial backups of the system. Each utility constructs a large file that contains, or *archives*, other files. In addition to file contents, an archive includes header information for each file it holds. Table 6.1 lists the parameters of the tar command.

TABLE 6.1   tar parameters

Option	Effect
--append (-r)	Appends files to an archive
--catenate (-A)	Adds one or more archives to the end of an existing archive
--create (-c)	Creates a new archive
--delete	Deletes files in an archive, not on tapes
--diff (-d)	Compares files in an archive with disk files
--extract (-x)	Extracts files from an archive
--help	Displays a help list of tar options
--list (-t)	Lists the files in an archive
--update (-u)	Like the -r option, but the file is not appended if a newer version is already in the archive

On Mac OS you can use Time Machine, discussed earlier in the section "Scheduled Backups." Figure 6.5 shows this tool and some of its options.

FIGURE 6.5 Time Machine

Restore/Snapshot

In Linux, the snapshot feature provides the ability to create a volume image of a device at a particular instant without causing a service interruption. When a change is made to the original device (the origin) after a snapshot is taken, the snapshot feature makes a copy of the changed data area as it was prior to the change so that it can reconstruct the state of the device. You can use the -s argument of the lvcreate command to create a snapshot volume.

To restore a snapshot, first change the directory to where the snapshots are located. Once there, change to the hidden subdirectory called .snapshot. There you will find directories such as nightly.0, nightly.1, ..., nightly.2, hourly.0, hourly.1, ..., and hourly.10 (use the ls to command to see them). Change to the directory that still contains your file and copy it to its original location.

You can use the Time Machine tool to restore files in Mac. The steps are as follows:

1. Select the Time Machine icon from the menu.

2. Select Enter Time Machine.

3. You'll be taken to the Time Machine window. Here you can navigate to the file or folder you need to retrieve.

4. Locate the file or folder and click the Restore button.

5. Time Machine will copy that file to its original location on your hard disk.

Image Recovery

Recovering an entire image in either system is not different from restoring a single file. In Linux, you can use the rsync utility to restore a snapshot. On Mac you use Disk Utility in conjunction with a backup of the system and the OS media. To do this, follow these steps:

1. Connect the external hard drive that contains the backup to the Mac to which you are restoring.

2. Insert the OS X CD and restart it.

3. Hold down the C key while booting to boot to the Mac OS X CD and select your language.

4. From the Utilities menu, select Disk Utility.

5. Select the drive the backup is stored on.

6. Select the Restore tab. Select that disk and drag that to the Source window. If you created a .dmg image, you'll need to click the drive you saved the image to (do not drag it), click Image, and select the disk image from the drive you stored it on.

7. In the left pane of Disk Utility, click your hard drive and drag it to the Destination window.

8. Check the Erase Destination check box to erase your old hard drive and replace it with the disk image you've selected as the source.

9. Click Restore. Click OK to verify.

Disk Maintenance Utilities

While I covered the disk maintenance utilities in the various sections earlier, Table 6.2 summarizes the tools discussed.

TABLE 6.2   Disk maintenance utilities

Tool	Function
rsync	Backs up and restores files
Time Machine	Backs up and restores files and images
fsck	Filesystem checker
Disk utilities	Verifies disk health and restores images
tar	Backs up files
lvcreate	Creates a snapshot volume

Shell/Terminal

In Linux, a shell is a command-line interface, of which there are several types. A terminal is a window that appears when you press Ctrl+Alt+T. They both accept commands, but they are two separate programs. The following are some differences:

- A terminal window can run different shells depending on what you have configured.
- Certain interactive applications can be run in the terminal emulator and they will run in the same window.
- Remote logins, using a program like SSH, can be run from inside a terminal window.

Mac OS calls the shell Terminal, and you can find it under Applications ➢ Utilities ➢ Terminal, as shown in Figure 6.6.

FIGURE 6.6   Mac terminal

Screen Sharing

In Linux, you can share a screen with others by using third-party tools, but you can also do it using the following procedure as a root user:

1. Change permissions to allow users to get added to the session by typing **chmod u+s / usr/bin/screen** (which allows a user to run an executable file of the specific owner who is launching the screen).

2. Change the access permission of the screen mode by typing **chmod 755 /var/run/ screen**.

3. Log out from SSH as a root user.

4. Type the command **Screen** to start the new screen.

5. Change the screen mode from single user to multiuser. Press Ctrl+A and then type `':multiuser on' //`.

6. Add the user into the screen (in this case the user is jack), press Ctrl+A, and then type `':acl name' // Ex: :acladd jack -`.

7. The user joins the screen so that both can work in the same terminal by typing **screen -x name_of_screen_session**.

In Mac, a screen-sharing tool is built in. In OS X Yosemite, the process is as follows:

1. Open Sharing preferences (choose Apple menu ➤ System Preferences and then click Sharing).

2. Select the Screen Sharing check box. If Remote Management is selected, you must deselect it before you can select Screen Sharing.

3. To specify who can share your screen, select one of the following:

   - *All users*: Anyone with a user account on your Mac can share your screen.

   - *Only these users*: Screen sharing is restricted to specific users.

4. If you selected Only These Users, click Add at the bottom of the users list, and then do one of the following:

   - Select a user from Users & Groups, which includes all the users of your Mac.

   - Select a user from Network Users or Network Groups, which includes everyone on your network.

5. To let others share your screen without having a user account on your Mac, click Computer Settings, and then select one or both of the following:

   - *Anyone may request permission to control screen*: Before other computer users begin screen sharing your Mac, they can ask for permission instead of entering a username and password.

   - *VNC viewers may control screen with password*: Other users can share your screen using a VNC viewer app—on iPad or a Windows PC, for example—by entering the password you specify here.

Force Quit

Force quit can be used on a Mac to stop an unresponsive application. To use this function, follow these steps:

1. Choose Force Quit from the Apple menu or press Command-Option-Esc.

2. Select the unresponsive app in the Force Quit Applications window, as shown in Figure 6.7, and then click Force Quit.

In Linux you can use the xkill feature to kill a program you click. To do this, follow these steps:

1. Press Alt+F2 and type in **gnome-terminal** to open a terminal session.

2. Inside the terminal type in **sudo xkill**, then click any window to kill it.

FIGURE 6.7   Force Quit Applications window

Features

Now that you have looked at maintenance on these systems, let's examine some of the key features you will find in the Mac OS and Linux variants. You can find many of these features in Windows with different names and different combinations of functions.

Multiple Desktops/Mission Control

In Apple, Mission Control provides a quick way to see everything that's currently open on your Mac. To use Mission Control, do one of the following:

- Swipe up with three or four fingers on your trackpad.
- Double-tap the surface of your Magic Mouse with two fingers.
- Click the Mission Control icon in the Dock or Launchpad.
- On an Apple keyboard, press the Mission Control key.

Regardless of how you invoke Mission Control, all your open windows and spaces are visible, grouped by app. You can also use the tool to create desktops that are called *spaces* and place certain apps in certain spaces. Moreover, you can switch between the spaces in the same session.

When you enter Mission Control, all your spaces appear along the top of your screen. The desktop you're currently using is shown below the row of spaces. To move an app window to another space, drag it from your current desktop to the space at the top of the screen.

To switch between spaces, do one of the following:

- Enter Mission Control and click the space you want at the top of the Mission Control window.

- Swipe three or four fingers left or right across your trackpad to move to the previous or next space.

- Press Ctrl+Right Arrow or Ctrl+Left Arrow on your keyboard to move through your current spaces. Then click a window to bring it to the front of your view.

In Linux you can do this using what are called *workspace switchers*, which must be activated. For example, Figure 6.8 shows the activation window in Ubuntu Unity. Once it's activated, you can create and populate workspaces and use Workspace Switcher to move from one to another, much like you do in Mac.

FIGURE 6.8 Enabling workspaces

Key Chain

Keychain is the password management system in OS X. It can contain private keys, certificates, and secure notes. In Mac OS X, keychain files are stored in ~/Library/Keychains/, /Library/Keychains/, and /Network/Library/Keychains/. Keychain Access is a Mac OS X application that allows a user to access the Keychain and configure its contents.

Spot Light

Spot Light is a search tool built into Mac systems. To open Spot Light, click the magnifying glass icon in the upper-right corner of the menu bar, or press Command+spacebar from any app. Spot Light results can include dictionary definitions, currency conversions, and quick calculations. It will search the Web as well, but you can limit its scope to just search the Mac.

iCloud

iCloud is Apple's cloud storage solution, much like OneDrive in Windows. It also allows for the automatic synchronization of information across all devices of the user. In addition, it can be used to locate an iPhone and can be a location to which a backup can be stored. All Mac users are provided with 5 GB of free storage and then can purchase additional storage for a monthly fee.

Gestures

Gestures are used in Mac to interact with a touchscreen. It is based on using multitouch, which allows you to touch the screen in more than one place and initiate specific subroutines called *gestures* such as when expanding or reducing a photo.

Finder

While Finder can also be used on a Mac to search for files, its main function is a filesystem navigation tool, much like Windows Explorer. To open a new Finder window, click the Finder icon in the Dock and then select File ➤ New Window. Figure 6.9 shows a Finder window.

FIGURE 6.9   Finder

Remote Disk

Remote Disk is an icon that appears under Devices as well as under Computer that allows you to see which computers on the same network have drives available to share. When computers on the same network have disk sharing enabled and are online, you can highlight that icon to see a list of them. To share optical discs from a Mac that has a built-in or external optical drive, use these steps:

1. On the Mac that has an optical drive, choose System Preferences from the Apple menu.

2. Click the Sharing icon in the System Preferences window.

3. Enter a name in the Computer Name field.

4. Enable the check box DVD Or CD Sharing.

5. You can also restrict who has access to your optical drive by selecting Ask Me Before Allowing Others To Use My DVD Drive.

Dock

The Dock is the series of icons that appear usually on the bottom of the screen on a Mac. It provides quick access to applications that come with the Mac, and you can add your own items to the Dock as well. In many ways, it is like the taskbar in Windows. It keeps apps on its left side. Folders, documents, and minimized windows are kept on the right side of the Dock. Figure 6.10 shows the Dock.

FIGURE 6.10   The Dock

Boot Camp

Boot Camp is a utility on a Mac that allows you to create a multiboot environment. While Apple only supports using the tool to install a version of Windows, it has been used to also create a bootable version of Linux. The Boot Camp Assistant, shown in Figure 6.11, guides the user through the process of setting up the system.

FIGURE 6.11   Boot Camp

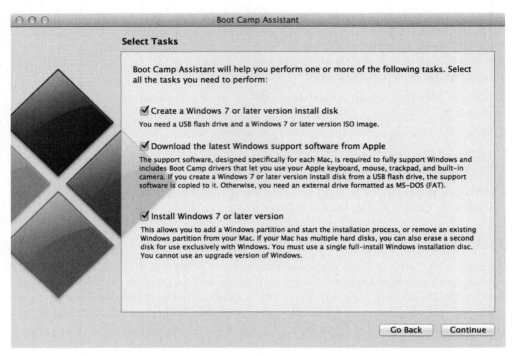

Basic Linux Commands

While you may not be expected to be an expert in Linux, you will be responsible for knowing some basic Linux commands. This section will go over the main ones you need to know.

ls

The ls command lists information about the files in the current directory. Its syntax is as follows:

```
ls [OPTION]… [FILE]...
```

While the file options are too numerous to mention here, they mostly specify the format of the output. For a complete listing and their use, see http://linuxcommand.org/man_pages/ls1.html.

grep

The grep command is used to search text or to search the given file for lines containing a match to the given strings or words. Its syntax is as follows, where PATTERN is the pattern you are trying to match:

```
grep [OPTIONS] PATTERN [FILE...]
```

It has options that govern the matching process as well as options that specify the output. For more information on the options and their use, see www.computerhope.com/unix/ugrep.htm.

cd

The cd command is used to change the current directory just as it does at the Windows command line. Its syntax is as follows:

cd [option] [directory]

The parameters that can be used with this command are as follows:

- -L: This option forces symbolic links to be followed. In other words, if you tell cd to move into a directory, which is actually a symbolic link to a directory, it moves into the directory the symbolic link points to.

- -P: This option uses the physical directory structure without following symbolic links. In other words, change into the specified directory only if it actually exists as named; symbolic links will not be followed. This is the opposite of the -L option, and if they are both specified, this option will be ignored.

- -e: If the -P option is specified and the current working directory cannot be determined, this option tells cd to exit with an error. If -P is not specified along with this option, this option has no function.

shutdown

The shutdown command brings the system down in a secure way. Its syntax is as follows:

shutdown [-akrhPHfFnc] [-t sec] time [message]

There are too many parameters to list here. For more information, see www.computerhope.com/unix/ushutdow.htm.

pwd vs. passwd

While the passwd command changes passwords for user accounts, the pwd command prints the full path name of the current working directory. The syntax for the passwd command is as follows:

passwd [options] [LOGIN]

For information on the numerous options that can be used, see www.computerhope.com/unix/upasswor.htm.

The syntax for the pwd command is as follows:

pwd [OPTION]…

The options that can be used are:

- -L, --logical: If the contents of the environment variable PWD provide an absolute name of the current directory with no . or .. components, then output those contents, even if they contain symbolic links. Otherwise, fall back to the default -P handling.

- ▪ -P, --physical: This prints a fully resolved name for the current directory in which all components of the name are actual directory names and not symbolic links.
- ▪ --help: This displays a help message and exits.
- ▪ --version: This displays version information and exits.

mv

While the mv command can be used to move or rename a file in Linux, it's usually used to move a file. In that scenario, the syntax is as follows:

```
mv [OPTION]... [-T] SOURCE DEST
```

For information on the parameters that can be used, see www.computerhope.com/unix/umv.htm.

cp

The cp command is used to copy files and directories. Its syntax is as follows:

```
cp [OPTION]… SOURCE… DIRECTORY
```

For information on the parameters that can be used, see www.computerhope.com/unix/ucp.htm.

rm

The rm command removes (deletes) files or directories when it is combined with the -r option. The syntax is as follows:

```
rm [OPTION]… FILE…
```

For information on using parameters, see www.computerhope.com/unix/urm.htm.

chmod

The chmod command is used to change the permissions of files or directories. Its syntax is as follows:

```
chmod options permissions filename
```

For information on using parameters, see www.computerhope.com/unix/uchmod.htm.

cmkdir

The cmkdir command is used to create a Cryptographic File System (CFS) directory. These directories are stored in encrypted format. The command will prompt you for a password that will be used to encrypt the directory. The syntax of the command is as follows:

```
Cmkdir  [option] directory
```

For information concerning possible options, see www.linuxcertif.com/man/1/cmkdir/.

chown

The chown command is used to change the ownership of a file. The syntax is as follows, where new_owner is the username or the numeric user ID (UID) of the new owner and object is the name of the target file, directory, or link:

chown [options] new_owner object(s)

The ownership of any number of objects can be changed simultaneously. The options are as follows:

- -R operates on filesystem objects recursively.
- -v (verbose) option provides information about every object processed.
- -c reports only when a change is made.

iwconfig/ifconfig

The ifconfig and iwconfig commands are used to configure network interfaces. While the ifconfig command is dedicated to wired connections, the iwconfig command is used on wireless interfaces. Here is the syntax of the two commands:

iwconfig interface [essid X] [nwid N] [mode M] [freq F] [channel C]
[sens S] [ap A] [nick NN] [rate R] [rts RT] [frag FT] [txpower T]
[enc E] [key K] [power P] [retry R] [commit]

For information on the options, see www.linuxcommand.org/man_pages/iwconfig8.html.

ifconfig interface [aftype] options | address …

For information on the options, see http://linux.die.net/man/8/ifconfig.

ps

The ps command displays information about a selection of the active processes. Its syntax is as follows:

ps [options]

For information on the use of the options, see http://linuxcommand.org/man_pages/ps1.html.

q

The q command is used to quit the Unix full-screen editor called vi. It can be used in two ways:

- :q (CR): Quits vi without saving, provided no changes have been made since the last save
- :q! (CR): Quits vi without saving, leaving the file as it was in the last save

su/sudo

The sudo command can be added at the front of a command to execute the command using root privileges. For example, to remove a package with root privileges, the command is as follows:

```
sudo apt-get remove {package-name}
```

The su command is used to change from one user account to another. When the command is executed, you will be prompted for the password of the account to which you are switching, as shown here:

```
$ su mact
password:
mact@sandy:~$
```

apt-get

apt-get is the command-line tool for working with Advanced Packaging Tool (APT) software packages. These tools install packages on your system. The syntax of the command is as follows:

```
apt-get [-asqdyfmubV] [-o=config_string] [-c=config_file]
[-t=target_release][-=architecture] {update | upgrade |
dselect-upgrade | dist-upgrade |install pkg [{=pkg_version_number |
/target_release}]… | remove pkg… | purge pkg… | source pkg
[{=pkg_version_number | /target_release}]… | build-dep pkg
[{=pkg_version_number | /target_release}]… | download pkg
[{=pkg_version_number | /target_release}]… | check | clean |
autoclean | autoremove | {-v | -version} | {-h | -help}}
```

For additional information on its use and the options, see www.computerhope.com/unix/apt-get.htm.

vi

The vi command is used to invoke the vi editor (mentioned in the section about the q command) which is a full-screen editor with two modes of operation: command mode that causes action to be taken on the file, and insert mode in which entered text is inserted into the file. To enter vi, you use vi *filename*. If the file named *filename* exists, then the first page (or screen) of the file will be displayed; if the file does not exist, then an empty file and screen are created into which you may enter text. To exit this mode when done, use one of the following commands, based on your intentions:

- :x<Return>: Quits vi, writing out the modified file to the file named in the original invocation
- :wq<Return>: Quits vi, writing out the modified file to the file named in the original invocation

- :q<Return>: Quits (or exits) vi
- :q!<Return>: Quits vi even though the latest changes have not been saved for this vi call

dd

The dd command copies a file, converting the format of the data in the process, according to the operands specified. Its syntax is as follows:

dd [OPERAND]...

or as follows:

dd OPTION

For information on the available operands and options, see www.computerhope.com/unix/dd.htm.

Exam Essentials

Describe the maintenance tasks that are considered best practices in Linux and Mac operating systems.   These tasks include scheduled backups, disk maintenance, system updates, patch management, driver and firmware updates, and antivirus and antimalware updates.

Identify tools used in the execution of maintenance and other routine tasks.   Some of these tasks include backup, Time Machine, restore, snapshot, image recovery, Disk Utility, screen sharing, and Force Quit.

Differentiate some of the features of the Linux and Mac operating systems.   Among these features are multiple desktops, Mission Control, Keychain, Spot Light, iCloud, gestures, Finder, Remote Disk, Dock, and Boot Camp.

Understand the use of basic Linux commands. These commands include ls, grep, cd, shutdown, pwd, passwd, mv, cp, rm, chmod, cmkdir, chown, iwconfig/ifconfig, ps, q, su/sudo, apt-get, vi, **and** dd.

2.2 Given a Scenario, Set Up and Use Client-Side Virtualization

A client-side virtualized computer is one that is an instance of an operating system that is managed centrally on a server and executed locally. One key feature of this approach is that while a constant connection to the server is not required for the system to function, the operating system disk image is updated and backed up by synchronizing regularly with a server. This section will look at the setup of a client-side virtualization scenario. The subobjectives covered in this section include the following:

- Purpose of virtual machines
- Resource requirements

- Emulator requirements
- Security requirements
- Network requirements
- Hypervisor

Purpose of Virtual Machines

Traditionally, workstations can have multiple operating systems installed on them but run only one at a time. By running virtualization software, the same workstation can be running Window 7 along with Windows Server 2008 and Red Hat Enterprise Linux (or almost any other operating system) at the same time, allowing a developer to test code in various environments as well as cut and paste between virtual machines (VMs).

From a networking standpoint, each of the VMs will typically need full network access, and configuring the permissions for each can sometimes be tricky.

Resource Requirements

The resource requirements for virtualization are largely based on what environments you are creating. The hardware on the machine must have enough memory, hard drive space, and processor capability to support the virtualization. You also need the software to make virtualization possible (discussed in the next section).

Emulator Requirements

XP Mode is a free emulator from Microsoft that you can download and use as a virtual emulator. A number of others are also available. In most cases, the motherboard and associated BIOS settings need no alteration to provide services to these VMs. Some of the newer virtualization products, however (such as Microsoft's Hyper-V, Windows 7 Virtual PC, and Windows 8 Client Hyper-V), require that the motherboard support hardware-assisted virtualization. The benefit derived from using hardware-assisted virtualization is it reduces overhead and improves performance.

 VMware Player allows you to work in multiple environments on one system. For more information, go to www.vmware.com/products/player.

Security Requirements

Tales of security woes that can occur with attackers jumping out of one VM and accessing another have been exaggerated. Although such threats are possible, most software solutions include sufficient protection to reduce the possibility to a small one.

Most virtualization-specific threats focus on the hypervisor (the software that allows the VMs to exist). If the hypervisor can be successfully attacked, the attacker can gain root-level access to all virtual systems. While this is a legitimate issue—and one that has been demonstrated as possible in most systems (including VMware, Xen, and Microsoft Virtual Machine)—it is one that has been patched each time it has appeared. The solution to most virtualization threats is to always apply the most recent patches and keep the systems up-to-date.

Network Requirements

Network access is not a requirement in every virtual environment (for example, if you were decoding an application that would run only locally) but is often needed in most. During implementation of the virtualization, you can configure the network functionality for the machine (known as *internal*) or combine elements of the network together to provide network virtualization (known as *external*). The difference between internal and external implementations is usually based on which software package you are using.

Hypervisor

The hypervisor is the software that allows the VMs to exist.

Exam Essentials

Be familiar with virtualization terminology.   The hypervisor is the software that allows the VMs to exist. VMs are separate instances of an operating system and function independently of one another on a host physical machine.

Know security concerns related to virtualization.   Most virtualization-specific threats focus on the hypervisor. If the hypervisor can be successfully attacked, the attacker can gain root-level access to all virtual systems.

2.3 Identify Basic Cloud Concepts

Increasingly, organizations are utilizing cloud-based storage instead of storing data in local data centers. The advantages to this approach include the ability to access the data from anywhere, the ability to scale compute resources to meet demand, and robust fault tolerance options. This section will look at various cloud models and some of the concepts that make it a viable option for the enterprise. The subobjectives covered in this section include the following:

- SaaS
- IaaS

- PaaS
- Public vs. private vs. hybrid vs. community
- Rapid elasticity
- On-demand
- Resource pooling
- Measured service

SaaS

When an enterprise contracts with a third party to provide cloud services, there is a range of options, differing mostly in the division of responsibilities between the vendor and the client. Software as a service (SaaS) involves the vendor providing the entire solution. This includes the operating system, the infrastructure software, and the application. The company may provide you with an e-mail system, for example, whereby it hosts and manages everything for you.

IaaS

Infrastructure as a service (IaaS) involves the vendor providing the hardware platform or data center, and the company installs and manages its own operating systems and application systems. The vendor simply provides access to the data center and maintains that access.

PaaS

Platform as a service (PaaS) involves the vendor providing the hardware platform or data center and the software running on the platform. This includes the operating systems and infrastructure software. The company is still involved in managing the system.

Public vs. Private vs. Hybrid vs. Community

When a company pays another company to host and manage this environment, it is called a *public* cloud solution. If the company hosts this environment itself, it is a *private* cloud solution.

There is trade-off when a decision must be made between the two architectures. The private solution provides the most control over the safety of your data but also requires the staff and the knowledge to deploy, manage, and secure the solution. A public cloud puts your data's safety in the hands of a third party, but that party is often more capable and knowledgeable about protecting data in this environment and managing the cloud environment.

When the solution is partly private and partly public, the solution is called a *hybrid* solution. It may be that the organization keeps some data in the public cloud but may keep more sensitive data in a private cloud, or the organization may have a private cloud that when overtaxed may utilize a public cloud for additional storage space or additional compute resources.

Finally, a community cloud is one that is shared by multiple organizations for some common purpose. This could be to share data for a joint project, for example.

Rapid Elasticity

One of the advantages of a cloud environment is the ability to add resources as needed on the fly and release those resources when they are no longer required. This makes for more efficient use of resources, placing them where needed at any particular point in time. These include CPU and memory resources. This is called rapid elasticity because it occurs automatically according to the rules for resource sharing that have been deployed.

On-Demand

In a cloud environment, it is typically possible for customers to add additional compute resources at any time to their cloud solution without involving the cloud provider. This is called on-demand resource utilization and results in the customer paying for what is used, rather than paying for unused resources.

Resource Pooling

Resource pooling is a cloud concept whereby collections of resources (CPU and memory) are stored in containers called *pools*. These pools can be configured to be shared by certain virtual systems. The relative priority to the usages of the resources is controlled by the configuration of what are called *resource shares*. It is also possible to use another concept in combination with resource shares called *resource guarantees*. These settings are used to ensure that certain systems always have required resources. Finally, resource limits can be used to prevent a system from monopolizing the resources in the pool.

Measured Service

Measured service is a term used to describe the process of tracking resource utilization by the customer for the purpose of charging for those resources. This works much in the same way that a utility company charges the organization only for the power used in a period. In this case, the customer is charged for the compute resources utilized in a period.

Exam Essentials

Describe the cloud service models.   These include SaaS, PaaS, and IaaS. Differentiate the models with respect to the various responsibilities of the vendor and the customer.

Differentiate cloud architectures.   Describe the architectural differences in the private, public, hybrid, and community cloud models.

Identify basic terms describing some of the benefits of cloud computing.   These include rapid elasticity, on-demand computing, and measured service.

2.4 Summarize the Properties and Purpose of Services Provided by Networked Hosts

To provide service to a network, you must be versed in the various roles that servers may play in the network. Armed with this knowledge, you can better ensure the proper function of these servers. There will also be a number of other network devices and appliances. This section will look at both topics. The subobjectives covered in this section include the following:

- Server roles
- Internet appliance
- Legacy/embedded systems

Server Roles

Servers are computers that provide some type of shared service to the hosts on the network. There are many roles that servers can play, but this section will discuss some of the more common server roles, focusing on those you are most likely to find in your network.

Web Server

Web servers are used to provide access to information for users connecting to the server using a web browser, which is the client part of the application. The browser uses HTTP as its transfer mechanism. These servers can be contained within a network and are available only within the network (called an *intranet server*), or they can be connected to the Internet where they can be reached from anywhere. To provide security, a web server can be configured to require and use HTTPS, which uses SSL to encrypt the connection with no effort on the part of the user.

File Server

File servers are used to store files that can be accessed by the users in the network. Typically, users are encouraged or even required to store any important data on these servers rather than on their local hard drives because these servers are typically backed up on a regular basis, whereas the user machines typically are not. These servers will have significant amounts of storage space and may even have multiple hard drives configured in a RAID system to provide quicker recovery from a drive crash than could be provided by recovering with the backup.

Print Server

Print servers are used to manage printers, and in cases where that is their only role, they will manage multiple printers. These servers provide the spooler service to the printers that it manages, and when you view the print queue, you are viewing it on the print server. Many enterprise printers come with a built-in print server, which makes using a dedicated machine for the role unnecessary.

DHCP Server

DHCP servers are used to automate the process of providing an IP configuration to devices in the network. These servers respond to broadcast-based requests for a configuration by offering an IP address, subnet mask, and default gateway to the DHCP client. While these options provide basic network connectivity, many other options can also be provided, such as the IP address of a TFTP server that IP phones can contact to download a configuration file.

DNS Server

DNS servers resolve device and domain names (website names) to IP addresses, and vice versa. They make it possible to connect to either without knowing the IP address of the device or of the server hosting the website. Clients are configured with the IP address of a DNS server (usually through DHCP) and make requests of the server using what are called *queries*. The organization's DNS server will be configured to perform the lookup of IP addresses for which it has no entry in its database by making requests of the DNS servers on the Internet, which are organized in a hierarchy that allows these servers to more efficiently provide the answer. When they have completed their lookup, they return the IP address to the client so the client can make a direct connection using the IP address.

Proxy Server

A proxy server is one that makes Internet connections on the behalf of users in a network. In doing so, it prevents them from making direct connections to the Internet and provides a point of exit at which you can control their access in a variety of ways. For example, you may allow certain users to have complete access to the Internet with no restrictions, while other groups of users may be restricted in the sites they can visit and the activities in which they may participate.

An additional feature of these servers is their role in web caching. Web caching is the process of retrieving a web page for a user and then caching that web page so that another request for the page by the same users or other users can be served locally without returning to the Internet to retrieve the page. It results in faster page retrievals in cases where the page has been cached.

Mail Server

Mail servers run e-mail server software and use SMTP to send and receive e-mail on behalf of users who possess mailboxes on the server. Those users will use a client e-mail protocol to retrieve their e-mail from the server. Two of the most common are POP3, which is a retrieve-only protocol, and IMAP4, which has more functionality and can be used to manage the e-mail on the server.

Authentication Server

An authentication server is one that accepts and verifies the credentials of users. Typically, it not only authenticates them but also provides them with access to resources using single sign-on. Single sign-on allows a user to authenticate once and *not* be required to authenticate again to access the resources to which they have been given access. One of the best examples of this is a domain controller in a Windows Active Directory domain. These servers are the point to which all users are directed when they need to log in to the network.

Internet Appliance

Beyond the roles that you can assign to servers by installing server software, there are network appliances that are dedicated to performing a particular function. In many cases, they perform better than a similar product that is software based. This section will look at several of the most common ones.

UTM

Unified threat management (UTM) is an approach that involves performing multiple security functions within the same device or appliance. The functions may include the following:

- Network firewalling
- Network intrusion prevention
- Gateway antivirus
- Gateway antispam
- VPN
- Content filtering
- Load balancing
- Data leak prevention
- On-appliance reporting

UTM makes administering multiple systems unnecessary. However, some feel that UTM creates a single point of failure and favor creating multiple layers of devices as a more secure approach.

IDS

An *intrusion detection system* (IDS) is a system responsible for detecting unauthorized access or attacks. It can verify, itemize, and characterize threats from outside and inside the network. Most IDSs are programmed to react in certain ways in specific situations. Event notification and alerts are crucial to IDSs. These notifications and alerts inform administrators and security professionals when and where attacks are detected. The most common way to classify an IDS is based on its information source: network based or host based.

The most common IDS, a network-based IDS (NIDS), monitors network traffic on a local network segment. To monitor traffic on the network segment, the network interface card (NIC) must be operating in promiscuous mode. An NIDS can monitor only the network traffic. It cannot monitor any internal activity that occurs within a system, such as an attack against a system that is carried out by logging on to the system's local terminal. An NIDS is affected by a switched network because generally an NIDS monitors only a single network segment.

IPS

An *intrusion prevention system* (IPS) scans traffic on a network for signs of malicious activity and then takes some action to prevent it. An IPS monitors the entire network. You need to be careful to set an IPS's filters in such a way that the generation of false positives and false negatives are kept to a minimum. False positives indicate an unwarranted alarm, and false negatives indicate troubling traffic that does not generate an alarm.

Legacy/Embedded Systems

An embedded system is a computer system with a specific function within a larger computing system. Embedded systems are present in many Internet-connected devices such as VoIP phones and routers, but they are also increasingly found in devices such as home appliances and automobiles. Legacy embedded systems are those that have been handed down from one version of a system to another with no major revision.

Exam Essentials

Identify the major server roles in a network.   These roles include DNS, DHCP, web, proxy, and authentication servers.

Differentiate various network appliances.   Describe the features and use of UTM, IPS, and IDS.

2.5 Identify Basic Features of Mobile Operating Systems

Computer operating systems are not the only type of operating system with which you will come into contact. Many tablets, smartphones, and other small devices will have operating systems that are designed to run on devices that have different resource capabilities and therefore require different systems. This section will look at operating systems for such mobile devices. The subobjective covered in this section includes the following:

▪ Android vs. iOS vs. Windows

Android vs. iOS vs. Windows

Although certainly not the only operating systems made for today's highly capable mobile devices, the Android and iOS operating systems are the most widely used. However, you may find that some mobile devices are running a Windows operating system. In this section, the three systems are compared and contrasted.

Open Source vs. Closed Source/Vendor Specific

The Android operating system from Google is built on a Linux kernel with a core set of libraries that are written in Java. It is an open source operating system, which means that developers have full access to the same framework APIs used by the core applications.

Apple iOS is a vendor-specific system made by Apple. Developers must use the software development kit (SDK) from Apple and register as Apple developers.

The Windows operating system, which is the most widely used for desktops and laptops, may also be found on some mobile devices such as smartphones and tablets, but it is not used as widely for these device types as iOS and Android. This is one of the best examples of closed source software.

App Source (Play Store, App Store, and Market)

Applications (*apps*) for mobile devices are where all the exciting functionality comes from on mobile devices. There are thousands of developers creating apps that will do everything but wash your car for you. Although many are free, some you must purchase.

Apps for Android systems can be obtained from Google Play Store or many other sites. Android Market is an app that can be installed on tablets that makes it easy to search for apps, games, and widgets.

Apple tightly controls the sale of apps (again, many are free) by making them available only on the Apple App Store site.

Screen Orientation (Accelerometer/Gyroscope)

Both accelerometers and gyroscopes can be used by mobile devices to determine the movement and tilt of the device. This means the device can tell which way the screen is being held. It uses this information to automatically adjust the display orientation appropriately with no action on the part of the user.

Either can be used, but since they exhibit slightly different characteristics, one works better for some types of movement and the other for other types of movement. The bottom line is that either will work, but they work better together.

The iOS operating system in the iPhone uses an accelerometer and a gyroscope to sense the movement and tilt of the device. The Android used only an accelerometer in earlier models, but since a gyroscope improves the performance, the newer models include both.

Screen Calibration

For a touchscreen device to operate correctly—that is, for it to properly interpret your touch and react accordingly—it must be calibrated correctly. When you touch an item on the screen and nothing happens or a movement that normally results in an expected reaction does not, the calibration of the device is off.

Many devices contain a built-in calibration tool. When you use the tool, it will ask you to touch the screen in various ways, which results in it relearning how to react to your touch. It can be a long process but will usually result in a solution to the problem. Consult the documentation for the device to locate the calibration tool.

GPS and Geotracking

Some devices use cell towers to get GPS information, while others (such as Android phones) get GPS information directly from satellites. The upside to getting this from a satellite is that no cell phone service is required for the GPS to work. It is worth noting, however, that when GPS is on, it is using the battery, so you might want to turn it off when you are not using it. The iPhone uses a combination of GPS, cell towers, and Wi-Fi towers to plot your location.

One thing that has caused some controversy is the issue of geotracking. Both iPhone and Android devices record the location of the device periodically and send this information to a central location. This upsets some users because U.S. Department of Homeland Security officials have disclosed that they retain the right to access this information when they deem necessary.

Wi-Fi Calling

Wi-Fi calling is a generic term that refers to extending mobile voice, data, and multimedia applications over IP networks. Generic Access Network (GAN) is another earlier term of which you may have heard that refers to the same general concept. It allows cell phone packets to be forwarded on an IP network when available rather than using the cellular network of which the device is also capable. This allows the user to use an 802.11 connection when available, conserving the use of their data plan and in some cases providing better performance.

Launcher/GUI

A launcher is a program that locates and starts another program. It provides shortcuts to computer programs and stores the shortcuts in one place so they are easier to find. Android can use many launchers, some of which are free and others that require a license. Many of these launchers are dedicated to a specific function such as viewing documents on the home page as on a desktop. These launchers are GUI based and usually provide the user with additional items in their menus and additional screens and functionalities.

Virtual Assistant

Virtual assistants are programs built into mobile devices that can assist in looking up information on behalf of the users. The best-known example is Siri, the assistant that can respond to voice requests and commands in the iPhone. Android also supports voice recognition with its voice actions, allowing you to dictate texts and e-mails, play music, or show a map with voice commands. Also, the Google Now feature has a voice command feature and can act as a simple virtual assistant by delivering weather and traffic updates, sports scores, and other information you may be interested in. Many more robust virtual assistant apps are available on Google Play.

SDK/APK

Software development kits (SDKs) and *application development kits* (ADKs) are sets of tools provided to third-party developers to assist in the development of applications that will run on the Google or Android operating system. It is in the interest of Google and Apple to support this effort because many users choose a system based on the available applications for the product. One of the reasons the Windows Phone has not seen the success many hoped is the dearth of applications created for the phone.

Emergency Notification

Wireless Emergency Alerts (WEA) are emergency messages sent by authorized government alerting authorities through your mobile carrier. The types of messages, some of which are already available, are as follows:

- Extreme weather warnings
- Local emergencies requiring evacuation or immediate action
- AMBER alerts
- Presidential alerts during a national emergency

Most mobile devices already come equipped to receive these messages, and in some models you can disable some of the messages that you do not want to receive. You cannot disable the presidential messages that may come in an emergency.

Mobile Payment Service

One of the newer uses of mobile devices is wireless mobile payment systems. With special software and a piece of hardware that attaches to the device and accepts the sliding of a credit card, the mobile device can become a cash register. Newer Android phones now have Near field communication (NFC) allowing Google Wallet to perform contactless payments too. Apple iPhone 6 and some iPads utilize NFC to enable Apple Pay to do the same. To merchants located in outdoor areas such as festivals and flea markets, this has given them another way to easily accept card charges.

Exam Essentials

Describe the major differences between the Android and iOS operating systems.   Android is an open source operating system, and iOS is a vendor-specific system made by Apple. Apps for Android systems can be obtained from Google Play or many other sites, whereas iOS apps are available only on the Apple Store site. Both use accelerometers and gyroscopes to track device orientation.

Identify the function of calibration.   For a touchscreen device to operate correctly, it must be calibrated correctly.

Describe some of the functions and features provided by mobile devices.   These features include GPS and geotracking, Wi-Fi calling, virtual assistants, emergency notifications, and mobile payment services.

2.6 Install and Configure Basic Mobile Device Network Connectivity and E-mail

For mobile devices to deliver the functionality that most expect, they must be connected to a network. To use e-mail (one of the most important functions to many users), the device must be set up properly as well. The subobjectives covered in this section include the following:

- Wireless/cellular data network (enable/disable)
- Bluetooth
- Corporate and ISP e-mail configuration
- Integrated commercial provider e-mail configuration
- PRI updates/PRL updates/baseband updates
- Radio firmware
- IMEI vs. IMSI
- VPN

Wireless/Cellular Data Network (Enable/Disable)

Like most computing devices, mobile devices provide more robust functionality when connected to a network (especially if that network is the Internet). Two types of networks can be used to gain access to the Internet: cell phone networks and Wi-Fi networks.

Cell phone networks have in the past been the second choice because the performance is not as good as an 802.11 Wi-Fi connection. With the introduction of 4G Long Term Evolution (LTE) technologies, however, the performance delivered by the cell network may become more competitive.

In either case, most mobile devices will have the ability to make an 802.11 connection or use the cell network. If you want to disable the automatic connection to the cell phone network or if it somehow got turned off and needs to be turned back on, you can do this through the settings. One example of the steps to access these settings is Settings

➤ Wireless ➤ Mobile ➤ Enable Data (select or deselect this). This is only one navigational example, and you should consult the documentation that came with the device.

Making a Wi-Fi connection is much like doing so with a laptop. In the settings of the device will be a section for Wi-Fi (in iPhone it's called Wi-Fi, and in Android it's called Wireless And Networks). When you access it, you will see all the Wi-Fi networks within range. Just as you would do with a laptop, select one and attempt to connect to the Wi-Fi network. If the connection requires a password, you will have to supply it. You also can preconfigure a wireless profile for commonly used secure wireless networks as well as those where the service set identifier (SSID) has been hidden.

Hotspot

Hotspots are publicly provided points of access to an 802.11 wireless network connected to the Internet. They typically have little or no security configured to make it as easy as possible for users to connect. There are also devices that have been created by vendors that allow a single device to act as a hotspot for other devices in the area. Sometimes these are called *mobile hotspots*. Some mobile devices can be turned into mobile hotspots with a software upgrade or an addition to the service plan.

Tethering

Tethering is the process of sharing the Internet connection of one device with another device. Connection of the phone or tablet with other devices can be done over wireless LAN (Wi-Fi), over Bluetooth, or with a physical connection using a cable, for example through USB. It also may be done by using a mobile hotspot or by using a similar feature on a mobile device.

Airplane Mode

Since airlines do not permit enabling the wireless connection on mobile devices during takeoff and landing, vendors created a mode called Airplane mode in which this function is turned off but all other functionality (games and other applications not requiring Internet access) is still fully functional.

Bluetooth

Bluetooth is a short-range wireless technology that is used to create a wireless connection between digital devices. One of its applications is to create connections between mobile devices and items such as speakers, headphones, external GPS units, and keyboards. Before you can take advantage of this technology, the devices must be configured to connect to one another. This section will discuss how to configure a Bluetooth connection.

Enable Bluetooth

On Android mobile devices, follow these steps:

1. From the Home screen, select the Menu button. From the menu, choose Settings ➤ Wireless And Networks ➤ Bluetooth.

2. Once Bluetooth is selected, wait until a check mark appears next to Bluetooth. Bluetooth is now enabled.

On iOS mobile devices, follow these steps:

1. On the main page, choose Settings ➤ General ➤ Bluetooth.

2. Tap the slider to enable Bluetooth.

Enable Pairing

Pairing a mobile device with an external device (speaker, headphone, and so forth) will enable the two devices to communicate. The first step is to enable pairing. This is much simpler than it sounds. For either mobile operating system, simply turn the external device on and you are ready for the next step. In some cases, you may need to make the external device discoverable. Check the documentation for the external device to see whether this is the case and how you do this.

Find Device for Pairing

Now that the external device is on and transmitting a signal, the mobile device is ready for pairing.

On an Android mobile device, follow these steps:

1. On the Settings menu, select Bluetooth Settings. The device will begin to scan for Bluetooth devices in the area.

2. When the external device appears in the list of detected devices, tap it. If no PIN code is required, the devices will pair.

On an iOS mobile device, when Bluetooth is enabled, it automatically starts scanning for Bluetooth devices. When your device appears in the list, select it. If a PIN is required, move on to the next step.

Enter Appropriate PIN Code

Many external devices will ask for a PIN when you select the external device from the list of discovered devices. In many cases, the PIN is 0000, but check the manual of the external device.

Test Connectivity

Once the previous steps are complete, test communication between the two devices. If you're using a headset, turn on some sound and see whether you can hear it in the headphones.

Corporate and ISP E-mail Configuration

E-mail is one of the most important functions that people access on their mobile devices. This section will discuss how to configure e-mail on the device. The following procedures are common examples, and your specific device may differ slightly. Please consult the documentation for your device.

Server Address

Before you can access e-mail on your mobile device, you must know the settings for the e-mail server of your e-mail provider. There are two protocols that can be used to access e-mail accounts: POP3 and IMAP. If your account offers the use of IMAP, you should select it in the following steps because IMAP accounts have more functionality.

You will need the following information to complete this setup:

- The FQDN of your POP3 server or IMAP server (this server receives the e-mails sent to you, so it's sometimes called *incoming*)
- The FQDN of your SMTP server (this server sends your e-mail to the recipient's e-mail server, so it's sometimes called *outgoing*)
- The port numbers used for both server types
- The security type used (if any)

POP3

On an Android mobile device, follow these steps:

1. Click your device's e-mail icon. On the page that follows, select Add Account.
2. Type your e-mail address and password and click Next.
3. Select POP3.
4. On the next screen, enter your username (your e-mail address), your password, the FQDN of the POP3 server, the port number, and the security type (if one is in use).
5. Enter the FQDN of your SMTP server, the port number, your username, and your password. Also select Require Sign In.

On an iOS mobile device, follow these steps:

1. Select Settings ➢ Mail, Contacts, Calendars ➢ Add Account.
2. Select Other.
3. Select Add Mail Account. Fill in your name, your e-mail address, your password, and a description. Click Next.
4. Select POP. Verify that the name, address, and description carried over from the last page.
5. Under Incoming Email Server, enter the FQDN of the POP3 server, your e-mail address, and your password.
6. Under Outgoing Mail Server, enter the FQDN of the SMTP server and your e-mail address.
7. Click Next. Click Save in the upper-right corner.

IMAP

On an Android mobile device, follow these steps:

1. Click your device's e-mail icon. On the page that follows, select Add Account.
2. Type your e-mail address and password and click Next.

3. Select IMAP.

4. On the next screen, enter your username (your e-mail address), your password, the FQDN of the IMAP server, the port number, and the security type (if one is in use).

5. Enter the FQDN of your SMTP server, the port number, your username, and the password. Also select Require Sign In.

On an iOS mobile device, follow these steps:

1. Select Settings ➤ Mail, Contacts, Calendars ➤ Add Account.

2. Select Other.

3. Select Add Mail Account. Fill in your name, your e-mail address, your password, and a description. Click Next.

4. Select IMAP. Verify that the name, address, and description carried over from the last page.

5. Under Incoming Email Server, enter the FQDN of the IMAP server, your e-mail address, and your password.

6. Under Outgoing Mail Server, enter the FQDN of the SMTP server and your e-mail address.

7. Click Next. Click Save in the upper-right corner.

Port and SSL Settings

With either operating system, you can (and should) select to use security if your e-mail server supports it. This will encrypt all traffic between the mobile device and the e-mail server. The choices offered are usually SSL or TLS, so you will need to know which of these is in use.

Exchange and S/MIME

In many cases, your work e-mail will be hosted on a Microsoft Exchange server. The setup is not so very different but does require more information.

- Exchange server address
- Username and password for account
- Domain name for account

On an Android mobile device, follow these steps:

1. Open the Mail application. Enter your e-mail address and password.

2. Click Next and then click Exchange Account.

3. Enter your domain/username, password, and Exchange Server address.

4. Check Use Secure Connection and Accept All SSL Certificates.

5. After authentication, check the boxes associated with the features you want to include, such as Push, Amount To Sync, Notifications, Sync Contacts, Sync Calendar, and Sync Calendar Amount. Be careful with the (Automatic) Push setting—it will run the battery down.

6. Click Next. On the next screen, you need to give an account name and your name (this will be displayed on outgoing e-mail messages).

On an iOS mobile device, follow these steps:

1. Select Settings ➢ Mail, Contacts, Calendars ➢ Add Account.

2. Select Microsoft Exchange.

3. Fill in your e-mail address, your domain, your username, your password, and a description if desired. Click Next.

4. Verify that the address carried over from the last page. Under Server, enter the FQDN of the Exchange Server or its IP address and click Next.

5. Finally, select the items you want to sync automatically with the e-mail server and click Done.

With respect to the S/MIME configuration, you need the following:

▪   A digital encryption certificate for yourself as the sender

▪   A copy of the digital public key from your intended recipient

▪   An e-mail program capable of handling S/MIME e-mail

Exchange supports S/MIME, so that part is taken care of. Once you have obtained your certificate, you must import it into your device and make it available to the e-mail program. Your certificate must be obtained from a certificate authority company such as VeriSign. The steps to this process will vary from organization to organization. Once you have downloaded the certificate, place it at a location on the device where you can find it during the import process.

Typically, the certificate will come to you in an e-mail that you should open on the Android device. When you click the enrollment link in the e-mail, you will be required to enter the password you set when you requested the certificate. Then you will create another password (called a PKCS#12 passphrase) that you will need during the certificate installation.

When the certificate downloads to the device, it will go into the Downloads folder. Now you have to add it to your credentials. Follow these steps:

1. Navigate to Settings ➢ Security and select Install From Storage.

2. Locate your downloaded certificate file (it's a `.pfx` file).

3. Enter your PKCS#12 passphrase (this is the one you created just before the downloads, not the one you created during enrollment).

4. Set the certificate name and its use (e-mail).

The certificate is now available to use to encrypt e-mail.

For iOS, follow the organizational steps to request a certificate. When the e-mail arrives, open it on the iOS device as you did in Android. Then follow these steps:

1. Open the Mail app and find the message that contains the `.p12` file. Tap the file icon to load it.

2. An Install Profile pop-up will appear for the identity certificate. Tap Install.

3. A warning that this is an unsigned profile may appear. If that happens, tap Install Now to acknowledge it.

4. You will be prompted for your passcode. Enter the passcode you use to unlock your iPad or iPhone when it's at the lock screen.

5. You'll then be asked for the password for the certificate. Enter the passphrase you came up with when you created the .p12 file on your Mac.

6. You may see a note that the certificate is Not Trusted. That's OK.

7. Push the Home button. Find the Settings app and start it.

8. In Settings, find Mail, Contacts, Calendars and select it.

9. In the list of accounts, find the account for this e-mail address and tap it.

10. Tap the Account line.

11. Scroll down until you see Advanced. Tap it.

12. Scroll down until you see the S/MIME section.

13. Make sure S/MIME is turned on.

14. Tap Sign. Make sure that the certificate for this account is selected and that Sign is turned on. (If you tap the (i) icon, you should see that the certificate is Trusted.)

15. Tap Advanced or Back to go back to the Advanced screen.

16. Tap Encrypt by Default. Again, select the correct certificate, and make sure Encrypt By Default is turned on.

17. Back out until you're at the Account screen and then tap Done to accept the changes.

Integrated Commercial Provider E-mail Configuration

You probably also want to set up your personal e-mail on a device from a commercial provider. This section will look at some of the major e-mail systems you may encounter.

Google/Inbox

On an Android mobile device, follow these steps:

1. Select the Gmail icon.

2. Select Already Have A Google account.

3. In the Sign In With Your Google Account field, enter your username and password and select Sign In.

On an iOS mobile device, follow these steps:

1. Select Settings ➤ Mail, Contacts, Calendars ➤ Add Account.

2. Select Gmail.

3. Fill in your name, address, password, and description if desired. Click Next.

4. Verify that the address carried over from the last page. Click Next.

5. Select the items you want to sync automatically with the e-mail server and click Done.

Yahoo

Because Yahoo recommends using IMAP as an e-mail client, these are the instructions for setting up IMAP on Android systems:

1. From the Android Home screen, tap the E-mail icon.

2. Enter your e-mail address and password and then tap Manual Setup.

3. Select IMAP Account.

4. On the next screen, Incoming Server Settings, enter your username and password and the following:

    ▪ **IMAP Server:** imap.mail.yahoo.com

    ▪ **Port:** Either 993 or 143 (or infrequently 585)

    ▪ **Security Type:** SSL (if selecting SSL, you choose port 993)

5. Tap Next.

6. On the next screen, Outgoing Server Settings, set the following:

    ▪ **SMTP Server:** smtp.mail.yahoo.com

    ▪ **Port:** Either 25 or 465 (or infrequently 2525)

    ▪ **Security Type:** SSL (if selecting SSL, you choose port 465)

7. Tap Next.

8. Select the e-mail check frequency interval and tap Next.

9. Name the account and input your display name.

10. Tap Done.

    On an iOS device, use these instructions:

1. Tap Settings ➢ Mail, Contacts, Calendars.

2. Tap Add Account.

3. Tap Yahoo.

4. Enter your name, your e-mail address, your e-mail password, and a description; then tap Next.

5. Optionally, disable aspects of Yahoo Mail from syncing.

6. Tap Save.

Outlook.com

To set up Outlook on Android, first, if required, install Outlook for Android. Follow these steps:

1. Download Outlook for Android from Google Play. Open the app.

2. If it is installed on your device, open the app and then tap the navigation control at the bottom of your device (or tap More ➢ Settings ➢ Add Account).

3. On the Add An Account page, tap Outlook.com if you have an Outlook e-mail account ending with @outlook.com, @hotmail.com, @msn.com, or @live.com. This includes international domains, such as @outlook.co.uk or any custom domains hosted on Outlook.com.

4. Enter your full e-mail address (for example <someone>@outlook.com), type your password, and then tap Sign In.

5. The account will be added, and Outlook for Android will begin to sync to the e-mail account.

On iOS, follow these steps:

1. Download the Microsoft Outlook app or search for Outlook in the App Store with your iOS device.

2. After the app has installed, tap Get Started.

3. Next, select the account you want to add.

4. Sign in to the account, and the Microsoft Outlook app will begin to sync with the account.

If you're unable to use the app for any reason, you can still set up Outlook.com on your iOS device.

1. Tap Settings and then tap Mail, Contacts, Calendar.

2. Tap Add Account in the Accounts page.

3. Select Hotmail.

4. Enter your Outlook.com address and password.

5. Select the fields that you want to sync. Tap Save.

iCloud

To set up iCloud e-mail on an Android device, follow these instructions:

1. Open the E-mail app and tap the menu button in the top-right corner. (If you've never used the E-mail app before, just open it and go to step 3.)

2. Tap Add Account.

3. Enter your iCloud e-mail address and password and then tap Next.

4. Select IMAP and tap Next.

5. When you see the Incoming Server Settings page, remove the @icloud.com from your username.

6. Change the IMAP server to **imap.mail.me.com**.

7. Set the security field to SSL/TLS (Accept All Certificates).

8. Make sure the port is set to 993 and then tap Next.

9. On the Outgoing Server Settings page, change the SMTP server to **smtp.mail.me.com**.

10. Change the security setting to STARTTLS and make sure the port is set to 587 and Require Sign-In is checked.

11. Tap Next to complete the process.

As you can imagine, setting up iCloud e-mail on an iOS device is simple because the applications all reside in the Apple ecosystem. First set up an iCloud e-mail account. If you have an e-mail address that ends with @mac.com or @me.com, you already have an equivalent address that's the same except it ends with @icloud.com. On your iOS device, simply go to Settings ➢ iCloud, turn on Mail, and then follow the onscreen instructions.

PRI Updates/PRL Updates/Baseband Updates

The *product release information* (PRI) is the connection between the mobile device and the radio. From time to time this may need updating, and when done, it may add features or increase data speed.

The *preferred roaming list* (PRL) is a list of radio frequencies residing in the memory of some kinds of digital phones. It lists frequencies the phone can use in various geographic areas. Each area is ordered by the bands the phone should try to use first. Therefore, it's a priority list for which towers the phone should use.

When roaming, the PRL may instruct the phone to use the network with the best roaming rate for the carrier, rather than the one with the strongest signal at the moment. As carrier networks change, an updated PRL may be required.

The baseband is the chip that controls all the GSM and 3G phone RF waves. An update makes the code in the chip current.

All mobile devices may require one or more of these updates at one point or another. In many cases, these updates will happen automatically, or "over the air." In many cases, you may be required to disable Wi-Fi and enable data for these to occur.

PRL

In Android phones, the location of the PRI update option will differ, but you'll generally find it in one of a few places in the Settings menu.

- Settings ➢ System Updates ➢ Update PRL
- Settings ➢ Sprint System Updates ➢ Update PRL
- Settings ➢ About Phone ➢ Update PRL

In iOS, there is no separate PRL update command on iOS devices, but running a profile update will force an update of the PRL.

PRI

A PRI update is a flash process. This usually occurs in over-the-air updates. When done manually, it involves acquiring the file and then performing a flash process with the bootloader, which in many cases also updates the radio (see the next section). The flash process can result in a useless device (bricked), so follow the vendor instructions.

Radio Firmware

The radios in mobile devices are equipped with firmware that, like all firmware, may need an update from time to time. In Android, follow these steps:

1. Download the Radio zip file.
2. Rename it to **update.zip**.
3. Copy it to the root of your phone's SD card.
4. Turn off your phone.
5. Start up in Recovery mode by holding Home and pressing Power.
6. Press Alt+S to apply the update.
7. Once the update is applied, press Home+Back to reboot the phone. The phone will start to boot up and then continue applying the update. Once this is completed, the Recovery menu will ask you for the second time to reboot the phone via Home+Back.
8. Double-check the baseband has been updated properly via choosing Menu ≻ Settings ≻ About Phone. Scroll down until you see the baseband version. You should see the radio version on this row. If not, you will need to update the radio again.

    In iOS, follow these steps:

1. After downloading the desired firmware, connect the device to your computer and select it in iTunes. Mac users hold down the Option key, while Windows users hold down the Shift key.
2. Click the Update or Restore button, select the IPSW file you recently downloaded, and click Choose. Your device should now begin to update. Take note that certain browsers may change the .ipsw file into a .zip file. If this should occur, just rename it to end in .ipsw, and iTunes will recognize it.

IMEI vs. IMSI

International Mobile Equipment Identification (IMEI) is used to identify a physical phone device, while *International Mobile Subscriber Identification* (IMSI) is used to identify a Subscriber Identification Module (SIM) card.

VPN

Many users need to use the mobile devices to connect to the corporate network. This should be done using a VPN connection. To set up a VPN connection in Android, follow these steps:

1. Open the Settings app and tap More under Wireless And Networks. (On Android 2.3, tap Wireless And Networks.)

2. Tap the VPN option on the Wireless And Networks screen. (On Android 2.3, tap VPN Settings.)

3. Tap the + button and provide the VPN's details. Enter a name for the connection, select the type of VPN server you're connecting to, and enter the VPN server's address (either an address like **vpn.example.com** or a numerical IP address).

In iOS, follow these steps:

1. Choose Settings ➤ General ➤ VPN.

2. Choose Add VPN Configuration.

3. Provide the VPN's details. Enter a name for the connection, select the type of VPN server you're connecting to, and enter the VPN server's address (either an address such as vpn.example.com or a numerical IP address).

Exam Essentials

Enable Bluetooth and pair a Bluetooth device with a mobile network.   Describe the process for both the iOS and Android operating systems.

Configure e-mail on a mobile device.   Describe the process of configuring e-mail, including both Exchange and Gmail for both the iOS and Android operating systems.

2.7 Summarize Methods and Data Related to Mobile Device Synchronization

Keeping information in sync between your desktop or laptop and your mobile device is one of the features that many users want to take advantage of. There are many types of information that can be synced, applications that can be installed to perform the synchronization, and a number of connection methods that can be used to do this. This section discusses mobile device synchronization. The topics addressed in this section include the following:

▪ Types of data to synchronize

▪ Synchronization methods

▪ Mutual authentication for multiple services

▪ Software requirements to install the application on the PC

▪ Connection types to enable synchronization

Types of Data to Synchronize

Users may be interested in maintaining a consistency between the state of data that exists on the laptop or desktop and the state of the same data on a mobile device. This section discusses common types of data.

Contacts

No one wants to enter a long list of contacts into a mobile device when that same list already exists in your e-mail account. Using push synchronization (*push* means it's automatic and requires no effort on the part of the user), you ensure that any changes made to the contact list either on the mobile device or on the desktop will be updated on the other device the next time you make a connection to the e-mail account from the other device. It will also update if the mobile device makes a direct connection to the desktop (covered later in "Connection Types to Enable Synchronization").

Programs

Program data from applications such as databases can also be synchronized between servers and mobile devices. A good example is the synchronization of the data entered into handheld devices used by the wait staff in restaurants and the server in the back room of the restaurant. Another example is the synchronization of data from handheld scanners in a warehouse with a server that may or may not be onsite. This seamless automatic updating makes the entire operation more productive.

E-mail

Even more important to users than their contacts is the state of their e-mail. The mobile device will synchronize the contacts, calendar items, and e-mail each time the mobile device makes contact with the e-mail account. This results in a consistent state between what is seen on the desktop and what is seen on the mobile device. Push synchronization will usually allow you to configure the push schedule, such as every 30 minutes. To preserve battery life, push sync should take place less frequently.

Pictures

Pictures are another item that users frequently want to view from their mobile device without going through the process of manually downloading them to the device. Synchronization allows the pictures stored on the desktop (or even a share on a server) to be available on the mobile device, even the one you just added an hour ago.

Music

Music files can also be included in the sync process. This helps to keep your library available on the mobile device. When you start talking about music and video files (see the next section), a word of a caution is in order. These large files can quickly add up and fill the hard drive and also add significantly to your data usage if the sync is happening over a wireless cell phone connection using a data plan. They can also be hard on the battery.

Videos

Video libraries can be kept consistent across devices using synchronization. Be aware of the effect of these large files on your drive space, battery level, and data usage if you are syncing wirelessly through a cell phone network.

Calendar

The calendar is a critical application for both work and play. All mobile devices support syncing the calendar between devices. In some cases, it may require a small application, especially when the e-mail system of which the calendar is part of is in a different ecosystem (for example, Google Mail and an iPhone).

Bookmarks

Bookmarks of frequently visited websites make everyone's day easier, and when the same ones are available in the browser of all your devices, including your mobile devices, it doubles the benefit. Bookmarks are another item that can be configured to sync automatically.

Documents

Technology to sync documents located in multiple locations has been around for some time now. Users have come to expect this functionality, and it is present in modern mobile devices as well. Users want to be able to work anywhere on any device and this facilitates that.

Location Data

In some cases, users may decide to allow an application to track their location for the purpose of tailoring search results. When this is done, it can be a onetime thing or the users can give the application ongoing permission to do so. Most device browsers will indicate this with some sort of icon or indicator on that page. These setting can also be synchronized between devices as well.

Social Media Data

While social media was once a guilty distraction, today even businesses and organizations use social media. When users have multiple accounts, many mobile platforms such as Google and Apple offer applications that can allow them to track and post to multiple accounts at once, reducing the time required to "check and update" the accounts.

e-books

Many users have accounts that give them access to books in digital format or e-books. Naturally, they want to have access to these books (and other content types) on all their devices. Not only can this be done, but the sync process can keep their various devices up-to-date with the latest position of a bookmark in the book or of new items that have been highlighted or notes that have been made.

Synchronization Methods

When synchronizing these various data types, there are two basic ways to make this happen. In this section, you'll look at both approaches.

Synchronize to the Cloud

One synchronization method that is gaining in popularity (as are all things "cloud") is synchronizing all your devices to a cloud server. This provides a central location for your data, settings, and all other items listed in the "Types of Data to Synchronize" section. This can be set up such that all devices update with the cloud as soon as they attain Internet access.

Synchronize to the Desktop

Another approach is to set up a sync process directly between two devices such as a smartphone and a desktop computer. In this case, the two devices will sync with one another at any time they find themselves on the same network such as a home wireless network.

Mutual Authentication for Multiple Services

Mutual authentication is a process whereby not only does the server verify the credential of the client but the client also verifies the credential of the server. It adds additional security to the process. Both Android and iOS devices support this type of authentication, typically using SSL. One of the challenges presented to performing this type of authentication in mobile devices is their relative lack of processing power when compared with desktop and laptop systems.

Software Requirements to Install the Application on the PC

Some devices come with a sync feature installed, but for the most robust functionality (for example, syncing between devices with different operating systems such as iPhone to Android and Android to BlackBerry), synchronization applications that will do a much better job than the built-in applications can be purchased either at the Apple Store site or in other app marketplaces.

When obtaining one of these, ensure that your device meets all the requirements of the application. These applications will call for certain minimum requirements on the mobile device to operate correctly, so observe these guidelines to ensure a successful installation and operation.

Connection Types to Enable Synchronization

The synchronization process can be carried out over several methods of connection between the devices. In some cases, you can connect the mobile device to the laptop or desktop using a USB connector. In other cases, you can establish a Bluetooth connection from the mobile device and the desktop. Finally, an 802.11 WLAN can also be used to establish this connection. In some instances, the synchronization application will allow you to introduce a shared folder into the scenario (like Dropbox, for example), which then allows you to use the Internet to sync from the laptop to the Dropbox and then from the Dropbox to the mobile device.

Exam Essentials

Identify the types of data usually synchronized on mobile devices. This includes but is not limited to contacts, programs, e-mail, music, pictures, and videos.

Describe the connection types available to enable synchronization. These include USB cables, cell phone networks, Bluetooth connections, and 802.11 networks and shared folders available through the Internet.

Review Questions

You can find the answers in the Appendix.

1. What utility is used to backup data in Linux?
   A. rsync
   B. Time Machine
   C. pwd
   D. chmod

2. What is the fsck command used for in Linux?
   A. to defrag
   B. to run a file system check
   C. to format a drive
   D. to perform backup

3. Which parameter when used with the tar command, creates a new archive?
   A. -r
   B. -A
   C. -c
   D. -d

4. What utility is used to create a snapshot volume in Linux?
   A. lvcreate
   B. rsync
   C. tar
   D. cpio

5. What is the shell called in Mac?
   A. command central
   B. terminal
   C. dock
   D. gateway

6. What tool can be used on a Mac to stop an unresponsive application?
   A. kill
   B. force quit
   C. end
   D. quit

7. What tool provides a quick way to see everything that's currently open on your Mac.?

   A. dock launch

   B. command central

   C. mission control

   D. mac view

8. What is password management system in OS X called?

   A. Spotlight

   B. Keychain

   C. iKey

   D. iLock

9. What is Spotlight used for in MAC?

   A. to filter output

   B. to search

   C. to identify malware

   D. to track access

10. What is the equivalent of Windows Explorer in MAC?

   A. Finder

   B. Spotlight

   C. Navigator

   D. Compass

Chapter

7

Security

COMPTIA A+ 220-902 EXAM OBJECTIVES COVERED IN THIS CHAPTER:

✓ **3.1 Identify common security threats and vulnerabilities.**

- Malware (spyware, viruses, worms, trojans, rootkits, ransomware)
- Phishing
- Spear phishing
- Spoofing
- Social engineering
- Shoulder surfing
- Zero-day attack
- Zombie/botnet
- Brute forcing
- Dictionary attacks
- Non-compliant systems
- Violations of security best practices
- Tailgating
- Man-in-the-middle

✓ **3.2 Compare and contrast common prevention methods.**

- Physical security (lock doors, mantrap, cable locks, securing physical documents/passwords/shredding, biometrics, ID badges, key fobs, RFID badge, smart card, tokens, privacy filters, entry control roster)
- Digital security (antivirus/antimalware, firewalls, user authentication/strong passwords, multifactor authentication, directory permissions, VPN, DLP, disabling ports, access control lists, smart card, email filtering, trusted/untrusted software sources)

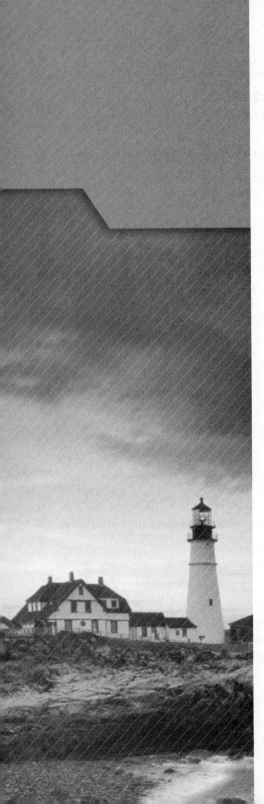

- User education/AUP

- Principle of least privilege

✓ **3.3 Compare and contrast differences of basic Windows OS security settings.**

- User and groups (administrator, power user, guest, standard user)

- NTFS vs. share permissions (allow vs. deny, moving vs. copying folders and files, file attributes)

- Shared files and folders (administrative shares vs. local shares, permission, inheritance)

- System files and folders

- User authentication (single sign-on)

- Run as administrator vs. standard user

- BitLocker

- BitLocker-To-Go

- EFS

✓ **3.4 Given a scenario, deploy and enforce security best practices to secure a workstation.**

- Password best practices (setting strong passwords, password expiration, changing default user names/passwords, screensaver required password, BIOS/UEFI passwords, requiring passwords)

- Account management (restricting user permissions, login time restrictions, disabling guest account, failed attempts lockout, timeout/screen lock)

- Disable autorun

- Data encryption

- Patch/update management

✓ **3.5 Compare and contrast various methods for securing mobile devices.**

- Screen locks (fingerprint lock, face lock, swipe lock, passcode lock)

- Remote wipes

- Locator applications

- Remote backup applications
- Failed login attempts restrictions
- Antivirus/antimalware
- Patching/OS updates
- Biometric authentication
- Full device encryption
- Multifactor authentication
- Authenticator applications
- Trusted sources vs. untrusted sources
- Firewalls
- Policies and procedures (BYOD vs. corporate owned, profile security requirements)

✓ **3.6 Given a scenario, use appropriate data destruction and disposal methods.**

- Physical destruction (shredder, drill/see note on page 499, electromagnetic/degaussing, incineration, certificate of destruction)
- Recycling or repurposing best practices (low-level format vs. standard format, overwrite, drive wipe)

✓ **3.7 Given a scenario, secure SOHO wireless and wired networks.**

- Wireless specific (changing default SSID, setting encryption, disabling SSID broadcast, antenna and access point placement, radio power levels, WPS)
- Change default usernames and passwords
- Enable MAC filtering
- Assign static IP addresses
- Firewall settings
- Port forwarding/mapping
- Disabling ports
- Content filtering/parental controls
- Update firmware
- Physical security

Given the ever-increasing need for security knowledge in the real world, CompTIA expects those who become A+ certified to have a basic knowledge and understanding of the principles behind it. The subobjectives in this category do a good job of providing a thorough overview of the topic.

3.1 Identify Common Security Threats and Vulnerabilities

This objective explores security threats and vulnerabilities. A number of important topics are discussed in this section that fall into the realm of two broad categories: social engineering and malware. You'll look at malware and then several different types of attacks, as well as some of the reasons your network is vulnerable. This list is far from inclusive because new variants of each are being created by miscreants on a regular basis. The list is, however, everything CompTIA expects you to know for the exam. Subobjectives covered in this section include the following:

- Malware
- Phishing
- Spear phishing
- Spoofing
- Social engineering
- Shoulder surfing
- Zero-day attack
- Zombie/botnet
- Brute forcing
- Dictionary attacks
- Noncompliant systems
- Violations of security best practices
- Tailgating
- Man-in-the-middle

Malware

We've all been battling malicious, invasive software since we bought our first computers. This software can go by any number of names—virus, malware, and so on—but if you aren't aware of their presence, these uninvited intruders may damage the data on your hard disk, destroy your operating system, and possibly spread to other systems.

You want to make certain that your systems, and the data within them, are kept as secure as possible. Security prevents others from changing the data, destroying it, or inadvertently harming it. In this section, I'll cover common types of malware.

Spyware

Spyware differs from other malware in that it works—often actively—on behalf of a third party. Rather than self-replicating, like viruses and worms, spyware is spread to machines by users who inadvertently ask for it. The users often don't know they have asked for it but have done so by downloading other programs, visiting infected sites, and so on.

The spyware program monitors the user's activity and responds by offering unsolicited pop-up advertisements (sometimes known as *adware*), gathers information about the user to pass on to marketers, or intercepts personal data such as credit card numbers.

Viruses

Viruses can be classified as polymorphic, stealth, retroviruses, multipartite, armored, companion, phage, and macro viruses. Each type of virus has a different attack strategy and different consequences.

Estimates for losses due to viruses are in the billions of dollars. These losses include financial loss as well as lost productivity.

The following sections will introduce the symptoms of a virus infection, explain how a virus works, and describe the types of viruses you can expect to encounter and how they generally behave. I'll also discuss how a virus is transmitted through a network and look at a few hoaxes.

Symptoms of a Virus/Malware Infection

Many viruses will announce that you're infected as soon as they gain access to your system. They may take control of your system and flash annoying messages on your screen or destroy your hard disk. When this occurs, you'll know that you're a victim. Other viruses will cause your system to slow down, cause files to disappear from your computer, or take over your disk space.

Because viruses are the most common malware, the term *virus* is used in this section.

You should look for some of the following symptoms when determining whether a virus infection has occurred:

- The programs on your system start to load more slowly. This happens because the virus is spreading to other files in your system or is taking over system resources.

- Unusual files appear on your hard drive, or files start to disappear from your system. Many viruses delete key files in your system to render it inoperable.

- Program sizes change from the installed versions. This occurs because the virus is attaching itself to these programs on your disk.

- Your browser, word-processing application, or other software begins to exhibit unusual operating characteristics. Screens or menus may change.

- The system mysteriously shuts itself down or starts itself up and does a great deal of unanticipated disk activity.

- You mysteriously lose access to a disk drive or other system resources. The virus has changed the settings on a device to make it unusable.

- Your system suddenly doesn't reboot or gives unexpected error messages during startup.

This list is by no means comprehensive. What is an absolute, however, is that you should immediately quarantine the infected system. It is imperative that you do all you can to contain the virus and keep it from spreading to other systems within your network or beyond.

How Viruses Work

A virus, in most cases, tries to accomplish one of two things: render your system inoperable or spread to other systems. Many viruses will spread to other systems given the chance and then render your system unusable. This is common with many of the newer viruses.

If your system is infected, the virus may try to attach itself to every file in your system and spread each time you send a file or document to other users. When you give removable media to another user or put it into another system, you then infect that system with the virus.

Most viruses today are spread using email. The infected system attaches a file to any email that you send to another user. The recipient opens this file, thinking it's something you legitimately sent them. When they open the file, the virus infects the target system. The virus might then attach itself to all the emails the newly infected system sends, which in turn infects the recipients of the emails. Figure 7.1 shows how a virus can spread from a single user to thousands of users in a short time using email.

Types of Viruses

Viruses take many different forms. The following sections briefly introduce these forms and explain how they work. These are the most common types, but this isn't a comprehensive list.

FIGURE 7.1   An email virus spreading geometrically to other users

 The best defense against a virus attack is to install and run antivirus software. The software should be on all workstations as well as the server.

Armored Virus   An *armored virus* is designed to make itself difficult to detect or analyze. Armored viruses cover themselves with protective code that stops debuggers or disassemblers from examining critical elements of the virus. The virus may be written in such a way that some aspects of the programming act as a decoy to distract analysis while the actual code hides in other areas in the program.

From the perspective of the creator, the more time it takes to deconstruct the virus, the longer it can live. The longer it can live, the more time it has to replicate and spread to as many machines as possible. The key to stopping most viruses is to identify them quickly and educate administrators about them—the very things that the armor intensifies the difficulty of accomplishing.

Companion Virus   A *companion virus* attaches itself to legitimate programs and then creates a program with a different filename extension. This file may reside in your system's temporary directory. When a user types the name of the legitimate program, the companion virus executes instead of the real program. This effectively hides the virus from the user. Many of the viruses that are used to attack Windows systems make changes to program pointers in the Registry so that they point to the infected program. The infected program may perform its dirty deed and then start the real program.

Macro Virus   A *macro virus* exploits the enhancements made to many application programs. Programmers can expand the capability of applications such as Microsoft Word and Excel. Word, for example, supports a mini-BASIC programming language that allows files to be manipulated automatically. These programs in the document are called *macros*. For example, a macro can tell your word processor to spell-check your document automatically when it opens. Macro viruses can infect all the documents on your system and spread to other systems via email or other methods.

Multipartite Virus   A *multipartite virus* attacks your system in multiple ways. It may attempt to infect your boot sector, infect all your executable files, and destroy your application files. The hope here is that you won't be able to correct all the problems and will allow the infestation to continue. The multipartite virus in Figure 7.2 attacks your boot sector, infects application files, and attacks your Word documents.

FIGURE 7.2   A multipartite virus commencing an attack on a system

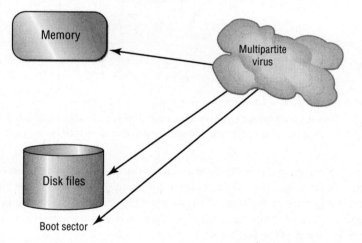

Phage Virus   A *phage virus* alters other programs and databases. The virus infects all these files. The only way to remove this virus is to reinstall the programs that are infected. If you miss even a single incident of this virus on the victim system, the process will start again and infect the system once more.

Polymorphic Virus   *Polymorphic viruses* change form in order to avoid detection. The virus will attempt to hide from your antivirus software. Frequently, the virus will encrypt parts of itself to avoid detection. When the virus does this, it's referred to as *mutation*. The mutation process makes it hard for antivirus software to detect common characteristics of the virus. Figure 7.3 shows a polymorphic virus changing its characteristics to avoid detection. In this example, the virus changes a signature to fool antivirus software.

FIGURE 7.3   The polymorphic virus changing its characteristics

A *signature* is an algorithm or other element of a virus that uniquely identifies it. Because some viruses have the ability to alter their signature, it is crucial that you keep signature files current, whether you choose to manually download them or configure the antivirus engine to do so automatically.

Retrovirus   A *retrovirus* attacks or bypasses the antivirus software installed on a computer. You can consider a retrovirus to be an anti-antivirus. Retroviruses can directly attack your antivirus software and potentially destroy the virus definition database file. Destroying this information without your knowledge would leave you with a false sense of security. The virus may also directly attack an antivirus program to create bypasses for itself.

Stealth Virus   A *stealth virus* attempts to avoid detection by masking itself from applications. It may attach itself to the boot sector of the hard drive. When a system utility or program runs, the stealth virus redirects commands around itself in order to avoid detection. An infected file may report a file size different from what is actually present in order to avoid detection. Figure 7.4 shows a stealth virus attaching itself to the boot sector to avoid detection. Stealth viruses may also move themselves from file A to file B during a virus scan for the same reason.

FIGURE 7.4   A stealth virus hiding in a disk boot sector

This is a disk

Present Virus Activity

New viruses and threats are released on a regular basis to join the cadre of those already in existence. From an exam perspective, you need be familiar with the world only as it existed at the time the questions were written. From an administrative standpoint, however, you need to know what is happening today.

To find this information, visit the CERT/CC Current Activity web page at www.us-cert .gov/current/current_activity.html. Here you'll find a detailed description of the most current viruses as well as links to pages on older threats.

Worms

A worm is different from a virus in that it can reproduce itself, it's self-contained, and it doesn't need a host application to be transported. Many of the so-called viruses that have made the news were actually worms. However, it's possible for a worm to contain or deliver a virus to a target system.

By their nature and origin, worms are supposed to propagate, and they use whatever services they're capable of to do that. Early worms filled up memory and bred inside the RAM of the target computer. Worms can use TCP/IP, email, Internet services, social media sites, or any number of possibilities to reach their target.

Trojans

Trojan horses are programs that enter a system or network under the guise of another program. A Trojan horse may be included as an attachment or as part of an installation program. The Trojan horse can create a back door or replace a valid program during installation. It then accomplishes its mission under the guise of another program. Trojan horses can be used to compromise the security of your system, and they can exist on a system for years before they're detected.

The best preventive measure for Trojan horses is to not allow them entry into your system. Immediately before and after you install a new software program or operating system, back it up! If you suspect a Trojan horse, you can reinstall the original programs, which should delete the Trojan horse. A port scan may also reveal a Trojan horse on your system. If an application opens a TCP or IP port that isn't supported in your network, you can track it down and determine which port is being used.

Rootkits

Rootkits have become the software exploitation program du jour. Rootkits are software programs that have the ability to hide certain things from the operating system. With a rootkit, there may be a number of processes running on a system that don't show up in Task Manager, or connections may be established/available that don't appear in a Netstat display—the rootkit masks the presence of these items. The rootkit does this by manipulating function calls to the operating system and filtering out information that would normally appear.

Unfortunately, many rootkits are written to get around antivirus and antispyware programs that aren't kept up-to-date. The best defense you have is to monitor what your system is doing and catch the rootkit in the process of installation.

Ransomware

Ransomware is a type of malware that usually encrypts the entire system or an entire drive with an encryption key that only the hacker possesses. Once he encrypts the machine, he will hold the data residing on the device hostage until a ransom is paid.

The latest version of this attack arrives as an attachment that appears to be a resume. However, when the attachment is opened, the malware uses software called Cryptowall to encrypt the device. What usually follows is a demand for $500 to decrypt the device.

Phishing

Phishing is a form of social engineering in which you simply ask someone for a piece of information that you are missing by making it look as if it is a legitimate request. An email might look as if it is from a bank and contain some basic information, such as the user's name. In the email, it will often state that there is a problem with the person's account or access privileges. They will be told to click a link to correct the problem. After they click the link—which goes to a site other than the bank's—they are asked for their username, password, account information, and so on. The person instigating the phishing can then use the values entered there to access the legitimate account.

One of the best counters to phishing is to simply mouse over the Click Here link and read the URL. Almost every time it is pointing to an adaptation of the legitimate URL as opposed to a link to the real thing.

The only preventive measure in dealing with social-engineering attacks is to educate your users and staff to never give out passwords and user IDs over the phone or via email or to anyone who isn't positively verified as being who they say they are.

When you combine phishing with Voice over IP (VoIP), it becomes known as *vishing* and is just an elevated form of social engineering. While crank calls have been in existence since the invention of the telephone, the rise in VoIP now makes it possible for someone to call you from almost anywhere in the world, without the worry of tracing, caller ID, and other features of the land line, and pretend to be someone they are not in order to get data from you.

Spear Phishing

Two other forms of phishing to be aware of are *spear phishing* and *whaling*, and they are similar in nature. With spear phishing, the person conducting it uses information that the target would be less likely to question because it appears to be coming from a trusted source. As an example, instead of Wells Fargo sending you a message telling you to click here to fix a problem with your account, the message that comes in appears to be from your spouse and it says to click here to see a video of your children from last Christmas. Because it appears far more likely to be a legitimate message, it cuts through the user's standard defenses like a spear and has a higher likelihood of being clicked. Generating the attack requires much more work on the part of the miscreant and often involves using information from contact lists, friend lists from social media sites, and so on.

Whaling is nothing more than phishing, or spear phishing, for big users. Instead of sending out a To Whom It May Concern message to thousands of users, the whaler identifies one person from whom they can gain all the data they want—usually a manager or owner—and targets the phishing campaign at them.

Spoofing

Spoofing is the process of masquerading as another user or device. It is usually done for the purpose of accessing a resource to which the hacker should not have access or to get through a security device such as a firewall that may be filtering traffic based on a source IP address.

Spoofing can take various forms. The hacker may change his IP address to one that belongs to a trusted user or device to get through a firewall filtering at the IP layer. In other cases, he might spoof the MAC address of a trusted device to defeat layer-two security applied on a switch or wireless access point (AP). It could also be the spoofing of a username and password to access a resource. Finally, it might be the spoofing of an email address to launch one of the email-based attacks.

Social Engineering

Social engineering is a process in which an attacker attempts to acquire information about your network and system by social means, such as by talking to people in the organization. A social-engineering attack may occur over the phone, by email, or by a visit. The intent is to acquire access information, such as user IDs and passwords. When the attempt is made through email or instant messaging, this is known as *phishing* (discussed earlier) and often is made to look as if it is coming from sites where users are likely to have accounts (eBay and PayPal are popular).

These types of attacks are relatively low-tech and are more akin to con jobs. Take the following example. Your help desk gets a call at 4 a.m. from someone purporting to be the vice president of your company. She tells the help-desk personnel that she is out of town to attend a meeting, her computer just failed, and she is sitting in a Kinko's trying to get a file from her desktop computer back at the office. She can't seem to remember her password and user ID. She tells the help-desk representative that she needs access to the information right away or the company could lose millions of dollars. Your help-desk rep knows how important this meeting is and gives the vice president her user ID and password over the phone.

Another common approach is initiated by a phone call or email from your software vendor, telling you that they have a critical fix that must be installed on your computer system. If this patch isn't installed right away, your system will crash and you'll lose all your data. For some reason, you've changed your maintenance account password and they can't log on. Your systems operator gives the password to the person. You've been hit again.

Shoulder Surfing

Shoulder surfing involves nothing more than watching someone when they enter their sensitive data. They can see you entering a password, typing in a credit card number, or entering any other pertinent information. The best defense against this type of attack is simply to survey your environment before entering personal data. Privacy filters can be used that make the screen difficult to read unless you are directly in front of it.

Zero-Day Attack

Vulnerabilities are often discovered in live environments before a fix or patch exists. Such vulnerabilities are referred to as zero-day vulnerabilities. A zero-day attack occurs when security vulnerability in an application is discovered on the same day the application is released. Monitoring known hacking community websites can often provide an early alert because hackers often share zero-day exploit information. Honeypots or honeynets can also provide forensic information about hacker methods and tools for zero-day attacks.

New zero-day attacks are announced on a regular basis against a broad range of technology systems. You should create an inventory of applications and maintain a list of critical systems to manage the risks of these attack vectors.

Zombie/Botnet

A bot is a type of malware that installs itself on large numbers of computers through infected emails, downloads from websites, Trojan horses, and shared media. Once installed, the bot has the ability to connect back to the hacker's computer. After that, his server controls all the bots located on these machines. At a set time, the hacker may direct the bots to take some action, such as direct all the machines to send out spam messages, mount a DoS attack, or perform phishing or any number of malicious acts. The collection of computers that act together is called a *botnet*, and the individual computers are called *zombies*. By recruiting many zombies to assist in the attack, the attacker greatly magnifies the effect of the attack.

Brute Forcing

A brute-force attack is a password attack that operates by attempting every possible combination of characters that could be in a password. These can be performed online or offline. While given enough time and enough processing power, any password can be cracked, so most enterprises use some sort of password policy that locks an account after a certain number of incorrect attempts. For this reason, online attacks are largely unsuccessful.

In contrast, the offline mode of the attack requires the attacker to steal the password file first but enables an unconstrained guessing of passwords, free of any application- or network-related rate limitations.

Dictionary Attacks

Dictionary attacks rely on the use of large files that contain words from the dictionary. These attacks are most often attempts to crack an encrypted password by encrypting each word in the dictionary file using the same algorithm used to encrypt the users' password and then comparing this value to the encrypted password for a match. These attacks are performed offline to eliminate the disabling of the account through password policies.

Noncompliant Systems

Upon infection, some viruses destroy the target system immediately. The saving grace is that the infection can be detected and corrected. Some viruses won't destroy or otherwise tamper with a system; they use the victim system as a carrier. The victim system then infects servers, file shares, and other resources with the virus. The carrier then infects the target system again. Until the carrier is identified and cleaned, the virus continues to harass systems in this network and spread.

You should use some type of enterprise-grade malware management system that scans the network for noncompliant devices. Most of these systems can automate the entire process of locating, isolating, and remediating noncompliant devices.

Violations of Security Best Practices

In a properly secured organization, securities policies should exist that define the minimum security measures expected of users. These policies will drive the development of the AUP. This policy describes in some detail the actions and functions that are allowed on the networks and those that are not. These rules should always be designed to follow and encourage the use of security best practices. A critical component of this document is the specification of consequences for noncompliance.

Tailgating

Tailgating is the term used for someone being so close to you when you enter a building that they are able to come in right behind you without needing to use a key, a card, or any other security device. Many social-engineering intruders needing physical access to a site will use this method of gaining entry. Educate users to beware of this and other social-engineering ploys and prevent them from happening.

Mantraps are a great way to stop tailgating. A mantrap is a series of two doors with a small room between them that helps prevent unauthorized people from entering a building. For more information see the section "Mantrap."

Man-in-the-Middle

A man-in-the-middle attack is one in which the hacker uses one of several techniques to position himself in the middle of a current communication session between two devices. One way he might do this is by polluting the arp cache (mappings of IP addresses to MAC addresses) such that the users on either end of the session think they are sending data to one another when in reality they are sending it to the hacker. This allows him to monitor the entire conversation.

Exam Essentials

Know the characteristics and types of viruses used to disrupt systems and networks.   Several different types of viruses are floating around today. The most common ones are polymorphic viruses, stealth viruses, retroviruses, multipartite viruses, and macro viruses.

Know the various types of social engineering.   Social-engineering variants include shoulder surfing (watching someone work) and phishing (tricking someone into believing they are communicating with a party other than the one they are communicating with). Variations on phishing include vishing and whaling as well as spear phishing.

3.2 Compare and Contrast Common Prevention Methods

A great many of the security issues that plague networks today can be solved through the implementation of basic security elements. Some of those elements are physical (locked doors) and others digital (antivirus software), but all share the goal of keeping out problems.

This objective is divided into four topic areas: physical security, digital security, user education/AUP, and the principle of least privilege. As you study for the exam, know what types of physical security elements you can add to an environment to secure it. Know as well what types of digital security you should implement to keep malware at bay. Understand that the first line of defense is the users and that you need to educate them to understand why security is important. You should follow the principle of least privilege to prevent users from inadvertently causing harm. The following are subobjectives covered in this section:

- Physical security
- Digital security
- User education/AUP
- Principle of least privilege

Physical Security

Physical security is a grab bag of elements that can be added to an environment to aid in securing it. It ranges from key fobs to retinal scanners. In this section, you will examine the list of components in the order given by CompTIA.

Lock Doors

One of the easiest ways to prevent people intent on creating problems from physically entering your environment is to lock your doors and keep them out. A key aspect of access control involves *physical barriers*. The objective of a physical barrier is to prevent access to computers and network systems. The most effective physical barrier implementations require that more than one physical barrier be crossed to gain access. This type of approach is called a *multiple-barrier system*.

Ideally, your systems should have a minimum of three physical barriers. The first barrier is the external entrance to the building, referred to as a *perimeter*, which is protected by burglar alarms, external walls, *fencing*, surveillance, and so on. An *access list* should exist to specifically identify who can enter and be verified by a guard or someone in authority. The second barrier is the entrance into the building and could rely on such items as *ID badges* to gain access. The third barrier is the entrance to the computer room itself (and could require fobs, or keys). Each of these entrances can be individually secured, monitored, and protected with alarm systems.

> **TIP**   Think of the three barriers this way: outer (the fence), middle (guards, locks, and mantraps), and inner (key fobs).

Although these three barriers won't always stop intruders, they will potentially slow them down enough that law enforcement can respond before an intrusion is fully developed. Once inside, a truly secure site should be dependent on a physical token for access to the actual network resources.

Mantrap

A mantrap is a series of two doors with a small room between them. The user is authenticated at the first door and then allowed into the room. At that point, additional verification will occur (such as a guard visually identifying the person), and then they are allowed through the second door. These doors are normally used only in very high security situations. Mantraps also typically require that the first door is closed, prior to enabling the second door to open. Figure 7.5 shows a mantrap design.

FIGURE 7.5   Arial view of a mantrap

Cable Locks

While not all devices support this, larger mobile devices such as laptops come with a notch where you can attach a cable lock and lock the device to something solid like you would lock a bicycle to a rack. This may even be advisable on some desktop systems if those systems are vulnerable to theft and they contain sensitive data. Users who carry company devices that support cable locks should be instructed to never leave the device unattended and, if necessary, lock the device to an immovable object.

Securing Physical Documents/Passwords/Shredding

It is amazing the information that can be gleaned from physical documents even in the age when there is such a push to go paperless. *Dumpster diving* is a common physical access method. Companies normally generate a huge amount of paper, most of which eventually winds up in dumpsters or recycle bins. Dumpsters may contain information that is highly sensitive in nature (such as passwords after a change and before the user has the new one memorized). In high-security and government environments, sensitive papers should be either shredded or burned. Most businesses don't do this. In addition, the advent of "green" companies has created an increase in the amount of recycled paper, which can often contain all kinds of juicy information about a company and its individual employees.

Biometrics

Biometric devices use physical characteristics to identify the user. Such devices are becoming more common in the business environment. Biometric systems include hand scanners, retinal scanners, and possibly soon, DNA scanners. To gain access to resources, you must pass a physical screening process. In the case of a hand scanner, this may include identifying fingerprints, scars, and markings on your hand. Retinal scanners compare your eye's retinal pattern to a stored retinal pattern to verify your identity. DNA scanners will examine a unique portion of your DNA structure to verify that you are who you say you are.

With the passing of time, the definition of *biometric* is expanding from simply identifying physical attributes about a person to being able to describe patterns in their behavior. Recent advances have been made in the ability to authenticate someone based on the key pattern they use when entering their password (how long they pause between each key, the amount of time each key is held down, and so forth). A company adopting biometric technologies needs to consider the controversy they may face (some authentication methods are considered more intrusive than others). It also needs to consider the error rate and that errors can include both false positives and false negatives.

ID Badges

ID badges can be any form of identification intended to differentiate the holder from everyone else. This can be as simple as a name badge or photo ID.

Key Fobs

Key fobs are named after the chains that used to hold pocket watches to clothes. They are security devices that you carry with you that display a randomly generated code that you can then use for authentication. This code usually changes quickly (every 60 seconds is probably the average), and you combine this code with your PIN for authentication.

RFID Badge

Radio Frequency Identification (RFID) is a wireless, no-contact technology used with badges or cards and their accompanying reader. The reader is connected to the workstation and validates against the security system. This increases the security of the authentication process because you must be in physical possession of the smart card to use the resources. Of course, if the card is lost or stolen, the person who finds the card can access the resources it allows.

Smart Card

A smart card is a type of badge or card that gives you access to resources, including buildings, parking lots, and computers. It contains information about your identity and access privileges. Each area or computer has a card scanner or a reader in which you insert your card.

Smart cards are difficult to counterfeit, but they're easy to steal. Once a thief has a smart card, that person has all the access the card allows. To prevent this, many organizations don't put any identifying marks on their smart cards, making it harder for someone to utilize them. Many modern smart cards require a password or PIN to activate the card, and they employ encryption to protect the card's contents.

Tokens

Physical tokens are anything that a user must have on them to access network resources and are often associated with devices that enable the user to generate a one-time password authenticating their identity. SecurID, from RSA, is one of the best-known examples of a physical token; learn more at `www.rsa.com/node.aspx?id=1156`.

Privacy Filters

Privacy filters are either film or glass add-ons that are placed over a monitor that prevent the data on the screen from being readable when viewed from the sides. Only the user sitting directly in front of the screen is able to read the data. This is a good mitigation to shoulder surfing.

Entry Control Roster

At any physical location where users are arriving and departing the facility, users should be authenticated through one of the mechanisms discussed in this section. There should be a recording of each user arriving and departing. This can be either a record of all successful and unsuccessful authentications on a log or, in the case of visitors who have no network account, a physical identification process of some sort. In any case, there should be an entry control roster in the form of a physical document that shows when each person entered and left the facility. This will serve as a backup in case the log is lost.

Digital Security

Whereas physical security under this objective focused on keeping individuals out, digital security focuses mostly on keeping harmful data/malware out. The areas of focus are antivirus software, firewalls, antispyware, user authentication/strong passwords, and directory permissions. Each of these is addressed in the sections that follow.

Antivirus/Antimalware

The primary method of preventing the propagation of malicious code involves the use of *antivirus software*. Antivirus software is an application that is installed on a system to protect it and to scan for viruses as well as worms and Trojan horses. Most viruses have characteristics that are common to families of a virus or viruses. Antivirus software looks for these characteristics, or fingerprints, to identify and neutralize viruses before they impact you.

More than 200,000 known viruses, worms, bombs, and other malware have been defined. New ones are added all the time. Your antivirus software manufacturer will usually work hard to keep the definition database files current. The definition database file contains all the known viruses and countermeasures for a particular antivirus software product. You probably won't receive a virus that hasn't been seen by one of these companies. If you keep the virus definition database files in your software up-to-date, you probably won't be overly vulnerable to attacks.

> The best method of protection is to use a layered approach. Antivirus software should be at the gateways, at the servers, and at the desktop. If you want to go one step further, you can use software at each location from different vendors to make sure you're covered from all angles.

Firewalls

Firewalls are one of the first lines of defense in a network. There are different types of firewalls, and they can be either stand-alone systems or included in other devices such as routers or servers. You can find firewall solutions that are marketed as hardware-only and others that are software-only. Many firewalls, however, consist of add-in software that is available for servers or workstations.

> Although solutions are sold as "hardware-only," the hardware still runs some sort of software. It may be hardened and in ROM to prevent tampering, and it may be customized—but software is present nonetheless.

The basic purpose of a firewall is to isolate one network from another. Firewalls are becoming available as appliances, meaning they're installed as the primary device separating two networks. *Appliances* are freestanding devices that operate in a largely self-contained manner, requiring less maintenance and support than a server-based product.

Firewalls function as one or more of the following:

- Packet filter
- Proxy firewall
- Stateful inspection firewall

> To understand the concept of a firewall, it helps to know where the term comes from. In days of old, dwellings used to be built so close together that if a fire broke out in one, it could easily destroy a block or more before it could be contained. To decrease the risk of this happening, firewalls were built between buildings. The firewalls were huge brick walls that separated the buildings and kept a fire confined to one side. The same concept of restricting and confining is true in network firewalls. Traffic from the outside world hits the firewall and isn't allowed to enter the network unless otherwise invited.

The firewall shown in Figure 7.6 effectively limits access from outside networks, while allowing inside network users to access outside resources. The firewall in this illustration is also performing proxy functions.

FIGURE 7.6   A proxy firewall blocking network access from external networks

 Although firewalls are often associated with outside traffic, you can place a firewall anywhere. For example, if you want to isolate one portion of your internal network from others, you can place a firewall between them.

The following list discusses three of the most common functions that firewalls perform:

Packet Filter Firewalls   A firewall operating as a *packet filter* passes or blocks traffic to specific addresses based on the type of application. The packet filter doesn't analyze the data of a packet; it decides whether to pass it based on the packet's addressing information. For instance, a packet filter may allow web traffic on port 80 and block Telnet traffic on port 23. This type of filtering is included in many routers. If a received packet request asks for a port that isn't authorized, the filter may reject the request or simply ignore it. Many packet filters can also specify which IP addresses can request which ports and allow or deny them based on the security settings of the firewall.

Packet filters are growing in sophistication and capability. A packet filter firewall can allow any traffic that you specify as acceptable. For example, if you want web users to access your site, then you configure the packet filter firewall to allow data on port 80 to enter. If every network were exactly the same, firewalls would come with default port settings hard-coded, but networks vary, so the firewalls don't include such settings.

Proxy Firewalls   A *proxy firewall* can be thought of as an intermediary between your network and any other network. Proxy firewalls are used to process requests from an outside network; the proxy firewall examines the data and makes rule-based decisions about whether the request should be forwarded or refused. The proxy intercepts all the packages and reprocesses them for use internally. This process includes hiding IP addresses.

The proxy firewall provides better security than packet filtering because of the increased intelligence that a proxy firewall offers. Requests from internal network users are routed through the proxy. The proxy, in turn, repackages the request and sends it along, thereby isolating the user from the external network. The proxy can also offer caching, should the same request be made again, and can increase the efficiency of data delivery.

A proxy firewall typically uses two network interface cards (NICs). This type of firewall is referred to as a *dual-homed* firewall. One of the cards is connected to the outside network, and the other is connected to the internal network. The proxy software manages the connection between the two NICs. This setup segregates the two networks from each other and offers increased security. Figure 7.7 illustrates a dual-homed firewall segregating two networks from each other.

The proxy function can occur at either the application level or the circuit level. *Application-level proxy* functions read the individual commands of the protocols that are being served. This type of server is advanced and must know the rules and capabilities of the protocol used. An implementation of this type of proxy must know the difference between GET and PUT operations, for example, and have rules specifying how to execute them. A *circuit-level proxy* creates a circuit between the client and the server and doesn't deal with the contents of the packets that are being processed.

FIGURE 7.7 A dual-homed firewall segregating two networks from each other

A unique application-level proxy server must exist for each protocol supported. Many proxy servers also provide full *auditing*, *accounting*, and other usage information that wouldn't normally be kept by a circuit-level proxy server.

Stateful Inspection Firewalls The last section on firewalls focuses on the concept of stateful inspection. *Stateful inspection* is also referred to as *stateful packet filtering*. Most of the devices used in networks don't keep track of how information is routed or used. After a packet is passed, the packet and path are forgotten. In stateful inspection (or stateful packet filtering), records are kept using a state table that tracks every communications channel. Stateful inspections occur at all levels of the network and provide additional security, especially in connectionless protocols such as *User Datagram Protocol (UDP)* and *Internet Control Message Protocol (ICMP)*. This adds complexity to the process. Denial-of-service (DoS) attacks present a challenge because flooding techniques are used to overload the state table and effectively cause the firewall to shut down or reboot.

User Authentication/Strong Passwords

You can set up many different parameters and standards to force the people in your organization to conform. In establishing these parameters, it's important that you consider the capabilities of the people who will be working with these policies. If you're working in an environment where people aren't computer savvy, you may spend a lot of time helping them remember and recover passwords. Many organizations have had to reevaluate their security guidelines after they've invested great time and expense to implement high-security systems.

Setting authentication security, especially in supporting users, can become a high-maintenance activity for network administrators. On one hand, you want people to be able to authenticate themselves easily; on the other hand, you want to establish security that protects your company's resources. In a Windows server domain, password policies can be configured at the domain level using Group Policy objects. Variables you can configure include password complexity, length, and time between allowed changes.

A good password includes both uppercase and lowercase letters as well as numbers and symbols. Be wary of popular names or current trends that make certain passwords predictable. For example, during the first release of *Star Wars*, two of the most popular passwords used on college campuses were C3PO and R2D2. This created a security problem for campus computer centers. Educate users to not use personal information that one could easily guess about them, such as their pet names, anniversary, or birthdays.

Multifactor Authentication

There are three factors of authentication: knowledge factors (something you know, such as a password), characteristic factors (some physical characteristic, such as a thumbprint), and behavioral factors (something you do, such a voice analysis).

When more than one of these factors is required to authenticate, it is called *multifactor authentication*. It is *not* multifactor authentication if it uses two forms of the same factor of authentication such as a password and a PIN (both knowledge factors). An example of multifactor authentication is the requirement of a PIN and a retina scan.

Directory Permissions

As a user, there is not much that can be done to improve or change the security of the directory services deployed. However, you *can* ensure that you don't become a tool for an attacker bent on compromising your organization's security.

- Ensure that your client is using the most secure form of authentication encryption supported by both your client and the authentication servers.

- Use encrypted software and protocols whenever possible, even for internal communications.

- Change your password according to the company's password policy.

- Use a company-established minimum character password that is unique for each account. While many companies set the minimum at 8 characters, it is not uncommon to see this set at 16.

- Never write your password down, or if you do, divide it up into several pieces and store each in a different secure location (such as a home safe, a gun cabinet, a chemical supply locker, or a safety deposit box).

- Never share your password or your logon session with another person; this includes your friends, spouse, and children.

- Verify that your client always interacts with an authentication server during the network logon process and does not use cached credentials.

- Allow all approved updates and patches to be installed onto your client.

- Ensure that all company data is copied back to a central file server before disconnecting from a logon session.

- Back up any personal data onto verified removable media.

- Never walk away from a logged-on workstation.

- Employ a password-protected screensaver.

- Don't use auto-logon features.

- Be aware of who is around you (and may be watching you) when you log on and when you work with valuable data.

- Never leave a company notebook, mobile phone, or PDA in a position where it can be stolen or compromised while you are away from the office. Cable locks should be used to keep notebooks securely in place whenever you are off site.

 NOTE As for the permission on directories themselves, that is governed by NTFS, which was discussed in Chapter 6, "Operating Systems."

The protection of a directory service is based on the initial selection of network operating system and its deployment infrastructure. After these foundational decisions are made, you need to fully understand the technologies employed by your selected directory services system and learn how to make the most functional yet secure environment possible. This will usually require the addition of third-party security devices, applications, services, and solutions.

VPN

Virtual private network (VPN) connections are remote access connections that allow users to securely connect to the enterprise network and work as if they were in the office. These connections use special tunneling protocols that encrypt the information being transferred between the user and the corporate network. Anywhere users, business partners, or vendors are allowed remote access to the network, VPN connections should be used. VPNs were discussed in Chapter 6.

DLP

Data loss prevention (DLP) solutions are designed to prevent sensitive material from purposefully or inadvertently escaping the organization. These solutions allow you to specify exactly what actions each user may take with respect to a document. For example, it may allow the document to be read but neither printed nor forwarded to another user.

Disabling Ports

One of the basic principles of security is to reduce the attack surface of all devices. This means shutting off all services and application that are not required and to close all ports not being used. With respect to switches and hubs, this means disabling any ports that do not have devices connected to them. If this is not done, anyone could walk up to any unused wall outlet, plug in a device, get an IP address through DHCP, and be on your network.

Access Control Lists

Access control lists are sets of rules configured on a router or firewall that control the type of traffic allowed to enter or leave an interface. These lists are what make packet filtering firewalls work. Using these lists, an administrator can at a granular level define who can send specific types of traffic to specific locations. For example, you could prevent a user from using Telnet to connect to the sales server, without preventing him from using Telnet to any other devices and without impacting any of his other activities.

Smart Card

Smart cards were discussed in the section "Physical Security" earlier in this chapter. While the emphasis there was on using smart cards for physical security, these cards can also be used to log on to the network and thus to access resources.

Email Filtering

While email filtering is typically discussed in the context of preventing spam, the organization must also be concerned about the contents and types of email sent by the users. Because the users are representing the organization in everything they do, you want them to follow certain guidelines. Email filtering allows for the recognition and the blocking of messages that contain content that is not compliant with these guidelines. Configuring the filtering solution in such a way that it recognizes and blocks noncompliant emails while leaving compliant emails unaffected can be a tremendous challenge.

Trusted/Untrusted Software Sources

Users frequently download and install software and not always from the safest sources. While policies should definitely reflect the desire of the organization to prevent unauthorized software downloads and installation, you may have to go beyond policies and implement a software restriction tool that prevents users from doing this. If you want to prevent all downloads and installations by users, you can use a Group Policy in Windows to require administrator privileges to do any downloading or installing. If your goal is to allow some installations but not others, you can use additional policies to define exactly which applications are allowed and which are not.

User Education/AUP

The most effective method of preventing viruses, spyware, and harm to data is education. Teach your users not to open suspicious files and to open only those files that they're reasonably sure are virus-free. They need to scan every disk, email, and document they receive before they open them. You should also have all workstations scheduled to be automatically scanned on a regular basis.

While education is important, in most cases you must attempt to control what users do. An acceptable use policy (AUP) is a document that specifies what users can and cannot do, and it should be signed by all during the hiring process. This creates a contract that can be used later to form the basis for disciplinary measures. These measures or consequences for noncompliance should be spelled out ahead of time.

Principle of Least Privilege

The concept of least privilege is a simple one: when assigning permissions, give users only the permissions they need to do their work and no more. This is especially true with administrators. Users who need administrative-level permissions should be assigned two accounts: one for performing nonadministrative, day-to-day tasks and the other to be used only when performing administrative tasks that specifically require an administrative-level user account. Those users should be educated on how each of the accounts should be used.

The biggest benefit to following this policy is the reduction of risk. The biggest headache with following this policy is trying to deal with users who may not understand it. A manager, for example, may assert that he should have more permission than those who report to him, but giving those permissions to him also opens up all the possibilities for inadvertently deleting files, crippling accounts, and so forth.

A least privilege policy should exist, and be enforced, throughout the enterprise. Users should have only the permissions and privileges needed to do their jobs and no more. ISO standard 27002 (which updates 17799) sums it up well: "Privileges should be allocated to individuals on a need-to-use basis and on an event-by-event basis, i.e., the minimum requirement for their functional role when needed." Adopting this as the policy for your organization is highly recommended.

Exam Essentials

Be able to describe why antivirus software is needed.   Antivirus software looks at a virus and takes action to neutralize it based on a virus-definition database. Virus-definition database files are regularly made available on vendor sites.

Understand the need for user education.   Users are the first line of defense against most threats, whether physical or digital. They should be trained on the importance of security and how to help enforce it.

3.3 Compare and Contrast Differences of Basic Windows OS Security Settings

There is an entire domain dedicated to security for A+. Add to that, CompTIA is heavily into security certifications with Security+ and CASP (CompTIA Advanced Security Practitioner), so you can see how important the topic is to those creating the exam. Because of that, make sure you have a good understanding of the topics covered here.

You want to make certain that your systems, and the data within them, are kept as secure as possible. The security prevents others from changing the data, destroying it, or inadvertently harming it. This can be done by assigning users the least privileges possible and hardening as much of the environment as possible. The following are the subobjectives covered in this section:

- User and groups
- NTFS vs. share permissions
- Shared files and folders
- System files and folders
- User authentication
- Run as administrator vs. standard user
- BitLocker
- BitLocker-To-Go
- EFS

User and Groups

There are a number of groups created on the operating system by default. The following sections look at the main ones of these.

Administrator

The Administrator account is the most powerful of all: it has the power to do everything from the smallest task all the way up to removing the operating system. Because of the great power it holds and the fact that it is always created, many who try to do harm will target this account as the one they try to break into. To increase security, during the installation of the Windows operating systems in question, you are prompted for a name of a user who will be designated as the Administrator. The power then comes not from being truly called Administrator (it might now be tmcmillan, mcmillant, or something similar) but from being a member of the Administrators group (notice the plural for the group and singular for the user).

Since members of the Administrators group have such power, they can inadvertently do harm (such as accidentally deleting a file that a regular user could not). To protect against this, the practice of logging in with an Administrators account for daily interaction is strongly discouraged. Instead, system administrators should log in with a user account (lesser privileges) and change to the Administrators group account (elevated privileges) only when necessary.

Power User

The Power Users group is not as powerful as Administrators group. Membership in this group gives read/write permission to the system, allowing them to install most software but keeping them from changing key operating system files. This is a good group for those who need to test software (such as programmers) and junior administrators. While the Power Users group exists in Windows Vista, Windows 7, and Windows 8 and 8.1, it is mostly there for legacy purposes and no longer has any more privileges than a standard user.

Guest

The Guest account is created by default (and should be disabled) and is a member of the Guests group. For the most part, members of Guests have the same rights as Users except they can't get to log files. The best reason to make users members of the Guests group is if they are accessing the system only for a limited time.

 As part of operating system security, we usually recommend you rename the default Administrator and Guest accounts that are created at installation.

Standard User

This group is the default that regular users belong to. Members of this group have read/write permission to their own profile. They cannot modify system-wide Registry settings or do much harm outside of their own account. Under the principle of least privilege, users should be made a member of the Users group only unless qualifying circumstances force them to have higher privileges.

NTFS vs. Share Permissions

The New Technology File System (NTFS) was introduced with Windows NT to address security problems. Before Windows NT was released, it had become apparent to Microsoft that a new filesystem was needed to handle growing disk sizes, security concerns, and the need for more stability. NTFS was created to address those issues.

Although FAT was relatively stable, if the systems that were controlling it kept running, it didn't do well when the power went out or the system crashed unexpectedly. One of the benefits of NTFS was a transaction tracking system, which made it possible for Windows NT to back out of any disk operations that were in progress when Windows NT crashed or lost power.

With NTFS, files, directories, and volumes can each have their own security. NTFS's security is flexible and built in. Not only does NTFS track security in ACLs, which can hold permissions for local users and groups, but each entry in the ACL can specify what type of access is given—such as Read, Write, Modify, or Full Control. This allows a great deal of flexibility in setting up a network. In addition, special file-encryption programs were developed to encrypt data while it was stored on the hard disk.

Microsoft strongly recommends that all network shares be established using NTFS. Several current operating systems from Microsoft support both FAT32 and NTFS. It's possible to convert from FAT32 to NTFS without losing data, but you can't do the operation in reverse (you would need to reformat the drive and install the data again from a backup tape).

If you're using FAT32 and want to change to NTFS, the convert utility will allow you to do so. For example, to change the E drive to NTFS, the command is `convert e: /FS:NTFS`.

Share permissions apply only when a user is accessing a file or folder through the network. Local permissions and attributes are used to protect the file when the user is local. With FAT and FAT32, you do not have the ability to assign "extended" or "extensible" permissions, and the user sitting at the console effectively is the owner of all resources on the system. As such, they can add, change, and delete any data or file that they want.

With NTFS as the filesystem, however, you are allowed to assign more comprehensive security to your computer system. NTFS permissions are able to protect you at the file level. Share permissions can be applied to the directory level only. NTFS permissions can affect users logged on locally or across the network to the system where the NTFS permissions are applied. Share permissions are in effect only when the user connects to the resource via the network.

Share and NTFS permissions are not cumulative. Permission must be granted at both levels to allow access. Moreover, the effective permission that the user has will be the most restrictive of the combined NTFS permission and the combined share permissions.

Allow vs. Deny

Within NTFS, permissions for objects fall into one of three categories: allow, not allow, and deny. When viewing the permissions for a file or folder, you can check the box for Allow, which effectively allows that group that action. You can also uncheck the box for Allow, which does not allow that group that action. Alternatively, you can check the box Deny, which prevents that group from using that action. There is a difference between not allowing (a cleared check box) and Deny (which specifically prohibits), and you tend not to see Deny used often. Deny, when used, trumps other permissions.

Permissions set at a folder are inherited down through subfolders, unless otherwise changed. Permissions are also cumulative: if a user is a member of a group that has read permission and a member of a group that has write permission, they effectively have both read and write permission.

Moving vs. Copying Folders and Files

When you copy a file, you create a new entity. When you move a file, you simply relocate it and still have but one entity. This distinction is important when it comes to understanding permissions. A copy of a file will generally have the permissions assigned to it that are placed on newly created files in that folder—regardless of what permissions were on the original file.

A moved file, on the other hand, will attempt to keep the same permissions as it had in the original location. Differences will occur if the same permissions cannot exist in the new location—for example, if you are moving a file from an NTFS volume to FAT32, the NTFS permissions will be lost. If, on the other hand, you are moving from a FAT32 volume to an NTFS volume, new permissions will be added that match those for newly created entities.

Folder copy and move operations follow similar guidelines to those with files.

File Attributes

Permissions can be allowed or denied individually on a per-folder basis. You can assign any combination of the values shown in Table 7.1.

TABLE 7.1   NTFS directory permissions

NTFS Permission	Meaning
Full Control	This gives the user all the other choices and the ability to change permission. The user also can take ownership of the directory or any of its contents.

TABLE 7.1   NTFS directory permissions *(continued)*

NTFS Permission	Meaning
Modify	This combines the Read & Execute permission with the Write permission and further allows the user to delete everything, including the folder.
Read & Execute	This combines the permissions of Read with those of List Folder Contents and adds the ability to run executables.
List Folder Contents	The List Folder Contents permission (known simply as List in previous versions) allows the user to view the contents of a directory and to navigate to its subdirectories. It does not grant the user access to the files in these directories unless that is specified in file permissions.
Read	This allows the user to navigate the entire directory structure, view the contents of the directory, view the contents of any files in the directory, and see ownership and attributes.
Write	This allows the user to create new entities within the folder, as well as to change attributes.

Clicking the Advanced button allows you to configure auditing and ownership properties. You can also apply NTFS permissions to individual files. This is done from the Security tab for the file. Table 7.2 lists the NTFS file permissions.

TABLE 7.2   NTFS file permissions

NTFS permission	Meaning
Full Control	This gives the user all the other permissions as well as permission to take ownership and change permission.
Modify	This combines the Read & Execute permission with the Write permission and further allows the user to delete the file.
Read	This allows the user to view the contents of the file and to see ownership and attributes.
Read & Execute	This combines the Read permission with the ability to execute.
Write	This allows the user to overwrite the file, as well as to change attributes and see ownership and permissions.

By default, the determination of NTFS permissions is based on the *cumulative* NTFS permissions for a user. Rights can be assigned to users based on group membership and individually; the only time permissions do not accumulate is when the Deny permission is invoked.

Shared Files and Folders

You can share folders, and the files beneath them, by right-clicking them and choosing Share With (Windows 7, Windows Vista, and Windows 8) from the context menu. In Windows 7, the context menu asks who you want to share the folder or file with (see Figure 7.8).

FIGURE 7.8   Sharing a folder in Windows 7

The options you see on the context menu will depend on the type of network you are connected to—a domain, a workgroup, or a Homegroup (the one shown in Figure 7.8). If you turn on password-protected sharing (the default), the person accessing the share has to give a username and password to access the shared entity.

The advanced sharing settings will come up if you try to share something in one of the Public folders or make other changes. This interface, shown in Figure 7.9, can also be accessed through the Network and Sharing Center applet in the Control Panel and is used to change network settings relevant to sharing.

FIGURE 7.9   Advanced sharing in Windows 7

Administrative Shares vs. Local Shares

Administrative shares are created on servers running Windows on the network for administrative purposes. These shares can differ slightly based on which OS is running but always end with a dollar sign ($) to make them hidden. There is one for each volume on a hard drive (c$, d$, and so on) as well as admin$ (the root folder, usually c:\windows), and print$ (where the print drivers are located). These are created for use by administrators and usually require administrator privileges to access.

Local shares, as the name implies, are those created locally and are visible with the icon of a group of two individuals.

Permission Propagation

As mentioned earlier in the discussion of permissions, permissions are cumulative. A user who is a member of two groups will effectively have the permissions of both groups combined.

Inheritance

Inheritance is the default throughout the permission structure unless a specific setting is created to override this. A user who has read and write permissions in one folder will have that in all the subfolders unless a change has been made specifically to one of the subfolders.

System Files and Folders

System files are usually flagged with the Hidden attribute, meaning they don't appear when a user displays a directory listing. You should not change this attribute on a system file unless absolutely necessary. System files are required for the OS to function. If they are visible, users might delete them (perhaps thinking they can clear some disk space by deleting files they don't recognize). Needless to say, that would be a bad thing!

User Authentication

You already know that users are authenticated by identifying themselves and providing credentials. You also have learned that these credentials can take many forms depending on the authentication factors in use. In the following section, you will be introduced to a feature found in almost all modern authentication systems, single sign-on.

Single Sign-On

One of the big problems that larger systems must deal with is the need for users to access multiple systems or applications. This may require a user to remember multiple accounts and passwords. The purpose of a single sign-on (SSO) is to give users access to all the applications and systems they need when they log on. This is becoming a reality in many environments, including Kerberos, Microsoft Active Directory, Novell eDirectory, and some certificate model implementations.

Single sign-on is both a blessing and a curse. It's a blessing in that once users are authenticated, they can access all the resources on the network and browse multiple directories. It's a curse in that it removes the doors that otherwise exist between the user and various resources.

Run as Administrator vs. Standard User

One of the security recommendations from Microsoft is to have administrative users log on with a standard user account and, when necessary, elevate the privileges of the account temporarily to perform a task and then remove those permission when the task is complete.

This is done by running the task, tool, or utility as an administrator. This can be done by right-clicking the tool and selecting Run as Administrator. Once the tool is closed, that security session ends, and the permissions are returned to those of a standard user. Having these highly privileged accounts logged in as infrequently as possible helps prevent hackers from gaining control of these accounts when they are live.

BitLocker

BitLocker is the whole drive encryption tool that can also seal a device such that it will not boot if any system files are altered. It can also lock the drive to a particular machine, preventing stealing the drive and connecting to another device. BitLocker was covered in Chapter 6.

BitLocker To Go

BitLocker To Go provides the same encryption technology to help prevent unauthorized access to the files stored on removable drives.

EFS

The Encrypting File System (EFS) is an encryption tool built into Windows Vista Business, Enterprise and Ultimate, Windows 7, and Windows 8 or 8.1 Professional or Enterprise. (EFS is not fully supported on Windows 7 Starter, Windows 7 Home Basic, and Windows 7 Home Premium.) It allows a user to encrypt files that can be decrypted only by the user who encrypted the files. It can be used only on NTFS volumes but is simple to use.

To encrypt a file in Windows 8.1, simply right-click the file, access the files properties, and on the General tab click the Advanced button. That will open the Advanced Attributes dialog box, as shown in Figure 7.10. On this page, check the box to Encrypt Contents To Secure Data.

FIGURE 7.10   Advanced attributes

Exam Essentials

Know the difference between single sign-on and multifactor authentication.   Single sign-on is the concept of having the user be authenticated on all services they access after logging in once. Multifactor authentication is not the opposite of single sign-on but merely requires more than one entity to be authenticated, for security purposes.

Know the NTFS permissions.   Permissions can be allowed or denied individually on a per-folder and per-file basis. Know the values shown in Tables 7.1 and 7.2.

3.4 Given a Scenario, Deploy and Enforce Security Best Practices to Secure a Workstation

In the previous objectives, the importance of user education has been mentioned. The user represents the weakest link in the security chain, whether the harm comes to them in the form of malware, social engineering, or simply avoidable mistakes. The workstation represents the digital arm of the user and must be properly and adequately secured to keep the user—and the network—protected.

A number of best practices are involved with securing a workstation. While a checklist could take many pages, depending on your environment, CompTIA has identified five that should appear on any roster. The following are the subobjectives covered in this chapter:

- Password best practices
- Account management
- Disable autorun
- Data encryption
- Patch/update management

Password Best Practices

One of the strongest ways to keep a system safe is to employ strong passwords and educate your users in the best security practices. In this section, you'll explore various techniques that can enhance the security of your user passwords.

Setting Strong Passwords

Passwords should be as long as possible. Most security experts believe a password of 10 characters is the minimum that should be used if security is a real concern. If you use only the lowercase letters of the alphabet, you have 26 characters with which to work. If you add the numeric values 0 through 9, you'll get another 10 characters. If you go one step further and add the uppercase letters, you'll then have an additional 26 characters, giving you a total of 62 characters with which to construct a password.

> Most vendors recommend that you use nonalphabetical characters such as #, $, and % in your password, and some go so far as to require it.

If you used a 4-character password, this would be 62 × 62 × 62 × 62, or approximately 14 million password possibilities. If you used 5 characters in your password, this would give you 62 to the fifth power, or approximately 920 million password possibilities. If you used a 10-character password, this would give you 62 to the tenth power, or 8.4×10^{17} (a very big number) possibilities. As you can see, these numbers increase exponentially with each position added to the password. The 4-digit password could probably be broken in a fraction of a day, whereas the 10-digit password would take considerably longer and consume much more processing power.

If your password used only the 26 lowercase letters from the alphabet, the 4-digit password would have 26 to the fourth power, or 456,000 password combinations. A 5-character password would have 26 to the fifth power, or more than 11 million, and a 10-character password would have 26 to the tenth power, or 1.4×10^{14}. This is still a big number, but it would take considerably less time to break it.

> To see tables on how quickly passwords can be surmised, visit www.lock-down.co.uk/?pg=combi&s=articles.

Mathematical methods of encryption are primarily used in conjunction with other encryption methods as part of authenticity verification. The message and the hashed value of the message can be encrypted using other processes. In this way, you know that the message is secure and hasn't been altered.

Password Expiration

The longer that a password is used, the more likely it is that it will be compromised in some way. It is for this reason that requiring users to change their passwords at certain intervals increases the security of their passwords. You should require users to set a new password every 30 days (more frequently for higher security networks), and you must also prevent them from reusing old passwords. Most password management systems have the ability to track previously used password and to disallow users from recycling old passwords.

Changing Default Usernames/Passwords

Default accounts represent a huge weakness in that every miscreant knows they exist. When an operating system is installed, whether on a workstation or a server, there are certain accounts created, and since the wrongdoer already knows the account name, it simplifies the process of getting into an account by requiring them to supply only the password. The first thing they will try, of course, is the default password if one exists.

Screensaver Required Password

A screensaver should automatically start after a short period of idle time, and that screensaver should require a password before the user can begin the session again. This method of locking the workstation adds one more level of security.

BIOS/UEFI

Passwords should be configured and required to access either the BIOS or UEFI settings on all devices. If this is not the case, it would be possible for someone to reboot a device, enter the settings, change the boot order, boot to an operating system residing on a USB or optical drive, and use that OS as a platform to access data located on the other drives. While this is a worst-case scenario, there is also much less mayhem a malicious person could cause in the BIOS and UEFI.

Requiring Passwords

Make absolutely certain you require passwords (such a simple thing to overlook in a small network) for all accounts, and change the default passwords on system accounts.

Account Management

While I touched on one account management technique previously (preventing the reuse of passwords), there are a number of additional account management best practices that you should know and implement.

Restricting User Permissions

When assigning user permissions, follow the principle of least privilege (discussed earlier) by giving users only the bare minimum they need to do their job. Assign permissions to groups, rather than users, and make users members of groups (or remove them from them) as they change roles or positions.

Login Time Restrictions

Most users have a set work schedule, and it is only during these works hours that the user should access the network and its resources. Since an active account is an account vulnerable to misuse, any time in which you can disable an account while still allowing users to do their jobs enhances security, since a disabled account cannot be used for malicious purposes.

For this reason, many administrators allow users to log in only during certain hours. Typically, access is allowed from about an hour before their workday until about an hour after the day ends (to allow some flexibility). For certain users who tend to work throughout the day and night, this system may not work.

Disabling Guest Account

To secure the system, disable all accounts that are not needed (especially the guest account). Next, rename the accounts if you can (Microsoft won't allow you to rename an account to Administrator). Finally, change the passwords from the defaults and add them to the cycle of passwords that routinely get changed.

Failed Attempts Lockout

Earlier you learned that a brute-force attack is a password attack that attempts all character combinations until the password is discovered. You also learned that the attacks are typically performed offline and not in a live environment. Why is that? Because almost all password systems are set up to allow only a set number of failed password attempts before the account is locked. While this policy may generate more password reset calls than you would like, that effect can be mitigated by implementing a complementary policy that allows the account to be automatically reenabled after a set amount of time (say five minutes). When this policy is communicated to the users, they know just to wait for five minutes and try again.

Timeout/Screen Lock

While the relative sensitivity of the data appearing on the screen of a user's computer can vary from time to time and from user to user, it is a good practice to protect that information when someone steps away from the device. Moreover, when the device is in an out-of-the-way location, it may even afford someone the chance to browse the device. For this reason, you should require a password-protected screensaver on all devices that kicks in after a short period of inactivity.

Disable AutoRun

It is never a good idea to put any media in a workstation that you do not know where it came from or what it is. The reason is that the media (CD, DVD, USB) could contain malware. Compounding matters, that malware could be referenced in the Autorun.inf file, causing it to be summoned when the media is inserted in the machine and requiring no other action. Autorun.inf can be used to start an executable, access a website, or do any of a large number of different tasks. The best way to prevent a user from falling victim to such a ploy is to disable the AutoRun feature on the workstation.

Microsoft has changed (by default, disabled) the AutoRun function on Windows Vista, Windows 7 and Windows 8, though running remains the default action for PCs using Windows XP through Service Pack 3. The reason Microsoft changed the default action can be summed up in a single word: security. That text-based Autorun.inf file not only can take your browser to a web page but can also call any executable file, pass along variable information about the user, or do just about anything else imaginable. Simply put, it is *never* a good idea to take any media that you have no idea where it came from or what it holds and plug it into your system. Such an action opens up the user—and their network—to any number of possible tribulations. An entire business's data could be jeopardized by such a minuscule act if a harmful CD were placed in a computer at work by someone with elevated privileges.

Data Encryption

While data encryption is possible both on a drive level (BitLocker) and on an individual file level (EFS), always keep in mind the cost of encryption and save this tool for instances where you really need it. By cost I mean that any encrypted file must be decrypted to be opened and encrypted again to be saved. This requires CPU cycles on the device. If you attempt to encrypt everything, the performance of the device may make it practically unusable. You must strike a balance between security and usability.

Patch/Update Management

While many patches and updates either repair something that doesn't work or add some additional functionality, many of them close a security hole. These are called *hotfixes* because they come out as soon as they are available and you need to apply them as soon as possible (after testing them in a nonproduction environment).

For best results in patch management, you should deploy an automated system that can check for, download, and make available to the network all patches and updates for all systems. A good example of such a system is Microsoft Windows Server Update Services (WSUS), which can manage the updates for both servers and clients and for other operating systems as well.

Exam Essentials

Understand the need for good passwords.   Passwords are the first line of defense for protecting an account. A password should be required for every account, and strong passwords should be enforced. Users need to understand the basics of password security and work to keep their accounts protected by following company policies regarding passwords.

List some techniques that enhance account management.   These techniques include but are not limited to disabling unused accounts, requiring frequent password changes, preventing the reuse of passwords, requiring complex passwords, and defining login hours for users.

3.5 Compare and Contrast Various Methods for Securing Mobile Devices

If laptops are easy to steal, smaller mobile devices are even more so. Because mobile devices are increasingly used to store valuable data and to perform functions once the domain of laptops and desktops, the need to secure these devices has grown. In this section, methods of securing mobile devices will be discussed. The topics addressed in objective 3.5 include the following:

- Screen locks
- Remote wipes
- Locator applications
- Remote backup applications
- Failed login attempts restrictions
- Antivirus/antimalware
- Patching/OS updates
- Biometric authentication
- Full device encryption
- Multifactor authentication
- Authenticator applications
- Trusted sources vs. untrusted sources
- Firewalls
- Policies and procedures

Screen Locks

One of the most basic (but not necessarily the most utilized) security measures you can take is to implement a screen lock on the device. This is akin to implementing the password you use to log on to your desktop or laptop, but it's amazing how few people use this basic security measure. This can prevent someone from using the mobile device if it is stolen. There are several ways screen locks can be implemented, and in the following sections you'll examine each method.

Fingerprint Lock

A fingerprint lock is one that uses the fingerprint of the user as credentials to authenticate the user and, when successful authentication completes, unlocks the screen. Because it relies on biometrics, it is for the most part more secure than using a passcode or a swipe.

Face Lock

A face lock is one that one that uses a facial scan of the user to authenticate the user and, when successful authentication completes, unlocks the screen. It also is more secure than a passcode or swipe process.

Swipe Lock

Swipe locks use a gesture or series of gestures, sometimes involving the movement of an icon to open the screen. In some cases, they require only knowledge of the mobile platform in use; they offer no security to the process because no authentication of the user is occurring. In other instances like Android, they require a pattern between nine dots to be swiped to unlock the device.

Passcode Lock

Setting the password on an Android phone is done by navigating to Settings Location & Security ➤ Change Screen Lock. On the Change Screen Lock page, you can set the length of time the device remains idle until the screen locks as well as choose a method from None, Pattern, PIN, or Password. Select Password and then enter the desired password.

On an iOS-based device, navigate to Settings ➤ Settings ➤ Passcode Lock to set the password and Settings ➤ General ➤ Auto-Lock to set the amount of time before the iPhone locks.

Remote Wipes

Remote wipes are instructions sent remotely to a mobile device that erase all the data when the device is stolen. In the case of the iPhone, this feature is closely connected to the locater application (discussed in the next section). To perform a remote wipe on an iPhone (which requires iOS 5), navigate to Settings ➤ iCloud. On this tab, ensure that Find My iPhone is enabled (set to On). Next, use the browser to go to iCloud.com and log in using the Apple ID you use on your phone.

Next, select the icon Find My iPhone. The location of the phone will appear on a map. Click the *i* icon next to the location. On the dialog box that opens, select Remote Wipe. You will be prompted again to ensure that is what you want to do. Select Wipe Phone.

The Android phones do not come with an official remote wipe. You can, however, install an Android app that will do this. Once the app, Lost Android, is installed, it works in the same way the iPhone remote wipe does. In this case, you log into the Lost Android website using your Google login. From the site, you can locate and wipe the device.

Android Device Manager, which is loaded on newer versions of Android, is available for download to any version of Android from 2.3 onward providing almost identical functionality to that of the iPhone.

Locator Applications

Locator applications like the Lost Android app for Android are available where apps are sold for Androids. These apps allow you to locate the device, to lock the device, and even to send a message to the device offering a reward for its return. Finally, you can remote wipe the device as well. The iOS devices and the newer Android devices have this feature built in, and it performs all the same functions.

Remote Backup Applications

Backing up your data with the iPhone can be done by connecting the device to a Mac and using iTunes to manage the content. (The data can also be backed up to a PC that has iTunes.) As users start to use the mobile device as their main tool, this may not be an optimal way to manage backups. New apps like Mozy are available that perform an online backup, which is attractive because the laptop or desktop where you backed up your data is not always close at hand but the Internet usually is.

Android has always taken a cloud approach to backups. There are many Android apps now that can be used to back up data to locations such as Dropbox or Box.net.

Failed Login Attempts Restrictions

Most of us have become accustomed to the lockout feature on a laptop or desktop that locks out an account after a certain number of failed login attempts. This feature is available on a mobile device and can even be set to perform a remote wipe of the device after repeated failed login attempts.

On the iOS, the Erase Data function can be set to perform a remote wipe after 10 failed passcode attempts. After 6 failed attempts, the iPhone locks out users for a minute before another passcode can be entered. The device increases the lockout time following each additional failed attempt.

The Android does not have this feature built in but does provide the APIs that allow enterprise developers to create applications that will do this.

Antivirus/antimalware

Mobile devices can suffer from viruses and malware just like laptops and desktops. Major antivirus vendors such as McAfee and Kaspersky make antivirus and antimalware products for mobile devices that provide the same real-time protection that the products do for desktops. The same guidelines apply for these mobile devices: keep them up-to-date by setting the device to check for updates whenever connected to the Internet.

Patching/OS Updates

Security patches and operating system updates are available on an ongoing basis for both the iOS and the Android. For the iPhone, both operating system updates and security patches are available at the Apple support site. Automatic updates can be enabled for the device in iTunes. Use the Check For Updates button located in the middle of iTunes.

An auto-update feature is built into Android, and you can also manually check for patches and updates by navigating to Settings ➢ About Phone ➢ System Updates. Selecting these options will cause the phone to check for, download, and install patches or updates.

Biometric Authentication

Most mobile devices now offer the option to incorporate biometrics as an authentication mechanism. The two most common implementations of this use fingerprint scans or facial scans or facial recognition technology. While there can be issues with both false negatives (the denial of a legitimate user) and false positives (the admission of an illegitimate user), they offer much better security than other authentication mechanisms.

Full Device Encryption

Full device encryption is available for smartphones and other mobile devices. Most companies choose to implement this through the use of an enterprise mobility management system since it can also manage the installation of updates, the tracking of devices, and the deployment of remote wipes and GPS location services when needed. There are also third-party applications that can provide full device encryption.

Multifactor Authentication

Authentication factors describe the method used to verify the user's identity. There are three available authentication factors:

- Something you know (such as a password)
- Something you are (such as a fingerprint)
- Something you have (such as a smart card)

When two different types of factors are required (such as something you know and something you have), it is called *multifactor authentication*. It is important for you to understand that using two or more of the same type of factors (such as a password and a PIN, both something you know) is *not* multifactor authentication. However, when multifactor authentication is used for mobile devices, the level of security is significantly increased.

Authenticator Applications

Authenticator applications, such as Google Authenticator, make it possible for a mobile device to use a time-based one-time password (TOTP) algorithm with a site or system that requires such authentication. In the setup operation, the site provides a shared secret key to the user over a secure channel to be stored in the authenticator app. This secret key will be used for all future logins to the site. The user will enter a username and password into a website or other server, generate a one-time password for the server using TOTP running locally, and type that password into the server as well. The server will then also run TOTP to verify the entered one-time password. While Google makes versions for multiple mobile platforms, there are also other third-party solutions.

Trusted Sources vs. Untrusted Sources

Applications and utilities for mobile devices can come from both trusted and untrusted sources. An example of a trusted source is the official Google Play site or the Apple Store. That doesn't mean these are the only trusted sources, but users should treat this issue with the same approach they have been taught with regard to desktop and laptop computers.

Any piece of software, be it an application, tool, or utility, can come with malware attached. Users should be trained to regard any software downloads with suspicion. It may be advisable to use an enterprise mobility management system to prevent users from downloading any software to a company-owned mobile device. You also may want to deselect the setting shown in Figure 7.11, which is an Android device setting. Apple devices warn users with a pop-up message when they download from an unknown source.

FIGURE 7.11   Allowing applications from unknown sources

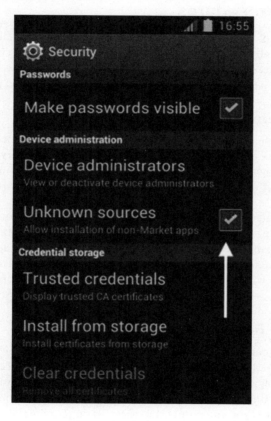

Firewalls

Because today's mobile devices function more like laptops and desktop systems, they need the same protection. Mobile device firewall products are those that install on the device and protect the device in the same way a personal firewall on a desktop system, such as the Windows Firewall, does.

The disadvantage to this approach is that the software runs continuously, thus placing an ongoing load on the battery. Likewise, intrusion prevention and intrusion detection software can be placed on mobile devices, again with the same effect on battery lifetime.

If you need another reason to invest in an enterprise mobility management system, this is it. Most solutions include a firewall product of some sort in the suite. One consideration when choosing a solution is to balance the features you need against the memory footprint of the solution because memory is a scarce resource in mobile devices.

Policies and Procedures

With the introduction of mobile devices to the network, changes and additions may be called for in the organizational security policy. As procedures are derived from broader policies, these changes will also impact the procedures that users are required to follow. In this section, you'll look at two issues that need to be considered with respect to policies and procedures.

BYOD vs. Corporate Owned

One of the decisions that must be made is whether to allow only company-owned mobile devices on the network or to allow personal devices as well. Many organizations have launched bring your own device (BYOD) initiatives. While this certainly makes the users happy, it brings with it new challenges in securing a wide range of user devices running on all sorts of platforms.

One of the ways enterprises have successfully implemented these initiatives without sacrificing the security of the network is by turning to enterprise mobility management systems. These systems can be used to control a wide variety of mobile devices and to manage the installation of updates, the tracking of devices, and the deployment of remote wipes and GPS location services when needed. Without one of these utilities, deploying BYOD can be a security nightmare.

Profile Security Requirements

The baseline or minimum security settings required on all mobile devices must be determined and standardized. This may require the creation of multiple security *profiles* based on different mobile device models and types, but the theory is the same. By defining a collection of security settings, implementing them on all devices, and constantly monitoring the settings for changes, you can ensure that these settings are maintained.

Exam Essentials

Describe the options available to secure the data on a mobile device. These options include passcode locks, remote wipes, locator applications, failed login attempt restrictions, and remote backup applications.

List other security guidelines for mobile devices. Always keep antivirus definitions up-to-date and set the mobile device to automatically check for OS updates and patches.

3.6 Given a Scenario, Use Appropriate Data Destruction and Disposal Methods

Think of all the sensitive data written to a hard drive. The drive can contain information about students, clients, users—anyone and anything. That hard drive can be in a desktop PC, a laptop, or even a printer (many laser printers above consumer grade offer the ability to add a hard drive to store print jobs). If it falls into the wrong hands, you can lose valuable data but also risk a lawsuit for not properly protecting privacy. An appropriate data destruction/disposal plan should be in place to avoid any potential problems.

Since data on media holds great value and liability, that media should never be simply tossed away for prying eyes to stumble upon. For the purposes of this objective, I'll talk about hard drives, and there are three key concepts to understand in regard to them: formatting, sanitation, and destruction. Formatting prepares the drive to hold new information (which can include copying over data already there). Sanitation involves wiping the data on the drive, whereas destruction renders the drive no longer usable. The subobjectives covered in this section include the following:

- Physical destruction
- Recycling or repurposing best practices

 While this objective is heavily focused on hard drives, it is also possible to have data stored on portable flash drives, backup tapes, CDs, or DVDs. In the interest of security, I recommend that you destroy them before disposing of them as well.

Physical Destruction

Physically destroying the drive involves rendering the component no longer usable. While the focus is on hard drives, you can also physically destroy other forms of media, such as flash drives and CD/DVDs.

Shredder

When it comes to DVDs and CDs, many commercial paper shredders include the ability to destroy them. Paper shredders, however, are not able to handle hard drives, and you need a shredder created for just such a purpose. Jackhammer makes a low-volume model that will destroy eight drives per minute and carries a suggested list price of just under $30,000.

Drill/Hammer

If you don't have the budget for a hard drive shredder, you can accomplish similar results in a much more time-consuming way with a power drill. The goal is to physically destroy the platters in the drive. Start the process by removing the cover from the drive—this is normally done with a Torx driver (while #8 does not work with all, it is a good one to try first). You can remove the arm with a slotted screwdriver and then the cover over the platters using a Torx driver. Don't worry about damaging or scratching anything because nothing is intended to be saved. Everything but the platters can be tossed away.

As an optional step, you can completely remove the tracks using a belt sander, grinder, or palm sander. The goal is to turn the shiny surface into fine powder. This adds one more layer of assurance that nothing usable remains. Always be careful to wear eye protection and not breathe in any fine particles that you generate during the grinding/destruction process.

Following this, use the power drill to create the smallest particles possible. A drill press works much better for this task than trying to hold the drive and drill it with a handheld model. Finally you can use a hammer to destroy the platters as well and it provides a certain level of satisfaction if the drive died and you had to restore it from backup.

Even with practice, you will find that manually destroying a hard drive is time-consuming. There are companies that specialize in this and can do it efficiently. One such company is Shred-it, which will pick it up from you and provide a chain-of-custody assurance and a certificate of destruction upon completion. You can find out more about what it offers here:

www.shredit.com/shredding-service/What-to-shred/Hard-drive-destruction.aspx

Electromagnetic/Degaussing

Degaussing involves applying a strong magnetic field to initialize the media (this is also referred to as disk wiping). This process helps ensure that information doesn't fall into the wrong hands.

Since degaussing uses a specifically designed electromagnet to eliminate all data on the drive, that destruction also includes the factory prerecorded servo tracks. You can find wand model degaussers priced at just over $500 or desktop units that sell for up to $30,000.

Degaussing hard drives is difficult and may render the drive unusable.

Incineration

A final option that exists for some forms of storage is to burn the media. Regardless of whether the media is a hard drive, CD, DVD, solid-state drive, or floppy disk, the media must be reduced to ash, or in the case of hard drive platters, the internal platters must be physically deformed using heat.

Certificate of Destruction

Certificates of destruction are documents that attest to either the physical destruction of the media on which sensitive data was located or a scientifically approved method of removing the data from a drive. In a later section of this chapter, you will be introduced to some methods of removal that are both approved and unapproved.

These documents are typically issued to the organization by a storage vendor or cloud provider to prove either that the data has been removed or that the media has been destroyed.

Recycling or Repurposing Best Practices

While destroying the media is certainly a way to safeguard the data, in some cases you want to reuse the media. It is possible to safely do so if you follow certain practices for removing the data while avoiding others. In this section, you'll learn about methods of removal, some of which are both recommended and others you should avoid.

Low-Level Format vs. Standard Format

Multiple levels of formatting can be done on a drive. A standard format—accomplished using the operating system's format utility (or similar)—can mark space occupied by files as available for new files without truly deleting what was there. Such erasing—if you want to call it that—doesn't guarantee that the information isn't still on the disk and recoverable.

A low-level format (typically accomplished only in the factory) can be performed on the system, or a utility can be used to completely wipe the disk clean. This process helps ensure that information doesn't fall into the wrong hands.

IDE hard drives are low-level formatted by the manufacturer. Low-level formatting must be performed even before a drive can be partitioned. In low-level formatting, the drive controller chip and the drive meet for the first time and learn to work together. Because IDE drives have their controllers integrated into the drive, low-level formatting is a factory process with these drives. Low-level formatting is not operating system dependent.

WARNING   Never low-level format IDE or SCSI drives! They're low-level formatted from the factory, and you may cause problems by using low-level utilities on these types of drives.

The main thing to remember for the exams is that most forms of formatting included with the operating system do not actually completely erase the data. Formatting the drive and then disposing of it has caused many companies problems when the data has been retrieved by individuals who never should have seen it using applications that are commercially available.

Overwrite

Overwriting the drive entails copying over the data with new data. A common practice is to replace the data with 0s. A number of applications allow you to recover what was there prior to the last write operation, and for that reason, most overwrite software will write the same sequence and save it multiple times.

Drive Wipe

If it's possible to verify beyond a reasonable doubt that a piece of hardware that's no longer being used doesn't contain any data of a sensitive or proprietary nature, that hardware can be recycled (sold to employees, sold to a third party, donated to a school, and so on). That level of assurance can come from wiping a hard drive or using specialized utilities.

If you can't be assured that the hardware in question doesn't contain important data, the hardware should be destroyed. You cannot, and should not, take a risk that the data your company depends on could fall into the wrong hands.

Exam Essentials

Understand the difference between standard and low-level formatting.   Standard formatting uses operating system tools and makes the drive available for holding data without truly removing what was on the drive (thus the data can be recovered). A low-level format is operating system independent and destroys any data that was on the drive.

Understand how to physically destroy a drive.   A hard drive can be destroyed by tossing it into a shredder designed for such a purpose, or it can be destroyed with an electromagnet in a process known as degaussing. You can also disassemble the drive and destroy the platters with a drill or other tool that renders the data irretrievable.

3.7 Given a Scenario, Secure SOHO Wireless and Wired Networks

CompTIA wants administrators of SOHO networks to be able to secure those networks in ways that protect the data stored on them. This objective looks at the security protection that can be added to a wireless or wired SOHO network. First you'll look at issues specific to a WLAN, and then you'll take a look at security considerations for wired and wireless networks. The subobjectives covered in this chapter include the following:

- Wireless specific
- Change default usernames and passwords
- Enable MAC filtering
- Assign static IP addresses
- Firewall settings
- Port forwarding/mapping
- Disabling ports
- Content filtering/parental controls

- Update firmware
- Physical security

Wireless Specific

Wireless networks present their own unique set of challenges that wired networks do not. The communication methods are somewhat different, as are the attack methods. In this section, security issues that are relevant only to a WLAN are discussed.

Changing Default SSID

Every wireless AP or wireless router on the market comes with a default SSID. Cisco models use the name *tsunami*, for example. You should change these defaults and create a new SSID to represent your WLAN. Typically, when hackers see a default SSID, they make the assumption (a reasonable one to make) that if the SSID was left to the default, the administrator password was as well. Moreover, if you also failed to change that, hackers can now log in, take over your AP, and lock you out.

Setting Encryption

The available types of wireless encryption (WEP, WPA, WPA2, and so on) were discussed in Chapter 2, "Networking." Know that you should always enable encryption for any SOHO network you administer and that you should choose the strongest level of encryption you can work with. Keep in mind that WEP is no longer considered secure and WPA is considered weak, so avoid their use if possible.

Disabling SSID Broadcast

One method of "protecting" the network that is often recommended is to turn off the SSID broadcast. The AP is still there and can be accessed by those who know about it, but it prevents those who are just scanning from finding it. This should be considered a weak form of security because there are still other ways, albeit a bit more complicated, to discover the presence of the AP besides the SSID broadcast.

Antenna and Access Point Placement

Antenna placement can be crucial in allowing clients to reach the AP. There isn't any one universal solution to this issue, and it depends on the environment in which the AP is placed. As a general rule, the greater the distance the signal must travel, the more it will attenuate, but you can lose a signal quickly in a short space as well if the building materials reflect or absorb the signal. You should try to avoid placing APs near metal (which includes appliances) or near the ground. Placing them in the center of the area to be served, and high enough to get around most obstacles, is recommended.

On the other end of the spectrum, you have to contend with the problem of the signal traveling outside your intended network (known as *signal leakage*) and being picked up in public areas by outsiders. To lessen this problem, use RF-absorbent materials on external walls, essentially shielding the surroundings.

Radio Power Levels

On the chance that the signal is actually traveling too far, some APs include *power-level controls* that allow you to reduce the amount of output provided.

 You can find a great source for information on RF power values and antennas on the Cisco site at http://www.cisco.com/c/en/us/support/docs/wireless-mobility/wireless-lan-wlan/23231-powervalues-23231.html

WPS

Wi-Fi protected setup (WPS) was a concept that was designed to make it easier for less knowledgeable users to add a new client to the WLAN without manually entering the security information on the client. One method involves pushing a button on the AP at the same time a client is attempting to join the network so that the settings are sent to the client. Other methods involve placing the client close to the AP, and near-field communication is used for the process.

Regardless of the details, as often happens when we try to make security simpler, we make it fail. It has been discovered that a hacker can identify the PIN used in a short period of time and with it the network's WPA/WPA2 preshared key. For this reason, the Wi-Fi Alliance has recommended against using this feature.

Change Default Usernames and Passwords

Default accounts not only include those created with the installation of the operating systems but are also often associated with hardware. Wireless APs, routers, and similar devices often include accounts for interacting with, and administering, those devices. You should always change the passwords associated with those devices and, where possible, change the usernames.

If there are accounts that are not needed, disable them or delete them. Make certain you use strong password policies and protect the passwords with the same security you do for any users or administrators (in other words, don't write the router's password on an address label and stick it to the bottom of the router).

In Windows, the Guest account is automatically created in Windows with the intent that it is to be used when someone must access a system but lacks a user account on that system. Since it is so widely known to exist, I recommend that you not use this default account and instead create another one for the same purpose if you truly need one. The Guest account leaves a security risk at the workstation and should be disabled to prevent it from being accessed by those attempting to gain unauthorized access.

Change *every* username and password that you can so they vary from their default settings.

Enable MAC Filtering

Most APs and network switches offer the ability to turn on *MAC filtering*, but it is off by default. In the default state, any wireless client that knows the values looked for can join the network, and any device connected to a switch port can send traffic. When MAC filtering is used, the administrator compiles a list of the MAC addresses associated with the users' computers and enters those. When a client attempts to connect and other values have been correctly entered, an additional check of the MAC address is done. If the address appears in the list, the client is allowed to join; otherwise, they are forbidden from doing so. On a number of wireless devices, the term *network lock* is used in place of MAC filtering, and the two are synonymous.

Adding port authentication to MAC filtering takes security for the network down to the switch port level and increases your security exponentially.

Assign Static IP Addresses

While DHCP can be a godsend, a SOHO network is small enough that you can get by without it issuing IP addresses to each host. The advantage to statically assigning the IP addresses is that you can make certain which host is associated with which IP address and then utilize filtering to limit network access to only those hosts.

While static IP addressing may not be scalable in a wired network with many devices, in a small network, using static IP addressing will make it impossible for someone to just plug into your network without knowing your IP address scheme.

Firewall Settings

All devices both wired and wireless should have personal firewalls enabled and configured to protect each system. In Windows, you can simply leverage the personal firewall that comes on all Windows Vista, Windows 7, and Windows 8 and 8.1 computers. For operating systems that don't come with personal firewall, third-party software should be implemented for this purpose. These firewalls help to prevent other devices from connecting to each station without the approval of the users.

The presence of personal firewalls on all the devices does *not* mean you don't need a network firewall at the edge of the network and between sections of the network that may have varying security levels. You can find more information on firewalls earlier in this chapter in the section "Digital Security."

Port Forwarding/Mapping

Another option to harden the entrance to the network is to deploy port forwarding or mapping. Port forwarding is a function typically performed on the same device that may be performing network address translation (NAT). One port number is set aside on the gateway for the exclusive use of communicating with a service in the private network, located on a specific host. External hosts must know this port number and the address of the gateway to communicate with the network-internal service. The purpose of this is to hide the real IP address of the destination device or server to protect it from connections outside the LAN.

Disabling Ports

Disable all unneeded protocols/ports. If you don't need them, remove them or prevent them from loading. Ports not in use present an open door for an attacker to enter.

> Many of the newer SOHO router solutions (and some of the personal firewall solutions on end-user workstations) close down the ICMP ports by default. Keep this in mind; it can drive you nuts when you are trying to see whether a new station, server, or router is up and running by using the ping command. This command depends on the use of ICMP.

Content Filtering/Parental Controls

Content filtering software examines all web connections, and in some cases emails, for objectionable content or sites that have been identified as off-limits by the administrator. While this can be helpful in preventing the introduction of malware or in screening objectionable content, you should be aware that these filters are making educated guesses about what to deny and allow.

A filter will invariably deny content that should be allowed and allow content that should be denied. Try to be as specific as possible when defining keywords that are used to identify sites and content and set the expectation among the users that the software is not perfect.

Parental controls operate on the same basic premise.

Update Firmware

In the past, updating firmware on devices such as APs, routers, and switches was considered to be desirable but optional. More and more security attacks are based on attacking the firmware, and for this reason firmware updates should be part of whatever automated update system you may be using (not to mention the additional functionality and bug elimination you may experience). It may be that you can get on a mailing list for each vendor so you can be notified when firmware updates are available. In any case, some systematic method must be developed to ensure these updates are maintained.

Physical Security

Just as you would not park your car in a public garage and leave its doors wide open with the key in the ignition, you should educate users to not leave a workstation that they are logged into when they attend meetings, go to lunch, and so forth. They should log out of the workstation or lock it. "Lock when you leave" should be a mantra they become familiar with. Locking the workstation should require a password (usually the same as their user password) to resume working at the workstation.

Moreover, don't overlook the obvious need for physical security. Adding a cable to lock a laptop to a desk prevents someone from picking it up and walking away with a copy of your customer database. Laptop cases generally include a built-in security slot in which a cable lock can be added to prevent it from being carried away easily, like the one shown in Figure 7.12.

FIGURE 7.12 A cable in the security slot keeps the laptop from being carried away easily.

When it comes to desktop models, adding a lock to the back cover can prevent an intruder with physical access from grabbing the hard drive or damaging the internal components. You should also physically secure network devices—routers, APs, and the like. Place them in locked cabinets, if possible. If they are not physically secured, the opportunity exists for them to be stolen or manipulated in such a way to allow someone unauthorized to connect to the network.

Exam Essentials

Know the names, purpose, and characteristics of wireless security.   Wireless networks can be encrypted through WEP and WPA technologies. Wireless controllers use special ID strings and must be configured in the network cards to allow communications. However, using ID string configurations doesn't necessarily prevent wireless networks from being monitored, and there are vulnerabilities specific to wireless devices.

Understand the basics of antenna placement and radio power levels.   Antenna placement can be crucial in allowing clients to reach the AP. Place APs near the center of the area to be served and high enough to get around most obstacles. Power-level controls allow you to reduce the amount of output provided.

Review Questions

You can find the answers in the Appendix.

1. Which type of virus covers itself with protective code that stops debuggers or disassemblers from examining critical elements of the virus?

   A. companion

   B. macro

   C. armored

   D. multipartite

2. What element of a virus uniquely identifies it?

   A. ID

   B. signature

   C. badge

   D. marking

3. How is a worm different from a virus?

   A. it isn't malicious

   B. doesn't need a host application to be transported

   C. it can replicate itself

   D. it is no longer a threat

4. Which of the following enters a system or network under the guise of another program?

   A. worms

   B. trojans

   C. viruses

   D. rootkits

5. Which type of virus alters other programs and databases?

   A. phage

   B. polymorphic

   C. multipartite

   D. companion

6. Which of the following is the process of masquerading as another user or device?

   A. shadowing

   B. spoofing

   C. duplicating

   D. masking

7. Which of the following is a vulnerability discovered in a live environment before a fix or patch exists?

   A. zero day attack

   B. day one attack

   C. stealth attack

   D. botnet attack

8. Which virus type attaches itself to legitimate programs and then creates a program with a different filename extension?

   A. companion

   B. macro

   C. armored

   D. multipartite

9. Which of the following is the term used for someone being so close to you when you enter a building that they are able to come in right behind you without needing to use a key, a card, or any other security device?

   A. shadowing

   B. spoofing

   C. tailgating

   D. keyriding

10. Which virus type attacks your system in multiple ways?

   A. companion

   B. macro

   C. armored

   D. multipartite

Chapter

8

Software Troubleshooting

COMPTIA A+ 220-902 EXAM OBJECTIVES COVERED IN THIS CHAPTER:

✓ **4.1 Given a scenario, troubleshoot PC operating system problems with appropriate tools.**

  - Common symptoms (proprietary crash screens [BSOD/pin wheel], failure to boot, improper shutdown, spontaneous shutdown/restart, device fails to start/be detected, missing DLL message, service fails to start, compatibility error, slow system performance, boots to Safe Mode, file fails to open, missing NTLDR, missing boot.ini, missing operating system, missing graphical interface, missing GRUB/LILO, kernel panic, graphical interface fails to load, multiple monitor misalignment/orientation)

  - Tools (BIOS/UEFI, SFC, logs, recovery console, repair disks, pre-installation environments, MSCONFIG, DEFRAG, REG-SRV32, REGEDIT, Event Viewer, Safe Mode, command prompt, emergency repair disk, automated system recovery, uninstall/reinstall/repair)

✓ **4.2 Given a scenario, troubleshoot common PC security issues with appropriate tools and best practices.**

  - Common symptoms (pop-ups, browser redirection, security alerts, slow performance, Internet connectivity issues, PC/OS locks up, application crash, OS updates failures, rogue antivirus, spam, renamed system files, files disappearing, file permission changes, hijacked email [responses from users regarding email, automated replies from unknown sent email], access denied, invalid certificate [trusted root CA])

  - Tools (antivirus software, anti-malware software, recovery console, terminal, system restore/snapshot, pre-installation environments, Event Viewer, refresh/restore, MSCONFIG/safe boot)

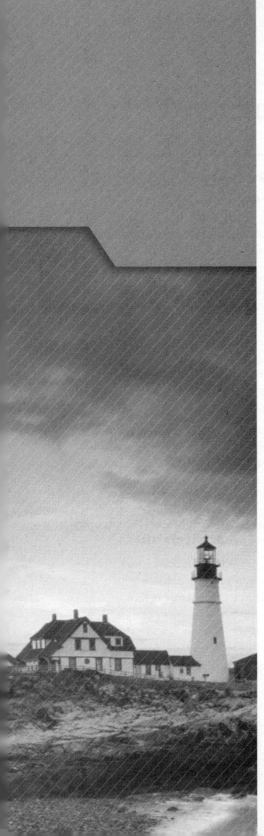

- Best practices for malware removal (identify malware symptoms, quarantine infected system, disable system restore [in Windows], remediate infected systems [update antimalware software, scan and removal techniques], schedule scans and run updates, enable system restore and create restore point [in Windows], educate end user)

✓ **4.3   Given a scenario, troubleshoot common mobile OS and application issues with appropriate tools.**

- Common symptoms (dim display, intermittent wireless, no wireless connectivity, no Bluetooth connectivity, cannot broadcast to external monitor, touchscreen non-responsive, apps not loading, slow performance, unable to decrypt email, extremely short battery life, overheating, frozen system, no sound from speakers, inaccurate touchscreen response, system lockout)

- Tools (hard reset, soft reset, close running applications, reset to factory default, adjust configurations/settings, uninstall/reinstall apps, force stop)

✓ **4.4   Given a scenario, troubleshoot common mobile OS and application security issues with appropriate tools.**

- Common symptoms (signal drop/weak signal, power drain, slow data speeds, unintended Wi-Fi connection, unintended Bluetooth pairing, leaked personal files/data, data transmission overlimit, unauthorized account access, unauthorized root access, unauthorized location tracking, unauthorized camera/microphone activation, high resource utilization)

- Tools (antimalware, app scanner, factory reset/clean install, uninstall/reinstall apps, Wi-Fi analyzer, force stop, cell tower analyzer, backup/restore [iTunes/iCloud/Apple Configurator, Google sync, One Drive])

In this chapter, I will focus on the exam topics related to troubleshooting. I will follow the structure of the CompTIA A+ 220-902 exam blueprint, objective 4, and explore the four subobjectives that you will need to master before taking the exam.

4.1 Given a Scenario, Troubleshoot PC Operating System Problems with Appropriate Tools

Because it's software and there are so many places where things can go wrong, the operating system can be one of the most confusing components to troubleshoot. Sometimes it seems a miracle that operating systems even work at all considering the hundreds of files that work together to make the system function. In this section, common operating system issues and their solutions are covered. The topics addressed in objective 4.1 include the following:

- Common symptoms
- Tools

Common Symptoms

What follows in this section can seem like a daunting list of symptoms the operating system can exhibit. With a proper plan of action and good backup (always have a backup!), you can approach any of these problems with confidence. In many cases today, technicians have ceased to spend significant amounts of time chasing operating system issues since the most important data is kept on servers and since computers can be reimaged so quickly that troubleshooting doesn't warrant the effort. Nevertheless, you should know these basic symptoms and the approach to take when they present themselves.

Proprietary Crash Screens/BSOD

Once a regular occurrence when working with Windows, blue screens (also known as the Blue Screen of Death, or BSOD) have become less common. Occasionally, systems will lock up; you can usually examine the log files to discover what was happening when this occurred and take steps to correct it. Remember, when dealing with a blue screen, always ask yourself "What did I just install or change?" In many cases, the change is involved in the BSOD. Also keep in mind that (as the instructions on the blue screen will tell you) a simple reboot will often fix the problem. Retaining the contents of the BSOD can help troubleshoot the issue. In most instances, you can find the BSOD error in Microsoft's knowledge base to help with troubleshooting.

The Apple pinwheel is displayed automatically by WindowServer when an application cannot handle all the events it receives. (WindowServer is the background process that runs the Mac OS X graphical user interface). To find out whether the CPU is a bottleneck on performance, use Activity Monitor (/Applications/Utilities) to monitor CPU usage. The pinwheel or beach ball may also appear if you don't have enough RAM.

Software can also cause the pinwheel. Open Activity Monitor's CPU tab and sort by the % CPU column in descending order; the apps at the top are the ones using the most CPU cycles. If an application is frozen, it will appear in red. If it is *not* a process with root listed as the user, quit it.

Failure to Boot

Booting problems can occur with corruption of the boot files or missing components. Common error messages include an invalid boot disk, inaccessible boot drive, missing NTLDR file, or missing BOOTMGR (some of which are discussed in more detail later in this section). Luckily, during the installation of the operating system, log files are created in the %SystemRoot% and %SystemRoot%\Debug folders (C:\WINNT for older systems and C:\ Windows for Windows 7, Windows Vista, and Windows 8). If you have a puzzling problem, look at these logs and see whether you can find error entries there. With Windows 7, for example, the following files are some of the log files created:

netsetup.log   This file differs from all the others in that it's in the Debug folder and not just %SystemRoot%. Entries in it detail the workgroup and domain options given during installation.

setupact.log   Known as the action log, this file is a chronological list of what took place during the setup. There is a tremendous amount of information here; of key importance is whether any errors occurred. The last lines of the file can show which operation was transpiring when the installation failed or whether the installation ended with errors. Like all the log files created during setup, this file is in ASCII text format and can be viewed with any viewer (WordPad, Word, and so on).

setuperr.log   The error log, as this file is commonly called, is written to at the time errors are noted in other log files. For example, an entry in setuperr.log may show that an error occurred, and you can find additional information about it in setuperr.log. Not only are the errors here, but also the severity of each is given.

You can configure problems with system failure to write dump files (debugging information) for later analysis when they occur by clicking Start ➢ Control Panel ➢ System and then clicking the Advanced System Settings option. The Advanced tab of the System Properties dialog box should open. Then click the Settings button in the Startup and Recovery section. Here, in addition to choosing the default operating system, you can configure whether events should be written to the system log, whether an alert should be sent to the administrator, and what type of memory dump should be written.

Improper Shutdown

Although not nearly the danger it once was, when the system is improperly shut down, either from a loss of power or by being forced to shut down without all programs closing, problems can result. For certain, anything that is still residing in memory and not saved to the disk will be lost (although Word may save you with its auto-recovery feature).

In other cases, though, important files may be corrupted or lost. In fact, if some files are lost, the computer may not even boot after the shutdown. If the system does boot and you have any doubts about the integrity of important system files, execute the command sfc/scannow. This program (called the System File Checker) will check the file structure. Another good command to execute if you have any doubts is chkdsk/R. This command will check the disk for errors and repair them if possible.

Spontaneous Shutdown/Restart

Some restarts are a function of hardware. (See Chapter 1 for more information about restarts.) In other cases, it is software related. If the system is automatically restarting, there is the possibility that it has a virus or is unable to continue current operations (in other words, it has become unstable). To solve issues with viruses, Trojans, and the like, install virus detection software on every client (as well as on the server), keep the definitions current, and run them often.

If the problem is with the system being unstable, examine the log files and try to isolate the problem. Reboot in safe mode (discussed in more detail in the "Tools" section) and correct any incompatibility issues. You can also deselect the Automatically Restart On Startup And Recovery option of the System applet (Advanced tab) in the Control Panel to prevent the system from rebooting.

Occasionally, systems reboot when they have been updated. This is a necessary process, and users are always given warning before the reboot occurs. If no one is present to choose to reboot later (it's the middle of the night, for example), the reboot will take place. Users who leave files open overnight in an unsaved state are at risk of losing work because of this process.

Device Fails to Start/Be Detected

Usually when devices fail to start or are not detected by the system and you have eliminated a hardware issue, the problem involves drivers. Drivers are associated with devices, and you can access them by looking at the properties for the device. The following, for example, are the three most common tabs of an adaptor's Properties dialog box in Device Manager (tabs that appear are always dependent on the type of device and its capabilities):

General   This tab displays the device type, manufacturer, and location. It also includes information regarding whether the device is currently working properly.

Driver   This tab displays information on the current driver and digital signer. Five command buttons allow you to see driver details, uninstall the driver, update the driver, or roll back the driver to the previous driver when a new driver causes an issue.

Resources   This tab shows the system resources in use (I/O, IRQ, and so on) and whether there are conflicts.

The most common driver-related device issue is device failure when a new driver is installed. If this occurs, you can use the Roll Back Driver option in Device Manager or boot into the Last Known Good Configuration.

Missing DLL Message

One of the more useful error messages you can receive is one indicating a missing DLL file. It's useful because it tells you exactly what's missing. DLL files are shared by various components. If they are missing or corrupted, you will receive an error message whenever you do something that requires the file. Make note of the name of the DLL and its location.

You can copy DLLs from another machine if the systems are at identical patch levels. Place them in the same location and the problem should be fixed. When you receive the error message, locate the missing DLL by searching for it. If it's gone completely, search for it on another system and copy it. Then just paste it into the proper location (that should be the system32 folder on the drive where the operating system is installed).

Services Fail to Start

Sometimes when the system is started, you receive a message that tells you a service failed to start. When that occurs, use the event log to determine the service that failed. Then to interact with service, access the Administrative Tools section of Control Panel and choose Services. This starts up the Services console. You can right-click any service and choose to start, stop, pause, resume, or restart it. You can also double-click the service to access its properties and configure such things as the startup type, dependencies, and other variables.

If the service refuses to start, it could be that a service on which it depends will not start. To determine what services must be running for the problem service to start, select the Dependencies tab of the service's Properties dialog box, as shown in Figure 8.1.

FIGURE 8.1   Service dependencies

In the figure you can see that the Remote Desktop service depends on both the RPC and Terminal Device Driver services to function. Try starting these services first. In some cases, you may need to trace the dependencies up several levels to get things going.

Compatibility Error

Some applications that function on an older operating system such as Windows 2000 or Windows XP experience problems when running on Windows Vista, Windows 7, or Windows 8. The problem is even more acute if the application was made to run on Windows NT or Windows 95/98.

When an application will not function for this reason, there are two solutions. It may even require using both measures to make the application function.

- Set the application to operate in the mode for which it was created. In the Properties dialog box of each application is the Compatibility tab. There you can use a drop-down box to select Windows XP mode, Windows 95 mode, or whatever is required. Figure 8.2 shows the Compatibility tab.

- Set the application to run as an administrator. Some older applications must run in the security context of an administrator to function, which is not generally allowed anymore in Windows Vista, Windows 7, and Windows 8. You may have to select the Run This Program As An Administrator box as well. The box is near the bottom of the Compatibility tab, as shown in Figure 8.2.

FIGURE 8.2   Compatibility tab

Slow System Performance

Slow system performance can come from many issues. For the purposes of this discussion, I will focus on performance that deteriorates after being acceptable as opposed to system performance that is poor from the outset (which could be a matter of insufficient resources such as RAM). Here is a list of possibilities:

- The first thing to check is the presence of a virus. If the system seems to have an over-abundance of disk activity, scan it for viruses using a virus program that resides externally on a CD/DVD or memory stick.

- Defragment the hard drive. The more fragmented it is, the slower the disk access will be.

- Check the space on the hard drive. When the partition or volume where the operating system is located becomes full, performance will suffer. This is why it is a good idea to store data and applications on a different partition from that holding the system files.

- Ensure the latest updates are installed. In many cases, updates help to solve performance problems, so make sure they are current.

- Use Task Manager to determine whether a process is using too much memory or CPU or is simply locked up (not responding), and if necessary, end the process.

Boots to Safe Mode

In many cases, a system will not boot in regular mode but will do so in safe mode. Safe mode loads the operating system but none of the drivers, with the exception of those absolutely essential to the system and those required for use of the keyboard, mouse, and the basic display (VGA mode).

If the system will start in safe mode but not otherwise, it is most likely a bad driver that is causing the system to hang during the bootup. One option to try for a quick fix is to perform a System Restore procedure to a point in time before the driver problem occurred. You can also use the Roll Back Driver feature to revert to the older but functional driver. The problem with this approach is that you have not identified the problem driver, so the issue may emerge again later.

If you go to Device Manager and check the status of all the devices, you should see a device that has a problem. Try updating the driver, which may be a better long-term solution. Another option is to look in the system log in Event Viewer; the problem driver may be specified in a message there as well.

File Fails to Open

Files will sometimes not open when you click them. In some cases, it's a problem of file association, which means the system doesn't know which application to use to open the file. Right-click the file and choose Open With. Then select the program to open the file. At that point, you may realize that the program required to open the file is not present, and you may have to install it.

If this occurs with EXE files, the culprit is usually a virus. Remove the virus first. If the EXE files still fail to function, there are EXE file association fixes available that can reassociate the files with the proper program.

Missing NTLDR

The NTLDR file loads the operating system files for Windows XP and 2000. In Windows Vista, Windows 7, and Windows 8, BOOTMGR performs this operation. If it is not present, the system will not boot.

The good news is that this file can be copied from any other system to the operating system drive. In Windows XP, follow these steps:

1. Insert the Windows XP installation disc into the computer.

2. When prompted to press any key to boot from the CD, press any key.

3. Once in the Windows XP setup menu, press the R key to repair Windows.

4. Log into the problematic Windows installations (if there are more than one) by pressing the number of the installation in the list presented. The number will be 1 if it is the only installation.

5. Enter the administrator password.

6. Copy the ntldr and ntdetect.com files to the root directory of the primary hard disk. Where the CD-ROM drive letter is E and your root directory is on the C drive, execute the following commands. Insert the proper drive letters for your CD and the root directory of your installation.

   ```
   copy e:\i386\ntldr c:\
   copy e:\i386\ntdetect.com c:\
   ```

7. Once both of these files have been successfully copied, remove the CD from the computer and reboot.

Missing boot.ini

The boot.ini file in Windows XP and Windows 2000 holds information about which operating systems are installed on the computer. In Windows Vista, Windows 7, and Windows 8, the boot configuration data (BCD) file holds this information. When the boot.ini file is missing, the system will not boot because the operating system files cannot be found.

Unfortunately, the boot.ini file is not a file you can copy from another system (unless that system is installed the same, which may be the case if the computers were imaged). For this reason, it is always a good idea to put the boot.ini file on an external drive or memory stick in case it becomes missing; then you can boot to the device, get the system running, and copy the boot.ini file to its proper location on the operating system drive.

Missing Operating System

The "no operating system found" message can result from a number of issues. Among them are the following:

- Nonsystem disk in the floppy drive
- Incorrect boot device order in the BIOS
- Corrupted or missing boot sector
- Corrupted boot files

In short, the operating system is not actually missing; the system is missing the file that can either locate it or load it. Follow the steps in this section with respect to the `ntldr` and `boot.ini` files for Windows XP.

In Windows Vista, Windows 7, and Windows 8, if using Startup Repair does not work, you may need to create a bootable disc to boot the device. The directions for this vary between the systems but can be found on the Microsoft site. Then you have two approaches. For Windows 8, one approach is to follow these steps:

1. Insert the installation DVD or USB and boot Windows 8 from it.

2. On the Windows Setup page, select the language to install, the time and currency format, and the keyboard or input method; then click Next.

3. Click Repair Your Computer and select Troubleshoot.

4. Click Advanced Options, select Automatic Repair, and select the operating system.

The other approach is to try to rebuild the boot configuration data, booting from the Windows 8 installation media and following these instructions:

1. Insert the installation DVD or USB and boot Windows 8 from it.

2. On the Windows Setup page, select the language to install, the time and currency format, and the keyboard or input method; then click Next.

3. Click Repair Your Computer and select Troubleshoot.

4. Click Advanced Options, click the command prompt, type the following commands, and press Enter after each command:

    ```
    Bootrec /fixmbr
    Bootrec /fixboot
    Bootrec /rebuildbcd
    ```

5. Restart the computer. Check whether you're able to boot now.

Missing Graphical Interface

The graphical user interface (GUI) is the method by which a person communicates with a computer. GUIs use a mouse, touchpad, or another mechanism (in addition to the keyboard) to interact with the computer to issue commands. A missing GUI or a GUI that fails to load (see the next section) usually results from a bad driver or something that is preventing the operating system from loading to the point where the GUI can load.

When the GUI is missing, try booting into safe mode. If the GUI appears for safe mode, you know it is a driver problem and can proceed with determining the offending driver, as discussed in the section "Boots to Safe Mode."

Missing GRUB/LILO

GRUB is the bootloader package on Linux and Unix systems. If it is not present, the system may not boot. In some cases when you install Windows, it will overwrite GRUB. If this occurs or in any case where you need to reinstall or recover GRUB, follow these steps, which are based on Ubuntu:

1. Mount the partition your Ubuntu installation is on.

2. Bind the directories to which GRUB needs access to detect other operating systems.

3. Using chroot, install, check, and update GRUB.

4. Exit the chrooted system and unmount everything.

5. Shut down and turn your computer back on, and you will be met with the default GRUB screen.

 For more detailed assistance with this process, go to http://howtoubuntu .org/how-to-repair-restore-reinstall-grub-2-with-a-ubuntu-live-cd.

While most distributions of Unix and Linux now use GRUB, some older systems use a bootloader called LILO. For some of the same reasons as with GRUB, LILO may become corrupted or may be missing after a Windows installation. This can also be recovered by reinstalling it. To do so, follow these steps:

1. Boot into Linux some other way, either using Loadlin or using a Linux boot floppy.

2. At the Linux command prompt, just type **/sbin/lilo**.

3. Reboot and LILO will be back.

Kernel Panic

On Unix and Mac, a kernel panic is a lockup of the entire system. A panic may occur as a result of a hardware failure or a software bug in the operating system. It occurs during the boot process. These incidents should occur infrequently, and you can reboot to escape the problem. However, if you find this is happening frequently, check the following items:

- Perform a safe boot.

- Update your software.

- Update your firmware.

- Make sure your startup disk has at least 10 GB of free space.

- Disconnect everything except the bare minimum (keyboard, pointing device, and display if those aren't built in).

- Check your RAM because defective RAM can cause kernel panics.

Graphical Interface Fails to Load

The approach to troubleshooting a GUI that won't load is basically the same as for a missing GUI since a GUI that won't load manifests itself as a GUI that is missing. Be aware that inappropriate or misinformed edits to the Registry can also delete files required for the GUI.

Sometimes restoring the Registry from a backup can solve the problem. Since the GUI will not be available, you must use the command line or the Recovery Console (discussed in the upcoming section "Recovery Console"). In Windows Vista, Windows 7, and Windows 8, this is called the Windows Recovery Environment (WinRE). WinRE can be accessed in Windows Vista or Windows 7 by pressing and holding the F8 key early in the system boot process and then selecting the Repair Your Computer option from the boot menu that appears. In Windows 8, you access WinRE by following these steps:

1. Press WinKey+I and click the Power icon.

2. Hold down Shift and click Restart.

3. Click Troubleshooting.

4. Click Advanced Options to bring up the repair options.

Multiple Monitor Misalignment/Orientation

More and more users are discovering the value of using multiple monitors to increase productivity. When multiple monitors are in use, it can become difficult to get all the monitors operating as well as each possibly can. Many times there are issues with the alignment and orientation.

Adjusting the alignment of the monitors refers to setting either the top or bottom edge of both displays at the same level in the Display properties. For example, in Figure 8.3, the two monitors have been aligned, so the top edges are on the same level. This will make it easier to move the cursor from one screen to the other by staying at the top of the screen when changing screens.

The display orientation refers to the how the content is spread across the monitor. Each screen can have its own orientation, and the four options are Landscape, Portrait, Landscape (Flipped), or Portrait (Flipped). To change this, select the desired orientation from the Orientation drop-down box, as shown in Figure 8.4.

FIGURE 8.3 Alignment of multiple monitors

FIGURE 8.4 Orientation of multiple monitors

Tools

A number of tools are available for troubleshooting operating system problems, some of which have been mentioned in passing in the earlier sections on common symptoms.

BIOS/UEFI

As you learned in Chapter 1, settings in both the BIOS and the newer UEFI can be used to troubleshoot hardware and boot problems. For more information, review the section "1.1 Given a Scenario, Configure Settings and Use BIOS/UEFI Tools on a PC" in Chapter 1.

SFC

The System File Checker (SFC) utility was discussed in the earlier section "Improper Shutdown." The purpose of this utility is to keep the operating system alive and well. SFC automatically verifies system files after a reboot to see whether they were changed to unprotected copies.

Logs

All operating systems collect information about events that have occurred that are stored in log files. There are typically log files for different components, such as a security log, an application log, or a system log. These file can be used to troubleshoot operating system issues, and events related to this are usually in the system log.

If the enterprise is large, you may want to have all the devices send their logs to a central server, where they can be stored and analyzed. In Windows, these logs can be viewed, filtered, and saved using a tool called Event Viewer. You'll look more closely at that tool later in this chapter.

In Linux, the following are some of the major log files and their locations:

- /var/log/messages: General and system related
- /var/log/auth.log: Authentication logs
- /var/log/kern.log: Kernel logs
- /var/log/cron.log: Crond logs (cron job)
- /var/log/maillog: Mail server logs
- /var/log/qmail/: Qmail log directory (with more files inside this directory)
- /var/log/httpd/: Apache access and error logs directory
- /var/log/lighttpd/: Lighttpd access and error logs directory
- /var/log/boot.log: System boot log
- /var/log/mysqld.log: MySQL database server log file
- /var/log/secure or /var/log/auth.log: Authentication log
- /var/log/utmp or /var/log/wtmp: Login records file
- /var/log/yum.log: yum command log file

Recovery Console

The Recovery Console isn't installed on a system by default. To install it, follow these steps:

1. Place the Windows disc in the system.

2. From a command prompt, change to the i386 directory of the CD.

3. Type **winnt32 /cmdcons**.

4. A prompt appears, alerting you to the fact that 7 MB of hard drive space is required and asking whether you want to continue. Click Yes.

Upon successful completion of the installation, the Recovery Console is added as a menu choice at the bottom of the startup menu. To access it, you must choose it from the list at startup. If more than one installation of Windows exists on the system, another boot menu will appear, asking which you want to boot into, and you must make a selection to continue.

To perform this task, you must give the administrator password. You'll then arrive at a command prompt. You can give a number of commands from this prompt, two of which are worth special attention: exit restarts the computer, and help lists the commands you can give.

For Windows Vista, Windows 7, and Windows 8, you must use the Windows Recovery Environment rather than the Recovery Console. See the section "Graphical Interface Fails to Load" for steps to access this tool.

Repair Discs

The Windows Backup and Restore tool allows you to create a system repair disc in Windows 7. As the name implies, this is a disc you can use to repair a portion of the system in the event of a failure. To create a system repair disc, follow these steps:

1. Open Backup and Restore by clicking the Start button, clicking Control Panel, clicking System And Maintenance, and then clicking Backup And Restore.

2. In the left pane, click Create A System Repair Disc, and then follow the steps. If you're prompted for an administrator password or confirmation, type the password or provide confirmation.

To use the system repair disc, follow these steps:

1. Insert the system repair disc into your CD or DVD drive.

2. Restart your computer using the computer's power button.

3. If prompted, press any key to start the computer from the system repair disc. (You might need to change your computer's BIOS settings to boot to the CD.)

4. Choose your language settings and then click Next.

5. Select a recovery option and then click Next.

Pre-installation Environments

Windows Preinstallation Environment (Windows PE) is a minimal operating system with limited services, built on the Windows Vista, Windows 7, or Windows 8 kernel. It is used to prepare a computer for Windows installation, to copy **disk** images from a network file server, and to initiate Windows Setup. It is also the environment in use when operating in the Windows Recovery Environment.

It can be used as a platform to repair issues with a system by booting to a disc with WinPE on it, somewhat like booting to a disc with DOS and system files on it. It includes much more functionality than a DOS boot disc but can be used in the same way to boot and access a drive with an operating system that will not boot.

MSCONFIG

The MSCONFIG utility helps you troubleshoot startup problems by allowing you to selectively disable individual items that normally are executed at startup. There is no menu command for this utility, so in Windows 8, for example, you use Start ➤ Run, type **msconfig**, and press Enter. It works in most versions of Windows, although the interface window is slightly different among versions. Figure 8.5 shows an example in Windows Vista.

FIGURE 8.5   MSCONFIG

DEFRAG

One of the biggest factors affecting hard drive performance over time is fragmentation. The more files are read, added to, and rewritten, the more fragmentation is likely to occur. The Disk Defragmenter utility (the defrag command) is the best tool for correcting fragmentation.

Disk Defragmenter reorganizes the file storage on a disk to reduce the number of files that are stored noncontiguously. This makes file retrieval faster because the read/write heads on the disk have to move less.

There are two versions of Disk Defragmenter: a command-line version and a Windows version that runs from within Windows. To locate and use the Windows version, follow these steps:

1. Swipe in from the right edge of the screen, tap Search (or if you're using a mouse, point to the upper-right corner of the screen, move the mouse pointer down, and then click Search), enter **Defragment** in the Search box, and then tap or click Defragment and optimize your drives.

2. Under Current Status, tap or click the drive you want to optimize, as shown in Figure 8.6.

3. To determine whether the drive needs to be optimized, tap or click Analyze. After Windows is finished, check the Current Status column to see whether you need to optimize the drive. If the drive is more than 10 percent fragmented, you should optimize the drive now.

4. Tap or click Optimize. Administrator permission is required.

FIGURE 8.6 Using Disk Defragmenter in Windows 8.1

If you are instead using the Windows 8.1 command-line version (defrag.exe), the available switches include the following:

/a Analyze only.

/c Perform the operation on all drives.

/v Verbose output.

REGSRV32

REGSRV32 (Microsoft Register Server) is a command-line utility in Windows operating systems for registering and unregistering DLLs and ActiveX controls in the Registry.

Many DLL files must be registered with the system to run. If you replace a missing DLL, you may need to also need to register the file. An example of registering a DLL looks like this:

```
regsvr32 shmedia.dll
```

REGEDIT

Windows configuration information is stored in a special configuration database known as the *registry*. This centralized database contains environmental settings for various Windows programs.

Windows Vista, Windows 7, Windows 8, and Windows 8.1 have two applications that can be used to edit the registry: REGEDIT and REGEDT32 (note the spelling with no *i*). In Windows XP and Vista, REGEDT32 opens REGEDIT. They work similarly, but each has slightly different options for navigation and browsing. In addition, REGEDT32 allows you to configure security-related settings for Registry keys, such as assigning permissions.

Registry edits are immediate and generate no warning message like you might get when making a change in Control Panel. Proceed with care because a mistake could render the system useless.

Event Viewer

During startup, problems with devices that fail to be recognized properly, services that fail to start, and so on, are written to the system log and can be viewed with Event Viewer. This utility provides information about what's been going on system-wise to help you troubleshoot problems. Event Viewer shows warnings, error messages, and records of things happening successfully. You can access it through Computer Management, or you can access it directly from the Administrative Tools in Control Panel.

Safe Mode

To access safe mode, you must press F8 when the operating system menu is displayed during the boot process. A menu of safe mode choices appears, and you can select the mode you want to boot into. This is the mode to boot into if you suspect driver problems and want to load with a minimal set while you diagnose the problem.

Command Prompt

You can find a complete discussion of the command prompt in objective 1.3 in Chapter 5.

Emergency Repair Disc

Emergency repair discs were discussed in the earlier section "Repair Discs."

Automated System Recovery

In Windows XP, the ERD has been replaced with Automated System Recovery (ASR), which is accessible through the Backup utility. It's possible to automate the process of creating a system recovery set by choosing the ASR Wizard on the Tools menu of the Backup utility (Start ➢ All Programs ➢ Accessories ➢ System Tools ➢ Backup). This wizard walks you through the process of creating a disc that can be used to restore parts of the system in the event of a major system failure.

The default name of this file is backup.bkf; it requires a floppy disk. The backup set contains all the files necessary for starting the system, whereas the floppy becomes a bootable pointer to that backup set and can access or decompress it.

A weakness of this tool is its reliance on a bootable floppy in a day when many new systems no longer include a 3.5-inch drive.

Uninstall/Reinstall/Repair

In some cases, the easiest way to repair an issue is to completely reinstall the operating system. This is one the biggest reasons you should encourage users to store data on servers rather than the workstation. However, operating system vendors are beginning to offer some options that are less drastic than that. They have also made it easier to perform various recovery types with no media.

For example, in Windows 8 and 8.1, there are several options presented when you choose to repair the computer. They are Refresh, Reset, and Restore. The effects of using the three options are as follows:

Refresh   This reinstalls Windows and keeps your personal files and settings. It also keeps the apps that came with your PC and the apps you installed from the Windows Store.

Reset   This reinstalls Windows but deletes your files, settings, and apps—except for the apps that came with your PC.

Restore   This is a way to undo recent system changes you've made by returning the system configuration to a previous point in time. It does not delete any files or applications, unless the application was installed after the restore point was taken.

To access these options, follow these steps:

1. Swipe in from the right edge of the screen, tap Settings, and then tap Change PC Settings. (If you're using a mouse, point to the upper-right corner of the screen, move the mouse pointer down, click Settings, and then click Change PC Settings.)

2. Tap or click Update And Recovery and then tap or click Recovery.

3. You will now see the three options shown in Figure 8.7.

FIGURE 8.7   Recovery

Exam Essentials

Identify the most common symptoms of operating system and system boot problems.   These include BSODs, boot failures, problems from improper shutdowns, spontaneous shutdowns/restarts, devices that fail to start, missing DLL messages, services failures, compatibility errors, slow system performance, files that fail to open, missing items (NTLDR, boot.ini, operating system, GUI), and invalid boot disk.

Describe the use of troubleshooting tools for operating system problems.   Among these tools are Recovery Console, sfc, preinstallation environments, msconfig, defrag, regsrv32, regedit, Event Viewer, safe mode, the command prompt, emergency repair discs, and Automated System Recovery.

4.2 Given a Scenario, Troubleshoot Common PC Security Issues with Appropriate Tools and Best Practices

System issues in many cases have security breaches at the root of the cause. It has become almost a given that any problem that cannot be traced to any other cause should be attacked by first scanning for viruses and malware. This section discusses common symptoms of security-related failures and tools that can be used to mitigate the damage. The topics addressed in objective 4.2 include the following:

- Common symptoms
- Tools
- Best practices for malware removal

Common Symptoms

Crazy things start to happen when malware is introduced to a computer. This section discusses some of the strange behaviors of computers that are infected.

Pop-Ups

Although relatively benign when compared with malware in general, pop-ups are annoying to users. They also use system resources as they open and in some cases can introduce additional malware when they open.

Fortunately, most browsers now contain pop-up blockers that can prevent unwanted pop-ups. In some cases, users want pop-ups to be allowed—in fact, some website functions fail when a pop-up blocker is enabled. For that reason, users can use the Pop-up Blocker Settings of Internet Explorer to allow pop-ups for certain websites, as shown in Figure 8.8. Other browsers usually have a similar setting.

FIGURE 8.8   Pop-up Blocker Settings dialog

Browser Redirection

A browser redirection is one of the most serious security problems. Browser hijacking software is external code that changes your Internet Explorer settings. It may include changing your home page or adding or removing items from your favorites. Some sites will be added that point to dubious content. In most cases, the home page will revert to the unwanted destination even if you change it manually because the hijacker made Registry changes to your system. To prevent this from occurring, remember these tips:

- Avoid suspect sites.
- Use and update an antivirus program regularly.
- Tighten your browser security settings.

Once you are a victim, you may have to apply antivirus software from an external source.

Security Alerts

Sometimes you can tell by security warnings that the site you are on is attempting to attack your computer. This is true if you have a personal firewall such as Windows Firewall. It can also occur when you have the phishing filter enabled in Internet Explorer. You will know when the system asks you whether you want to allow access to your machine from the site. Unless you initiated a download, don't allow it.

Slow Performance

A reduction in performance is one of the classic signs of malware infection. When no other reason can be isolated for the slowing of a system, scanning for malware is always recommended. All types of malware eat up significant system resources, starving the normal processes of the computer of the power they need.

Internet Connectivity Issues

Some malware will affect your Internet access. It may disallow you from accessing certain sites, or it may allow access to only a small number of sites. It has been reported that viral programs block access for certain programs and browsers while still allowing others to function. When access is denied, the following message is generated:

```
Unable to connect to HTTP Proxy. Your proxy may be misconfigured or
offline. -336
```

Moreover, this occurred even after the virus was supposedly cleaned from the system.

PC/OS Locks Up

It is quite common for the system to lock up when the malware is attacking. You may notice when this occurs that the hard drive is very busy, although nothing appears to be going on. In some cases, you can use Task Manager to end the process that is locking everything up, and in other cases you simply must shut down the computer to break out of the lockup.

Application Crashes

Another possible symptom of a malware infection is the crashing of applications. While this will occur from time to time for other reasons, when it is occurring repeatedly, you should suspect malware. When the application that is crashing is your antivirus software, this is an even stronger indication of malware because disabling or damaging your antivirus protection is the first thing that some types of malware attempt to do.

OS Updates Failures

Malware may take certain measures to protect itself. One of these is to block you from accessing operating system update sites like Windows Update. You never notice this because these updates can be set to run automatically, so when they fail, it may not be obvious that they did.

Another action the malware can take along the same lines is to disable your antivirus software. For this reason, any time your antivirus program notifies you that it is not functional or cannot update itself, you should consider this possibility and get it back up and running (if you can) as soon as possible.

Rogue Antivirus

If you receive messages (again usually at a suspect website) warning you that your system is infected, it will also usually offer to clean the system. At a minimum, they are trying to sell you anti-malware software through the bogus warning.

Worse, though, is that executing the "cleaning" sometimes results in the introduction of malware to the system—which was the whole point of the message to begin with. In general, pay no attention to these messages and try to close them and exit the website that generated them as quickly as possible.

Spam

A sudden increase in spam may indicate that adware has been installed on the machine. This type of malware monitors your activities so that it can more accurately target spam email. This is not particularly dangerous, but you have to wonder—if that malware got on your system, what *else* might lurk on your computer?

Renamed System Files

Many viruses will rename system files and adopt the name of the system file. This can help the virus escape detection when scanning occurs since most virus definitions identify the virus by the name of the file that introduced the virus. This renaming of the system file can cause big problems when the file is required and the virus file is incapable of providing the required functionality.

Files Disappearing

Another symptom of a viral infection is the deletion of files in the system. Many viruses delete key files in your system to render it inoperable. This could be one of the ways it renders any existing antivirus programs inoperable. It also can be part of disabling Internet access either completely or selectively.

File Permission Changes

If the malware is a rootkit or Trojan horse, it can change permissions to key files. The permissions would then allow access to remote systems. This can help to enhance the functionality of backdoors, which allow the computer to be controlled remotely.

Hijacked Email

Viruses can also make changes to the email client that sends a copy of all emails to another system. Depending on the content of email, this can make the user open to identity theft and can also be used in corporate espionage. It is especially harmful if the account is an IT administrator passing key enterprise security details through email.

The following are examples of evidence of email highjacking:

- Responses to email never sent by the user
- Automated replies from unknown people

Access Denied

This can be a symptom of the file permission changes discussed in Chapter 7. It can also be a message you get when you try to access the Internet in general or try to access specific sites such as those used for security updates and antivirus definitions.

Invalid Certificate (Trusted Root CA)

When you are bombarded with certificate error messages at every website you visit, it's another sign of malware. Some types of malware interface with the certificate authentication process.

Tools

Fortunately there are tools at your disposal to help you in the fight against malware of all types. This section discusses the major items in this toolbox.

Antivirus Software

The first line of defense against malware of all types is antivirus software kept up-to-date with the latest antivirus engine and definition files. Antivirus software is an application that is installed on a system to protect it and to scan for viruses as well as worms and Trojan horses. Most viruses have characteristics that are common to families of viruses. Antivirus software looks for these characteristics, or fingerprints, to identify and neutralize viruses before they impact you.

More than 200,000 known viruses, worms, bombs, and other malware have been defined. New ones are added all the time. Your antivirus software manufacturer will usually work hard to keep the definition database files current. The definition database file contains all the known viruses and countermeasures for a particular antivirus software product. You probably won't receive a virus that hasn't been seen by one of these companies. If you keep the virus definition database files in your software up-to-date, you probably won't be overly vulnerable to attacks.

Terminal utility

The terminal utility is the command prompt in any operating system we have discussed. Not only can this utility be used to do many things that could not be done using the GUI, it can be used to troubleshoot malware issues. In many cases you can locate malware files at the command prompt that cannot otherwise be located. You also can delete files that the antivirus can sometimes only quarantine.

Anti-malware Software

Since all types of harmful software discussed in this section are classified as malware, anti-malware software is any that identifies and protects your system from viruses, worms, Trojans, and spyware.

Recovery Console

The malware may not allow you to take steps such as deleting the programs while in the GUI. Oftentimes you can boot to the Recovery Console and delete the files you need to delete.

In many cases, you can identify the files in question by using Task Manager to view the processes that are running. However, identifying them and deleting them may be another matter. Using the Recovery Console, you may be able to do this once you know the names of the files or programs.

System Restore/Snapshot

The Recovery Console that existed in Windows 2000 and Windows XP has been removed from Vista and Windows 7. In its place is the System Recovery Options menu that appears on the installation disc. While renamed, it serves the same purpose of allowing you to troubleshoot startup problems or restore your system.

To access this feature, restart your system using the installation disc. At the language settings, choose your language and click Next. In the following menu, choose Repair Your Computer. Choose which operating system you are having a problem with (if more than one is installed) and click Next. The System Recovery Options menu will open, and you can then choose any tool from the menu and run it. Table 8.1 describes the tools available on the System Recovery Options menu. The most useful ones for removing malware are the command prompt and Windows Complete PC Restore. When you use this tool to make a backup of the entire PC, you can then re-create the entire computer without the virus.

The System Restore option allows you to take a snapshot of the system files and save that snapshot. Later, if the installation of an application or update causes a problem, you can return the computer system files to the state they were in prior to the installation.

TABLE 8.1   System Recovery Options menu

Tool	Purpose
Command Prompt	Offers access to the tools that were available in the Recovery Console
Startup Repair	Fixes problem with startup, such as missing operating system files
System Restore	Allows you to restore the system to a saved restore point
Windows Complete PC Restore (Vista) System Image Recovery (Windows 7)	Copies all the files from a backup and overwrites anything currently on the system
Windows Memory Diagnostic Tool	Checks the memory for errors

Pre-installation Environments

Pre-installation environments such as Windows PE were discussed in the "Given a Scenario, Troubleshoot Operating System Problems with Appropriate Tools" section. Just as you can use Windows PE to access the hard drive when a system won't boot, you can also use it to access and delete viral programs using the same identification and removal techniques discussed in that section.

Event Viewer

Many times a viral program is intelligent enough to prevent its activities from being recorded in Event Viewer, but it is still worth the effort to see whether there are events recorded that are related to its operation. You may be able to determine its name and what it's doing. Information you glean here could be helpful in identifying and removing the malware.

Refresh/Restore

Earlier in this section you learned about a system restore. In Windows 8 and 8.1, there is another option called Refresh. This option allows you to reinstall the operating system without removing any of your data. It is a good option when the system has been installed for a long time and is running slowly. While it does not remove the data, it will remove all applications with the exception of those that came with the system and those you got from the Windows Store.

MSCONFIG/Safe Boot

MSCONFIG can be used to boot the computer into modes that can be helpful during troubleshooting. For example, booting the device with only basic services may allow you to determine that a particular service or application is causing the problem you are experiencing. MSCONFIG was discussed in the section "1.4 Given a Scenario, Use Appropriate Microsoft Operating System Features and Tools" in Chapter 5.

Best Practices for Malware Removal

Over time best practices have been developed through trial and error that help minimize the chances of getting viruses and reduce the effort involved in getting rid of malware. Some of these practices are discussed in this section.

Identify Malware Symptoms

First identify the symptoms the malware is producing as clearly as you can. This can help identify the exact virus in some cases. In many scenarios, identifying the symptoms can help establish the severity of the infection, which is good to determine when IT resources are stretched thin and battles must be chosen.

Quarantine Infected System

The infected system should be quarantined—removed from the network to prevent a spread of the infection to other systems. This is why it is a good practice to keep data on servers so that when user systems need to be quarantined, a new machine can be quickly imaged for the user to reduce the impacts on productivity while the infected machine is cleaned.

Disable System Restore (in Windows)

System Restore is a useful tool in many cases, but when a virus infection occurs, it can be an ally of the virus. Virus scanners cannot clean infections from restore points, making reinfection possible. If a system restore is performed after running an antispyware utility, viral objects may reappear. Disable System Restore before attempting to clean a system. When you do this, you will delete all restore points in the system, including any that may have an infection.

Remediate Infected Systems

Once the infected system has been quarantined, you must take steps to clean it. This two-step process is discussed in this section.

Update Anti-malware Software

Before scanning the system with antivirus software, update the software and the engine if necessary. Definition files can change daily, and the virus may be so new that it is not contained in your current definitions file even if it is only a week old.

Scan and Removal Techniques (Safe Mode, Pre-installation Environment)

Although you can run the scan and removal from the GUI, it is a best practice to do this either after booting to safe mode or from a pre-installation environment like Windows PE. Viruses that evade detection in the GUI are not as easily able to do so in either of these environments.

Schedule Scans and Run Updates

The antivirus software can be scheduled to perform a scan of the system. You should set this up to occur when the system is not in use, like at night. The scanning process will go faster then and will not affect users. Also, set the software to automatically check for and install any updates to the definition files and to the engine when available.

Enable System Restore and Create Restore Point (in Windows)

Although it is recommended that you disable System Restore before cleaning an infection, it is a good idea to create a restore point after an infection is cleaned. This gives you a clean restore point going forward in case the system becomes infected again at some point.

Educate End User

In many cases, users are partly responsible for the virus infection. After an infection occurs is a great time to impress on users the principles of secure computing. They should be reminded that antivirus software and firewalls can go only so far in protecting them and that they should exercise safe browsing habits and refrain from opening any attachments in email from unknown sources, regardless of how tempting.

Exam Essentials

Identify the symptoms of malware infection.   Some of the symptoms are pop-ups, browser redirection, security alerts, slow performance, Internet connectivity issues, lockups, Windows Update failures, spam, renamed and disappearing system files, file permission changes, hijacked email, and access denied messages.

List the tools available to prevent and address virus infections.   Among the tools used for prevention and removal are antivirus, anti-malware, and antispyware software; Recovery Console; System Restore; pre-installation environments; and Event Viewer.

Implement best practices for malware removal.   According to best practices, the steps to address malware removal are

1. Identify malware symptoms.
2. Quarantine infected system.
3. Disable System Restore.
4. Remediate infected systems.
5. Update antivirus software.
6. Scan and remove the malware.
7. Enable System Restore and create a restore point.
8. Educate end users.

4.3 Given a Scenario, Troubleshoot Common Mobile OS and Application Issues with Appropriate Tools

Mobile devices have their own unique sets of issues that may not be encountered with desktop computers. In this section, I'll discuss common issues and their solutions. The topics addressed in objective 4.3 include the following:

- Common symptoms
- Tools

Common Symptoms

Not all mobile device issues are unique to mobile devices. They suffer from many of the same issues as desktop machines. However, some problems are unique to mobile devices or at least more prone to occur with them, as you will learn in this section.

Dim Display

With respect to laptops, the backlight and inverter can cause dimming problems, but in most cases the screen has been dimmed inadvertently with the function keys. It is also possible that the switch on the laptop that tells the system the lid is closed may be held down by some obstruction. Check that as well.

On smartphones you should first check the brightness settings to ensure they have not been inadvertently changed. Many Android devices force you to choose between manual settings of brightness and auto-brightness; you may have changed that to use manual settings. Apple's iOS allows you to adjust brightness levels on an iPhone even when auto-brightness is turned on. To recalibrate the setting, turn auto-brightness off in the Brightness & Wallpaper settings. Then go into an unlit room and drag the adjustment slider to make the screen as dim as possible.

Intermittent Wireless

Almost all mobile devices today include an internal wireless card. This is convenient, but it can be susceptible to interference (resulting in low signal strength) between the device and the access point or cell tower. Do what you can to reduce the number of items blocking the signal between the two devices, and you'll increase the strength of the signal. It is also possible that the cable that connects the antenna to the laptop needs to be reseated. Smartphones can connect to a WLAN as well. These devices will suffer from blockage and interference issues the same as laptops.

No Wireless Connectivity

When there is no wireless connectivity, it is usually because of one of two things:

- The wireless capability is disabled (enabling and disabling this function is usually done with a key combination or a function key) because this is easy to disable inadvertently. This can also be a hardware switch on the side, front, or back of the case.

- The wireless antenna is bad or the cable needs to be reseated.

Try the following steps when troubleshooting no wireless connectivity:

1. Power cycle the AP or wireless router.
2. Power cycle the device.
3. On a laptop, check the hardware wireless button (if the laptop has one).
4. On a smartphone or tablet, check your wireless settings to ensure that Wi-Fi is on. Also make sure that Airplane mode is off.
5. Disconnect and reconnect.
6. Verify that the wireless device is using the correct password.

No Bluetooth Connectivity

Bluetooth is also enabled and disabled with a key combination and can be disabled easily. The first thing to try is to reenable it. The second thing in a laptop to try is to reseat the antenna cable. If all else fails, try a new antenna. Like the WLAN NIC, this can also be a hardware switch on the side, front, or back of the case.

In smartphones and laptops, the problem also can occur after an upgrade or update of some sort. In these cases, it can be that the proper driver is missing from the upgrade or was somehow corrupted or overwritten during the upgrade process. Here are some additional things you might try on a smartphone:

1. Power cycle the device.
2. Remove the battery and put it back in.
3. Clear the Bluetooth cache. While each device is different, a common way to access this setting and clear the cache on Android is to open the phone's Settings, tap the More tab, tap Application Manager, select to view ALL, select Bluetooth Share, and tap Clear Cache.
4. Clear the Bluetooth data. While each device is different, a common way to access this setting and clear the data is to go to Settings, tap the More tab, tap Application Manager, select to view ALL, Bluetooth Share, and select Clear Data.
5. Reboot the device in safe mode.
6. Make sure the device to which you are pairing has no issues.
7. As a last resort, perform a hard reset (covered later in the section "Tools").

Cannot Broadcast to External Monitor

It's always possible that a hardware issue is causing an external monitor to not work when connected to a mobile device, but, again, in most cases the problem is an incomplete understanding of the key combination to use to send the output to the external monitor.

On some devices you need to use the Fn key in combination with the keys on the top row; on others you simply use the top-row keys. Before spending too much time troubleshooting, consult the documentation and ensure you are using the correct procedure. In some models, this can also be controlled from the video control panel or from within PowerPoint or other presentation software.

Another issue with both smartphones and laptops is a mismatch in screen resolution between the source device and the destination. Finally, check the port used to connect the device and ensure that it is functional and enabled.

Touchscreen Nonresponsive

In some cases, a touchscreen is simply broken and must be replaced, or in some cases the device must be replaced. In other cases, the issue is much less serious. If the screen still has the protective cover that comes on it, remove it. It can interfere with the operation of the screen. Make sure the screen is clean by cleaning it with a soft microfiber cloth. Ensure the user hands are dry because wet hands will cause an issue. Check these items first.

Then, before assuming the worst, try the following to solve the issue with laptops:

1. Perform a full shutdown of the device.
2. If it is a device that uses Windows, perform a Windows update. For other systems, check for an update at the vendor website.
3. Ensure that the system is set to consider your screen a touchscreen (laptop). This is a setting in Windows. Search for *tablet PC settings*.
4. Some devices support a touchscreen diagnostic test. Perform the test.
5. If the problem occurs after returning from sleep mode, check to see whether the screen is set to be functional while in sleep mode in power settings.

With smartphones, consider the following as well:

1. Reset the device. If your device does not have this function, remove the battery, memory card, or SIM card; then reinstall them.
2. Delete any applications you recently installed. Some third-party applications can cause your device to lock up or freeze.
3. Recalibrate the touchscreen. Look in the device's Settings menu for a calibration option.

Apps Not Loading

When an app will not load on a mobile device, the first item to check is that the app is the right version for the device. Not all apps work on all devices. When an app has been working and now won't open or load when you access it, try the following items:

- Check to see whether there is an update for the app.
- Force the app to quit. In Android, for example, in the multitask menu, swipe it away and then reopen it.

- If the issue involves downloading the app, check to make sure you have enough space for the app.

- If the app is resource intensive, ensure that your device has the resources to run the app.

Slow Performance

The first thing to suspect when performance slows is insufficient internal storage space. This begins to occur over time and will only get worse until the issue is solved by removing something to free up some space.

Another issue is apps that run all the time. Close these apps and clear the app cache. While you can do this manually, third-party apps are available that can do this for you on a schedule. The following are some other items you may try:

- If an update is available, update your firmware.

- Reset the phone (back up the data first!).

Unable to Decrypt Email

While there are services that can encrypt your email messages for you, many users choose to do this themselves using third-party tools. This allows more control but also requires an understanding of how it works and what the recipient needs to decrypt your email messages.

When a user receives an email that cannot be decrypted, check these items:

- Ensure that the sender and the recipient are using the same encryption standard. If one user is using S/MIME and another PGP, there will be a problem.

- Both users need to be in possession of the public key of the other user.

- Both users will need to have imported their respective private keys to their devices.

Considering the level of understanding that most users have of the way encryption works and its requirements, it is not surprising that services that handle all the keys are gaining in popularity.

Extremely Short Battery Life

One of the biggest complaints users lodge against their mobile devices is short battery life. When a battery is nearing the end of its life cycle, it will begin to exhibit this behavior, so it could be you need a new battery. However, there are a number of other things you can do to mitigate the problem.

- Change the location and brightness settings because these components really eat power.

- Turn off Bluetooth and Wi-Fi when not needed. These also take power.

- Disable push notifications for nonessential apps.

- Close apps not in use.

- Prevent the device from overheating, which is bad for the battery.

Overheating

Mobile devices get hot from time to time. An inherent problem is a lack of ventilation. The following are some activities that will worsen this:

- Excessive gaming
- Continuous online browsing
- Old battery
- Using the device while charging the device

Some tactics that can help prevent overheating are as follows:

- Disable any unwanted functions.
- Turn it off when not in use.
- Don't leave the device in places like a hot car.
- Clean the battery contacts.

Frozen System

Dealing with a frozen device takes a similar approach to dealing with a slow device. Try the following items:

- Plug the phone into a charger and see whether it unlocks.
- Delete any unused apps or photos.
- Delete the data cache.

No Sound from Speakers

When a speaker on a mobile device is not functioning, in most cases it has simply been inadvertently turned off. After checking the settings described later in this section, you can assume that there is a hardware problem. In that case, with smartphones, it is typically advisable to send the device to the manufacturer, but with laptops, it is possible to replace the internal speakers.

To determine whether the settings are the issue, ensure that the speaker volume is up and the speaker is not disabled. On an Android, first test the loud speaker by following these steps:

1. Go to the Home screen and tap the Phone icon.
2. Type *#7353# into the dialer as though you are dialing a phone number. A list of options will appear.
3. Tap Speaker, and music should start to play. You can tap Speaker again to silence the music.

To test the internal speaker, follow the same steps, but in step 3, tap Melody.

Music should start to play from the earpiece on the phone and allow you to see whether the speaker that you hold up to your ear to talk with people is working properly as well.

On an iPhone, follow these steps:

1. Go to Settings ➤ Sounds and drag the Ringer and Alerts slider to turn the volume up.

2. If you can hear sound from the speaker, then the speaker works.

3. If the device has a Ring/Silent switch, make sure it's set to ring. If you can see orange, it's set to silent.

Inaccurate Touchscreen Response

In cases where the touchscreen is working but not responding correctly, the action you should take depends on the vendor. With Apple devices, try the following, and if there is no relief, contact Apple so the warranty is not voided:

1. If you have a case or screen protector on your device, try removing it.

2. Clean the screen with a soft, slightly damp, lint-free cloth.

3. Unplug your device.

4. Restart your device. If you can't restart, force your device to restart.

With Android devices, first restart the phone. If that doesn't work, perform a factory reset using these steps:

1. Make a backup of personal data such as email and photos because the process will erase all your files.

2. Open the Applications tab and tap Settings.

3. Tap Privacy and then Factory Data Reset.

4. Tap Reset Phone.

On a laptop, this issue may be solved by recalibrating the screen. While systems vary, the steps using Windows 7 are as follows:

1. Click Start, Control Panel, and Hardware And Sound.

2. Under Tablet PC Settings, tap Calibrate The Screen For Pen Or Touch Input.

3. On the Display tab, under Display options, tap Calibrate and then Yes to allow the program to make changes.

4. Follow the onscreen instructions to calibrate your touchscreen.

System Lockout

When a user gets locked out of a device from typing too many incorrect passwords (or *patterns*) on Android phone, there are several things you can try before resetting the device (which will delete all the data). First try this:

1. Enter your email address in to the device.

2. In the password field, enter **null**.

3. If this works, you will then be prompted to enter a new pattern, and once again you have your phone back in action with all data intact.

If that fails, you will need to perform a factory reset, as described in the section "Inaccurate Touchscreen Response."

On an iPhone, you can go to iForgot to unlock it with your existing password or reset your password. You can also click the Reset Password or Forgot Password button in the alert. Type your full email address when you're asked to enter your Apple ID.

Tools

You can utilize a number of tools to solve these problems, many of them already referenced in the section covering the various issues. In this section, the options will be formally addressed.

Hard Reset

You can perform a hard reset to solve many but not all of the issues covered in the section "Common Symptoms." Each device will have a different way to perform this reset, but the key thing you need to know is that before you do this you should back up all data because it will be removed. This process returns the device to its factory defaults. On a laptop running Windows, this process is equivalent to resetting the operating system.

Soft Reset

A soft reset is a less drastic action you take with the mobile device. It is simply a matter of restarting the device. While the list of problems this action can solve is smaller than that for resetting, there were several problem listed in the section "Common Symptoms" that may react favorably to soft reset, and considering the consequences of using the hard reset, it is always advisable to try a soft reset first.

Close Running Applications

In some cases, mobile devices are running slowly simply because you are asking the device to do too many things at once. In this case, close some of the open applications on the device. In many cases, users may not even be aware that an app is running. Another issue that may respond to this approach is when the device is frozen. If the device is frozen because of a problem with an app, closing the app will break the lockup.

Reset to Factory Default

Resetting a mobile device to the factory defaults differs from a hard reset in one way. After a factor reset, you will be presented with the activation screen, and you will have to go through the activation process again. So, there is really nothing to be gained by using this process over a hard reset.

Adjust Configurations/Settings

As you found while reading the "Common Symptoms" section, in many cases all that needs to be done to a device is to adjust the settings. For specific setting changes that will solve specific issues, please refer to the section "Common Symptoms."

Uninstall/Reinstall Apps

Some apps just don't play well with a particular model or type of phone. In some cases, it is an issue with the application itself, and in others it is a compatibility issue you have discovered. Moreover, the problem app may not just malfunction; it may cause the device to lock up. In these situations, you can try uninstalling it and reinstalling it, and the app may fix itself. If that doesn't work, remove the app.

Force Stop

In some cases, when you stop an application on a mobile device, it does not stop completely. In other cases, it will not respond to attempting to stop it. If you go to the list of apps (Settings ➤ Applications ➤ Manage Applications ➤ Downloaded On ANDROID) on the device, the Force Stop setting is made available to you for each app that is running. Using this button provides you with an option to end a locked app.

Exam Essentials

Identify common symptoms of mobile device issues.   Some of the symptoms include a dim, flickering, or blank display; intermittent or nonexistent wireless or Bluetooth connectivity; battery and power issues; indicator lights; and an inability to use an external monitor.

Describe tools available to troubleshoot mobile device issues.   These tools include hard reset, soft reset, closing running applications, resetting to factory defaults, adjusting configurations/settings, uninstalling or reinstalling apps, and using a force stop.

4.4 Given a Scenario, Troubleshoot Common Mobile OS and Application Security Issues with Appropriate Tools

Mobile devices may use different operating systems than desktop systems, and their applications may be packaged a bit differently, but they still can suffer from security issues. It logically follows that they must be secured as well. In this final section of Chapter 8, I'll talk about the symptoms of security issues and describe some tools you can use in the struggle to protect these devices and their data. The following are the subobjectives covered in this section:

- Common symptoms
- Tools

Common Symptoms

Just as desktop systems do, mobile devices will exhibit certain symptoms when security issues manifest themselves. This section surveys some of the more common symptoms of a security issue with a device.

Signal Drop/Weak Signal

All mobile devices are going to experience some dropped calls and weak signals from time to time. However, a device that is fully charged and close to its cell tower or Wi-Fi access point that suffers these symptoms on a regular basis is probably infected with malware. You should scan the device using a malware product designed specifically for mobile devices.

Power Drain

Another sign of a malware infection on a mobile device is rapid draining of the battery. This occurs because the malware is performing operations in the background. If the device is also suffering signal loss, this only increases this possibility. If the device is also rapidly eating all the data in your plan, it is almost certain the device has malware.

Slow Data Speeds

When malware is present and running in the background, it is using resources as well as running down your battery. That's means when you are downloading or uploading data, the process is competing with the malware for resources. Therefore, slow data speeds may also be a sign of a malware infection.

Unintended Wi-Fi Connection

Some models of mobile devices such as smartphones will automatically connect to any available open WLAN (an open WLAN is one that does not require authentication). In most cases, users will be aware of this because they may be presented with a browser screen requiring the user to accept terms of service. Not all networks do this, however, and if you have connected to a rogue access point managed by a malicious individual, you can be almost certain your connection will be so seamless you may not know you are connected.

The danger in this is that after the access point issues your device an IP address, you will find yourself residing in the same subnet as the malicious hacker, and the hacker can now launch a peer-to-peer attack on your device. To prevent this, set the mobile device to *not* automatically connect to any available wireless network. For example, on an iPhone, use these steps:

1. Launch the Settings app.
2. Tap Wi-Fi.

3. Tap the blue arrow to the right of a network.

4. Switch the Auto-Join tab to OFF.

Unintended Bluetooth Pairing

Unintended Bluetooth connections or pairings can also occur with mobile devices. This is also a security issue because several wireless attacks are made through a Bluetooth connection. Many users leave their Bluetooth settings in a state that makes connections to their peripheral devices easier to make. However, leaving them in a discoverable state makes it also easier for malicious individuals to create a Bluetooth pairing with your mobile device that makes wireless attacks through the Bluetooth connection possible.

In spite of the fact it adds a step to the process of pairing a new device to the mobile device, users should make their mobile devices undiscoverable as a default setting and enable this setting only when they need to create a new pairing with a trusted device. Many new devices unfortunately (for example, iPhone 6) don't have a setting to turn off discovery without disabling Bluetooth entirely. While the logic behind this is that the iPhone automatically prevents access to personal data through the Bluetooth connection, on any devices that make turning off discovery possible, it should be done.

Having said all this, if a device that is supposedly secured makes an unintended Bluetooth connection, this could be a clue that the device has been compromised through either malware or social engineering.

Leaked Personal Files/Data

Obviously, if personal files located on a mobile device suddenly are gone or suddenly are found to be leaked, it is also a clue that the device has been compromised through either malware or social engineering.

Data Transmission Overlimit

When certain types of malware begin to operate on a mobile device, they may transmit data from the device to the hacker, or vice versa. Since this uses your data plan without your knowledge, you may suddenly find yourself over your data limit. You may not find this out until you receive a data bill that exceeds your mortgage payment. In any cases such as this, the device should be immediately scanned for malware.

Unauthorized Account Access

Another sign that a mobile device has been compromised is when changes are made to your account that can be made only by the account holder, such as adding a feature or disabling a security function. In some cases, the carrier will notify you of changes of this nature, in case you weren't the one to make the change.

Unauthorized Root Access

While mobile devices grant the owner control over all available settings on the device, they do not grant the owner total control over the device. Total control or root access allows the user to customize the device far beyond what the user could normally do. This is why many advanced users "root" their device so that they can attain this level of access. Consequently, if changes begin to appear on the device that could be made by a user with only root permissions, it is a sign the device has been compromised.

Unauthorized Location Tracking

Location tracking allows the device to determine your location for the purpose of tailoring search results. Location tracking can be disabled on a mobile device. In most cases, disabled location tracking is the default, and users will be asked by certain applications if they want to enable it. When a user has either never enabled this feature or has disabled this feature and it suddenly begins to track the location of the device, it is another indication that the device has been compromised.

Unauthorized Camera/Microphone Activation

Cameras and microphones can be either enabled or disabled on a mobile device. When a user either has never enabled these components or has disabled these components and the components begin to function, it is another indication that the device has been compromised.

High Resource Utilization

In any case where the device appears to be utilizing CPU and memory at a rate that is not consistent with the activities of the user, it is a sign that malware is possibly at work on the device. Malware will utilize resources in the process of performing whatever functions it has been deigned to perform. When unexplained excessive resource usage is going on, it is another indication that the device has been compromised.

Tools

While the issues with mobile devices may seem innumerable, you do have tools to help you address them. In this section, I'll talk about tools that can address the symptoms discussed in the section "Common Symptoms."

Anti-malware

As with any computing device, mobile devices should be protected with anti-malware software. All the major antivirus and anti-malware vendors create versions of their product for smartphones and tablets. You should ensure that this is the case and that the devices are all updated with the latest malware and engine updates. This will be made simpler if the enterprise invests in a mobile device management solution that can scan the devices and ensure that all anti-malware is up-to-date.

App Scanner

While apps are what bring functionality to a mobile device, some apps come with security flaws of which not only the user may be unaware but the developer of the app may be unaware. An app scanner is one that scans your apps for flaws and reports them. An example of an app scanner for Android is Appvigil, but there are scanners for Apple devices as well.

Factory Reset/Clean Install

Several of the issues discussed in the section "Common Symptoms" had as a possible solution performing a factory reset or a clean install. Both approaches are drastic in that they delete all the data and settings on the device but are sometimes unavoidable. You should understand the consequences before you use this approach.

Uninstall/Reinstall Apps

Just as with desktop and laptop systems, sometimes the only way to get an app to function correctly is to uninstall the app and reinstall it. When the app doesn't respond to other solutions, this is a good approach to take.

Wi-Fi Analyzer

Mobile devices operate almost exclusively as wireless devices. For this reason, network issues with mobile devices typically end up in many cases being wireless issues. A Wi-Fi analyzer is a tool that can be used to scan and troubleshoot a WLAN. While these products can vary in the features they provide and (naturally) in cost, the following are among the functions that can be performed with these tools:

- Determine current performance
- Isolate and troubleshoot security issues
- Identify rogue wireless devices
- Determine sources of interference

Force Stop

A force stop can be used to terminate an application that is either locked up or simply won't close. For more information, see "Force Stop" for objective 4.3 in this chapter.

Cell Tower Analyzer

While a wireless analyzer will tell you information such as the SSIDs of other WLANs in the area, the channel being used, and the signal strength, a cell tower analyzer gives you information such as the following:

- Available towers from a location
- Signal strengths
- Tower to which you are currently connected
- Tower owner information (Verizon, Sprint, and so on)

Backup/Restore

If you are ever faced with an issue for which the only solution is to reinstall the operating system or to reset the device to the factor defaults, all settings and data will be removed.

Therefore, it makes good sense to back up the settings and data on the device in case you need to restore this information after a factory reset.

Some device vendors such as Google make this easy by offering to do it automatically for you on a schedule. In an enterprise, this is another function you may be able to automate using enterprise mobility management software (which is another reason to invest in this software). In this section, I'll cover some solutions.

iTunes/iCloud/Apple Configurator

In the Apple ecosystem, several tools are available to hold your backed-up data and settings. iTunes can maintain all your music so that if you do a reset, the device will sync with iTunes and make your music available on the new or reset device.

iCloud provides its users with the means to store data such as documents, photos, and music on remote servers for download to iOS, Macintosh, or Windows devices. This is another option for storing your data and settings. An additional feature it provides is the ability to locate a lost phone. Currently Apple users get 5 GB of free storage and can purchase additional storage.

The Apple Configurator is an app that can be used to mass-configure iOS devices. It is an example of an enterprise mobility management solution that provides remote management to help set up and maintain standard configurations and software across a number of devices.

Google Sync

Google Sync allows you to synchronize mail, contacts, calendar, and more across multiple devices. It is available to anyone with a Google account and an Android or Chrome device.

One Drive

One Drive is a cloud-based storage service by Microsoft that operates somewhat like iCloud. Users can store data in this cloud solution. This feature is also available as an app on Google Play and Apple iTunes.

Exam Essentials

Describe common mobile device issues.   Some of the symptoms include signal drop/weak signal, power drain, slow data speeds, unintended Wi-Fi connections, and leaked personal files/data.

Describe tools available to troubleshoot mobile devices.   These tools include performing a hard reset, performing a soft reset, closing running applications, resetting to factory defaults, adjusting configurations/settings, uninstalling or reinstalling apps, and using force stop.

Review Questions

You can find the answers in the Appendix.

1. Which operating system may experience a BSOD?

   A. Linux

   B. Unix

   C. Mac

   D. Windows

2. What is the proprietary crash screen called in Mac?

   A. pin wheel or beach ball

   B. blue screen of death

   C. red dawn screen

   D. black death

3. Which Windows 7 log file is a chronological list of what took place during the setup?

   A. setuperr.log

   B. setupact.log

   C. netsetup.log

   D. chrono.log

4. Which type of file can NOT be copied from another machine if missing or corrupted?

   A. .dll

   B. boot.ini

   C. ntldr

   D. bootmgr

5. Which tool can be used to determine if a process is using too much memory or CPU or is simply locked up?

   A. event viewer

   B. task manager

   C. computer management

   D. safe mode

6. Which of the following is NOT a possible cause of a "no operating system found" message?

   A. Nonsystem disk in the floppy drive

   B. Incorrect boot device order in the BIOS

   C. Corrupted or missing boot sector

   D. System disk in the DVD drive

7. Which of the following commands is not used to repair the BDC?

   A. Bootrec /fixmbr

   B. Bootrec /fixbcd

   C. Bootrec /fixboot

   D. Bootrec /rebuildbcd

8. What is the bootloader package in Linux?

   A. grub

   B. strap

   C. GILO

   D. boot

9. Which utility helps you troubleshoot startup problems by allowing you to selectively disable individual items that normally are executed at startup?

   A. ipconfig

   B. msconfig

   C. netconfig

   D. bootconfig

10. Which of the flowing is a command-line utility in Windows operating systems for registering and unregistering DLLs?

   A. regedit

   B. regedt32

   C. regsrv32

   D. regsrv

Chapter
9

Operational Procedures

COMPTIA A+ 220-902 EXAM OBJECTIVES COVERED IN THIS CHAPTER:

✓ **5.1 Given a scenario, use appropriate safety procedures.**

- Equipment grounding

- Proper component handling and storage (antistatic bags, ESD straps, ESD mats, self-grounding)

- Toxic waste handling (batteries, toner, CRT)

- Personal safety (disconnect power before repairing PC, remove jewelry, lifting techniques, weight limitations, electrical fire safety, cable management, safety goggles, air filter mask)

- Compliance with local government regulations

✓ **5.2 Given a scenario with potential environmental impacts, apply the appropriate controls.**

- MSDS documentation for handling and disposal

- Temperature, humidity-level awareness, and proper ventilation

- Power surges, brownouts, blackouts (battery backup, surge suppressor)

- Protection from airborne particles (enclosures, air filters/mask)

- Dust and debris (compressed air, vacuums)

- Compliance to local government regulations

✓ **5.3 Summarize the process of addressing prohibited content/activity and explain privacy, licensing, and policy concepts.**

- Incident response (first response, use of documentation/documentation changes, chain of custody)

- Licensing/DRM/EULA (open source vs. commercial license, personal license vs. enterprise licenses)

- Personally identifiable information
- Follow corporate end-user policies and security best practices

✓ 5.4 Demonstrate proper communication techniques and professionalism.

- Use proper language—avoid jargon, acronyms, slang when applicable
- Maintain a positive attitude/project confidence
- Actively listen (taking notes) and avoid interrupting the customer
- Be culturally sensitive (use appropriate professional titles, when applicable)
- Be on time (if late, contact the customer)
- Avoid distractions (personal calls, texting/social media sites, talking to co-workers while interacting with customers, personal interruptions)
- Dealing with difficult customer or situation (do not argue with customers and/or be defensive, avoid dismissing customer's problems, avoid being judgmental, clarify customer statements [ask open-ended questions to narrow the scope of the problem, restate the issue, or question to verify understanding], do not disclose experiences via social media outlets)
- Set and meet expectations/timeline and communicate status with the customer (offer different repair/replacement options if applicable, provide proper documentation on the services provided, follow up with customer/user at a later date to verify satisfaction)
- Deal appropriately with customers' confidential and private materials (located on a computer, desktop, printer, etc.)

✓ 5.5 Given a scenario, explain the troubleshooting theory.

- Always consider corporate policies, procedures, and impacts before implementing changes (identify the problem, establish a theory of probable cause, test the theory to determine cause [question the obvious], establish a plan of action to resolve the problem and implement the solution, verify full system functionality and if applicable implement preventive measures, document findings, actions, and outcomes)

If you looked back over the history of the A+ certification, you would be hard-pressed to find any domain or topics that have changed as much as this one. Much of what is here is common sense, but don't dismiss the chapter based on that. Since these topics are worth 13 percent of the weighting, doing well on this portion of the exam can increase your chances of acing the 220-902 exam.

5.1 Given a Scenario, Use Appropriate Safety Procedures

This objective deals with potential hazards, both to you and to the computer system. It focuses on protecting humans from harm due to electricity and on protecting computer components from harm due to electrostatic discharge. The subobjectives included in this section are as follows:

- Equipment grounding
- Proper component handling and storage
- Toxic waste handling
- Personal safety
- Compliance with local government regulations

Equipment Grounding

Electrostatic discharge is one of the most dangerous risks associated with working with computers. Not only does ESD have the potential to damage components of the computer, but it can also injure you. Not understanding the proper way to avoid it could cause you great harm.

The ESD that we are speaking about here does not have the capability to kill you since it doesn't have the amperage. What does represent a threat, though, is using a wrist strap of your own design that does not have the resistor protection built into it and then accidentally touching something with high voltage while wearing the wrist strap. Without the resistor in place, the high voltage would be grounded through you!

Electrostatic discharge (ESD) is the technical term for what happens whenever two objects of dissimilar charge come in contact—think of rubbing your feet on a carpet and then touching a light switch. The two objects exchange electrons in order to equalize the electrostatic charge between them. If the device receiving the charge happens to be an electronic component, there is a good chance it can be damaged.

The likelihood that a component will be damaged increases with the use of complementary metal-oxide semiconductor (CMOS) chips because these chips contain a thin metal oxide layer that is hypersensitive to ESD. The previous generation's transistor–transistor logic (TTL) chips are more robust than the CMOS chips because they don't contain this metal-oxide layer. Most of today's integrated circuits (ICs) are CMOS chips, so ESD is more of a concern lately.

The lowest static voltage transfer that you can feel is around 3,000 volts (it doesn't electrocute you because there is extremely little current). A static transfer that you can *see* is at least 10,000 volts! Just by sitting in a chair, you can generate around 100 volts of static electricity. Walking around wearing synthetic materials can generate around 1,000 volts. You can easily generate around 20,000 volts simply by dragging your smooth-soled shoes across a carpet in the winter. (Actually, it doesn't have to be winter to run this danger; it can occur in any room with very low humidity. It's just that heated rooms in wintertime generally have very low humidity.)

It would make sense that these thousands of volts would damage computer components. However, a component can be damaged with as little as 80 volts. That means if your body has a small charge built up in it, you could damage a component without even realizing it.

Just as you can ground yourself by using a grounding strap, you can ground equipment. This is most often accomplished by using a mat or a connection directly to a ground.

Proper Component Handling and Storage

When handling computer components, such as motherboards, network cards, and such, it is easy to damage the delicate circuitry with the static electricity that builds up in your body in certain environments. In this section, we'll talk about how you can protect these components and how you should store these components when not in use.

Antistatic Bags

When working with components and when storing them, it is a good idea to store them in antistatic bags. Although you can buy these bags, replacement parts usually come in antistatic bags, and if you keep these bags, you can use them later. These bags also can serve as a safe place to lay a component temporarily when working on a device.

ESD Straps

There are measures you can implement to help contain the effects of ESD. The easiest one to implement is the *antistatic wrist strap*, also referred to as an *ESD strap*. You attach one end of the ESD strap to an earth ground (typically the ground pin on an extension cord) and wrap the other end around your wrist. This strap grounds your body and keeps it at a zero charge. Figure 9.1 shows the proper way to attach an antistatic strap.

FIGURE 9.1 Proper ESD strap connection

Pin connects to ground pin
(small round hole) or
earth ground

ESD strap

Outlet

If you do not have a grounded outlet available, you can achieve partial benefit simply by attaching the strap to the metal frame of the PC case. Doing so keeps the charge equalized between your body and the case so that there is no electrostatic discharge when you touch components inside the case.

> **WARNING** An ESD strap is a specially designed device to bleed electrical charges away *safely*. It uses a 1 megaohm resistor to bleed the charge away slowly. A simple wire wrapped around your wrist will not work correctly and could electrocute you!

> **WARNING** Do not wear the antistatic wrist strap when there is the potential to encounter a high-voltage capacitor, such as when working on the inside of a monitor or power supply. The strap could channel that voltage through your body.

ESD Mats

It is possible to damage a device simply by laying it on a bench top. For this reason, you should have an *ESD mat* (also known as an *antistatic mat*) in addition to an ESD strap. This mat drains excess charge away from any item coming in contact with it (see Figure 9.2). ESD mats are also sold as mouse/keyboard pads to prevent ESD charges from interfering with the operation of the computer.

FIGURE 9.2 Proper use of an ESD mat

Component being worked on

Connect mat to ground pin
(small round hole) or earth ground

ESD mat

Outlet

You can also purchase ESD floor mats for technicians to stand on while performing computer maintenance. These include a grounding cord, usually 6 to 10 feet in length.

Vendors have methods of protecting components in transit from manufacture to installation. They press the pins of ICs into antistatic foam to keep all the pins at the same potential, and circuit boards are shipped in antistatic bags, discussed later. However, keep in mind that unlike antistatic mats, antistatic bags do not drain the charges away—they should never be used in place of antistatic mats.

Self-grounding

Grounding is the electrical term for providing a path for an electrical charge to follow to return to earth. This term was mentioned earlier as it relates to ESD straps and mats, but it is the element of those that saves you from harm in the event of an electrical discharge—the charge passes to ground. The easiest way to ground yourself is to use a grounding strap.

Toxic Waste Handling

Many of the components that are in a computer should not be simply thrown in the trash because they contain toxic materials. In this section, you'll learn about proper handling and disposal of these components and materials.

Batteries

Batteries can contain a number of compounds and materials that should not make their way into landfills. The following are some examples:

- Rare earth metals
- Lead
- Cadmium
- Lithium
- Alkaline manganese
- Mercury

You should make battery recycling a standard procedure and follow local regulations for battery disposal when the time comes to dispose of the batteries.

Toner

Toner cartridges are another item that should not be thrown away. They should be recycled. Moreover, in any case where toner has been spilled you should clean up with a special vacuum made for that purpose. If you use a regular vacuum, the metal toner will damage the vacuum.

CRT

While most CRT monitors have been disposed of already, you may find yourself with a number of them that you need to get rid of. These cannot be thrown in the trash. The contents of the device are under pressure, and if something breaks the glass screen, there will glass and other materials sprayed out with a force that could injure someone.

The monitor uses a lot of power as it directs electrons on the screen via a strong magnet. The electrons and magnet require a considerable amount of voltage to be able to do their task. Like power supplies, monitors have the ability to hold their charge a long time after the power has been disconnected.

You should never open a power supply or a monitor for the reasons discussed here. The risk of electrocution with these two devices is significant.

If you question the presence of electricity, or the voltage of it, use a voltmeter. Figure 9.3 shows a simple voltmeter capable of working with both AC and DC currents.

FIGURE 9.3   A simple voltmeter

Many states have laws that govern the disposal of monitors since they are often classified as hazardous. CRT monitors contain high amounts of lead and other harmful materials such as arsenic, beryllium, cadmium, chromium, mercury, nickel, and zinc. To dispose of a monitor, contact a computer recycling firm and let them get rid of the monitor for you. CRT monitors must be disposed of according to the environmental regulations.

Personal Safety

There is nothing on a computer, a server, a router, and so on, that cannot be replaced or repaired. The same, however, is not true for you. It is imperative that you protect yourself from harm and follow safety procedures when working with computers.

Disconnect Power Before Repairing PC

You should never attempt to remove a case, open a case, or work on any element that is carrying electricity without first disconnecting it. If removing power on the device you are working on is more complicated than just unplugging it (requiring circuit breakers to be thrown, fuses to be removed, and so forth), then use a voltmeter to make sure the current is off at the device before proceeding.

Remove Jewelry

Gold and other metals are great conductors of electrical current. The last thing you want while working on a problem is for the gold chain around your neck to fall against a capacitor. Take it off. While not all jewelry is metallic, all jewelry is a snagging hazard.

Lifting Techniques

An easy way to get hurt is by moving equipment in an unsafe or improper way. Here are some safe lifting techniques to always keep in mind:

- Lift with your legs, not your back. When you have to pick something up, bend at the knees, not at the waist. You want to maintain the natural curve of the back and spine when lifting.
- Be careful to not twist when lifting. Keep the weight on your centerline.
- Keep objects as close to your body as possible and at waist level.
- Where possible, push instead of pull.

The goal in lifting should be to reduce the strain on lower back muscles as much as possible since muscles in the lower back aren't nearly as strong as those in the legs or other parts of the body. Some people use a back belt or brace to help maintain the proper position while lifting.

Weight Limitations

Closely related to lifting and moving equipment is the topic of weight limitations. If you believe the load is too much for you to carry, don't try to pick it up. Get help!

When possible, use a cart and always be aware of the environment. While you may be able to carry 80 pounds on a level surface without trouble, that number will lessen if there are stairs, uneven floors, or narrow doorways. Map out the path you are going to take before you begin lifting and moving items.

Electrical Fire Safety

Repairing a computer is not often the cause of an electrical fire. However, you should know how to extinguish such a fire properly. Three major classes of fire extinguishers are available, one for each type of flammable substance: A for wood and paper fires, B for flammable liquids, and C for electrical fires. The most popular type of fire extinguisher today is the multipurpose, or ABC-rated, extinguisher. It contains a dry chemical powder that smothers the fire and cools it at the same time. For electrical fires (which may be related to a shorted-out wire in a power supply), make sure the fire extinguisher will work for class C fires. If you don't have an extinguisher that is specifically rated for electrical fires (type C), you can use an ABC-rated extinguisher.

Cable Management

It can be time-consuming to tie up cables, run them in channels, and snake them through walls, but it is time well spent when it keeps one person from harm. It is all too easy to get tangled in a cable or trip over one that is run across the floor. Exposed cables should be routed properly and covered using cable-throughs and pass-throughs to reduce the likelihood of tripping as well as damage to the cables themselves.

Take the extra time to manage cables, and it will increase your safety as well as that of others who work in that environment.

Safety Goggles

In any environment where you may get dust or harmful materials in your eyes, you should wear safety goggles. For example, when working in a dusty shop area where a computer is located, this might be advisable. Another example might be when you are cleaning up printer toner.

There are also safety glasses that can be used when spending long hours staring at a computer screen that will reduce the eye strain that comes with this type of activity.

Air Filter Mask

While safety goggles will protect your eyes from dust and other harmful particulates, they will do nothing to protect your lungs. Air filter masks should always be available, and technicians should be encouraged to wear them in any situation where safety goggles are called for or in any scenario where you have reason to believe that the surrounding air may contain harmful compounds.

Compliance with Local Government Regulations

It is your responsibility, as an administrator and a professional, to know (or learn) the regulations that exist for dealing with safety. You should know them from the local level to the federal level and be familiar with the reporting procedures for incidents you are faced with.

If employees are injured, for example, you may need to contact the Occupational Safety and Health Administration (OSHA). On their website (www.osha.gov), you can find links to information on issues of compliance, laws and regulation, and enforcement.

When it comes to disposal, you can find a list of state laws here:

www.electronicsrecycling.org/public/ContentPage.aspx?pageid=14

The Environmental Protection Agency (EPA) offers basic information here:

www.epa.gov/osw/conserve/materials/ecycling/index.htm

Exam Essentials

Understand ESD.   Electrostatic discharge occurs when two objects of unequal electrical potential meet. One object transfers some charge to the other one, just as water flows into an area that has a lower water level.

Understand the antistatic wrist strap.   The antistatic wrist strap is also referred to as an ESD strap. To use the ESD strap, you attach one end to an earth ground (typically the ground pin on an extension cord) and wrap the other end around your wrist. This strap grounds your body and keeps it at a zero charge, preventing discharges from damaging the components of a PC.

Know the fire extinguisher types.   Class C is the type of fire extinguisher needed for electrical fires.

Know that you may need to report incidents.   When incidents happen, you must always document them, and every attempt should be made to do so both fully and truthfully. Depending upon the type of incident, you may also need to report it to other authorities, such as OSHA.

5.2 Given a Scenario with Potential Environmental Impacts, Apply the Appropriate Controls

Environmental harms can come from many sources. Not only are temperature and humidity elements that must be controlled, but administrators need to also carefully monitor power, air, and particulates that can harm humans and computers. Not understanding environmental impact and controls can cause great harm. The following are the subobjectives covered in this section:

- MSDS documentation for handling and disposal
- Temperature, humidity-level awareness, and proper ventilation
- Power surges, brownouts, blackouts
- Protection from airborne particles
- Dust and debris
- Compliance to local government regulations

MSDS Documentation for Handling and Disposal

It is important that you know the potential safety hazards that exist when working with computer elements and how to address them. It is imperative that you understand such issues as *material safety data sheets (MSDSs)* and know how to reference them when needed. Any type of chemical, equipment, or supply that has the potential to harm the environment or people has to have an MSDS associated with it. These are traditionally created by the manufacturer, and you can obtain them from the manufacturer or from the Environmental Protection Agency at www.epa.gov.

These sheets are not intended for consumer use but are aimed at emergency workers and employees who are exposed to the risks of the particular product. Among the information they include are such things as boiling point, melting point, flash point, and potential health risks. They also cover storage and disposal recommendations and the procedures to follow in the case of a spill or leak.

Temperature, Humidity-Level Awareness, and Proper Ventilation

Three items closely related to an environmentally friendly computing environment are temperature, humidity, and ventilation. We will cover the most important elements with all three.

Temperature Heat and computers don't mix well. Many computer systems require both temperature and humidity control for reliable service. The larger servers, communications equipment, and drive arrays generate considerable amounts of heat; this is especially true of mainframe and older minicomputers. An environmental system for this type of equipment is a significant expense beyond the actual computer system costs. Fortunately, newer systems operate in a wider temperature range. Most new systems are designed to operate in an office environment.

If the computer systems you're responsible for require special environmental considerations, you'll need to establish cooling and humidity control. Ideally, systems are located in the middle of the building, and they're ducted separately from the rest of the heating, ventilation, and air conditioning (HVAC) system. It's a common practice for modern buildings to use a zone-based air conditioning environment, which allows the environmental plant to be turned off when the building isn't occupied. A computer room will typically require full-time environmental control.

Humidity Level Another preventive measure you can take is to maintain the relative humidity at around 50 percent. Be careful not to increase the humidity too far—to the point where moisture starts to condense on the equipment! It is a balancing act keeping humidity at the right level since low humidity causes ESD and high humidity causes moisture condensation. Both extremes are bad but have completely different effects.

Also, use antistatic spray, which is available commercially, to reduce static buildup on clothing and carpets. In a pinch, a solution of diluted fabric softener sprayed on these items will do the same thing.

At the least, you can be mindful of the dangers of ESD and take steps to reduce its effects. Beyond that, you should educate yourself about those effects so you know when ESD is becoming a major problem.

Ventilation Rounding out temperature and humidity is ventilation. It is important that air—clean air—circulate around computer equipment to keep it cool and functioning properly. Server rooms require much more attention to ventilation than office spaces but are the subject of other exams (Server+, for example) and not test fodder for A+.

What is test fodder is the topic of ventilation within the computer itself—an inadequate flow of internal air within a computer is a common cause of overheating. To prevent this, know that all slot covers should remain in place and be replaced if a card is removed from the system. Know as well that internal fans should be periodically cleaned to ensure proper air flow. A missing slot cover or malfunctioning fan can lead to that inadequate flow of internal air.

Power Surges, Brownouts, Blackouts

A number of power-related threats can harm computers. Among them are the following:

Blackout   This is a complete failure of the power supplied.

Brownout   This is a drop in voltage lasting more than a few minutes.

Sag   This is a short-term voltage drop.

Spike   The opposite of a sag, this is a short (typically under 1 second) increase in voltage that can do irreparable damage to equipment.

Surge   This is a long spike (sometimes lasting many seconds). Though a surge is typically a less intense increase in power, it can also damage equipment.

The two solutions to know for the power issues on the exam are battery backups and surge suppressors.

Battery Backup

A battery backup, or *uninterruptible power supply (UPS)*, keeps the system up and running when the normal power is removed (because of blackout, brownout, and so on). Even in installations that use generators to keep the systems running, battery backups are usually still used so they can keep the machines running while the generators come up to speed.

Most UPS units come with software that can be used to configure the actions to take when the battery backup is active. The software, for example, can be configured to shut the connected devices down when the battery begins to get low.

Surge Suppressor

A surge suppressor keeps a spike from passing through it and onto the equipment that could be damaged. *Tripping* occurs when the breaker on a device such as a power supply, surge protector, or UPS turns off the device because it received a spike. If the device is a UPS, when the tripping happens, the components plugged in to the UPS should go to battery instead of pulling power through the line. Under most circumstances, the breaker is reset, and operations continue as normal. Figure 9.4 shows a surge-protector power strip, with the trip button to reset at the top.

FIGURE 9.4   The reset button on the top of a surge-protector power strip

Nuisance tripping is the phrase used if tripping occurs often and isn't a result of a serious condition. If this continues, you should isolate the cause and correct it, even if it means replacing the device that continues to trip.

Surge suppressors (also known as *surge protectors)*, either stand-alone or built into the UPS, can help reduce the number of nuisance trips. If your UPS doesn't have a surge protector, you should add one to the outlet before the UPS in order to keep the UPS from being damaged if it receives a strong surge. Figure 9.5 shows an example of a simple surge protector for a home computer.

FIGURE 9.5   A simple surge protector

All units are rated by Underwriters Laboratories (UL) for performance. One thing you should never do is plug a UPS or computer equipment into a ground fault circuit interrupter (GFCI) receptacle. These receptacles are intended for use in wet areas, and they trip very easily.

WARNING   Don't confuse a GFCI receptacle with an isolated ground receptacle. Isolated ground receptacles are identifiable by orange outlets and should be used for computer equipment to avoid their picking up a surge passed to the ground by any other device.

Protection from Airborne Particles

Computers don't do well with airborne particles. To protect them from such, you can use *enclosures* for your sensitive equipment and *air filters* to condition the air.

Enclosures

Enclosures can be considered the first line of defense against particulates. Enclosures are available that can filter the air, keep air out, and so on. Make certain that the enclosure you turn to for a solution still offers the necessary ventilation needed to prevent overheating.

Air Filters

Most enclosures incorporate an air filter to clean the air before allowing it to enter. An analogy to think of is the air filter on a car, which keeps dirt, dust, bugs, and other things from the intake. When working with air filters, make certain they are kept clean and are changed per the manufacturer's requirements.

Dust and Debris

One of the most harmful atmospheric hazards to a computer is dust. Dust, dirt, hair, and other airborne contaminants can get pulled into computers and build up inside. Because computer fans work by pulling air through the computer (usually sucking it in through the case and then pushing it out the power supply), it's easy for these items to enter and then become stuck. Every item in the computer builds up heat, and these particles are no exception. As they build up, they hinder the fan's ability to perform its function, and the components get hotter than they would otherwise. Figure 9.6 shows the inside of a system in use for only six months in an area with carpeting and other dusty surroundings.

FIGURE 9.6   Dust builds up inside the system

Compressed Air

You can remove dust and debris from inside computers with *compressed air* blown in short bursts. The short bursts are useful in preventing the dust from flying too far out and entering another machine, as well as in preventing the can from releasing the air in liquid form. Compressed air cans should be held 2–3 inches from the system and always used upright so the content is released as a gas. If the can becomes cold to the touch, discontinue using it until it heats back to room temperature.

It's possible to use an air compressor instead of compressed-air cans when you need a lot of air. If you take this approach, make sure you keep the pounds per square inch (PSI) at or below 40, and include measures on the air compressor to remove moisture.

Vacuums

Dust can build up not just within the computer but also in crevices on the outside. Figure 9.7 shows USB ports on the back of a system that have become a haven for small dust particles. These ports need to be blown out with compressed air, or cleaned with an electronic *vacuum*, before being used, or degradation with the device connected to them could occur.

FIGURE 9.7   Dust collects in unused ports as well

Compliance to Local Government Regulations

As careful as you try to be, there is always the possibility for accidents to occur. Accidents can be environment-related (for example, a flash flood no one could predict suddenly overtakes the server room and shorts out the wiring) or caused by humans (someone mixes the wrong cleaning chemicals together to try to make their own concoction). Regardless of the cause or circumstances, one thing is written in stone: you must fully and truthfully document the problem.

That documentation must be seen by internal parties (managers, human resources, and so on), and it may also need to be seen by external parties. The latter depends on the type of industry you are in and the type of incident that occurred. For example, if a large amount of battery acid is spilled on the ground, you should contact the Environmental Protection Agency (see reporting procedures at www.epa.gov).

Exam Essentials

Know what an MSDS is.   An MSDS is a material safety data sheet containing instructions for handling an item. It can be acquired from the manufacturer or from the EPA.

Know that you may need to report incidents.   When incidents happen, you must always document them, and every attempt should be made to do so both fully and truthfully. Depending on the type of incident, you may also need to report it to other authorities, such as the EPA.

Know what components are not suitable for a landfill.   Batteries, CRTs, and circuit boards are all examples of items that should not be thrown away normally because of the elements used in them. Batteries contain metals such as lead and nickel, circuit boards contain lead solder, and CRTs contain phosphors.

Know the safety procedures to follow when working with computers.　Be careful when moving computers or working around any electrical components. Know that liquids and computers don't mix, and keep the systems as clean and dust-free as possible to ensure optimal operation.

5.3 Summarize the Process of Addressing Prohibited Content/Activity and Explain Privacy, Licensing, and Policy Concepts

Working in the IT profession, it is entirely plausible that you will encounter a situation where you find proof of a user, or a number of users, engaging in activities that are prohibited. Those activities can include any number of things, and the prohibition may range from a company policy (you cannot use social media during working hours) all the way up to a federal law (you cannot traffic in child pornography). You have an obligation to respond appropriately and accordingly.

Regardless of whether you agree with a prohibition, when you encounter instances wherein activities are in violation of it, you must respond in a professional and legal manner. The following are the subobjectives covered in this section:

- Incident response
- Licensing/DRM/EULA
- Personally identifiable information
- Follow corporate end-user policies and security best practices

Incident Response

The extent to which a security event causes harm to your network largely depends on the speed and quality of your response to the incident. By following a structured incident response policy, the chances of minimizing the damage and the likelihood that you will be able to bring parties to justice in the case of illegal activity are greatly enhanced. The following sections cover some important guidelines regarding the incident response process.

First Response

There are three crucial components to the first response: identifying the problem, reporting it through the proper channels, and preserving the data.

Identify

A part of identifying the problem involves identifying what policy or law prohibits such an action. Prohibited content generally falls within the following categories (this list should not be considered to represent everything prohibited because many companies have other policies):

- Exploiting people (in any way, such as sexually, violently, and so on)
- Promoting harassment of any person or group
- Containing or promoting anything illegal or unauthorized
- Promoting racism, hatred, bigotry, or physical harm
- Containing adult content involving nudity or sexual acts
- Violating privacy rights, copyrights, contract rights, or defamation rights
- Viruses or malware of any sort
- Impersonation
- Soliciting information from anyone younger than 18
- Involving pyramid schemes, junk mail, chain letters, spamming, or the like

Report Through Proper Channels

Once you have identified prohibited content or activity, you must report it through the proper channels. If the violation is one only of company policy, then usually the company's human resources department is the proper channel. If the violation is of a law, then often you must contact legal authorities—notifying the appropriate internal resources as well. If the violation is of a federal law and you tell only an internal resource (HR manager, for example), it does not absolve you of the responsibility if that person does not continue to report it up the appropriate chain.

Law enforcement personnel are governed by the rules of evidence, and their response to an incident will be largely out of your control. You need to carefully consider involving law enforcement before you begin. There is no such thing as dropping charges. Once they begin, law enforcement professionals are required to pursue an investigation.

Data/Device Preservation

You have as well an obligation to preserve the content found until it is turned over to the appropriate authority. Doing so may require commandeering anything from a flash drive up to a network server. Until someone in a position of authority relieves you of the responsibility, you must preserve the data or device in the state in which you discovered it. If you are ever unsure of how to proceed, you should immediately contact your supervisor.

Because knowing what to do when something is discovered is something that may not come naturally, it is a good idea to include the procedures you'll generally follow in an *incident response plan (IRP).* The IRP outlines what steps are needed and who is responsible for deciding how to handle a situation.

> Your policies should clearly outline who needs to be informed in the company, what they need to be told, and how to respond to the situation.

Use of Documentation/Documentation Changes

During the entire process, you should document the steps you take to identify, detect, and report the problem. This information is valuable and will often be used should the problem escalate to a court of law. Many help-desk software systems provide detailed methods you can use to record procedures and steps.

Chain of Custody (Tracking of Evidence/Documenting Process)

An important concept to keep in mind when working with incidents is the *chain of custody.*

When you begin to collect evidence, you must keep track of that evidence at all times and show who has it, who has seen it, and where it has been. The evidence must always be within your custody, or you're open to dispute about whether it has been tampered with.

Licensing/DRM/EULA

While many in the IT community would like to think that software, music files, and movie files should be free, that is not the case. Using any of these items without paying for them is *illegal.* Operating systems, application software, and many third-party utilities require a license to legally use the software. It also requires that you accept an end-user license agreement (EULA) whereby you agree to use the software as described in that agreement.

Music and movie files, on the other hand, are protected by digital rights management (DRM). This is a system that maintains control over these files and ensures that they are installed only on devices that belong to the person who purchased the file with the end goal being to prevent users from sharing and giving these away without paying for them.

Not all software required a license. In the next sections, we'll talk about software that doesn't require a license and also discuss the differences between personal and enterprise licenses.

Open Source vs. Commercial License

Open source software is software that is free and available to all. Commercial software, on the other hand, requires the purchase of a license to legally use the software. While there is the obvious monetary advantage to using open source software, the organization or user must typically have a deeper understanding of the software than may be required to use commercial software successfully. Another advantage of commercial software is the ongoing support the vendor can provide in using the software, while a user of open source software is pretty much on their own when issues arise.

Personal License vs. Enterprise Licenses

While an individual software license entitles a single user to install and use a piece of commercial software, an enterprise license purchase is based on a number of seats or devices on which the software can be legally installed. Also, while each individual license will come with installation media, the purchase of an enterprise license comes with a single version of the installation media, which can be installed on the number of devices specified in the license agreement.

Personally Identifiable Information

Personally identifiable information (PII) is any piece of information about a user that can be used alone or in combination with other pieces of information to identify an individual user. While it is the responsibility of all organizations to protect PII that they may possess, it is especially important in certain regulated industries such as healthcare and finance.

The danger of leaking PII is that much of this information, such as address, Social Security number, and place of employment can be used to perform identity theft, a growing concern worldwide.

Follow Corporate End-User Policies and Security Best Practices

Every organization should have a security policy that drives all security-related activities and clearly spells out how sensitive data is handled and what specific operations the users are allowed to perform. The acceptable use policy is a document that each user should sign when hired that serves as a contract between the user and the company in detail. Moreover, this document, as well as the security guidelines that network technicians must follow, should be driven by well-established best practices. The following are some of the guidelines that should be included:

- Password policy
- Acceptable use policy
- Access control policy
- Remote access policy

As an A+ technician, part of your job is to educate users about the importance of these security policies and to monitor the environments for any violations of the policies.

Exam Essentials

Report prohibited content and activities.   You have an obligation to report prohibited activities and content to the appropriate authorities when you uncover them. You must ascertain which authority is prohibiting the actions and notify them.

Document and preserve the evidence. It is imperative that the evidence be documented and preserved until turned over to the appropriate authority. In some cases, this can include commandeering a removable drive, a computer, or even a server. Failure to do so can leave you facing fines and other punishments.

5.4 Demonstrate Proper Communication Techniques and Professionalism

It's possible that you chose computers as your vocation instead of public speaking because you want to interact with people on a one-on-one basis. As unlikely as that possibility may be, it still exists.

Some have marveled at the fact that CompTIA includes questions about customer service on the A+ exam. A better wonder, however, is that there are those in the business who need to know these items and don't. Possessing a great deal of technology skill does not immediately endow one with great people skills. A bit more on appropriate behavior as it relates to the IT field follows. The following are the subobjectives covered in this section:

- Use proper language (avoid jargon, acronyms, and slang when applicable).
- Maintain a positive attitude/project confidence.
- Actively listen (taking notes) and avoid interrupting the customer.
- Be culturally sensitive.
- Be on time (if late, contact the customer).
- Avoid distractions.
- Deal with difficult customers or situations.
- Set and meet expectations/timelines and communicate status with the customer.
- Deal appropriately with customers' confidential and private materials.

Use Proper Language: Avoid Jargon, Acronyms, Slang When Applicable

Avoid using jargon, abbreviations, slang, and acronyms. Every field has its own language that can make those from outside the field feel lost. Put yourself in the position of someone not in the field, and explain what is going on using words they can relate to.

Be honest and fair with the customer, and try to establish a personal rapport. Tell them what the problem is, what you believe is the cause, and what can be done in the future to prevent it from recurring.

Alert your supervisor if there is a communication barrier with the customer (for example, the customer is deaf or does not speak the same language as you do). This is particularly important if the barrier will affect the problem resolution or the amount of time it will take.

If you're providing phone support, do the following:

- Always answer the telephone in a professional manner, announcing the name of the company and yourself.

- Make a concentrated effort to ascertain the customer's technical level, and communicate at that level, not above or below it.

Maintain a Positive Attitude/Project Confidence

Maintain a positive attitude. Your approach to the problem, and the customer, can be mirrored back. Moreover, project confidence in dealing with the issue because that engenders more cooperation and patience from the customer, both of which have a direct impact on the success of your troubleshooting efforts.

Actively Listen (Taking Notes) and Avoid Interrupting the Customer

Good communication includes listening to what the user, manager, or developer is telling you and making certain that you understand completely what they are trying to say. Just because a user or customer doesn't understand the terminology, syntax, or concepts that you do doesn't mean they don't have a real problem that needs addressing. You must, therefore, be skilled not only at listening but also at translating. Professional conduct encompasses politeness, guidance, punctuality, and accountability. Always treat the customer with the same respect and empathy you would expect if the situation were reversed. Likewise, guide the customer through the problem and the explanation. Tell them what has caused the problem they're currently experiencing and offer the best solution to prevent it from recurring.

Listen intently to what your customer is saying. Make it obvious to them that you're listening and respecting what they're telling you. If you have a problem understanding them, go to whatever lengths you need to in order to remedy the situation. Look for verbal and nonverbal cues that can help you isolate the problem. Avoid interrupting the customer because that telegraphs that what he has to say is not important enough to listen to.

Be Culturally Sensitive

It is important as well to be culturally sensitive—not everyone enjoys the same humor. Moreover, be mindful of the difference in the way business is conducted in different cultures and be flexible in your approach based on this. When you sense that the customer prefers a more formal relationship with you, try to reflect that in your approach.

Use Appropriate Professional Titles, When Applicable

While many folks are not put off at all when you address them by their first name, in many cultures it is considered rude to do so, and you should also address the customer using the appropriate title when applicable. Not all cultures are as informal as what you may have become accustomed to. Again, sensitivity to the customer's approach to you can be a valuable clue to how the customer would prefer to interact with you.

Be on Time (If Late, Contact the Customer)

Punctuality is important and should be part of your planning process before you ever arrive at the site. If you tell the customer you'll be there at 10:30, you need to make every attempt to be there at that time. If you arrive late, you have given them false hope that the problem would be solved by a set time. That false hope can lead to anger when you arrive late and appear to not be taking their problem as seriously as they are. Punctuality continues to be important throughout the service call and doesn't end with your arrival. If you need to leave to get parts, tell the customer when you'll be back, and then be there at that time. If for some reason you can't return at the expected time, alert the customer and inform them of your new return time.

In conjunction with time and punctuality, if a user asks how much longer the server will be down and you respond that it will up in five minutes only to have it remain down for five more hours, you're creating resentment and possibly anger. When estimating downtime, always allow for more time than you think you'll need, just in case other problems occur. If you greatly underestimate the time, always inform the affected parties and give them a new time estimate. Here's an analogy that will put it in perspective: if you take your car to get the oil changed and the counter clerk tells you it will be "about 15 minutes," the last thing you want is to be sitting there 4 hours later.

Avoid Distractions

It is important that you avoid distractions while working on a customer's or user's problem. Those distractions can come in the form of personal calls, talking to co-workers, or personal interruptions.

If you arrive at the site to troubleshoot a problem and there are distractions there of the customer's making (children present, TV on, and so on), you should politely ask the customer to remove the distractions if possible. If the area you will be working in is cluttered with personal items (mementos from the state fair, stuffed animals, and so on), ask the customer to relocate the items as needed or ask them if it is OK to do so before you relocate the items.

Personal Calls

Taking personal calls while working with a customer can make the customer feel as if their problem is being minimized. Spend time solving the problem and interacting with the customer and then attend to the personal calls when you leave.

If you are anticipating an important call that cannot be avoided, let the customer know beforehand so they will understand that this interruption is coming.

Texting/Social Media Sites

Keep in mind that when you are supporting a customer, you are working on their time and not your own. You are also using their equipment, not your own. Consequently, avoid any use of the customer's equipment or time for personal texts or visits to social media sites. It is allowable to use the time and the equipment for legitimate research or other activities that are directly related to solving the customer issues.

Talking to Co-workers While Interacting with Customers

Just as taking personal calls can seem to minimize the importance of interacting with the customer, so too can talking to co-workers. The customer needs to be the focus of your attention until their problems have been addressed, and then you can attend to other matters.

If you must contact someone else while troubleshooting, always ask the customer's permission.

Personal Interruptions

The broad category of personal interruptions includes anything that takes you away from focusing on the customer and is not job related. Spend your time dealing with the customer first and solving their problems before attending to personal issues.

Dealing with Difficult Customers or Situations

Handle complaints as professionally as possible. Accept responsibility for errors that may have occurred on your part, and never try to pass the blame. Remember, the goal is to keep them as a customer, not to win an argument.

Do Not Argue with Customers and/or Be Defensive

Avoid arguing with a customer because doing so serves no purpose; resolve their anger with as little conflict as possible. Moreover, don't be defensive when the customer questions your approach and thought process. While they may clueless about troubleshooting, they deserve to understand why you are doing what you are doing.

Avoid Dismissing Customer's Problems

Just as personal calls and interruptions can make it seem as if you are not taking the customer seriously enough, so too can dismissing their problems as less important than they believe they are. It is important to put yourself in their shoes and see the issue from their perspective. What may seem trivial to you may be a vital issue for them.

Avoid Being Judgmental

It is important to not minimize their problem or appear as if you are being judgmental.

Clarify Customer Statements (Ask Open-Ended Questions to Narrow the Scope of the Problem, Restate the Issue, or Question to Verify Understanding)

The most important skill you can have is the ability to listen. You have to rely on the customer to tell you the problem and describe it accurately. They can't do that if you're second-guessing them or jumping to conclusions before the whole story is told. Ask questions that are broad and open-ended at first and then narrow them down to help isolate the problem. This is particularly necessary when you are trying to solve the problem remotely.

It's your job to help guide the user's description of the problem. Here are some examples:

- Is the printer plugged in?
- Is it online?
- Are any lights flashing on it?

Restate the issue to the customer to make sure that you correctly understand what they are telling you (for example, "There is only one green light lit, correct?"). Ask questions as needed that verify your understanding of the problem. The questions you ask should help guide you toward isolating the problem and identifying possible solutions.

Do Not Disclose Experiences via Social Media Outlets

Although it might make you feel better about a particularly trying experience with a customer to vent about it on social media, don't do that. Not only is it remotely possible that the post may somehow find its way to the attention of the customer, it reflects poorly on you as someone who shares his business dealings with the world.

Set and Meet Expectations/Timeline and Communicate Status with the Customer

Customer satisfaction goes a long way toward generating repeat business. If you can *meet* the customer's expectations, you'll almost assuredly hear from them again when another problem arises. If you can *exceed* the customer's expectations, you can almost guarantee that they will call you the next time a problem arises.

Customer satisfaction is important in all communication media—whether you're onsite, providing phone support, or communicating through email or other correspondence.

Share the customer's sense of urgency. What may seem like a small problem to you can appear to the customer as if the whole world is collapsing around them.

Offer Different Repair/Replacement Options If Applicable

If there are multiple solutions to the problem the customer is encountering, offer options to them. Those options often include repairing what they already have or replacing it. If the repair could lead to a recurrence of the situation but the replacement will not, then that should be explained to them clearly.

The ramifications of each choice should be clearly explained along with costs (estimates, if necessary) so they can make the decision they deem in their best interest.

If you are unable to resolve the issue, explain to the customer what to do and make sure to follow up properly to forward the issue to appropriate personnel.

Provide Proper Documentation on the Services Provided

Document the services you provided so there is no misunderstanding on the part of the customer. Supply them with the documentation and keep a copy handy to refer to should any questions arise. Explain clearly the cause of the problem and how to avoid it in the future.

It is important that the documentation be complete so that if you do not refer to it for quite some time (years), you will still be able to understand and explain what was done.

Follow Up with Customer/User at a Later Date to Verify Satisfaction

When you finish a job, notify the user you're done. Make every attempt to find the user and inform them of the resolution. If it's difficult to find them, leave a note for them to find when they return, explaining the resolution. You should also leave a means by which they can contact you, should they have a question about the resolution or a related problem. In most cases, the number you leave should be that of your business during working hours and your pager, where applicable, after hours.

If you do not hear back from the customer, follow up with them at a later date to verify that the problem is resolved and they are satisfied with the outcome. One of the best ways to keep customers is to let them know that you care about their success and satisfaction.

Deal Appropriately with Customers' Confidential and Private Materials

The goal of *confidentiality* is to prevent or minimize unauthorized access to files and folders and disclosure of data and information. In many instances, laws and regulations require specific information confidentiality. For example, Social Security records, payroll and employee records, medical records, and corporate information are high-value assets. This information could create liability issues or embarrassment if it fell into the wrong hands. Over the last few years, there have been several cases in which bank account and credit card numbers were published on the Internet. The costs of these types of breaches of confidentiality far exceed the actual losses from the misuse of this information.

> Confidentiality entails ensuring that data expected to remain private is seen only by those who should see it. Confidentiality is implemented through authentication and access controls.

Just as confidentiality issues are addressed early in the design phase of a project, you as a computer professional are expected to uphold a high level of confidentiality. Should a user approach you with a sensitive issue—telling you their password, asking for assistance obtaining access to medical forms, and so on—it's your obligation as a part of your job to make certain that information passes no further.

Located on a Computer, Desktop, Printer, Etc.

Technicians may come into contact with confidential information in the course of performing their job duties. That information could come in the form of data stored on a computer, information on a desktop, data (in any form) on a printer, and many other locations. When the possibility exists, ask users to remove such confidential information or close the application that displays it (saving their work before they close).

If the area where you will be working is cluttered with personal information (printed customer lists, and so on), ask the customer to relocate the items if possible. No confidential information should ever be disclosed to outside parties.

Exam Essentials

Use good communication skills.   Listen to the customer. Let them tell you what they understand the problem to be, and then interpret the problem and see whether you can get them to agree to what you're hearing them say. Treat the customer, whether an end user or a colleague, with respect, and take their issues and problems seriously.

Deal appropriately with confidential data.   You—as a computer professional—are expected to uphold a high level of confidentiality. No confidential information should ever be disclosed to outside parties.

5.5 Given a Scenario, Explain the Troubleshooting Theory

Most of those employed in the IT field who will be seeking CompTIA's A+ certification are regularly in positions where they need to know how to troubleshoot, repair, and maintain computer systems. The following subobjective is covered in this section:

- Always consider corporate policies, procedures and impacts before implementing changes

Always Consider Corporate Policies, Procedures, and Impacts Before Implementing Changes

When implementing the steps in the troubleshooting theory discussed in this section always keep in mind that before you make any changes or take any actions, you should always ensure the changes are consistent with your corporate policies. You should also determine whether a particular change you are considering has an established procedure defined in the corporate guidelines. Finally, have a clear understanding of the potential impact of any change you make, and always ensure that a rollback plan has been established in advance. Whenever you determine that a change has the potential to cause widespread issues, try to make the change in a test environment or on a small, low-impact section of the network.

Identify the Problem

Although it may sound obvious, you can't troubleshoot a problem without knowing what the problem is. In some cases, the problem will be obvious. But in others, especially when relying on the description of the problem by the user, it will appear to be one thing on the surface when in actuality the issue the user is experiencing is a symptom of a different, possibly larger problem. In this section, processes that can help bring clarity to the situation are discussed, and a cautionary note about this step is covered as well.

Question the User and Identify User Changes to Computer and Perform Backups Before Making Changes

Identify the problem by questioning the user and identifying user changes to the computer. Before you do anything else, ask the user the following:

- What the problem is
- When the last time was that the problem didn't exist
- What has changed since

Be sure that you do a backup before you make any changes so that all your actions can be undone, if necessary.

When performing this step, be wary of accepting the user's diagnosis of the problem at face value. For example, a user may start the conversation with the statement "The email server is down." At this point, ask the question, "Is there anything else you cannot do besides open your email?" Ask them to try accessing a shared folder or the Internet. If either of those tasks fails, the problem is probably not the email server but basic network connectivity of their computer.

Establish a Theory of Probable Cause (Question the Obvious)

As you get answers to your initial questions, theories will begin to evolve as to the root of the problem. Analyze the problem, including potential causes, and make an initial determination of whether it's a software or hardware problem. As you narrow down the problem, determine whether it's hardware or software related so you can act accordingly.

Once you have developed a list of possible causes, develop a list of tests you can perform to test each to narrow the list by eliminating each theory one by one. Don't forget to consider the obvious and make no assumptions. Just because the cable has worked every day for the last five years doesn't mean the person cleaning the office may not have caught the vacuum cleaner on the cable and damaged its connector last night.

If Necessary, Conduct External or Internal Research Based on Symptoms

You are not expected to immediately know the solution to every issue the user may have. You are, however, expected to perform whatever research is required to solve the issue. That can include using the Internet, calling trusted fellow technicians, and contacting vendors for assistance. Later in this section you will learn that when a resolution is found, you should always documents these lessons learned in a form that you can use later to solve the same or similar issues.

Test the Theory to Determine Cause

Test related components, including connections and hardware and software configurations. Also use Device Manager and consult vendor documentation. Whatever the problem may be, the odds are good that someone else has experienced it before. Use the tools at your disposal—including manuals and websites—to try to zero in on the problem as expeditiously as possible.

Once Theory Is Confirmed, Determine Next Steps to Resolve Problem

If your theory is confirmed, then determine the next steps you need to take to resolve the problem. In cases where you have determined the device where the problem lies but you have no expertise in that area, escalate the problem to someone as needed. For example, if you have narrowed down the problem to the router and you don't understand or manage the router, escalate the problem to the router administrator.

If Theory Is Not Confirmed, Reestablish New Theory or Escalate

If your theory is not confirmed, then come up with a new theory or bring in someone with more expertise (escalate the problem). If you make changes to test one theory, make sure you reverse those changes before you test another theory. Making multiple changes can cause new problems and make the process even more difficult.

Establish a Plan of Action to Resolve the Problem and Implement the Solution

Evaluate the results and develop an action plan of steps to fully resolve the problem. Keep in mind that it's possible that more than one thing is causing the problem. If that is the case, you may need to solve one problem and then turn your attention to the next.

Once you have planned your work, work your plan. Methodically make the required changes while always having a back-out plan if your changes cause a larger problem.

Verify Full System Functionality and If Applicable Implement Preventive Measures

When the problem is believed to be resolved, verify that the system is fully functional. If there are preventive measures that can be put in place to keep this situation from recurring, take those measures on this machine and all others where the problem may exist. Also keep in mind that times like this are great learning moments to teach users what role they may have played and what actions they may be able to take on their own in the future to prevent the problem, if that is appropriate.

Document Findings, Actions, and Outcomes

Document your activities and outcomes. Experience is a wonderful teacher, but only if you can remember what you've done. Documenting your actions and outcomes will help you (or a fellow administrator) troubleshoot a similar problem when it crops up in the future.

In some cases, you may think you have solved a problem only to find it occurs again later because you only treated the symptom of a larger problem. When this type of thing occurs, documentation of what has occurred in the past can be helpful in seeing patterns that otherwise would remain hidden.

Exam Essentials

Know the six main steps in the troubleshooting process. The six steps are as follows: identify the problem; establish a theory of probable cause; test the theory to determine the cause; establish a plan of action to resolve the problem and implement the solution; verify full system functionality and if applicable implement preventive measures; and document findings, actions, and outcomes.

Review Questions

You can find the answers in the Appendix.

1. Which of the following is the technical term for what happens whenever two objects of dissimilar charge come in contact?

    A. RFI

    B. EMI

    C. ESD

    D. LED

2. Which of the following is NOT a safe lifting technique to keep in mind?

    A. Lift with your back, not your legs

    B. Be careful to not twist when lifting

    C. Keep objects as close to your body as possible

    D. Where possible, push instead of pull.

3. What class of fire extinguisher is used for paper fires?

    A. A

    B. B

    C. C

    D. D

4. Any type of chemical, equipment, or supply that has the potential to harm the environment or people has to have what document associated with it?

    A. SOW

    B. MSDS

    C. SLA

    D. MOU

5. What humidity level should be maintained for computing equipment?

    A. 50 percent

    B. 40 percent

    C. 60 percent

    D. 30 percent

6. Which of the following is a complete failure of the power supplied?

    A. sag

    B. spike

    C. blackout

    D. brownout

7. How should you use compressed air to clear duct?

    A. in long bursts

    B. in slow steady burst

    C. in short bursts

    D. never use it

8. Which of the following is a drop in voltage lasting more than a few minutes?

    A. sag

    B. spike

    C. blackout

    D. brownout

9. Which of the following outlines what steps are needed and who is responsible for deciding how to handle a situation?

    A. SOW

    B. SLA

    C. MOU

    D. IRP

10. Which of the following is a very short-term voltage drop?

    A. sag

    B. spike

    C. blackout

    D. brownout

Appendix

Answers to Review Questions

Chapter 1

1. Answer: A

UEFI (Unified Extensible Firmware Interface) is a standard firmware interface for PCs, designed to replace BIOS

2. Answer: B

NVRAM is memory that does not lose its content when power is lost to the machine.

3. Answer: C

Cylinders, heads, and sectors (CHS) is also called the drive geometry, because together these three numbers determine how much data the disk can hold.

4. Answer: D

Read only memory (ROM) is memory that cannot be written to and usually resides on a chip on the board.

5. Answer: A

This can be set by accessing the BIOS or UEFI settings.

6. Answer: B

When the proper CPU speed is known, you must make sure the relationship between the speed of the CPU and that of the motherboard bus is correct. This is done with a value called the multiplier.

7. Answer: C

When the device has a Trusted Platform Module (TPM) chip present on the motherboard, additional security and options become available.

8. Answer: A

Lo-jack is a product made by Absolute Software that allows you to remotely locate, lock, and delete the data on a mobile device when it is stolen. It is a small piece of software that embeds itself on the computer and is difficult to detect.

9. Answer: B

Secure Boot is a standard adopted by many venders that requires the operating system to check the integrity of all system files before allowing the boot process to proceed. By doing so it protects against the alteration or corruption of these system files.

10. Answer: C

Every computer has a diagnostic program built into its BIOS called the power-on self-test (POST). When you turn on the computer, it executes this set of diagnostics.

Chapter 2

1. Answer: C

    A BNC connector is used with coaxial cabling not fiber.

2. Answer: B

    Unshielded twisted Pair (UTP) lacks the shielding required. YTH types either have the shielding or are impervious to EMI and RFI.

3. Answer: A

    While RJ-45 is for data, the RJ-11 connector is for a phone or modem connection.

4. Answer: A

    When the same standard is used on both ends, it is a straight through cable and when different standards are used on each end, it is a crossover cable

5. Answer: D

    Coax supports both baseband and broadband signaling. Baseband signaling means that a single channel is carried through the coax, and broadband refers to multiple channels on the coax

6. Answer: C

    1000BaseLX operates at 1 Gb and will go up to 550 meters.

7. Answer: B

    CAT5 transmits data at speeds up to 100 Mbps and was used with Fast Ethernet (operating at 100 Mbps) with a transmission range of 100 meters.

8. Answer: D

    Category 6 cable typically is made up of four twisted pairs of copper wire, but its capabilities far exceed those of other cable types. Category 6 twisted pair uses a longitudinal separator, which separates each of the four pairs of wires from each other and reduces the amount of crosstalk possible.

9. Answer: C

    RG-58 is the type traditionally used in Thin Ethernet networks (10Base2). Thick coax (10Base5) utilized RG-8, was used primarily for backbone cable.

10. Answer: C

    IP addresses with a first octet value between 128-191 are Class B addresses.

Chapter 3

1. Answer: D

    The maximum transmission speeds are as follows:

    280 Mbit/s effective (USB 2 mode)

    1.6 Gbit/s effective (PCIe 1 mode)

    3.2 Gbit/s effective (PCIe 2 or USB 3 mode)

2. Answer: C

    Laptop memory comes in smaller form factors known as small outline DIMMs (SoDIMMs).

3. Answer: A

    Of the listed options, the only one that is used in laptops is MicroDIMM.

4. Answer: C

    Thunderbolt ports are most likely to be found on Apple laptops, but they are now showing up on others as well.

5. Answer: C

    DisplayPort is a digital interface primarily used to connect a video source to a display device such as a computer monitor or television set. It resembles a USB port and has an icon that looks like a D with one arrow pointing up and another pointing down to its left.

6. Answer: B

    Some models of notebook PCs require a special T-8 Torx screwdriver. Most PC toolkits come with a T-8 bit for a screwdriver with interchangeable bits, but you may find that the T-8 screws are countersunk in deep holes so that you can't fit the screwdriver into them. In such cases, you need to buy a separate T-8 screwdriver, available at most hardware stores or auto parts stores.

7. Answer: B

    When replacing the keyboard, one of the main things you want to keep in mind is to not damage the data cable connector to the system board.

8. Answer: C

    If required, remove the connector attached to the old drive's signal pins and attach it to the new drive. Make sure it's right side up and do not force it. Damaging the signal pins may render the drive useless.

9. Answer: C

    The 2.5 inch hard drives are smaller (which makes them attractive for a laptop where space is at a minimum) but in comparison to 3.5 inch hard drives, they have less capacity and cache and they operate at a lower speed.

10. Answer: A

The advantage of solid state drives is that they are not as susceptible to damage if the device is dropped, and they are generally speaking faster as no moving parts are involved. They are, however, more expensive, and when they fail they don't generally give some advance symptoms like a magnetic drive will do.

Chapter 4

1. Answer: A

One common reason for shutdowns is overheating. Often when that is the case, however, the system reboots itself rather than just shutting down.

2. Answer: D

A bad NIC driver would cause the NIC not to work but would not cause a system lockup.

3. Answer: B

During the boot-up of the system, a power-on self-test (POST) occurs and each device is checked for functionality.

4. Answer: B

If you find that you are continually resetting the system time, it could be that the CMOS battery is dying.

5. Answer: B

Power supply problems can cause reboots as well. The power supply continually sends a Power_Good signal to the motherboard and if this signal is not present momentarily the system will reset.

6. Answer: A

Take care to keep the ambient air within normal ranges (approximately 60–90 degrees Fahrenheit) and at a constant temperature.

7. Answer: B

Once a regular occurrence when working with Windows, blue screens (also known as the Blue Screen of Death) have become much less frequent.

8. Answer: A

While Microsoft users have the BSOD to deal with Apple users have also come to have the same negative feelings about the "Pin Wheel" of death. This is a multicolored pinwheel mouse pointer.

9. Answer: B

If the other variable match, it need not be from the same manufacturer.

10. Answer: C

Loopback plugs are used to test the functionality of various types of ports, but their most common use is to test a network card.

Chapter 5

1. Answer: B

The Aero interface offers a glass design that includes translucent windows. It was new with Windows Vista.

2. Answer: A

Windows 7 renamed these Windows Desktop Gadgets.

3. Answer: C

For removable drives, BitLocker To Go provides encryption technology to help prevent unauthorized access to the files stored on them.

4. Answer: B

Windows XP Mode (XPM) is a virtual client (emulating Windows XP Professional with Service Pack 3), which requires that you also download and install Windows Virtual PC to use.

5. Answer: D

This feature allows you to use free space on a removable drive to speed up a system by caching content and is used when you are running low on available memory.

6. Answer: A

Rolled into the Action Center in Windows 7, this interface shows the status of, and allows you to configure, the firewall, Windows Update, virus protection, spyware and unwanted software protection, Internet security settings, UAC, and network access protection.

7. Answer: B

The System log file displays alerts that pertain to the general operation of Windows.

8. Answer: B

In both Windows and Windows 8.1, the user interface is very different from earlier versions of Windows. The start menu was removed and the desktop replaced with a new look called Metro.

9. Answer: C

Pinning is the process of configuring an icon for a program on the taskbar so that it is easier to locate. It was introduced in Windows 7 and continued in Windows 8 and Windows 8.1 and for frequently used applications, it saves navigating through the Start menu or Start screen to locate the application.

10. Answer: C

One Drive is the cloud based storage feature formerly known as Sky Drive that is Microsoft answer to other cloud -based storage solutions like Dropbox.

Chapter 6

1. Answer: A

In Linux backups of data can be scheduled using the rsync utility from the command line.

2. Answer:B

As Linux systems manage the disk differently than Windows they need NO defragmentation. There is a maintenance task you may want to schedule in Linux. From time to time you should run a file system checker called fsck. This is a logical file system checker.

3. Answer: C

The -c option creates a new archive.

4. Answer:A

You can use the -s argument of the lvcreate command to create a snapshot volume.

5. Answer: B

Mac calls the shell "Terminal" and you can find it under Applications >Utilities >Terminal.

6. Answer: B

Force quit can be used on a Mac to stop an unresponsive application.

7. Answer: C

In Apple, Mission Control provides a quick way to see everything that's currently open on your Mac.

8. Answer: B

Keychain is password management system in OS X. It can contain private keys, certificates, and secure notes.

9. Answer: B

Spot Light is a search tool built into Mac systems.

10. Answer: A

While Finder can also be used in Mac to search for files its main function is a file system navigation tool, much like Windows Explorer.

Chapter 7

1. Answer: C

An armored virus is designed to make itself difficult to detect or analyze. Armored viruses cover themselves with protective code that stops debuggers or disassemblers from examining critical elements of the virus.

2. Answer: B

A signature is an algorithm or other element of a virus that uniquely identifies it. Because some viruses have the ability to alter their signature, it is crucial that you keep signature files current, whether you choose to manually download them or configure the antivirus engine to do so automatically.

3. Answer: B

A worm is different from a virus in that it can reproduce itself, it's self-contained, and it doesn't need a host application to be transported.

4. Answer: B

Trojan horses are programs that enter a system or network under the guise of another program. A Trojan horse may be included as an attachment or as part of an installation program.

5. Answer: A

A phage virus alters other programs and databases. The virus infects all of these files.

6. Answer: B

Spoofing is the process of masquerading as another user or device. It is usually done for the purpose of accessing a resource to which the hacker should not have access or to get through a security device such as a firewall that may be filtering traffic based on source IP address.

7. Answer: A

Vulnerabilities are often discovered in live environments before a fix or patch exists. Such vulnerabilities are referred to as zero-day vulnerabilities.

8. Answer: A

A companion virus attaches itself to legitimate programs and then creates a program with a different filename extension. This file may reside in your system's temporary directory. When a user types the name of the legitimate program, the companion virus executes instead of the real program.

9. Answer: C

Tailgating is the term used for someone being so close to you when you enter a building that they are able to come in right behind you without needing to use a key, a card, or any other security device. Many social engineering intruders needing physical access to a site will use this method of gaining entry.

10. Answer: D

A multipartite virus attacks your system in multiple ways. It may attempt to infect your boot sector, infect all of your executable files, and destroy your application files.

Chapter 8

1. Answer: D

Once a regular occurrence when working with Windows, blue screens (also known as the Blue Screen of Death) have become less common.

2. Answer: A

The Apple pin wheel is displayed automatically by the window server when an application cannot handle all of the events it receives. (WindowServer is the background process that runs the Mac OS X graphical user interface).

3. Answer: B

Known as the action log, this file is a chronological list of what took place during the setup.

4. Answer: B

The boot.ini is specific to the machine.

5. Answer: B

Use Task Manager to determine if a process is using too much memory or CPU or is simply locked up (not responding) and if necessary end the process.

6. Answer: D

Were there a disk with system files in the DVD drives the system would boot to it.

7. Answer: B

There is not bootrec/fixbcd command.

8. Answer: A

The GRUB is the bootloader package in Linux and UNIX systems. If it is not present the system may not boot.

9. Answer: B

The MSCONFIG utility helps you troubleshoot startup problems by allowing you to selectively disable individual items that normally are executed at startup.

10. Answer: C

REGSRV32 (Microsoft Register Server) is a command-line utility in Windows operating systems for registering and unregistering DLLs and ActiveX controls in the Registry.

Chapter 9

1. Answer: C

Electrostatic discharge (ESD) is the technical term for what happens whenever two objects of dissimilar charge come in contact—think of rubbing your feet on a carpet and then touching a light switch.

2. Answer: A

Lift with your legs, not your back. When you have to pick something up, bend at the knees, not at the waist.

3. Answer: A

A for wood and paper fires, B for flammable liquids, and C for electrical fires.

4. Answer: B

Any type of chemical, equipment, or supply that has the potential to harm the environment or people has to have a material safety data sheets (MSDS) associated with it. These are traditionally created by the manufacturer, and you can obtain them from the manufacturer or from the Environmental Protection Agency.

5. Answer: A

Another preventive measure you can take is to maintain the relative humidity at around 50 percent. Be careful not to increase the humidity too far—to the point where moisture starts to condense on the equipment!

6. Answer: C

There are a number of power-related threats that can harm computers. Among them are the following:

- Blackout: A complete failure of the power supplied.
- Brownout: A drop in voltage lasting more than a few minutes.
- Sag: A very short-term voltage drop.
- Spike: The opposite of a sag, this is a short (typically under 1 second) increase in voltage that can do irreparable damage to equipment.

- Surge: A long spike (sometimes lasting many seconds). Though they are typically a less intense increase in power, they can also damage equipment.

7. Answer: C

The short bursts are useful in preventing the dust from flying too far out and entering another machine, as well as in preventing the can from releasing the air in liquid form.

8. Answer: B

There are a number of power-related threats that can harm computers. Among them are the following:

- Blackout: A complete failure of the power supplied.

- Brownout: A drop in voltage lasting more than a few minutes.

- Sag: A very short-term voltage drop.

- Spike: The opposite of a sag, this is a short (typically under 1 second) increase in voltage that can do irreparable damage to equipment.

- Surge: A long spike (sometimes lasting many seconds). Though they are typically a less intense increase in power, they can also damage equipment.

9. Answer: D

Because knowing what to do when something is discovered is something that may not come naturally, it is a good idea to include the procedures you'll generally follow in an incident response plan (IRP). The IRP outlines what steps are needed and who is responsible for deciding how to handle a situation.

10. Answer: A

There are a number of power-related threats that can harm computers. Among them are the following:

- Blackout: A complete failure of the power supplied.

- Brownout: A drop in voltage lasting more than a few minutes.

- Sag: A very short-term voltage drop.

- Spike: The opposite of a sag, this is a short (typically under 1 second) increase in voltage that can do irreparable damage to equipment.

- Surge: A long spike (sometimes lasting many seconds). Though they are typically a less intense increase in power, they can also damage equipment.

Index

Note to the reader: Throughout this index boldfaced page numbers indicate primary discussions of a topic. Italicized page numbers indicate illustrations.

E

O

P

Q

R

Comprehensive Online Learning Environment

Register on Sybex.com to gain access to the comprehensive online interactive learning environment and test bank to help you study for your CompTIA A+ certification.

The online test bank includes:

- **Chapter Tests** to reinforce what you learned
- **Practice Exams** to test your knowledge of the material
- **Electronic Flashcards** to reinforce your learning and provide last-minute test prep before the exam
- **Searchable Glossary** gives you instant access to the key terms you'll need to know for the exam

Go to `http://sybextestbanks.wiley.com` **to register and gain access to this comprehensive study tool package.**